BEYOND THE MISSOURI

Also by Richard W. Etulain
A Selective Listing

AUTHOR

Owen Wister

Ernest Haycox

Re-imagining the Modern American West: A Century of Fiction, History, and Art

Telling Western Stories: From Buffalo Bill to Larry McMurtry

COAUTHOR

Conversations with Wallace Stegner on Western History and Literature

The American West: A Twentieth-Century History

EDITOR

Jack London on the Road: The Tramp Diary and Other Hobo Writings

Writing Western History: Essays on Major Western Historians

Basques of the Pacific Northwest: A Collection of Essays

Contemporary New Mexico 1940–1990

Does the Frontier Experience Make America Exceptional?

César Chávez: A Brief Biography with Documents

New Mexican Lives: Profiles and Historical Stories

Western Lives: A Biographical History of the American West

COEDITOR

The Popular Western: Essays Toward a Definition

The Idaho Heritage

The Frontier and American West

Basque Americans

Fifty Western Writers: A Bio-Bibliographical Guide

A Bibliographical Guide to the Study of Western American Literature

Faith and Imagination: Essays on Evangelicals and Literature

The Twentieth Century West: Historical Interpretations

Religion and Culture

The American West in the Twentieth Century: A Bibliography

Researching Western History: Topics in the Twentieth Century

Religion in Modern New Mexico

By Grit and Grace: Eleven Women Who Shaped the American West

Portraits of Basques in the New World

With Badges and Bullets: Lawmen and Outlaws in the Old West

The Hollywood West

The American West in 2000: Essays in Honor of Gerald D. Nash

Wild Women of the Old West

Chiefs and Generals

BEYOND THE MISSOURI

The Story of the American West

RICHARD W. ETULAIN

UNIVERSITY OF NEW MEXICO PRESS * ALBUQUERQUE

©2006 by the University of New Mexico Press

All rights reserved. Published 2006

10   09   08   07   06   1   2   3   4   5

LIBRARY OF CONGRESS CATALOGING-IN-PUBLICATION DATA

Etulain, Richard W.

Beyond the Missouri : the story of the American West / Richard W. Etulain.

  p. cm.

Includes bibliographical references and index.

ISBN-13: 978-0-8263-4032-0 (cloth : alk. paper)

ISBN-10: 0-8263-4032-6 (cloth : alk. paper)

ISBN-13: 978-0-8263-4033-7 (pbk. : alk. paper)

ISBN-10: 0-8263-4033-4 (pbk. : alk. paper)

  1. West (U.S.)—History. I. Title.

F591.E85 2006

978—dc22

 2006013707

COMPOSITION AND DESIGN: MELISSA TANDYSH

FOR

ROBERT (BOB) C. WOODWARD
&
EDWIN R. (BING) BINGHAM
Encouraging mentors

DAVID V. HOLTBY
Superlative editor

JOYCE OLDENKAMP ETULAIN
Understanding, supportive mate

Contents

Preface

THE PERSONAL STORIES OF THE ETULAIN FAMILY IN THE PAST THREE generations reflect familiar ingredients of a long western past. My family has experienced several of the quick changes and increasing complexities that define much of the American West. In the roughly eighty years stretching from World War I to the beginning of the twenty-first century, my parents and their three sons saw their West rapidly transition from a primarily agricultural place into a region dotted with highly mechanized and commercial farms and ranches, military and high-tech installations, and burgeoning tourist sites. Those swift transformations and mounting complexities shaped and shifted our lives.

My Basque father immigrated from Spain to the American West in 1921. After a decade of herding sheep, he bought his own sheep ranch in eastern Washington. By World War II Dad had amassed nearly ten thousand acres of grazing land and in the next two decades diversified his investments to include a wheat ranch, a motel, and apartments. Changing residences, he and our family moved to an agricultural hub at the edge of an expanding cold war airbase. Before his death in 1983, my father also became involved in a mushrooming western tourist industry.

My mother, of sod-house frontier heritage, experienced similar sharp shifts in her western surroundings. As a girl she lived with her family on a small rented farm in the State of Washington, but as a young mother she experienced the new impacts of commercial irrigation, booming agricultural markets, environmental innovations, and more sophisticated educational opportunities for herself and her sons. Before the end of her life in 1999, my mother had lived through nearly a full century of a rapidly changing West.

The careers of the three sons followed similar paths of change. Reared in a rural, agricultural West, we soon became part of the rising influx to western cities. After gaining college degrees, all of us worked for cold war–related industries or in areas reliant on government-funded projects. Nearly all Etulains in the next generation are western urbanites, some work with new technologies, and all have been impacted by the swift socioeconomic changes sweeping through the West.

From the earliest societies into the twenty-first century the American West has experienced profound changes and transformations. Particularly since the first European contacts in the sixteenth century, economic, social, cultural, and environmental forces from without and within altered the West. All global regions feature change and complexity, of course; but, as we shall see in the following pages, unique transformations and resulting regional shifts have defined the American West in unexpected ways.

~

A few words about the empirical and intellectual origins of this book. In the longer view the research for this volume began on an isolated sheep ranch in eastern Washington. In that outback of channeled scabrock surrounded by fertile wheat farms I experienced a place much different from most of the early twenty-first-century West. Boyhood on that stock ranch, earliest education in a one-room school with five students, and a farm town twenty-two miles distant—those were the molding experiences of my first years. Later laminations included public schools in town, undergraduate liberal arts education at Northwest Nazarene College (now University) in Idaho, and graduate work in history and English at the University of Oregon. Then a career as a college and university teacher of American and western history.

More specifically, the primary impetus for this narrative history came in the early 1980s when two other western historians and I began working on a full-scale history of the American West. Our collaborator could not complete his assigned chapters, so Michael P. Malone and I published the third part of the projected history, *The American West: A Twentieth-Century History* (1989). When Professor Malone became a college president and was unable to finish the jointly authored overview, I decided to take on the task. The project was delayed until an early retirement enabled me to focus on this book.

Meanwhile, for more than twenty years I taught a full run of western history courses at the University of New Mexico. A stimulating graduate seminar in western historiography that balanced readings in the classics in the western field with new monographs fresh off the presses allowed me to keep up with the field. Work with some fifty master's and doctoral students in western history also greatly expanded my knowledge of the field. I was surrounded too by a group of superb colleagues in what may have been the strongest program in western history in the United States.

This book is based on a wide reading of pertinent sources. In the "Suggested Readings" section appended to each chapter, I list both the sources on which I built this work and books and essays useful for each chapter's topics.

This is a center-of-the-road book, with the author happily accepting his designation as a "radical middler." I have tried to prepare a balanced, blended story rather than one that follows a specific agenda.

~

In researching and writing this book, I have piled up various debts to university and commercial presses and their editors for allowing me to use phrases, paragraphs, and pages from my previous writings. Editors at the University of New Mexico Press, University of Nebraska Press, University of Arizona Press, Bedford Books, and Fulcrum Publishing have granted such permissions. So have journal editors at *Montana: The Magazine of Western History*, *The Historian*, and *Western Historical Quarterly*.

Also on my thanks list are several people who have supported this project over several years. Early on Katherine Kurzman, Tisha Rossi, and Mary Dougherty kept me at the task. Louise Townsend and later Jill Root did their best to straighten out my thinking, writing, and organization. Joan Feinberg and Jane Knetzger were encouraging. I am also indebted to my western pard and collaborator, Glenda Riley, for reading and commenting on the entire manuscript. More recently David Holtby once again took on a project that needed his direction. I appreciate the help of all these diligent editors and readers. Finally, this book is dedicated to four persons who have given me many years of support, warmth, and friendship.

Introduction

∼

BETWEEN 1848 AND 1853, THOUSANDS OF NEWCOMERS INVADED CALIFORNIA. Overnight, this distant and recently Mexican territory became a state, with the population of its chief "instant city," San Francisco, booming from less than 1,000 to nearly 50,000. It was the California Gold Rush, with its rumors of quick and easy riches, that enticed nearly all the new immigrants. In this dramatic half-decade, cultural change and a new social complexity transformed the racial-ethnic, family, and class makeup of northern California.

Nearly a century later another torrent of new arrivals flooded to the Far West. Drawn by a different kind of rumored gold—the promise of high-paying, war-related jobs—thousands of families from all parts of the United States relocated to the Pacific Coast states to take new positions, especially those in aircraft- and ship-building factories. The gears of change again spun out of control, as they had in California in the mid-nineteenth century. From the viewpoint of the twenty-first century the California Gold Rush and World War II clearly transformed the American West.

The recent phenomenal growth of Las Vegas, Nevada, provides still another example of an ever-changing, diverse American West. A city of only 126,000 residents in 1970, Las Vegas had more than doubled in size a decade later. Booming to 740,000 in 1990, the city gained 650,000 new residents in the following decade and became the fastest-growing metropolis in the United States by 2000. Futurists were predicting more than two million residents in the Las Vegas area before 2010. Obviously gambling and tourism had fueled most of the city's swift leap ahead. With this mushrooming expansion came diverse problems. Sprawling suburbs, swelling water demands, transportation needs, additional institutions for an expanding senior citizen population, and larger requirements for schools, hospitals, and police and fire stations—they were all in exploding Las Vegas.

But the American West, here the continental region stretching from the North Dakota–to-Texas range of states to the Pacific Coast, has always been a region of rapid, constant change. These three illuminative happenings, as well as dozens of other dramatic events, transformed economic, social, and cultural life within the West. As a result, the stories historians tell about the American West must, of necessity, focus on the two hallmarks of western identity: change and complexity. This book is a new overview of the America West, and it emphasizes these two interrelated regional themes.

The ideas of change and complexity need further explanation. Even though the interconnected themes of quick change and persisting complexity mark many regional and national histories, they hold particular import for understanding the western past. The sudden, tragic impact of European diseases on Native tribes, the overnight transformation of several subregions of the West during nineteenth-century mining rushes and World War II, as well as the explosion of population in recent Las Vegas—all these dramatic transformations tell us much. They and numerous other happenings illustrate the ongoing, headlong changes repeatedly altering the West. Change has coursed through the American West as a result of the meeting of competing cultures, of changes in how people labor and produce goods for sale, and of varying human responses to the environment.

A lasting diversity also marks the western past: First the differences among prehistoric peoples and among hundreds of Indian tribes and cultures at the time of first white contact; then the varied western subregions that emerged in the nineteenth and twentieth centuries; next the racial and ethnic complexities of the West in the late twentieth and early twenty-first centuries. The American West has always hosted diverse sociocultural groups. The modern West, still reflecting this diversity, is home to more racial and ethnic minorities than any other section of the United States, especially in its numbers of Indian, Hispanic, and Asian Americans. Consider too that in its rapid development, California has become the most urban American state, with most of its population residing in towns, cities, and metropolitan cores; it is also the richest state agriculturally. At once and at the same time the American West remains the most urban region of the United States yet also contains more open spaces between those areas than other U.S. regions. The main purpose of this history is to tell the story of these changes and complexities so central to understanding the American West.

~

In the past three generations, scholars have fundamentally altered their histories of western change and complexity. During the first half of the twentieth century, most authorities on the American West followed the ideas of historian Frederick Jackson Turner and accepted the Turner or "frontier" thesis. Turnerians argued that the western past was part of a frontier experience gradually moving from the eastern to the western coasts of the United States. These histories emphasized the achievements of westward-moving pioneers, although by the 1950s frontier specialists were admitting that Indians had been pushed aside and mistreated in this coast-to-coast movement.

In the late 1960s and early 1970s, other historians began revising Turnerian interpretations of the western past. These scholars emphasized minority racial and ethnic groups, with women and families also frequently playing larger roles in their stories. Within the next decade and a half—by the mid-1980s—additional attention was devoted to these subjects as well as to environmental topics and clashes between classes in the West.

Western historiography then moved in a significant new direction in the years from the mid-1980s to the mid-1990s. In this decade, the provocative New Western history was born. Especially revealing of this emerging movement were Patricia Nelson Limerick's path-breaking synthesis, *Legacy of Conquest: The Unbroken Past of the American West* (1987); the Trails Conference in 1989—engineered in large part by Professor Limerick and eventuating in a widely cited collection of essays, *Trails: Toward a New Western History* (1991); and Richard White's massive overview, *"It's Your Misfortune and None of My Own": A History of the American West* (1991). Increased emphases on race, class, and gender; stress on the greedy, destructive nature of capitalism and its adherents; and extensive discussions of environmental depredations—these were key flashpoints in the histories of Limerick, White, and other writers such as Donald Worster, Peggy Pascoe, and Ramón Gutiérrez. In addition, the works of these New Western historians were much less optimistic than earlier accounts of the West. Even though a few critics scored these works as excessively negative, most students of the American West accepted the New Western history. Its advocates seemed to have captured the western field by the mid-1990s.

∼

But soon, by the turn of the twenty-first century, the New Western history appeared to be less dominant. Dissenting rivals pointed to what they considered the one-sided, presentist, and negative tone and conclusions of these revisionist writers. More importantly, however, other historians, neither apologists for the earlier frontier thesis of Frederick Jackson Turner nor proponents for the New Western history, were publishing books displaying increasing complexity in their coverage of the West. Two examples of these new works should suffice. Elliott West's *The Contested Plains: Indians, Goldseekers, and the Rush to*

Colorado (1998) provides a wonderfully written, stimulating account of Native American and Anglo American interactions with their changing environments and with one another. After contact, these peoples compete and conflict, but sometimes they even combine their cultures in West's superbly balanced and intricate story. Without taking sides, without denigrating either society, West's book symbolizes what a complex western story can and should be.

Walter Nugent's thorough demographic history of the American West, *Into the West: The Story of Its People* (1999), tells an equally attractive and complicated story. Beginning with prehistoric times and carrying his account to the present, Nugent discusses the numerous groups of people who have relocated to the West in more than four centuries of immigration. Like Elliott West, Nugent spins an appealingly complex narrative, treating the conflicts as well as the conversations that took place among these groups. Both writers provide a nuanced western past, refreshingly devoid of new heroes and old villains. As one reviewer put it, in treating all these varied peoples and cultures, writers like Elliott West and Walter Nugent avoided writing triumphalist *or* condemnatory history. Their books provide the kinds of complex, varied accounts we need in western history. Revealingly, both volumes were given the Caughey Prize, the coveted book-of- the-year award from the Western History Association.

~

This western history also aims at a complex narrative of the American West. I am convinced that this is the most realistic and defensible view one can now take of this subject. For example, as historians David Weber, and more recently James F. Brooks, and other Borderlands scholars remind us, we must avoid viewing the eighteenth-century Southwest as solely a series of ongoing conflicts. Instead, we should realize that after the Pueblo Revolt of 1680 and de Vargas's Reconquest in the mid-1690s, Pueblo Indians and the Spanish found they were inextricably linked to one another—economically, militarily, religiously, and sometimes racially. Indeed, out of these contacts evolved a new society, the Hispanic culture, neither Old World nor New World but a complex combination of the two.

Nineteenth-century figures such as Padre José Martínez, doña Tules, John McLoughlin, and Brigham Young were similarly complicated figures. Kit Carson also remains an intriguingly complex western figure. Although scholars and popularizers in the late nineteenth and early twentieth centuries usually saluted Carson as an adventurous frontier hero, outspoken revisionists of the past generation have harpooned him as little more than an "Indian killer." Truth to tell, Carson's story is more entangled than either side suggests. Yes, he killed Indians, as did most scouts and many others on the frontier, and he was involved in the unfortunate and tragic relocation of the Navajo to the Bosque Redondo. Still, Carson married and had a child with one Indian woman, was considered a superb agent by the Ute Indians, and opposed the relocation of the Navajo. Later, he married a Hispanic woman, and they were parents of seven living children. Kit Carson, then, was a culture broker, the kind of complex figure this text will emphasize.

Or, consider the labyrinthine careers of twentieth-century figures like Hiram Johnson, Sister Aimee McPherson, Georgia O'Keeffe, Lyndon B. Johnson, and César Chávez. They too led lives too untidy to be easily forced into molds of heroism or villainy. Utilizing the sociocultural messiness of historical characters like these, this history follows the mediating stance of Wallace Stegner, our Wise Man of the West, on history: "I have been convinced for a long time," Stegner wrote, "that what is mistakenly called the middle of the road is actually the most radical and the most difficult position—much more difficult and radical than either reaction or rebellion."

In short, this book follows neither the too-optimistic, homogenized perspective of the Turnerian school of historians or the less optimistic, conflictual approach of the New Western historians. To abandon the former to take up the latter is to exchange one narrowness for another. My devotion to complexity leads me to draw on both views, noting successes as well as failures in the western past. In every chapter of the text, in numerous pen portraits, I provide examples of the complexities and persistent changes that characterize the history of the American West. When historians place as much emphasis on cultural crossroads, compromises, and communities as on confrontations and conflicts, they write more comprehensive, persuasive—and useful—western history.

CHAPTER ONE

Western Landscapes and First Peoples

~

IMAGINE THE FIRST HUMAN AS AN AMBITIOUS, CURIOUS TRAVELER CRISS-crossing the earliest American West, seeing and pondering the region's chief physical features. Send the visitor back through the West in the coming centuries, asking that traveler to tell of the changes he or she saw and experienced. Our peripatetic wanderer begins at the Mississippi River, before it and other places had names, and moves westward, zigzagging across the northern Plains and Rockies to the Pacific Coast. Then, moving down the coast, the indefatigable wayfarer returns through the Southwest, to the southern Plains, and on to the Mississippi. Our intrepid traveler will encounter vast prairies and plains, jagged mountains, plateaus, interior valleys and basins, the West Coast, the arid Southwest, and subhumid southern Plains. In passing through these varied landscapes, our sightseer will be forced to skirt natural barriers, cross several rivers, traverse the highest mountains in what will become the United States, and challenge the region's demanding deserts.

Our inquisitive vagabond will also visit many of the distant, out-of-the-way western spots, as well as well-known sites like the Badlands, the Grand Canyon, the Great Salt Lake, and Death Valley. He or she will discover what hundreds of thousands—even millions—of later explorers, travelers, immigrants, and tourists have realized: physically, the American West is several regions, varying greatly in topography and landscapes from subregion to subregion.

If our journeyer could revisit the West each half-century thereafter, a second truth would come into focus about this huge space. Notable changes continually disrupt and transform the landscapes, peoples, and cultures of the American West. Despite stereotypes to the contrary, thousands of years ago humans were already beginning to plant their footprints on western terrains. These first peoples, and many subsequent generations, transformed the region century after century. These two hallmarks, diversity and change, have marked the American West from prehistoric times, through first European contacts, through the nineteenth and twentieth centuries, and up to the present. If both a time and geographical traveler, our wanderer would realize an additional truth: from the earliest inhabitants to the most recent immigrants, humans have added still another ingredient to western identity by continually revisioning and redefining the American West. So, clear differences, rapid transformations, and shifting interpretive viewpoints remain important for helping us to understand the western past.

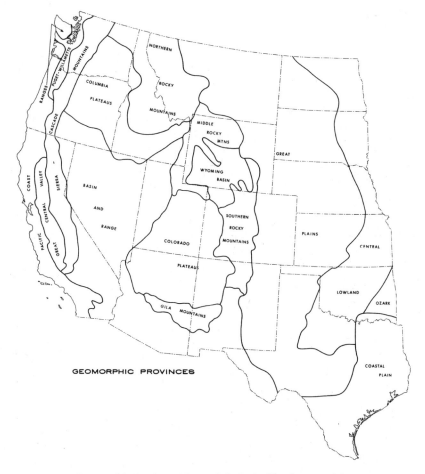

FIGURE 1:1. *Geomorphic Provinces.* The varied physical landscapes of the American West are a powerful force in influencing the number and kind of settlements in the region. From Warren A. Beck and Ynez D. Haase, *Historical Atlas of the American West*, map 2. Copyright © 1989 by the University of Oklahoma Press, Norman. Reprinted by permission of the publisher. All rights reserved.

~

The American West encompasses four major topographical regions from the Mississippi River to the Pacific Coast. These regions, moving from east to west, are (1) the Plains and prairies; (2) the Rocky Mountains; (3) the intermountain region between the Rockies and coastal mountains, including the Columbia and Colorado plateaus; and (4) the Pacific Coast, consisting of coastal ranges, valleys, and coastlines. Stretching across the southern reaches of the Rockies and the intermountain area and into the Pacific Coast region is the region's largest desert. Except for the earliest humans (and later, Canadians) arriving from the north and those moving north from Mexico, most migrants to the American West have arrived from the American East or the Asian Far East. The majority of the newcomers faced the taxing challenges of crossing the Plains, mountains, and deserts—whether from the east or from the Orient. Until well into the twentieth century, new arrivals to the West had to learn how to navigate through or surmount these natural barriers if they were to traverse the West in a direct route. But in the past half-century, air travel, superhighways, irrigation empires, new forms of technology, and increasing emphases on "footloose industries" (high-tech and computer companies) have aided migrants in overcoming these earlier natural impediments. Built landscapes also have begun to dominate many sections of the West. Still, during most of the region's history its varied natural landscapes have profoundly shaped the kinds of settlements made here. To comprehend the West's history is to understand human interactions with the varied contours of its natural setting.

~

Travelers from the east experienced forbidding new terrain and landscapes once they crossed what became the first tier of states west of the Mississippi. Passing over the 100th meridian stretching from North Dakota to Texas, newcomers discovered ground cover different from that of their previous experiences. Trees were nearly nonexistent, except for those small but notable stands lining scattered river and creek banks. Generally water was scarce, rainfall light, and soils resistant to plowing. At the eastern edges of the Great Plains were the grasslands where more than adequate rainfall fell, allowing those fertile soils to produce abundant tall grasses. Farther west were the short grasslands, subhumid areas with less than twenty inches of rainfall. Mountains to the west of the Plains blocked moist winds blowing in from the Pacific, limiting most of the Plains to about fifteen inches of rain, insufficient precipitation to support widespread row-crop agriculture. These level lands, sometimes visualized as a sea of grass, inclined upward on their western edges, leading very gradually toward the Rocky Mountains. On the drier, southern edges of the Plains, grasses disappeared, leaving mesquite or desert grass coverage.

The Plains hosted an unusual cast of animals. The most exotic species for newcomers was the buffalo, or bison. For centuries, these heavy, clumsy, hairy beasts served as four-legged commissaries for earlier inhabitants and later for Plains Indians, furnishing meat, cloth, tools, and fuel ("buffalo chips," or dung). Perhaps as many as twenty-five million buffalo roamed the eastern Plains before their slaughter began in the mid-nineteenth century. Indeed, until the 1860s the buffalo were the most significant species of western animal life. Twenty years later nearly all buffalo were gone, an unmistakable example of how rapidly the West could change. The disappearance of the buffalo greatly diminished Indian abilities to withstand nature's other demands on the Plains. Two other animals, the jackrabbit and the coyote, noted pests and scavengers in many parts of the Plains, plagued pioneer farmers and ranchers well into the twentieth century. One Texan, following tenaciously held western beliefs, asserted that a jackrabbit could "eat as much as a horse" and that coyotes were "arrant cowards," "outlaws of the Plains," and "enemies of all animals, especially those in misfortune."

The size, height, and appearance of the Rocky Mountains astounded firstcomers. If their extensions north into Canada and Alaska and south into Mexico are included, the Rockies are the earth's longest mountain chain. Towering often more than 8,000 feet, the Rockies included more than fifty peaks soaring above 14,000 feet. With the tallest peak east of the Mississippi limited to 6,290 feet above sea level, the Rockies struck eastern travelers and tourists as stony edifices looming into the clouds. These lofty heights, laden with snow and featuring jagged facades, were the original water source for several of the West's most notable river systems. The Rocky Mountains captured much of the moisture missing from lands immediately to the east and west. Once melted, the immense snow cover of the Rockies, sometimes twenty-five feet deep, fed the Missouri, Mississippi, and Rio Grande systems to the east and the Snake and Columbia rivers to the west. The streams flowing down both sides of the Continental Divide also provided water for other individual rivers: the Yellowstone to the east, the Colorado and Green to the southwest, the Arkansas and Platte to the southeast, and the Rio Grande to the south. The huge snow accumulations and other precipitation in the Rockies became the greatest water reservoir for the American West.

The Rockies were not an alpine chain of equal width from north to south. Up and down their length the mountains expanded or narrowed to include the fertile valleys and upland meadows of Montana, Wyoming, and Colorado. An unusual east-to-west passageway, later named the South Pass, also snaked through the mountains in south-central and southwestern Wyoming. This high plateau allowed wagoners and later highway builders to cross the one open route through the seemingly impenetrable northern Rockies.

The Rockies also displayed a variety of ground coverage from north to south and east to west. In the lower elevations of the Plains Zone (4,000 to 6,000 feet) short grasses predominated, with scattered smaller willows, pines, and cottonwoods growing near sources of water. Ponderosa pines character-ized the drier areas of the Montane Zone (6,000 to 9,000 feet). The Subalpine (9,000 to 11,000) and Alpine zones (11,500 and up) hosted spruce trees at their lower levels but not much higher up because trees could not survive at those elevations. The stands of timber at the lower levels became resources widely utilized by pioneer woodsmen and miners.

For others the Rockies proved to be a gold mine, sometimes literally. Rich in gold, silver, and other precious mineral deposits, the mountain slopes and streambeds also yielded up enormous finds in copper, coal, and a variety of

FIGURE 1:2. *The Rocky (or "Great Stony") Mountains.* The Rocky Mountains astounded first-time visitors to the West. These travelers also rarely understood that melting snow packs in the mountains were a major water source for the river systems of the northern West. Courtesy Idaho State Historical Society, 63–35.19.

other minerals. In addition, for three or four decades in the first half of the nineteenth century, incoming hunters and trappers found the mountains alive with beaver, deer, goats, and a large assortment of birds. But mountain men and fur trappers, miners, and exuberant boomtowners wreaked havoc on the Rockies in the nineteenth century. Streams were quickly stripped of their beaver, creek and river beds destroyed by avaricious miners, and pristine mountain meadows overrun with boomtowns. Although these nineteenth-century events tragically altered Rocky Mountain landscapes, hard-learned lessons from these environmental disasters and changed attitudes about them did not come about until much later in the twentieth century.

~

West of the Rockies, a series of plateaus, basins, and deserts alternated from north to south. For the most part these areas contained some of the hottest, semiarid, arid, and least peopled sections of the American West. Hemmed in by mountains to the west, east, and north, this intermountain subregion received little rainfall. The natural landscapes of these interior sections of the West clearly reflected this aridity.

The intermountain region divided into four major parts. The Columbia Plateau in the north included much of eastern Washington and Oregon and southern Idaho. The Basin and Range section spread over most of Nevada and western Utah. The Colorado Plateau included southern Utah and western Colorado along with extensive parts of northeastern Arizona and northwestern New Mexico. The desert rim stretched across the southern edge of the Intermountain West, from west Texas to the eastern edges of southern California.

The flora and fauna of the intermountain area varied markedly from north to south. Forested lands covered large parts of northern Washington and northeastern Oregon. Eastern Oregon contained fertile farm areas in the north, with drier grazing areas predominating in the south. The Snake River plain was also arid country, but since the early 1900s irrigation systems have provided much-needed water for potato, cereal, and other row crops of southern Idaho farmers. Most of Nevada and much of the Colorado Plateau was even more arid, as in northern Arizona and New Mexico. The intriguing natural wonders of these areas, including the Grand Canyon, Zion and Bryce Canyons, Capitol Reef, and Canyonlands, became tourist destinations as well as getaway sites for backpackers and river runners.

Extending across the southern reaches of the Rocky Mountain and Intermountain regions, stretching from Texas to California, was the largest desert country of the United States. This arid section covered large parts of New

Mexico, Arizona, Nevada, California, and Utah. Other desert-like subregions extended into smaller areas of Oregon, Idaho, Colorado, Wyoming, and Texas. Most of these western desert areas betrayed one overwhelming characteristic: they were arid, often experiencing less than ten inches of unpredictable rainfall. Sometimes these desert areas received more than half of their annual rainfall in summer thunderstorms, sending flash torrents roaring down arroyos and canyons. In addition the high temperatures in the desert regions often evaporated the scarce rainfall before it was available to plants and animals. Plants like the ocotillo, paloverde, and mesquite accommodated to these drought-like or arid conditions. Members of the cactus family were particularly adept at storing water. It is estimated, for instance, that a fifty-foot-high saguaro cactus, after a downpour, might weigh ten tons, nine of which were stored water. On more than a few occasions thirsty persons were able to wet their parched throats by tapping into water stored in a cactus.

Farther west the Pacific Coast area encompassed the Sierra Nevada and Cascade mountain chains, the Pacific Northwest and California interior valleys, the coastal range of mountains, and the coastal plains and shores. The Cascade–Sierra Nevada ranges included several of the country's highest mountains: Mt. Whitney (14,495 feet) in California, Mt. Rainier (14,408), in Washington, and Mt. Hood (11,225) in Oregon. Between these lofty ranges and the coastal mountains lay the fertile valleys of the Northwest and California. These verdant troughs included the Willamette Valley in Oregon and Washington and the fertile but drier central valleys of California. California's spectacular Yosemite Valley (now national park) and Oregon's beautiful, deep Crater Lake were natural jewels of this intermountain channel.

The far-western coastal areas from central California north to the Canadian border were among the wettest regions of the United States. Like the eastern ends of the American West, the northern Pacific Coast enjoyed heavy annual rainfalls. On the coast north of the Bay Area in California, storms from November to March often dropped more than 50 inches of rain on heavily forested areas; some sections received as much as 100 inches of rain. In these moist and cool locations one found some of the world's tallest trees (the coastal redwoods) and the bulkiest (sequoias).

At the other end of the coastal ranges in the state of Washington was the Olympic Peninsula, covered with lush green forests and a rich variety of ferns and other plant life. Here lay one of the wettest regions of the entire earth with annual rainfall averaging 120 to 140 inches, and a few places deluged with 180 inches. The Peninsula, writes one regional historian, was "a veritable evergreen jungle."

The diverse subregions of California provided yet another example of the complexity of the West. The Sierra Nevada proved that California was a mountainous region, the redwood forests proved it was a richly forested area, the central valleys proved (once they were watered) that California was fertile valleys, and, finally, the southern interior deserts proved that California was a desert. Truth to tell, California was all these. And the terrains and climates that made up California were generally true of the Pacific Coast region. It too was rainy, forested, and fertile, but it too contained arid and infertile areas.

The varied animal and plant life of the Pacific Coast region illustrated the distinct landscapes of the area. Early visitors to the coastal regions spoke of the teeming beaver of the inland streams, the abundant sea otter along the coasts of Oregon and Washington, and the trout- and salmon-filled streams of the northern Pacific Coast. Once non-Indians arrived in California and the Pacific Northwest, the meadows and hillsides became rich grazing lands for hundreds of thousands of cattle and sheep. From the mid-nineteenth century onward American miners discovered and mined the abundant lodes of gold, silver, and other minerals that many coastal states contained. Probably these hordes of undisciplined miners did more to ruin pristine mountainsides and creeks and rivers and to befoul clean, limpid streams than any other newcomers to the West.

The variety of forests and plants in the Pacific Coastal areas greatly impressed tens of thousands of first-time visitors. Of course the gigantic redwoods and sequoias of California and the mammoth Douglas firs of the Northwest have attracted attention throughout the centuries. East of the coastal and Cascade ranges in the Pacific Northwest one encountered scattered forests as well as near-desert scablands covered with sagebrush and other semiarid ground coverage. But farther east the fertile Palouse Country of eastern Washington has spawned some of the most abundant wheat crops in the entire world.

A similar complexity characterizes the landscapes of California. Moving eastward and once beyond the heavily forested areas on the northern coastal areas, one discovers the interior valleys of California. They too have become a veritable farmers' market, producing a larger variety of fruit, vegetables, and other crops than any other region in the United States. It is here in the cornucopia of these interior, irrigated valleys that California has become our richest agricultural state. Before the Spanish and Americans arrived in the eighteenth and nineteenth centuries, Native groups found the valleys and mountains of California overflowing with fish, small animals, and acorns. The coastal and valley Indians of California particularly benefited from an abundance of marine animals, birds, and small mammals. It is not surprising that some of the very areas where Indians found so much to sustain them before contact have become the most populated areas of modern California.

∽

)

Native Americans and scholars furnish divergent accounts of human beginnings in the American West. One of these important sources of information about the region's first peoples is the stories Indians tell about their ancestors in the American West. Like Judeo-Christian people who believe the Genesis narrative of the Bible, many Indians accept their individual creation stories as the most believable accounts of their tribal origins. For these Native Americans, creation stories provide veracious narratives of Indian origins, furnish powerful and hopeful reminders of their people's sacred history, and include cherished celebrations of their much-loved homelands.

At the end of the nineteenth century a Wichita Indian man of the southern Plains told the story of his tribe's origins in this way. "When the earth was created it was composed of land and water," he began, "but they were not separated. The land was floating on the water, and darkness was everywhere." The only person in existence, Man Never Known on Earth, created the world, including a male named Having Power to Carry Light and a female companion, Bright Shining Woman. These two traveled to villages where other humans "knew neither where they had come from nor how to live." Having Power to Carry Light showed men how to construct bows and arrows and become hunters, and Bright Shining Woman taught women to plant and harvest corn. After carrying out their missions they disappeared into the sky to become a star and the moon.

Several ingredients of the Wichita creation story are common to other Indian stories of the world's origins and human beginnings. In these narratives a god-like figure usually brings order out of chaos or at least out of an inchoate, partially finished world. That newly created world includes a man and woman who frequently conceive the first child. It is the parents' duty to teach their children—or other humans they encounter—their responsibilities as the world's first citizens. Often there is an opposing evil force that challenges the world's first family for supremacy.

Readers with Judeo-Christian backgrounds will recognize intriguing parallels between the Garden of Eden story of the Old Testament and the plot lines of many Indian creation stories. Like the first chapters of the book of Genesis, creation stories attempt to answer the compelling questions of human existence: Is there a God? If so, how did He create the world? Who were the first humans, what were they like, and what were their duties? How did evil become part of this God-created world?

Even though nearly all creation stories addressed some of these central cosmological questions, their content varied from tribe to tribe throughout the American West. In the Southwest, the Pueblos told emergence stories in which the first humans entered this world from a dark underground cavern, something like a womb or a kiva (a site of religious celebration). For the Kiowas humans entered the world through a hole in a log until a pregnant woman swollen with child blocked the passage and kept others from coming into this world. That was the reason there were so few Kiowas. The Brulé Sioux of the northern Great Plains told of a huge flood that destroyed the world except for a beautiful young woman saved by an eagle. They mate, produce twins, and that boy and girl become the father and mother, the progenitors, of the Lakota nation. The Modocs of southern Oregon and northern California tell the story of Kumush, the Old Man of the Ancients, who descends into "the underground world of the spirits" with his daughter. They gather up the bones of the underground spirits, and, after several tries, scatter the bones abroad in the "upper world." Some of these bones come alive as Modocs. They "will be the bravest of all . . . [Kumush's] chosen people."

The creation stories not only speak of the world's origins, they also reveal much about how the created world should operate. Just as the Wichita story made clear that Indian men were to be hunters and Indian women farmers, so in the Brulé Sioux narrative the mother nurtures and instructs the children. In the Zuni creation story of the Southwest, the Sky-father impregnates the world, helping to create Earth-mother. They become parents and discuss how to teach their children the lessons they will need to survive. In these and other narratives the offspring are instructed to plant corn and carefully till and thankfully utilize the earth's fecundity.

These stories reveal still other worldviews of Native Americans, for instance, Indian convictions about the unities of human, animal, and natural worlds. Frequently the male and female creators are Father Sky and Mother Earth. Male humans sometimes mate with female animals, female humans with birds or animals. Animals also represent human characteristics. White Rabbit, Wolf, Toad, Raven, and a host of other animals, like characters out of the ancient Aesop fables or the American Br'er Rabbit and Br'er Fox tales, epitomize the light and dark of human actions. The most notorious of these people-like animals is Coyote. Sometimes a lustful, evil trickster, sometimes a courageous leader, as in the Nez Perce story of the Pacific Northwest, Coyote appears as a major figure in many tribal stories.

The creation stories likewise suggest much about a tribe's relations with neighboring Native Americans, even before contacts with Euroamericans. In the Modoc story, when Kumush and his daughter arrive in this world with the bones of the underworld spirits, they scatter the bones and create the Shasta and Warm Springs tribes. These tribes will be strong warriors. But when the father and daughter throw out the bones to begin the Klamath tribe, Kumush says of these people, "You'll be as easy to frighten as women are. You won't be good warriors."

Like the Modoc narrative, most of the Indian creation stories are pregnant with meanings about human origins, the unities of human and natural worlds, and the divergent roles men and women are to play in this life. Read sympathetically and analytically, the Indian creation narratives help us to understand, more fully, important features of Native worldviews and cultures.

~

Many archaeologists and historians tell different stories. They argue that the first westerners migrated from Siberia, crossing the Bering Strait toward the end of the Pleistocene, or Ice, Age. They then roamed south to the American West. A few anthropologists speculate that these migrations began as far back as 75,000 years ago; even more argue that the movements across the Bering came as recently as 18,000 to 15,000 years in the past. Nearly all conclude that the earliest Americans crossed over a land bridge, known as Beringia, which connected Asia and North America during a time of lower ocean levels. These prehistoric people, whose southward route was blocked for centuries by a gigantic ice sheet covering much of present-day Canada, possibly found a western passageway through the glaciers, or they may have traveled south by water along the far-western coasts. Most scholars conclude that substantial groups of these newcomers had arrived in the American West by 12,000 to 11,000 BC. Fanning out, they occupied several subregions of the West, stretching from the Mississippi Valley to the Pacific Coast. Recent discoveries in Chile suggest that humans may have arrived in North and South America even earlier.

Who were these Paleo-Indian or Pleistocene people who first came to the trans-Mississippi West? Why did their ways of life seem to disappear by about 8000 BC? Archaeological discoveries near Folsom and Clovis, New Mexico, help answer some of these hotly disputed questions. At these two sites, as well as at others in the Southwest, bison and mammoth (large, elephant-like creatures) bones; a collection of spear "points"; and other skeletal and implement remains reveal that these ancient Paleo-Indians were big-game hunters, known later as Folsom Man or Clovis People. Using spears with intricately fluted points, these ancient peoples ranged over expansive territories, hunting mammoths, sloths, bison, and other huge animals. The meaty bison, perhaps weighing as much as one thousand pounds, served these early men and women much as the all-purpose buffalo did the Plains Indians centuries later. One archaeologist estimated that if a bison were killed twice a week, hunters would gain one thousand pounds of meat, providing a group of twelve to fifteen persons with about fifteen pounds of meat each day. Quite possibly the megafauna (the big-game animals) determined the locations of base camps and kill sites; as the quarry migrated, so did their trackers. Kill sites have been discovered in several parts of North America. The slightly earlier remains of Clovis People

Early Cultures in New Mexico

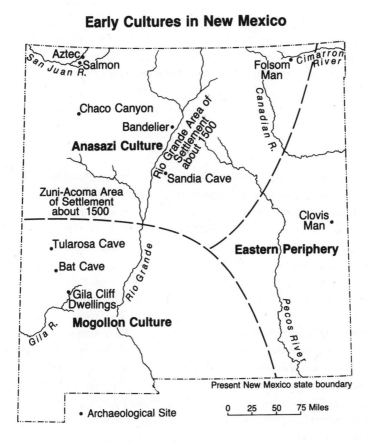

FIGURE 1:3. *Early Cultures in New Mexico.* Archaeologists made important discoveries about the Folsom Man and Clovis People in the Southwest. Anasazi and Mogollon cultures also emerged in what is modern-day New Mexico. From Calvin A. Roberts and Susan A. Roberts, *New Mexico* (Albuquerque: University of New Mexico Press, 1988), 7.

are widely scattered, with the Folsom remains largely in the Southwest, Plains, and southern Rockies. The Pleistocene people were also gatherers of varied kinds of plant food.

Most of our limited understanding of these Paleo-Indians comes from their kill sites and base camps. We know them primarily as skilled users of stone and bone implements, their "tool kits." Perhaps like other late Stone Age people they traveled in small bands of twenty-five to fifty persons. Spear points, bones, hearths, and other debris at excavations suggest that these Pleistocene peoples probably lived much of their lives as nomadic hunters. The spear points discovered at Clovis, Folsom, and other southwestern sites are often similar to those found elsewhere in North America for this era. Even though these groups may have had contacts with humans nearby, they seemed primarily to set up base camps close to their hunting and killing areas. Often the kill sites were near rivers, other watered areas, and bogs; the hunters undoubtedly drove the megafauna into these places, where they were easier to trap and kill.

~

Toward the end of the Pleistocene and the beginning of the Holocene or Archaic period (about 9000 to 8000 BC) the big-game animals disappeared. Had the hunters killed off their major food source? Some anthropologists think so. Other scholars argue that dramatic climatic shifts transformed land surfaces and vegetation, drastically reducing food supplies for the megabeasts, thus changing the lives of the hunters. As a result, fewer kill sites are evident; more contain the remains of earlier, larger bison; and settlements were now closer to water and grass, implying that plant gathering became more important to these ancient men and women.

So marked were these transformations that archaeologists call the centuries following 8000 the Archaic or Holocene period. Peoples of the Archaic Era turned to new sources of food to survive. To replace the big-game animals, they searched for smaller quarry such as rabbits, deer, and birds. They also fished. But the largest adjustment came in their gathering habits. Archaic men and women became "gathering gourmets," collecting numerous seeds, roots, berries, and nuts.

Other changes in Holocene material culture and lifeways resulted from these shifts in their food chain. Stones for grinding seeds and baskets for gathering plant foods began to appear. Snares likewise reveal the growing dependence of Archaic hunters on rabbits. These seed-gathering and snaring efforts probably involved men and women alike, possibly closing the previous divisions of sexual labor in earlier societies.

Over the many centuries of the middle and later Holocene periods (6000–5000 BC to 300–200 BC) the lifestyles of Archaic men and women, although undergoing continual change, nonetheless solidified into a few recognizable patterns. Rather than following the nomadic living patterns of the Pleistocene peoples, most Archaic communities settled closer to well-watered areas, small lakes, or canyons where they could capture animals and gather plant foods. Learning the rhythms of smaller animals, birds, and fish, these ancient people adapted to those cycles, migrating to take advantage of annual patterns. Archaic residents were obviously suiting their lives to the seasonal cycles of their food sources. Perhaps new waves of migrants from Asia, Alaska, or Canada also moved into the American West during the Archaic period, bringing with them other implements and experiences and adding to the complex transitions taking place during the long Holocene period.

In the Southwest the most important common ingredient among Archaic men and women was a gradual, clear turn toward agriculture. Perhaps as early as 1500 BC, or possibly even earlier, crops from Mexico were being introduced into the Southwest. First Mexican corn and then later squash and beans were the most widely cultivated crops. Still, the step-by-step transition to agriculture did not mean the end of earlier hunting and gathering systems. Cultivation began as an endeavor to supplement the other food supplies of the hunters and gatherers. In the centuries following 1000 BC, late Archaic peoples continued hunting small animals and collecting wild plants. With the megafauna now extinct, deer, antelope, a wide variety of birds and fishes, and rodents were targeted quarry. Even as they continued hunting, Archaic peoples were betraying their increasing reliance on horticulture. They built storage pits for corn and other products. They dug wells, suggesting the need for more water for burgeoning populations and agricultural efforts. Other signals of the more sedentary ways were the technical advancements in pottery and basket making.

New forms of housing also reveal the in situ ways of the villages of the last centuries BC and the first centuries AD. Families usually moved from campsites to pit houses and on to permanent villages. These new types of homes were clustered in small towns of aggregated family huts or pit houses. Settlements now expanded in numbers beyond the twenty-five to fifty people who had inhabited the earlier, more nomadic camps.

≈

In the later stages of the Archaic era and in the centuries immediately following, these early human settlements began to exhibit more regional varieties. Eventually these areas or subregions (anthropologists call them *culture areas*) evolved into identifiably different cultures. Holocene communities, for the most part, became increasingly tied to the varied food sources of their locations. Northwest Coast persons enjoyed a particularly rich diet of fish and shellfish. They also hunted sea animals such as seals, otters, and whales. Those living along the California coast also enjoyed abundant food from the sea, such as oysters, clams, fish, sea lions, and dolphins. Both of these areas were served well with food sources close at hand. Western Archaic peoples in the Great Basin areas (Nevada, Utah, and parts of California, Oregon, Idaho, and Wyoming) faced larger challenges. In these semiarid areas families had to migrate to find food, foraging for rather than growing food. In a southeastern area near the confluence of the Mississippi and Arkansas rivers, later labeled Poverty Point, gourds and squashes, fish and shellfish were important food sources.

Centuries before first European contact, the early peoples developed trade systems that crisscrossed large sections of the West. Networks of exchange carried shells, for example, from the California coast to the Great Basin and returned obsidian to the Pacific Coast. When the Spanish did arrive in the sixteenth century in the Southwest they found that the Pueblo Indians of that region were trading their corn for the buffalo meat and hides of the Plains peoples. Trade fairs were also in place in precontact times. Pueblo communities at Taos and Pecos had already been established as important trade centers. Most often this intercultural trade in varied parts of the West involved the exchange of agricultural products of the horticultural people for the foods that hunters and gatherers collected.

Because of its dry climate and relatively undisturbed archaeological sites, the Southwest provides the richest traces of these trade networks as well as evidences of the evolving cultural areas leading to more stable village life. In the period from about 200 BC to AD 600–800 the Hohokam, Mogollon, and Anasazi cultures emerged. Living in the arid, demanding environment of southern Arizona, the Hohokam people created "the largest permanent irrigation systems in ancient North America to bring water to the desert and grow crops, and they built communities and developed regional exchange networks." Farther east in southwestern and south-central New Mexico, the Mogollon people often situated their villages on tops of mesas, allowing for a greater measure of protection. They too were farmers but did not utilize irrigation. Gradually the Mogollon people transformed their crude pit houses of wood, brush, and mud to aboveground, joined houses much like those the historic Pueblo people erected.

By approximately AD 800 the northern Mogollon communities were gradually losing out to an expansive, stronger group of newcomers. These flourishing peoples were the Anasazi, the most widely discussed village culture of the Southwest. In the language of the Navajo, the modern-day Native Americans who inhabit much of the earlier Anasazi homelands, the word *Anasazi* means "old ones." Like the Hohokam and Mogollon, the Anasazi emerged at the end of the Archaic period. At AD 1000 they were the dominant culture of the Southwest.

Anthropologists, attempting to make sense of the long period from the end of the Archaic period (200 to 100 BC) to the first contacts with invading Europeans in the 1500s, divide Anasazi history into two lengthy epochs. These are the Basket Maker periods from about 100 BC to AD 700 and the Pueblo periods from AD 700 to European contact. During the eight hundred years or so of Basket Maker history, the Anasazi became increasingly sedentary, building subterranean homes with smoke holes in their ceilings and beginning to produce their first decorated pottery. Their homes often included a *sipapu* indentation in the floor, indicating that, like the later Pueblo Indians, the Anasazi may have believed that they emerged through a hole in the ground from an otherworld to life aboveground. At the end of the Basket Maker periods, sizable numbers of Anasazi lived in the Chaco Canyon of northwestern New Mexico. They had constructed kivas, underground ceremonial and religious areas; dogs had been adopted as hunting companions or pets; and animal hides and plant fibers continued to be the main sources for clothing and sandals.

During the Pueblo period after AD 700 the Anasazi became even more rooted and increasingly village-situated. They also began living in aboveground homes, clustered in villages of apartment-like dwellings. These congregated villages were usually located near water sources and farmlands. During the century or so following AD 1000, Anasazi culture flourished. The Anasazi built new or expanded existing large buildings for which they became particularly noted: the cliff dwellings of Mesa Verde in Colorado and Canyon de Chelly in Arizona, the extensive buildings near Aztec, New Mexico, and the sprawling villages in Chaco Canyon.

The Anasazi culture in the Southwest reached the pinnacle of its achievement in Chaco Canyon. By the time of the Classic Bonito Phase (AD 1020–1120) the Anasazi towns in the canyon area had expanded to sixteen. The nearly four hundred settlements scattered up and down the canyon hosted probably as many as five or six thousand inhabitants. Much of the population was centered in a few large towns on the canyon floor.

In several ways Pueblo Bonito (pretty town), the most spectacular of these settlements, represents the major achievements of Anasazi culture in the Southwest. Built in the two centuries after AD 900, the D-shaped Pueblo Bonito covered nearly five acres, loomed up four or five stories at its back, contained almost seven hundred rooms at its largest size, and may have housed up to 1,200 people. As one anthropologist notes, "no other apartment block of this scale was built in North America until the 1880s—nearly 800 years later."

In addition to its immense size and impressive architecture, the Great House at Pueblo Bonito, a town in itself, reverberated with other notable meanings. Archaeologists carefully analyzing the layout of Pueblo Bonito and other Great Houses up and down Chaco Canyon point to the symmetry of these amazing buildings. These scholars argue that the architectonic balance of the edifices' walls, rooms, and kivas illustrates the Anasazi desire for equilibrium in all things—in their creation stories, in their culture, and in their spirituality. Still other students marvel at the number of kivas at Pueblo Bonito—more than thirty—and suggest that the Great House may have been more important as a site for religious rituals than as a residence for multitudes of people.

Whatever one concludes about the exact meaning of Pueblo Bonito, and the controversies among scholars have been as fractious and combative as a series

FIGURE 1:4. *Pueblo Bonito, Chaco Canyon.* These huge, sprawling ruins of the grand Pueblo Bonito represent the magnificent achievements of the Anasazi culture that flourished from about AD 1000 to 1200. Courtesy Palace of the Governors (MNM/DCA), 36177.

of vicious dogfights, one conclusion seems acceptable to all: the immense Great House of Pueblo Bonito and the other Chaco Great Houses are an irrefutable illustration of the remarkable endurance and achievements of the Anasazi people. Together, they are commonly known as the "Chaco Phenomenon." Here in a forbidding desert (the average annual rainfall is about nine inches), the Anasazi erected a set of immense buildings, skillfully balanced and impressively constructed. The remote and demanding Chaco Canyon became, in the words of one scholar, "the setting for arguably the most breathtaking suite of buildings of the entire prehistoric epoch in the Southwest."

Then a dramatic change took place. Despite all its magnificence and strength, the Anasazi culture was at the mercy of an uncertain climate. Growing numbers of families moving to the villages also added to pressures on precarious food supplies. When a series of sustained droughts descended on the Anasazi they were forced out of their homelands, unable to feed mushrooming populations when rains failed to fall. Too many people with too little food and too much demand on a fragile agricultural environment brought an end to the Anasazi culture. Although the settlements in Chaco Canyon deserve their reputation "as the culmination of Anasazi accomplishment," they could not ward off the huge negative impacts of crop failures, the destruction of their environment, and the mounting hunger when rainfall dwindled year after year. Beginning in the 1200s the Anasazi scattered, searching for new environments that could sustain them. They moved in several directions, but the largest numbers immigrated to the upper Rio Grande valley and nearby areas. Over the next two centuries, they built new towns in these regions. There they were living when the first Spanish explorers, missionaries, and settlers marched into the far-northern frontier of New Mexico in the sixteenth century.

$\backsim$

If our peripatetic visitor, after viewing western landscapes and examining pre-historic settlements, had returned to the West for another trip through the region just before Europeans arrived, he or she would have realized again the complexity and change that have characterized western history throughout its course. The diversity of Indian cultures from east to west and north to south illustrates once again the varieties of peoples who have lived in and continually reshaped the region. Our hypothetical traveler, moving east from the Pacific Coast to the Mississippi Valley, would have encountered hundreds of tribes inhabiting varied physical and cultural regions.

The cultures of Pacific Northwest Indians living up and down the coastline from southern Alaska to northern California provide another illustration of the dissimilarities of the western past. Among those peoples of the northern half of the coast, and moving south, were the Tlingits, Haidas, Kwakiutls, the Salish coastal groups, the Chinooks, and the Tillamooks. Unlike most other western tribes, these Natives were not agriculturalists or pottery makers. But most were stable, independent, and wealthy. Their proximity to the Pacific Ocean and its abundance of food and other supplies was key to the affluent lives of these northwestern coastal tribes. Harvesting the nearby salmon, halibut, other ocean fish, and whales, the coastal tribes also made use of the rich resources of proximate rivers, streams, and forests. They likewise impressed first visitors as superb seamen, able to navigate and stay afloat on waterways in the worst of storms. The tribes to the north lived in large, solid houses of planks that contained several rooms and ornately decorated doorposts.

Early observers often mentioned the vigorous religious life of the coastal Indians. As animistic believers they saw bears, beaver, whales, and many other animals as symbols of the spirit world. These spirits must be appeased, tricked, or worshipped through elaborate rituals, ceremonies, and belief systems. Some tribes employed brightly colored masks for participation in these religious functions. Later, others erected the unique carved totem poles that served in part as historical accounts, narrating stories of past tribal deeds and family histories.

Natives of the Pacific Northwest coast likewise exhibited much stronger class concerns than many other western tribes. Even though blessed with abundance, they seemed insecure about their wealth and adopted the "potlatch" system to share and circulate their riches. At celebrations of births, weddings, or other special events a well-to-do Native man might give away his slaves, break valuable implements or personal items, or burn his food supplies. The more he destroyed the more prestige he brought to his family, clan, or tribe. But the system contained a protective feature: when others participated in similar give-aways, they in effect resupplied the goods and other belongings of the first potlatch. These ceremonies of material and social circulation struck early white visitors as curious roundabout events. For the coastal Indians, however, they were important gestures providing needed socioeconomic balance.

Whites were slow in contacting these Pacific Northwest tribes, much later than the first Europeans who came to the Southwest. True, a few European sailors touched on the northern coasts before the 1700s, but Russian fur men of the eighteenth century were the first to move in among the Northwest Indians. Tragically the cultural fallout from those fur traders and other European competitors was swift and disastrous. Conflicts among the European traders and trappers and fast-spreading diseases soon nearly wiped out several of the coastal tribes. Yet cultural survivals evidenced tribal tenacity. The Chinook Jargon, a mixture of language from the Salish and Chinook combined with French and English words, endured well into the nineteenth century as a means of verbal communication. Pierced noses and flattened heads also remained physical symbols of beauty among some tribes of the northern region. Although archaeological evidence is slim and written accounts late, these sources of information reveal that the Pacific Northwest tribes were people of material and cultural abundance at the time of first white contacts.

Native life to the south in California both resembled and differed from that of Indians in the coastal Northwest. In fact California Indians presented several cultural faces. Perhaps as many as 300,000 Indians resided in California in the mid-eighteenth century. Gathered in five hundred or more "village states," they made up one of the most populous Native areas in North America. Sebastián Vizcaíno, a Spanish explorer of the early 1600s, reported that he had traveled "more than eight hundred leagues [roughly 2,500 miles] along the coast" and that "the coast [was] populated by an endless number of Indians." Like Natives in the Northwest, California tribal groups along the Pacific Ocean were affluent, living well off the marine bounty of fish and mammals. Sustained by the natural abundance of their fertile setting, coastal Indians such as the Miwoks, Yokuts, and Chumash impressed first visitors as skilled hunters and gatherers, as peaceful, nonagressive people. They had developed complex methods of plant cultivation and utilized fire ecology to burn chaparral and other brush to encourage new buds for animal grazing and the gathering of acorns. Other tribes such as the Pomo wove intricate baskets, mats, and fish traps. The Pomo women particularly developed an elegant sense of basket artistry. Despite myths to the contrary, in no way were these California coastal lands devoid of human culture or cultivation before the arrival of Europeans.

Farther to the south dissimilar Native cultures evolved. Gabrielino, Serrano, Luiseño, and Diegueño peoples formed more complex social structures, practiced ground painting, and created a lunar calendar. They also organized a "*toloache* cult," utilizing the jimson weed for both medicinal and ritualistic purposes. Indian peoples on the eastern edge of California, including the Mohaves and the Yumas, inhabiting a more arid and forbidding terrain, planted crops to add to their limited diets. Pressured by strong competitors along the Colorado River, these Indians were forced to adopt militaristic strategies to protect their homelands.

No Native groups in the West felt the brunt of invading European and American peoples more decisively and destructively than the Indians of California. Roughly eighty years after the Spanish arrived in the 1760s and 1770s and instituted their mission and *encomienda* policies, Indian population in California had been reduced by nearly two-thirds, to about 100,000 persons. This decimation continued with the invasion of Gold Rushers in the late 1840s and 1850s and the near-genocidal attacks on Indians and their ways of life. By the end of the nineteenth century only about 15,000 Indians remained. The story of European and American contact with California Natives and its aftermath is a tale of unremitting tragedy.

~

Indians of the Columbia Plateau often followed sociocultural patterns similar to those of their Native neighbors, but the tribes of the Great Basin exhibited novel forms. Like coastal groups, Plateau peoples such as the Nez Perce, Flatheads, Yakimas (now Yakamas), Umatillas, and Walla Wallas relied heavily on fish, especially salmon, for their main food supply. One of the finest salmon fisheries in North America, where the Columbia River narrowed at The Dalles in Oregon, became a huge Native American trade fair, attracting thousands of Indians from the Pacific Northwest. For these peoples the salmon were a sacred food source, with important religious rituals encouraging their annual cycles of coming up the Columbia and returning to the sea.

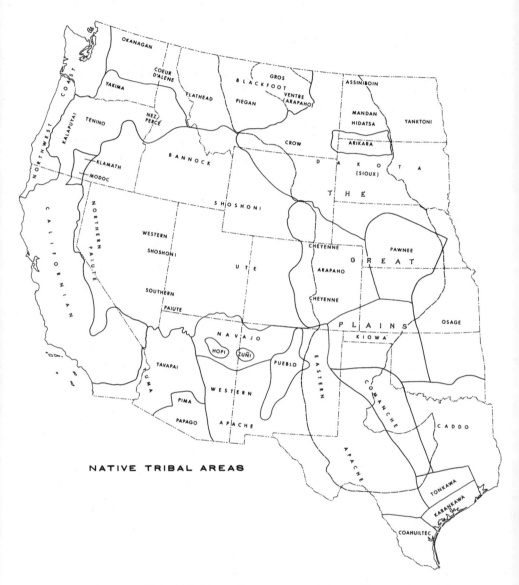

FIGURE 1:5. *Native Tribal Areas.* The numerous tribal areas illustrate the varied Indian cultures Europeans encountered in their first contacts with Natives in the West. From Warren A. Beck and Ynez D. Haase, *Historical Atlas of the American West*, map 8. Copyright © 1989 by the University of Oklahoma Press, Norman. Reprinted by permission of the publisher. All rights reserved.

If the Yakamas, Umatillas, and Wascos relied on fishing and rivers and looked west for cultural cues, the Flatheads, Nez Perce, and Shoshones were hunters and more closely linked to other Natives to the east. Of vital import for these eastward-leaning groups were their yearly buffalo hunts across the Rockies to the Plains. These annual trips not only provided necessary food but also buffalo skins for clothing, tepees, and ropes, and bones for tools and weapons. The hunting forays also triggered intertribal conflicts between Plateau and Plains Indians. Well before large numbers of Europeans appeared, Mandans and Blackfeet, among others, raided the Shoshones and the Flatheads. One of these raids at the end of the eighteenth century included the capture and selling of the Shoshone girl Sacagawea, who eventually returned west, accompanying the American explorers Lewis and Clark to the Pacific.

The most widely known of the Plateau groups were the Nez Perce. They lived in the verdant valleys at the juncture of present-day Oregon, Washington, and Idaho. One version of their creation story tells of Coyote (often a trickster figure in Indian mythology) fighting with a huge, malevolent monster that devours Indians. By his wiles, Coyote gets inside the monster and quickly kills the beast by cutting loose his heart. Coyote then carves up the monster's gigantic body and scatters the parts around the region. Wherever a body part lands, ancestors of modern tribes—for instance the Yakamas, the Spokans, and the Flatheads—arise. But when Coyote sprinkles the beast's blood where the three modern states converge, the Nez Perce or Nimipu ("The Real People") spring up. In this beautiful location the Nez Perce remained a holistic, stable society until disruptive American forces invaded their homelands in the nineteenth century.

Horses, guns, and then Euroamerican explorers brought quick, dramatic changes to the Nez Perce and other Plateau peoples. In the mid-to-late eighteenth century, before any substantial groups of whites arrived, horses traded or stolen from the Spanish Southwest and guns gained from the French and English had spread among the Plateau Indians. These animals and weapons intensified the existing struggles among tribes of the northern interior West. For the most part, the Plains groups were the most forceful; their superior numbers and weapons helped them overcome opponents. Plateau Indians increasingly worried about their powerful Native competitors to the east.

When the American explorers Meriwether Lewis and William Clark and their Corps of Discovery arrived among the Nez Perce in 1805, the Nimipu feared the newcomers. Yet the Indians provided the expedition with much-needed horses and helped them on their trip west. The Nez Perce furnished the same hospitality and aid when the explorers returned in the spring and early summer of 1806. The Nez Perce, hoping the newcomers would supply guns and ammunition to be used against their Plains opponents, were disappointed when Lewis and Clark had none to sell or trade. In turn, members of the Corps spoke of the "good hearts" among the Nez Perce and praised their hospitality, horses, and women.

Although the Plateau groups spoke different languages, similar social and cultural customs often linked the tribes. Most resided in small villages or often traveled in roving bands—to trade at The Dalles fair or to hunt buffalo east of the Rockies. Moving about by canoe or newly acquired horses, the Indians of the Plateau region were much less isolated than Great Basin Natives to the south.

The lives of Great Basin Indians reflected the dry, sparse, demanding landscapes of their homelands. Living in Nevada, Utah, and parts of Idaho, Oregon, Wyoming, and California, the Basin Natives included the Klamaths and Bannocks in the north and, moving south, the Modocs and Shoshones, and the Paiutes and Utes. These and other Indian groups occupied the 400,000-square-mile area between the Rocky and Sierra Nevada mountains and north of the desert Southwest. Their arid and semiarid regions and diverse climates kept these nomadic Natives on the move, trying to locate scarce food and water supplies. Crisscrossing these relatively infertile areas, Indians of the Great Basin often gathered piñon nuts and wild plants and hunted small game during the spring and summer and then in the winter congregated in small villages near lakes.

The unyielding Basin habitats demanded much of their Native residents. To survive, the Paiutes and Shoshones became adept at trapping jackrabbits and rodents, roasting grasshoppers and crickets, and constructing decoys to capture ducks and other game birds. One cave in northwestern Nevada yielded an unusual example of Basin diligence and ingenuity. Centuries after its construction a blanket made from six hundred mouse skins, neatly sewed together, remained in good shape to ward off a cold winter.

The earliest white explorers, travelers, and settlers in the Great Basin often haughtily dismissed these Natives as "digger" Indians, as subhumans who feasted on anything that crept or crawled. Chief among the most supercilious reporters was noted writer Mark Twain, who described the "Goshoot" (Gosiute) group as "the wretchedest type of mankind . . . [he had] ever seen"; they were "inferior to all races of savages on our continent." Twain continued that they were "a thin, scattering race . . . who produce nothing at all, and have no villages . . . a people whose only shelter is a rag cast on a bush to keep off a portion of the snow." Because the Basin Indians followed very simple lifestyles and did not exhibit the warrior-like social system of the Sioux, Blackfeet, or Comanche tribes, they were frequent targets of the most negative descriptions of European and American visitors.

~

The popular and enduring stereotypes of Plains Indians are often barriers to more factual, realistic descriptions of these tribes at the arrival of white men and women. Many of these tribal groups, for example, did not gain horses until the first decades of the eighteenth century, well after the earliest contacts between Europeans and Native Americans in the Southwest. Indeed, not until after the pathbreaking Pueblo Revolt of 1680 did horses spread out, through intertribal trade and raiding, from the Southwest to the northern Plains Indians. After horses arrived, the Plains Natives became much more nomadic, utilizing horses and portable tepees in their pursuit of the all-purpose buffalo.

When the initial Europeans made their way onto the Plains in the sixteenth and seventeenth centuries, they encountered dissimilar Indian groups. The Siouan speakers, such as the Mandans, Hidatsas, and Dakota or Lakota (Sioux), resided on the northern Missouri River; the Caddo speakers, the Arikaras, on the middle Missouri; and nearby the Pawnees and Wichitas (Caddo). Nearly all these tribes lived in circular or square earth-covered lodges located near rivers or streams. Most were part-time agriculturalists, planting yearly crops of corn, beans, and squash. Native hunters also pursued the large buffalo herds, primarily to the west. The Indian women were the farmers, the men the hunters.

At the western end of the Plains, where the land was less fertile, tribes were more nomadic. There they retained their predominant hunter-gatherer ways. By the mid-eighteenth century the Blackfeet, Piegans, Bloods, Gros Ventres ("Big Bellies"), and Crows were largely horsed Indians, hunting buffalo and gathering berries and other plants. Before they gained horses from the south, these tribes moved about with dog-drawn *travois*, or sleds. They hunted on foot, using disguises, surprises, and surround techniques to capture their quarry or driving them over cliffs. Once horses and guns became available to these Natives, and even before they met any sizeable groups of whites, the Plains Indians had become more mobile and efficient hunters.

The tribal groups that ultimately became some of the fiercest opponents of incoming Europeans were the varied peoples known as the Sioux, also the Dakota or Lakota. Occupying parts of modern-day Minnesota, the Dakotas, and adjacent areas to the south and west, the Sioux hunted buffalo, planted corn and other crops, and raided nearby competing tribes. By the eighteenth century the varied Siouan groups had gradually moved farther west and become hunters on the Plains, employing horses and guns to pursue their major game, the buffalo. Their nomadic lifestyles were closely tied to the giant buffalo herds they followed. Explorers like Lewis and Clark crossing the northern Plains in the early nineteenth century found the Santee, Yankton, and Teton Dakota (or

Sioux) valiant opponents. They were nimble riders armed with guns. Farther west on the upper reaches of the Missouri, the varied Blackfoot tribes were equally feared foes, for Natives and whites alike.

Most of the Sioux and other Plains Indians organized themselves into loosely confined bands. Following band leaders whose courageous exploits they might admire, Plains peoples retained their independence and individual freedom rather than closely adhering to the orders of one chief or a tribal council. Native men and women of the Plains were expected to know tribal traditions, with murder and other serious crimes punished by shunning or sometimes ejection. Young men were often encouraged to seek visions during questing journeys, including self-torture and several hours or even days without food or drink. Afterwards they rejoined their bands as men, perhaps now ready to become warriors. But courageous deeds on the battlefield, including leading a charge, counting coup (touching an enemy without receiving an injury), scalping an opponent, or stealing horses, sealed a budding warrior's reputation.

Religious beliefs and rituals were central to Plains Indian life. In addition to the vision quests that many young Indians undertook, adult Natives sought supernatural guidance for their everyday beliefs and actions. Dances, songs, dreams, and medicine bundles (wrapped sacred objects) provided instruction and totems for Indians in their search for spiritual teaching and encouragement. One of these demanding rituals was the Sun Dance. In this ceremony a Native, often a youth abstaining from food or drink, danced around a specially selected pole until he fainted from exhaustion or fell into a trance. A more stringent version of the ritual called for the celebrant to insert skewers, attached to something above his head, through the pectoral muscles of his chest and to dance until those skewers broke free. This ordeal of self-torture was intended to prove the dancer's courage and his search for new spiritual insights.

The Plains Natives varied greatly in economic power by the end of the eighteenth century. The semiagricultural and hunting towns of the Mandans, Hidatsas, and Arikaras situated along the Missouri and in present North Dakota drew hundreds—even thousands—of Indians to trade each year. The visitors, often from the nomadic tribes to the west, exchanged bison products and horses for foodstuffs and guns. The buffalo hunters from the west, including the Crows, the Shoshones (Snakes), and the varied Blackfeet groups, were less financially secure. Tied almost entirely to the buffalo, they usually lacked the agricultural or fishing base that added to the economies of other Plains groups.

∾

The expansive, varied terrains stretching from the California border to east Texas and extending into southern Colorado and Oklahoma hosted dozens of dissimilar Indian cultures. The deserts, mountains, plateaus, and plains of this vast region, as well as its diverse climates, shaped the lives of a welter of Native groups. In addition, the initial contacts between Natives and Europeans occurred earlier in this section of the West. These pioneering encounters led to the later transport of horses, guns and ammunition, and deadly diseases to other parts of the region.

Indian groups in modern-day Arizona and New Mexico had well-developed cultures by time the first whites entered the region in the early to mid-sixteenth century. In Arizona the Akimel O'odhams (Pimas) and Tohono O'odhams (Papagos), descendents of the earlier Hohokam and Mogollon cultures, had constructed intricate irrigation systems, allowing them to plant crops and thus establish more permanent communities. In their hot desert homelands these Indians gathered in small villages of brush and dirt houses, wore little clothing, and made colorfully decorated pottery. Before the first Spanish explorers arrived in the Southwest in the early 1500s the Hohakam and Mogollon cultures gave way to the expanding, increasingly powerful Anasazi culture to the north.

The Anasazi (ancestors of the modern Pueblo Indians) and the surrounding Athapascan people (forerunners of the present-day Navajo and Apache tribes) were the major groups of eastern Arizona and New Mexico. Cultural, social, and linguistic differences, among others, distinguished these groups from one another. These dissimilarities provided a rich, complex spectrum of Native identities in this central part of the Southwest.

The Pueblos were the best known of the southwestern tribal groups. Living along the northern Rio Grande from below modern-day Albuquerque north to Taos in New Mexico and across areas east of the river and west into Arizona, the Pueblos were primarily sedentary Indians. Situated along the Rio Grande or in other areas sufficiently well watered to raise crops, the Pueblos were the most rooted of the southwestern Natives of the 1500s.

By time of contact with the Spanish in the 1500s the Pueblos had worked out recognizable patterns of cultural and social organization. Without giving up their skills in hunting and gathering, the Pueblos had also become horticulturists, raising crops such as corn, squash, and beans. Their fields and crops, situated near pueblos (villages) and water sources and tilled by men and women alike, greatly aided the Pueblos in attaining a stable and even expanding society. In the late 1500s the Pueblos numbered between 30,000 and 50,000 people.

The Pueblos were community-minded Natives. Rather than emphasize individual deeds, as the neighboring Navajos and Apaches were more inclined to do, the Pueblos celebrated accomplishments that aided and buttressed the group.

Religious beliefs, as well as rites and rituals associated with these beliefs, served as unifying elements to the Pueblo communitarian culture. The creation story of Pueblos living at the Acoma Pueblo illustrates these unities. For Acomans, their story began at Sipapu, a mysterious underground location. There Tsichtinako (Thought Woman) nursed the sisters Nautsiti and Iatiku and helped prepare them to live in a new world above. With the aid of Badger and Locust, the sisters climbed through a hole in the ground (Sipapu) and created the Pueblo country. Even though Snake and Magpie instigated discord and Nautsiti departed, Iatiku remained, giving birth to many children. Iatiku taught the Acoma people, with the aid of spirits and kachinas (ancestral gods), how to erect homes, construct a village, and build a kiva. Over time, the people of Acoma believed their pueblo, joining earth and sky, was the center of the world.

Living in nearby sections of the Southwest were two other Native groups, the Navajos and the Apaches. These two peoples had something of a common heritage: both were Athapascan speakers who, over the centuries, had migrated from western Canada to the Southwest. They probably arrived in the 1200s or 1300s and moved into former Pueblo settlements when drought and other pressures drove many of those Indians into the Rio Grande valley. The Navajos, the larger of the two groups, settled and remained in the present-day Four Corners area where New Mexico, Arizona, Utah, and Colorado meet. The Navajos were nomads, more often hunters than gatherers. Even though they eventually raised corn, the Navajos, or Diné, never became as thoroughly agricultural as the Pueblos.

Living arrangements among the Navajos differed from those of the Pueblo. The Navajos resided in helter-skelter clusters of hogans, round or hexagonal structures of mud and wood. Sometimes these clustered hogans evolved into clans, with headmen as leaders. The clans elected war leaders, but each of the units could make decisions separately from the others. Navajo religious beliefs seem also to have been more open-ended than those of other Natives. Perhaps they seem less structured because we know less of them. The Diné believed in nature gods and chanted and recited hundreds of songs and prayers like the Pueblo but exhibited less interest than their neighbors in Christianity when missionaries entered their homelands.

Most of the Apache tribes were even more nomadic than the Navajo. They too were initially hunters and gatherers and then tillers of a few crops. The Apache, primarily situated on the Plains and in eastern New Mexico, also roamed as far as the northern canyons and forested areas of Arizona and New Mexico. They most often inhabited temporary brush shelters, like those of the Great Basin peoples, but also moved about from place to place. The Apaches gained reputations as incredible fighters. Revenge, it is said, was often the driving force that motivated these skillful warriors. Moreover, they could and did

FIGURE 1:6. *Comanche Indians.* This painting of a Comanche war leader
depicts the military prowess that warriors of this southwestern and
Plains tribe gained in the eyes of Native and European opponents.
Painting by Roy Anderson. Courtesy Pecos National Historical Park.

exist on almost any food source. Early observers also were astounded at how the Apaches lived nearly naked in freezing temperatures.

The nomadic Apaches rarely stayed long in one location. They traveled often, taking advantage of the cycles of food and forage in several sites. Their tepee-type brush houses, called wickiups, were easily and quickly erected. Apaches frequently moved about in small groups, were often matrilineal in organization, and placed more importance on individuals and their deeds than did the community-minded Pueblos. Later, once they gained horses, the Apaches, particularly those located near Plains cultures, became superb horsemen. It was one of the great ironies of early southwestern history that the Spaniards inadvertently revolutionized early Native societies in the region by supplying the horses that the Apache and other Indian raiders used so successfully in devastating the livestock herds of the Spanish and the Pueblo Indians.

Indian experiences on the southern Plains, mainly in Texas and Oklahoma, reflected the varied terrains, climates, and soils in which they lived. Along the Texas coast, tribes like the Karankawa benefited from a surplus of fish and marine animals. Nearby the numerous Caddoan peoples of eastern Texas became skilled agriculturists. These Natives, living well on the natural abundance of their homelands, developed complex social systems, including specialists in religion and politics who did not work in the fields. To the south, in the more arid landscapes of south Texas and northern Mexico, life was more demanding. There the Coahuiltecan Natives had to adopt rigorous subsistence patterns to survive. Unable to withstand the impacts of early Spanish military entradas and disease-carrying settlers, these Indians soon disappeared as a separate tribe.

The Indian groups of north Texas and southern Oklahoma displayed more endurance, more tenacious military and cultural power. First the Apaches and later the incoming Comanches from the north dominated these buffalo-hunting areas. Once the Comanches obtained horses in the eighteenth century, they drove the Apaches west and became *the* mounted Indians of the southern Plains. The Comanches and the nearby Kiowas were indefatigable nomads, traveling and raiding throughout north Texas and Oklahoma. The more sedentary Wichitas, attempting to maintain their agricultural ways in river bottoms dotting the southern Plains, were eventually forced to make peace with the more militaristic Comanches in order to survive. The Comanches, like the Sioux, Blackfeet, and Apaches elsewhere, were some of the fiercest opponents of other Natives and European invaders. They held out longer against competitors and white newcomers than most other Native opponents.

The roving first human we sent out at the opening of this chapter would have much to talk about at the end of his or her periodic travels. Our traveler would have seen, close up, the varied landscapes that characterize the American West. In addition, our visitor, understanding the passage of time, would tell us about the large changes that characterized prehistoric cultures in the region. Finally, he or she could describe at length how Native American tribes greatly differed in their first contacts with invading Europeans and Americans from the sixteenth century onward. Undoubtedly our intrepid reporter would have stopped for an extended period in the Southwest where the Spanish first settled and were the first Europeans to intermingle with Native Americans in the areas stretching from California to Texas.

Anderson, Gary Clayton. *The Indians of the Southwest, 1580–1830: Ethnogenesis and Reinvention.* Norman: University of Oklahoma Press, 1991.

Barrett, Elinore M. *Conquest and Catastrophe: Changing Rio Grande Settlement Patterns in the Sixteenth and Seventeenth Centuries.* Albuquerque: University of New Mexico Press, 2002.

Binnema, Theodore. *Common and Contested Ground: A Human and Environmental History of the Northwestern Plains.* Norman: University of Oklahoma Press, 2001.

Calloway, Colin G. *First Peoples: A Documentary Survey of American Indian History.* 2nd ed. Boston: Bedford/St. Martin's, 2004.

———. *One Vast Winter Count: The Native American West before Lewis and Clark.* Lincoln: University of Nebraska Press, 2003.

Deverell, William F. *A Companion to the American West.* Malden, MA: Blackwell, 2004.

Erdoes, Richard, and Alfonso Ortiz, eds. *American Indian Myths and Legends.* New York: Pantheon, 1984.

Etulain, Richard W. "Prehistoric Man and Woman in New Mexico." In *New Mexican Lives: Profiles and Historical Stories,* edited by Richard W. Etulain, 5–18. Albuquerque: University of New Mexico Press, 2002.

———, ed. *Western Lives: A Biographical History of the American West.* Albuquerque: University of New Mexico Press, 2004.

Fagan, Brian. *Ancient North America: The Archaeology of a Continent.* New York: Thames and Hudson, 2000.

Farb, Peter. *Face of North America: The Natural History of a Continent.* New York: Harper and Row, 1963.

Fiedel, Stuart J. *Prehistory of the Americas,* 2nd ed. Cambridge, UK: Cambridge University Press, 1992.

Hunt, Charles B., and Stanley W. Trimble. "Physiography of the United States." In *The New Encyclopedia of the American West,* edited by Howard R. Lamar, 864–84. New Haven, CT: Yale University Press, 1998.

Hurt, R. Douglas. *Indian Agriculture in America: Prehistory to the Present.* Lawrence: University Press of Kansas, 1987.

Iverson, Peter. *Diné: A History of the Navajos.* Albuquerque: University of New Mexico Press, 2002.

Lamar, Howard R., ed. *The New Encyclopedia of the American West.* 1977; New Haven, CT: Yale University Press, 1998.

Lister, Robert H., and Florence C. Lister. *Chaco Canyon: Archaeology and Archaeologists.* Albuquerque: University of New Mexico Press, 1984.

Mann, Charles C. *1491: New Revelations of the Americas Before Columbus.* New York: Knopf, 2005.

Meinig, D. W. *The Shaping of America: A Geographical Perspective on 500 Years of History*. Vol. 1, *Atlantic America, 1492–1800*. New Haven, CT: Yale University Press, 1986.

Momaday, N. Scott. *The Way to Rainy Mountain*. Albuquerque: University of New Mexico Press, 1969.

Nichols, Roger. *American Indians in U.S. History*. Norman: University of Oklahoma Press, 2003.

Plog, Stephen. *Ancient Peoples of the American Southwest*. New York: Thames and Hudson, 1997.

Prucha, Francis Paul. *The Great Father: The United States Government and the American Indians*. 2 vols. Lincoln: University of Nebraska Press, 1984.

Ramsey, Jarold, ed. *Coyote Was Going There: Indian Literature of the Oregon Country*. Seattle: University of Washington Press, 1977.

Riley, Carroll L. *Rio del Norte: People of the Upper Rio Grande from Earliest Times to the Pueblo Revolt*. Salt Lake City: University of Utah Press, 1995.

Sokolow, Jayme A. *The Great Encounter: Native Peoples and European Settlers in the Americas, 1492–1800*. Armonk, NY: M. E. Sharpe, 2002.

Stegner, Page, ed. *Marking the Sparrow's Fall: Wallace Stegner's American West*. New York: Henry Holt, 1998.

Stegner, Wallace. *The American West as Living Space*. Ann Arbor: University of Michigan Press, 1987.

Stuart, David E. *Anasazi America: Seventeen Centuries on the Road from Center Place*. Albuquerque: University of New Mexico Press, 2000.

Thomas, David Hurst. *Skull Wars: Kennewick Man, Archaeology, and the Battle for Native American Identity*. New York: Basic Books, 2000.

Wishart, David J., ed. *Encyclopedia of the Great Plains*. Lincoln: University of Nebraska Press, 2004.

CHAPTER TWO

Spain in the Southwest

~

THE SPANISH CARAVAN MOVED SLOWLY UP THE RIO GRANDE VALLEY IN the sun-baked midsummer of 1598. The travelers, consisting of more than five hundred men, women, and children, were on their way to settle the far-northern frontier of New Spain. Led by the redoubtable Spanish Basque Juan de Oñate and accompanied by their large herds of livestock, the immigrants especially dreamed of quickly gathering the rich minerals that they were told awaited them. Once in north-central New Mexico, Oñate's group hurriedly established the first Spanish settlement; it was situated near the Pueblo Indian village of San Juan. The resulting encounters between the Spanish and Native Americans, at first cautiously friendly, soon became strained and later turned violent. It was not an auspicious beginning for the first permanent European colony in the North American West.

Oñate's difficulties in settling New Mexico in the late sixteenth and early seventeenth centuries foreshadowed many of the dilemmas the Spanish experienced in the next two centuries in the Southwest. Natives usually welcomed the European newcomers to New Mexico, Texas, Arizona, and California. But as the Spanish forcefully imposed their governmental, religious, and military systems, Indians across the region grew increasingly discontent. That mounting disagreement boiled over in the enormously important Pueblo Revolt of 1680. After that momentous event and once the Spanish recaptured New Mexico in the mid-1690s, they learned to rule the Indians less coercively. From Oñate's initial entrada (entry) in 1598 until Spain's loss of the Southwest in 1821, the story of Spanish-Indian interchanges in the region is a complex one of conflicts, cultural conversations, and sometimes combinations.

~

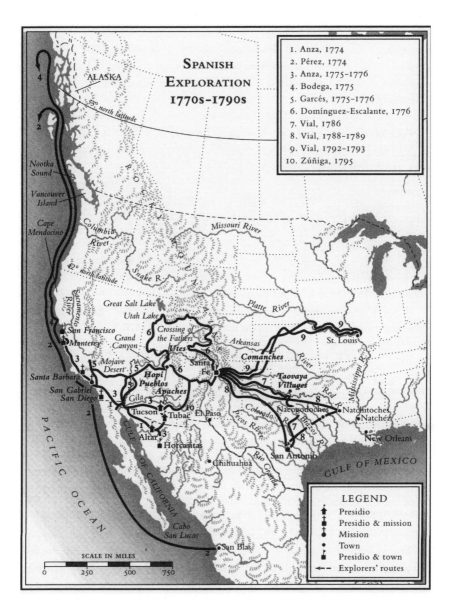

FIGURE 2:1. *Spanish Exploration, 1770s-1790s.* The Spanish explored much of the inland Southwest and the maritime Pacific Coast between the early 1770s and the beginning of the nineteenth century. From John L. Kessell, *Spain in the Southwest: A Narrative History of Colonial New Mexico, Arizona, Texas, and California.* Copyright © 2002 by the University of Oklahoma Press, Norman. Reprinted by permission of the publisher. All rights reserved.

The Spanish played central roles in European exploration and settlement of the New World from the 1400s onward. They were major actors in the drama enacted up and down the east and west coasts of North and South America. The earliest Spanish explorations took place in the late fifteenth century and in the following decades fanned out to Florida, Mexico, and South America. By the mid-sixteenth century, bold Spanish conquistadors were marching across the deserts of what became the American Southwest.

The Spanish believed the New World was ripe with riches, chiefly in minerals, fertile lands, and pagan souls needing conversion to Christianity. As we shall see in the next chapter, most other Europeans of the time shared some of these beliefs. But Spain was one of the first European powers to move decisively. Within a half-century after Christopher Columbus's voyages to Hispañola in 1492–93, the Spanish launched expeditions into New Mexico. In the intervening decades, men such as Juan Ponce de León, Pánfilo de Narváez, and Hernando de Soto explored Florida and other parts of the southeastern United States. Concurrently, Hernán Cortés pushed into Mexico and Francisco Pizarro into Peru. If the forays into Florida and nearby areas ended in failure, those by Cortés and Pizarro gave Spain strong, enduring footholds in Mexico and South America by the 1530s and 1540s.

Even though Narváez's expedition to Florida in 1527–28 proved unsuccessful, it opened the way for later Spanish entry into the Southwest. One survivor of that tragic voyage, Alvar Núñez Cabeza de Vaca, escaped from captivity among Indians in Texas and made his way across large parts of the Southwest before reuniting with other Spanish comrades on his way to Mexico. The dramatic story that Cabeza de Vaca told reinforced Spanish beliefs that the Strait of Anián (a "northwest passage" from the Atlantic to the Pacific) and the rumored Seven Cities of Cíbola lay within the grasp of explorers and settlers bold and courageous enough to seek them. In 1638–39, the Franciscan fray Marcos de Niza set out northward from Mexico with several others and with the black Moor Esteban as their guide. The African slave met his end among the Pueblo Indians of northern New Spain (New Mexico) when he reportedly overstepped cultural boundaries in his treatment of Native women. But fray Marcos believed that he had truly seen the magical Cíbola in the hazy valleys lying before him. He returned to Mexico City with exaggerated fables, igniting the fervor of many others to journey north.

The most significant of these Spanish conquistadors entering New Mexico was Francisco Vázquez de Coronado. He set out in February 1540 with high hopes and a retinue of nearly three hundred Spaniards and perhaps as many as one thousand Indians. Unfortunately nothing worked as Coronado dreamed. He found no legendary Cíbola, but instead thousands of miles of sun-parched terrain. The Natives were increasingly unfriendly after Coronado made large demands on them, cruelly mistreating those who failed to obey his commands. Coronado's flawed expedition of 1540–42 should have raised questions among the Spanish about their misguided notions concerning New Mexico. In fact, none of their exaggerated dreams proved true; some became nightmares. But the expeditions continued to roll up the Rio Grande in the second half of the sixteenth century, with others determined to find the riches that had eluded earlier explorers.

~

At the end of the sixteenth century, Juan de Oñate seemed an ideal candidate for mounting a successful expedition of settlement into northern New Spain. An experienced leader, courageous to a fault, and, even more important, a rich man, Oñate was also well connected. On his father's side he was the son of a Spanish Basque immigrant; on his mother's, he had ties to the great Native leader of Mexico, Moctezuma. Besides, Oñate knew how to fight Indians and was a devout Catholic. These necessary backgrounds bode well for don Juan.

But his errand into the northern wilderness seemed ill-fated from the outset. Competitors for the right to settle New Mexico libeled Oñate's good name, the Spanish administrator who gave him permission to lead the immigrants northward was transferred, and other delays undermined the expedition. By the time Oñate finally crossed the Rio Grande in early May 1598, his group had dwindled from 200 to 130 fighting men and their families and servants. Mounting expenses from the frustrating delays also forced him to borrow from his wealthy family. Still Oñate moved on, hoping to recoup his fortunes once in New Mexico.

Oñate acted with characteristic energy and direction after his expedition arrived in northern New Mexico in July and August 1598. First, he and his followers moved in with the Pueblos in their village of Ohke, which Oñate renamed San Juan. Soon the settlers relocated across the Rio Grande and established San Gabriel on the western side of the river. Quickly Oñate built and dedicated the San Gabriel church and set up an administration by which to govern the settlers and rule the nearby Indians. Using the new settlement as his launching spot, the governor sent out friars to nearby pueblos and began to explore the area, planning, of course, to discover rich mineral deposits and thereby ensure the success of his colony.

In its first years, Oñate's settlement suffered major setbacks. Several officers and soldiers mutinied, and the Pueblos quickly grew restive. Their hostility erupted in December 1598 when residents at the Acoma Pueblo attacked and killed eleven Spanish soldiers under the command of Oñate's nephew Juan de Zaldívar. Oñate reacted quickly and harshly, sending Juan's brother, Vincente

FIGURE 2:2. *Juan de Oñate, Spanish Explorer and Founder.* The prime mover of the first Spanish settlement in the Southwest, Oñate was a strong leader, but his harsh treatment of Pueblo Indians and his inability to please his fellow settlers led to his resignation as governor. Photo courtesy of Rick Hendricks.

de Zaldívar, to attack the Acomans. Using a clever ruse, Zaldívar gained access to the nearly impregnable mesa-top pueblo and, after three days of vicious fighting, stormed to victory. Perhaps more than half of the pueblo's 1,500 inhabitants were killed. In a quick trial, Oñate declared residents of Acoma guilty of murder. He sentenced captives between ages twelve and twenty-four to slavery for twenty years, directed that children be taken from their parents and given as wards to the Spanish, and ordered that all males over twenty-five were to have a foot cut off. This brutal penalty was not unusual in Spanish and other European treatment of Indian opponents (nor of Indian treatment of Indian foes), but in Oñate's case he sowed seeds of discontent that grew into veritable thickets of opposition and hatred.

The debacle at Acoma was but prologue to an unending string of difficulties and disappointments for Oñate's beleaguered colony in the next decade. Colonists took umbrage with what they considered their leader's harsh leadership. The political and military leaders squabbled over policies, and both groups differed with the Franciscans about how Indians ought to be treated. Oñate's frequent absences from the colony to explore other parts of the Southwest also undermined his leadership. But most troublesome of all, the colony could find no successful way to support itself. No rich mineral deposits were discovered, many of the colonists were unable (or unwilling) to plant, till, and harvest crops, and additional support from Mexico was late and inadequate. With his colony crumbling and near total chaos, Oñate resigned his governorship on August 24, 1607. Explaining his actions to the Spanish viceroy in Mexico, Oñate wrote, "Finding myself helpless in every respect, because I have used up on this expedition my estate and the resources of my relatives and friends . . . I find no other means . . . than to renounce my office."

≈

A successor was sent, of course, but problems similar to those Oñate encountered vexed the Spanish throughout seventeenth-century New Mexico. These frustrations fused into one large dilemma: how might the Spanish organize and administer the institutions necessary to govern settlers and Natives in the New World. Four evolving institutions and their changing modes of operation clarify how the Spanish tried to control the Southwest. All help to define Spanish administration; all also illuminate Spanish-Indian relations in New Spain.

The *encomienda*, or trust, system attempted to establish a mutual working relationship between Spanish invaders and the Indians. In return for tribute that *encomenderos* received from Indian pueblos or individual groups of Indians, the Spanish were to protect the sedentary groups like the Pueblos from nomadic tribes such as the Navajos and Apaches and to provide religious instruction. The tribute could be in the form of maize (corn), a blanket, or an animal skin but also in field labor or personal domestic service. The encomienda system echoed an earlier feudal king-vassal relationship in which the king rewarded leaders (*ricos*) or military commanders with a form of largesse in return for their loyalty to and defense of the monarch. Even though the regional Spanish administrator in Mexico, the viceroy, limited the number of encomiendas in New Mexico to about thirty-five, the institution became increasingly oppressive and often greatly harmed Indians rather than protecting them. Indian women working as domestic servants, for example, sometimes suffered heinous sexual assaults from their Spanish "protectors." Linked to the encomienda and thus not a separate institution was the *repartimiento de indios*. It called for Indians to work on public projects thought to be for everyone's benefit, including, for instance, the building of the town of Santa Fe.

A second Spanish institution, the mission, more important in several ways than the encomienda, provided religious instruction for the Indians. Usually staffed with Franciscan priests, the missions in New Mexico often consisted of one or two friars assigned to a pueblo, for the most part in the upper and central regions of the province. The missions included schools to teach reading, writing, and Christian doctrine. Even though many Spaniards thought Indians uncivilized barbarians, they nonetheless were motivated to convert the Natives in order to save their own souls from hell. Clearly, Spanish leaders were also convinced that until Indians abandoned their Native beliefs and became Christians they could not be useful parts of the Spanish empire and its dominions. By the mid-seventeenth century perhaps as many as twenty thousand Indians were being ministered to. The number of Franciscan friars in New Mexico remained small, however, with about 250 in the province in 1680.

Meanwhile, the Spanish relied heavily on a third institution, the *presidio*, to protect their settlers and borders from invaders and treasonous residents. These military installations resembled English or French forts, although a presidio also referred to the soldiers themselves stationed within a province or on its borders. Distance and maintenance costs kept the number of presidios much smaller than Spanish colonial officials and settlers wished. In New Mexico, which remained isolated from any European invasion in the seventeenth century, no presidios were established until after the Pueblo Revolt of 1680. After that notable event and because encomiendas were not reestablished following the revolt, presidios took up the task of protecting the colony from *indios bárbaros*, the nomadic groups who frequently attacked Spanish and Pueblo Indian towns.

The fourth major Spanish institution was the town, or *pueblo*. Towns were an important part of Spanish settlement in the Southwest, even though Spanish society there was overwhelming rural. Towns often hosted missions, administrative headquarters, and sometimes presidios. There were even attempts to relocate the Pueblo Indians, already in their own towns, to Spanish pueblos to enlarge and strengthen urban numbers, make protection of Indians less difficult, and possibly offset some of the drawbacks resulting from distances between missions. In New Mexico, Oñate's San Gabriel, later Santa Fe, and even later El Paso, Santa Cruz de la Cañada, and Albuquerque were the first villas, or towns. From the 1620s to the end of Spain's control in 1821, Santa Fe was the political, religious, and cultural center of northern New Mexico. In the eighteenth century, after the displacement of many New Mexicans following the Pueblo Revolt, El Paso became *the* Spanish town in the southern region of the province.

In the seventeenth century, Pueblo Indian discontents with Spanish aggressive and coercive control began to mount. These dissatisfactions bubbled to the surface periodically in small and brief rebellions. Finally, the lid blew off in 1680 when the Pueblos rose up and drove the Spanish from New Mexico.

The Pueblos learned early on that the Spanish newcomers often brought more difficulties than blessings. Although the number of Pueblo towns in the Rio Grande region remained constant during the roughly sixty years following

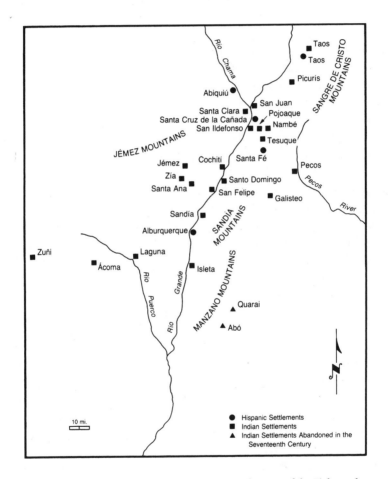

FIGURE 2:3. *Principal Indian and Hispanic Settlements of the Eighteenth Century.* The close physical proximity of and the resulting cultural contacts between Native Americans and the Spanish settlements in early New Mexico led to both conflicts and accommodations from the seventeenth into the nineteenth centuries. From Charles Cutter, *The Protector de Indios* (Albuquerque: University of New Mexico Press, 1986), 59.

Coronado's expedition, those numbers dropped off precipitously after Spanish setters arrived in 1598. About 60 percent of the pueblos were abandoned in the first eighty years of the seventeenth century. Spanish incursions into Pueblo farmlands, their pressures on Indian towns, and the attack of deadly diseases disrupted and destroyed Pueblo populations. Diseases were particularly virulent. Epidemics of smallpox, measles, and other European-introduced maladies killed off thousands of Pueblos. Adding to the Pueblo woes were the increased attacks of the Apaches and other nomadic opponents. Together these ruinous forces brought about a rapid population decline. Pueblo numbers, estimated to be about 60,000 in 1600, plummeted 75 percent to about 15,000 in 1680.

Like all other Europeans, the Spanish believed in their own superiority and the inferior status of Indians. Although moderns have difficulty understanding such attitudes, no European power thought much differently about the Natives of the New World. Indeed, of the imperial forces that invaded and settled portions of North America in these centuries—the British, the French, the Russians, the Dutch, and the Spanish—the Spanish were probably as enlightened in their treatment of Indians as any other Europeans. Still, even these attitudes led to coercive colonization that brought much suffering to the Pueblos.

Opposing attitudes between the two societies concerning land, labor, and religion were at the root of most clashes. Even though the dean of early historians of the Spanish Borderlands, Herbert Eugene Bolton, concluded in 1921 that "for eighty years Spaniards and Indians dwelt at peace with each other," most recent historians point to many more conflicts than accommodations between the two groups.

∾

After 1660, the discontents especially began to rumble. One of the events that heightened Indian distresses occurred in 1675 when Governor Juan Francisco Treviño cracked down on Native healers. Hearing that a group of *hechiceros* (medicine men) were meeting in Taos, the governor sent forces to invade the meeting. The Spanish then detained forty-seven Indian men. Three of the Native leaders were killed. The remainder were released, but not before they had been harshly punished and admonished to cease their resistance to Spanish religious and political control. Among those severely beaten was Popé (or PO´PAY), a Pueblo leader and medicine man from the San Juan Pueblo. From that time forward, Popé began to organize the rebellion of what became the dramatic Pueblo Revolt of 1680.

Popé remains a mysterious figure in southwestern history. Some think of him as more legendary than human, but most scholars agree that this middle-aged man from the San Juan Pueblo became the leader of those who planned and

FIGURE 2:4. *Popé (or PO'PAY), Pueblo Indian Leader.* Popé, from the San Juan and Taos pueblos, led the Pueblo Indians in the Pueblo Revolt of 1680, during which the Spanish were driven out of New Mexico. Sculpture by Clifford Fragua. National Statuary Hall, Washington, D.C. Photo courtesy David Pike.

launched the revolt of 1680. One Native American historian, providing an imaginative recreation of what Popé might have been like, writes that he "undoubtedly grew up like any other Pueblo boy of his time. Probably he followed the rules and rhythms of the community, in which religion was woven into the patterns of Pueblo life." After Popé reached adulthood, he would have taken part in the dances of his people, participated in religious ceremonies, and been appointed a war captain. As a Pueblo leader, Popé would have become aware of how much Spanish officials and religious leaders disapproved of tribal practices and religious customs.

After Governor Treviño's harsh whipping of the Indian leaders in 1675, Popé moved to Taos and began planning his revenge. There, isolated from the Spanish leaders in Santa Fe, he began meeting with other Pueblo leaders to foment rebellion. Sometime between 1675 and the summer of 1680, they hit upon a coordinated plan to surprise and overthrow the Spanish. In early August of 1680, strings of knotted deer hide were secretly sent to sympathetic Pueblo villages in northern New Mexico, with knots on the strings representing each day before the scheduled uprising. When rumors about the rebellion leaked out, Popé and the other Pueblos launched an early attack.

On August 10, 1680, under Popé and other able leaders, the angry Pueblos arose early in the morning to rid themselves of the overbearing Spanish. In the next three or four days nearly all of northern New Mexico flamed into rebellion. Village priests were killed, churches desecrated, and Spanish farmers and ranchers and their families murdered. Those able to escape fled to Santa Fe, areas to the south, or even as far away as El Paso on the Mexican border. Governor Antonio de Otermín held out for ten days in Santa Fe. Glad to be rid of their conquerors, the besieging Pueblos finally allowed the governor and Spanish survivors to march out of the city on August 21, unmolested. The bedraggled Spanish moved slowly down the Rio Grande, arriving and taking refuge in El Paso by late September.

The Pueblo Revolt is the key event for understanding Spanish-Indian encounters in the Southwest in the sixteenth and seventeenth centuries. Those bloody days of August 1680 proved that Spanish control of Native Americans in New Mexico had been unsuccessful. Those times also revealed that the Pueblos would no longer be satisfied to live under "submissive resentment." New policies based on changed attitudes would have to be formulated and put to work. But these shifts did not occur overnight; they occurred gradually during the next few decades.

In fact, the next two decades after the Revolt were years of adjustment. The Pueblo consensus favoring rebellion soon splintered after the Spanish retreated to El Paso, with Popé's dictatorial leadership a probable cause of the breakdown. Finding that the Spanish absence did not solve most problems in New Mexico, some Indians began calling for a return of their recent overlords. In 1692 a Spanish leader, the valiant don Diego de Vargas, surveyed New Mexico. In the next two years, in a series of sometimes brutal conflicts, he reasserted Spanish control of New Mexico. Putting down another revolt in 1696, Vargas could rightfully claim the reconquest of the colony by 1700.

But in the early 1700s New Mexico became a quite different place from that in earlier decades. The Spanish, finally realizing the negative impact of their harsh policies, reconsidered and reformed some of their institutions. The encomienda system was eliminated, fewer demands were made for Indian labor, and the

Franciscans became less evangelical in eradicating Native religious rituals. The Pueblos, meanwhile, sensing their need of military protection from the Navajos and the Apaches, accepted some Spanish demands in return for aid against their enemies. Throughout the next century, the Spanish and Pueblos gradually arrived at a shaky accommodation. As we shall see, those rather uncertain agreements helped bring about a new hybrid Hispanic-Indian society and culture in the Southwest by the early nineteenth century.

≈

The Spanish came later to Texas and California than to New Mexico. Their experiences in these new regions also differed from those in New Mexico. True, Texas and California became part of the Spanish Borderlands, they too felt the shaping influences of Spanish institutions, and they also experienced the European-Native encounters known elsewhere in the Southwest. But their locations at the far ends of the western Borderlands, their history under other kinds of leaders, and the shifting fortunes of Spain sent Texas and California in different directions from New Mexico.

Most of all, Texas became a defensive colony. Unlike the populated settlements of New Mexico or of mission-dominated California, Spanish experiences in Texas illustrate the reactive nature of Spanish policies. Often stretched too far and too thin to send large numbers of families, priests, or soldiers to the Gulf Coast from the mouth of the Rio Grande to the Mississippi River, Spain instead tried to dispatch small groups to Texas to ward off their European competitors. That stop-gap policy did not work very well.

In 1519 as Ponce de León (Florida), Hernán Cortés (Mexico), and Francisco Pizarro (Peru) invaded or were planning to enter other parts of the Americas, Alonso Alvarez de Pineda sailed along the Texas coastline. Nearly a decade later, in 1527, Pánfilo de Narváez's tragic expedition, including the notable traveler Alvar Núñez Cabeza de Vaca, set out to explore the Florida coast and to move inland. Poor decisions, unexpected illnesses, Indian attacks, and disastrous storms destroyed the expedition, but Cabeza de Vaca survived. After years of wandering, he encountered other Spaniards to the west in 1536. When Cabeza de Vaca's dramatic tale of his wanderings (*Adventures in the Unknown Interior of America*, 1542) became known, the report helped to spur renewed Spanish efforts at exploration. At much the same time, from 1539 to 1543, Hernando de Soto marched and pillaged his way across the Southeast to the eastern edge of Texas and northern boundary of Louisiana. In 1541–42 Coronado crossed and then recrossed the Texas and Oklahoma panhandles in his fruitless search for the mythic Quivira, a rumored rich and exotic land in the interior of the continent. But in the sixteenth century, these explorations brought no settlers to Texas.

The first Spanish settlements in Texas were founded in the late seventeenth century. When learning in the 1680s that the Frenchman René Robert Cavelier La Salle was helping establish French settlers on the Texas Coast, the Spanish were driven into action. Commencing in 1686, Spanish explorers and colonizers moved along the coast and inland up the Trinity River. Also, encouraged by the apparent interest of the Caddo Indians in their Christianizing efforts, Franciscans traveled up the Neches River to begin several missions among these friendly Natives in 1690. The Spanish Crown chose to move into Texas with missions more than with presidios, even though a military leader, Domingo Terán de los Ríos, was named governor of the new province in 1691.

But the Spanish failed to support or protect the missionaries. Neither settlers nor soldiers came to Texas. And the once-friendly Hasinai of the Caddo confederacy turned against the Franciscans and worried them out of the new mission stations. After the missionaries fled, Spain lost interest in Texas—until the French seemed ready once again to pounce on the region.

This time the Frenchman was Louis Juchereau de Saint-Denis. In 1713, the experienced, intrepid Saint-Denis entered northwestern Louisiana and east Texas, marched across the plains, and encountered the surprised Spanish in midsummer 1714 at their frontier outpost San Juan Bautista on the Rio Grande. The lethargic Spanish stirred themselves, beginning to reoccupy Texas two years later. Returning to the Teja Indians and other tribes of the Hasinai confederacy, the Spanish reestablished four missions and a presidio between the Trinity and Neches rivers in east Texas.

Of more lasting significance was the site established in the modern San Antonio region. There, on May 1, 1718, Padre Antonio de San Buenaventura de Olivares laid the foundations of a mission, eventually known as San Antonio de Valero. Five days later, the recently named governor of Texas, don Martín de Alarcón, established nearby the Presidio de Béjar. Overnight, the mission and presidio, and the few settlers who came and stayed, made San Antonio the center of the Texas province.

But Spanish involvement in Texas was based more on the shaky proposition of heading off competitors than on compassion and commerce. That meant the geopolitics of European empires drove the Spanish Crown. Competition stretched Spain too far and too thinly, thereby leading to small, weak settlements in Texas. In 1731, only five hundred or so Spaniards resided in Texas, with about three hundred of these in San Antonio. By 1790, San Antonio had grown to nearly thirteen hundred residents. Thirty years later, at the end of Spanish rule, about three thousand full- and mixed-blood Hispanics lived in Texas, with half the population in San Antonio. At the same time, Spanish population in "crowded" New Mexico approached thirty thousand.

Texas remained a sparsely populated province for several reasons. Located too far from other centers of colonial Spanish strength, its establishment as a barrier to French expansion was insufficient reason to draw many settlers. Although the earliest missionaries, soldiers, and other colonists to Texas repeatedly pleaded with the Crown to send reinforcements, they could not demonstrate to Spanish leaders that Texas had abundant precious minerals or promised other financial rewards. The necessary soldiers and other Spaniards needed to help and protect settlements against invading Indians, competing Europeans, and internal squabbles never arrived. Bureaucratic and financial difficulties, lessening interest in Texas, and mounting competitors elsewhere in the Americas kept the Spanish reinforcements from coming. At the end of Spanish rule and the beginning of Mexican control in 1821, the Texas region was also vulnerable to expansionistic Americans to the east.

~

The Spanish were even more tardy in moving into California. As was the case in Texas, early Spanish contacts along the West Coast resulted from Spanish fears of competition from other Europeans. A half-century or so after Columbus sailed into the Caribbean, Spanish captains were plying the Pacific Coast along Baja (lower) and Alta (upper) California. Rumors of rich pearl and metal deposits as well as of an exotic island inhabited by Amazon women who entertained and seduced men so as to perpetuate the race seemed to draw a number of intrepid sailors to the area. In 1642, the veteran Captain Juan Rodríguez Cabrillo sailed up the California coast as far as Santa Catalina Island, north of San Diego. After Cabrillo died from an injury, his successor, Bartolomé Ferrar, moved north to the region of the California-Oregon border and then returned to Mexico the next year. Sixty years later, hearing of possible English competition in the person of Sir Francis Drake, the Spanish sent sailor Sebastían Vizcaíno up the California coast in 1602–3 to look for a suitable settlement site. He recommended a Spanish settlement in Monterey Bay, but his suggestion was not immediately followed. Eight decades later the redoubtable Jesuit Eusebio Francisco Kino also urged expansion into California, although he advocated missions rather than military or political establishments. His recommendation also lay unheeded for a long while.

Still another eighty years elapsed before two occurrences in the 1760s brought Spanish settlers to California. In 1765, José de Gálvez, a dynamic and experienced Spanish administrator, came to New Spain as *visitador general*, or inspector general. Immediately, Gálvez called for strengthened frontier areas, reorganized administrative structures, and expansion to the Pacific as soon as settled regions became stronger. Even as he began to carry out these plans, the alarming rumor came that a Russian force had already landed in California. Gálvez's dream of moving into California now took on new, larger meanings as a way to head off the Russians.

Gálvez chose two extraordinary men to launch Spanish settlement of Alta, or present-day, California. In 1767, Captain Gaspar de Portolá, with thirty years of European military experience, arrived in Baja California. Two years later, he led a group of seventy men overland, north to San Diego Bay. Indefatigable and courageous, Portolá not only helped settle San Diego, arriving there on July 1, 1769, but he also set out within two weeks to examine the suitability of the Monterey Bay, just south of modern San Francisco, as the site for an important Spanish colony. By the following December he was back in San Diego, having carried out his two orders. These were difficult journeys up new trails, going where Spaniards had never been before—so arduous and taxing that the commander and his troops were forced to eat their own pack animals. They arrived back, as Portolá remembered, "smelling of mules."

A key member of Portolá's team of explorers was Father Junípero Serra. Although small (5' 2") and unhealthy, Serra was a zealous man of inexhaustible energy who pushed himself with taxing journeys and self-flagellation. From 1769 until his death in 1784, Serra was a central figure in establishing nine missions along the southern California coast. Early historians and Hispanophiles lionized Serra as a founding father of California, but more recently other scholars and Native leaders have criticized Serra for what they consider his paternalistic and unsympathetic treatment of California Indians. Whatever the ups and downs of Serra's reputation and the controversies surrounding his attitudes toward Native Americans, he was unquestionably a leading figure in the Spanish settlement of California.

Before 1821, twenty missions dotted the California coastal landscape from San Diego in the south to the Bay Area in the north. Around these stations gathered mission Indians, who were taught to read and write and instructed in Christian doctrine. As we shall see more extensively in chapter 4, the mission system was not very successful; deaths there often exceeded births. In addition it soon became clear that the missions, exceedingly fragile on their own, needed other Spanish institutions for support. The help came before long. At Father Serra's prodding, and with the advice of the viceroy in Mexico, one of the giants of southwestern history, Juan Bautista de Anza, blazed an overland trail in 1774 from Sonora in northern Mexico to Monterey, the most important settlement in Spanish California. The next year he returned on the difficult journey, bringing along nearly 250 colonists, including dozens of families. The settlers arrived on September 17, 1776, and shortly thereafter founded Mission Dolores and the town of San Francisco.

For almost a half-century, Spanish California continued to expand. More

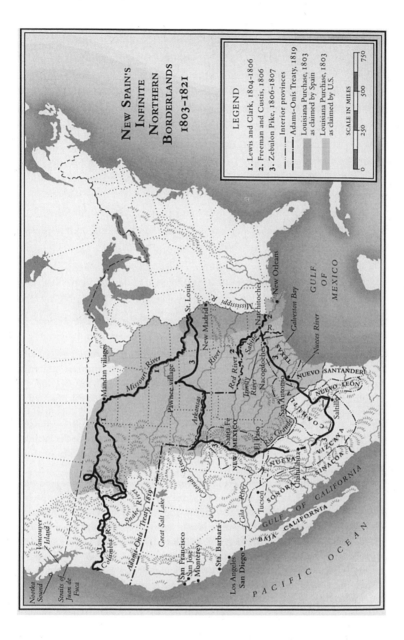

FIGURE 2:5. *New Spain's Infinite Northern Borderlands, 1803–1821.* By the end of Spanish control of the Southwest and Mexico in 1821, American explorations and diplomatic agreements with other nations had defined the northern and eastern boundaries of New Spain. From John L. Kessell, *Spain in the Southwest: A Narrative History of Colonial New Mexico, Arizona, Texas, and California.* Copyright © 2002 by the University of Oklahoma Press, Norman. Reprinted by permission of the publisher. All rights reserved.

missions were added, towns were established at San Jose and Los Angeles, and presidios opened. Mission Indians were taught to grow crops and to tend livestock. When the overland route from Sonora through Arizona closed because of Indian depredations, the missions were forced to provide most of the foodstuffs for the entire province, except those coming via undependable sea transport. Most of the farming and ranch economy, on which California depended until the Gold Rush and which brought thousands of newcomers in the mid-nineteenth century, was in place before the end of Spanish dominance.

Even though the Spanish lacked the wherewithal to populate and adequately support California as a major colony, they tried to protect it from other Europeans hungering and thirsting for colonies on the West Coast. Spanish attempts to ward off competitors came to a head in the so-called Nootka Sound Controversy from 1789 to 1794. This time the presence of the British, as well as rumors about Russian and American expansion, served as catalysts for Spanish reactions. Adopting the questionable position that earlier Spanish voyages north of the California border allowed them to claim all the Pacific Northwest, Spanish officials seized British ships at Nootka Sound on Vancouver Island (see chapter 3).

These precipitous actions nearly led to war. But wishing to avoid further conflict, the Spaniards, once they learned that the French (themselves involved in a tumultuous revolution) would not support Spanish demands, backed down and agreed to joint occupation with the British. The Spanish also paid damages and returned the English vessels. This retreat symbolized Spanish difficulties at the end of the eighteenth and beginning of the nineteenth centuries. Unable to stand by its international threats, falling behind the expanding British, the Spanish were headed for disaster. Scarcely a quarter-century later, Spanish colonies, beginning in Mexico, began to revolt and declare their independence. A weakening Spanish Crown was unable to head off these movements of colonial separation.

∼

Before those dramatic events occurred, complex sociocultural arrangements in the Spanish Borderlands had been evolving up through 1821. An important ingredient in this developing society was encounters between the Spanish and Native Americans, contacts that led to conflicts as well as combinations. The outcomes revealed early on how complex the history of the American West might become. The voices of both the Spanish and Indians speak to the complexities of this new society.

Like other Europeans expanding into the New World, the Spanish wrestled with appropriate definitions of and policies dealing with the Native Americans.

FIGURE 2:6. *Fandango*. This popular, lively dance provided sociocultural connections among Spanish, Mexican, Indian, and (later) American societies in the Southwest. Painting by Theodore Gentiliz. Courtesy the Daughters of the Republic of Texas Library at the Alamo.

The Spanish too began with unanswered questions: Were the Indians of the Americas like other humans? Did they have souls? If Native Americans were human and had souls, did Christians have a responsibility to convert these "savages" to Christianity? Gradually, in the sixteenth century, the Spanish answered each question affirmatively, attempting to make a place for Indians in New World Spanish society. "Throughout the colonial experience," writes one scholar, "the essence of Spanish policy for sedentary natives was that of inclusion, rather than exclusion." Particularly influential in leading the Spanish to a more enlightened policy on Native peoples was Father Bartolomé de Las Casas. A Dominican priest, Las Casas urged Spanish officials to formulate laws to protect the rights of indigenous people. As a result of his pleas for the Natives of the Americas, he was named to the office of *protector de indios*, or protector of the Indians. In this decision the Spanish became more idealistic in their attitudes toward Natives than most other Europeans. No other empire established an office for protecting the Indians. The Spanish clergy particularly favored this position, hoping the person named to the office would be an advocate for Indian rights. But, on the faraway frontiers of gritty reality, sympathy and justice were like large stones in a farm field, difficult to deal with. Differences of opinion among civil and religious leaders, jealousy among church officials, and the arduous work of colonists to gain satisfactory livings undercut the generous attitudes Las Casas and his brethren hoped to foster in the Western Hemisphere.

Like a sharply shifting kaleidoscope, Indian reactions to Spanish policies differed according to the places and times in which they experienced those policies. Early accounts of Spanish-Indian contacts often spoke entirely of Spanish designs and directions. More recently, we have realized the importance of understanding Native resistance as well as accommodation, their rebellions and their agreements. At this point a generalization seems in order: if Natives showed initial friendliness and eagerness to help the European newcomers, large and insistent Spanish demands for Indian food, land, and clothing, as well as for Native obedience and conversion, fostered increasing dissatisfaction among Indians across the southwestern Borderlands. No Indian reaction was total acceptance; a few groups exhibited near total rejection. Still, over time, with the pressing weight and strength of Spanish economic, military, political, and cultural dominance, Native Americans found it increasingly difficult to remain separate from the European invaders. Bit by bit, many Indians became increasingly Hispanicized, even to the point of conversion, intermarriage, and the acceptance of Spanish institutions. Most Native Americans did not go that far, however. A range of reactions, from negative to partial acceptance, provides a multifaceted story of these contacts.

≈

Even though most historical accounts do not contain Indian voices speaking in reaction to Spanish incursions or policies, they frequently deal with Native responses. The Pueblos in New Mexico, for example, often fled to the hills rather than meet with Spanish explorers after their disastrous experiences with Coronado in the early 1540s. In coastal Texas, the Teja Indians soon turned against the Franciscans after Christian doctrine did little to ward off the smallpox that seemed to have arrived with the missionaries. The Tejas told the friars in the 1690s that they must get out or die. Sometimes the mission system obviously failed. In San Antonio, falling Indian numbers, intermarriage, and other forces so changed Native culture that by the late eighteenth century San Antonio de Valero ceased as a Franciscan-dominated entity. One friar urged that the mission be secularized, transferred from the Franciscan order to a parish organization funded by the Roman Catholic Church rather than by a separate brotherhood. That secularization occurred in the 1790s. Most other missions near San Antonio were secularized before the Spanish left Texas.

In California, a similar train of events took place. As historian David Weber writes, "California's coastal peoples . . . had received Spaniards with cautious but friendly curiosity. Growing familiarity, however, soon bred contempt." Over time, it became clear that unless Indians obeyed Spanish demands, followed the teachings of the friars, and provided labor for Spanish missionaries, officials, and farmers, they were in for a difficult time.

Yet one can easily oversimplify Indian experiences in the Borderlands. Too often Native reactions are forced into two categories: those who gradually joined the Spanish through the mission system or another institution, becoming "Hispanicized" Indians; or those who resisted, like the Apaches and Comanches, and became in Spanish eyes *bárbaros*, nomadic, non-Christian, and "wild" Indians. Setting aside these oversimplifications, one must see further complexities in Indian reactions to the Spanish—including those, for example, who remained separate from Spanish society through redefining themselves culturally.

Native groups in Texas illustrated some of these methods of ethnogenesis, of reinventing themselves and recreating tribal identities to avoid totally losing their ways of living under the onslaught of the Spanish. When diseases and warfare nearly decimated Indian groups, tribes had to make difficult decisions that would help them rebound from these terrible losses. Sometimes they fled from Spanish demands for slavelike labor; sometimes they learned from the Spanish how to raise livestock and applied these lessons to their own expanding horse herds. Even more often *ladino* Indians (those who had learned Spanish ways) worked to reconfigure Indian bands. The Comanches, for example, adopted Shoshone and other peoples into their bands, thereby expanding their presence and power on the Plains. Like the Comanche, other tribes, in acts of ethnogenesis, combined fragmented groups, reinvented tribal identities, and incorporated into the newly formed Native groups, hybrid in religious and cultural beliefs. These were survival techniques, compromises aimed at retaining at least a modicum of Indian individuality in the face of increasingly heavy pressures from the invading Spanish.

For Indian women, the pressures were frequently more difficult than for Indian men. As servants or slaves, the women were too often victims of Spanish abuse or moral lapses. Even though increasing numbers of Spanish families came to the Southwest, presidios, farms and ranches, and other outlying areas were male-dominated, containing few Spanish women. This gender imbalance in the early Borderlands sometimes led to sexual abuse, with Native women victimized by rapacious Spanish men. For example, in a horrendous incident in New Mexico, when one Alejandro Mora raped his domestic named Juana, he brazenly said he had done so, "'to determine if she was a virgin.'" Because she had resisted, reported Juana, "'he hung me from a roof-beam and beat me.'" Even the padres occasionally broke their oaths of chastity and fathered children with Native women, married and unmarried. Indians were not blind to these lustful double standards of priests who preached sexual purity and yet preyed on mission women.

~

The sociocultural story of the Spanish Southwest is much more complicated than abusive Spanish men and victimized Indian women, however. In these more than two centuries of contact new kinds of racial, ethnic, and gender identities and relationships emerged. Indeed, one of the most revealing indicators of Spanish presence in the Southwest was the development of a mixed, ever-evolving society. The Spanish, especially those born in Spain (*peninsulares*) or to Spanish parents in the New World (*criollos*), considered themselves *gente de razón* (people of reason) and thought of those farthest from them on the racial/ethnic spectrum as *gente sin razón* (people without reason). This perspective meant that Spaniards considered Indians part of this second category, as people lacking "reason." But, over time, since the Spanish were unable to replicate the racial and class divisions they knew in Europe, they were forced to accept the inevitable, which usually included intermarriage or cohabitation with Indians or people of other races.

What men felt free to do on the isolated frontier of the New Spain changed family traditions and revolutionized sexual expectations. Even though the Spanish were conservative on religious and moral practices, their deeds in the Borderlands often bruised or even broke several of these traditions. In a land where men greatly outnumbered "acceptable" women (of similar racial and class backgrounds), Spanish men often married relatives or without benefit of clergy. Others married what the Spanish considered below their class, meaning they took Indian women as wives or mistresses. Those couples of lower-class origin (*gente baja*) often lived together, unwilling to pay fees to sanctify their unions or to satisfy priests who were themselves breaking their oaths of chastity. Men who could not find socially acceptable women sometimes resorted to prostitutes, were guilty of rape, or even indulged in sodomy or bestiality. Clearly, the Borderlands, devoid as it was of sufficient Spanish women for the Spanish men stationed or living there, led to deeds well beyond those considered usual or acceptable for Spanish males.

As a result, a welter of racial and ethnic identities characterized the Borderlands. The most typical of the new combinations was a man of Spanish heritage marrying or living with a Native American woman. Their mixed-blood children were classified as *mestizos*. Eventually, from the mid-nineteenth century forward, these mixes became widespread. In addition to the numerous mestizo offspring, there were *mulattos*, the products of European and Indian or African parentage. Over time, racial and ethnic combinations became even more complex, with *lobos* coming from the mixing of Indian and mestizo peoples and *coyotes* from combinations of mestizos and mulattos. Finally, in New Mexico, there were also *genízaros*, captured or detribalized Indians who became Hispanicized and an underclass.

These racial and ethnic blends, and the class divisions resulting from them, left their imprint on the Southwest in the more than two centuries of Spanish domination. The area became, and remains today, the predominant Spanish-speaking section of the United States. Spanish was the language of communication, trade, and civil records. Over the years, Native leaders learned Spanish and sometimes took Spanish names. The Roman Catholic Church also flourished, as it still does in Spanish-speaking and Native regions throughout the country. Yet Native groups also retained, or returned to, their own languages, dialects, and religious views and practices. Not much changed religiously in the Southwest until floods of non-Catholic immigrants poured into the region in the twentieth century.

In other cultural trends Spanish styles also came to dominate the architecture and art of the region. Mission architecture, as well as the Pueblo style, became popular for church, official, and other public buildings. Although the Spanish tried to imitate ecclesiastical and domestic architectural styles they knew in Spain, they also frequently adapted the construction and styles of their buildings to local circumstances. Lacking builders and materials needed to replicate Old World structures, Spanish builders erected public edifices and residential dwellings, for example, that utilized adobe rather than stone. Travelers from Europe and Mexico often recognized and commented on the carryover of European architectural traditions, but they also noted the plainness of church and home interiors.

~

On the eve of the Spanish departure from the Southwest and Mexican independence in 1821, demographic patterns had begun to jell across the Borderlands. In Texas, now bordering on Louisiana, which the Americans had purchased in 1803 from the French leader Napoleon, 1,500 persons resided in the largest town of San Antonio. A few others lived in La Bahía del Espíritu Santo (later Goliad) and Nacogdoches, with no more than 2,500 non-Indian persons in the entire province. In New Mexico, the population included 30,000 gente de razón, with El Paso (then a part of New Mexico) boasting a population of 8,000 and Santa Fe 5,000, as the largest towns in the most populous Spanish colony. In addition 10,000 acculturated Pueblo Indian farmers or town dwellers lived in the province. Meanwhile, about 1,000 Hispanic or mixed-race gente de razón resided in modern-day Arizona, with nearly 400 living in Tucson. Alta California was home to about 3,200 gente de razón, with most of these persons living on the coastal plain stretching from San Diego to San Francisco. The three major towns in California were Los Angeles, San Jose, and Santa Cruz (then Branciforte). The presidio at Monterey, then the provincial capital, numbered about 700 gente de razón in the town and nearby areas. In all, about 35,000 to 40,000 persons who considered themselves Spanish or gente de razón lived in the Spanish Borderlands from Texas to California.

The diminishing numbers of Indians in these same areas amply demonstrates the negative demographic impact of the Spanish on Native populations. Above all other influences were deadly diseases. Although census figures for Native Americans in the western Borderlands are notoriously hazy and vary widely, some historians think there may have been about 400,000 Indians there at the time of first Spanish settlements: New Mexico, 1590s; Texas, 1680s–90s; California, 1760s–70s. Periodic smallpox and other epidemics sent a contagion of killing diseases like a deadly tsunami flooding across the Southwest, wiping out tens of thousands of Indians. Ironically those nomadic Natives farthest removed from the Spanish suffered least, although the dispersal of horses spread diseases faster and farther. Once Natives gathered in Spanish pueblos and missions, and near presidios, they died by the multitudes. Pueblo Indians in New Mexico, numbering about 80,000–100,000 when Oñate and the first Spanish settlers arrived in the late 1590s, had dwindled to no more than 10,000 in 1820. In California, the nearly 300,000 Native Americans there before the first Spanish missionaries arrived in the 1760s and 1770s numbered fewer than 200,000 in 1821. Native Americans in Texas and Arizona areas suffered equally high losses of population.

∼

When Spain withdrew more than two centuries after its invasion of the Southwest, it left behind a diverse sociocultural heritage. Of all the subregions of the American West, the Southwest or western Borderlands area has retained more non-English-speaking legacies than in any other western subregion. By the time the Spanish exited in 1821, the Southwest already exhibited many of the complex social and cultural features that remain to this day a part of the region's identity. At the same time that Spain was controlling the Southwest other European imperial rivals were attempting to set up their colonial empires in eastern and northern sections of the American West.

Anderson, Gary Clayton. *The Indians of the Southwest, 1580–1830: Ethnogenesis and Reinvention*. Norman: University of Oklahoma Press, 1999.

———. "Wakantapi and Juan Sabeata: Indian Leadership and Early European Invasion in the New World." In *Western Lives: A Biographical History of the American West*, edited by Richard W. Etulain, 5–28. Albuquerque: University of New Mexico Press, 2004.

Barrett, Elinore M. *Conquest and Catastrophe: Changing Rio Grande Pueblo Settlement Patterns in the Sixteenth and Seventeenth Centuries*. Albuquerque: University of New Mexico Press, 2002.

Bolton, Herbert Eugene. *The Spanish Borderlands: A Chronicle of Old Florida and the Southwest*. New Haven, CT: Yale University Press, 1921.

Bouvier, Virginia M. *Women and the Conquest of California, 1542–1840: Codes of Silence*. Tucson: University of Arizona Press, 2001.

Brooks, James F. *Captives and Cousins: Slavery, Kinship, and Community in the Southwest Borderlands*. Chapel Hill: University of North Carolina Press, 2002.

Bustamante, Adrian. "'The Matter Was Never Resolved': The *Casta* System in Colonial New Mexico." *New Mexico Historical Review* 66 (April 1991): 143–64.

Cabeza de Vaca, Alvar Nuñez. *Cabeza de Vaca's Adventures in the Unknown Interior of America*. Edited and translated by Cyclone Covey. New York: Crowell-Collier, 1961.

Chávez, Thomas E. *Spain and the Independence of the United States: An Intrinsic Gift*. Albuquerque: University of New Mexico Press, 2002.

Chávez-García, Miroslava. *Negotiating Conquest: Gender and Power in California, 1770s to 1880s*. Tucson: University of Arizona Press, 2004.

Chipman, Donald D. *Spanish Texas, 1519–1821*. Austin: University of Texas Press, 1992.

Cutter, Charles R. *The Protector de Indios in Colonial New Mexico, 1659–1821*. Albuquerque: University of New Mexico Press, 1986.

Cutter, Donald C., and Iris Engstrand. *Quest for Empire: Spanish Settlement in the Southwest*. Golden, CO: Fulcrum, 1996.

Forbes, Jack. *Apache, Navaho, and Spaniard*. Norman: University of Oklahoma Press, 1960.

Frank, Ross. *From Settler to Citizen: New Mexican Economic Development and the Creation of Vecino Society, 1750–1820*. Berkeley: University of California Press, 2000.

Gutiérrez, Ramón A. *When Jesus Came, the Corn Mothers Went Away: Marriage, Sexuality, and Power in New Mexico, 1500–1846*. Stanford, CA: Stanford University Press, 1991.

Hurtado, Albert L. *Indian Survival on the California Frontier*. New Haven, CT: Yale University Press, 1988.

John, Elizabeth A. H. *Storms Brewed in Other Men's Worlds: The Confrontation of Indians, Spanish, and French in the Southwest, 1540–1795.* College Station: Texas A&M University Press, 1975.

Jones, Oakah L. *Los Paisanos: Spanish Settlers on the Northern Frontier of New Spain.* Norman: University of Oklahoma Press, 1988.

Kessell, John L. *Spain in the Southwest: A Narrative History of Colonial New Mexico, Arizona, Texas, and California.* Norman: University of Oklahoma Press, 2002.

Sando, Joe. "Popé, the Pueblo Revolt, and Native Americans in Early New Mexico." In *New Mexican Lives: Profiles and Historical Stories,* edited by Richard W. Etulain, 19–44. Albuquerque: University of New Mexico Press, 2002.

Simmons, Marc. *The Last Conquistador: Juan de Oñate and the Settling of the Far Southwest.* Norman: University of Oklahoma Press, 1991.

Spicer, Edward H. *Cycles of Conquest: The Impact of Spain, Mexico, and the United States on the Indians of the Southwest, 1533–1960.* Tucson: University of Arizona Press, 1962.

Weber, David J. *Bárbaros: Spaniards and Their Savages in the Age of Enlightenment.* New Haven, CT: Yale University Press, 2005.

———. *The Spanish Frontier in North America.* New Haven, CT: Yale University Press, 1992.

CHAPTER THREE

Imperial Rivalries and Colonial Empires

∼

ON A GRAY, SODDEN MORNING IN NOVEMBER 1805, A NEW AMERICAN window to the west swung wide open. On that memorable day on the lower Columbia River members of the Lewis and Clark Expedition glimpsed the Pacific Ocean for the first time. Catching the stirring emotion of that illuminative moment, Captain William Clark, one of the expedition's two leaders, recorded in his journal, "Ocian in view! O! the joy." Lewis and Clark and their Corps of Discovery were the first American white men to see the western sea stretching to the horizon. They had looked through a vast watery door, open to the west.

That dramatic discovery on the Columbia was freighted with large meanings. American was only one of the ambitious countries vying for dominance west of the Mississippi and along the Pacific Coast. In the decades stretching from the mid-eighteenth to the early nineteenth century, the British, Russians, and Spanish (and then the Americans) competed for control of the West Coast of North America. The French were still another European competitor in the interior West. The story is one of expansive imperial rivals hoping to enlarge their colonial empires in an international West. Their story also bears news of numerous and varied contacts with Native groups whose lives would never be the same after the invading Europeans arrived. Together these stories illustrate again the complexities and changes that typify the western past.

∼

In the late fifteenth century, several European countries crouched in readiness to move outward. They were poised for new ventures, like a set of runners at the starting blocks. Freed from the shackles of medieval feudalism and gaining new riches through trade and plunderings of the Middle East, Europe readied itself for fresh contests. Ambitious kings and hungry merchants, hearing of possible riches in the Far East, already dreamed of the power and profits that might derive from bountiful trade with the Orient. The exotic goods flowing in from the eastern Mediterranean—wines, silks and linens, and especially spices—whetted the appetites of the Europeans hungering and thirsting after larger worlds of investment, domain, and notoriety.

The race to the New World began in earnest in the 1480s and 1490s. In the first competitions the Portuguese forged ahead of other new nations. Ambitious Prince Henry the Navigator (1394–1460) of Portugal, like a modern CEO, worked tirelessly at encouraging exploration of the Atlantic Ocean. First, he sent seamen to scout along the coast of Africa, to look for new trade routes. He also made use of the newest kinds of ships, known as caravels, and exploited the most recent technology for safer and more expansive sailing. By the end of the fifteenth century, Portuguese sea captains Bartolomeu Dias had sailed to the Cape of Good Hope and Vasco de Gama to India and back. Others were pushing farther into the Atlantic.

The Spanish, under the leadership of the dual monarchs Fernando and Isabel, followed closely in the wake of the Portuguese. As we learned in the previous chapter, Columbus sailed into the Caribbean in 1492, just six months after the Spanish chased the last Moors out of Spain and back to Africa. Three or four decades later the Spanish were in Florida, Mexico, and Peru. Throughout the 1500s and well into the 1600s the Spanish plied the Atlantic and Pacific Oceans. Then, in a showdown battle in Europe in 1588, the British defeated the vaunted Spanish Armada in the English Channel, indicating that English navies were replacing the Spanish as the leading European sea power.

Even before these pivotal events, England was also engaged in exploring the Western Hemisphere. As early as 1497, Tudor King Henry VII sent out John Cabot to the New World. Cabot explored the coast of Newfoundland, pointing out the abundance of fish there, and later may have sailed into Hudson's Bay. But not until the second half of the sixteenth century, under the strong, dynamic leadership of Queen Elizabeth I, were the British a strong presence on the high seas. With Elizabeth's encouragement Sir Francis Drake sailed along the Pacific Coast and perhaps entered San Francisco Bay in 1578. Other British captains and explorers were scouting the East Coast for possible settlements. Two centuries later Captains James Cook and George Vancouver made notable voyages in the 1770s and 1790s along the West Coast as far north as present-day Canada. These voyages and the overland trips of the intrepid explorer Alexander Mackenzie in the 1780s and 1790s established English claims to the Canadian coast and western mainland. In his second and more famous trip in 1793, Mackenzie became the first white man to complete a transcontinental trip across North America to the Pacific Ocean.

Meanwhile the French embarked on their first explorations. French adventurers, like other European explorers, were looking for a fabled Northwest Passage that would lead directly from Europe through the New World to the Orient. In the mid-1530s Jacques Cartier scouted for the passageway along the St. Lawrence River. Three decades later Captains Jean Ribault and René de Laudonnière and other Frenchmen coasted Florida until the worried Spanish chased them away. By the 1570s and 1580s, numerous European ships were gathering along the coast of Newfoundland to plunder its rich fisheries. In 1578 alone, 200 ships were in the area, with 150 of them French vessels. Frenchman Samuel de Champlain continued these explorations and moved on to the next stage of European expansion by establishing the first permanent French settlement in the New World at Quebec in 1608.

By the opening decades of the seventeenth century, several European nations had explored large sections of the New World. The Portuguese, Spanish, English, French, and, in a more limited way, the Dutch could claim a stake in European expansion into North and South America through their voyages of exploration. Next came the initial settlements. As we have seen, the Spanish first settled the Southwest in 1598. European competitors were soon on their heels. Over time the Portuguese and Dutch dropped out of the race to explore and settle the American West, but the Russians took their place in the competition to claim the West Coast as imperial territory. Another two centuries elapsed before the newest entrants in the contest, the ambitious Americans, joined the competition.

≈

Like a series of steady waves, the French rolled westward from the Atlantic seaboard in the 1600s and 1700s. Explorers opened the way for French entry into North America, and missionaries and fur traders soon followed. Sometimes missionaries and traders traveled with the explorers. Together, they facilitated French expansion onto the frontier. By 1763, the French knew the Canadian East Coast, the Great Lakes, and much of the Mississippi Valley.

Samuel de Champlain was the French founding father. In 1608, and later in the 1630s, Champlain and his followers established New France and Quebec along the St. Lawrence before others pushed on to the Great Lakes. Roughly two decades later the aggressive Pierre-Esprit Radisson and his brother-in-law Médard Chouart des Grosseilliers moved farther west, perhaps into the eastern Dakotas. In the next quarter-century, other redoubtable Frenchmen turned south, making their way down the Mississippi. In 1673, Louis Jolliet and Father Jacques Marquette descended the Mississippi to the confluence of the Arkansas River.

The most important of the French explorers on the lower Mississippi, however, was René-Robert Cavelier, Sieur de La Salle. In the early 1680s he not only found the mouth of the Mississippi but also established a French colony on the Texas coast. The ambitious and forward-looking La Salle claimed all the Mississippi Valley for the French, naming it Louisiana in honor of his king. As we learned in the previous chapter, La Salle's bold steps west of the Mississippi did much to rekindle Spanish interest in making Texas and eastern Louisiana a barrier against French expansion. But a return trip for La Salle in the late 1680s proved a disaster. Tiring of their leader's strange and autocratic actions, La Salle's men rose up and murdered him.

Missionaries and traders pushed the claims of the French farther into frontier Indian country. Indeed, religious motivations often competed with—and complicated—French efforts to explore and establish trade agreements in the interior. Beginning in 1615, missionaries of the Recollect order, which was linked to the Franciscans, tried to use the same methods of conversion and discipling that priests employed among Native Americans of New Mexico and the Southwest. Neither these efforts nor those of the Jesuits led to numerous conversions. When the Jesuits moved farther west and lived among the Indians in their villages and traveled nomadic routes with them, the missionaries achieved much more. But conflicts among various groups, the Iroquois against the Hurons, for example, disrupted Jesuit efforts in the mid-seventeenth century.

Missionaries, like the explorers, then moved west to the western Great Lakes and upper Midwest areas. There they established missions and quickly descended the Mississippi River, setting up other stations. In these and earlier missions the friars, especially the Jesuits, experimented with the "Reduction" system. Less centralized and regulated than the Spanish missions in New Mexico and California, these Jesuit-operated stations in New France tried to be less coercive and to adopt more Native traditions into the new religious mix. As one authority has written, "their basic principle of 'accommodation,' reflected to a lesser degree in some other Roman Catholic missions, counseled assimilation to native language and culture, minimal adaptation of Indians to white ways, and naturalizing a society to Christianity rather than 'civilizing' or westernizing it." Later, religious orders established schools in the Mississippi Valley. For example, Rose Philippine Duchesne, a French nun (recently canonized), founded convent schools for Indian girls in Kansas and other academies in Missouri and Louisiana.

Before long the French realized that the fur trade could be even more important than landholding in ensuring economic successes in New France. Looking for ways to compete with other European powers colonizing the New World, the French discovered that lucrative profits were possible in the fur trade. They not only pioneered the fur trade across Canada, but the systems they utilized

FIGURE 3:1. *Robert Cavelier, Sieur de La Salle.* La Salle was a notable French explorer. He traveled through much of southern Canada, the Mississippi Valley, and other frontier areas before his soldiers murdered him in the outback wilderness of eastern Texas in 1687. Painting by George P. A. Healy, 1882. Courtesy Chicago Historical Society, P and S–1883.002.

became models adopted by their major competitors, first the British and then the Americans. Within the bounds of the fur trade the French also made their largest, most significant contacts with Native Americans.

New France founder Samuel de Champlain laid the foundations for the colony's expansive and very successful fur trade. His formative plans called, first of all, for trade with the Huron Indians nearer Quebec and then for their roles as middlemen in the expansion of the trade deep into the continent's interior. Later, the Ottawa Indians replaced the Hurons as agents between Quebec fur merchants and other Indian trappers to the west. This two-part scheme—trade with Indians near Quebec and commerce through intermediaries with far-western Natives—became the blueprint for later British and American trade efforts.

The key link to the second, more expansive part of the fur trade system was the energetic *coureurs de bois* ("woods runners"). These adventuresome businessmen and fur traders traveled to Indian villages in the Great Lakes or farther west, often living with the groups with which they traded. There they married or lived with Native women. They fathered mixed-blood (*metís*) children whose diverse racial and cultural backgrounds helped cement French alliances with tribes in the interior West, particularly along what is now the Canadian-U.S. border. The coureurs de bois served complex purposes. As a group—and there were hundreds in the field—they linked together a far-flung economic system. But they also became exotic, romantic figures whose courage and derring-do made them legends in their own time. Later, British and American free trappers thought of themselves as inheritors of this French trapper tradition. What the mythic cowboy became to the more recent American cattle kingdom, the coureurs de bois were to the French fur trade.

Unfortunately for the French, they lacked the power and resources to move much beyond the Mississippi Valley. There were a few small victories, however. In 1720, when the Spanish leader Pedro de Villasur attempted to drive the competing French out of the eastern Plains, a contingent of Indian warriors, armed with French guns, destroyed the Spanish invaders. The European squabbles that ate up Spanish energies and ambitions also shadowed French dreams of empire. When the French were forced to cede Louisiana (the present state of Louisiana and the frontier territory of the Louisiana Purchase of 1803) to the Spanish and Canada to the British at the end of the French and Indian War (the Seven Years' War) in 1763, those cessions signaled the end of French domination in North America. Even though the Spanish, by secret treaty, re-ceded the Louisiana territory to the French in 1800–1801, the French government never returned in force to the Mississippi area or lands farther west.

Yet French influence remained alive in the West. The important Mississippi River towns of St. Louis and New Orleans and their surrounding regions retained the French language, the Catholic Church, and other vestiges of French culture. French impact on the fur trade and the roles of the colorful coureurs de bois remained in the West long after French governing elite left. More than a few French trappers and fur traders took up with British companies expanding westward on both sides of the Canadian-U.S. boundary. Even the famed Chinook jargon—the polyglot language of French, English, Indian words, and hand signs of many Indians, mountain men, and fur traders—illustrated the staying power of the French language on the western frontier. And, as we shall see, French unions with Indian women, leading to the mixed-blood *metís* people, had lasting impact on the social patterns of the West, particularly on the Canadian side, after France left North America.

~

The hunger of expansion that infected other nations struck Russia in the eighteenth century. Like the covetous monarchs of Spain, France, and England, the Russian czar Peter the Great wanted to expand his influence. Listening to rumors from Russian traders about the rich furs available in Siberia and farther east, the czar dreamed of exploring eastern Russia and discovering a possible waterway between Siberia and Alaska. Peter wrote, "In my last travels I discussed the subject with learned men and they were of the opinion that such a passage could be found." In 1728, Vitus Bering explored Russia's eastern coast. Another expedition in 1741, led by Bering and Aleksei Chirikov, touched on Alaska, preparing the way for Russian fur trade efforts in the next decades south from Alaska, along the Canadian coast, and into the Oregon Country. A generation later, the Russians were still interested in the northern West Coast of North America. In the 1780s, the Russian leader Catherine II even hired a British sailor, Joseph Billings, to scout out these coastal areas to reinforce Russian territorial claims there.

Russian explorations continued in the eighteenth and early nineteenth centuries. Concerned that European competitors would claim and settle the North Pacific coast, the Russians sent explorers as far south as the Bay Area in California. Even as the Russian sea captains plied the coastal waters, fur traders and other Russian entrepreneurs were beginning to kill off the sea otter for their pelts and to exploit the Natives as helpers in their economic efforts. As early as the 1780s, Russian trade posts and settlements were being established in Alaska. In 1812 the Russians founded Fort Ross, just north of San Francisco, but the post never amounted to much. It was too far from Alaska, too distant from Russian lines of communication and support.

~

Every American student knows the British settled the Atlantic seaboard in the seventeenth century. Late in that century and early in the next, a series of European wars between England and France spilled over into the New World, pitting English and French colonies against one another. By the mid-1760s, the British had driven the French out of Canada, the Great Lakes, and areas between the seaboard British colonies and the Mississippi. Although England lost the Revolutionary War (1775–83) and failed to decisively defeat the Americans in the War of 1812 (1812–15), they kept hold of Canada.

Canada served as one launching point for British expansion to the Far West. Another came through British explorations along the Pacific coast. In May 1670, the Governor and Company of Adventurers of England was established as a trade company in the Hudson's Bay area of northern Canada. Known thereafter as the Hudson's Bay Company (HBC—or cynically by its critics as "Here Before Christ"), the corporate company expanded westward in Canada in the seventeenth and eighteenth centuries. More than a century after the founding of the HBC, a second firm, the North West Company (NWC or Nor'Westers), was organized in 1784 and soon competed with the HBC in a series of bloody, destructive battles for supremacy in the North American fur trade.

Of the two companies the Nor'Westers arrived first at the West Coast. Searching for a passage to the Pacific in 1789, the ambitious and courageous Alexander Mackenzie, an employee of the NWC, traveled along the northwest-flowing river now bearing his name, the Mackenzie River, to the Arctic Circle. Four years later Mackenzie tried again and succeeded. This time he reached the Pacific through a series of arduous, demanding journeys on the Peace, Fraser, and Bella Coola rivers. There, on the Pacific Coast, the tireless Scots explorer recorded on the face of a rock: "Alexander Mackenzie, from Canada, by land, the twenty-second of July, one thousand seven hundred and ninety-three." A dozen years before the Americans Meriwether Lewis and William Clark, the indomitable Mackenzie became the first white man to cross North America to the Pacific.

Two centuries before Mackenzie's magnificent jaunt across the continent, British captains had sailed along the Pacific Coast of North America. As early as the 1570s, Sir Francis Drake plied the coastal waters off California, hoping to capture Spanish galleons loaded with riches stolen from New World Natives. The Spanish, fearing that Drake and other British privateers might discover the much-sought-after Northwest Passage (the Spanish Strait of Anián), sent several of their own maritime explorers up the coast of what became Mexico, the United States, and Canada. Although voyagers coasted the western shores throughout the seventeenth and first half of the eighteenth centuries, none led to a Spanish or British settlement on the Pacific Coast.

From the 1760s through the 1790s, the British dominated maritime exploration of the Pacific Northwest. The leaders in these signal efforts were James Cook and George Vancouver. A seasoned and ambitious sailor, Captain Cook had already charted much of the South Pacific, including New Zealand and Australia. He had completed two voyages to the Pacific in the 1760s and 1770s when he set out for a third trip to North America in 1776. Hoping to prove

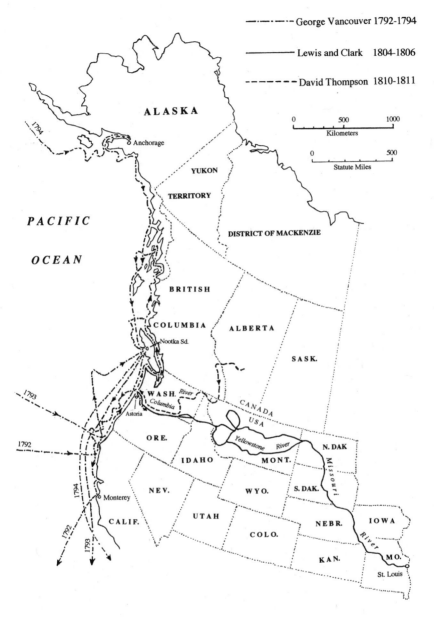

FIGURE 3:2. *Sea and Land Explorations in the Early Pacific Northwest.* Two Englishmen, Captain George Vancouver and trapper/pathfinder David Thompson, explored much of the coast and inland Pacific Northwest. Meanwhile Americans Meriwether Lewis and William Clark and their Corps of Discovery journeyed from the Missouri River country to the West Coast and returned. © Map copyright Herbert K. Beals. Courtesy Herbert K. Beals.

whether a Northwest Passage connected the Atlantic and Pacific, Cook sailed into Pacific Northwest waters in 1778. Trading with coastal Indians and attracted to the coast's scenery and mild climate, Cook and his two vessels moved north to Nootka Sound (on present Vancouver Island) in March and April. Cook then proceeded northward, still searching for the illusive Northwest Passage. Finding his way clogged with ice, he changed course, sailing south and west to Hawai'i. There, tragically, a violent struggle between Cook's men and the islanders led to the commander's death. But his men sailed on to China, where they learned of the abundant riches to be obtained by selling sea otter pelts to wealthy Chinese merchants. When news of these possible fur trade bonanzas reached London, investors and political leaders determined to send other sea-borne expeditions to the Pacific Northwest.

Fourteen years after Cook cruised into the Pacific along the northwest coast, Captain George Vancouver sailed into the same waters. Vancouver's *Discovery*, a sloop of war, and the armed tender *Chatham* moved along the Oregon and Washington coasts in April and May 1792. British officials had instructed Vancouver to continue the search for a Northwest Passage and to pay special attention to the Strait of Juan de Fuca. The captain was to survey the inlets, bays, and river mouths along the coast. "The obvious purpose of his voyage," two historians write, "was exploration that would facilitate Great Britain's commerce in the Pacific . . ." Vancouver was also to study the region's Natives, examining their societies and cultures.

Meanwhile the Spanish and English were at loggerheads over sailing rights in the northern Pacific and control of the Nootka Sound on what became known as Vancouver Island. Each side claimed rights based on earlier voyages. In the late 1780s the Spanish attempted to lock out their British competitors. But afraid of setting off an international imbroglio, the faltering Spanish caved in to the British. At a series of meetings at the Nootka Sound, half way up the western coast of Vancouver Island, the Spanish and British, while avoiding war, could not agree by 1793 on all sailing and settlement rights in the area.

As a British representative in some of these negotiations, George Vancouver helped solidify England's claim to the contested area. His extensive coastal explorations in 1792 did even more to substantiate those claims. Following his sound instincts, the capable and industrious Vancouver made nearly twenty anchorages and named several of the bays and waterways along the northern coast, including Puget Sound for Lieutenant Peter Puget. Although Vancouver missed the Columbia River on his way north, he had encountered American Robert Gray, whose vessel *Columbia* had just exited from its difficult entry into the mouth of the Columbia. After Vancouver left for California, his second in command, Lieutenant William Broughton, took the smaller *Chatham* carefully into the estuary of the Columbia. He spent more time than Gray examining the lower Columbia, thus buttressing English claims that the American captain had merely stuck his toe in the waters that Broughton and his men later thoroughly explored.

The British overland and maritime explorations by Mackenzie, Cook, and Vancouver provided some of Great Britain's major claims to what became known as the Oregon Country. Meanwhile, English fur traders came into the region—on the shirttails of the explorers.

~

The two great British fur trade firms, the Hudson's Bay Company and the North West Company, and their stable of energetic administrators and able traders and trappers were in the vanguard of actual British entry into the far northern West. Decade by decade and fort by trading post, the HBC moved across Canada, particularly after the French presence was eliminated at the end of the French and Indian War in 1763. By 1810, HBC operatives were as far west as the Saskatchewan plains, but they had not yet moved over the Rockies into the Pacific Northwest. After the two companies bloodied themselves in hand-to-hand brutal competition east of the Rockies, the Nor'Westers came first to the Oregon Country.

A dozen years after Alexander Mackenzie glimpsed the Pacific in 1793, the NWC sent other parties from 1805 to 1807 to establish posts near the coast. The Nor'Westers had heard that the Americans were expanding in the region and hoped they could head off their ambitious former colonists in the race to capture the rich fur trade of the Pacific Northwest. The most important of the early NWC partners to arrive was David Thompson. This stocky, sturdy Scotsman, formerly an employee of the HBC, explored much of the Columbia River drainage system. On his trip down the Columbia in 1811, Thompson stopped at the juncture of the Columbia and Snake rivers to write an important notice: "Know hereby that this country is claimed by Great Britain as part of its territories, and that the N. W. Company of Merchants from Canada, finding the factory for this people inconvenient for them, do hereby intend to erect a factory in this place for the commerce of the country around." Thompson also mapped much of the northern West along the current Canadian-U.S. boundary and helped establish trade posts in Idaho and Montana. Marrying a métis (Indian and French mixed-blood) woman, Thompson fathered a large family, which accompanied him on his travels and to his numerous homes. Later, he served on the British commission named to settle the boundary conflict between England and the United States. Throughout his career, Thompson helped expand the British fur trade into the Pacific Northwest and thereby greatly enlarged that country's claims to the region.

The vicious competition between the Nor'Westers and the HBC erupted into violence in 1816. In a deadly confrontation in the Red River Valley, just north of the Canadian boundary, a group of NWC men murdered twenty-one HBC employees. Hearing of this disastrous conflict, British officials forced the two companies in 1821 to merge under the aegis of the HBC. The new combination, signaling a turning point in English influence in the Far West, also created a vacuum in the Pacific Northwest because the HBC had not yet moved into the region. It soon did.

In the 1820s the HBC worked diligently to expand its dominion on the northern Pacific slope. Since a Joint Occupation agreement in 1818 allowed Americans to compete with English companies in the Oregon Country, the HBC, under the energetic and insightful leadership of George Simpson, attempted to head off their American rivals. After quick inspection trips to the Columbia Department, which extended from the Russian settlements in the north to Spanish sites in California and from the Pacific to the ridge of the Rockies, Simpson implemented plans of immediate and far-ranging goals. In the first place, to discourage American expansion of its fur trade, Simpson decided to "trap out" the Snake River area, stripping the area of all beaver. The British would also develop elaborate trade systems with Indians, enmeshing Natives like colonists in a complex trade web favorable to London. Moreover, agricultural settlements would be established north of the Columbia. If it worked as planned, this intricate system would not only further British economic developments in the Oregon Country, it would gradually squeeze out American competitors.

Even though the British maintained a trade and clandestine diplomatic presence in the far-northern Plains after the War of 1812, the center pivot of their expansive and elaborate design on control was the establishment of Ft. Vancouver on the northern shore of the Columbia, across the river from present Portland, Oregon. As many as seventeen posts were to be built or maintained in the interior of the Pacific Northwest, but Ft. Vancouver would be the headquarters for the far-flung HBC empire. The name of the post was selected, writes historian Frederick Merk, "to associate the Columbia River explorations of the Vancouver expedition with England's claim to the soil north of the river."

The lord and master of Ft. Vancouver was the magnificent Dr. John McLoughlin. A giant of a man towering six feet seven, McLoughlin exhibited a commanding personality. His bushy and prematurely white hair, his kindly but flashing eyes, his friendly disposition that could turn hostile—these characteristics drew and repelled visitors at the fort. For twenty-one years, from 1824 to 1845, as chief factor of the HBC headquarters in Ft. Vancouver, McLoughlin administered a domain larger than all of Great Britain. He worked endlessly to maintain English control in the Oregon Country by emphasizing the fur trade, expanding agricultural settlements north of the Columbia, and opening fair and just dealings with Indians. Related through his mother to well-known fur traders, experienced in the fur trade since his teenage years, and married to a métis woman, McLoughlin came well prepared and ideally suited for his work in the Northwest.

DR. JOHN M?LOUGHLIN.

FIGURE 3:3. *Dr. John McLoughlin of the Hudson's Bay Company.* Chief factor for the Hudson's Bay Company at Fort Vancouver, Dr. McLoughlin was a powerful British merchant and leader who often aided American missionaries and settlers coming up the Oregon Trail. A drawing from *History of the Pacific Northwest: Oregon and Washington* (1889). Courtesy Idaho State Historical Society, 77–2.5.

The White-Headed Eagle, as McLoughlin became known, was an able leader, but his generosity got him into trouble with his London bosses when the winds of change blew in new directions. Trappers brought in rich loads of fur pelts, agricultural lands up and down the valleys of western Washington produced abundant crops of wheat and other cereals, and the HBC gained the confidence of Indian trappers with whom the firm traded. But McLoughlin, disobeying company orders, also helped needy American missionaries and settlers who began to arrive in the 1830s and 1840s. He furnished these newcomers with food, places to stay, and even much-needed transportation. Americans quickly learned that Dr. McLoughlin at Ft. Vancouver could be counted on to aid pioneers. Gradually, by the early 1840s, it was becoming evident that England could not compete on equal footing with the incoming Americans. Feeling these pressures, HBC officials voted to transfer company headquarters north to Vancouver Island. Rather than follow company decisions, McLoughlin retired in 1845–46 to land he owned south of Portland.

The removal of the HBC to Canada and the settlement of the Canadian-American border in 1846 at the 49th parallel confirmed what many already knew. The Americans, by force of numbers, had become the sole owners of the Oregon Country. For nearly forty years Americans from the east had placed their footprints on this faraway northwest corner of the continent. Newcomers now began following their tracks west.

~

"In the annals of American exploration," writes historian William Cronon, "no single journey looms larger in either history or myth than the celebrated expedition that between 1804 and 1806 carried Meriwether Lewis, William Clark, and more than three dozen companions from the Mississippi River to the mouth of the Columbia and back again." The remarkable journey of the Lewis and Clark Corps of Discovery was all that—and more. True, sailor Robert Gray had established a tenuous American claim to the Pacific Northwest when his ship *Columbia* crossed over the bar into the mouth of the Great River of the West near present-day Astoria in 1792. But the Lewis and Clark Expedition serves as a watershed in American far-western history. Before their journey from 1804 to 1806, Americans were a weak player in the region's history; after the expedition, they were not only seated at the center table of negotiation, they were beginning to hold valuable trump cards.

Even before Thomas Jefferson became the third president of the United States in 1801, he evinced considerable interest in the American frontier. The curiosity of this red-haired, erudite, Enlightenment man from Virginia knew no borders. In addition to a thirst for history, literature, law and government, and the classics, Jefferson hungered after knowledge of flora and fauna, Indians, lands yet undiscovered. While serving as secretary of state in the first George Washington administration, Jefferson pushed for exploration of the West. In the 1790s he supported travelers who wanted to traverse the region. Those efforts came to nothing. Then, as president, he felt the increasing pressures of European and New World geopolitics. He wanted to secure the trans-Mississippi West before other nations actually settled the area. When Jefferson read British explorer Alexander Mackenzie's account of his trip to the Pacific Coast, he was goaded into further action. As president he could pull different levers and fire the engine of discovery in a more direct way.

When Jefferson in 1802 turned again to mounting an exploration of the West, he faced one large problem: the area west of the Mississippi and north of the Missouri did not belong to the United States. But the president was addressing that dilemma. Even as planning for the expedition moved ahead, Jefferson was negotiating with French leader Napoleon Bonaparte for the purchase of Louisiana (all the large land area from east Texas north to Canada and from the Mississippi to the Rockies). In January 1803, Jefferson sent Congress his rationale for the Lewis and Clark Expedition. Accepting the president's plan, the national assembly appropriated $2,500 for the expedition. Jefferson named his personal secretary Meriwether Lewis to head up the team of explorers, and Lewis requested that his long-time friend William Clark, a seasoned frontiersman, serve as coleader. Even as Lewis began to spend the congressional appropriation, American agents in Europe were dealing with France for the purchase of Louisiana. Two months after the successful transaction in France in late spring of 1803, the president received notice, and the news appeared in the *National Register* the next day, July 4. Now the expedition could traverse American territory up the Mississippi and Missouri rivers to the ridge of the Rockies. But from there to the Pacific they would be crossing contested terrain.

Jefferson gave explicit instructions to Lewis. The president asked the expedition, first of all, to explore the Missouri River and, if possible, find "the most direct & practical water communication across the continent, for the purpose of commerce." Lewis and Clark were also to explore trade possibilities with western Indian tribes. Jefferson likewise instructed the expedition to gather thorough scientific information about the Indians, landforms, plants and animals, natural resources, and rivers they encountered. In addition, the explorers must keep extensive records, which several did.

By spring 1804 the expedition was ready to embark on its momentous journey west. Lewis and Clark had journeyed down the Ohio and up the Mississippi to St. Louis, at the confluence of the Mississippi and Missouri rivers. They had recruited American and French frontiersmen and army enlisted men. During the winter of 1803–4, the two leaders had trained the new recruits, weeded out a few undesirables, and instituted military discipline. On May 14, 1804, they set off, day after day poling up the Missouri, pulling their boats by towlines along the bank or in shallow water, or hoping for strong winds that would billow the sails and help send them upstream. It was difficult, exhausting work. Along the way, Lewis and Clark attempted to establish peaceful relations with Natives and gather useful information about landforms near the Missouri. Except for the touchy and tricky contacts with the Teton Sioux near modern Pierre, South Dakota, these negotiations and the daily work pattern went smoothly. By early fall 1804 the Corps had arrived among Mandan and Hidatsa villages in present North Dakota, where they established Ft. Mandan and stayed for the winter.

April 7, 1805, dawned bitingly cold, with a frigid wind blowing in from the north. The expedition now included thirty-four persons: Captains Lewis and Clark, the twenty-seven young male recruits, Clark's slave York, a mixed-blood interpreter (who shortly turned back), and trader Touissaint Charbonneau,

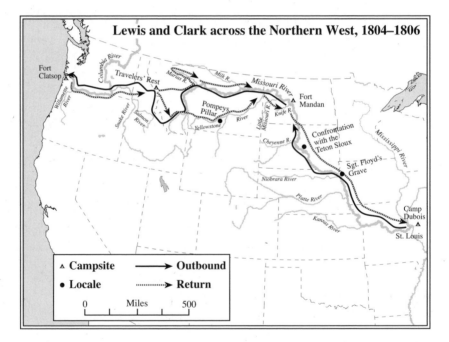

FIGURE 3:4. *Lewis and Clark across the Northern West, 1804–1806.* Explorers Meriwether Lewis, William Clark, and thirty-one other members of their expedition spent more than two years exploring from the mouth of the Missouri River to the Pacific Coast and back to St. Louis. In traversing the river systems, mountains, and plains of the northern West, they helped establish American claims to this area. Map by Robert Pace.

his Shoshone wife, Sacagawea (also Sacajawea), and their newborn son, Jean Baptiste. It was an auspicious moment in western history. The Corps was now 1,500 miles up the Missouri. On that day they headed west in two larger pirogues and six smaller canoes. They also sent back down the Missouri the large keelboat laden with collected flora and fauna specimens as well as Corps members who failed to measure up to the captains' tough discipline. Before the year was out, they were at Ft. Clatsop at the mouth of the mighty Columbia. They had had little sound information about the dangerous route ahead, almost nothing about the northern plains, the rugged Rockies, the treacherous streams, and the rivers running west to the sea. But they were nothing if not intrepid, superbly led, and vigorous young men. It was surely a journey of "undaunted courage."

By mid-June the expedition was at the Great Falls in Montana. In roughly nine weeks they had come nearly 1,000 miles and yet had not seen a single Indian since leaving Ft. Mandan. But the portage around the gigantic falls exhausted the men. For several days they stumbled over and through difficult terrain carrying their supplies. Clark, impressed with their diligent work during the portage, wrote in his peculiar spelling about the expedition's men, "The men has to haul with all their Strength wate [weight] & art. . . . Some become fant for a few moments, but no man Complains all go Chearfully on. . . ." They moved past the Three Forks of the Missouri and a nearby site that Sacagawea recognized as the place where Plains Indians had attacked her Shoshone people and she had been taken captive.

In mid-August, the Corps faced large new challenges. They had used up nearly all food supplies from St. Louis, they needed to find a way over and through the Rockies, and they must find a water route to the Pacific. Fortunately for the expedition, they came upon the Shoshone (or Snake) Indians. Although not an affluent tribe and themselves much in need of meat, these Natives were rich in horses and willing to sell or trade for those needed animals, especially after Cameahwait, a Lemhi Shoshone leader, recognized Sacagawea as his sister. Obtaining the necessary mounts and pack animals, the expedition labored across the high, rugged mountains in Montana, stumbled through the difficult Lolo Pass on the Idaho-Montana border, and headed farther west. Helped along by the friendly Nez Perce Indians, by mid-October the Corps was on the Columbia, their watery highway to the Pacific.

Expedition members did not react well to Native groups living along the lower Columbia. They thought of these Indians as dirty, as foul smelling from their dried salmon, and as unrepentant thieves. In turn some of the tribal groups abhorred the expedition's feasting on roast dog. But these Indians, the Corpsmen admitted, were splendid canoe makers and superb oarsmen. Soon moving by present-day Portland at the confluence of the Columbia and Willamette rivers, the explorers pushed on to the Pacific. Although Clark's journal entry "Ocian in view! O! the joy," anticipated their arrival by a few days, they were soon at the mouth of the Columbia on the Pacific, the first Americans to arrive at that spot.

The expedition spent a miserable winter at Ft. Clatsop in 1805–6, near present-day Astoria, Oregon. It was a soggy three months at the continent's end, perched as they were, rain-drenched visitors waiting for the deluge to stop. But on March 23, 1806, the sun came out and the Corps headed home, making the return trip much more quickly since, except for the miles up the Columbia and Snake systems, they were heading downstream. They also knew more about the mountains and clearances to cross.

Retracing much of their earlier trail coming west, the expedition had to wait at the Lolo Pass across the Idaho panhandle because the high mountain snowdrifts had to break up before they could pass eastward. At the end of June, Lewis and Clark divided their command in order to explore additional territory. Lewis and nine men went directly east, over the Continental Divide and on to the Great Falls of the Missouri. The most violent events of the journey transpired when Lewis, after splitting off from Clark to scout new country, went farther north with his companions. In a deadly conflict with the Blackfeet, two tribesmen were killed, and Lewis and his men galloped eastward to escape the Indians. Meanwhile, Clark and the larger group of men traversed paths similar to their westward route. Refloating their boats and reopening their buried supplies and following some of Sacagawea's knowledge of the route, Clark's contingent blazed a new section of the trail just north of Yellowstone Park.

On August 12, 1806, the two groups joyously reunited, even though Lewis lay wounded from an accidental gunshot wound from one of his nearsighted companions. The expedition moved quickly down the Missouri. At high noon on September 23, they nosed into the western bank of the Mississippi River at St. Louis. Soon thereafter, Lewis and Clark, York, and a group of Indians went to Washington to meet with President Jefferson.

News of the expedition's safe return brought jubilant headlines. Many feared they had been lost because their whereabouts and condition had been unknown for nearly eighteen months. The expedition had returned with an abundance of information about unknown flora and fauna, previously unmapped routes of rivers, and locations of mountains. Lewis and Clark also learned much about Indians. If we "listen to Indian voices and watch native people as active participants in the venture," writes James Ronda, the leading authority on the expedition, we have much to learn. The expedition should be seen, Ronda adds, as "a microcosm for the larger world of cultural relations in North America."

Although early nineteenth-century Americans might not have understood the important ethnic-racial implications of the expedition, they soon recognized its diplomatic importance. For an ambitious young country, the Lewis

FIGURE 3:5. *Sacagawea/Sacajawea.* This Native American woman, who accompanied the Lewis and Clark Expedition, made worthy contributions as a linguist and helped to secure much-needed horses from her Shoshone people. By the early twentieth century, images of Sacagawea depicted her as a larger-than-life heroine, as the virtual guide for the expedition in its arduous journey. Statue in Washington Park, Portland, Oregon. Courtesy Idaho State Historical Society, 68–45.1.

and Clark Corps of Discovery established a "right" to a piece of the Oregon Country. Now the Americans could compete on stronger grounds with the Spanish and Russians, and perhaps the British, for ownership of the Pacific Northwest. Dreams of empire quickly flashed into view soon after Lewis and Clark completed their successful errand into the western wilderness. But two centuries had to fly by before many Americans realized that the Lewis and Clark Expedition had its downside too, opening troublesome doors to deadly diseases, demanding fur traders and mountain men, and greedy and extractive overlanders, all of which invaded far-western Indian lands.

~

Reactions of Native Americans to European and American invaders illustrate the varied, shifting dimensions of the western past. Too often these Indian responses get lost in tales of Euroamerican high adventure sailing to or travel-ing overland to conquer the American West. But as one authority notes, when Americans tell such stirring yarns as the Lewis and Clark story, we "need to get out of the boat and onto the bank." Native American scholar Roberta (Bobbie) Conner suggests the same necessity when she calls for putting Indian tribes back into the Lewis and Clark and other frontier and western stories.

These stories of Native-white contact must include differences and changes since hundreds of Indian tribes and several European nations were involved in the international West. Along with differences and conflicts, compromises were also large parts of these stories. Even new conversations and combina-tions emerged from these cultural contacts. Stories of Native reactions to their encounters with incoming whites must include all these diverse ingredients.

European and American preconceptions of Indians often led to conflict— at first contact and later. Europeans, including the Spanish, French, British, and Russians, as well as the later Americans, arrived in the American West convinced of their superiority culturally and socially over Native Americans. These supercilious attitudes meant that white invaders, even before they met Indians, believed that New World tribes needed large doses of civilization and Christianity. If the Natives resisted they must be persuaded or coerced to accept the "higher culture" of the newcomers.

By contrast, Indian attitudes toward incoming whites were often ones of curiosity, hesitancy, or wariness. Most did not hold notions of superiority or entertain bellicose attitudes toward whites. When Europeans made their initial entries into western Indian country, they were often seen as mysterious new-comers mounted on four-legged animals and dressed in clothes that Indians had never before seen. The Spanish, for instance, although viewed as enigmatic visitors, were nonetheless offered food and hospitality. But later in the sixteenth century when conquistadors like Coronado and Juan de Oñate demanded and even took food that the Pueblo Indians needed, Native attitudes swiftly changed from curiosity to discontent to hostility. Repeatedly when Europeans and Americans refused to treat the Indians as equals and pressured Indian groups to provide food and other sustenance, Natives become unfriendly if not determinedly hostile toward the invaders. In addition to wondering why the newcomers were so demanding about food and housing, Indians rebelled at the mistreatment of their women. They also wondered why whites wanted to "own" land when it should be available to all. One Nez Perce man spoke for many other Natives when he asked Americans in the mid-nineteenth century why did they want so much land, and why were they trying to steal lands that first belonged to Indians?

From other Indian and white contacts came compromises rather than deadly conflicts. Refusing to be crushed or pushed aside, tribes negotiated with the white imperialists instead of declaring war or passively submitting to defeat or dominance. Among the negotiators were the Quapaws of Arkansas, the Choctaws of the Mississippi Valley, and several tribes of the upper Mississippi, all of whom became allies of the French in their competitions with the British. In the Southwest, the Comanches, Apaches, and other horsed Indians raided neighboring tribes for captives, which they sold as slaves to the Spanish. In the Great Lakes, Ohio Valley, upper Plains, and Mississippi Valley regions such tribes as the Sioux, Choctaws, Chickasaws, and several others, playing off rival French and British empire builders, were able to gain compromise agreements with their European allies rather than suffer defeat. Indians in east Texas and adjacent areas to the north, particularly the Caddos, Lipan Apaches, and Wichitas, found themselves caught between the Spanish and French and tried to wrest the best deals for trade, alliance, and support rather than to affront either European power.

But these attempts at negotiation and coexistence often foundered on the shoals of rapid, traumatic change. The arrival and dispersal of horses from the late seventeenth through the mid-eighteenth century, when nearly every Plains tribe had mounts, revolutionized tribal relations with other Natives as well as with incoming Europeans. The availability of horses transformed some tribes like the Shoshone and Nez Perce from essentially sedentary to mobile and more nomadic Natives. According to Native American author N. Scott Momaday, when his Kiowa ancestors gained horses "their ancient nomadic spirit was suddenly free of the ground." Indeed the appearance of horses impacted tribes throughout the West. Spanish horses from the Southwest, once they became available to tribes of the Pacific Northwest and the northern Rockies, allowed Indians from those areas to move regularly into the northern Plains to hunt buffalo, trade, and compete with other Indians and whites. By the end of the eighteenth century most Plains tribes also had guns. With horses and guns the Comanches, Sioux, and Blackfeet, among others, became the most powerful mounted warriors on the Plains, beating back Native competitors and holding off European and American invaders well into the nineteenth century. Invading Europeans, chiefly the British and Americans, impacted Indians in still another way. As they pushed west, these whites forced such tribes as the Cheyenne and Sioux farther west. When those tribes entered homelands of other Indians, fresh competitions broke out among western Natives.

Other kinds of invasions could not be put off, compromised, or defeated. The worst of these invaders were the deadly diseases that followed Europeans into the West. Total up the numbers of Natives who died in violent conflicts with other Indians, with Europeans, and from accidents; many more died from diseases than from all these other causes combined. In the "Columbian Exchange" following 1492 and lasting at least halfway through the nineteenth century, hundreds of thousands—even millions—of Indians fell victim to vicious European maladies. They "died like fish in a bucket," wrote one Spanish observer. A German missionary at the end of the seventeenth century spoke of the huge losses in another way. He said, "the Indians die so easily that the bare look and smell of a Spaniard causes them to give up the ghost."

Virulent pathogens (germs) did not appear immediately on the heels of incoming Europeans and Americans. But they were not far behind. The century immediately following first contacts usually was the most deadly. Even though Europeans and Americans had built up immunity to many of the germs they carried, those pathogens struck down susceptible Natives by the hundreds of thousands. In the decades after these Indian-white contacts, epidemics of smallpox often broke out, wiping out large portions of entire tribes. From the late eighteenth to the mid-nineteenth century possibly as many as one-quarter to one-half of all Plains tribes died from smallpox and other killing diseases. In addition to killing off tens of thousands of Indians, the epidemics undermined tribal coherence, driving Natives from their homelands, dispersing them, and pushing them into unfamiliar new areas. The Mandans suffered as much as any tribal group. With about 15,000 members when the French made first contact in the 1730s, the Mandans were decimated by smallpox epidemics in the next century, numbering about 2,000 in spring 1837. By the next fall only 138 Mandans were still living.

Diseases among tribes varied because their contacts with other Indians, Europeans, and Americans differed. Ironically, those whites who chased Indians from their homelands, chiefly the British and Americans, spread fewer diseases than those who resided in Native villages. The Spanish and French, living chiefly with southwestern, upper Plains, and Mississippi Valley Indians, evidently spread diseases more rapidly and thoroughly than those whites who separated themselves from Indians. When Americans began to explore and settle the West in the first half of the nineteenth century, they too brought other diseases that killed off thousands of Natives. Scarlet fever, measles, and cholera were particularly bad along the travel routes such as the Oregon Trail. Speaking of the deadly spread of cholera, one Cheyenne man wrote in anguish, "If I could see this thing, if I knew where it came from, I would go there and fight it." Understanding these debilitating losses among Indians from diseases helps one to realize why some Natives were unable to defeat or fend off invaders, let alone determine their own destinies. Once Europeans and Americans moved in force into the American West, the Native American world turned upside down.

Considering the astounding losses of life and power because of the ravages of disease and the mounting influence of Euroamerican newcomers, it is surprising how much of their destiny Native Americans were able to shape and control. When Pueblo Indians chased the Spanish out of New Mexico in the Pueblo Revolt of 1680, they helped convince the Spaniards to become better and more accepting rulers when they returned a dozen or so years later. Indeed, through intermarriage with the Spaniards and the influences of their mestizo offspring, Pueblos greatly influenced the configurations of sociocultural, political, and economic life in eighteenth-century New Mexico. Other Native women, via their marriages and other liaisons with the French coureurs de bois that produced metís children in the northern West and along the Canadian border, helped shape the fur trade and social relations in those regions from the seventeenth through the nineteenth centuries. Likewise Indian women who cohabited with or married American mountain men in the first half of the nineteenth century provided influential links between Native and white economies and cultures.

In general, stories of European entry into the American West too often overlook the cultural middle grounds that formed and existed between white and Native American societies. In these sociocultural crossroads, mestizo, metís, and other mixed-blood peoples served as cultural brokers among the competing societies in the West. When Native or mixed-blood women married Europeans such as the conquistadors and other Spanish settlers, the French fur men, British leaders like Dr. John McLoughlin and David Thompson, and American frontiersmen such as William Bent, Kit Carson, and Granville Stuart, they originated or cemented kinship, alliance, or trade connections and thus links of understanding between Indian and white westerners. Even as Indians were gradually defeated and herded onto reservations in the nineteenth century, they were able to define, through their agency, some of the terms of their traumatic transition.

~

The Lewis and Clark Expedition began to shape the history of the northern West and Pacific Northwest even before the Corps completed its journey. On the return trip, John Colter, one of the most valuable members of the expedition, left his fellows in North Dakota to return to the Rockies with fur traders already racing up the Missouri. Even more significant, the Corps's contact with Native groups along the routes from 1804 to 1806 disrupted previous alliances, forged new ones, and, unfortunately, helped spread contagious diseases among several Indian groups.

As part of his instructions President Jefferson had asked Lewis and Clark to report on the possibilities of expanded trade opportunities in the new country. The American president knew, like any insightful leader, that the nation that controlled trade networks in the West was likely to control and win the area. Rumors that the mountains and coastal areas teemed with valuable fur-bearing animals like the beaver and sea otter whetted the appetites of several ambitious leaders and eastern entrepreneurs in the United States. Among these businessmen was John Jacob Astor, said to be the country's richest person in the opening years of the nineteenth century. Astor hoped to capitalize on the new possibilities afforded in the western fur trade and to compete with the British already rumored to be pushing into these frontier areas. To establish his trade beachhead, Astoria founded in 1808 the American Fur Company, which later became the most powerful U.S. fur company. Two years later he also established the Pacific Fur Company to help expand his fur empire in the West.

Before other Americans, Astor realized he must display a strong presence in the Pacific Northwest if he were to realize his economic dreams there. But Astor's ambitious efforts in the Far West seemed jinxed from the beginning. In 1810, he sent maritime and overland expeditions to meet at the mouth of the Columbia and to form a trade post at Astoria. Distance, disorganization, and difficult weather and terrain confused and nearly defeated both groups. Setting sail in September 1810, the *Tonquin*, captained by the martinet Jonathan Thom, barely made it over the bar at the Columbia's entrance, but not before several men lost their lives in the effort. The survivors straggled ashore on the southern banks of the river and established Ft. Astoria in late March 1811.

The overlanders, led by the ill-prepared Wilson Price Hunt, struggled across the country from St. Louis to the Pacific. Often sick, hungry, and sometimes lost, Hunt's party limped into Astoria in January 1812. Ironically, despite all the arduous travel of Astor's expeditions and the difficult circumstances in beginning trade in the Pacific Northwest, Astoria was soon in British hands. When the War of 1812 broke out, the Astorians, fearing the British would capture the fort as war booty, sold out in 1813 to the English North West Company. Although Astor's post was restored to him after the war, he never returned to the Pacific Northwest, convinced the United States would not protect his valuable posts on the far-distant Pacific Coast.

The Astor experience, a failure in most respects, nonetheless strengthened American claims to the region. In the next three decades, as fur traders, missionaries, and pioneers up the Oregon Trail added to the numbers of Americans living in Oregon, a series of diplomatic agreements solidified the increasingly strong U.S. presence in this far corner of the West.

~

Between the Treaty of Ghent (1815) at the end of the War of 1812 and the mid-1820s, Americans made agreements with all the major powers vying for control of the Pacific Northwest. In this string of diplomatic decisions the Americans greatly benefited from the strong, nationalistic leadership of such luminaries as Albert Gallatin, John Quincy Adams, and James Monroe. These chauvinistic Americans not only wanted to protect lands the United States occupied, they looked for ways to expand their nation's boundaries. Well before the idea of Manifest Destiny bubbled up in the 1840s, these leaders were thinking of the future destinies of the United States.

The peace at the end of the War of 1812 only glancingly impacted the American West. Several events soon thereafter were much more influential. At war's end in 1815, Astoria was returned to the Americans, Andrew Jackson's defeat of the British at New Orleans strengthened American presence at the mouth of the Mississippi, and a commission was named to negotiate boundary questions with British Canada. Three years later, in the Convention of 1818, the British and the United States signed a treaty establishing the 49th parallel from Minnesota to the ridge of the Rockies as the U.S.-Canadian boundary. No boundary was decided upon stretching from the Rockies to the coast, but it was agreed for the next ten years to allow joint occupation of the Pacific Northwest by the British and Americans. That agreement could be renewed at the end of the decade. Neither the Treaty of Ghent nor the Joint Occupation agreement was a large victory for the Americans, although the negotiations settled vexing controversies between the two English-speaking countries. These agreements allowed the United States to move in other directions and to deal with equally difficult diplomatic dilemmas, some of which directly impacted the Oregon Country.

The next piece of the diplomatic puzzle turned up the following year, 1819, in the Adams-Onís Treaty (Transcontinental Treaty) with Spain. In this treaty, the weakening Spanish, fearful of losing all their holdings north of Mexico, gave way on several American demands. Luis de Onís, the Spanish minister to Washington, understood this necessary strategy when he told the Spanish king, "I think it would be best not to delay making the best settlement possible, seeing that things certainly won't be better for a long time." For the Spanish, that meant giving up their claims to Florida and the Pacific Northwest north of the 42nd parallel (the current California-Oregon border). But Spain did save Texas, despite the efforts of the ardent nationalist John Quincy Adams to make that area American. Two years later, in 1821, Spain lost the Southwest in Mexico's successful revolution against its mother country.

American diplomatic decisions vis-à-vis the West increasingly became part of a larger picture. That near-global perspective came into focus in the 1820s. President James Monroe, in his well-known Monroe Doctrine in 1823, enunciated the doctrine of two spheres, calling for an end to any new European colonization in the Western Hemisphere (the first sphere) and promising the United States would not "interfere in the internal concerns of any . . . [European] powers . . ." (the second sphere). For the American West, the doctrine meant Russian designs on the northern Pacific Coast must end, and no other European power, especially Spain, should meddle in the affairs of Mexico and its possessions in the present American Southwest. Less than six months after the Monroe Doctrine was enunciated in December 1823, Secretary of State Adams negotiated a treaty with Russia calling for that country to withdraw from all territory below 54° 40', the southern tip of Alaska.

With the Spanish and Russians out of the picture, only the British remained as competitors with the Americans for domination of the Pacific Northwest. In 1827, Britain and the United States renewed the Joint Occupation agreement they had signed in 1818. Then, as we shall see in chapter 5, the situation in the Oregon Country changed markedly during the 1830s and 1840s. First, American traders, trappers, and missionaries began to trickle in during the 1830s. Early in the next decade that trickle quickly became a full stream. By the mid-1840s about five thousand Americans resided south of the Columbia River in present-day Oregon, with only about five hundred British living north of the Columbia. In March 1845 the new president, James K. Polk, motivated by a rising spirit of Manifest Destiny, announced in his forceful inaugural address that the United States should take Oregon, to which Americans' title of ownership, he said, was "clear and unquestionable." At first, the British refused to yield to such blustering. But neither country wanted war, so pragmatic and wise British and American diplomats pushed for accommodation. In 1846, an agreement was hammered out calling for the U.S.-Canadian border to follow the 49th parallel to the Pacific, as it does today. Here was still another example of how often compromise more than deadly conflict shaped the history of the American West.

≈

In the half-century from the 1790s to the 1840s, several diplomatic agreements settled ownership of and boundaries along the northern American West. The aggressive, opportunistic Americans were the clear winners in these negotiations. Although arriving well after the European powers of Spain, France, and England had vied for at least two centuries for control of the West, the near-at-hand Americans pushed aside their European competitors to gain dominion over the northern West. In doing so the United States expanded its northern boundary to the Pacific along the 49th parallel. It also nailed down a southern boundary between the United States and Spanish (later Mexican) territories. Even before the ink was dry on these northwestern and southwestern treaties, the ambitious, expansive Americans were pondering other ways to move into Texas, New Mexico, and California.

Ambrose, Stephen. *Undaunted Courage: Meriwether Lewis, Thomas Jefferson, and the Opening of the American West*. New York: Simon and Schuster, 1996.

Anderson, Gary Clayton. *The Indian Southwest, 1580–1830: Ethnogenesis and Reinvention, 1580–1830*. Norman: University of Oklahoma Press, 1999.

Boyd, Robert. *Coming of the Spirit of Pestilence: Introduced Infectious Diseases and Population Decline among Northwest Coast Indians, 1774–1874*. Seattle: University of Washington Press, 1999.

Calloway, Colin G. *First Peoples: A Documentary Survey of American Indian History*, 2nd ed. Boston: Bedford/St. Martin's, 2004.

———. *One Vast Winter Count: The Native American West before Lewis and Clark*. Lincoln: University of Nebraska Press, 2003.

Carlson, Laurie Winn. *Seduced by the West: Jefferson's America and the Lure of the Land Beyond the Mississippi*. Chicago: Ivan Dee, 2003.

Crosby, Alfred W. *The Columbian Exchange: Biological and Cultural Consequences of 1492*. Westport, CT: Greenwood, 1972.

D'Arcy, Jenish. *Epic Wanderer: David Thompson and the Mapping of the Canadian West*. Lincoln: University of Nebraska Press, 2004.

DeVoto, Bernard. *The Course of Empire*. Boston: Houghton Mifflin, 1952.

Eccles, William J. *France in America*. New York: Harper and Row, 1972.

Fisher, Robin. *Vancouver's Voyage: Charting the Northwest Coast, 1791–1795*. Seattle: University of Washington Press, 1992.

Gitlin, Jay. "Empires of Trade, Hinterlands of Settlement." In *The Oxford History of the American West*, edited by Clyde A. Milner II, Carol A. O'Connor, and Martha Sandweiss, 79–113. New York: Oxford University Press, 1994.

———. "On the Boundaries of Empire: Connecting the West to Its Imperial Past." In *Under an Open Sky: Rethinking America's Western Past*, edited by William Cronon, George Miles, and Jay Gitlin, 71–89, 285–91. New York: Norton, 1992.

Goetzmann, William H. *New Lands, New Men: America and the Second Great Age of Discovery*. New York: Viking, 1986.

Golay, Michael. *The Tide of Empire: America's March to the Pacific*. New York: Wiley, 2003.

Gough, Barry. *Distant Domain: Britain and the Northwest Coast of North America, 1579–1809*. Vancouver: University of British Columbia Press, 1980.

Haycox, Stephen W. *Alaska: An American Colony*. Seattle: University of Washington Press, 2002.

Lang, William. "George Vancouver, Lewis and Clark, and David Thompson: Exploring the Pacific Northwest by Tide and Trail." In *Western Lives: A Biographical History of the American West*, edited by Richard W. Etulain, 89–116. Albuquerque: University of New Mexico Press, 2004.

Mackie, Richard. *Trading Beyond the Mountains: The British Fur Trade in the Pacific Northwest, 1793–1843.* Vancouver: University of British Columbia Press, 1997.

Mancall, Peter C., and James H. Merrell, eds. *American Encounters: Natives and Newcomers from European Contact to Indian Removal, 1500–1850.* New York: Routledge, 1999.

Meinig, D. W. *Atlantic America, 1492–1800.* Vol. 1, *The Shaping of America: A Geographical Perspective on 500 Years of History.* New Haven, CT: Yale University Press, 1986.

Momaday, N. Scott. *The Way to Rainy Mountain.* Albuquerque: University of New Mexico Press, 1969.

Moulton, Gary, ed. *The Journals of the Lewis and Clark Expedition.* 13 vols. Lincoln: University of Nebraska Press, 1983–2001.

Reed, John Phillip. *Contested Empire: Peter Skene Ogden and the Snake River Expeditions.* Norman: University of Oklahoma Press, 2002.

Ronda, James P. *Finding the West: Explorations with Lewis and Clark.* Albuquerque: University of New Mexico Press, 2001.

———. *Lewis and Clark among the Indians.* Lincoln: University of Nebraska Press, 1984.

Sleeper-Smith, Susan. *Indian Women and French Men: Rethinking Cultural Encounter in the Western Great Lakes.* Amherst: University of Massachusetts Press, 2001.

Thornton, Russell. *American Indian Holocaust and Survival: A Population History since 1492.* Norman: University of Oklahoma Press, 1987.

White, Richard. *The Middle Ground: Indians, Empires, and Republics in the Great Lakes Region, 1650–1815.* Cambridge, UK: Cambridge University Press, 1991.

CHAPTER FOUR

Opening the Southwest

∾

THE LID FLEW OFF THE SOUTHWEST IN EARLY 1821. THE SPANISH EMPIRE, which had dominated large sections of the region since the early seventeenth century, was collapsing. The Mexicans were poised to chase out the Spanish and take over the sprawling region stretching from Texas to California and extending north to Utah and Colorado. Also waiting in the wings of change were the Americans, ready to enter Texas and New Mexico in pathbreaking ways. By the end of the year, Spain was gone, Mexico in charge, and Americans on the move. For the next quarter-century, Mexico tried to control her new northern provinces. When Mexico's shortcomings as the new landlord became clear, Americans began infiltrating all parts of the Mexican Southwest. Twenty-five years after Mexico had assumed control of the region, another conflict—the Mexican-American War—erupted in 1846. Two years later, the Americans had won that war and had taken huge chunks of territory from Mexico in the Treaty of Guadalupe Hidalgo. By the middle of the nineteenth century, the Southwest had passed from Mexican to American control. That meant in less than three decades two different countries had ruled the Southwest, and now a third was in control. The legacies of these rapid transfers, especially in the shifting racial-ethnic makeup of the region, as well as complex American attitudes toward these sociocultural changes, would impact the Southwest for the next century—and more.

∾

News of the dramatic transition from Spanish to Mexican dominion pulsated north in 1821. In Mexico, revolutionaries, including General Augustín de Iturbide, proclaimed independence from Spain in February. But Spanish sympathizers governing Texas, New Mexico, Sonoma, and California hesitated to join the treason. Still, through the spring and summer, governors of the *Provincias Internas* (internal provinces) gave way, swearing allegiance to the new Mexican government. California delayed until April 1822 before capitulating to the untried rulers in Mexico City. On July 25, 1822, the feast day of Spain's patron saint Santiago (St. James), General Iturbide "reached for the golden ring," writes historian John L. Kessell, and "had himself crowned Augustín, emperor of Mexico. His reign lasted not a year. Further struggle ensued, as factions convulsed the new nation's center and ignored its periphery." These extraordinary events of 1821–22 foreshadowed many of the complexities and dilemmas that vexed Mexico and its provinces to the north in the next twenty-five years.

Revolutions are often like youths coming of age: declarations of independence and a change in official status frequently do not solve preexisting difficulties and dilemmas. Although Mexico had achieved its independence, it faced enormous odds in trying to unify diverse, widely scattered peoples. Only a strong, insightful leader with a large loyal following could have solidified the new Mexican republic. That leadership and unity were missing in Mexico in the 1820s.

Distance, perplexing diversity, and faulty administration marked the Mexican provinces from Texas to California in the early 1820s. During the previous years Spain had never overcome the dilemmas of communication between Mexico City and its far-northern frontier. Important messages and crucial decisions often took weeks—if not months—to reach the provinces. Sometimes legislative enactments had already been repealed before the initial legislation reached Texas, New Mexico, or California. The tyranny of distance also exacerbated church relations. At the end of the Spanish period, approximately 40,000 to 50,000 persons resided in New Mexico, but *nuevomexicanos* had not seen a presiding bishop, then residing in Durango, Mexico, for more than fifty years. On this faraway frontier only twenty-four priests were available to deal with all the *mestizos* (mixed bloods) and Indians, meaning each pastor served more than 1,500 to 2,000 parishioners. In the next decades, the Mexican government and the Catholic Church were no more successful than the Spanish in overcoming the distance and inadequate communication separating the core from the peripheries of the new Republic.

Mexicans faced other problems that eventually divided the country into warring federalist and liberal political camps. Several large political dilemmas perplexed the new government. How would monarchical rule be replaced in the New World? Should Mexico adopt a centrist government with political power emanating from Mexico City, or should it allow, as others wished, more control at the provincial level? In 1824, through a new constitution, Mexico attempted to address these knotty problems.

Equally vexing were relations with Indians. In the closing years of Spain's rule, the Spanish made two important changes in its dealings with Native

Americans, hoping to ameliorate if not solve the large questions challenging their Indian programs. Spanish administrative policies were revised, and their treatment of Indians was readjusted. In revising its course, Spain trusted that the use of gifts and other inducements might forge new understandings with nomadic tribes such as the Utes, Arapahos, Kiowas, Pawnees, Navajos, Apaches, and especially the Comanches. These Native raiders had large impacts on the far-northern territorial rim, forcing the Spanish and their Pueblo Indian allies to expend more money and energy on military missions than planned, and discouraging immigration and investment in a chancy environment. The Mexican government inherited this unsolved problem.

Other dilemmas on ethnic, class, and economic issues remained. In New Mexico, for example, Spanish upper-class *ricos* often discriminated against *los pobres* (the poorer ones), especially those of Indian or African heritage. This racial and class hostility made it difficult for mixed-race mestizos to gain political, economic, or social power or leadership. When don Pedro Bautista Pino became the first New Mexican representative to the Spanish Cortes (Congress) in 1810, he tried to counter Spain's ethnocentric criticism that New Mexicans were largely mixed-bloods: mestizos (Spanish and Indian), *mulattos* (mixes of Spanish, Indian, and perhaps black Africans), and *coyotes* (children of Indian slave women and non-Indian fathers). But in responding that all New Mexicans were either full-blood Spanish or Pueblo Indians, Pino lied, asserts historian John Kessell. In falsifying the makeup of New Mexican society, Pino "revealed the mindset of a New Mexico rico, not the truth." New Mexican society remained much more complex than Pino averred. Later, Pino could have argued that at least Mexico, in contrast to Spain, tried to deal with these major racial and class tensions soon after it wrested control from the Spanish.

Finally, a host of economic questions faced the new Mexican government. In the first place, an unfavorable balance of trade existed. Residents of the far north were importing much more than they were exporting. The result was often fiscal chaos for the provincials, who were being treated like colonists in a mercantilist imperial system. The continuing military difficulties with Indians also ladled off funding for other needs, disrupted trade with other Natives, and encouraged smugglers, who resorted to numerous dodges to avoid poorly enforced government regulations. Spain had not been able to get solid, middle-class citizens to settle on uncertain frontiers like east Texas or California because those citizens saw few safe economic possibilities there. They likewise feared for their lives. Here again the new Mexican government moved in novel directions to address existing difficulties.

Three years after gaining its independence, Mexico adopted the Constitution of 1824. The new constitution, which remained in effect until 1835, dealt with several of the vexations apparent in the new country. First, it established a federated political system of states and territories. Although none of the far-northern areas became a separate state under this new system, Alta California (present California) and New Mexico were denominated territories, and Texas and the Arizona region were linked to Mexican states south of them. But the constitution writers wanted to allow the territories and states more local jurisdiction, to be freer than under the Spanish. In theory the document also decreed the end to all class and race distinctions. Yet it also gave special *fueros* (rights or privileges) to the military and clergy and allowed for only the Roman Catholic religion, even while declaring universal freedom of speech.

The Constitution of 1824 was a grand, idealistic document and not surprisingly failed to solve the dilemmas facing Mexico. Two bickering factions quickly emerged: the centrists or conservatives, including the clergy, the ricos (largely landowners and businessmen), and the military, called for a stronger central government; and the liberals, consisting primarily of liberal *criollos* (Spaniards born in Mexico) and mestizos, stood for less domination by religious and centrist forces and more power for citizens in the states and territories. These factions, and the fractious disputes separating them, hamstrung well-organized, thoughtful administration of the provinces. Like many former colonies becoming new independent states, Mexico had decided on home rule (Mexico rather than Spain) but not on who should rule at home (centrists or liberals). These large, persisting divisions and the chaos resulting from them obviously shaped Mexican policy, or the lack of it, vis-à-vis the northern areas. Snapshots of Texas, New Mexico, and California during the Mexican period (1821–46) reveal the shaky, inadequate linkages between the core and the peripheries of the Mexican state.

Other threatening agents of change crouched nearby. In 1821, the year Spanish control ended in the Southwest, two American men waited to enter different parts of the region. Immediately after the Spanish left, Stephen F. Austin moved to Texas to assume the negotiations his late father, Moses Austin, had begun in 1819 with Spain. At the same time, William Becknell organized a group of traders to set out for Santa Fe, after hearing that the new Mexican government might welcome traders and even allow immigrant settlers within its borders. These two men and their pathbreaking journeys in 1821 help to explain the complex transitions taking place in the Southwest in the 1820s.

~

In the closing years of Spanish rule Texas experienced more discontent and turmoil than New Mexico or California. For nearly a dozen years before Mexican independence Texas was in constant confusion. One revolutionary attempted to throw out the Spanish in 1811, and in the next year an adventurer, in command of a ragtag army, overran the province and declared it the Republic of Texas. In the absence of strong Spanish control, pirates and smugglers also infested the Texas coasts, including the notorious swashbuckler Jean Laffite. Then in 1819 when the Adams-Onís Transcontinental Treaty between Spain and the United States retained Texas for the Spaniards, a group of angry Americans, under the leadership of renegade James Long, attempted unsuccessfully to capture the

FIGURE 4:1. *The United States of Mexico, 1824.* Three years after its independence from Spain, Mexico adopted a new constitution reorganizing all its states and territories, including those that later became part of the United States. From David J. Weber, *The Mexican Frontier 1821–1846: The American Southwest* (Albuquerque: University of New Mexico Press, 1982), 23.

area. These rebellions and invasions were short-lived and ultimately failed, but they kept Texas in chaos on the eve of Mexican independence.

The Spaniards then made a fateful decision, which the Mexicans later repeated. Spain—and then Mexico—allowed immigrants to settle on Texas lands, providing the newcomers pledged obedience to Spanish—and then Mexican—laws. Among the applicants for a Spanish land grant was Moses Austin, an American from Missouri. Promised land on which he could settle as many as three hundred families, Austin returned to the United States, but he died in 1821 before he could complete his *empresario* grant. His son, Stephen F. Austin, renegotiated the grant in the same year with the Mexicans, added other similar grants, and began bringing in as many as fifteen hundred American families to Texas. Eventually he controlled huge expanses of land. More than forty empresario grants were handed out, most to residents of the United States. At first the Mexicans and incoming Americans seemed satisfied with these land policies. But as more and more of the rapacious Yankees appeared with their slaves and exhibited clear designs on additional land, discontents mounted between the Mexicans and the Americans.

In the 1820s, Americans, especially Southerners, flooded into east Texas, transforming the economic and cultural life of the region. Heads of families could obtain a *sitio*, about 4,400 acres of grazing land, and a *labor*, about 177 acres of farming land. In return for these land grants, immigrants had to swear allegiance to the laws of Mexico, follow Christian teachings (interestingly, Roman Catholicism was not mentioned in the agreements), and prove themselves morally upstanding. Notably, the statements on slavery were so vague as to allow slavery to exist on the grants. Americans from the South were soon bringing their slaves and establishing plantations, especially along the Guadalupe, Colorado, and Brazos river valleys in southeastern Texas. A few Americans arrived soon after the Louisiana Purchase of 1803–4, with their numbers greatly expanding in the 1820s. By 1830, more than seven thousand Americans had inundated Texas, more than twice as many as *tejano* (Texas Mexican) residents in the area. The Anglo-American population doubled again in the next four years, and on the eve of the Texas Revolution in 1835, Americans and their slaves may have totaled 35,000, ten times the tejano population. American slavery, and controversies surrounding it, quickly became a major reason for the 1835 conflict.

Predominately from the South, these invading Americans dramatically altered the sociocultural life of Texas between the early 1820s and the mid-1830s. The result was a multicultural society that illustrates the complex racial and ethnic mixes in the southern half of the American West. The Anglo-American population, drawn primarily by the empresario grants and other immigration ventures, boomed several new urban areas in Texas, including San Felipe de Austin, Gonzales, Velasco, and Matagorda. Although subsistence agriculture was widespread among Anglos, a few were beginning to grow cotton for market. The Catholic religion was the only recognized faith, but many Anglos were, at best, nominal in that church, with a shortage of priests encouraging their lukewarm religiosity. Gradually, too, since few Mexican troops were stationed in the area and residents felt unprotected, Anglos developed their own volunteer and extralegal militias.

The African American population in Texas consisted primarily of slaves arriving with their Anglo plantation owners. Although slavery had begun to disappear in the last years of Spanish domination, Americans imported thousands of slaves. By the mid-1830s perhaps as many as 5,000 slaves resided in Texas. In fact, observers began to point out similarities between slavery in the American South and in Mexican Texas. As one history of Texas reveals, "runaways were common; fugitives sought their freedom among the Indian tribes of East Texas or in the Mexican settlements of the interior." Rumors of several slave rebellions worried Anglos, but no major uprising among slaves occurred in the 1820s or 1830s.

For Hispanic Texans, primarily descendants of the earlier Spanish and mixed-race population, the Mexican era was one of rapid, often traumatic change. This tejano population lived both in towns and on farms. Men living outside urban areas usually worked as stockmen or subsistence farmers. Women in Hispanic families enjoyed a few rights unknown outside the Southwest. They could buy and sell land and inherit benefits from their deceased military husbands. Conversely, a vicious double standard remained in place: women guilty of adultery were severely ostracized and sometimes lost their property whereas philandering men experienced no such penalties.

Many of the traumatic changes in Hispanic society resulted from the impact of Anglos who poured into Texas. As American numbers mushroomed, they increasingly took control of local affairs, often to the detriment of traditional Hispanic rights and customs. As one tejano official complained, the Americans were "restless people—scheming, haughty, and rash." When mounting numbers of Anglos arrived, tejanos found themselves unable to decide political, economic, or social questions in their own homeland. Upper-class, well-to-do Hispanics might agree that American capitalistic enterprises, particularly the expanding cotton economy based on slavery, helped Texas profits. Yet in adapting American capitalism to their nonmarket economies, tejanos had welcomed in the snake of disruption, as they soon discovered to their dismay in the next generation.

For Indians, the Mexican period was also one of marked transformation. Gone were nearly all the Spanish missions and Catholic efforts to evangelize at those institutions. When the remaining missions were closed in the first decade after Mexican independence, mission lands were given to new landowners. To their detriment, mission Indians, without the priestly support and encouragement they once knew, seemed to get lost in the transition. Concurrently, nonmission and nomadic Indians continued their raiding, attempting to remain independent from Mexican forces and American settlements. Apaches, Comanches, and other nomads stole horses and mules, chiefly from Mexicans, and found markets for these purloined animals among shady Americans living in east Texas. Another change came in the form of Cherokee bands arriving after fleeing from the American South, largely Georgia and Alabama. Attempting to settle on the Trinity River in east Texas, the incoming Cherokees were driven off by Plains Indians and forced to move farther to the north. More than any other tribal group, the Comanches, the proud riders of the plains, remained *the* Native raiding force in Texas and New Mexico, and even into parts of northern Mexico.

~

The Anglo-induced disruptions aside, equally upsetting were the political clashes between liberal and centrist forces in Mexico City during the 1820s and 1830s, which spread into Texas. This virus of instability infected all the provinces on the northern rim, Texas with the rest. In late 1832 and early 1833 Antonio López de Santa Anna, a key figure in Mexican history, engineered a revolt against the military centrist, or conservative, leadership. After a chaotic year in which he served as president and then abruptly retired, Santa Anna made a comeback in May 1834, this time as a reborn conservative centrist. Earlier, his liberal or federalist leadership had alienated the Church and the military, two powerful Mexican institutions; now, Santa Anna returned as their advocate. Once in power, he terminated the Constitution of 1824, held new elections, and organized a centrist state in 1835.

Revolts in several states soon erupted against Santa Anna's new government. The centrists were clearly much more unsympathetic than the liberals to American immigration and rising Anglo power. In Texas rumors circulated that Americans were raising an army to invade Mexico. More real were American discontents with the constantly changing Mexican governments and the labyrinthine legal details that complicated land holdings in Texas. Conversely Mexicans in Texas and farther south were increasingly upset with the growing numbers of slaves American brought to Texas. By September 1835 a Mexican force was quickly organized and marched toward Texas. Reports that the invading forces would free slaves, take over Texas, and clear the area of resisters hardened the opposing factions into warring groups. In the first skirmishes that fall, American-backed forces won most of the conflicts, and Texans sympathetic to the Anglos began to call for a Texas declaration of independence from Mexico.

Early the next year, in 1836, President Santa Anna led a substantial Mexican force north to put down the rebellion in Texas. The Mexican troops swarmed into southern Texas and marched into San Antonio to surround the Alamo, a former mission where two hundred men were barricaded to meet the Mexican assault. On March 6, 1836, Santa Anna threw his nearly two thousand men head-long against the Alamo. In vicious, hand-to-hand fighting the Mexicans gradually stormed and captured the fortress. All of the defenders, including the legendary Davy Crockett from Tennessee, William Travis, and a few tejanos, perished that day or were executed soon after the battle. Santa Anna had won a major victory but lost nearly one-third of his men, including many of his troop command-ers. Flushed with success, Santa Anna moved southeast toward the coast to clear Texas of other revolutionaries. At Goliad, his forces surrounded and captured nearly four hundred resisters. On March 20, about 350 of the captives were sum-marily executed, on orders from Santa Anna.

The defeats at the Alamo and Goliad crystallized opposition to Santa Anna. Cries of "Remember the Alamo," "Remember Goliad," and "Death to Santa Anna" became rallying calls for a new force organized under the leadership of hard-nosed Sam Houston. When Houston retreated eastward with nine hundred men, many Anglo Texans feared Santa Anna would drive them entirely out of the prov-ince. The Mexican leader, confident of total victory after the Alamo and Goliad, followed Houston to San Jacinto, near present Houston. In a surprise attack on April 21, the Houston-led troops, some under the able leadership of tejano Juan N. Seguín, took the Mexican forces unawares during their afternoon *siesta* and in less than an hour defeated Santa Anna's command. The fury of the Texans drove them to continue killing Mexicans until nightfall. More than half of the Mexican troops were killed or wounded, with but thirty to thirty-five Texan casualties.

Total defeat at San Jacinto ended Mexican control of Texas. Taken prisoner, Santa Anna was forced to sign a treaty giving Texas its independence and stipu-lating withdrawal of all Mexican troops from the region. Mexico never ratified the treaty, but independence stood. From 1836 to 1845, Texas existed as a separate country, the Lone Star Republic, before its annexation into the United States in 1845. Distance, the unsteadiness and relative impotence of the Mexican state, the chaos of Mexican politics, and the rising numbers, power, and independent individualism of incoming Americans led to the successful Texas Revolution in 1835–36.

~

In 1821, New Mexico was the oldest and most populous of the former Spanish provinces. But by the end of the Mexican-American War in 1848 or soon there-after, New Mexico had been surpassed in several ways by Mexican cousins to the east and west. Texas became a part of the United States in 1845, and five

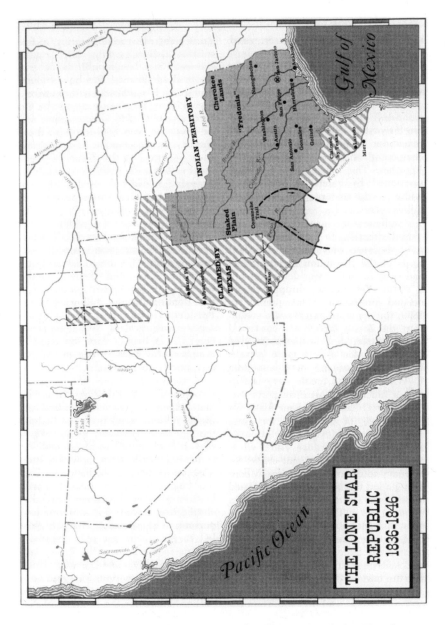

FIGURE 4:2. *The Lone Star Republic, 1836–1846.* After the Texas Revolution, Texas became and remained a separate country—an independent republic—for a decade before being annexed into the United States. From Lynn I. Perrigo, *The American Southwest: Its People and Cultures* (Albuquerque: University of New Mexico Press, 1971), 125.

years later California was also a new state. Conversely more than a half-century elapsed, until 1912, before New Mexico transitioned from a U.S. territory to statehood. Although nuevomexicanos experienced many of the changes that transformed Texas and California during the Mexican period, nothing like the Texas Revolution or the decimation of Native population in California swept through New Mexico. Mexican instability and American incursions were the major outside shaping forces; inside, racial, political, and religious tensions functioned as the most important agents of change.

When the Mexican period began in 1821, New Mexico was a far-off colony of scattered farms and towns. Most residents were of mixed race (mestizos), Catholic, and subsistence farmers. Pueblo Indians lived in their twenty-six towns scattered, in a crosslike formation, vertically up and down the Rio Grande Valley and horizontally from near the present Arizona border in the west to beyond the Sangre de Cristo Mountains in the east. "Wild," or nomadic, Indians such as the Apaches, Navajos, Utes, and Comanches surrounded the Pueblos and continued as daily threats to the stability of New Mexico.

The 1820s were a decade of both continuity and change for nuevomexicanos. Most residents continued to work their small plots of land, providing sufficient food for their families and a bit more to barter for needed household and agricultural supplies. Their most apparent ties were to the local *patron* (large landowner), to a *pueblo* (village), or sometimes to a *villa* (larger town) like Santa Fe. Many residents were *peones* (common workers), and some adopted the *partido* system of receiving their wages in livestock rather than in cash so as to become herders or part-owners of small flocks for a nearby patron. Their wives and children shared in this fairly stable agricultural, ranching, or small-town style of life. True, a few ricos like the Chávez, Martínez, or Pino families were dominant forces in the Rio Arriba (upriver) areas, but they were a very small group.

Beginning in 1821, the Americans invaded this land of *poco tiempo* (little time) and helped redraw its economic configurations during the next twenty-five years. Even before Mexican independence, a few Americans had sneaked into New Mexico. The most notorious of these visitors was explorer Zebulon Pike, who arrived in 1807. Sent by the U.S. government to explore relations with Indian tribes in Nebraska and Kansas in 1806, Pike wandered outside the United States (perhaps on purpose) and early the next year down into New Mexico. There, on a tributary to the Rio Grande, the Spanish captured Pike, took him to Santa Fe and on to Chihuahua, Mexico, before sending him back to Louisiana in midsummer 1807. Pike's account of his travels, published in 1810, whetted American trade interests in the Southwest. Other Americans, including several traders, had tried unsuccessfully to open dealings with the Spanish.

The door of trade and commerce swung open wide in 1821. That year William Becknell, a nearly bankrupt Missouri trader, advertised for men to accompany him "for the purpose of trading Horses & Mules, and catching Wild Animals of every description." When Becknell and his men arrived in Santa Fe in late 1821 they were warmly received and found Mexicans anxious to engage in trade. Returning quickly to Missouri, Becknell and others soon reappeared on what became known as the Santa Fe Trail. Often the traders gained huge returns. Becknell boasted he might make a 2,000 percent profit on his trade items of domestic goods, household implements, and small farm tools. When news of these astronomical earnings became known, the stampede down the trail was on. Hundreds of trader wagons wore deep ruts in the trail routes from Missouri to Santa Fe.

The Santa Fe Trail notably impacted New Mexico. Not only did the American traders gradually refocus New Mexico's major commercial links to the east and the United States; they also moved the region, bit by bit, toward a market economy and capitalistic society, away from subsistence patterns. The newly forged Missouri–Santa Fe connections weaned New Mexico increasingly away from its connections to the south through El Camino Real (the Royal Road) and the Chihuahua trade system. At first, many New Mexicans, sensing the new trade goods available to them, opened their arms to the Americans. Others were certain that an American fox had been invited into a Hispanic hen house.

The Santa Fe Trail, the growing impact of the fur trade system soon thereafter, and other Anglo incursions helped, in the words of one historian, to "Americanize Mexican frontier society." Down the trail came Americans such as Lucien Maxwell, Kit Carson, and a host of others who married Hispanic or Indian women and integrated into New Mexican society, changing it as they did so. Other American travelers flashed their supercilious attitudes toward native New Mexicans. Susan Shelby Magoffin, a Kentuckian and the eighteen-year-old bride of a trader, revealed much about herself in her diary, published much later as *Down the Santa Fe Trail and Into Mexico*. One of the first Anglo women to travel the Santa Fe Trail, Magoffin praised the politeness of New Mexicans and drew appealing word pictures of their food and dances but was repulsed by other scenes. "The women slap about with their arms and necks bare, perhaps their bosoms exposed (and they are none of the prettiest or whitest)," she wrote; and when Mexican women crossed a creek, she added, "they pull their dresses . . . up above their knees and paddle through the water like ducks. . . . I am constrained to keep my veil drawn closely over my face all the time to protect my blushes."

American presence in New Mexico continued to expand. Merchants or traders like Charles Beaubien, Ceran de St. Vrain, the Bent brothers, and James Magoffin, of varied backgrounds but also Americans, invaded New Mexico in the 1820s and 1830s. Some married daughters of important New Mexico families and began to exert clear influence in the region's economic and political circles. As the importance of these and other Americans waxed, lines of dominance from Mexico waned. Separation, political inconstancy, and the lack of resources led to the lessening

Mexican influence, with much the same outcome in Texas and California. Not surprisingly events in Santa Fe mirrored the unsteadiness of Mexican governments, where the presidency changed hands an incredible thirty-six times from 1833 to 1855. The lack of clear, peaceful direction from Mexico City encouraged and abetted expanding local control. As one New Mexican complained, "Mexico has never been able to protect us because, unfortunately, of continuous revolts . . . opportunism has smashed the union to pieces."

~

The lives of politician Manuel Armijo and entrepreneur doña Tules (María Gertrudis Barceló) illustrate the changes taking place in territorial New Mexico. Armijo served three times as governor of New Mexico (1827–29,

FIGURE 4:3. *La Doña Tules*. María Gertrudis Barceló, or doña Tules, represented the independent Hispanic woman during the Mexican period of southwestern history. Courtesy Palace of the Governors (MNM/DCA), 50815.

1837–44, 1845–46). Rising from humble backgrounds, he became a military leader, dispenser of governmental largesse (especially to his family and friends), and participant in the Santa Fe trade. Biased Americans pictured him as corpulent, crooked, and without courage. To be fair, Armijo ruled in impossible times when the lack of clear direction from Mexico led to many conflicts among local factions and fractious disputes over how to deal with the incoming Americans. In 1841, Armijo decisively led New Mexican forces who defeated invaders from Texas, the Texas–Santa Fe expedition; but in 1846, he seemed unwilling to rally other troops against the Americans, thus allowing them easily to capture New Mexico. In the words of one scholar, the career of Manuel Armijo reflected the "ambivalent loyalties" of his time. He governed in a "disaffected periphery" as it "had begun to drift away."

The career of the vivacious doña (or la) Tules illustrates similar ambiguities. Born in 1800 in Mexico as María Gertrudis Barceló, doña Tules moved with her family to New Mexico about 1820. She married and eventually bore two children, both of whom died as infants. Even before she became a wife and mother la Tules may have become a gambler, dealing faro and other games of chance. When Americans encountered Tules in the 1830s and 1840s, they described her as rather unattractive but with a good figure and lively eyes, and as a wonderful dancer. Others were less complimentary. Josiah Gregg, an American visitor and author who despised doña Tules, viciously libeled her as "a woman of shady character," "a common prostitute," and a "whore and gambler." No one else pictured her as such, although some accused her of adultery with Governor Armijo.

All Americans agreed, however, that doña Tules was a powerful, revealing force in Mexican New Mexico. She had earned a great deal of money through gaming and her gambling salon in Santa Fe. She moved easily through male society, and visitors often gathered at her *sala* (living room) for conversation and dancing. Even serving as a hostess for incoming Americans, she accepted the *gringo* entry much as she had other changes in her eventful life. Free, vivacious, ambitious, and charming, doña Tules demonstrated that Mexican women of her time could not be stereotyped merely as invisible housewives. As one historian notes, doña Tules "was the ultimate woman of Republican New Mexico, taking her independence to the limits possible to New Mexico women, stretching her opportunities as far as they would go. She lived her life exactly the way she chose . . ."

The elasticity and complexities of New Mexican life during the Mexican period led to endless puzzles. For one, the persisting clashes between liberal and conservative elements in Mexican political and social arenas diminished the power of Catholic religious orders and encouraged the emergence of local religious societies. By 1846, there were only ten Franciscans in all of the far north, nine of whom were in California. Under the growing influence of the Mexican secular liberals, Spaniards, including most priests, were ordered out of Mexico soon after they lost control of the area. In New Mexico isolation from church headquarters and the distinct lack of priests abetted the local development of *Los Hermanos de los Penitentes*, or simply the *Penitentes*. Rejecting church direction of their activities and keeping their pageants secret or at least out of public view, this religious fellowship of laypersons provided important rituals for an isolated province. Later, conflicts between a powerful local priest, José Antonio Martínez (Padre Martínez), and the church hierarchy under the unyielding leadership of Bishop Jean Baptiste Lamy revealed how much Catholics in New Mexico differed from those in other areas of the Southwest.

The most vexing decision facing New Mexicans, however, was how to deal with the wandering tribes surrounding and often harassing the province. As the Spanish before them, the Mexicans were not very successful in dealing with these Native groups. Neither a "velvet glove" nor an "iron fist" policy worked in treating with the peoples New Mexicans called *indios bárbaros* ("barbaric Indians"). Complicating the situation was the disarray of Mexican military organizations. Poorly paid and badly led, the military was unable to deal with the nomadic Natives. In the two decades following Mexican independence, Apache and Comanche raiders kept travelers, the scattered settlers, and even soldiers worried about their plunderings. One New Mexican complained, "We are surrounded on all sides ... by many tribes of heartless barbarians, almost perishing, and our brothers instead of helping us are at each other's throats in their festering civil wars."

At first Mexicans tried to utilize earlier Spanish techniques of gifts, trade agreements, and promises to control the nomadic tribes. When these policies failed, New Mexicans tried to battle their Native foes. But, with new sources of advanced weapons—some purchased from unscrupulous American traders—the raiders grew stronger and bolder. By the mid-1850s the Apaches, Comanches, and other wanderers seemed a more threatening force than the ambitious Americans.

Not surprisingly, the instability of Mexican governance, divisive class and ethnic factors, and pressing defense problems encouraged frequent political turmoil in New Mexico. After several previous squabbles, a violent rebellion broke out in August 1837 in the northern part of the territory. Lower-class New Mexicans, perhaps supported by Pueblo Indians, rose up in sudden revolt against centrist governor Albino Pérez. The insurrectionists murdered Pérez and replaced him with their own José Angel Gonzales, an illiterate, mixed-race buffalo hunter. Failing to gain support from the ricos and fighting a thrown-together force under Manuel Armijo, the rebels were soon crushed. But the complexities and deep divisions remained in New Mexico. Discontent with Mexican and New Mexican leadership paved the way for American military entry in 1846.

≈

Predicaments similar to those in New Mexico faced California soon after the end of Spanish rule. Isolation, flawed leadership, internal divisions among *Californios* (Mexican Californians), and new American encroachments defined much of California's history in the next two decades. But the secularization of the missions and the terrible loss of Indian life also sent California in different directions. From 1821 to 1846, California suffered through difficulties parallel to those in Texas and New Mexico but ones that differed in intensity and character.

At the beginning of the Mexican period, a small non-Indian population of less than 3,000 lived in California, primarily along the Pacific coast. The bulk of residents settled near the more than twenty missions scattered from San Diego to San Francisco or in nearby pueblos (towns) or presidios. Estimates of Indian population vary widely, but perhaps as many as 100,000 to 150,000 Natives lived in California, with nearly 21,000 congregated in and around the missions. Because few Spaniards immigrated to California before 1821, only twenty land grants had been given out before Mexican independence. But change was in the air, and it came quickly. Once Spanish dominance disappeared and strong Mexican control did not arrive, local discontents and divisions quickly surfaced. So did the Americans.

For Californians, what to do about the church, Indians, and political control became interlocking puzzles by the mid-1820s. Over time complex Indian-white and Indian-Indian relations had evolved. Although at times seemingly reluctant to do so, large numbers of Indians had moved to the missions sites—sometimes as a result of Franciscan encouragements to do so, sometimes to avoid the ongoing conflicts between them and "foothill peoples" like the Yokuts and Miwoks, who resisted priests' pressures to relocate to the missions. These differing responses to the Spanish and their mission programs, historian Albert Hurtado points out, "illustrate the variety of Indian-white relations in the interior" of California. Once the Spaniards left, the Franciscans lost power as their numbers diminished. Meanwhile, the rising liberal force emanating out in Mexico City increasingly pushed for the secularization of the missions. But what should be done with mission Indians if the missions were closed? These overlapping events and questions faced California well into the 1830s.

Even before the Spanish exited, the missions were in trouble. Although most of the Indians coming to the missions did so largely of their own choice, tragedies awaited them there. The numbers of Native deaths were beginning to surpass the birthrate at the missions. Epidemic, nonepidemic, and venereal diseases wiped out hundreds—even thousands—of Indians living within or near the missions. As journalist-historian Carey McWilliams observed, the Indians who remained isolated from the missions, including the Cahuillas and Diegueños, maintained a better survival rate than the Chumash, Luiseños, and Juaneños who became mission Indians and perished at an astonishing rate. "So far as the Indian was concerned,"

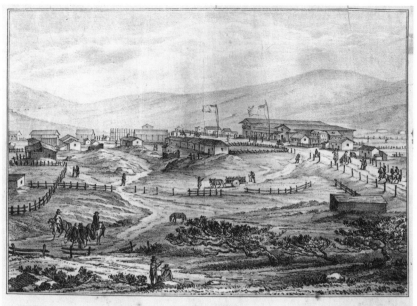

MISSION DOLORES.

FIGURE 4:4. *Mission Dolores of California.* The missions of the Southwest, especially those in California, illustrated efforts of the Spanish to Christianize, "civilize," and control Indian peoples of the region. Courtesy of The Bancroft Library, University of California, Berkeley, 1963,002:0100–A.

wrote McWilliams, "contact with the Missions meant death." Discontents among the Native neophytes often spilled over, with as many as one or more in ten at missions attempting to run away.

At first Mexicans tried to emulate the Spanish in utilizing the mission system to help colonize and control their far-northern provinces. Employing Indians as forced laborers, the priests—with the support of government officials—coerced the neophytes to plant crops of corn and cereals and to tend orchards and vineyards. Natives also became skilled herdsmen. Just before secularization in 1833–34, the missions owned more than 800,000 head of livestock, with Indians as their primary keepers. Although mission Indians helped produce beef, fruit, vegetables, and crafts, the Mexicans, like the Spanish before them, ruled more than "civilized" the missionized Indians. Conversion rates to Catholic Christianity were never very high, and once the mission system collapsed, not many Natives remained devout church men and women.

These mounting difficulties and clear failures encouraged critics to call more vociferously for the secularization of the missions. Other Californians, more unscrupulous and coveting the church-controlled lands, also urged the dismantling of the missions. Concurrently, liberals in Mexico and California joined in the chorus for secularization. As plans for shifting the missions from order-led (Franciscans) to secular institutions (control by parish, or secular, priests) were being formulated, a new Mexican government in 1833 mandated the secularization of the California missions. Chaos resulted momentarily, until California Governor José Figueroa worked out a plan for new secular leadership of the missions and the division of the mission-held lands among Indians, leading Californio families, and soldiers and their families. Unfortunately, the governor lacked the power to control the cupidity of los ricos and to impede their drive to exploit the Natives. Few Indians gained control of good lands, leading Hispanic families did, and administrators pledged to divide the mission holdings equitably rarely did so. If the mission system had been, at best, a mixed experience for the neophytes, their post-secularization lives were even worse. *Rancheros* and other new owners gobbled up most of the best mission lands, leaving Indian holdings too small to support their families. The former neophytes were forced to become farmer laborers and to abandon the mission areas for new homes in the interior. For nearly all California Indians, the next three or four decades were unremitting tragedy. They lost their mission status (unsatisfactory though it might have been), they succumbed to waves of diseases decimating Indian populations, or, even worse, they became targets for "Indian hunters" during the California Gold Rush and soon thereafter.

≈

The secularization of the missions allowed for the expansion of the rancho system already in place. Much of the land and livestock of the former mission stations quickly ended up in ranchero hands. Under Spanish rule only twenty land grants were given out, but under the Mexicans (particularly after 1833), more than five hundred grants were scattered among leading citizens. Many of these grants were carved out of the mission lands.

Attitudes toward the rancho society ran the gamut from idealistic and romantic to viciously negative. Guadalupe Vallejo, a woman from an old Californio family, wrote of the rancho life, "It seems to me that there never was a more peaceful or happy people on the face of the earth." But Richard Henry Dana Jr., the acerbic Harvard man who traveled to California in the mid-1830s as a common sailor, presented a more jaundiced view: "The Californians are an idle, thriftless people," he wrote, "and can make nothing for themselves. The country abounds in grapes, yet they buy bad wine made in Boston . . ." Despite the abundant cattle hides available to them, Dana added, Californios bought shoes from New England merchants at horrendous prices.

The rancho system encouraged an extravagant, short-lived society. Killing off their cattle solely for their hides at an alarming rate and failing to plan for the longevity of their herds, the rancho dons frequently lived showy and impractical lives. Before the term was coined, many rancho families were guilty of "conspicuous consumption." More and more in the late 1830s and into the 1840s, they found that the money they received from the hides and tallow they sold to Boston traders was inadequate to support their costly tastes. Their huge holdings were too often mortgaged to buy the expensive clothes and fund the extravagant entertainment and lavish holidays and weddings the rancheros desired. Even before the American takeover in 1846, the Californio rancho society was on shaky grounds.

Americans coming to California, as they had in Texas and New Mexico, wrought marked changes to the area. By the late 1820s they had replaced the British as the leading traders. At first Americans worked in the sea otter trade, as the Boston merchants had in the Pacific Northwest. As the otter began to disappear, American merchants turned to the half-wild mission and rancho cattle for their hides and tallow. If the Mexicans became the landowners after the Spanish left and the missions were secularized, the Americans became the men of commerce. As historian Earl Pomeroy concludes, by the early 1840s, "the Americans were rapidly becoming economic masters" of California.

Although increasingly powerful in California's economic affairs, Americans were never very numerous before 1846. A few Yankees, including fur trapper Jedediah Smith, wandered through the area, but not until the Boston companies established their hide and tallow connections were more than a handful or two of Americans living in California. Once such firms as Bryant and Sturgis and McCulloch and Hartnell appeared, American influence expanded in numbers and power. Agents for these companies usually became California residents, often marrying Californio women. For example, Abel Stearns, a New Englander, came to California in 1829, married the beautiful doña Arcadia Bandini of a well-known family, and became perhaps the richest resident of southern California. Another Massachusetts man, Alfred Robinson, arrived in 1829, became an agent for the Bryant and Sturgis firm, and married into the distinguished de la Guerra family of Santa Barbara. Perhaps the most important American immigrant was Thomas O. Larkin. Also from Massachusetts, Larkin came to California in 1832. Marrying an American widow whom he met on shipboard to the West Coast, Larkin set up residence in the California capital of Monterey, where he raised his family and built a two-story house that became the model for the Monterey colonial style of architecture. From 1844 to 1848, he served as the American counsel to California and helped midwife the territory into American control.

Not surprisingly, these transformations—the secularization of missions, the rapid rise and decline of the rancho culture, and the increasing presence of the influential Americans—added to the political precariousness of California. As in Texas and New Mexico, California politics in the Mexican period were as turbulent and nearly as frequent as monthly dogfights. In the vacuum arising from the lack of strong, decisive, and timely control from Mexico City, political leadership in Monterey and the rest of California descended into a series of "revolutions." Governors, military leaders, and increasing numbers of rancho families competed for political hegemony. Complicating the situation was an emerging sectionalism in which northern Californio leaders like Juan Bautista Alvarado, Mariano Guadalupe Vallejo, and José Castro battled southerners José Antonio Carrillo, Pío Pico, and Juan Bandini. Governors appointed from Mexico City now faced this additional vexation of a badly divided California.

From 1821 to 1847, nearly twenty governors (almost one a year!) tried to direct the chaotic politics of the province. The political career of one of these governors, José Figueroa, illustrates the challenges leaders encountered. An able man of strong character, Figueroa was named governor in 1832. He assiduously tried to solve the secularization crisis. Within his first few months in office, leadership changed in Mexico City. Figueroa received orders from the Mexican legislature to yield his governorship to his replacement and then, almost overnight, to reassume control. Even after getting mixed signals from the Mexican government, Figueroa tried to implement his own rational, fair-minded plan of secularization. But Californios lusting after the mission lands for themselves undermined Figueroa's plans in such a way as to deny Indians their rights and the land ownership the governor wanted for them. Caught in the complicated web of regional-national, class, religious, and family complexities, Figueroa lacked the funding and needed military support to carry out secularization in a deliberate, even-handed manner. In bad health, Figueroa resigned shortly before his death in September 1835. Although a man of ability and integrity willing to lead California through a difficult period of transition, his brief governorship (1832–35) symbolized the barriers even men of Figueroa's talents faced. Few others tried as diligently as he.

In fact, by the mid-1840s, California was on the verge of falling apart. Rival capitals in Los Angeles and Monterey accentuated divisions. As a result, politics, the justice system, fiscal affairs, and military organization were at a standstill, virtually collapsing. Then, on the eve of the Mexican-American War (1846–48), the turmoil in the region and the struggle for domination became clear in the Bear Flag Revolt of 1846. Hearing that Mexican leaders might be rounding up horses to attack Anglos, a ragtag collection of Americans and their supporters captured those horses and then moved on to Sonoma. There, under the leadership of one William Ide, the Americans surrounded the home of the well-known Californio Mariano Vallejo, arrested him, and took him to jail at nearby Sutter's Fort. Ide and his nondescript colleagues then declared California a republic and fashioned a flag of cotton that featured a lone red star and a grizzly bear. The Bear Flag rebellion had succeeded. Mexican opposition came to nothing, with California seemingly ripe for the plucking.

In the spring of 1846 boiling discontent pushed the Southwest toward the edge of chaos. The previous year, following a decade of independence, the United States annexed Texas. The Mexican government, declaring the annexation an act of war, withdrew its minister to the United States. In New Mexico, political bickering, difficulties with nomadic Indians, and anti-Yankee sentiments weakened an already unsteady provincial government. In California, disorder reigned. Two other happenings—one, the rise and flowering of Manifest Destiny, and the other, the election of 1844—provided the additional spark needed to ignite the fuse of war in May 1846.

∼

American historian Bernard DeVoto once argued that events in and surrounding the year 1846 made it a "Year of Decision" in American history. For DeVoto, several monumental occurrences—the settlement of the Oregon Country dispute, the coming of the Mormons to Utah, and the California Gold Rush—transformed the American West. Added to these pathbreaking events was the Mexican-American War. That conflict engaged American attention and energies from 1846 to 1848, and in the latter year the Treaty of Guadalupe Hidalgo transferred enormous new tracts of land and diverse peoples from Mexico to the United States. DeVoto was correct: the war and its aftermath was a defining period of the nineteenth-century American West, especially in its impact on the Southwest.

Long-run and short-range influences converged to precipitate the outbreak of war in 1846. As we have seen, Mexico's inability to govern the Southwest led to regional instability. Conflict with Indians, notable changes in Catholic Church organization, class and racial clashes, and conflicts between conservatives and liberals in Mexico and her northern provinces—all these unsolved questions kept the Southwest in turmoil. American incursions in Texas, New Mexico, and California added unsettling influences. Stephen F. Austin and other empresarios in Texas, Santa Fe Trail entrepreneurs and fur traders in New Mexico, and the hide and tallow companies in California illustrate the growing American economic presence in the Southwest.

Other trends and events as well pointed toward conflict. Mexicans continued to fear the slavery system Americans had introduced and expanded. Some Americans, especially commercial interests thirsting after desired trade ports on the Pacific, encouraged efforts to push the Mexicans aside in California. Other Yankees, thinking of Mexico as a second- or third-rate nation, haughtily dismissed Mexican resistance to American settlements in Texas and the Southwest. These superior attitudes probably lay behind the clumsy and inadequate American diplomatic efforts to solve border conflicts emerging between the two countries.

Additionally, by the early 1840s Americans became increasingly sensitive to what they considered their rightful role in world affairs. Expansionists and ardent continental nationalists such as Thomas Jefferson, John Quincy Adams, James Monroe, and Andrew Jackson were forerunners of the expansionistic mood of the 1840s. Then in 1845 Brooklyn journalist John L. O'Sullivan provided the needed catchword phrase to define this new marriage of American expansion and mission. O'Sullivan coined the phrase "manifest destiny." It was, he said, "the right of our manifest destiny to overspread and to possess the whole continent which providence has given us for the development of the great experiment of liberty and federated self government." Quite simply these words meant that God had foreordained a nation of English-speaking peoples to carry out their mission to spread their superior ideas and traditions to lesser societies and cultures. It was their manifest destiny to do so.

In the previous year of 1844, James K. Polk, the Democratic candidate for the presidency, had run on a platform of "the reannexation of Texas" and "the reoccupation of Oregon." Although neither phrase was entirely accurate, Polk's successes at the polls signaled that Americans were ready to solidify their territory, brook no competition from others, and perhaps take new lands lying at their borders. The annexation of Texas in 1845 and the settlement of the Oregon Country boundary in 1846 epitomized the Democratic platform promises. But might there be more? Advocates of expansion and lock-step disciples of Manifest Destiny doctrine thought so. When the Mexicans refused to recognize Texas as a new American state, contested the Rio Grande as the established boundary between the two countries, and recalled their ambassador, they played into the hands of President Polk and other nationalists. Polk sent envoy John Slidell to Mexico City to smooth over the difficulties. When that mission utterly failed—the Mexican government snubbed Slidell and refused to recognize him—the president ordered General Zachary Taylor into the disputed region between the Nueces and Rio Grande rivers, probably hoping that conflict might erupt. In late April 1846, Mexican forces crossed the Rio Grande and attacked American troops for entering an area the Mexicans claimed as theirs. When Congress heard of the attack, they declared war on May 13, 1846, with President Polk clearly pushing the legislators toward that declaration.

Soon after war began American military leaders implemented two strategic plans. One force, under Taylor's leadership, would veer south into Mexico; the other would move west, taking New Mexico, and then march to the coast to capture California. In August 1846, Stephen Watts Kearny entered Santa Fe with 1,600 men. Curiously, Governor Manuel Armijo, after acting as if he would oppose the invaders, retreated south without firing a shot. Kearny promised that all rights of New Mexicans would be protected under a new U.S. provincial government. As later events would show, Kearny's promise proved untrue. Moving west, Kearny crossed the Colorado River and entered California, where Californios attacked his command. Recovering from this engagement at San Pascual and joined by reinforcements from San Diego, Kearny marched into that town. There he combined forces with Commodore Robert F. Stockton, who had failed in his earlier efforts to defeat the Mexicans, and established a temporary government in southern California. Together Kearny and Stockton defeated a Mexican force at San Gabriel on January 8–9, 1847, and moved on to take Los Angeles.

In northern California, John Frémont, taking control after the Bear Flag Revolt, became the unappointed leader of that region. When Stockton, without grounds for doing so, appointed Frémont governor of California, Kearny and Frémont clashed for the right to govern. Kearny arrested Frémont, and the latter was later court-martialed and declared guilty of disobedience and mutiny, although President Polk leniently allowed Frémont back into the service. By the time this squabble for leadership was solved in January 1847, California was in the hands of the Americans. No one could have predicted, of course, that in the next two years the Gold Rush would explode and that California would enter the union just three years later in 1850.

During these months of conflict in New Mexico and California, Zachary Taylor drove into northern Mexico. After defeating Mexican forces north of the Rio Grande in May 1846, Taylor moved south. The Mexicans put up a stiff fight when the American invaded below the Rio Grande. Nonetheless by mid-September Taylor had captured Monterry, after which he declared a cessation of hostilities. Five months later, Taylor's forces were attacked by Santa Anna and his twenty thousand men at Buena Vista, about seven miles south of Satillo. In this momentous battle the left flank of the nearly five thousand American troops seemed about to crumble when Taylor arrived with reinforcements to drive off the Mexicans. The vicious conflict and victory at Buena Vista on February 22, 1847, which some consider the turning point of the war, ended Taylor's major role in the embroilment. In less than a year Taylor had defeated superior Mexican numbers four times and taken control of three Mexican provinces south of Texas. These large achievements were too much for President Polk. As a Democrat, the president feared the rising popularity of Taylor, a Whig already being touted as a presidential candidate for 1848.

So Polk turned to another man, Winfield Scott, to lead the invasion into Mexico City. In March 1847, Scott landed his twelve thousand troops on Mexico's eastern coast and quickly subdued Vera Cruz. A man of ample girth and fastidious ways—his troops dubbed him "Old Fuss and Feathers"—Scott was a skilled, able general. Marching inland, he avoided Santa Anna's force at Cerro Gordo Pass and moved on to Puebla. With the help of reinforcements, Scott swung south of the nation's capital where he captured outlying towns. Calling for an armistice rather than an all-out attack on Mexico City, Scott waited for the outcome of possible peace negotiations between U.S. envoy Nicholas Trist (who traveled with Scott) and the Mexican government. When Santa Anna refused to treat with Trist, Scott invaded the capital. On September 14, 1847, after heavy fighting, Scott entered the city's Grand Plaza. For the first time in U.S. history, its flag flew over the capital of a foreign country. The fall of Mexico City effectively ended Mexican resistance.

~

More than four months transpired before a peace treaty was signed on February 2, 1848. Even though President Polk had become disillusioned with peace commissioner Trist and recalled him, General Scott urged Trist to push on with the peacemaking. The Treaty of Guadalupe Hidalgo (signed in a small town near Mexico City) granted extraordinary concessions to the victors. Mexico ceded California and New Mexico outright to the United States and recognized Texas as American territory. The relinquished territory also included the present states of Nevada, Utah, Arizona, and parts of Colorado and Wyoming. In all (including Texas) the United States had gained nearly one million acres of new lands, more than in the original states and territories or in the Louisiana Purchase. In contrast, including Texas, Mexico lost nearly half its territory. In return, the United States agreed to pay $15 million as part of the treaty and to underwrite more than $3 million in damages U.S. citizens claimed from the war. The Rio Grande would become the new boundary between Mexico and the United States. Despite Polk's disdain for envoy Trist and his treaty, the president reluctantly supported the agreement and urged the Senate to ratify it, which they did. By July 1848, American troops had withdrawn from Mexico.

The Mexican-American War had not been uniformly popular in the United States. Critics, chiefly those in the opposing Whig party, claimed Polk had led the country into war. In December 1847 one tall, homespun Whig congressman from Illinois challenged the president to show the exact "spot" where fighting had begun. Thereafter he was known as "spotty [Abraham] Lincoln."

In New England, writer Henry David Thoreau spent a night in jail for refusing to pay taxes to support the war. Thoreau's resulting essay, "Civil Disobedience," became a rallying cry for resisters down through the decades, including East Indian leader Mahatma Gandhi and Americans Martin Luther King Jr. and César Chávez.

The war and the acquisition of vast new territories also added to the ongoing fiery national debate over slavery. Most northerners wanted to exclude the

FIGURE 4:5. *Territorial Adjustments after the Mexican War.* After the Treaty of Guadalupe Hidalgo in 1848 ended war with Mexico, and following other American territorial agreements with England in 1846, nearly all the West had become American territory. From Warren A Beck and Ynez D. Haase, *Historical Atlas of the American West*, map 41. Copyright © 1989 by the University of Oklahoma Press, Norman. Reprinted by permission of the publisher. All rights reserved.

peculiar institution from the former Mexican areas, a position they advanced in the so-called Wilmot Proviso of 1847. Slave-holding southerners wished to open the new southwestern lands to slaves. After a series of complex and heated debates, the Compromise of 1850, largely engineered by Senator Stephen A. Douglas of Illinois, limped through Congress. The compromise stipulated that California would come into the union as a free state and the territories of Utah and New Mexico (then including Arizona) would be organized under the principle of popular sovereignty, allowing voters there to decide for or against slavery. A fractious boundary dispute between Texas and New Mexico was settled by the U.S. government paying Texas $10 million to quiet its demands. Slave-trading was disallowed in the nation's capital, but the South got its much-desired harsher fugitive slave law. Neither antislavery nor proslavery advocates were satisfied with the compromise, but its passage put off a possible civil war for another decade.

One final act completed the southern boundary between the United States and Mexico. Jefferson Davis, U.S. secretary of war in 1853 (and later president of the Confederacy), coveted a sliver of land overlapping the southern sections of what became the states of Arizona and New Mexico on the U.S. side and northern Mexico. He wanted the land for a possible transcontinental railroad from the South to the West Coast. President Franklin Pierce, yielding to Davis, sent James Gadsden to negotiate for the desired land. When Gadsden arrived in Mexico, he found Santa Anna much in need of funds. The $10 million American offer was quickly accepted, and the Gadsden Purchase agreement was signed on December 30, 1853, and ratified by the U.S. Senate and President Pierce in June 1854. With this purchase the boundary of the United States was completed across the Southwest.

~

The outcomes of the Mexican War and the subsequent rapid transfer of the Southwest from Mexican to American territory left several complex and unresolved legacies. For many persons of Mexican heritage in the newly acquired American areas, the aftereffects of war and treaty were decidedly negative. The loss of nearly half its territory scarred Mexico economically and psychologically. For Mexico, the Colossus of the North had invaded and stolen Mexican lands. For many mestizo residents from Texas to California, the fallout was different. Although the Treaty of Guadalupe Hidalgo promised to recognize and protect the rights and lands of people living in what became the American Southwest, those rights and properties were often unprotected, and sometimes lost. Like noted tejano Gregorio Cortez or Californio Mariano Vallejo, many formerly Mexican citizens were pushed aside by the American juggernaut that rolled into the Southwest after 1848. Thousands of Native Americans, including such notable Indians as Mangas Coloradas, Victorio, and Geronimo, would also suffer negative experiences resulting from the Mexican-American War and resulting American takeover.

For expansionist Americans, the legacies were quite different. Texas, New Mexico, California, and adjacent areas, as new American lands, now beckoned settlers, particularly farmers, traders, and adventurers. Manifest Destiny had won the battle, and the huge new southwestern areas from the Louisiana border to the Pacific yawned invitingly for ambitious Americans.

For all those involved and for later generations, the Mexican War was one of the transforming events of western history. Geographically, politically, economically, and especially socioculturally the war transferred what had been northern Mexico into the American Southwest. But the Treaty of Guadalupe Hidalgo promised much more than it accomplished. Troubled legacies of the war remained. Indeed, a century and a half after the treaty was signed unresolved dilemmas continue. Many Mexicans and Hispanics who became U.S. residents in 1848 believed, like their descendants today, that other Americans did not accept them as equals.

Meanwhile in another region to the north fur traders and mountain men, missionaries, and overlanders on the Oregon Trail were migrating into the Pacific Northwest. Even though these intrepid pioneers had little knowledge of events occurring in the Southwest, they too were agents of American Manifest Destiny in the Far West.

Brands, H. W. *Lone Star Nation: How a Ragged Army of Volunteers Won the Battle for Texas Independence and Changed America*. New York: Doubleday, 2004.

Brooks, James F. *Captives & Cousins: Slavery, Kinship, and Community in the Southwest Borderlands*. Chapel Hill: University of North Carolina Press, 2002.

Calvert, Robert A., and Arnoldo De León. *The History of Texas*. Arlington Heights, IL: Harlan Davidson, 1990.

Cantrell, Gregg. *Stephen F. Austin: Empresario of Texas*. New Haven, CT: Yale University Press, 1999.

Dana, Richard Henry, Jr. *Two Years Before the Mast*. 1840; New York: Penguin Books, 1981.

Dary, David. *The Santa Fe Trail: Its History, Legends, and Lore*. New York: Alfred A. Knopf, 2000.

Davis, William C. *Lone Star Rising: The Revolutionary Birth of the Texas Republic*. New York: Free Press, 2004.

DeVoto, Bernard. *Year of Decision: 1846*. Boston: Little, Brown, 1943.

Drumm, Stella M., ed. *Down the Santa Fe Trail and Into Mexico: The Diary of Susan Shelby Magoffin, 1846–1847*. 1926; Lincoln: University of Nebraska Press, 1982.

Eisenhower, John S. D. *So Far from God: The U.S. War with Mexico 1846–1848*. New York: Random House, 1989.

Foote, Cheryl J. "Stephen F. Austin and Doña Tules: A Land Agent and a Gambler in the Mexican Borderlands." In *Western Lives: A Biographical History of the American West*, edited by Richard W. Etulain, 59–88. Albuquerque: University of New Mexico Press, 2004.

González, Deena. *Refusing the Favor: Spanish-Mexican Women of Santa Fe, 1820–1880*. New York: Oxford University Press, 2000.

Griswold del Castillo, Richard. *The Treaty of Guadalupe Hidalgo: A Legacy of Conflict*. Norman: University of Oklahoma Press, 1990.

Hackel, Steven W. *Children of Coyote, Missionaries of Saint Francis: Indian-Spanish Relations in Colonial California, 1769–1850*. Chapel Hill: University of North Carolina Press, 2005.

Hurt, R. Douglas. *The Indian Frontier, 1763–1846*. Albuquerque: University of New Mexico Press, 2002.

Hurtado, Albert L. *Indian Survival on the California Frontier*. New Haven, CT: Yale University Press, 1988.

Kessell, John L. *Spain in the Southwest: A Narrative History of Colonial New Mexico, Arizona, Texas, and California*. Norman: University of Oklahoma Press, 2002.

Lamar, Howard R. *The Far Southwest 1846–1912: A Territorial History*. 1966; Albuquerque: University of New Mexico Press, 2000.

Lecompte, Janet. "La Tules: The Ultimate New Mexican Woman." In *By Grit and Grace: Eleven Women Who Shaped the American West*, edited by Glenda Riley and Richard W. Etulain, 1–21. Golden, CO: Fulcrum, 1997.

McWilliams, Carey. *Southern California Country: An Island on the Land*. New York: Duell, Sloan and Pearce, 1946.

Merk, Frederick. *Manifest Destiny and Mission in American History*. New York: Random House, 1963.

Montejano, David. *Anglos and Mexicans in the Making of Texas, 1836–1986*. Austin: University of Texas Press, 1977.

Pomeroy, Earl. *The Pacific Slope: A History of California, Oregon, Washington, Idaho, and Nevada*. New York: Alfred A. Knopf, 1966.

Reséndez, Andrés. *Changing National Identities at the Frontier: Texas and New Mexico, 1800–1850*. New York: Cambridge University Press, 2005.

Rice, Richard B., William A. Bullough, and Richard J. Orsi. *The Elusive Eden: A New History of California*. New York: Alfred A. Knopf, 1988.

Sandos, James A. *Converting California: Indians and Franciscans in the Missions*. New Haven, CT: Yale University Press, 2004.

Silbey, Joel H. *Storm Over Texas: The Annexation Controversy and the Road to Civil War*. New York: Oxford University Press, 2005.

Stephanson, Anders. *Manifest Destiny: American Expansion and the Empire of Right*. New York: Hill and Wang, 1995.

Weber, David J. *The Mexican Frontier, 1821–1846: The American Southwest under Mexico*. Albuquerque: University of New Mexico Press, 1982.

———. *Myth and the History of the Hispanic Southwest*. Albuquerque: University of New Mexico Press, 1988.

———. *The Spanish Frontier in North America*. New Haven, CT: Yale University Press, 1992.

West, Elliott. "Reconstructing Race." *Western Historical Quarterly* 34 (Spring 2003): 7–26.

CHAPTER FIVE

Mountain Men, Missionaries, and the Trail to Oregon

◦≈◦

THE STRING OF WAGONS, LIKE A SMALL ARMY OF MIGRATING, WHITE-TOPPED tents on wheels, moved slowly along the rough trail beside the Snake River. It was 1843, and they were on their way to Oregon. "Oregon Fever" had infected these nine hundred immigrants, as it had hundreds of other Midwesterners. Traveling with the wagon train were missionary Marcus Whitman, returning west from a recruiting trip to the East, and Peter Burnett, later to become the first governor of the state of California. This Great Migration would be later celebrated as the pioneers who helped win Oregon from the British and for the United States. They were indeed an important ingredient in that victory, preparing the way for annual wagon trains up the Oregon Trail.

In the 1840s between fifteen thousand and twenty thousand immigrants traveled the Oregon Trail to the Willamette Valley. Before the sensational California Gold Rush redirected the traffic southward beginning in 1849, the immigrants went to the Oregon Country to take up rich lands rumored to be available south of the Columbia River. Even as these ambitious, sturdy pioneers gained the farmable lands they sought, they were also pathmakers for later settlers. Before the early 1840s, travelers to the northern West came as explorers, visitors, fur traders and trappers, and missionaries; but they were as a trickle compared to the waves that washed up the trail in the 1840s. It was these later arrivals who did most to win the Pacific Northwest for the United States.

◦≈◦

Three overlapping, interrelated strains of influence were prologue and stimuli to the first large groups of settlers moving into the Oregon Country. Enthusiasts and promoters like Hall Jackson Kelley and Nathaniel Wyeth, American fur traders and mountain men competing with the British Hudson's Bay Company, and missionaries such as Jason Lee, Marcus and Narcissa Whitman, and Father Pierre-Jean De Smet were instrumental in advertising the Oregon Country and northern West as ripe for settlement. Between 1820 and 1840, these men and women promoted a Pacific Northwest ready for the plucking, rich in fur trade and farming possibilities, a prime location for Indian missions, and a region ready for American rather than British occupation. These tub-thumpers prepared the way for the thousands who came up the Oregon Trail in the 1840s and in that decade won the territory for the Americans.

When diplomatic negotiations between 1819 and the mid-1820s cleared away all competitors except the British, Americans began to think more expansively about the future of the Oregon Country. Propagandists, much like modern real estate developers, trumpeted the virtues of the Pacific Northwest, overlooked Natives in the area (except as candidates for religious and cultural conversion), and downplayed the arduous trip of two thousand to three thousand miles. But, of course, romantic dreams without substantiating facts have never stopped enthusiastic if misinformed true believers.

~

The first of the cheerleaders for Oregon was Dr. John Floyd. As early as December 1820, this congressman from Virginia urged his colleagues to consider the rich possibilities of the Oregon Country, especially "the expediency of occupying the Columbia River." Floyd's efforts were as successful as a woodpecker working a marble quarry. Most congressmen thought the Pacific Northwest was too far away, too difficult to link to eastern interests. When Floyd's ideas failed to win over his colleagues, his legislation died a quick death.

Hall Jackson Kelley, an enthusiastic Massachusetts teacher, was another of the early promoters of Oregon. Having become rich from writing textbooks (obviously a more lucrative profession then than two centuries later), Kelley could nourish his avocation—boosting Oregon. Kelley had read the Nicholas Biddle edition of the Lewis and Clark journals published in 1814 and talked to seamen and hunters. Once bitten by the Oregon bug, Kelley could find no cure for his affliction. Preparing pamphlets and circulars, he preached sermons extolling the blessings of Oregon to all who would listen. Also keeping in mind British competition for the region, Kelley wrote that Americans ought to take the territory rightfully theirs because it had been "planned by Providence, made easy by nature." Oregon was "the most valuable of all the unoccupied parts of the earth." In a moment of propagandistic overkill, Kelley catalogued for members of Congress the "Great benefits [that] must result to mankind" if Oregon were settled. In that open country "Science and the Arts, the invaluable privileges of free and liberal government, and the refinements and ordinances of

Christianity, diffusing each its blessing, would harmoniously unite in meliorating the moral condition of the Indians, in promoting the comfort and happiness of the settlers, and in augmenting the wealth and power of the Republic."

Kelley did most of his trumpeting from a distance. In 1829 he established the American Society for Encouraging the Settlement of the Oregon Territory, but he made his only trip to the Pacific Northwest in 1832. It was a personal disaster. After a difficult, long journey to Oregon via Mexico, Kelley arrived to an unusually cold reception from Dr. John McLoughlin, chief factor of the Hudson's Bay Company at Ft. Vancouver. Kelley had hoped that Congress would fund his travel expenses. When it did not and when, in fact, some Oregonians thought him a horse thief from California, Kelley had had enough. Following four months of frustration in the Northwest, he retreated east.

Kelley's mantle as the self-appointed evangelist of Oregon virtues fell on the more able shoulders of his neighbor Nathaniel J. Wyeth. Also from Massachusetts, Wyeth had read Kelley's writings and caught the fire of the latter's fervor. A businessman, Wyeth failed in his initial efforts to establish a trade site in the Pacific Northwest in 1832, but with renewed funding and rekindled interest, he returned two years later to plant a small post on Sauvie Island on the Columbia and Willamette rivers, near Ft. Vancouver. At first fishermen and farmers working for Wyeth achieved minor successes, but the rainy climate and the illness of his workers dampened Wyeth's enthusiasm. He too received no help from Dr. McLoughlin, who told his superiors, "We opposed him [Wyeth] . . . as much as was Necessary." By summer 1836, Wyeth had left the Pacific Northwest, but his dreams and even his unsuccessful endeavors had interested others in Oregon. Senator Lewis F. Linn and Senator Thomas Hart Benton, both of Missouri, were loyal disciples. In the 1830s and 1840s they too spoke of Oregon as a Promised Land, an agricultural paradise.

~

Hard-headed fur traders and their intrepid mountain men workers did more than the idealistic propagandists to prepare the way for the eventual tide of settlers to the Pacific Northwest. The fur trade brought hundreds of— perhaps a few thousand—men into the northern West who eventually scattered up and down the Rockies. The fur business also became an entrepreneurial force that aided in heading off British competition in the northwest corner of the West. The trappers were catalysts of transformation in two other ways: in their exploitation of resources they displayed the darker side of environmental despoliation in the Far West; they also served later as guides for overland travel expeditions.

Until the early 1820s the British dominated the fur trade in much of the northern West. The Americans had barely begun to compete there with their English cousins. In 1821, because of ruinous, violent competition, the British government forced the marriage of its two fur trade behemoths in North America—the North West and Hudson's Bay companies. Then in 1824–25, the new entity, the Hudson's Bay Company, erected Ft. Vancouver on the northern side of the Columbia River, across from present Portland, as the headquarters for its Columbia Department. Selected as chief factor of the department was the huge, indefatigable Dr. John McLoughlin. As we have seen, he became a major figure in the history of the Pacific Northwest from the 1820s into the 1840s.

The British had gradually moved farther west, shifting their attention and efforts to western Canada and the Pacific Northwest following their losses in the east at the end of the War of 1812. Once in the Far West, the British largely abandoned the "factory," or post, system and replaced it with the "brigade" organization. The North West Company had pioneered the brigade system by sending teams of seasoned trappers into the Canadian mountains to trap beaver and bring in their pelts to company agents. As long as the redoubtable Donald McKenzie directed the brigade system, it worked extraordinarily well.

Mounting competition with the Americans impelled the British in new, more destructive directions. Once the joint occupation agreement between Great Britain and the United States was signed in 1818, the British embarked on a "trapping out" campaign to harvest all the beaver pelts in areas where American trappers might work. Operating like a powerful vacuum cleaner, Peter Skene Ogden and his Hudson's Bay Company brigades sucked the Snake River basin clear of beaver. Ogden's successes from 1824 to 1831 testified to the ruinous power of competitive capitalism in regards to the fauna of the area. At the same time Ogden traversed large sections of these isolated, intermountain areas and became the company's most widely traveled explorer.

In the 1820s and 1830s, after a shaky start, the Americans became powerful rivals of the British fur traders. During the era of the War of 1812, John Jacob Astor had lost his post at Astoria, and it had become part of the Hudson's Bay trade empire. But Astor then proceeded to dominate the fur trade in the Old Northwest, utilizing the earlier factory system in which Indian trappers brought furs to forts or posts to be traded to American businessmen. Another American trader, Manuel Lisa, who helped supply the Lewis and Clark Expedition, went upstream in 1807 to establish new trade links with Indians on the upper Missouri. Two years later, he and the Chouteau family of St. Louis founded the Missouri Fur Company. Still other American fur traders were beginning to work the upper Arkansas River.

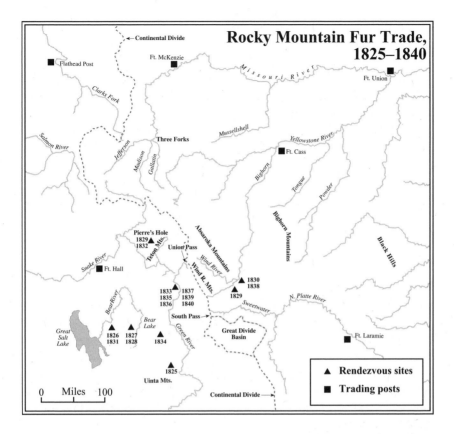

Rocky Mountain Fur Trade, 1825–1840

← Continental Divide

Flathead Post

Ft. McKenzie

Missouri River

Ft. Union

Clarks Fork

Salmon River

Jefferson

Madison

Gallatin

Three Forks

Mussellshell

Yellowstone River

Ft. Cass

Bighorn

Tongue

Powder

Bighorn Mountains

Black Hills

Pierre's Hole
1829 ▲
1832

Teton Mts.

Union Pass

Absaroka Mountains

Wind River

Wind R. Mts.

Snake River

Ft. Hall

▲ 1830
1838

1833 ▲ 1837
1835 ▲ 1839
1836 ▲ 1840

▲ 1829

Sweetwater

N. Platte River

South Pass →

Bear
Lake

Great
Salt
Lake

▲ ▲ ▲
1826 1827 ▲
1831 1828 1834

Bear River

Green River

Great Divide
Basin

Ft. Laramie

▲
1825

Uinta Mts.

Continental Divide →

0   Miles   100

▲ **Rendezvous sites**

■ **Trading posts**

FIGURE 5:1. *The Rocky Mountain Fur Trade 1825–1840.* American mountain men trapped beaver and other fur-bearing animals in the northern Rockies and sold their pelts to fur merchants in annual rendezvous meetings in the Rocky Mountains. Map by Robert Pace.

The American presence in the northern Rockies notably changed in the early 1820s. In 1822, William H. Ashley and Andrew Henry, two traders, advertised in a St. Louis newspaper for "Enterprising Young Men . . . to ascend the Missouri to its source, there to be employed for one, two, or three years" as fur trappers. Ashley and Henry were breaking with tradition: the men they hired were not to be company men but "free trappers," on short-term contracts with the two businessmen. Later in the decade, the number of free trappers greatly expanded as they made informal agreements to provide furs for the St. Louis merchants. Ashley and Henry established a post (Fort Henry, later renamed Fort Union) on the Yellowstone River, but difficulties in that region forced the Ashley-Henry Company to try something new. They sent two parties of men moving directly overland into the mountains rather than up the Missouri to face off in deadly conflict with the Arikara and Blackfeet Indians.

The next logical step in the American fur trade organization was to transfer large parts of the system to the mountains. The Ashley-Henry Fur Company established a new framework for trapping beaver in the Rockies and transporting the pelts to businessmen in St. Louis or to the east. This novel arrangement contained three parts and became known as the "rendezvous" system. (1) "Skin trappers" worked on credit; they were "free trappers," separate and on their own. They gathered their furs in the mountains and brought them to a yearly rendezvous in the northern Rockies. (2) There, a representative of the Ashley-Henry firm (or other later companies) purchased the furs or provided trade goods for the trappers in exchange for their pelts. (3) The company representative then transported the gathered pelts to the third part of the system, a St. Louis warehouse.

The rendezvous system contained romantic as well as negative features. The trappers, or mountain men, quickly became sensational figures in the mythology of the American West. In some respects, rightfully so. Their work was demanding, dangerous, and uncertain. Only courageous, energetic, and rigorous men could withstand the requirements of life in the Rockies. The trappers began their work in the fall before the bitter cold struck the mountains. Holing up in the Rockies during the snow-clogged winter, the mountain men resumed their beaver trapping in the icy streams in the spring and early summer. Then, off to the rendezvous in midsummer before returning to the mountains for the next year.

Travelers and writers who saw the mountain men in the mountains or at a rendezvous were struck with the dress and mannerisms of the individualistic trappers. A mountain man was usually clothed in greasy buckskins with numerous colorful fringes and in durable moccasins. His hair was long, often plaited; and he wore a beard. Around his neck hung his "possible" sack, containing tobacco, shot, and pipe. But, as one historian has written, "romantic as these clothes were, they could be best appreciated at a distance, for . . . from the time they were put on," they were rarely removed.

Some observers thought of the mountain men as "white Indians." "To cope with the wilderness and its human and animal adversaries," Robert Utley has noted, the trappers "imbibed deeply of Indian technology, tools and weapons, costume, practice, and even thought and belief." But contacts with Native Americans were more complex and transitory than wholesale adoption of Indian dress and ways. At one end of the spectrum, some mountain men closely identified with Indians, marrying or living with Native women, residing with tribal groups, or even helping one nation to fight against traditional enemies. At the other end of the gamut, some trappers were sworn enemies of

THE SUMMER RENDEZVOUS.

FIGURE 5:2. *The Summer Rendezvous.* The yearly rendezvous gatherings were important times of economic and social contact and interaction among mountain men, Native American men and women, and fur traders from the East. From Frances Fuller Victor, *The River of the West* (1870), 49. Courtesy Idaho State Historical Society, 76–2.88.

all Indians, killing them on sight. A majority of the trapper-Native contacts were at neither extreme, however. Although many trappers took Indian women as their mates, those unions were often as pragmatic as romantic or lustful. The "many tender ties," as one writer describes these relationships, cemented important trade linkages between Native and white groups. Marriage and other connections with Indian tribes provided the entrée American and Canadian traders and trappers needed to work on the fur frontier. In turn, Indian women's ties to mountain men and traders opened needed relations with incoming English-speaking men. In subsequent generations, the mixed-blood offspring of these unions, such as the Hyde brothers of Colorado, were frequently culture brokers in ongoing Indian-white relations in the pioneer West. They were also important reminders of the complexity of the western past.

From the mid-1820s to the end of the trapper era in the mid-1840s, perhaps as many as three thousand persons worked as mountain men. Most of the trappers lived rather anonymous, nomadic lives in the mountains. A few, however, like Jim Bridger, Thomas Fitzpatrick, Old Bill Williams, Jim Beckwourth, Kit Carson, and Jedediah Smith became legends. Bridger and Fitzpatrick, often partners, traveled over much of the interior West and were superb leaders of men and, later, important guides for settlers. Williams, formerly a Baptist minister, was as independent and valiant as any of the mountain men. Beckwourth, the mulatto son of a Virginia aristocrat and slave woman, lived with Indian groups, marrying several Native women. His dictated autobiography *The Life and Adventures of James P. Beckworth, Mountaineer, Scout, Pioneer, and Chief of the Crow Nation* (1856), though shot through with exaggerations, remains a revealing account of one trapper's life. Kit Carson worked as a trapper early in his extraordinarily active, varied life. A fearless, small, illiterate man of gargantuan energies, Carson traversed enormous sections of the West, particularly in the southern Rockies, California, and the Southwest. Carson's extensive knowledge of much of this terrain made him an ideal guide for explorer John C. Frémont after Carson left the trapper trade.

Of all the mountain men Jedediah Strong Smith may have been the most notable. Born in New York State in 1799, Smith joined the Ashley-Henry firm in 1822 and soon was leading brigades of men into the mountains. In 1826, he and two others bought out Ashley, and thereafter Smith perhaps explored larger sections of the West than any of his contemporaries, looking for new trapping areas and leading parties to the Far West. On several occasions he nearly died of hunger and thirst, at the hands of Indians, or, once, from a severe mauling from a gigantic grizzly. After the violent encounter with the bear, Smith sat calmly while a companion sewed up his scalp and reattached a nearly severed ear—all without any deadening. Unlike many other mountaineers, Smith was literate, a refined gentleman, and deeply religious. After many narrow escapes, he met his demise in 1831 at the hands of the Comanche Indians along the Cimarron River, but not before he had become a widely known and respected trapper, guide, and businessman. Jedediah Smith, in the words of his biographer, was an "opener" of the American West.

The mountain men linked several western experiences. Trappers like Jedediah Smith, Jim Bridger, and Kit Carson, for example, were also pathmaking explorers, scouting out important trails in the West and rediscovering sites like the South Pass in Wyoming. In their ongoing interactions with Native groups, they served as significant culture brokers between two societies. In addition, the mountain men furnished connections between St. Louis, the Rockies, points farther west, and fur trading south into Taos, New Mexico. Of equal importance were the trapper roles as guides for missionaries like Jason Lee, Marcus and Narcissa Whitman, and Henry and Eliza Spalding. In the 1840s, mountain men also led several pioneer groups up the Oregon and California trails. Finally, some of the trappers became pivotal settlers themselves in scattered areas like French Prairie, Oregon, and Taos, where beginning or growing communities were being formed. In these multiple ways, fur traders and trappers built bridges, over time, to westerners that followed them.

There were also negative sides to the fur trade and mountain men. In their treatments of other humans and animals, the trappers were frequently harsh, violent, and exploitative. The mountain men's destructive, headlong pursuit of fur-bearing animals largely led to the end of the fur trade in the northern West. True, changing styles in European hats lessened the demand for beaver pelts, but even more significant, the beaver had been trapped out of the Rockies. By the mid-to-late 1830s intense competition among the Hudson's Bay brigades moving east from Fort Vancouver, the free trappers and rendezvous mountain men of the upper and southern Rockies, and the increasing pressure from members of Astor's American Fur Company in the upper Missouri country led to ruthless exploitation of the beaver. In 1840, the year of the last rendezvous, few beaver remained. To twenty-first-century Americans, the mountain men seem heartless and mindless abusers of animal life. In frontier times, the response was more likely than not a shrug of acceptance and the decision to move on. For nineteenth-century Americans, whether trappers, miners, or farmers, natural resources were to be used. The clear, strong recognition of abuses of land, water, and animals was still a century in the future.

～

Ironically, the mountain men, although themselves often nonreligious and even antisocial, escorted some of the first missionaries and settlers to the northern West. As scouts and guides, the trappers obviously served as agents of westward expansion. In the 1830s, they led missionaries to the Oregon Country; in the 1840s and 1850s, they guided wagon trains west. Once the beaver were stripped from mountain streams, the mountain men scattered into raw, emerging settlements throughout the far West.

Other influences were also at work to prepare the Pacific Northwest for its first wave of missionaries. Catholic missionaries had been serving in the Spanish Borderlands areas for more than two centuries, opening the way for later expansion into the northern West. In the 1820s and early 1830s Protestant missionaries had launched their evangelistic work in Hawai'i. Then, in 1829, thinking that the Oregon Country was ripe for proselytizing, an agent from the American Board of Commissioners for Foreign Missions (ABCFM, serving Presbyterian, Congregationalist, and Dutch Reform denominations) surveyed the Pacific Coast of the Northwest as a possible mission site. Two years later the Methodists also began considering expansion of their missionary work into Oregon.

But perhaps the most dramatic event to spur missionaries to the Pacific Northwest came in the early 1830s. Although the facts remain obscure and possibly distorted, evidently four Indians—three Nez Perce and one Flathead—

traveled to St. Louis in 1831–32 asking for more information about the white man's religion, especially its "power" for healing and success. When an overly dramatized story of this pilgrimage appeared in 1833 in the Methodist paper *Christian Advocate and Journal*, several Protestant groups quickly organized mission efforts, particularly to the Flathead and other tribal groups of the interior West.

~

In 1834, Jason Lee, a member of the Methodist Episcopal Church, arrived as a pioneer missionary to Oregon. Sent to serve the Flathead Indians in present-day Montana, Lee soon changed his focus after a conversation with Dr. McLoughlin at Ft. Vancouver. The chief factor of the Hudson's Bay Company urged Lee to establish his mission in the Willamette Valley, which Lee did in fall 1834, about ten miles north of Salem. For nearly ten troubled years Jason Lee tried to organize and expand his mission in the Oregon Country. Little seemed to work out as he planned.

Born in Canada in 1803, Lee converted to Methodism in 1826. In 1833, the Methodists selected Lee to direct the "Mission to the Flathead Indians of Oregon." Although Lee exhibited clear signs of sincerity and devotion to his evangelical cause, he lacked the requisite leadership skills to establish and administer a new mission station three thousand miles from its denominational headquarters in New England. Timid, irresolute, and self-deprecating, Lee seemed unable to handle the flawed humans sent to his mission. His inadequacies quickly undercut the effectiveness of his mission.

Lee's decision to locate his work near the Willamette River rather than among the interior tribes also changed the focal point of his efforts. At first, Lee's energies were spent in Christianizing and "civilizing" Indians who lived near his station. But those efforts soon ran aground on the shoals of reality. Lee needed farmers and other workers if the mission were to become self-sustaining. Out of necessity he gradually devoted more time to tilling the soil than to cultivating unconverted Indians. Financial pressures, the distaste of some missionaries for Natives, the persisting squabbles among mission members, and Lee's inability to administer his staff led to major problems. By 1837–38, the Methodist mission seethed with discontent, wobbling without clear direction.

In 1838, Lee returned east, ostensibly to raise additional funding but also under pressure to gain leadership training. As his biographer writes, Lee likely received "a vote of no confidence and a recommendation for a forced vacation." Lee himself recalled his own doubts, saying, "I have never yet seen the time when I would not have been glad to relinquish the Superintendency." Two years later, Lee returned with fifty-one additional helpers, as part of the "great reinforcement" of 1840. But the old squabbles broke out like a reopened sore soon after Lee's return. He and Elijah White, a determined, opinionated mission doctor, clashed on station policies, particularly about White's unauthorized expenditures in Lee's absence. White was soon expelled from Lee's mission.

In 1843, the Methodist board recalled Lee. He was charged with being too secular, of putting farming and colonization before the Christianizing of Indians. But the reasons for his failure were more complex. By the time of Lee's dismissal, more than $100,000 had been raised for Methodist missions in the Oregon Country. Six stations scattered throughout present Oregon and Washington had been established by 1840–42. They were staffed with nine ministers, twelve laymen, and several helpers with varied duties. Two mills, one store, a school, and other landholdings were also part of the mission's operations. But problems outweighed Methodist successes. Several ministers and other workers abandoned their stations, factions divided the mission, and Lee himself furnished no adequate reports of the mission's performance. The results were confusion—and then chaos. In 1845, two years after Lee's withdrawal from Oregon, his mission had collapsed. Lee had failed to Methodize Oregon, although the school he established eventually became Willamette University, and subsequent settlers were drawn to the area by virtue of Lee's high-minded if unsuccessful missionary efforts.

The experiences of two other Protestant missionary couples, the Whitmans and the Spaldings, differed notably from those of Jason Lee and the Methodists. Their motivations were similar, however. In 1835, Marcus Whitman, a medical doctor, traveled to the West looking for a satisfactory site for a mission among the interior Indian tribes. Returning east, he quickly married Narcissa Prentiss (who, like Marcus, felt a call to Indian missions), and the newly married couple set out for Oregon in early 1836. Traveling with the Whitmans were Henry and Eliza Spalding; all were sponsored by the ABCFM. The Whitmans located among the Cayuse Indians at Waiilatpu, near present Walla Walla, whereas the Spaldings established their station at Lapwai, close to Lewiston, Idaho, among the Nez Perce Indians.

As with Lee, the personalities of the Whitmans and Spaldings did much to determine the outcome of their missionary efforts. So did their ambivalent attitudes toward Native Americans. Trained as a physician rather than a minister, Marcus had practiced medicine for more than a dozen years before he applied for appointment as a medical missionary. A devout Presbyterian, energetic, and persevering, Marcus nonetheless was shaped—even scarred—by his cold, distant, unsympathetic mother and his rather joyless boyhood. Conversely, Narcissa Prentiss Whitman, an equally committed evangelical, was raised in a loving, idealistic—and sheltered—home. Early on, she fell in love with the idea of becoming a missionary. Without much knowledge of foreign fields or other cultures, Narcissa nonetheless convinced herself that as God's handmaiden she could love and nurture any "benighted heathen," no matter the location or people. But the ABCFM discouraged her from serving as a foreign missionary as a single woman. Marcus's need for a wife on the mission field led to his quick proposal of marriage, and Narcissa's equally fervent wish to become a missionary led to her swift acceptance. Both saw the fortuitous marriage as a sign of God's providence in their lives.

The Spaldings resembled and yet differed from the Whitmans. Henry Spalding, enormously devoted to his work, was born out of wedlock, experienced an unhappy childhood, and drove himself unmercifully. For Spalding, hard work and diligence seemingly solved most problems. He carried other emotional baggage as well. Before the two missionary families came west, Spalding had proposed marriage to Narcissa and had been rejected. That rejection rankled in Spalding's soul, quite possible causing him to question Narcissa's suitability for the mission field. Eliza Spalding may have been the best fitted of the quartet for mission work. A gifted teacher and willing to abide her driven husband, the plain-appearing Eliza accepted the Native sociocultural differences that alarmed and alienated Narcissa Whitman. The Nez Perce came to love Eliza in a way the Cayuse never appreciated Narcissa.

Dr. McLoughlin had warned the Whitmans about the difficulties of working with the Cayuse, whom the HBC leader considered an excessively independent, contentious tribe. But Marcus's tireless labors helped to establish a mill and a productive farm. He also traveled widely to doctor Natives, other missionaries, and mission workers. For Narcissa, a string of disappointments began early with the drowning death of the Whitmans' two-year-old daughter Clarissa, their only child, born in their first year at Waiilatpu. Increasingly, Narcissa found her idealistic attitudes about Indians severely tested. Her ambivalences shone through in a revealing letter to her mother in 1840. The Cayuses "are an exceedingly proud, haughty and insolent people," she wrote. "We feed them far more than any of our associates do their people, yet they will not be satisfied. Notwithstanding all this there are many redeeming qualities in them, else we should have been discouraged long ago. We are more and more encouraged the longer we stay."

The Whitmans gradually lost their optimism about the Indians as their dilemmas and distresses mounted. Convinced that the Cayuse had to be Christianized and "civilized," Marcus and Narcissa learned some Nez Perce (a language the Cayuse understood) but gave nearly all religious instruction in English and seemed little interested in learning or appreciating Cayuse worldviews. Nor did the Whitmans hold out much hope that the converted Indians would acculturate until they became farmers and adopted other white ways. Over time, the Whitman mission station devoted more and more of its resources to helping

FIGURE 5:3. *Marcus Whitman and Narcissa Whitman.* The Whitmans were motivated, diligent, but ultimately unsuccessful missionaries to the Cayuse Indian before their martyrdom in 1847 in the Pacific Northwest. Paintings by Drury V. Haight. Courtesy Whitman Mission National Historic Site.

other whites, especially after immigrants began coming up the Oregon Trail from 1843 onward and stopped at Waiilatpu for rest and supplies.

The work of the Spaldings among the Nez Perce took a divergent path. First of all Henry tried to put off direct white-Indian contact, hoping to prepare his Native charges for these eventual cultural interactions before other whites arrived. He also worked assiduously with the Indians to plow fields and plant crops, fruit trees, and gardens. In fact, more than a few Nez Perce had taken up farming on their own by the early 1840s. Concurrently, utilizing Eliza's talents as a contented, friendly teacher, the mission school enrolled more than two hundred students.

Despite these successes, frictions among the missionaries grew. Whitman wanted to encourage white-Indian contacts, Spalding wished to defer them. They also disagreed on how much the stations should aid incoming settlers. These differences of opinion and other complaints were relayed to the American Board in Boston. Reacting to these rumors and criticisms, the board recalled some missionaries, dismissed Spalding, and commanded the Whitmans to relocate their mission to northeastern Washington. This stunning news alarmed all missionary factions and impelled Whitman east to save their stations. His quick trip east accomplished their goal. But once he returned in 1843, traveling with the nearly nine hundred immigrants who came up the Oregon Trail that year, old problems resurfaced and new ones boiled up.

As the numbers of white settlers stopping at the Whitman mission mounted annually, so did Cayuse discontents. The Indians had hoped the white man's Christianity would achieve what they wished from their own beliefs—protection from the world's inexplicable events and added material wealth. That had not happened, with the Natives increasingly dissatisfied with the Protestants' emphases on the afterworld's satisfactions. Nor were the Cayuse happy with missionary and other white attacks on their Indian views. They also felt, to a great extent correctly, that the Whitmans were now focusing most of their attention and energies on the new immigrant settlers.

When a measles epidemic in 1847 struck down many Cayuse, the Indian discontent reached a bursting point. They were convinced that Marcus Whitman was poisoning them. Rumors of a Cayuse uprising began circulating, eventually reaching Whitman. He admitted that he might "have to leave in the spring" if things did "not clear up," but he also thought he could "quell any trouble." Whitman greatly underestimated his opponents. On the dreary, foreboding day of November 29, the Cayuse broke into the Whitman home, tomahawked Marcus, murdered Narcissa, and ransacked much of the mission. Thirteen persons, included the Whitmans, were martyred. Hearing of these tragic events, the Spaldings fled their station in Lapwai for Oregon. Although Spalding returned to his charges a few years later, it was clear that the American Board missions had largely failed as religious establishments. But, as we shall see, on immigrants trudging up the trail to Oregon the stations would have a larger, more positive impact.

~

By the 1830s, the Catholics had established mission stations in the central and northern plains and were looking farther west for other suitable locations. Some trappers with Catholic backgrounds worked for the HBC; other French Canadian Catholics had retired near the Willamette River and Lee's Methodist mission and urged the company to send priests to the Pacific Northwest. But company administrators were reluctant to do so, thinking evangelistic priests might stir up Catholic-Protestant controversies and further confuse Indians working with the company. After Dr. McLoughlin's strong pressure—he argued that priests might strengthen the Catholic and HBC presence in the Oregon Country—the company relented and sent Fathers François Norbet Blanchet and Modeste Demers to open a Catholic mission in Oregon in 1838. The following year Father Blanchet traveled to the French Prairie area to establish St. Paul's mission, not far from Lee's station. By the early 1840s, with the arrival of other priests and nuns, Catholic missions were formed at several locations throughout Oregon and Washington. Other missions, under the leadership of Jesuit fathers, were established to the east in Idaho and Montana.

The most dynamic of the missionary "black robes" was Father Pierre-Jean De Smet, who first came west in 1840 to meet with the Flatheads about founding a mission in the northern Rockies. A Jesuit from Belgium, the sturdy, energetic

FIGURE 5:4. *Father Pierre-Jean De Smet.* This Belgian-born Catholic priest crisscrossed the northern West as an energetic religious leader and fair-minded diplomat with Indians. During his busy lifetime Father De Smet may have traveled as much as two hundred thousand miles. Courtesy Idaho State Historical Society, 1895-B.

Father De Smet did more than any other missionary, Catholic or Protestant, to serve Indians of the northern West as spiritual guide and diplomat. Indians, government officials, military leaders, and even many of his religious competitors often recognized—even saluted—De Smet's religious, diplomatic, and cultural roles in the tension-filled middle ground between Indian and non-Indian peoples. Probably as intimately acquainted with the varied tribes of the northern West as any person of his time, the Belgian priest could serve as a go-between, a cultural mediator, for religious, governmental, and military institutions interested in communicating with Indians and possibly winning their approval of European and American beliefs and actions. For more than thirty years De Smet moved tirelessly back and forth dealing with numerous vexing problems among Indians and whites, Catholics and Protestants, and within Catholic circles. It is estimated that during his lifetime he made nearly twenty trips to Europe, traveling as much as two hundred thousand miles.

In two important ways, the Catholics were able to forge ahead of the Protestants in communicating Christianity to Native Americans. First, the black robes moved west and established missions as single men. Without wives or children, they were freer to live among the Indians, accompany their nomadic charges, and avoid the frictions between Indian and white families. Even more significant, Blanchet and De Smet devised a superb instruction tool, the Catholic Ladder, to teach Indians the long, complicated history of Christianity. De Smet, writes his biographer, used this "vertical-shaped visual device" "to explain to natives the progression of Christianity from Adam and Eve to the present." This teaching aid functioned for Native Americans much as the well-known sculpted images on the façade of the famous Notre Dame Cathedral in Paris did for illiterate Europeans. In pictorial images, resembling later graphic novels, both narratives attempted to simplify and make clear a complex story and to motivate viewers to convert to Christianity.

The Catholic Ladder, the herculean efforts of De Smet and other priests, and the positive responses of many Native groups greatly encouraged the Catholics. By the mid-1840s, more than five hundred persons attended services at St. Paul's and possibly twice as many a half-dozen years later. In the 1840s, Catholic missions were also planted across Idaho and Montana. Even though in the next decade the California Gold Rush redirected Catholic missions southward, priests remained throughout the northern West. After Jason Lee left and the martyred Whitmans were gone, few Protestants missionaries stayed in the Pacific Northwest, but the black robes remained. As Dorothy Johansen, an authority on the Pacific Northwest, correctly notes, "If continuous missionary service were the final test for success of the two religious groups among the Indians, the laurels would go to the Catholics."

Unfortunately, the Protestants and Catholics often squabbled for dominance like two hungry dogs at an early morning feeding. As part of the Protestant Crusade that swept across the eastern United States from the 1820s to the 1840s, Methodist and American Board missionaries to Oregon set out to blacken the reputations of Catholics and to dissuade Indians from following Catholic doctrines. Some referred to the black robes as "semi-Christian Catholics" and as false teachers. Catholics, exhibiting equal talents at vituperation, responded in kind. De Smet considered the Methodists uneducated and especially spiteful toward Catholics. He was notably hard on the Mormons, referring to them as an "abomination of abominations," as "polygamous fanatics." One can only guess what Native Americans thought when two groups claiming to be Christians expended so much time and energy libeling one another. Amazingly, however, the Christianizing influences often took hold. Many Natives of the northern West converted to Christianity or clearly exhibited, in later years, Christian sociocultural influences.

One unexpected consequence of the first missionary endeavors needs mention. Although the numbers of converted Natives and particularly the numbers of permanent mission stations were far less than eastern supporters of the missions hoped, the Protestant and Catholic evangelists nonetheless greatly encouraged westward migration. When eastern promoters of the Oregon Country heard that Narcissa Whitman and Eliza Spalding safely made the trip to the Pacific Northwest—they were the first white women to make the trip overland—the enthusiasts urged other families to undertake the long, difficult, but achievable trip to Oregon. Like the mountain men who served as scouts and guides, the missionaries as travelers to and residents in the early Far West were catalysts for pioneers who followed them in the next decade.

~

Stand at the South Pass crossing of the Rockies in southwestern Wyoming, and think of how many immigrants on the Oregon, California, and Mormon trails traversed this space in the decades following 1840. The first whites to locate the South Pass were John Jacob Astor's men between 1811 and 1813; later, in the 1820s, mountain men rediscovered the important passage through the Rockies. Through this wide, flat opening, about midway between their "jumping-off" points near the Missouri and their new homes in the Willamette Valley or in California passed hundreds of thousands of pioneers and forty-niners before the completion of the first transcontinental railroad in 1869. Nearly all the Mormons who went west from the 1840s to the 1860s also crossed through the South Pass. For nearly another generation after 1869, before railroads connected all parts of the Pacific Northwest to major points east, multitudes of immigrants trudged up the Oregon Trail and over the South Pass to the coast.

Before the tracks of the iron horse replaced the ruts of covered wagons and other horse- and oxen-driven and human-pulled carts, the dusty trail across South Pass was the major pioneer pathway to the West.

Several pull and push factors were at work in sending the first large groups up the Oregon Trail and over the South Pass. The beckoning letters of missionaries and the stories of enthusiasts like Hall Jackson Kelley and Nathaniel Wyeth motivated itchy-footed pioneers drawn to the Oregon Country. Tales from other visitors about the verdancy of the Willamette Valley and the bucolic nature of the Northwest also appealed to covetous agriculturalists hoping for new lands to till. By the 1830s, but particularly in the 1840s and 1850s, "Oregon Fever" infected thousands of farm families, especially those living in the northern Mississippi Valley.

Then in 1837 a disastrous depression struck. The Panic of 1837 devastated Americans all across the country but particularly hammered midwestern farmers in the next few years. Epidemics of malaria and other diseases disillusioned and defeated others. To these discontented sons of the soil, the Oregon Country seemed a true Eden, a land of milk and honey awaiting ambitious and courageous immigrants. Families by the thousands increasingly felt these pull and push influences by the early 1840s.

A few scattered pioneers ventured up the Oregon Trail before 1841, but in that year the first organized groups of more than 50 persons set out in the spring for Oregon and California. That company embarked from Independence, Missouri. The next year about 120 overlanders in 18 wagons also "jumped off" from Independence. In 1843, the Great Migration attracted nearly 900 persons in 100 wagons headed for Oregon. Accompanying the travelers were as many as 5,000 cattle and oxen. The numbers to Oregon mounted in the next years, with nearly 1,500 in 1844, about 2,500 in 1845, and perhaps 4,000 to 5,000 in 1847. After gold was discovered in California in 1848, the numbers of those going up the trail exploded to 50,000 in 1850 and 60,000 in 1852.

Over time embarking travelers from the Mississippi Valley learned more about details of the arduous trip that stretched out before them. They would travel nearly two thousand miles to Oregon in a trip that would take four to six months. The overlanders tried to start as early as conditions allowed and hoped there would be sufficient grass for the livestock. Early April was often considered the ideal starting date. Getting off early was important because delays could lead to tragedy, as in the case of the Donner Party caught in early snows of 1846 in the Sierra Nevada. Several of that group perished or resorted to cannibalism to survive.

The Oregon Trail leading from the jumping-off spots along the Missouri River to the Willamette Valley was neither direct nor unchanging. After leaving Independence, St. Joe, or Westport Landing on the Missouri, or other nearby frontier towns, pioneers usually headed for Ft. Kearny on the Platte River. Traveling along the south bank of the Platte, they forded the river and moved westward to Ft. Laramie in eastern Wyoming, a third of the way to Oregon. After arching northward, they dropped south through South Pass and down to Ft. Bridger. Then the travelers turned north again to Ft. Hall in eastern Idaho. Near Ft. Hall, California-bound immigrants cut south to travel along the Humboldt River, over the towering and dangerous Sierra Nevada Mountains, and down into northern California. Those headed for Oregon followed the Snake River to Ft. Boise before crossing the troublesome Blue Mountains and on to the Whitman mission near Walla Walla. Then they moved westward along the Snake and Columbia rivers to The Dalles, where hastily constructed and hazardous rafts floated them to the juncture of the Columbia and Willamette rivers. By 1846, the pioneer Sam Barlow had pushed through a toll road along the southern slopes of Mt. Hood, allowing immigrants to travel overland and avoid the dangerous watery journey down the Columbia to their stopping point—Oregon City, just south of Portland.

~

Challenges to the overlanders were unique to each part of the journey and often changed over time. Along the Platte, dust storms, quicksand, and overloaded wagons vexed travelers. So, eventually, did the traffic. Consider, for example, the exceptional years of 1850 and 1852 when fifty thousand to sixty thousand pioneers headed up the trail. That meant an average of nine hundred to one thousand pioneers were departing from the jumping-off places each day in the months of April and May. Virtual traffic jams, let alone inadequate feed for oxen and cattle, faced travelers on both sides of the Platte. When the immigrants reached the halfway point at South Pass, they might not have realized that the largest difficulties lay ahead. The blazing sun along the Snake, the dangerous path up and over the Blue Mountains, and the perilous route down or alongside the Columbia nearly paralyzed some travelers. Once safely in the Willamette Valley, overlanders rarely forgot the challenges of *the* trip of their lifetime. Oregonians also had their unique spin on the route westward. Where one branch of the trail turned south in Idaho for California, Oregonians noted, the sign pointing to California displayed an alluring picture of gold, the one pointing west only the word "Oregon." Those who could read went to Oregon; those materialists after the almighty dollar went to California!

A decade after the first overlanders traveled to Oregon, the trail had changed considerably. Guidebooks continued to warn of nature's challenges at river and mountain crossings, but stopover places providing much-needed rest and refurnishing were available at Forts Laramie, Bridger, Hall, Boise, and The

Dalles. As one scholar notes, "the immigration experience was ever changing; each travel year evidenced distinctive patterns, unique dramas of triumph and tragedy, new contributions to the mosaic of western development."

Despite these changes over time, immigrants always had to pay close attention to the costs of their "outfit." The expenses for strong draft animals, a sturdy wagon, and the essential food supplies quickly added up. Travel guides often estimated the costs as $100 to $200 per traveler, although families of more than four might bring down these averages. Oxen, the pull animals used by most pioneers, usually cost about $50 per animal for the needed yoke of four (eight animals). A wagon might set one back $100 and other necessary gear another $100. Foodstuffs like flour, bacon, coffee, and sugar were essential from the beginning since they might cost as much as $1 per pound at Ft. Laramie or any other trail stops. Fortunately for farm families, they might have to spend less because they already had some of the needed animals. But one must keep in mind these totals when a laborer's daily wage was $1.50, and land in Illinois might cost $3 to $6 per acre. The cost of moving to Oregon was extremely dear because an overlander might expend one year's wages for his outfit ($400 to $600) and lose another year's income because a summer of travel precluded raising a crop that year. Obviously, relocation to the Northwest via the Oregon Trail was impossible for poor easterners or midwesterners.

Often immigrants mistakenly overloaded their wagons with prized furniture, keepsakes, and other cherished goods. They soon realized their oxen could not pull much more than the ideal load of about 2,500 pounds, and the abandonment began. One traveler reported seeing "bar iron, large grindstones, and baking ovens dumped on the trail. He rode past cooking stoves, kegs, and barrels scattered among harnesses, clothing, bacon, and beans." Another "counted two thousand abandoned wagons" along the trail. Still others found enough castoffs along the trip to refit their own needs.

Through this winnowing process, overlanders came to understand the wisdom of following recommended provisions for each person. Each adult would need about two hundred pounds of flour, one hundred pounds of bacon, fifteen of coffee, fifty of beans, fifty of lard, thirty of bread and biscuits. So much for the modern-day suggested healthy diet of fresh fruit, vegetables, and whole wheat bread. Some families brought along a milk cow, hoping fresh milk would nourish children and stave off trail diseases. During the 1840s, other travelers relied on the newly killed game that veteran guides sometimes provided. Even if fresh meat, fruit, and vegetables were mostly unavailable, overlanders relished their whiskey. As one pioneer noted, he often hungered for a bit of "bread soaked with a little whiskey."

Trail parties also quickly realized that, to survive, they needed more than pell-mell travel up the trail. In the earliest trail years, mountain man guides,

FIGURE 5:5. *Inside an Immigrant Wagon.* A covered wagon traveling up the Oregon Trail might contain a family's clothing, a bed, a spinning wheel, and dozens of other small household items crammed into a small space. Courtesy National Archives.

scouts, or missionaries like Marcus Whitman led the trains; later the yearly jaunts produced interesting experiments in democracy and community forma-tion as well as revealing gender divisions of labor. In most trips, either before the train jumped off or after a few days of travel, participants elected a captain or an informal council to list and enforce laws. The noted frontier mother Sarah Royce commented on the gender divisions on one trip west: as the men made the governing decisions, "the few women in the company were busy meantime in cooking, washing, mending up clothes, etc." Decisions about organization usually dealt with group needs and individual responsibilities. These included communal grazing, night guard duty, and the traveling order of the wagons. But sometimes the rule-makers went too far, imposing Sabbath restrictions on nonbelievers, military-style regimentation, and even vigorous guidelines for personal behavior. The problem was, of course, inherently American. Clearly, conflicting impulses of community-making and rampant individualism were at work on the way west. That so many trains arrived at their destination with-out falling into warring factions suggests that necessity and group pressures won out over the particularism of divisive, individualistic overlanders.

The largest portion of, although not all, travelers coming up the Oregon Trail were parts of families. Not until the California Gold Rush did the yearly immigration trains take on a decidedly masculine cast. The adaptability of these families to trail travel reveals much about mid-nineteenth-century America as well as about the unique experiences of overlanders. On the trail, men usually drove the wagons, took care of livestock, hunted for game, and stood guard. As expected, women were involved in domestic chores: preparing meals, caring for children, and washing clothes. Older children were also supposed to do their part, tending animals, hauling wood and water, and helping with their parents' duties.

Women kept most of the accounts of these westward journeys. Their diaries show women both reinforcing and breaking with their expected duties. Wives and mothers were particularly upset with the wrenching decision to leave their own mothers, sisters, and other family members. Yet the lure of economic prosperity, the wishes of their husbands, and the expectations of society that they should follow their families pressured women to go west when they often wished to stay east. As one reluctant woman wrote in her journal, "Agreeable to the wish of my husband I left all my relatives . . . although it proved a hard task to leave them but still harder to leave my children buried in . . . [a] graveyard but such is our lot on earth [;] we are divided." Another wife told her husband, after expressing her reservations about going west, "We are married to *live together.* . . . *You have no right* to go where I cannot, and if you do, you need never return for I shall look upon you as dead."

Not all women were hesitant emigrants, however. Indeed many, remarkably flexible in adjusting to new experiences, enthusiastically followed their menfolk up the trail. "Ho for California. . . . We are off to the Promised Land," wrote one exuberant woman. Another told her daughter that she "was always ready and willing to do." Once on the trail, women learned the difficult tasks of cooking over open fires, keeping their children away from life-threatening dray animals and wagon wheels, and wearing practical clothes that affronted their eastern-generated sense of style. Changes came by the dozens. Women hesitant to use buffalo chips (dung) for fuel gradually, grudgingly accepted this unpleasantness. Indeed, it was rumored that some pragmatic trail wives, abandoning earlier repugnances, moved quickly from gathering chips to kneading bread—without washing their hands between tasks.

Numerous dangers threatened the overlanders, but not always those they feared most. For example, Indians were never the menace that the "prairie telegraph" (rumor mill) suggested. In the twenty years from 1840 to 1860, only an estimated 362 immigrants and 426 Indians were killed in interracial battles, about twenty annually from each culture. (Revealingly, mythmakers in twentieth-century movies or novels have killed more than that total in a single episode.) Despite their inbred fears of Indians, trail women, often needing the help of Natives and steeped in a tradition of nurturing rather than violent reactions to competitors, "often found relationships for mutual support with Indians." Exchanges of necessary goods and services forged tradition-breaking linkages between pioneer women and Native women and men. Although early entries in women's trail diaries described fears about "savage" Indians, later passages in the same writings spoke of more numerous peaceful and helpful encounters than violent confrontations.

Other dangers proved more malignant. Chief among these were diseases, especially deadly cholera. This Asian disease ravaged overland trains, particularly those passing along the Platte and Humboldt rivers, headed for California. Carrying the germs of the disease from their midwestern beginning points and infecting many others, immigrants sometimes died by the hundreds. As many as twenty thousand, or one out of every seventeen pioneers who went up the trail, succumbed to cholera. Hundreds of graves lined the trail, several with grim gravestones stating "Died of Cholera." Mountain fever, measles, diarrhea, and scurvy were other deadly afflictions. Equally tragic were trail accidents. Children fell under wagon wheels, adults and younger pioneers drowned in river crossings, and the careless handling of guns led to fatalities. Even though alarmists may have warned pioneers about marauding Indians, diseases and accidents stuck down many more overlanders than did conflicts with Natives.

All told, more than 300,000 immigrants went west between 1840 and 1860. About 65,000 traveled to Oregon, nearly 200,000 to California, and more than 40,000 to Utah. It was a dramatic human movement that in one generation sent multitudes of Anglo people into areas that only Native Americans and Hispanics had inhabited. Undoubtedly many of the immigrants would have identified with one woman's reactions: it is, she noted, "a constant source of wonder to me how we . . . were able to endure it." Endure the arduous trip they did and in doing so peopled large sections of the West as farmers, miners, and Mormons.

~

In the Oregon Country, the incoming tides of settlers washed over and redirected the few nascent settlements already established there. In 1840, about 150 Americans resided in Oregon; by 1844, the number had mushroomed to about 2,500. A clear pattern was emerging: as the yearly newcomers spilled out of the immigration pipeline looking for tillable fields, earlier residents felt threatened since no laws protected the lands on which they squatted. Jealous too of the HBC's presence and power in the Pacific Northwest, recent arrivals soon pushed for a provisional government favoring the Americans. In 1843, during

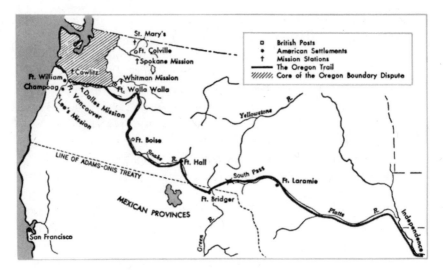

FIGURE 5:6. *The Oregon Country.* Competitions with the British, involvements in an expanding fur trade, and journeys up the Oregon Trail defined the experiences of many Americans in the Pacific Northwest from the 1820s to the 1840s. From Ray Allen Billington and Martin Ridge, *Westward Expansion: A History of the American Frontier,* 6th ed., abr. (Albuquerque: University of New Mexico Press, 2001), 161.

a series of "wolf" meetings ostensibly called to provide protection against wild predators, the new American settlers urged the U.S. Congress to organize a provisional government of Oregon. But Washington, D.C., dragged its feet.

In the mid-1840s, other developments drove the settlers in new directions. With nearly 3,000 residents in the Willamette Valley now petitioning for some kind of local government, pioneer Jesse Applegate (who had arrived with the Great Migration in 1843) formulated a compromise that recognized both British and American rights in the territory. In 1846, as we have seen, the joint occupation agreement between the two countries for the control of Oregon ended, with American residents again asking Congress to provide a territory government for the region. Startled by the murder of the Whitmans in 1847 and the Cayuse War that followed, the federal government realized that something must be done in the Pacific Northwest. In the midst of the Mexican-American War and wishing to avoid further confusion in the Far Northwest, Congress, after considerable partisan wrangling, passed a bill to establish the Oregon Territory. President Polk signed the bill in the summer of 1848. On March 3, 1849, Oregon was officially recognized as a new territory with Joseph Lane as its first governor. Other internal squabbles and the signal impact of the

California Gold Rush, which stole away much of Oregon's male population in the early 1850s, delayed statehood for a decade.

⌇

The frenetic years between the Great Migration of 1843 and Oregon's becoming a territory in 1849 demonstrated how rapidly western history changed. In those six years, Oregon's population burgeoned from less than 1,000 to about 9,000 persons. The annual reinforcements who came up the Oregon Trail made up the lion's share of this population boom. But, of course, Oregon's story included much more than the overlanders. In the previous two or three decades, propagandists like Hall Jackson Kelley and Nathaniel Wyeth, the mountain men as pathfinders and scouts, and the missionaries as promoters had prepared the way for the immigrant road to Oregon. And the arrival of so many easterners disrupted Native communities across the Pacific Northwest, sewing seeds of discontent that led to several conflicts between whites and Indians in subsequent decades. Meanwhile American diplomats had cleared the way for sole American control of the Pacific Northwest.

As Oregonians were gaining territorial status in 1849, pathbreaking events to the east and south were already transforming other parts of the Far West. Mormons were forging their own trail to Utah, and hordes of hungry gold miners were inundating California. These changes seemed even more swift and varied than those that marked the Oregon country between 1810 and 1850.

Barbour, Barton H. *Fort Union and the Upper Missouri Fur Trade.* Norman: University of Oklahoma Press, 2001.

Bowen, William A. *The Willamette Valley: Migration and Settlement on the Oregon Frontier.* Seattle: University of Washington Press, 1978.

Carriker, Robert C. *Father Peter John De Smet: Jesuit in the West.* Norman: University of Oklahoma Press, 1995.

Clark, Malcolm Jr. *Eden Seekers: The Settlement of Oregon, 1818–1862.* Boston: Houghton Mifflin, 1981.

Dary, David. *The Oregon Trail: An American Saga.* New York: Alfred A. Knopf, 2004.

DeVoto, Bernard. *Across the Wide Missouri.* Boston: Houghton Mifflin, 1947.

Dodds, Gordon B. *The American Northwest: A History of Oregon and Washington.* Arlington Heights, IL: Forum, 1986.

Drury, Clifford M. *Marcus and Narcissa Whitman and the Opening of Old Oregon.* Glendale, CA: Arthur H. Clark, 1973.

Dunlay, Tom. *Kit Carson and the Indians.* Lincoln: University of Nebraska Press, 2000.

Faragher, John Mack. *Women and Men on the Overland Trail.* New Haven, CT: Yale University Press, 1979.

Furtwangler, Albert. *Bringing Indians to the Book.* Seattle: University of Washington Press, 2005.

Goetzmann, William H. *Exploration and Empire: The Explorer and the Scientist in the Winning of the American West.* New York: Alfred A. Knopf, 1966.

Hafen, Le Roy R., ed. *Mountain Men and Fur Traders of the West.* 10 vols. 1965–72; Lincoln: University of Nebraska Press, 1982.

Hurt, R. Douglas. *The Indian Frontier, 1763–1846.* Albuquerque: University of New Mexico Press, 2002.

Jeffrey, Julie Roy. *Converting the West: A Biography of Narcissa Whitman.* Norman: University of Oklahoma Press, 1991.

———. *Frontier Women: "Civilizing" the West? 1840–1880.* Rev. ed. New York: Hill and Wang, 1998.

Johansen, Dorothy O., and Charles M. Gates. *Empire of the Columbia: A History of the Pacific Northwest.* 2nd ed. New York: Harper and Row, 1967.

Lavender, David. *Land of Giants: The Drive to the Pacific Northwest, 1750–1950.* Garden City, NY: Doubleday, 1958.

———. *Westward Vision: The Story of the Oregon Trail.* New York: McGraw-Hill, 1963.

Loewenberg, Robert J. *Equality on the Oregon Frontier: Jason Lee and the Methodist Mission, 1834–43.* Seattle: University of Washington Press, 1976.

Meinig, D. W. *The Great Columbia Plain: A Historical Geography, 1805–1910.* Seattle: University of Washington Press, 1968.

Morgan, Dale L. *Jedediah Smith and the Opening of the West*. Indianapolis: Bobbs-Merrill, 1953.

Morrison, Dorothy Nafus. *Outpost: John McLoughlin and the Far Northwest*. Portland: Oregon Historical Society Press, 1999.

Riley, Glenda. *Women and Indians on the Frontier 1825–1915*. Albuquerque: University of New Mexico Press, 1984.

Ronda, James P. *Astoria & Empire*. Lincoln: University of Nebraska Press, 1990.

Schoenberg, Wilfred P. *A History of the Catholic Church in the Pacific Northwest*. Washington, D. C.: Pastoral Press, 1987.

Schwantes, Carlos A. *The Pacific Northwest: An Interpretive History*. Lincoln: University of Nebraska Press, 1989.

Unruh, John D. *The Plains Across: The Overland Emigrants and the Trans-Mississippi West, 1840–60*. Urbana: University of Illinois Press, 1979.

Utley, Robert M. *A Life Wild and Perilous: Mountain Men and the Path to the Pacific*. New York: Henry Holt, 1997.

Van Kirk, Sylvia. *Many Tender Ties: Women in the Fur Trade Society, 1670–1870*. Norman: University of Oklahoma Press, 1980.

Wishart, David J. *The Fur Trade of the American West, 1807–1840: A Geographical Synthesis*. Lincoln: University of Nebraska Press, 1979.

CHAPTER SIX

Mormons, Miners, and the Search for Western Community

≈

IN JULY 1847 WHEN MORMON LEADER BRIGHAM YOUNG FIRST GLIMPSED the Salt Lake Valley he reportedly prophesized, "It is enough. This is the right place. Drive on." The next year in San Francisco, another Mormon, Samuel Brannan, raced excitedly through the city's streets shouting that gold had been discovered on the western slopes of the Sierra Nevada Mountains in northern California. These two dramatic events, less than a year apart, foreshadowed new waves of populations deluging the mid-nineteenth-century American West and forever changing life in the region. The arrival of the Mormons in the central Mountain West and the booming mining rushes that spilled out from northern California into other parts of the West were but trickles compared to the tides of settlers that rolled in during the next decades. These two currents of newcomers, so different in backgrounds and outlook, became part of the complex search for community in the American West from the 1840s to the 1890s.

≈

When the Mormons entered the Salt Lake Valley in the mid-1840s, they were a young church, less than two decades old. Yet they were already a bruised, hardened people. Established in upstate New York in 1830 and led by the charismatic, idealistic prophet Joseph Smith, the Church of Jesus Christ of Latter-day Saints (Mormon) had already been driven out of New York, Ohio, and Missouri before moving to Illinois in 1839. There, the Mormons set up another New Jerusalem in Nauvoo, near the banks of the Mississippi River, and attempted to reestablish their communal ways. Strong opposition again boiled up. Mormon isolationist tendencies and their advocacy of what opponents considered strange doctrines alienated their gentile (non-Mormon) neighbors.

When rumors surfaced of Smith's intention to run for the presidency of the United States and of the practice of polygamy among the Saints, the Nauvoo area roiled in conflict. On June 27, 1844, a viciously anti-Mormon mob stormed the jail where Joseph and Hyrum Smith were being held and brutally assassinated the prophet and his brother.

The next three years were a crucial period in Mormon history. In the months immediately following Smith's murder, it looked as if the church might falter. But soon the Mormons chose a new leader, moved many miles westward in a dramatic exodus, and established a new Eden in the West. Several men claimed the right to bear Brother Joseph's mantle, but by the late summer and early fall of 1844 the Saints decided to back the Brigham Young–led Quorum of the 12. With that decision, it became clear that Young would be the next Mormon prophet.

By force of will and able leadership, Brigham Young gradually calmed the worried Saints in Nauvoo, helped them to regroup, and initiated plans for relocation in the West. Young's accomplishments in these dark days proved his leadership talents and foretold how much his organizational genius and determination would spark the Mormons. The notable months of his guidance at Nauvoo were but a brief interlude in the life of one of the most remarkable of all westerners.

Brigham Young's background and earliest years gave few hints that he would become the skilled leader of a major religious movement. Born in Vermont in 1801, the ninth of eleven children, he grew up in a family of few socioeconomic means and was poorly educated. Still, he was tireless and dependable, establishing his livelihood by his teenage years as a painter and carpenter. Something of an independent religious seeker like Joseph Smith, Young nonetheless joined the Methodist Church when he was twenty-one and demonstrated his adherence to the moral and social order of most contemporary conservative Protestants. Several years later, however, Young chanced to read the *Book of Mormon* (1830) soon after its publication, was converted, and came into the church in 1832.

Although Young was no intellectual, he was a determined and practical man. Obviously his commonsense talents, once recognized by his church, were greatly useful to the Saints during the next years when Young served as a missionary in Europe and then held increasingly responsible positions among Mormons in the United States. By the middle 1840s Brigham Young, tried in the fires of competition and adversity, had proved his mettle.

Even before his death, Joseph Smith had thought of relocating the church farther west, away from gentile influences and harassments. Smith knew—as Young learned—that the West might be the place to escape the Mormons' persecutors. Under Smith's leadership, the Saints began, in the words of one of the best-known Mormon hymns, "Come, Come Ye Saints," to look for a place "Far away in the West / Where none shall come to hurt or make afraid." As Young

FIGURE 6:1. *Brigham Young, Mormon Moses.* This courageous, energetic, if autocratic leader of the Latter-day Saints brilliantly directed and controlled Mormon settlement in the Great Basin area for thirty years. Courtesy Idaho State Historical Society, 79–2.21.

took over plans for the westward trek, he also made sure that church members worked at growth and unity—by finishing the temple at Nauvoo, by continuing foreign and home missions, and by solidifying the hierarchy of the church.

≈

The Mormon move west was unique. It was better planned and more smoothly carried out than any other nineteenth-century westward movement. Organized like a great chain of community-minded honeybees aiding one another, the Mormon exodus spread across the West from Illinois to Iowa to Utah with the first Saints breaking the way and planning for the needs of their brothers and sisters coming later. Building on the Old Testament parallels of exodus from Egypt to the Promised Land, the Mormons systematically organized their stopping-off camps and trail leadership with careful emphasis on the needs of the group. (Only the tragic deaths of two hundred immigrants in 1856 in a delayed and inadequately planned handcart company stand as a blotch on the remarkably successful Mormon trail record.) In the earliest journeys westward, Young was everywhere, leading, driving, and encouraging his people. As two Mormon historians have written, "It was in Iowa in 1846 that Young learned to be the Moses his people needed."

Religiously motivated, centrally controlled, and implemented in stages, the Mormon errand into the wilderness West was another indication of the pronounced spirit of community that infused the Latter-day Saints (LDS) throughout the nineteenth century. It also set them apart from other overlanders and settlers in the West. The emphases on cohesion and cooperative organization, so evident in the early Mormon settlements and in the camps along their westward trek, also characterized LDS pioneering in the Salt Lake Valley. Young made use of a fresh crop of leaders along the way west, and those trail-toughened and experienced veterans became a new cadre of leaders in Utah. By the end of 1847 when the Mormons' membership totaled about 50,000, several settlements were underway in the Salt Lake area to serve a population there that grew quickly to nearly 5,000—equivalent to the numbers of pioneers moving to Oregon in a full decade of settlement (1834–44). Mormons moved quickly and steadily into Utah, and by 1852 the exodus from Nauvoo was virtually complete.

Brigham Young drew extensively on the designs of Joseph Smith and his own experiences in reestablishing the communal form of Mormon organization in Utah. On July 25, 1847, a Sunday—and only one day after his arrival—Brother Brigham called the faithful together and told them that the land, water, and trees of the valley and surrounding hills belonged "to the people; all the people." Laying out Salt Lake City in a plan reminiscent of a New England town, Young also divided nearby lands into small acreages. Land was chosen by lot but given out according to the size and needs of individual families. Although individuals would work separate parcels of land, water and other resources would be under church control and used to benefit the cooperative community.

Once laid out in the Salt Lake Valley, these farm villages became the pattern for Mormon towns throughout the Rocky Mountain West. Before Young left the next month for Winter Quarters in Nebraska to help lead other Saints into Eden, the first ground in the valley had been broken and crops planted—nearly all of which failed, unfortunately, because of the lateness of the season. A temple site had been located, and all adults were rebaptized in order to "renew their covenants" to the church. When Young returned the following September with nearly 2,500 settlers, more than four hundred adobe and log houses had been erected, the first crop harvested, and almost a dozen towns established in the valley, including Salt Lake City with a population of more than 1,500.

If Mormon plans for the Salt Lake Valley were workable and well coordinated, their dreams for far-flung western and international harvest fields were even more visionary. The Saints were convinced that God expected them to extend their limits "to a wider field." Spurred by these convictions, church leaders spoke of expanding throughout the West, of obtaining seaports in Mexico, California, and the Pacific Northwest, of establishing landholdings stretching one thousand miles from north to south, and eight hundred miles from east to west. To maintain this expansive empire, Mormon colonists would be sent to establish an "outer cordon" of settlements from California to Nevada, to Idaho, and throughout Utah. In the early 1850s many of these colonies were founded—ninety-five between 1847 and 1857—and expansion continued in the late nineteenth century into nearby states, and eventually into Canada and Mexico. Concurrently, thousands of new converts poured into Utah from Europe, where the indefatigable efforts of diligent missionaries won tens of thousands of converts, chiefly in England and Scandinavia.

As American and European Mormons inundated Utah and nearby areas, Young and other LDS leaders realized the pressing necessity for additional church organizations as well as changes in traditional structures to meet the novel experiences of their new location. Organizational efforts began shortly after the Treaty of Guadalupe Hidalgo in February 1848 ended the Mexican-American War and before the Compromise of 1850 included territorial status for Utah. Since no formal secular government existed in Utah from 1847 to 1849 and because Young wanted to provide unity for the spreading Mormon settlements and to retain central powers in Salt Lake City, he called a constitutional convention in March 1849 to establish the State of Deseret ("honeybee"). It would encompass parts of Oregon, Idaho, Wyoming, Colorado, Arizona, California, and New Mexico.

Before 1849 the church controlled governmental activities. Now theocracy (an overlap of religious and political leaders) seemed imminent when Young and his lieutenants were elected leaders of the State of Deseret while maintaining their church offices. The dream of Deseret was delayed, however, when the federal government rejected its petition for statehood and instead gave territorial status to Utah (which included Utah, Nevada, and parts of Colorado and Wyoming). Mormon leaders were disappointed with this decision, but when President Millard Fillmore selected Brigham Young as territorial governor in 1850, they quietly accepted their new status.

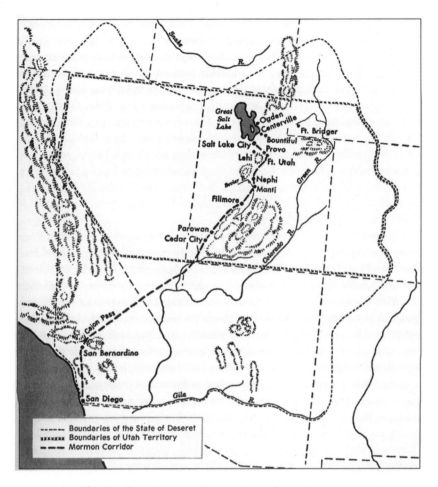

FIGURE 6:2. *The Great Basin Frontier.* The outer boundaries of the Mormon frontier covered much of the Great Basin region in the 1840s and 1850s. From Ray Allen Billington and Martin Ridge, *Westward Expansion: A History of the American Frontier*, 6th ed., abr. (Albuquerque: University of New Mexico Press, 2001), 189.

Conflict soon arose when the federal government named nonresident gentiles (non-Mormons) to major territorial offices, and these new appointees frequently imported to Utah their undisguised antipathy toward the Saints. During the early and middle 1850s, Mormon leaders and government-appointed territorial officials frequently clashed over questions of taxation, Indian policy, and the territorial court system. Mormons, sometimes opposing all directives by outsiders, did everything within their power to maintain home rule whereas federally appointed leaders, frequently selfishly motivated and party hacks, often attacked the Saints as guilty of immorality, excessive church loyalty, and even treason. The continuing territorial squabbles, exaggerated by both sides and further exacerbated by the national sectional conflicts of the 1850s, took an ugly turn in 1857 and almost led to an armed conflict. When James Buchanan became president in 1857, he inherited the troubles in Utah, but instead of examining both sides of the conflict he quickly sided with those denouncing the Mormons and decided to send a federal military force to bring the Saints in line. When news of impending invasion reached Salt Lake on July 24, 1857, just as the Saints celebrated their first decade in the valley, Brigham Young hastily raised an army of Saints and waited for the arriving federal soldiers in the mountains east of Salt Lake. These offensive moves on the part of the federal government and the resulting defensive countermoves by the Utah Mormons set off the so-called Utah or Mormon War in 1857. Although no pitched battle took place after cooler heads talked both sides into less warlike actions, these were tense days in Utah.

While the Mormons and their defenders waited, many of their memories alive with the harassments and mistreatments of earlier years in Ohio, Missouri, and Illinois, the most unfortunate event of western Mormon history, the Mountain Meadows Massacre, took place in southern Utah. The massacre was not explicitly a part of the Mormon War, but similar hatreds and emotions helped lead to this horrendous event. In the bloody incident in September 1857, a united force of Indians and Mormons from southern Utah attacked the Fancher wagon train, an immigrant group on its way from Arkansas to California. The attackers killed more than 120 adults. Even though a charged atmosphere of impending war and other local tensions and the presence of the perceived threatening immigrants help explain the causes of the massacre, they do not excuse the tragedy, which remains a dark blot on the Mormon record. Although Salt Lake church leaders may not have been directly to blame for the attack—local church and military leaders probably were—Mormon officials at all levels were in part responsible through their emotional attacks on gentiles, their abuse of Indian allies, and the tone of antagonism and alarm they maintained throughout this period. Non-Mormons added to the discontent by blackening the reputations of Saints in any way they could. Fortunately, in the Salt Lake City area, emotions began to cool on both sides, and the so-called Mormon War was over nearly as quickly and as easily as it threatened to begin. Church officials also tried to quiet the ugly rumors surfacing from the Mountain Meadows Massacre.

Although separation from other Americans and internal conflicts and adjustments characterized the first decade in Utah, in the next forty years the

Mormons were drawn increasingly into the maelstrom of national sociocultural conflicts. The first gentiles who came through Utah were an ambiguous gift. Even before the Gold Rush brought a cresting ripple of immigrants to the West Coast in the 1850s, overlanders traveled through Utah, trading with Mormon settlers or staying over for a much-needed rest. Salt Lake City as a trade center or stopping-off place became increasingly important once the forty-niners began their treks westward, sometimes numbering as many as 15,000 travelers per year. Many Saints were fair and helpful to the overlanders. Others, after Brigham Young allowed that it was "no sin to gull" a gentile, quickly set up a favorable balance of trade—buying low and selling high. The first of what Mormon historian Leonard Arrington has called "windfall opportunities," the Gold Rush was followed by the Mormon War, new modes of transportation and communication, and the arrival of the first transcontinental railroad in 1869 as a series of events that economically benefited Utah.

At the same time, these economic windfalls brought into Utah increasing numbers of outsiders in search of financial gain. The Mormon War, for example, drew several non-Mormon merchants who, although supplying the army stationed in Utah, also traded with the Saints by providing goods not available in the valley. During the Civil War other troops had to be supplied, so the new merchants continued to do well. As mines opened in Idaho and Montana in the 1860s, gentile traders bought goods in the East and additional merchandise in Salt Lake City, traded these items in the northern mining camps, and returned with the exchanged gold to Utah. Such well-known merchants as Russell, Majors and Waddell and Ben Holladay did a thriving if short-lived business in the Salt Lake area.

Even more momentous was the completion of the Central Pacific and Union Pacific railroads in 1869. Now the Mormons were adjacent to the direct route between the East and West coasts, and the closed, self-sufficient economy that they had pursued for nearly two decades was thrown open to two new dynamic forces, railroads and mining. Ironically, the Saints hastened the coming of the railroads by contracting to level grades, cut ties, lay track. In addition, when the railroad chose to pass through Ogden rather than Salt Lake City, the brethren completed a spur line between the two cities within the next year. Throughout the next decade or two Mormons were involved in building other railroads in varied parts of the territory, thus encouraging the new and foreign economic and social elements that arrived with the railroads.

Although some gentile or former Mormon investors such as the Walker brothers and William Godbe helped finance the railroads and mining ventures, even more aid came from national or international sources. British investors, as they did throughout the West, backed Utah mining in the 1870s, and other European bankers and businessmen followed suit. Even though the Panic of

1873, mine scandals, and other financial problems kept these investors from realizing sensational profits, mining succeeded in Utah, gradually and steadily adding to the economic livelihood of the region, and, by extension, bringing new ethnic groups as workers and residents of the territory.

Brigham Young's efforts illustrate Mormon desires to dominate economic affairs in Utah and their tendency to follow eastern experiences and organizations. Brother Brigham also reinstituted the earlier ideas of Joseph Smith, known variously as the Law of Consecration, the Order of Enoch, or the United Order. In these controversial church policies Smith had asked the faithful to deed over their property to a church leader, a bishop, who would return sufficient land or property for each church member to work and to support his family. The remainder of land or property would remain with the church. Generally, churchmen were not inspired participants in this demanding law. In the competitive air of the 1870s, Brigham Young tried again, urging members to give their property to local "orders" and to work for the benefit of the community. Some communities joined together on specific projects; others, like the best-known example in Orderville (1875–85), attempted a village commune, in which residents lived together, ate at a common table, and shared expenses and profits. Again, however, church members were less enthusiastic than the church apostles about the order movement. Young's death in 1877 removed the major cheerleader for such Mormon communities.

∾

No aspect of Mormon social life was more controversial and engendered more opposition than their practice of plural marriage, or polygamy. Although Joseph Smith vigorously denied that he and the church apostles participated in polygamy in the 1830s and 1840s, they clearly had in Nauvoo—and perhaps earlier. Not until 1852 did the church openly admit that polygamy was an official church doctrine and had been practiced for some time. For the next forty years Mormon leaders urged their followers to participate in this "new and everlasting covenant of celestial marriage," while gentiles in Utah and non-Mormons continually petitioned the federal government to destroy what they considered a pernicious institution.

It is not difficult to understand why most Americans, traditionally monogamous, reacted so strongly against polygamy. The institution affronted their moral, social, and cultural standards. Neither they nor later observers much understood the institution. For example, most Mormons were not involved in plural marriages. Although percentages varied dramatically over time and place, rarely were more than 25 percent of Mormon men and women polygamous, and only those whose spiritual and economic achievements and capabilities

FIGURE 6:3. *Mormon Polygamy, a Cartoon.* Nineteenth-century cartoonists often ridiculed the Mormon practice of plural marriage (polygamy). Here the humorist portrays Brigham Young atop a cabinet, safe from the bedlam among his wives and babies in his bed and in a nearby crib. Courtesy Denver Public Library, Western History Collection, F29933.

won permission from the church leader could marry a second wife. In addition, husbands had to gain permission from their first wife before they married again. In spite of Smith and Young's exhortations for Mormon men to take multiple wives, as Old Testament patriarchs had, not many did; in fact, rapid church growth from the 1840s to the 1880s was not paralleled by an increase in plural marriages. More than two-thirds of polygamous men married but a second time, and many chose a younger sister of their first wife. Usually marrying in their twenties or early thirties, these polygamous men most often married women twenty-five or younger, and these wives produced fewer children per marriage than nonpolygamous wives. The two prophets practiced what they preached, however, with Smith marrying as many as sixty or more wives, and Young united to twenty-seven and sealed to an equal number of living women and perhaps to more than one hundred deceased women.

In the decade following the official announcement of polygamy in 1852, opposition quickly arose. When John C. Frémont declared plural marriage one of the "twin relics of barbarism" in his Republican campaign for the presidency in 1856, he illustrated this early, strong antipolygamy stance. Six years later the Morrill Anti-Bigamy Act declared polygamy illegal in the territories, but the legislation was not enforced in Utah for at least a decade. In 1874, George Reynolds, secretary to Brigham Young, decided to test the constitutionality of this and other antipolygamy laws. It was a case the Mormons thought they could win handily. But the Supreme Court in 1879, after seeming earlier to favor the Saints, upheld the laws tested and opened the way for a heightened attack on the church's peculiar institution. When that attack came, Mormon President John Taylor, who had succeeded to the presidency in 1880 three years after the death of Young, refused to budge, asserting that plural marriages were God-inspired doctrine that he must uphold. Federal officials were not following the same doctrine, however. Here was the substance of an irrepressible conflict, which the Edmunds Act (1882) brought to a boiling point when it disallowed plural marriages and disenfranchised those who participated in them. Mormon leaders, including President Taylor, denounced the act and went into hiding. Five years later the Edmunds-Tucker Act tightened the legal collar on the Saints by dissolving the corporate status of the LDS Church, abolishing woman's suffrage in Utah, and undermining the property holdings of the church. When Wilford Woodruff replaced Taylor as the Mormon president, he at first vowed to continue the church's hard line. As it became clear, however, that continued resistance might lead to the destruction of the church, Woodruff, speaking for his beleaguered Mormons, issued on September 25, 1890, a manifesto declaring he would abide by the laws of the land concerning marriage and would urge his fellow members to "do likewise." Although a few minor questions remained, the conflict over the divisive issue of polygamy was at an end; accommodation was just beginning.

~

In the years after leaving Nauvoo in 1846, the Mormons tried to build a separate, covenanted community on the frontier. Although the first generation in the West, under the powerful, hardheaded, and pragmatic leadership of Brigham Young, were able to carry out much of their idealistic design, they were much less successful after the coming of the railroad in 1869 and the death of Young in 1877. As more and more gentiles crowded west and traveled through Salt Lake City or traded with the Saints, the Mormons found themselves changing, within and without. In the generation from Young's death until statehood in 1896, the Mormons became more and more like those from whom they wished to be isolated. In fifty years, the Saints had shifted from being a frontier people apart to becoming part of a New West linking Mormon and gentile.

Along the way the Mormons made unique but also typical contributions to the formation of the pioneer West. Travelers through Utah in the first decades of Mormon settlement often commented on the differences between these communities and others in the Far West. They marveled at the equitable divisions of land, the equity of the Mormon irrigation systems, their novel villages, and the general communal organization of the Mormons. In noting these balanced divisions of land and water and the signs of symmetry and community in Mormon villages and towns, tourists focused on outward symbols of the cohesion and cooperation that united Mormons and characterized their first years in the West. Less apparent to outsiders was the organizational structure of the church that led directly to the covenanted communities. The church doctrine of continuous revelation—but only to the prophet—kept power in his hands and in the church hierarchy: the twelve apostles and the Council of the 50. Unlike so many other early settlers in the West, Mormons followed the dictates of their autocratic leaders, and thus the Utah experience, although not entirely theocratic, was less democratic and individualistic than any other major far-western settlement in the nineteenth century. Their Zion, their New Jerusalem, was remarkably different from other western experiences; it became something of a "near-nation"—almost a separate Holy City in the Rocky Mountain West.

Even though many early visitors to Utah recognized the Saints as a community apart, they did not seem to comprehend several other important ingredients of Mormon society. No one did more, for example, than Mormon women to provide stability and continuity in these communities. As notable parts of a thoroughly patriarchal society that reserved political and economic leadership—as well as church direction—to men, LDS women were expected to provide secure, comfortable homes for their husbands and to raise large families. To help in the fields, too—if necessary—was not an unexpected duty. Most frontier women faced similar challenging circumstances, but Mormon women carried additional burdens. Church leadership responsibilities—particularly stints as overseas missionaries—often removed fathers, husbands, and brothers from farming and business operations, leaving these responsibilities in the hands of their women, who soon proved equal to managing the sometimes difficult tasks involved. Those women involved in polygamous marriages carried added weights unknown to other frontier women. Although most Mormon women—as one might expect—claimed these burdens were light and their yokes easy, they were called to go with the church and their families an extra mile—or two or three. In the words of western historian and novelist Wallace Stegner, the Mormon women "were incredible." All the more extraordinary, then, that these hardy, hard-working, and dependable women viewed their roles as usual and commonplace, not in the least extraordinary.

Despite the exterior appearances of community and social and moral order, Mormons experienced the incoming winds of change blowing into and throughout the West as the nineteenth century wore on. As the velocity and rapidity of these winds increased, the Saints faced a perplexing dilemma. Like New England Puritans whom the Saints wished to imitate and so often paralleled, the Mormons had fled intolerance and persecutions in their early years. Once ensconced in their New Jerusalem, however, Mormons too resented gentiles and their ways much as New England Puritans castigated those troublers within their Israel, Roger Williams and Anne Hutchinson. Still, even though separation and isolation were keys to the Mormons' original move west in the 1840s, signs of accommodation and social intercourse with outsiders were apparent by the 1870s, and those signs grew increasingly evident in the generation between Young's death and Utah statehood in 1896.

Revealingly, although scholars often emphasize the agricultural and rural nature of Mormon settlements in the Rockies, Mormon society has been more urban than many observers have thought. Indeed, as historian Earl Pomeroy has noted, Salt Lake City and other Utah cities, after San Francisco, were the "largest urban concentration in the Far West just after the Civil War." Brother Brigham urged agricultural pursuits and rural settlements on the faithful, but the growing power of the metropolis—Salt Lake City—as church headquarters, as supply center, as depot for newcomers, and as a symbol for the gathering gave it increasing hegemony over an expanding region from Idaho to California. In spite of itself, the Mormon community was becoming more urban and urbane than the patriarchs had planned.

By the closing years of the nineteenth century, Mormons had made a separate peace with some of the ideals that impelled them west a half-century earlier. They had given up their central doctrine of plural marriage, they were no longer an isolated, separate community, and they had embraced the new economic doctrines of Gilded Age America. Still, they had not abandoned other traditions. If Salt Lake City was their new counting house, it also remained their religious meeting place. The LDS Church dominated sociocultural life in Utah, and even if politics and political parties were undergoing change in the 1890s, Mormons still controlled most elections. Utah and its Mormons—like other sections of the West—illustrated the conflicting forces of change and continuity that characterized the West at the end of the nineteenth century.

California Gold Rush

A different set of communities was rapidly emerging in other parts of the American West. These were the mining towns scattered throughout the frontier. One month before California became a U.S. territory in February 1848, gold was discovered at Sutter's Mill on the western slopes of the Sierra Nevada Mountains. News of that strike triggered one of the most remarkable people movements in

American history. The California Gold Rush inaugurated a series of mining stampedes during the next half-century that drew hundreds of thousands of miners, suppliers, hangers-on, and many others to far-flung parts of the West. From California to Colorado and Nevada in 1859–61, to Idaho and Montana in the 1860s, to South Dakota and Arizona in the 1870s, and finally north to Alaska in the 1890s, the mining strikes popped up like a series of planned explosions. In those decades, Virginia City, Nevada; Deadwood, South Dakota; Tombstone, Arizona; and Nome, Alaska, flashed on and then off the scene as notorious boom-and-bust mining towns. Of most lasting, powerful significance were the instant cities of San Francisco and Denver, which began as supply centers for mining bonanzas but evolved into major western urban places.

The gold and silver rushes transformed several sections of the West in the second half of the nineteenth century. Individual prospectors and mining corporations, especially driven by the desire to uncover new lodes of rich minerals, ripped up the terrain of scattered sites. Working like powerful magnets, the booms peopled remote subregions of the western frontier and helped establish important economic and transportation networks. Not surprisingly, the hordes of newcomers also dramatically altered the previous ethnic and gender makeup of these places. The mining booms and resultant boomtowns helped transform the American West in 1900 into a much different region than it had been in 1850.

∾

The discovery of gold in California happened almost by accident. James Marshall, a partner of the famed Swiss immigrant and entrepreneur John Sutter, was constructing a mill and mill race at Sutter's Mill (or Coloma) on the American River, about fifty miles east of present Sacramento. On the morning of January 24, 1848, Marshall spied what looked like small pieces of gold at the bottom of the mill race. Preliminary examinations of the rocks proved Marshall's guess to be true, but he was unaware he had uncovered a rich lode. News of his discovery leaked out downriver in California and then quickly spread around to Mexico, into the Pacific area, and down to South America. A bit later the news reached the East Coast of the United States and across the Atlantic to Europe. The stampede was on. The closest and first to arrive were the Californians, but Mexicans and South Americans, and others around the Pacific, soon followed. Once other Americans heard of the sensational strike, they too headed for El Dorado. The wild rush populated the gold region overnight. By the end of 1849, less than two years after Marshall's initial discovery, there were probably 100,000 people in California, but 250,000 at the end of 1852. All this in a region that had numbered perhaps 14,000 souls, plus Indians,

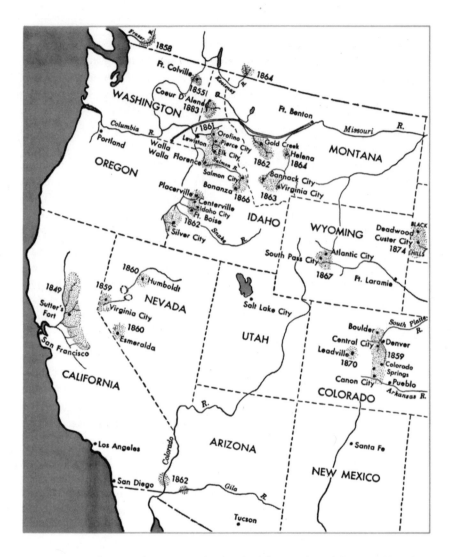

FIGURE 6:4. *The Miners' Frontier.* In the decades following the California Gold Rush of 1849 miners rushed to several other mining areas scattered throughout the Far West. From Ray Allen Billington and Martin Ridge, *Westward Expansion: A History of the American Frontier*, 6th ed., abr. (Albuquerque: University of New Mexico Press, 2001), 263.

at the beginning of 1848. There had been nothing like it in the history of the United States.

Chaos reigned. In a matter of weeks, tens of thousands of prospectors crowded the original strikes and other boom areas up and down the western slopes of the Sierra Nevada. Adequate food and safe drinking water, satisfactory living quarters, protected claims, and healthy conditions were all in jeopardy. The pick-and-shovel work proved to be taxing and endless. One might find some gold, but how was one to bring in needed supplies? At first nothing was available, except at exorbitant costs.

The experiences of many early miners in the California camps were repeated throughout mining booms of the West. Although optimistic miners sometimes enthused, "Gold is where you find it," many prospectors later lamented, "Gold is where I ain't." Forty-niners gradually learned some of the secrets of nature in producing rich mineral deposits. Over time, through the weight of surface soil and rocks, minerals had solidified into "veins." If enough of these veins existed in one area, prospectors spoke of a "lode." Through erosion veins became exposed, particularly where rivers or creeks wore away valley walls as well as parts of veins or lodes and deposited these heavy materials in streambeds below. Prospectors "panned" for this gold by shoveling dirt and mineral-bearing rocks into their large pans, sloshing water around in the pans, and hoping that some "pay dirt" settled into the bottoms of their pans. This process was known as placer mining. Another, later system, allowing miners and their backers to burrow after the veins or lodes in valley walls or deep into the ground, was labeled quartz or lode mining. A more corporate style of mining replaced earlier placer stages when the expenses of building and shoring up mining shafts demanded more capital than prospectors commanded. A third method, hydraulic mining, called for water to be pressurized, sent down a hose, and directed at sides of valleys or mountains. This complicated system, leading to the washing away of huge sections of dirt and rock in a short time, was particularly costly, financially and environmentally. In a few other mining areas, huge dredges moved snail-like up streambeds, scooping up the streambed, spitting out the useless gravel, and separating the precious minerals. All these methods, destroying creek and river beds, muddying water sources, and dumping huge piles across the landscape, did irreparable damage to mining sites throughout the West.

In the halcyon years of the California Gold Rush from 1848 to 1852, miners, government officials, financiers, and suppliers worked out patterns later adopted elsewhere in western mining areas. From Nevada City in the north to Sonora in the south (along appropriately numbered State Highway 49), dozens of jerry-built mining towns sprang up to house the incoming prospectors. Probably only half of the new population, about 100,000, actually worked as miners, but those numbers overran any legal, economic, community, and social systems and traditions already in place. Haste, flimsiness, imbalance, and rapid change characterized the regulations thrown up to try to deal with this avalanche of population and resultant problems.

Immediately officials were faced with vexing legal dilemmas. In 1848–49, California was not yet a state—statehood arrived in 1850—meaning that an inchoate mix of Spanish-Mexican institutions and American military regulations were under pressure to deal with complex issues the Gold Rush triggered. In the absence of a well-coordinated system of local and regional legal and governmental regulations, the miners and mining communities had to improvise. Following precedents of eastern frontiers lacking needed local administration, the camps organized locally through self-initiated gatherings. They set up "districts" and selected "recorders," through which law codes were established, mining claims recorded, and disputes adjudicated. Out of this process emerged a shaky, often-changing but necessary web of rules that provided a modicum of legal organization for the fly-by-night communities and mining areas. In addition, a vague feeling of association seemed to emerge in these predominately male populations, a feeling that encouraged preliminary agreements needed to foster a sense of community for otherwise atomistic, individual miners.

The California Gold Rush camps provide an illuminating illustration of the rapid change and diversity that characterized much of the nineteenth-century American West. In 1850, two years after Marshall's incredible discovery of gold at Coloma, California had become a state, its population booming to more than 100,000. San Francisco and Sacramento blossomed as supply cities, with newcomers, former prospectors and miners alike, realizing that by "mining the miners" they could do better economically than enduring the daily drudgery of pick and pan. Merchants sold mining tools and clothing; cooks—or what passed for cooks—furnished meals; saloonkeepers and prostitutes provided recreational and sexual services; and others found jobs transporting a panoply of goods to the Gold Rush towns. But, above all, a spirit of "get rich and get out" or a tendency to move on undermined attempts at fostering a "settled," ongoing community spirit.

New Englander Dame Shirley (Louise A. K. S. Clappe) captured that footloose malady in a letter home from Indian Bar in California on April 10, 1852: "Our countrymen are the most discontented of mortals. They are always longing for 'big strikes.' If a 'claim' is paying them a steady income, by which, if they pleased, they could lay up more in a month than they could accumulate in a year at home, still they are dissatisfied, and, in most cases, will wander off in search of better 'diggings.'"

Out of these frenzied, swiftly changing experiences evolved a fragmented, multicultural society. It was endlessly shifting and ill at ease with itself. The majority of the rushers were young white males. By and large, they were in their twenties, from New England and the East Coast. Women and children—indeed stable families generally—were often nearly nonexistent in the first flush years of the strike. Even though many of the men did not strike it rich, they were not poor. It had cost nearly $500 to travel overland or around Cape Horn to San Francisco. Even if they did not find a bonanza, most of the young miners were sufficiently well off to return home in a few months or a year or two, which many of them did.

EFFECT ON NATIVES

The sudden influx of the Gold Rush populations conspicuously altered existing racial and ethnic arrangements and imposed new ones on California. Above all, the Indians of northern California were displaced or marginalized, as were other groups in the mining camp societies. Caught in the deluge of immigrants, California's Indians, unable to protect themselves, suffered tragic consequences. About 150,000 in 1850, their numbers precipitously declined to about 30,000 at the end of the decade. Murderous attacks of all sorts—including "Indian hunting"—wiped out whole tribal groups. The Yana and Yahi tribes located near the mines included about 1,800 men and women in 1852; two decades later only 20 members survived. Indian women, often victims of the lusts of young male miners, disappeared even more rapidly than Indian men. Nowhere in the American West was the story of Indian decimation more bloody and brutal than in mid-nineteenth-century California.

The magnet of the Gold Rush drew several other racial and ethnic groups. Some of the first to arrive were Sonorans, experienced miners from northern Mexico. Soon thereafter came the "Kanakas," Natives from Hawai'i, and by late 1848 and early 1849, miners from Chile and Peru. Perhaps as many as five or six thousand South Americans had come to California by the mid-1850s. Australians soon followed. Thousands of Europeans fleeing the continental disruptions of 1848 also headed for the diggings. As many as 25,000 Europeans, with a heavy influx of Frenchmen, had arrived by 1852. The Chinese came later, with most of the 35,000 that immigrated coming after 1852. Many Chinese came as contract laborers, signing work agreements with other Chinese contractors, who paid for the workers' trip and extracted a portion of the immigrants' wages until their debt was paid. In 1860, more than 30,000 Chinese resided in California, meaning that one of five miners in the state was Chinese.

These varied ethnic groups, even while flavoring California's sociocultural stew, felt the sting of racial prejudices. In addition to the horrific violence visited upon Native Americans, legal and social restrictions were heaped on other groups. As part of these barriers, the state of California enacted a Foreign Miners' Tax in 1850 and other taxes in the next years, aimed chiefly at the "Sonorans" (Mexicans and Chileans) and later at the Chinese. Sometimes as high as $20 per month, the tax became nearly prohibitive for these two

RACIAL PREJUDICES

• MINERS TAX 1850

groups. On other occasions Chinese, often exploited and victimized, were simply excluded from areas, allowed as workers on but not owners of claims.

These groups cheated by exclusionary mining laws suffered in other ways from other Anglo animosities. The stories surrounding bandit Joaquín Murrieta (also Murieta) illustrate the strife and violence of the mining camps in the Gold Rush area. Oral tradition says Joaquín and his family emigrated from northern Mexico to Sonora town in the southern mines about 1849. Soon he began to feel the ostracism Anglos heaped on Mexican miners and horsemen. It was said that Anglos raped his wife, Rosa, lashed Joaquín, and lynched his brother, accusing him of horse stealing. Joaquín's desire for revenge sent him, or several other men named Joaquín, on months of retribution for the violent deeds repeatedly visited on him and his family. Sometimes he attacked and robbed Chinese miners, more often he and his riders retaliated against Anglos. Contrasting accounts accused Joaquín of attacking the weak—Chinese, women, and children. As hysteria over "Joaquín attacks" mounted, rewards for his capture encouraged posses to pursue him relentlessly. Captain Harry Love and his state-funded rangers caught up with a gang of Mexican riders on July 25, 1853, killed several, and cut off the head of one raider they believed was Murrieta and preserved it in alcohol. For Anglo Californians, Joaquín represented the disruptive elements of a ragged frontier that needed to be quelled. For Mexicans of the Gold Rush era—and for Chicanos of later generations—Joaquín became a hero, a social bandit riding for his people. Driven by prejudices and outraged by violence, he used guerilla tactics to offset the coercive power of a dominant Anglo society. Whatever one concludes about the shadowy Joaquín Murrieta, his story illustrates the difficulties of establishing a stable, just society on a new, rambunctious, constantly changing frontier.

By the end of the 1850s, a modicum of economic and social permanence was evident in California. Ever-booming San Francisco, the main entry point for international immigrants and suppliers for the Gold Rush, began to exhibit shaky signs of stability. For the most part, the disruptive fallout from violent vigilante forays had ended in San Francisco, and a vigorous, multicultural society was in the making. The arrival of the first transcontinental trains in 1869 brought even more yeasty elements to leaven San Francisco. The instant city on the coast, continuing to mushroom each year, began to rival New York and Boston as a cultural center. By 1880, "Baghdad by the Bay," which San Francisco was soon dubbed, had grown to 234,000, acquiring in thirty years the population that it took Boston 250 years to achieve. Throughout the nineteenth century no western city came close to duplicating the awesome economic and cultural dominance of San Francisco. What Los Angeles would become in the post-1900 West San Francisco achieved in the nineteenth century. Most of that early dominance was linked directly to the shaping power of the California Gold Rush.

The dramatic growth and expanding regional power of San Francisco was but one legacy of the Gold Rush. Seen in larger context, it is now clear that the explosive movement to California in the decade after the discovery of gold transformed the Far West. California's overnight transfiguration from a sleepy Spanish outpost to a new state boasting a population of 380,000 in 1860 represented the spectacular economic and social forces unleashed on and revolutionizing the Pacific Slope. Perhaps of larger regional significance, this avalanche of newcomers set off other reactions. In the 1850s and 1860s, freighters and stagecoach lines hustled to connect the West Coast with points east, and when the transcontinental railroad arrived the Atlantic and Pacific coasts had been truly linked. The California Gold Rush was a gigantic people mover luring hundreds of thousands from all points of the globe. A movement reshaping the West for years to come, the Gold Rush, combined with later mining booms, was clearly the most important transforming event of the nineteenth-century American West.

~

Before long, other gold and silver strikes surfaced eastward like a flat rock skipping on a pond. These new discoveries, although less momentous than the California Gold Rush as long-range shaping forces, rapidly drew miners hungry for new strikes and the riches they promised. Between the late 1850s and the mid-1860s bonanza rushes erupted in Nevada, Colorado, Idaho, and Montana. They both duplicated and broke from the patterns of the mining camps of the western Sierra Nevada Mountains.

In the 1850s Mormon prospectors had surveyed the eastern slopes of the Sierra Nevada but gave up after mediocre returns. Then, on June 10, 1859, almost by happenstance, two prospectors uncovered what became known as the Ophir vein of the Comstock Lode. Their find was located in the Washoe Mountains, where the Sierra Nevada juts out toward the Great Basin. Within a few days the miners turned up a huge quartz vein that, after a few initial assays, proved to be immensely rich, worth nearly $4,000 a ton of ore. Much of the vein was almost pure silver and gold. "The Ophir Mine," writes one historian, "was the richest in mining history." The original discoverers, plus Henry T. P. "Old Pancake" Comstock, quickly sold their claims for up to $40,000, without realizing the immense wealth that lay below the surface at the Ophir. All the initial miners died in poverty, but the purchasers, especially Judge James Walsh and George Hearst, became "Comstock Kings" from the region's abundant mineral wealth.

The Comstock Lode and the later "Big Bonanza" of the 1870s in the same region illustrate the quick changes occurring in western mining. When it became clear that individual prospectors ("lone Alkali Ikes") could not furnish the capital and technological skills to develop the Comstock, capitalists and companies took over. The latter could finance the costly lode-mining system of driving shafts hundreds of feet into the earth or into mountainsides. This capitalized, mechanized system demanded expensive equipment and more skilled miners. Hard rock drills and stamp mills needed to separate the precious minerals from the surrounding ore were hauled up over the Sierra and utilized at the Comstock. Skilled Cornish, Welsh, and German miners were hired to build and shore up the extensive system of shafts that honeycombed the area. In the 1870s the Consolidated Virginia company drove a shaft several hundred feet underground to mine a vein more than fifty feet wide of nearly pure silver and gold. More than $200 million was taken from this Big Bonanza strike. It was clear to most observers, however, that it was not the individual or small-time miners who "cashed in" on the Comstock. Rather, the larger, fully capitalized companies reaped most of the huge profits of the Big Bonanza.

Within months of the 1859 discovery, Virginia City, the center for the Comstock Lode, exploded to 15,000 inhabitants. It grew to 20,000 in the 1870s but by the 1890s was a virtual ghost town. Here was a story happening over and over in the West: in the few months after a mining strike, isolated frontier sites teemed with newcomers. The appearance of thousands of hopeful, acquisitive, and hungry miners quickly drew hoteliers and housekeepers, cooks, and suppliers of pleasure. Newspapers, churches, and schools soon followed. The lively, sometimes frenzied lifestyles of boomtowns like Virginia City lured all sorts of travelers, tourists, and curiosity seekers. Among those who ventured to the Comstock was author Mark Twain. He had arrived in Carson City, Nevada's territorial capital, in 1861 as a companion to his brother Orion, who had been named secretary of the territory for his support of Abraham Lincoln in the election of 1860. By turns Twain served as clerk, unsuccessful miner, mill worker, speculator, and then reporter and editor of Virginia City's *Territorial Enterprise*. He wrote seriocomic letters to his family describing the pell-mell life of the boomtown. Like so many other newcomers, he was both drawn and repelled by what he saw and experienced. Yet he confided to his mother and sister, "I had rather die in Washoe than *live* in some countries." What Twain felt replicated what thousands of others sensed about Virginia City and other mining towns.

One year before the strike at the Comstock, scattered gold deposits were discovered on the Front Range of the Rockies at the confluence of the South Platte River and Cherry Creek. Although near Denver and eighty miles distant from Pike's Peak, the stampede in 1858 and 1859 became known as the Pike's Peak Gold Rush. Rumors of earlier findings in the area, the disastrous economic fallouts from the Panic of 1857, and the fanciful puffery of Mississippi

Valley newspapers attracted as many as 100,000 people to the area. But when much of the hyperbole proved disappointingly false, nearly half of the miners turned back or stayed but a few days. Perhaps no more than a quarter of the boomers actually plied pick and shovel in the diggings.

The fifty-niner rush duplicated other mining experiences in the West and differed from still others. Like the forty-niners to California, most of the early Colorado prospectors worked at panning. But the diggings were much less rich than on the Sierra foothills and soon played out. As on the Comstock, the largest deposits were in underground lodes, necessitating more complicated technology and expensive smelting processes to gain the gold. Companies soon pushed out individual miners in the Colorado mines.

Still, many would-be miners stayed on. The Denver area developed agriculturally, as early prospectors became farmers to support the growing town. Like San Francisco, Denver was quickly transformed into an instant city by a gold rush. Unlike Virginia City, Deadwood, and Tombstone, both San Francisco and Denver became developing towns and major urban places by the end of the century. Because they were located near fertile croplands and accessible transportation grids (rushers to Colorado came up the Oregon or Santa Fe trails and cut south or north to Denver), the California and Colorado cities built on valuable hinterlands not available to boomtowns in Arizona and South Dakota.

A similar story unfolded in Idaho and Montana. Between 1860 and 1865, beginning in Idaho and then spreading east to Montana, a series of strikes stampeded miners to both sides of the northern Rockies. The first discoveries in 1860 to 1863 were in Idaho on the Clearwater and Salmon Rivers, not far from modern Lewiston. As those diggings began to play out, discoveries to the south in the Boise Basin in 1863, with Idaho City as their focal point, proved even richer in gold deposits than the northern Idaho mines. In Montana, a quartet of strikes prompted an influx of miners to the Rockies: Bannock (July 1862), Alder Gulch/Virginia City (May 1863), Last Chance Gulch/Helena (July 1864), and Confederate Gulch/Diamond City (January 1865). A large portion of these camps was peopled by miners from within the West, with California prospectors particularly flooding to the new strikes.

The Idaho and Montana boomers faced a number of problems. The first was distance and difficulty of access. A miner or supplier in the Lewiston area had to descend the Snake and Columbia Rivers to Portland, travel south to San Francisco, go east to Salt Lake City, and then north to the Montana camps. That was the most direct route because no others were yet open through the Rockies. These gold and silver towns enticed tens of thousands of miners and even some of their families, but few permanent settlers. Population centers shifted so rapidly that territorial capitals should have been made portable and on wheels, to be transferred overnight to the next boomtown. Lewiston

FIGURE 6:5. *Hydraulic Mining*. This ruinous form of mining utilized high-pressure streams of water to pinpoint, break down, and quickly wash away hillsides and valley walls to uncover deposits of precious metals. Courtesy Idaho State Historical Society, 3308.

and Boise in Idaho and Bannock, Virginia City, and Helena in Montana served as temporary territorial capitals in the 1860s and 1870s.

The remoteness of these camps made law and order and community building difficult. Road agents, robbers, and vigilante mobs convulsed both areas. One notorious highwayman, Henry Plummer, disguised as a sheriff, plundered Idaho and then Montana camps. Vigilantes finally caught up with him and his henchmen, hanging them in 1864 without much attempt at careful legal proceedings. Although both regions hosted transient populations in the thousands early on and became territories in 1863–64 (Idaho nearly as large as Texas until the territorial lines were drawn), neither became a state until 1889 (Montana) or 1890 (Idaho). In the long intervening periods, both territories experienced frequent political difficulties under third-rate hacks or crooked appointees. If the mineral rushes to Idaho and Montana drew thousands at the outset, they did little to ensure an orderly procession toward well-organized communities later in the century.

The last of the largest rushes occurred in the mid-1870s in Deadwood, in the Black Hills of South Dakota. In 1870, the population of Dakota Territory (then North and South Dakota) numbered about 15,000; ten years later it had boomed to 135,000. Most of that demographic burst resulted from mining bonanzas, much less from farming and new forms of transportation. And a large part of that notable influx derived from the rush to the Black Hills. Rumors of rich mineral deposits sent a federal government–sponsored exploration, led by General George Custer, in the summer of 1874 to evaluate these sensational stories. His confirmation of the mineral deposits infected thousands of prospectors and hangers-on with gold fever. Although the Black Hills were protected Indian territory, hordes of avaricious miners, paying no heed to legal barriers, stampeded into the Hills.

By the end of 1875, 15,000 people were encamped in the Hills, most crowded into the towns of Deadwood and Custer City. Contacts soon led to conflicts between the invaders and the Sioux and Cheyenne peoples attempting to protect their sacred territories. Social turmoil within the inchoate mining communities compounded the chaos. These tensions, without and within, argues western historian Howard R. Lamar, caused the Dakota Territory to become "the most violent of American frontiers."

The Black Hills mining communities waxed and waned from 1875 forward. The Deadwood diggings, as well as those in other Hills areas, dropped off. But the huge Homestake Mine in nearby Lead, begun in the late 1870s, continued to draw miners and mining operations throughout the twentieth century. This sprawling mine, as well as a few others, enticed farmers and ranchers to these areas to help supply needed foodstuffs. The arrival of these newcomers put increasing pressures on the Teton Sioux to cede more land, which they did, to open additional territory for agriculturists. Yet the remoteness of the Black Hills, the continuing presence of strong Indian cultures, and the lateness of needed transportation kept the Black Hills areas from experiencing the kind of expanding growth that characterized San Francisco and Denver.

~

In the first years of nearly all frontier mining camps, youth, physical mobility, and transience worked crossways against developing a cohesive community spirit. Young white males rarely stayed rooted to one set of diggings. When a reputed boom proved less than its advertisements or a lode played out, energetic prospectors moved on, quickly and often. As historian Robert Hine notes in his provocative study of community building on the American frontier, *Gemeinshaft* ("unity stemming from emotions, beliefs, and shared life experiences") and *Gesellschaft* (a spirit more derived from "cities and states, public opinion, and industry") were both difficult to achieve in mining camps. Instead, fragmentation, fractiousness, and rapid turnover marked the rush

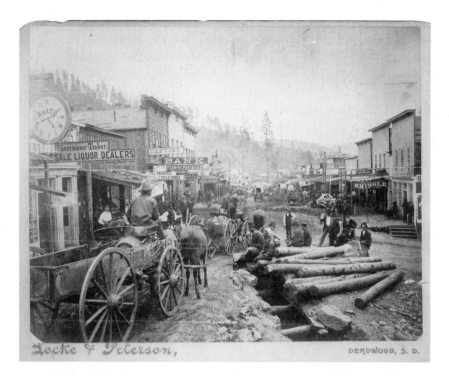

FIGURE 6:6. *Deadwood, Dakota Territory.* Mining rushes and the overnight
appearance of boomtowns like Deadwood illustrated how quickly socioeconomic
systems changed and fragile environments were damaged or destroyed in the
West. Courtesy Nebraska State Historical Society, RG 3573. PH:3–1.

camps. In the California Gold Rush towns of Grass Valley and Nevada City,
for example, only about 10 percent of the resident population in 1850 remained
there in 1856. This impermanence and outmigration were replicated in dozens
of frontier mining sites.

The determined efforts of Sarah Royce reveal much about attempts to foster community in the frontier West. The wife of an unlucky frontier farmer
and businessman and the mother of the eminent philosopher Josiah Royce,
Sarah Royce battled against rootlessness in Grass Valley. Protecting her own
expanding brood against the rough, masculine society of her town, she tried to
bring culture by teaching school, supporting church groups, and encouraging
sound marriages. A committed evangelical, Sarah Royce also helped launch
attacks on Grass Valley saloons, Hurdy Gurdies (dance halls), and other modes
of recreation and entertainment she considered immoral. Despite Royce's

energetic efforts, she and her cohorts seemed unable to divert the tide of social disruptions that infected Grass Valley. Many other ambitious community builders in western mining camps were similarly unsuccessful in creating a strong sense of unity and place in the earlier years of these swiftly changing towns.

A major key for the developing stability of a mining town was often the close proximity of an expanding hinterland. San Francisco and Denver, the products early on of mining rushes, were transformed into instant cities because nearby regions in California and Colorado could support and supply these two urban places. As the entry point for Pacific travelers, as the supply source for the Comstock and much of the Pacific Northwest, and as the terminus for the first transcontinental railroad, San Francisco quickly became "the city" on the West Coast. A decade after its beginning, Denver was also connected to a nourishing agricultural hinterland and linked to the transcontinental rail line. To a lesser extent, Sacramento and Stockton in California, Helena and Butte in Montana, and Lewiston in Idaho also established economic livelihoods that expanded well into the next century. But for all these towns and cities there were hundreds of mining camps that vanished as quickly as they appeared or gradually died like a malnourished animal. The get-in, dig-it-out, and move-on nature of most mining rushes precluded their ever developing into full-fledged, expanding western cities.

Other economic developments also militated against unified, coherent mining communities. Class divisions among camp residents were evident from the start of these places, and these splits often persisted, even widened. In the early California camps, which so often served as schools for later rushes, social stratification developed based on wealth, occupational differences, and ethnic identity. Similar separations divided mining towns throughout the second half of the nineteenth century. Few miners struck it rich; many departed from diggings with less than when they arrived. One journal at the end of the century spoke of the "hundreds of lives" that "were sacrificed" and the "remnant of this great army" that left many miners "poor in pocket, with shattered constitutions and wrecked hopes." Only a small number of self-made entrepreneurs like George Hearst of the Far West, Horace Tabor of Colorado, or William Andrews Clark of Montana became gold and silver kings. As we have seen, many mining rushes quickly moved from individual to corporate control, as in Virginia City, Nevada, and Deadwood, South Dakota. The powerful dominance of these paternalistic, and often absentee, companies like the Guggenheims and Rockefellers in the northern West, the Anaconda Company in Montana, and Phelps Dodge in the Southwest led workers and labor unions to fight bitterly and sometimes violently against what they considered coercive and deadly company policies. These labor-company conflicts were as prologues to the intense battles that erupted between the more radical Western Federation of Miners and Industrial Workers of the World ("Wobblies") and companies in the twentieth century.

Mining towns also excluded miners on the basis of their racial or ethnic identity. Beginning with the violent and sometimes murderous displacement of Indians in California and Colorado, dozens of mining camps systematically kept minority peoples from participating in their social, economic, and political institutions. In numerous locations, the Chinese, Mexicans, African Americans, and Europeans such as the Irish, Italians, and Cornish felt the sting of illegal and informal laws and traditions. The Chinese ("Celestials" or "Orientals") were particularly discriminated against and relegated to inferior social and economic status, even though—or perhaps because—they were unusually hard-working and ambitious miners able to wrest livings from many mining areas that others had abandoned. Negative stereotypes of all these groups were usual fare in mining camp laws, organizational bylaws, and newspaper stories.

One can easily make too much of the transitory and fragmentary nature of the frontier mining camps, however. Another story needs airing. Sociocultural contacts, conversations, some combinations, and even a few communities also emerged from the western mining camps.

The nascent camps needed time and the concomitant longings and energies of their residents to achieve a modicum of unity. Generally, if a mining camp endured for a decade without exhausting its mineral base, that was sufficient time to establish the needed institutions on which to build some sense of cohesion. Over time, elementary schools, Protestant and Catholic churches, and fraternal organizations materialized, symbolizing and encouraging permanence. In the space of ten years, many mining camps had moved from a gathering of haphazard tents to a town of timber and brick buildings. In the first months of Deadwood, Dakota, for instance, Methodist "Preacher" Smith harangued street dwellers even as Wild Bill Hickok and Calamity Jane wandered those streets. The Congregationalists, Catholics, and Episcopalians came soon thereafter. Within a year or two after the camp's founding in 1875, primary schools were accepting miners' children. By the early 1880s, the Masons, Old Fellows, Civil War associations, women's clubs, and a library association were established. These groups, writes one historian, illustrate "the overwhelming need of individuals [in Deadwood and other camps] to become, as quickly as possible, parts of their new community."

Other ties aided in unifying the mining camps. None was more important than families and relatives. A few wives and children accompanied their husbands and fathers to the mining sites, and increasing numbers came after a few years. Preconditioned in nineteenth-century America to act as agents of social and moral order, women often founded schools and helped establish churches. They also provided hearths of hospitality—homes away from home for many lonely and womanless men. In Leadville, Colorado, noted Local Color writer and artist Mary Hallock Foote, although isolating herself from the pell-mell life of main street and labor strife at the mines, nonetheless entertained engineers, surveyors, and mine managers with her engineer husband, A. D. Foote. Visitors saluted Mrs. Foote's graciousness, her genteel ways, and the comforts of her rustic mountain cabin. Her home became a meeting and gathering place for elite engineers and other guests. Later, in the Boise Basin in Idaho, Foote and her husband relied heavily on their extended families and his engineering fraternity to survive several financial and physical crises.

Camp residents found other ways to establish and celebrate their common sociocultural connections. Traveling shows provided welcome entertainment and gathering times for many of the isolated mining towns. Theater groups performing Shakespearean and other elite plays, tent shows, and circuses drew out crowds, as did boxing matches, baseball games, and even cockfights and bullfights, on which there was vigorous betting. Locally sponsored activities like church socials, picnics, weddings, and dances also attracted large numbers of guests. But other celebrations, particularly on the Fourth of July, were even more popular avenues for displaying community patriotism.

The communal spirit of these gatherings helped to offset the restless impermanence that infected so many of the mining camps. The safety nets of family, fraternities, and church associations served as protections against the corrosive forces threatening to undermine all communal spirit. Indeed, the impulses of unity and disintegration often vied for dominance without either winning control of the camps. "Education, culture, and religion," one mining historian reminds us, "flourished in the same environment as vice and gambling."

~

By the end of the nineteenth century, the Mormons and miners provided clear evidence of their shaping impact on the western scene. They also illustrate the West's molding power of those who entered its gates. The Mormons, first establishing their strong Zion in the Mountain West, had founded other settlements from Canada to Mexico, and even launched missionary programs across the Atlantic and Pacific. Although the Saints hoped to remain isolated and safe from non-Mormon influences, they were drawn bit by bit into American affairs by the end of the century. Increasingly, their story would be linked to that of the United States. Concurrently, dozens of scattered mining camps drew ambitious, adventuresome populations westward from the mid-century to 1900. Some of these camps became the spearheads of further frontier settlement, including the overnight cities of San Francisco and Denver, while others like Sacramento, Helena, and Lewiston developed into territorial or state capitals. Still others, such as Deadwood, Leadville, and Tombstone, after initial booms, dwindled into small towns. But all the camps had been strong magnets in drawing hundreds of thousands of people west. In so doing, they added to the yeasty mix of a diverse and swiftly changing region.

Alexander, Thomas G., and James B. Allen. *Mormons & Gentiles: A History of Salt Lake City.* Boulder, CO: Pruett Publishing, 1984.

Arrington, Leonard J. *Brigham Young: American Moses.* New York: Alfred A. Knopf, 1985.

———. *The Great Basin Kingdom: An Economic History of the Latter-day Saints, 1830–1900.* Cambridge, MA: Harvard University Press, 1958.

Arrington, Leonard J., and Davis Bitton. *The Mormon Experience: A History of the Latter-day Saints.* New York: Alfred A. Knopf, 1979.

Bagley, Will. *Blood of the Prophets: Brigham Young and the Massacre at Mountain Meadows.* Norman: University of Oklahoma Press, 2002.

Brands, H. W. *The Age of Gold: The California Gold Rush and the New American Dream.* New York: Doubleday, 2002.

Bushman, Richard Lyman. *Joseph Smith: Rough Rolling Stone.* New York: Knopf, 2005.

Clappe, Louise Amelia Knapp Smith [Dame Shirley]. *The Shirley Letters. . . .* 1854–55; Santa Barbara, CA: Peregrine Smith, 1970.

Eifler, Mark A. *Gold Rush Capitalists: Greed and Growth in Sacramento.* Albuquerque: University of New Mexico Press, 2002.

Greever, William S. *The Bonanza West: The Story of Western Mining Rushes, 1848–1900.* Norman: University of Oklahoma Press, 1963.

Griswold del Castillo, Richard. "Joaquín Murrieta: The Many Lives of a Legend." In *With Badges and Bullets: Lawmen & Outlaws in the Old West*, edited by Richard W. Etulain and Glenda Riley, 106–22, 208–9. Golden, CO: Fulcrum Publishing, 1999.

Hine, Robert V. *Community on the American Frontier: Separate But Not Alone.* Norman: University of Oklahoma Press, 1980.

———. *Josiah Royce: From Grass Valley to Harvard.* Norman: University of Oklahoma Press, 1992.

Holliday, J. S. *The World Rushed In: An Eyewitness Account of a Nation Heading West.* New York: Simon and Schuster, 1981.

Hyde, Anne F. "Sam Brannan and Elizabeth Byers: Mormons and Miners at Midcentury." In *Western Lives: A Biographical History of the American West*, edited by Richard W. Etulain, 147–76. Albuquerque: University of New Mexico Press, 2004.

Johnson, Susan Lee. *Roaring Camp: The Social World of the California Gold Rush.* New York: W. W. Norton, 2000.

Mann, Ralph. *After the Gold Rush: Society in Grass Valley and Nevada City, California, 1849–1870.* Stanford, CA: Stanford University Press, 1982.

Marks, Paula Mitchell. *Precious Dust: The True Saga of the Western Gold Rushes.* New York: William Morrow, 1994.

O'Dea, Thomas F. *The Mormons.* Chicago: University of Chicago Press, 1957.

Paul, Rodman Wilson, and Elliott West. *Mining Frontiers of the Far West, 1848–1880*. Rev. exp. ed. Albuquerque: University of New Mexico Press, 2001.

Peterson, Charles S. *Utah: A History*. New York: W. W. Norton, 1977.

Roberts, Brian. *American Alchemy: The California Gold Rush and Middle-Class Culture*. Chapel Hill: University of North Carolina Press, 2000.

Rohrbaugh, Malcolm J. *Days of Gold: The California Gold Rush and the Making of California*. Berkeley: University of California Press, 1999.

Royce, Sarah. *A Frontier Lady: Recollections of the Gold Rush and Early California*. New Haven, CT: Yale University Press, 1932.

Shipps, Jan. *Mormonism: The Story of a New Religious Tradition*. Urbana: University of Illinois Press, 1985.

Smith, Duane A. *Mining America: The Industry and the Environment, 1800–1980*. Lawrence: University Press of Kansas, 1987.

——. *Rocky Mountain Mining Camps: The Urban Frontier*. Bloomington: Indiana University Press, 1967.

Stegner, Wallace. *The Gathering of Zion: The Story of the Mormon Trail*. New York: McGraw-Hill, 1964.

Zhu, Liping. *A Chinaman's Chance: The Chinese on the Rocky Mountain Mining Frontier*. Niwot: University Press of Colorado, 1997.

CHAPTER SEVEN

Ranching, Farming, and Transportation Networks

∼

WHEN EASTERN WRITER OWEN WISTER CAME WEST TO WYOMING FOR THE first time in 1885, he reacted enthusiastically to what he saw and experienced, like a schoolboy on the first day of vacation. Little did he know that the cow country that so intrigued him in the mid-1880s—and that he would romanticize in his classic western novel *The Virginian* (1902)—was headed for big trouble. Within the next few years Wister's Wyoming fell into the deadly Johnson County War, pitting large ranchers against smaller stockmen. Elsewhere in the West cattle and sheep raisers locked horns for grazing rights, and in still other areas hordes of bib-overalled farmers had already pushed into the West, threatening the domain of livestock ranchers. The decades between the Civil War and the turn of the century witnessed the rise and decline of open-range cattle kings as well as the emergence of the farmer to new dominance; the competition for land included a major struggle between ranchers and farmers. Of vital importance to these agricultural and other developing economies were the first transcontinental railroads that crisscrossed the West from the 1860s onward. Nearly overnight the railroads and other forms of frontier transportation not only connected producers to their markets, they linked many parts of the West to the larger nation during the Gilded Age. Seen as a whole, the swift changes in agricultural and transportation grids played notable parts in the western story of the second half of the nineteenth century.

∼

Even though the grazing and herding of livestock were important ingredients in Hispanic societies, large-scale livestock businesses in the West did not commence until after the Civil War. One line of influence derived from livestock that European immigrants had brought to the southeastern coast of the United

States. Gradually herds descended from these immigrant cattle, needing new, larger pastures, spread across the lower Southwest. By the early nineteenth century cattle raisers following this route were in Louisiana and Arkansas searching for fresh grazing areas. In immigrating farther westward they encountered another cattle-raising tradition, inherited from the Spanish and maturing in Texas and the Southwest.

The Spanish had included cattle-raising as part of their Mexican and southwestern mission efforts. As early as 1598, colonizer Juan de Oñate brought cattle into New Mexico. Although the Hispanic cattle business endured many vicissitudes and transitioned to private enterprise before American entry, it had generally done well. Bit by bit cattle became a medium of exchange between Hispanics and the first Anglos into the Southwest. Meanwhile in California, in the late 1840s and the 1850s, a few rancheros drove cattle from the ranges of southern California to the Gold Rush mining camps in the north, but these drives were short-lived and small affairs compared to the more dramatic and sustained efforts that flourished later on the Great Plains.

The most publicized segment of the Cattle Kingdom—trail drives from open ranges of Texas to the cattle towns in Kansas and Nebraska—began almost immediately after the end of the Civil War. When Texas veterans returned home in the summer of 1865, their lives and livelihoods were often in shambles, but new opportunities soon beckoned. Even though the families of many of the ranchers were scattered and their houses and outbuildings needed extensive repairs, land and grass were available. For the most part their cattle, which had run nearly untended during the war, had not been destroyed. Rumors spread quickly that cattle worth but $5–$6 a head in south Texas could command a princely price nearly ten times that in northern urban areas where customers were willing to pay 25–35 cents a pound for sirloin steak. The challenge: how to get the semiwild Texas longhorns to the waiting northern markets, where demand far outdistanced supply in the years immediately after 1865.

These stories of huge beckoning markets sounded promising and, if true, very rewarding. In the early spring and summer of 1866 several of the hardworking Texas cowmen decided to test the rumors and rounded up as many as 260,000 head of cattle, in several herds, to drive north to Missouri and Kansas. The drovers had a difficult time. Bands of renegade bushwhackers and Jayhawkers (raiders, especially in Kansas) stole nearly half of the cattle before they reached railroad connections. Things went so badly in 1866 that the Texans realized they would need better and safer trails north, ones that avoided rocky areas and brushy hills often hiding the thieves. At the same time Texas cattlemen began their first drives north, Joseph G. McCoy and his brothers, stockmen from Illinois, heard about the Texas drovers and decided to develop the semisettled site of Abilene, Kansas, as a meeting point for Texas herds

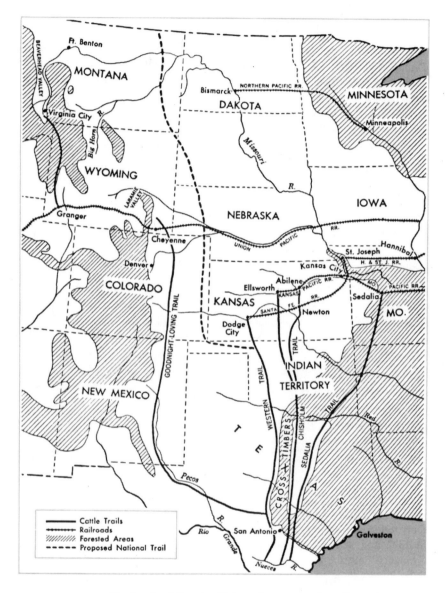

FIGURE 7:1. *The Ranchers' Frontier.* Linkages between cattle trails moving
north and railroad lines reaching west provided necessary transportation grids
on which to expand the ranchers' frontier. From Ray Allen Billington and
Martin Ridge, *Westward Expansion: A History of the American Frontier,*
6th ed., abr. (Albuquerque: University of New Mexico Press, 2001), 325.

and new railroads moving west. McCoy bought land near Abilene, built large holding pens for several thousand cattle, and sent messengers south to direct Texas drives to his new railhead. Abilene became the first well-known cattle town, with 35,000 head moving through there in 1867. This route from Texas to Abilene became known as the Chisholm Trail, named after Jesse Chisholm, a notable mixed-blood trader in the area.

The number of yearly herds headed to Abilene from Texas quickly expanded. In 1868, 75,000 cattle passed through Abilene, and in 1869 and again in 1870, 350,000 each, and finally twice as many—700,000—in 1871, the largest and last year of Abilene's halcyon era. In the early 1870s citizens and businessmen of Abilene, tiring of conflicts with Texans, closed their town to drives, forcing drovers to find new railheads such as Wichita and Ellsworth in 1872 and thereafter. By this time the long-trail system was well organized and could gradually shift west when the railroads and incoming farmers pushed cattlemen in that direction.

If the organization at the end of each trail drive was fine-tuned by the 1870s, so was the system along the trail. Ranchers often combined their herds, hired an experienced trail boss, and allowed him to employ the necessary men to make the trip. Usually trail herds consisted of 2,000 to 2,500 cattle with ten to twelve cowboys, a man in charge of the *remuda* (extra horses), and a cook ("doughbelly" or "sourdough"). A trail boss might earn $90 a month for his responsibilities; cowboys, paid $30 to $45 monthly, were expected to work as many as fourteen hours a day for a trip of about 1,200 miles lasting three to four months.

Drovers tried to establish a well-organized routine for their trail drives. After the herd had been on the trail for a few days, and had become accustomed to the drive, cattle were allowed to spread out over several miles, five or six animals abreast. The boss and the chuck wagon driver usually rode point in front of the herd, the swing and flank riders alongside, and most often the greenhorn cowboys riding drag, eating the dust of the herd on long, hot summer days. Steers that had been on the trail before often helped herds to move the needed ten to twelve miles per day. The cowboys took turns night riding, hoping that their riding and singing would head off any stampedes. The work was dirty, tiring, and demanding—and sometimes dangerous if a herd was unruly or attacked by renegades. By the end of long, arduous drives, trail bosses and cowboys alike were ready to let out their cinches more than a notch or two at awaiting cow towns.

But the sensational sides of cattle towns at the end of the trail have often been overemphasized. Popular novels and movies usually depicted the cow towns as solely rip-roaring, devil-may-care places for cowboys to squander their wages and assuage their passions. The reality is less sensational. Trail towns such as Abilene, Ellsworth, Wichita, Dodge City, and Caldwell were established primarily as exchange points that drovers and shippers needed to transport Texas cattle to markets or stockyards. The towns were that—and more. Beginning with the cattle McCoy enticed to Abilene in 1867 and for most of the next two decades, the cattle towns rose and fell as drovers gradually moved west in search of better grazing areas and in front of farmers swarming in from the east.

Important as these spots were for business transactions, they soon gained melodramatic reputations for activities besides shipping cattle. Cowboys found many saloons selling whatever they wanted: drinks to satisfy their thirst, gambling tables to snatch away their dollars, and nearby dancers and prostitutes to release their trail-suppressed passions. Because these hired men on horseback often viewed the trail towns as a place to let off steam, fistfights, knifings, and gunfights occasionally enlivened steamy, late-summer nights.

These tales of drinking, wenching, and gunslinging can be exaggerated— and often have been. Businesses in the cow towns tried to walk the narrow line between allowing cowboys free rein on the one hand and closing up all the saloons and houses of pleasure on the other. Most often they tried to hire men of known abilities—Wild Bill Hickok, Wyatt Earp, and Bat Masterson, for example—whose force of will or quick guns could maintain law and order. Another marshal, Bear River Tom Smith, kept the lid on Abilene for a few months—without guns—before a man resisting arrest bludgeoned him to death. Still, the cattle towns were not nearly as violent as they were reputed to be. As historian Robert Dykstra has shown, homicides were few, and standup gunfights rarely if ever occurred. Even if cow towns allowed young cowboys "to let things out a notch or two" at the end of several months on the trail, they certainly were not the wide open, shoot-'em-up towns inhabiting hundreds of Wild West novels and films.

∾

Cattleman and cowboys were central protagonists in this open-range cattle business on the plains. Typical of many Texas stockmen—one authority calls him the "almost perfect illustration of the cattleman"—was Charles Goodnight, who returned from the Civil War to find that his cattle herds, left to run wild during the war, had grown to seven thousand head. A man of insight and courage, Goodnight and his partner Oliver Loving pioneered in 1866 what later became known as the Goodnight-Loving Trail from Texas to New Mexico and on to Colorado. After Loving's death, Goodnight worked with New Mexico cattle king John Chisum on several deals and finally threw in with John George Adair, a British investor, who loaned Goodnight $50,000 at 18 percent interest.

So successful was the Goodnight-Adair partnership that at one time they ran 100,000 cattle on perhaps a million acres of land in the Texas panhandle.

Like most successful cattlemen, Goodnight was not an empty-headed romantic. He was a stubborn realist, a business-minded man who used sound economic principles to realize his goals. Convinced that eastern and European investors were needed to help develop the West, he set out to bring that capital into his cattle dealings. He was also as demanding of himself as of others. On one occasion he drove his herd eighty miles without water, without sleep, for three days and nights. In another circumstance when a group of Coloradans tried to head off his trail drive, Goodnight, with his buckshot-loaded shotgun in hand and backed by his rifle-toting men, told his confronters, "I've monkeyed as long as I want to with you sons of bitches." He went through with no further problems.

More exceptional for its size and location was the sprawling ranch of Henry Miller and Charles Lux. Their mammoth Double H ranch, the result of at least fifteen combined ranches, spread over northern California and spilled into Oregon and Nevada. An emigrant from Germany, Miller became a successful butcher in San Francisco but then joined forces with his major competitor, Charles Lux, an Alsatian, and together they bought up holdings in the San Joaquin Valley and nearby areas until they owned the largest ranch in the coastal states. At one time running nearly one million head of cattle, Miller and Lux also used giant irrigation systems to cultivate as many as 500,000 acres on which they grew vegetables and many other crops. For a time the two men dominated agriculture in several areas of northern California, but Lux's death initiated several court fights with his heirs before Miller was able to gain control of the giant estate. Although the Double H was unusual in its size, it did demonstrate what strong-willed, ambitious livestock owners could accomplish in the Gilded Age West.

Despite the central importance of these and other large cattlemen to the western livestock business, they have excited much less interest than their workers, the cowboys. Who were these men, these hired men on horseback, the primary symbol of the Old West? Few cowboys fit the fantastic, larger-than-life portraits in so many twentieth-century Westerns. Most were young—in their teens or early twenties—and many were illiterate. Most did not stay on one job for long, for they were men with needed skills and often drifted from ranch to ranch. Some were ex-Confederates, whereas many others were not Anglo-Saxons. Of the estimated 35,000 to 50,000 riders who went up the long trails from Texas, as many as 20 to 30 percent may have been blacks or Mexicans. In addition, Indians, Chinese, and even a few women served as riders or worked on trail-driving crews.

Most individual cowboys remain shadowy, indistinct figures, but a few became notable for one reason or another. Perhaps the best known of those

FIGURE 7:2. *Nat Love.* Black cowboy Nat Love represented
the large number of African American, Native American,
and Mexican/Hispanic riders who worked in the open-range
cattle business. From Nat Love, *The Life and Adventures
of Nat Love . . .* (Los Angeles: Wayside Press, 1907).

who later wrote about their cattle-trailing days was Charles Siringo. He began
cowboying in the early 1870s and spent more than twenty years on the range.
Siringo wrote his autobiography, *A Texas Cowboy: Or, Fifteen Years on the
Hurricane Deck of a Spanish Pony* (1885), which Texas historian J. Frank Dobie
called "the most-read non-fiction book on cowboy life." Another cowpuncher
who became a notable author was Andy Adams, a trail-toughened veteran

who began his range experiences in the 1880s. A Texas cowboy, he trailed several herds of horses and cows. After Adams hung up his spurs and moved to Colorado, he wrote his classic novel *The Log of a Cowboy* (1903) and several other works of fiction. Adams's novels, based largely on his own experiences as a working range rider, struck most readers as but one step removed from actual history.

E. C. "Teddy Blue" Abbott, an English immigrant, also began his cowboying on the lower plains. Later he roamed north to Montana, where he married the daughter of his well-known boss Granville Stuart and himself gradually moved from cowboy to cowman. His published reminiscences, *We Pointed Them North* (1939), depict the lively but demanding ways of the cattle kingdom stretching from Texas to Canada. Living among rangemen, Teddy Blue learned and perceptively described their codes of honor and value systems. Siringo, Adams, and Abbott, however, were exceptions; for each of these well-known writing cowboys there were thousands who rode day after day without leaving their brands on the pages of written history.

~

The full story of the western cattle kingdom includes much more than open-range cattle businesses in Texas and the resulting long-trail experiences northward to waiting railroad cattle cars in the cow towns of Kansas. Other regions of the West were also participating in the larger story. As early as the 1850s, for example, immigrants west had taken along small herds to Oregon, where these cattle had fattened on the rich and abundant grasslands of the Oregon Country's interior valleys. By the 1860s and 1870s surplus cattle from these herds were available to the hungry miners in Idaho and Montana as well as to those establishing ranches in Montana. At the same time, a few long drives from Texas continued into Montana territory for the same purposes. By and large, however, difficulties with Indians, who were feeling the pinch of diminishing buffalo herds in the upper Plains and Rockies, closed off trade with Texas and forced new ranchers in the north to rely on Oregon stock to replenish their herds. Indeed, between 1869 and 1875 more than 250,000 cattle were trailed from Oregon to the waiting ranges of Montana. Although these drives are less well known than those from Texas to the Kansas cattle towns, they were often more difficult, with dangerous mountains to cross and more hazardous weather to brave.

Even though Oregon Country cattle were available for stocking or replenishing northwestern herds, few open-range cattle businesses flourished in the north until the railroad reached Cheyenne in 1867. Then in the early 1870s Texas herds began to flow into western Kansas and Nebraska, eastern Colorado, and southeastern Wyoming. During this time Wyoming herds, for example, greatly expanded, and when a treaty with the Cheyenne and Sioux after General George Custer's defeat in 1876 opened verdant grazing lands north of the Platte and east of the Bozeman trail, a push northward was on. The new, extensive ranges opened just in time, so Texas cattlemen thought. Even though 200,000 to 300,000 cattle moved into Montana from the Oregon country between 1879 and 1881, blizzards on the northern ranges wiped out much of this stock, and with the oversupply from the west depleted, ranchers turned to new sources to restock their ranges.

In the early 1880s not only Texas cattle but also animals from the ranches and farms of the upper Midwest ("barnyard stock" and "states cattle") resupplied northern herds. These eastern cattle had difficulty, however, weathering the devastating winters of the north country, and ranchers there also became increasingly discouraged with the moody, unfattened, and unwieldy longhorns from Texas. Despite these problems, northern ranchers quickly enlarged their herds, with the number of Montana beeves jumping from 250,000 in 1880 to 600,000 by 1883. The gradual disappearance of the buffalo, the corralling of Indian tribes on reservations in the area, and the thousands of immigrating miners and military personnel combined to help bring about these quick changes.

Toward the mid-1880s, then, everything seemed just right—abundant grass, dependable weather, inviting markets, and more than sufficient capital flowing from the east and Europe. Animals worth $5 as newborn calves could be sold as marketable steers for $45 to $60. With success stories like these to be told, westerners excited nonresident investors, and new capital flowed into the West in search of Texas-sized profits. Possibilities like these plunged still other capitalists headlong into the race with western cattlemen for huge and quick returns. As Gene Gressley, the leading student of bankers and cattlemen, has noted, the western "range cattle industry during the last two decades of the nineteenth century was operated basically on borrowed capital."

Then, just as barbed wire and westward-moving farmers began to spell the doom of the Texas long drives in the 1880s, a combination of problems threatened to end the newly baptized cattle kings of the northern ranges. Indeed, the open-range cattle kingdom rapidly crumbled and fell in the 1880s and 1890s. In these years many observers seemed to think the range inexhaustible, but others cautioned against overstocking the northern grasslands. Several years elapsed before still other voices joined the earlier warnings. At the same time, small-time cowmen felt crowded out by European and eastern financiers who underwrote the large spreads that seemed to be pressing their smaller brethren on every side. Additional tensions mounted when northerners thought they could not walk out of their cabins without bumping into a braggart Texas (a "Rawhider," as Texans were often called), and they resented the southerners' referring to them as "sagebrush men" and "knock-kneed Oregonians."

More problems beset northerners. So large were mounting debts and losses to bad weather and predators that some northern foremen and partners underreported their difficulties to owners or investors. Signs of disaster loomed ahead. Grazing areas were already overstocked, and ranchers knew they owed much of their cattle and land to alien financiers, but few could have predicted the force that blew stockmen off their feet: the vicious and unpredictable weather. During the winter of 1885, freezing snow and cold destroyed a majority of many herds, and the following dry summer left little grass for remaining cattle. Yet more cattle arrived, from Texas and from the Northwest, to fight for the diminishing pastures.

Even worse times were to come. Snow began in November 1886, and for a month after Christmas intermittent storms piled on more. Then in late January chinooks (warm winds from the north) blew across the northern plains, melting much of the snow, but immediately the chilling blast of a subzero cold front froze the newly melted white cover and the grass beneath it, leaving the already hungry and bewildered cattle cold and starving. And then more snow. Ranchers were stunned—even before spring broke over the northern ranges they could already count their sickening losses.

The Big Die-up of 1886–87 decimated more than half of many northern herds. Some owners lost more than 70 to 80 percent of their cattle. Most of the free-grass-and-open-range cattle business on the Plains and in the Rockies was at an end. Bad weather, shifting markets, uncertain financial arrangements, and competition for land with nesters (farmers) had conspired, along with disastrous winters, to put an end to the heyday of one of the West's most romantic experiences. Despite all the difficulties, some cowmen were able to retain their sense of humor. Riding the trail on a hot day the following July, one old-time cowboy looked up at the sun and chuckled, "Where the hell was you last January?"

∽

Although less romantic, the story of sheepmen and their herds is an integral part of the western livestock narrative. The Gold Rush and subsequent mining booms were turning points in western sheep-raising. The new miners, especially those accustomed to mutton, were a waiting market for sheep bands trailed overland from New Mexico to California. Such well-known southwesterners as Miguel Otero, Lucien Maxwell, and "Uncle Dick" Wootton—along with several other sheepmen—may have driven more than a half-million sheep to California and Nevada during the 1850s.

Not until during and after the Civil War, however, did sheepmen in the

Orange County area of California begin to deliver their flocks to miners in the northern Rockies. In the next two or three decades, when the pastures of the interior West were discovered to be rich grazing areas on which to fatten lambs and to produce abundant clips of wool, prime bands from the West Coast were driven eastward to stock new sheep-raising areas in the Great Basin and up and down the Rockies. Other flocks were brought in from the East, and thus these two staging areas helped to stock the interior West via east-west trails or, later, by railroads when rails crisscrossed many subregions of the West.

Although many Anglo-Saxons raised farm flocks east of the Mississippi, open-range sheepherding was often considered a low-status occupation in much of the trans-Mississippi West. As one former sheepherder noted wryly, "You could not fire a shotgun into the average crowd in the range country without hitting a man who had at one time herded sheep, but it would probably take the charge in the other barrel to make him admit it."

More often than not Hispanics and Indians tended flocks in the Southwest whereas a smattering of Irish, Greeks, and Scots herded elsewhere in the West. But increasingly toward the end of the century and in the early 1900s Basques from northern Spain and southern France became the most notable western herders. The ubiquitous Basques became particularly well known in California, Nevada, Idaho, and parts of Oregon and Wyoming.

As sheepmen moved into areas thought traditionally to be cattle-raising regions, conflict inevitably arose. In Arizona the famed Graham-Tewksbury feud (1886–92) was in part a struggle between sheepmen and cowmen, and in Wyoming during the 1880s cattlemen on several occasions shot up sheep camps and destroyed flocks, some numbering in the thousands. Ironically, the wicked winters of the 1880s killed off so many cattle in the northern Rockies that in some sections of Wyoming (already becoming known as the "Cowboy State"), sheep outnumbered cattle 8 to 1.

Although sheepmen expanded into many sections of the West during the early 1890s, economic hard times of that decade and the loss of a protective tariff on wool in 1894 hurt sheep raisers until the Dingley Tariff (1897) reinstated protection. By 1900, even though the standing of herders and sheepmen was considered greatly inferior to the growing mythic status of cowboys and cattlemen, more than thirty million sheep grazed the abundant pastures of the West. Sheep ranchers were caught between two nearly overwhelming forces: (1) the hatred of the cowman and his desire to rid the land of these "hoofed locusts" and (2) the growing needs of farmers for more land. In several ways beset by the animosities of these two groups, the sheepman was seldom victorious in head-on struggles with either foe. Still, if the sheepman's social and cultural status was uncertain, his economic livelihood was fairly secure by 1900—and would be well into the next century.

FIGURE 7:3. *Sheep Shearing.* Spring shearing was an important segment of the yearly schedule sheep raisers followed on their ranches in the northern, southwestern, and Pacific Coast sections of the West. Courtesy Idaho State Historical Society, 60–120.21.

≈

Explorers, mountain men, and miners laid out the first routes west, and ranchers were among the first to make their living off the land, but farmers did more than any other group to populate the rural West. Indeed, between 1870 and 1900 more land was settled than in all of America's previous history. In these three decades, 430 million acres—mostly in the West—were claimed and 225 million put under cultivation. Agriculture was obviously the dominant occupation in the West in the last decades of the nineteenth century.

Before sizeable groups of Anglo-American farmers began moving into the West, Indians and Hispanics had carried on agricultural endeavors in parts of the region. Several southwestern tribes, including the Hopis, Navajos, Pueblos, Apaches, and other groups in east Texas, supplemented their gathering and hunting economies with crops. Some Native Americans used irrigation to raise such crops as corn, beans, and squash. More rudimentary was the agriculture of Indians in California and Great Basin Indians, with many coastal Indians and Natives of the Rockies and much of the upper Great Plains raising few if any crops.

When the Spanish entered the Southwest from the sixteenth through the eighteenth centuries, they set up missions that virtually enslaved Indians to serve as farmers of mission lands or as herders of their flocks. Other Spaniards, under the *encomienda* system, used Indians to carry out horticultural activities. These tasks continued throughout most of the Spanish and Mexican periods of southwestern history up to the 1840s, but few Anglos followed Hispanic agricultural practices or utilized the same lands for farming. That meant a large break occurred between previous agricultural practices and those that Anglo-American farmers followed when they first came into the trans-Missouri West.

The initial American farmers were the advance cadres of the much larger agricultural units that marched into the West after the Civil War. The first arrivals were those under the leadership of Stephen F. Austin in east Texas in the 1820s, those who settled the valleys of Oregon and California in the 1840s and 1850s, and those who came with Mormons into Utah in the late 1840s.

≈

By the early 1860s several subregions of the West had been opened to farmers, but no federal system was in place to deal with land problems. Agriculturists west of the Mississippi and others interested in moving west called for a land system that would provide free or cheap land. Out of these clamorings came the Homestead Act of 1862 and other legislation intended to aid farmers in acquiring new land.

Westerners argued for inexpensive or free land because they considered their hard work and personal investments a fair trade for a parcel of the public domain. They concluded that having to purchase land, in addition to buying livestock and implements and building homes and outbuildings, would lead to failure. So they urged legislators to make land available as inexpensively as possible in order that they might become landowners without having to pay high prices to speculators or large corporations who had used their financial resources to gobble up the most arable lands. Congress heeded these calls for free or cheap land and passed a series of acts in the late nineteenth century enabling thousands of farmers to become landowners.

The most important piece of legislation for farmers was the Homestead Act of 1862. Passed during southern secession and as part of the Republican Party's campaign promises of 1860, the Homestead Act pledged 160 acres (a quarter section) of surveyed but unclaimed land to adult citizens—male or female—or to those promising to become citizens. If settlers lived on the land for five years, improved it, and paid a small registration fee, they could have the land free and clear. Or if settlers wished, they could pay $1.25 per acre after six months of residence and then borrow against the land that they now owned.

In several ways this act laid out an incongruous land system. It was, first of all, a system inappropriate for much of the West, especially in rocky, alkaline, or other arid regions. It was also frequently poorly administered, allowing speculators, dummy representatives, railroads and other large corporations, or other landowners to snap up large areas of excellent farming land. Still, here was the best available way for small-time farmers to obtain land, and hundreds of thousands of homestead applications were filed between the 1860s and 1890s. However much speculators and corporations misused the specifications of this and other land acts, the Homestead Act provided a means by which farmers could own land and avoid the tenancy so characteristic of many eastern areas.

Farmers could gain parcels of land in several other ways. In the Preemption Act of 1841, Congress allowed for preemption on most surveyed land. This meant that squatters who had settled on and improved unsold areas had first priority in purchasing that land at the minimum price when it was put up for sale. Congress also passed the Timber Culture Act of 1873, which allowed farmers 160 acres over and above their original quarter section under the Homestead Act if they planted at least 40 acres of the new land to timber. A second amendment to the Homestead Act—the Desert Land Act of 1877—stipulated that an individual could purchase for a small sum 640 acres (a section) of desert country if he or she promised to irrigate a portion of the land. Sometimes the Timber Culture and Desert Land acts were misused, but they did provide additional land for farmers who could afford to plant the necessary timber, bring water to the new land, or outsmart speculators and other investors bent on snatching up any available good land.

Despite the abuses, these acts, by and large, achieved the purposes for which they were intended. Millions of free or inexpensive acres were made available to hundreds of thousands of settlers who swarmed west from the 1860s to 1900. Even though these land policies were not the economic safety valve that historian Frederick Jackson Turner and some of his disciples claimed they were—many eastern urban workers could not afford to make the trip west and to purchase the necessary machinery to begin farming—they did advertise the West and encourage Americans and immigrants to test the riches of this frontier Eden.

New legislation, however, did not solve all the problems confronting would-be farmers. By the late 1860s the Homestead Act was in place, railroads were inching across the plains, and Indians were gradually receding west under the pressures of advancing settlers; but many dirt farmers still had to be convinced that the Plains were not the Great American Desert, a rumor that had been bandied about for almost a half-century. Indeed, in 1860 the area between the Sierra Nevada and the Cascade Mountains on the west and the prairie settlements on the east contained 50 percent of the country's land but only 1 percent of its population. In the next three decades farm families were willing to test the fruitfulness of land lying near the western edges of prairie settlements, and they found, for the most part, that these farmlands in eastern Dakota, Nebraska, and Kansas were suited for farming. These areas often produced bountiful crops, especially those planted with cereal grains. Some enthusiastic farmers were even ready to argue that they had discovered the Garden of the West.

A number of special circumstances and events impelled large numbers of farmers into new areas beyond the 95th meridian. New steel plows, reapers, binders, and threshers as well as several other much-needed implements were available to farmers in the 1860s and 1870s. At the same time many prospective settlers were convinced of the correctness of the popular mythology that rain followed the plow. If they moved onto the plains and turned over the soil, so this myth ran, they could expect added precipitation. It is true that large newly cultivated areas in eastern Dakota, Kansas, and Nebraska experienced increased rainfall in the 1870s, thereby convincing farmers that their predispositions had been correct.

To capitalize on this popular mythology, railroad promoters hired journalists and other propagandists to "puff" the northern plains as ripe for cultivation. These tub-thumpers pointed to burgeoning crops in the new areas and obtained testimonies from hundreds of intrepid settlers that the desert was now "blossoming as a rose." When the first farm families experienced the higher than average rainfalls of the 1870s, their enthusiastic reports encouraged settlers hungering and thirsting after land to move west. As one observer has noted, so successful were the propagandists that by 1885 "they had practically reduced the Great American Desert to a small area southwest of Salt Lake City."

Others were warning against the rapid, enthusiastic movement of settlers onto the Plains. The most authoritative of these spokesmen was John Wesley Powell. A long-time naturalist and in charge of the U.S. Geographical and Geological Survey of the Rocky Mountain region (in 1881 Powell became chief of the U.S. Geological Survey), he warned in his speeches and in his notable *Report on the Lands of the Arid Region of the United States* (1878) that farmers should not move west of a line that ran from the western boundary of Minnesota south through central Kansas and the middle of present-day Oklahoma into central Texas. These areas could provide useful grazing lands, Powell asserted, but they would not, over time, be good regions for farming.

If farmers refused to heed his warnings, Powell told his listeners and readers, the government should alter the homestead laws to make them more suitable for conditions west of the line he had drawn (he excepted, of course, the fertile lands along the Pacific Coast).

In the same year that Powell's report was published, a new frenzy—the "Dakota Boom"—touched off. Commencing in 1878, this boom into the Dakota Territory and later into the central Plains lasted for nearly a decade. Enthusiasm, promotion, good weather and abundant crops, and swelling numbers of immigrants from Europe—all these factors underlay these years of spectacular westward expansion. It seemed, one editor wrote, that "the Almighty . . . had preceded us and prepared a quarter section already to sow."

During the 1880s, the population of Dakota surged from 135,000 to 512,000, at the same time that the number of farms jumped from 17,000 to 95,000. Much the same happened in Kansas and Nebraska, where despite bad years in the early 1880s, farmers moved well beyond the 100th meridian when better times returned from 1884 to 1887. Generally speaking, farmers followed more the enthusiastic reports they heard from other farmers and boomers than what they considered the dour warnings of Powell and other pessimists. Although every decade from 1870 to 1900 had its bad years in which hard-pressed farmers asked for and even received relief from county and state sources, they rarely remembered these experiences during the enthusiastic, booming years. And many farmers were able to succeed despite all the problems they faced.

The fortunes of Dakota farmer Fred A. Fleischman illustrate how a man with little cash and a 160-acre homestead might become a successful farmer. In June 1879 Fleischman filed on his quarter section and had twenty acres of his quarter section plowed at a cost of $60. The following spring he borrowed $200, which, added to his savings of $225, allowed him to move to his homestead and to build a frame house. Luckily, prices in the fall were good, and he sold his 1880 crop of wheat and oats for $170. The next year prices jumped, and he received $223 for 213 bushels of wheat and $128 for oats and other crops. Plowing up more land, Fleischman sold $1,241 of produce in 1882. In less than three years with but $225 in savings, Fleischman had a decent home and farm. Admittedly, good weather and favorable prices worked much to his benefit, but many other farmers also gained a measure of success through hard work and judicious choices of land, livestock, and implements, and by a close watch on their expenditures.

Even more exciting to agriculturists were the stories they heard about bonanza farming. Although exceptional, these large bonanza farms in the Dakota Territory and California in the 1870s and 1880s were nonetheless significant and revealing parts of the western agricultural experience. In Dakota the best known of the bonanza farms was that which Oliver Dalrymple managed for absentee owners. They had purchased lands from the Northern Pacific Railroad at about 20 percent of their cash value, about 50 cents to $1.00 per acre. Later, Dalrymple operated additional wheat lands for other owners of bonanza farms, tending perhaps as much as 100,000 acres in all. When the farms he managed produced 25 bushels per acre in the second year of operation in 1877, several other bonanza operators began to follow his large-scale operations.

Throughout the first decade of their existence, many of these sprawling farms in the Red River Valley of present-day North Dakota and Minnesota were bonanzas indeed. Their reported successes gained headlines of national magazines and newspapers. But less favorable weather, higher railroad rates and taxes, and a drop in prices soon put the squeeze on the big-time operators. Many of them, including Dalrymple in 1896, broke up their large-scale farms. Still, in the long run the bonanza operations helped to advertise farming areas in the West and to promote settlement of such areas as the Red River Valley. They also helped stabilize the finances of the Northern Pacific Railroad, which in turn provided necessary transportation to the Pacific Northwest and thus encouraged settlement of that area. Bonanza farms likewise reflected the boosterism of Gilded Age America and thus helped build the reputation of the West as a land of milk and honey ready for settlement and exploitation.

~

At the other end of the West, California agriculture, from the perspective of the 1850s and 1860s, seemed to be heading in unique directions. The agricultural efforts of the previous Hispanic-Mexican missions, the new kinds of soil and climate, and the varieties of landscape in the huge new state encouraged unusual forms of agriculture. And immigrants with a variety of agricultural experience and training had arrived by the early 1850s. Innovations did occur, and yet a majority of the predominant patterns and experiences in California agriculture were modeled after "back home" precedents rather than on innovations arising from the unusual characteristics of California.

Vegetable and fruit farmers in California found a ready market early on for their produce in the Gold Rush populations flowing into San Francisco and the Bay Area, but wheat growers soon outstripped them in nearby areas to the east. In this quick, early domination of wheat, California was following the patterns evident in New York and Pennsylvania and concurrent developments on the Great Plains. Hindsight clarifies this early dominance of wheat. Since orchards and vineyards took several years to mature and since farmers were interested in a quick return on their investments and work, they turned to wheat—rather than to oranges and grapes, for example—as their principal crop. The process of wheat-raising was also less labor-intensive. As soon as a steady, remunerative market in England was discovered in the 1860s, Californians were convinced of the wisdom of their emphasis on wheat.

The large bonanza wheat farms that arose in northern California during the late nineteenth century demanded innovative solutions for management, technology, and labor problems. From the beginning, managers turned to newly invented farm machinery from California and eastern manufacturers to avoid gargantuan labor costs. Even though the large success of these vast wheat farms was temporary, they did provide important returns on California land from the 1860s through the 1890s. They also helped to people the rural areas of California and to finance the tremendous growth of the state during this era.

Wheat was not the only crop developed in the late nineteenth century. During the 1850s and 1860s farmers experimented with grapes and with other fruits such as peaches, pears, and apples. Agoston Haraszthy, Hungarian-born father of the California grape industry, was especially important in showing vintners how European methods and cuttings might be utilized in California. Other leaders pioneered in growing and pruning techniques, suiting vineyards to California's semiarid lands and bright sun.

Although Californians drew on their "back home" experiences in growing wheat and fruit, the marketing system they established for selling wheat abroad and the innovative methods growers utilized reveal their willingness to experiment in a new, semiarid climate. By the end of the century, California agriculture had developed so rapidly, had utilized mechanization and irrigation to such an extent, that in 1899 only Texas, Kansas, and Nebraska of the western states ranked above it in the value of farm products raised.

In the Pacific Northwest, the earliest white settlers, arriving in the 1840s after the missionaries, bragged about the region as an agricultural paradise. These newcomers soon discovered that many crops grew easily and well in the fertile Willamette Valley. In fact, so profitable was farming there that some agriculturists who thought of leaving Oregon for the California mines in the late 1840s and 1850s stayed on when they realized that the agricultural lode farmers were mining was frequently richer than that prospectors found in panning and sluicing. At first vegetables, grains, and other crops grew more rapidly and dependably in Oregon than in California, even if inadequate transportation and marketing remained major vexations. Where Oregonians might receive $1.00 per pound for apples in the 1850s, they later sold their apples to miners for as much as $1.00 each. Overall, northwesterners did well as farmers. By the 1860s they had produced a surplus of several crops and, per capita, were more productive than the industrious Mormons in the Great Basin.

A rising tide of population to the Pacific Northwest in the 1880s and 1890s followed completion of transcontinental railroads, and the availability of several new labor-saving farm implements transformed agricultural endeavors in the region. These changes were particularly evident in eastern Washington and on the northwestern edge of Idaho. Once the major barriers of transportation and markets were hurdled, wheat production boomed, especially in this rich Palouse Country area. Although farmers were at first slow to move into this region of rolling, fertile hills, they flooded in during the 1880s. Few if any areas could match the quick mechanization of farming that took place in this portion of the Inland Empire, and by the turn of the century the Palouse Country was recognized as one of the major wheat-growing areas of the nation.

In other parts of the West, farming was a less well-developed although still important activity. For example, one California county produced more wheat and more than half as much barley as all the Rocky Mountain areas together. Even though mining strikes in Colorado, Idaho, and Montana lured thousands of hungry miners, none of these states developed an agricultural base as large or as notable as those in the plains or coastal areas. Isolation, distance, the lack of well-placed railroads, and the limited size of good farming areas also slowed agricultural development in New Mexico and Arizona. If farmers settled near a dependable water source, a homestead of 160 fertile acres was more than sufficient to make a good living. But this was often not possible in many areas of the Rockies and Southwest. Not until the Newlands Act of 1902 did the federal government show what could be accomplished in utilizing public lands

FIGURE 7:4. *Threshing in the Palouse.* One of the most productive wheat-growing areas of the West developed in the Palouse Country, a region that overlaps the states of Idaho, Washington, and Oregon. Courtesy Idaho State Historical Society, 60–52.806.

sales to finance notable irrigation projects in the arid West. These large-scale irrigation projects and the resultant opening of extensive agricultural areas of the West for hordes of new farmers proved to be a central feature of western agriculture early in the twentieth century.

The events surrounding land rushes into Indian Territory (present-day Oklahoma) in the late 1880s and early 1890s are prime illustrations of the complex contests for land that characterized the last half of the nineteenth-century American West. During the early 1880s David L. Payne and other "boomers" pressed for white entrance into the Indian lands of the territory. After the Dawes Severalty Act (1887) promised land for individual Indians and allowed the remaining lands to be sold, expansionists lobbied for the opening of these areas. The first dramatic land run came in spring 1889. On April 22, at high noon, pistols fired, and the boom was on, with tens of thousands of settlers rushing in and overnight tossing up tent cities such as Oklahoma City, Norman, and Guthrie. Some farmers had sneaked into the territory ahead of time ("sooners") and staked out prime farmland, but many other settlers took up town lots while additional farmers settled on quarter sections of land. Further runs continued in the early 1890s with the largest on September 16, 1893, when nearly 100,000 settlers raced into the Cherokee Outlet in search of one of the 40,000 available claims totaling six million acres of land.

Although many of the earliest farmers arriving in Oklahoma were poor and did not fare well, those who arrived between 1891 and 1893 did much better. No part of the farmer frontier had been settled so quickly, and during the 1890s these rushes into the newly opened Oklahoma lands represented acquisition of the remaining best parts of the agricultural frontier. After those events, other kinds of lands were claimed, ones that demanded new farming techniques such as irrigation and innovative plowing.

≈

What can one conclude about the experience of these farmers? Generally their lives were, by turn, satisfying and difficult—sometimes even tragic—but always demanding. Indeed, the daily duties of western agriculturists rarely if ever resembled the lifestyles of Wild West heroes and heroines whose lives were romanticized in the latter half of the nineteenth century. Closer to the essence of the West, the activities of the farmer—along with experiences of town and city dwellers—reflected the concerns of a majority of westerners in the second half of the nineteenth century.

Often beset by problems and perplexities, farmers, not surprisingly, began to formulate a series of organizations to deal with their social and economic difficulties. In 1867, Oliver H. Kelley founded the National Grange or the Order of the Patrons of Husbandry, whose meetings were intended to allow farmers to discuss mutual problems as well as to serve as social gatherings to break the monotony of farm families. Although not planned as such, the Grange quickly became politically active in the early 1870s, sponsoring reform legislation to curb what Grangers considered the exorbitant prices of middlemen and the outrageous rates of railroads. When the Grange lost popularity in the mid-1870s, farmers turned first to the Greenback Party and then to Farmers' Alliances to remedy the difficulties they experienced. Initially, the alliance groups were also established to address sociocultural ills, but they too soon became vehicles for political organization. Eventually farmers' desires and demands were such that they swung their organized, political support in the 1890s behind the Populist Party. As we shall see in chapter 8, the Populists became the major political spokesmen for agricultural grievances in the last decade of the nineteenth century.

If men found farming a demanding and sometimes numbing occupation, the tasks of their wives, sisters, and daughters were equally—perhaps even more— onerous. The wife of a dirt farmer was expected to keep house, rear their children, provide meals, and take a turn with out-of-doors tasks since most farmers could not afford to hire laborers—even if they had been available. In addition to these difficult obligations, women were often separated from other women, except during weekends, holidays, or other community gatherings. Isolated and carrying heavy responsibilities as part-time doctors and teachers, farm women found their daily lives demanding. Even though most did not crack under these large demands—as do the fictional heroines in Dorothy Scarborough's *The Wind* (1925) and in Ole Rölvaag's *Giants in the Earth* (1927)—they were often sorely tested and close to a breaking point. The lives of pioneer farm women reflect another side of the early frontier too often omitted in narrating the history of the West.

Thus from the 1860s to the end of the nineteenth century the competition for land in the American West had shifted from dominance by stock raisers to a clear-cut victory for farmers. Although cattle and sheep raisers were not driven from their lands, they were no longer involved in the long drives that moved cattle from Texas to the Midwest and northern Plains and sheep from the West Coast inland. Instead, they had to be content with the numerous rich grazing areas of the West that they already controlled. On the other hand, farmers were on the move, flooding into many new areas unknown to agriculturists in 1860. By the end of the century farmers greatly outnumbered ranchers and dominated the western agricultural scene. Their expansion continued into the next century, with more land taken up between 1898 and 1917 under the Homestead Act than in the previous three decades from 1868 to 1897.

If an observer could have viewed the West from a central prominence during the final decades of the nineteenth century, he or she would have seen the spread of livestock holdings into western sections of Texas and the Plains states as well as into portions of Rocky Mountain states and territories and the eastern slopes and grasslands of California, Oregon, and Washington. Even more obvious would have been the movements of thousands of farmers into the eastern and central regions of the Plains states, along the Mormon corridor to the Great Basin, and to the rich, fertile valleys of the coast states and the Palouse Country of the Pacific Northwest. In the contest to people the western countryside the farmers had raced past the livestock people.

~

The morning of May 10, 1869, broke cold and dreary, but the sun soon emerged, warming a gathering, expectant crowd. That day at Promontory Summit, about fifty miles west of Ogden, Utah, a waiting audience witnessed one of the great wonders of the American West. When the wood-burning "Jupiter" engine of the Central Pacific and the coal-burning No. 119 of the Union Pacific pulled together, just yards apart, all was in readiness. Officials from each railroad drove the last spike, and the first transcontinental railroad connected the East and West.

The momentous events at Promontory worked like the two-faced Janus figure of ancient times, one backward, the other forward. Earlier developments in transportation trail- and road-building culminated in the auspicious happening in May 1869. This happening also presaged the important new railroads that ribboned the West before the end of the nineteenth century. Clearly, Promontory provides another revealing symbol of the rapid change that characterizes western history. It likewise demonstrates how much federal government policies shaped the pioneer West.

When Europeans settled in the American West, they tried to retain connections with their families, friends, and supporters. From the Spanish in the late sixteenth century through the first Americans to Oregon, Utah, and California in the mid-nineteenth century, colonists utilized several modes of transportation and communication to keep these connections intact. The squeaky Spanish carts, American pioneer covered wagons, Mormon handcarts, freighters' heavy wagons, steamships on the Mississippi, Missouri, and other larger rivers—all served as means of transportation and communication. As the numbers of settlers coming west grew, so did their demands for better transportation. The establishing of military posts during and after the Mexican-American War added to the need for overland transportation.

In the quarter-century from the first sizeable migrations to Oregon until the completion of the initial transcontinental railroad in 1869, several new kinds of transportation served the Far West. Private companies, usually with federal government support, provided these new services. In the early 1850s, following the first rushes to California, mail was delivered semimonthly via ships sailing from the East Coast, around the Cape, to San Francisco. A person could send a one-ounce letter for twelve cents, but a passenger was charged $500 for his trip by steamship from New York to the West Coast. The great expense of traveling around the southern tip of South America or even the shorter route across Panama led to increased calls for overland routes. By the mid-1850s, horse- or mule-drawn express company wagons were delivering mail to Santa Fe, Salt Lake City, and San Francisco. None of these deliveries seemed entirely satisfactory, so westerners increased their demands for better contact between the East and West.

Heeding these calls, the federal government issued mail contracts, funded road construction, and continued its support of military posts in several western subregions. By the early 1850s, federal contracts for delivering freight and mail to the West and congressional subsidies to build or improve wagon roads greatly improved frontier transportation. These actions also set off sometimes brutal competitions among several freight and stagecoach companies. In 1855, Russell, Majors and Waddell, a freighting combine, began operations by carrying goods to military posts. Expanding too rapidly into a stage line and then into the Pony Express in 1860–61, the partnership teetered and then collapsed. In 1862, the company sold out to Ben Holladay.

Holladay loomed large in frontier transportation. A crude man with the social refinement of a porcupine and the soul of a shark, he lied, cheated, bullied—and prospered. Gaining a reputation as a get-it-done freighter and stage operator, he established the Overland Stage Line after taking over Russell, Majors and Waddell. Holladay often squeezed out his stage competitors and then charged exorbitant fees once he monopolized a freight or stage route. He achieved enormous financial success until the Panic of 1873 undermined his investments, and then retired.

The most successful and long-lasting of all the transportation firms, Wells, Fargo, and Co., bought out Holladay's mail contract and his stages in 1866. Wells, Fargo had begun operation in California in 1852. Buying up other lines, it became the premier "fast freight" company running between San Francisco and the Comstock in Nevada. By 1860, Wells, Fargo had expanded to nearly 150 offices and gained a freight monopoly in the Far West, especially in mining districts. A few years later, the firm opened passenger lines, which continued until the railroads came in 1869.

The gleaming stagecoaches were the most romantic ingredient of the pre-railroad transportation system. Improvements in coach design, the establishment of stop stations at needed intervals, and the promise of reasonably satisfactory schedules made the stagecoach the ultimate mode of transportation in the 1860s. Instead of the arduous four-month trip by covered wagon that Oregon or California pioneers experienced in the previous two decades, stagecoach passengers were promised a trip of about twenty days, traveling at about ten miles an hour, from the Missouri River to Sacramento. But the jolting ride, the inedible if not deadly food, the ever-present dust, and the unregulated heat and cold were enough to sicken even the most persisting passengers. Half seriously, Mark Twain praised his stagecoach journey in 1861 to Nevada as "a fine pleasure trip" on which his party "fed fat on wonders every day." Yet he also complained of the steady inconveniences of climate and travel, the dangerous drivers, and the obnoxious travelers. But the trip that cost him $150 was never dull: twenty sleepless days and nights of cease-less "bowling along."

～

Although plans for a transcontinental railroad began in the 1850s, sectional rivalries that led to the Civil War delayed further planning. Once the Confederate states seceded, however, Congress passed the Pacific Railroad Act of 1862 that outlined the federal government–private enterprise partnership for constructing the railroad from the Midwest to the West Coast. The act had the strong backing of President Abraham Lincoln, yet another clear evidence of how much Lincoln influenced important policies shaping the West. The Central Pacific Railroad (CP) would build east from California, and the Union Pacific Railroad (UP) from roughly the 100th meridian to an undetermined meeting place with the CP. In the form of a loan subsidy, both companies would receive $16,000 per mile of track laid in flat areas, $32,000 per mile in hilly areas, and $48,000 per mile in the mountains. In addition, the firms would be given ten sections (a section equals 640 acres) of land for each mile of completed track. When the companies hesitated even after this astounding offer, Congress doubled the size of the land grants in 1864 and allowed even more favorable terms on the subsidies.

Unfortunately, most of the principal builders of the CP and UP were unprincipled. In California, the Big Four—Leland Stanford, Collis P. Huntington, Mark Hopkins, and Charles Crocker—secretly manipulated their funding through a construction company and thus lined their own pockets. UP financiers were equally avaricious. Congressman Oakes Ames and others organized the Credit Mobilier, a phony construction business, to overcharge the government, the UP itself, and other stockholders. To keep government investigations at bay, Ames used his influence, and gifts of Credit Mobilier stock, to get special favors from other congressmen and even Cabinet members of the Grant administration. Once uncovered, the scandal of Ames's

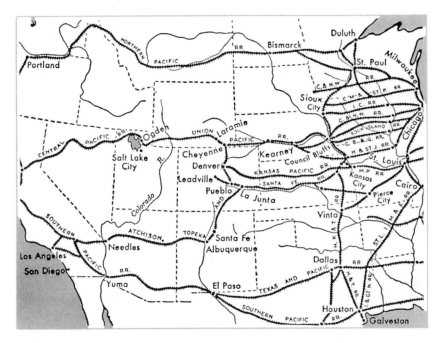

FIGURE 7:5. *Principal Pacific Railroads in 1883.* By the mid-1880s, most of the major transcontinental railroads stretching to the Pacific had been completed. These rail lines provided a new transportation network that facilitated the rapid settlement of the West.

From Ray Allen Billington and Martin Ridge, *Westward Expansion: A History of the American Frontier*, 6th ed., abr. (Albuquerque: University of New Mexico Press, 2001), 294.

doings shocked Congress and the Executive Branch. Censorship of Ames and his cronies and considerable embarrassment of government officials followed, but funding and construction continued.

The CP faced the daunting task of laying track over the mighty rock fastness of the Sierra Nevada. In need of an army of workers to undertake the demanding work, and finding them unavailable, the company reluctantly hired resident and immigrant Chinese by the thousands for the taxing labor. Eventually, more than 90 percent of the CP workers were Chinese. They cleared land, built roadbeds, and laid track, but they particularly worked at the most difficult of tasks, erecting snow sheds and tunneling through the Sierra. Working like a crew of high-wire acrobats, the Chinese drilled and blasted their way through the mountains. Even the tough-minded Mark Hopkins had to admit that "without them [the Chinese] it would be impossible to go on with the work." More ambivalently, Charles Crocker's brother reported that the Chinese "prove nearly equal to the white men in the amount of labor they perform, and are far more reliable." Day by exhausting day, the CP inched agonizingly forward. By late summer 1867, after two years of excruciating labor, the CP was crossing the Sierra summit, poised to descend its eastern slopes.

The UP started more slowly but moved quickly across the plains. Employing hundreds of Irish laborers to lay track, the UP had built five hundred miles of track (nearly four hundred more than the CP) as their rivals topped the Sierra. With the energetic Casement brothers, Jack and Dan, directing most of the building, hosts of UP workers laid track mile by rapid mile, trying to win a major portion of the subsidy away from the CP. All during 1868 the two companies raced toward one another. Along the UP, "hell on wheels" rail construction towns sprang up, catering to the workers' seemingly unquenchable thirsts and passions. During the construction railroad and army men helped to guard workers from rumored Indian attacks. As the two lines quickly approached one another in early spring 1869, they even began preparing competing, parallel roadbeds, but Congress stopped this nonsense, ordering the meeting place at Promontory Summit, north of Salt Lake City. As the celebrating took place

FIGURE 7:6. *Trestle on Central Pacific Railroad.* Chinese laborers were a major workforce in the completion of the Central Pacific Railroad in the 1860s and in later reconstructions of that rail line. Carleton E. Watkins photo, ca. 1880. Courtesy The J. Paul Getty Museum, Los Angeles, 94.XA.113.26.

on May 10, one wag, explaining the ethnic makeup of the two groups of railroad workers, observed that the CP had been built on tea, the UP on whiskey.

The completion of the first transcontinental railroad immediately impacted western travel and transportation. Covered wagons took four months and stagecoaches twenty days to carry their passengers and freight from the Missouri River to Oregon or California. Now, one could make the trip in about four days, in much more comfort. Indeed, ambitious and adventuresome travelers could, if willing to undertake risks of limb and life, travel from the East Coast to San Francisco in about ten days. This notably shortened travel time in one generation seemed an amazing feat of technological achievement to Americans in 1870.

UP & CP RR's COMPLETION

The successful linking of the CP and UP in 1869 greatly encouraged the building of other transcontinental railroads across other parts of the West. Between 1870 and 1893 four other such lines were completed. By the end of the century, transcontinental railroads connected the most populated areas of the country west of the Mississippi.

Two of the new cross-country railroads stretched through the Southwest, two across the northern West. The southernmost line, the Southern Pacific (SP), linked previously built western and eastern segments. In the 1860s and 1870s, the SP in California, headed by the ambitious, strong-willed Collis P. Huntington, laid tracks south from the Bay Area to Los Angeles and then cut east through Needles, California, and over the Arizona and New Mexico deserts in the 1870s and early 1880s. From the east came the Texas and Pacific Railroad, presided over by the charming but shrewd Thomas A. Scott. After a good deal of entrepreneurial dirty dancing and feinting, Huntington crushed Scott and brought the two lines together just east of El Paso, Texas, in 1882.

In the 1870s and 1880s, the second of the southern transcontinentals, known eventually as the Atchison, Topeka and Santa Fe, wobbled westward through Kansas, the southeastern corner of Colorado, and then dipped down to Albuquerque. Surviving near-deadly competition with Huntington's SP, the Santa Fe then drove its own tracks west, arriving in California in the mid-1880s. Along its line, the Santa Fe, under the leadership of energetic and tight-fisted Ford F. (Fred) Harvey, established the memorable Harvey House depots and restaurants, in which Harvey Girls ("Young women of good character, attractive and intelligent, 18–30") served and charmed the railroad's customers. Fred Harvey's dying words, one story goes, were "Slice the ham thinner."

Congress had chartered the first of the northern transcontinentals, the Northern Pacific Railroad (NP), as part of the Pacific Railway Act of 1864. Awarded even larger land grants than the CP or UP to lay tracks from Lake

Superior to the Puget Sound, the NP seemed dormant for a long while, slowed particularly by the Panic of 1873 and the failure of the railroad's chief financer, Jay Cooke and Company. Only when the industrious German immigrant Henry Villard gained control of the NP did the railroad rouse itself and push on to the West Coast, first to Portland in 1883 and then directly to Tacoma one year later.

The fourth transcontinental line was the Great Northern Railroad (GN), the brainchild of Canadian investor James J. Hill. Perhaps the most dynamic—and honest—of the railroad men, the risk-taking Hill engineered the GN across the north from St. Paul to Seattle, arriving there in 1893. By careful planning and sound financing, Hill built his rail line without a land grant or government subsidy. In the words of biographer Michael Malone, Hill was an "empire builder," a man whose "quick intelligence and power of analysis" "demonstrates the impact one willful individual can have on the course of history."

This expanding network of western transcontinental railroads, and the branch lines build out from them, helped transform the late-nineteenth-century West. The rail lines greatly assisted ranchers and farmers in shipping their livestock and crops to markets and mills; they connected hundreds of isolated areas within the West, helped launch new urban sites, and sped up communication between the West and the nation. By the mid-1890s all western states and territories save South Dakota and Oklahoma hosted at least one transcontinental line. Through this web of railroads, the East and West, as well as much of the interior West, had been connected. As one transportation historian has concluded, "the railroad, more than any other single agency, brought to a rapid end the frontier of the trans-Mississippi West."

But there were also darker sides to the western railroad story. Too often overbuilt, inadequately funded, and ripped off by their Gilded Age "robber baron" owners and directors, most of the railroads were in shaky conditions by 1900. Some had been so hastily and shoddily built, such as the CP and UP, that their roadbeds and ties soon had to be replaced. Others like the Southern Pacific squeezed customers so tightly that it became known as "the Octopus." Still other lines implemented short haul–long haul policies that allowed railroads to charge shippers all the market would bear and extort outrageous fees from customers on short routes for which there was no competition. These manipulations and injustices and their impacts on agriculturalists and other westerners helped ignite the Populist and Progressive political fires that broke out and blazed across the West in the 1890s and early twentieth century.

Ambrose, Stephen E. *Nothing Like It in the World: The Men Who Built the Transcontinental Railroad 1863–1869*. New York: Simon and Schuster, 2000.

Athearn, Robert G. *Union Pacific Country*. Chicago: Rand, McNally, 1971.

Atherton, Lewis E. *The Cattle Kings*. Bloomington: Indiana University Press, 1961.

Bain, David H. *Empire Express: Building the First Transcontinental Railroad*. New York: VikingPenguin, 1999.

Carlson, Laurie Winn. *Cattle: An Informal History*. Chicago: Ivan Dee, 2001.

Deverell, William. *Railroad Crossing: Californians and the Railroad, 1850–1910*. Berkeley: University of California Press, 1994.

Dick, Everett. *The Sod-House Frontier 1854–1890*. New York: Appleton-Century, 1937.

Drache, Hiram M. *The Day of the Bonanza: A History of the Bonanza Farming in the Red River Valley of the North*. Fargo: North Dakota Institute for Regional Studies, 1964.

Dykstra, Robert R. *The Cattle Towns*. New York: Alfred A. Knopf, 1968.

Fite, Gilbert C. *The Farmers' Frontier 1865–1900*. New York: Holt, Rinehart and Winston, 1966.

Fradkin, Philip L. *Stagecoach: Wells Fargo and the American West*. New York: Free Press, 2001.

Gressley, Gene M. *Bankers and Cattlemen*. New York: Alfred A. Knopf, 1966.

Hurt, R. Douglas. *American Agriculture: A Brief History*. Ames: Iowa State University Press, 1994.

Igler, David. *Industrial Cowboys: Miller & Lux and the Transformation of the Far West, 1850–1920*. Berkeley: University of California Press, 2001.

Jackson, W. Turrentine. *Wagons Roads West*. Berkeley: University of California Press, 1952.

Jeffrey, Julie Roy. *Frontier Women: "Civilizing" the West? 1840–1880*. 1978; rev ed. New York: Hill and Wang, 1998.

Jordan, Terry G. *North American Cattle-Ranching Frontiers: Origins, Diffusion, and Differentiation*. Albuquerque: University of New Mexico Press, 1993.

Lamar, Howard R. *Charlie Siringo's West: An Interpretive Biography*. Albuquerque: University of New Mexico Press, 2005.

McGregor, Alexander Campbell. *Counting Sheep: From Open Range to Agribusiness on the Columbia Plateau*. Seattle: University of Washington Press, 1982.

Malone, Michael P. *James J. Hill: Empire Builder of the Northwest*. Norman: University of Oklahoma Press, 1996.

Orsi, Richard J. *Sunset Limited: The Southern Pacific Railroad and the Development of the American West, 1850–1930*. Berkeley: University of California Press, 2005.

Osgood, Ernest Stapes. *The Day of the Cattleman*. Minneapolis: University of Minnesota Press, 1929.

Riley, Glenda. *Taking Land, Breaking Land: Women Colonizing the American West and Kenya 1840–1940*. Albuquerque: University of New Mexico Press, 2003.

Schwantes, Carlos Arnaldo. *Long Day's Journey: The Steamboat and the Stagecoach Era in the Northern West*. Seattle: University of Washington Press, 1999.

Settle, Raymond, and Mary L. Settle. *Empire on Wheels*. Stanford, CA: Stanford University Press, 1949.

Siringo, Charles A. *A Texas Cowboy: or, Fifteen Years on the Hurricane Deck of a Spanish Pony*. Chicago: Siringo and Dobson, 1886.

Webb, Walter Prescott. *The Great Plains*. Boston: Ginn and Company, 1931.

Wentworth, Edward Norris. *America's Sheep Trails: History, Personalities*. Ames: Iowa State College Press, 1948.

Winther, Oscar Osburn. *The Transportation Frontier: Trans-Mississippi West, 1865–1890*. New York: Holt, Rinehart and Winston, 1964.

Worcester, Don. *The Chisholm Trail: High Road of the Cattle Kingdom*. Lincoln: University of Nebraska Press, 1980.

CHAPTER EIGHT

Conflicts, Compromises, and Accommodations

~

THE MORNING OF JUNE 25, 1876, DAWNED COLD ON THE LITTLE BIGHORN River, but by midmorning the sun was warming, the weather increasingly sultry. Although spring had arrived late to the valleys and mountains of eastern Montana, summer was now in full bloom. In the early months of 1876, notable changes had invaded the northern plains; even more dramatic transformations loomed. Just eight days before, Crazy Horse and his Oglala Sioux and Cheyenne warriors had held off General George Crook's force of 1,300 troops on the nearby Rosebud. After Crook withdrew, Crazy Horse moved north to join Sitting Bull on the Little Bighorn.

Perhaps as many as 8,000 Indians, including 2,000 to 2,500 warriors, were now camped at the Little Bighorn. It was, writes one authority, the "largest gathering of Indians ever to occur on the northern plains." After the brutal battle with Crook, the Native Americans had not expected the "blue coats" to reappear soon. Many in the encampment were resting in their tepees or gathering food when the cry rang out that soldiers were coming. At high noon on June 25, General George Custer, with his usual decisiveness, decided to attack. Even though he did not know the number of Native Americans he faced, Custer divided his famed Seventh Cavalry into three groups and plunged ahead. Warriors poured out of their encampments to face the soldiers and soon drove one group to retreat. Meanwhile, Custer had galloped onward to his own destiny. He was soon surrounded, and he and his 250 men quickly killed. The Battle of the Little Bighorn lasted but two to three hours, with the Indians in every way victorious.

Despite the momentous victory of Native Americans at the Little Bighorn, the tide of conflict on the northern Plains and elsewhere soon turned against the tribes. Within a decade, nearly all Indian resistance in the West had melted away. Crazy Horse was killed in captivity in 1877, Chief Joseph ended his valiant retreat in 1877, Sitting Bull returned to a reservation in 1881, Geronimo finally gave up in 1886, and the Dawes Act of 1887 announced the federal government's plans to transform Indians into farmers and American citizens. Little Bighorn symbolized the peak of Native American military success against white Americans, but it also demonstrated how quickly the tables turned. Only ten years separated Little Bighorn from Geronimo's ultimate surrender.

The second half of the nineteenth century overflows with a plethora of military, social, and economic confrontations among peoples in the West. Some resemble that violent conflict on June 25, 1876, in faraway Montana. Others reflect less violent encounters. But all illustrate the competitions between Native and white groups as well as intra-American factions. They occurred in every subregion of the West. These contests often led to conflict, but sometimes they also ended in compromise and accommodation or even new combinations. The numerous competitions helped shape Indian-white relations, Civil War disputes, the rise of a Wild West, and labor and political disputes toward the end of the nineteenth century.

~

By the mid-1840s, Native Americans had learned a great deal about Europeans and Americans through several decades—sometimes centuries—of contacts. Based on these encounters, and the varied experiences resulting from them, these competing groups had begun to formulate conceptions of and policies toward one another. Some notions and actions persisted over centuries, but the pathbreaking events of the 1840s revolutionized other Indian-white relationships.

Contacts between Native Americans and Europeans and Americans differed within each western subregion. As we've seen, in the Borderlands of Texas and New Mexico, nomadic tribes like the Comanches, Apaches, and Navajos continued to raid Mexican settlements after 1821. These Native wanderers also warred on the Puebloan peoples of New Mexico, who by the mid-nineteenth century became allies with the Spanish and later the Mexicans and sometimes intermarried with them. In California, virtual decimation—some call it genocide—of Indians took place. Indian population there, estimated at less than 200,000 in 1821, had dwindled to about 100,000 in 1848. The contacts between Native Americans and non-Indians elsewhere, although of long duration along the Pacific Coast and in parts of the northern and Plains West, were less numerous than those along the southern reaches of the region.

During the 1840s the nature of Indian-white contacts notably changed throughout the West. The annexation of Texas and Oregon, the opening of the Oregon and Mormon trails, and, most of all, the Gold Rush to California forced new relationships on the two groups. These diplomatic agreements and the subsequent trails westward greatly expanded the size of the West and lured hundreds of thousands of immigrants. In California, overnight; in Utah and the Oregon Country during the next decade; and elsewhere in the 1860s through the 1880s, the incoming migrants wanted land. What earlier had seemed a solid barrier between Indians and whites was now a permeable, see-through curtain with several large openings.

The surging populations invading California and Oregon in the 1840s and 1850s and the resultant white hunger for living space and land led quickly to

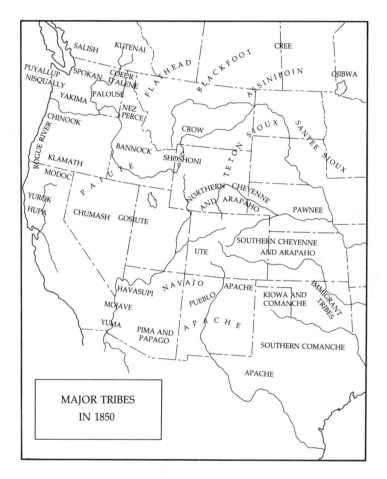

FIGURE 8:1. *Major Tribes in 1850.* The variety of the Indian tribes scattered across the West added much to the sociocultural complexities of the region. From Robert M. Utley, *The Indian Frontier of the American West 1846–1890* (Albuquerque: University of New Mexico Press, 1984), 5.

disasters for Indians. As miners and farmers pushed into California after 1849, the destruction of Native living spaces and their lifeways, and the dramatic loss of Indian lives required that something be done. Yet the results were disappointing for Natives. By the end of the 1850s, fewer than ten treaties had been negotiated, setting aside less than ten thousand acres for Indians. These agreements establishing reservations for Natives came too little and too late for most California Indians. Indian populations in California plummeted to 35,000 by 1860.

Natives and whites also signed treaties setting up reservations in the Pacific Northwest. But the U.S. Senate's unwillingness to ratify some of the treaties and understandable Indian reluctance to relocate from fertile western valleys to more arid areas in eastern parts of Washington and Oregon stymied most efforts to establish reservations. When miners overran tribal lands, violence erupted. Between 1855 and 1858, the Rogue War in southern Oregon, the Yakima (now Yakama) War in central Washington, and conflicts with the Palouse and Spokane Indians in eastern Washington resulted in defeats for the Indians. After winning these conflicts, whites confiscated Native lands and removed Indians to newly established reservations.

Similar attempts to arrange treaties with Indian tribes in the Southwest were unsuccessful. Texans, refusing to set aside lands for reservations, favored chasing all Native groups from their state. In New Mexico, government agents were unable to make treaties with the Apaches, Navajos, and Utes that both sides would honor and that the U.S. Senate would support. Meanwhile, the Pueblos were left unprotected and neglected and suffered as much from nomadic Native raids as from the Mexicans and Americans. As one Zuni elder wryly remarked, "perhaps if the Pueblos stole like the Navajos they might get something from the Americans."

The story of the Five Civilized Tribes (Cherokees, Creeks, Choctaws, Chickasaws, Seminoles) casts dark and then lighter shadows. At first, driven west under President Andrew Jackson's harsh removal policies in the 1830s, these tribes suffered greatly in the relocation process. These initial tragedies included the Trail of Tears march in 1838 when 2,000 of 13,000 Cherokee men, women, and children died on the way from the South to Indian Territory (present eastern Oklahoma). But these tribes recuperated quickly and showed great resilience once in their new homes. Despite bitter tribal disagreements over removal and other factual disputes, the Civilized Tribes became more unified in the 1850s. They set up strong tribal organizations, embraced Christianity, farmed, and accepted compromises and accommodations with one another and whites that other Natives stoutly resisted.

Indians living on the sprawling Great Plains were among those most resistant to change. Treaties such as that at Ft. Laramie, Wyoming, in September 1851, which lured more than 10,000 Sioux, Cheyennes, Arapahos, Crows, Gros

Ventres, Assiniboines, and Shoshones for a "big talk" on the Platte River, accomplished little for federal policy makers and military leaders who wished to control Indians and place them on reservations. Indian leaders did not want to move, they still had abundant lands and buffalo, intertribal warfare continued, and frontier military power was insufficient to carry out federal goals of quarantining Natives on reservations. Indians on the Plains, as well as those in the Apache country of the Southwest, held out longest against the "concentration," or reservation, policy attempted after the Mexican-American War.

Yet the decisions of the 1850s foreshadowed events to come. In that decade, federal government policy makers tried to negotiate treaties that included Indian relocation, reservations, and annuities (food and supplies) for Indians. Most of these attempts failed before the Civil War because of insufficient support from western residents, military leaders, and the U.S. Congress. After 1865, a heightened military presence, increasing immigration, the growing support of reform groups aiding Indians, and congressional attention stiffened the backs of treaty makers. Meanwhile, Indians were beginning to feel mounting pressures. Washakie, a Shoshone chief, spoke for increasing numbers of Natives when he lamented in 1855, "Since the white man has made a road across our land . . . and has killed off our game, we are hungry, and there is nothing for us to eat. Our women and children cry for food and we have no food to give them." Washakie's complaint would become part of a larger and louder chorus among Indians in the next twenty-five years.

≈

In the two generations before the Civil War broke out in April 1861, the South and North had designs on the West. Both regions hoped to capture and bring under their economic and political domination the area west of the Mississippi. The South wanted the western frontier primarily for expansion of its slavery and cotton kingdom whereas the North coveted the West for agricultural and commercial exploitation.

Whether the West would become slave or free dominated national political considerations in the first half of the nineteenth century. In the Missouri Compromise of 1821 Congress maintained a balance of the free and slave states by bringing in Missouri as a slave and Maine as a free state. The compromise also stipulated that, except for Missouri, slavery would be disallowed in western lands of the Louisiana Purchase north of 36° 30' (the southern boundary of Missouri). Three decades later the Compromise of 1850, attempting to balance southern and northern interests, brought California in as a free state but stated that the principle of popular sovereignty (allowing residents to choose) would obtain on the slavery issue in the territories of Utah and New Mexico. Neither the South nor the North found these compromises satisfactory but acceded to them to keep peace and avoid war.

The Kansas-Nebraska controversy of 1854 reopened the fractious debate of whether slavery would expand into the West. More than anyone else, Senator Stephen A. Douglas, dubbed the Little Giant of Illinois because of his small stature, reintroduced the angry quarrel. Driven by ambiguous professional and personal motives, Douglas wanted to organize the Kansas-Nebraska area to help develop the West. He hoped for a transcontinental railroad route through that region, he wished to gain additional political support from the area, and he sought to profit from his own investments there. Desiring southern backing for his legislation, the pragmatic Douglas included popular sovereignty in his bill, allowing residents of Kansas and Nebraska to decide for or against slavery. By including popular sovereignty, the bill organizing Kansas and Nebraska territories had, in effect, repealed the balancing provisions of the Missouri Compromise. When the Kansas-Nebraska Bill passed Congress in 1854, negative reactions across the North were immediate and vociferous. It was said that Douglas could have traveled from Illinois to Maine in the light of his own burning effigies.

For the next few years "Bleeding Kansas" convulsed in a mini–civil war. The North and South attempted to win the area to the opposing positions on the controversial extension of slavery into the territories. Northerners sent "Beecher's Bibles" (rifles) by the hundreds, and southerners made certain that thousands of nonresident, proslavery men from Missouri showed up for Kansas elections to keep it a slave territory. The violent confrontations included antislavery fanatic John Brown's murderous attack on Pottawatomie Creek in May 1856 and proslavery forces' burning of Lawrence. The bloodshed continued into the 1860s. The Kansas-Nebraska controversy and the resultant "war" there proved how incendiary the issue of slavery in the West could be.

Once the Civil War began, however, the West played an important yet not decisive role in the military actions of the war. But other issues had been added to northern and southern desires to dominate the West. These ambitions stirred new ingredients into the Civil-War-in-the-West mix.

Most of the military conflict west of the Mississippi took place in the first range of states from Minnesota to Louisiana. Missouri, badly divided between Union and Confederate supporters, remained a cockpit of warfare throughout the Civil War. More battles took place in that state than in any other save Virginia. When John C. Frémont, without permission, issued proclamations confiscating property and setting slaves free in Missouri he exacerbated an already volatile situation. After President Lincoln removed Frémont from leadership of the Department of the West, Missouri descended into guerilla warfare, with northern and southern ragtag forces chasing one another back and forth across the state. In addition, Confederate "bushwhackers" in Missouri spilled west, where they and Kansas "Jayhawkers" engaged in unending depredations on one another and on innocent settlers. Among the most violent of the bushwhackers was Confederate William C. Quantrill, who launched vicious attacks on Missouri and Kansas settlements. Riding with Quantrill was the young Jesse James.

The most notable Confederate invasion of the West took place in 1861–62. Southerners had become increasingly aware of the strategic and economic importance of the Southwest and California to the Confederacy. They hoped for a quick victory in New Mexico and then a march into Colorado, and perhaps on to California, to capture the mineral wealth of both areas and open Pacific seaports to Confederate control. In early 1862 a Confederate force of Texans under the command of General Henry H. Sibley invaded New Mexico, was victorious at Valverde in the southern part of the territory on February 16, and moved quickly up the Rio Grande and took Albuquerque and Santa Fe without opposition. Only Fort Union to the northeast of Santa Fe remained under Union control. Marching toward that holdout, Sibley's forces on March 26–28 engaged northern soldiers under Colonel John Slough at Glorieta Pass. Just as the Confederates seemed on the verge of another victory, a group of Colorado volunteers led by Major John M. Chivington (later a villain at the Sand Creek Massacre of 1864) discovered and destroyed the Confederate supply train while on a flanking maneuver. With their supplies gone and worried by rumors that the California Column of Union men was proceeding to New Mexico, the Confederates retreated in disorder to Texas. Although the battle at Glorieta has been mistakenly dubbed "the Gettysburg of the West" (it in no way measured up to the turning-point events in faraway Pennsylvania in July 1863), the Confederate loss there stymied their designs on the Southwest and California.

~

The Civil War did not, meanwhile, end confrontations between Indians and whites in the West. Some of those conflicts displayed new kinds of clashes; others followed familiar patterns of Indian-white competition. Events in Indian Territory (Oklahoma), New Mexico, and Colorado illustrate these changing and continuing kinds of struggles.

What happened with the Five Civilized Tribes represented a break with the past. Unlike most other western tribes, these nations in the Southwest included an unusually large slave population. In 1860, 10 percent of the Creeks and nearly 30 percent of the Seminoles were slaves. Not surprisingly, these Indian groups favored the southern position on slavery. But the situation was messy. Soldiers from the Cherokee, Creek, and Seminole nations fought for both the Union and Confederate sides, leading to what historian Alvin Josephy calls the "little civil war." Other troops switched from southern to Union forces during the war. Considerable numbers of fugitive slaves also joined the northern army. The struggle over slavery, the divided loyalties of tribes, and federal accusations against the "treasonous" actions of the Civilized Tribes created a welter of confusion in the Indian Territory. Clearly the Civil War greatly disrupted the progress the tribes had made in the 1850s and led to chaotic conditions during the postwar years.

Other military engagements in Colorado and New Mexico followed earlier patterns but also brought about increasingly tragic and violent conflicts between Indians and the frontier military. Tens of thousands of settlers invaded Colorado after the gold strike of 1858–59, spilling into and disrupting Indian lands, especially their hunting grounds. Sporadic Indian raids in retaliation alarmed white Coloradans and sent territorial governor John Evans on the warpath. Conversely, desiring peace rather than war, bands of Cheyennes and Arapahos, under the leadership of Black Kettle, turned in their weapons and moved north near Sand Creek. But on the morning of November 28, 1864, Colonel John Chivington led a surprise attack of cavalry forces against the peaceful Indians. Even though Black Kettle hoisted a white flag of surrender and peace, the soldiers stormed the camp, slaughtering and mutilating the bodies of more than 250 Native men, women, and children. The Sand Creek battle quickly became a symbol of the hell-bent, hate-the-Indians sentiments that drove soldiers and volunteers to wantonly kill Natives.

A different kind of tragedy took place in New Mexico. After the Confederates experienced defeat at Glorieta Pass and withdrew, Brigadier General James H. Carleton assumed control of Indian affairs. As historian Francis Paul Prucha writes, Carleton was a "man of ability and zeal, [but] he was also arrogant and arbitrary." First Carleton drove the Mescalero Apaches to their knees and forced them to relocate to the Bosque Redondo reservation, near Fort Sumner. There the four hundred or so Apaches were to become farmers and be provided government assistance until they became self-sufficient.

Carleton then went after the Navajos. The nearly 10,000 Navajos must surrender and move to the Bosque Redondo, the general told them, or they would be relentlessly pursued and run to the ground. When the Navajos refused to give up, Carleton sent Christopher "Kit" Carson and his soldiers in midsummer 1863 to Navajo country to bring in the tribe, whatever the cost. Carson followed his orders and launched attacks on the Navajos and destroyed their crops and animals. Unable to survive, the Navajos capitulated and in the deadly Long Walk trudged across New Mexico to the Bosque Redondo. Nearly 8,000 of the Navajo were crowded onto this cramped, arid space—and proceeded to starve and die off. Finally understanding the near-desperate circumstances of the Navajos, the federal government negotiated a treaty with the tribe, allowing them to return to a newly formed reservation carved out of their homeland spreading across northwestern New Mexico and northeastern Arizona. After their return the Navajos never again participated in military rebellion against the U.S. government.

~

In the quarter-century stretching from 1865 to 1890 relations between Indians and whites reached a violent climax and then settled into a less stormy period. But the unsolved dilemmas continued. In these years Indian leaders such as Sitting Bull, Crazy Horse, Chief Joseph, and Geronimo arose to lead their tribes in major battles against the frontier military, or, in the case of Joseph, to retreat from the incoming soldiers. Concurrently the U.S. government tried to implement new policies to end conflicts with Indians and transform them into tillers of the soil. By 1890 tribal groups lived on reservations throughout the West and began to experience the stipulations of the Dawes Act of 1887. Some sent their children to schools for Indians. These changes shaped experiences of Indians well into the twentieth century.

Viewed from Native American perspectives, the years between the Civil War and 1890 look much different. As William T. Hagan, well-known historian of American Indians, notes, "If any organization can be imposed on this [period of] history, it must be in terms of the Indian response to white occupation of the West and to white attempts to convert the Indian into the white man's image of himself." Many of these reactions were defensive, others assertively offensive.

The responses of Native Americans varied throughout subregions of the West. In the coastal areas of California, Oregon, and Washington, nearly all Indians were subdued, some demoralized, and most lived on reservations. The exceptions were the brief uprisings among Snake (Shoshone) and Paiute groups in 1867–68 in northern California, Nevada, and southern parts of Oregon and Idaho. By late summer 1868, nearly eight hundred of these tribal members had surrendered to General George Crook. More notably, the Modocs in southern Oregon resisted a return to a reservation in 1872–73. When a commission arrived to talk peace, a small group of warring Modocs, led by Captain Jack, attacked and killed the peace commissioners. Having reluctantly led the war faction against the commissioners, Captain Jack then was betrayed by those he led. He was captured and hanged, whereas they went free. Ironically, on several previous occasions, Captain Jack had tried to avoid war with whites.

Native groups in the northern Rockies and Plains were more numerous and warlike, and thus experienced other kinds of contacts with whites. Their story, central as it is to understanding Indian-white relations after the Civil War, merits larger coverage. Environmental, political, and military factors add to the complexity of their story.

By the 1860s, Indian groups such as the Arapahos, Shoshones, Cheyennes, and the varied clans of the Lakota Sioux were feeling mounting pressures from several sources. For centuries Native Americans of the Plains had relied on the bison for their sustenance. Once these tribes gained horses and guns from Europeans and from other Natives, they were better able to count on the buffalo, their four-legged commissaries, for their very existence. As historian Elliott West has written of the buffalo's place in Indian life, "No animal was more useful and widely revered. It walked prominently through Native American cosmologies. Various parts of the bison were eaten, worn, fought with, slept on, traded with, and worshiped." Even mountain tribes such as the Flatheads, Nez Perce, and Coeur d'Alenes traveled far to hunt and kill the bison to fulfill their yearly needs.

By the mid-1860s these patterns of living, of hunting and travel, were under threat. Diseases the explorers and later pioneers and their animals brought to the Plains had decimated tens of thousands of Indians. Epidemics of smallpox wiped out large populations of Mandans, Hidtsas, Pawnees, Comanches, and Sioux. Later, cholera, measles, and scarlet fever were virulent invaders and killed off multitudes of Native Americans. Then the settlers came. For two decades wagons had crossed the Plains, upsetting the migration patterns of buffalo, dividing up the herds into northern and southern groups, and using up the grass that the bison and Indian ponies needed. One Sioux chief, seeing these disastrous changes that followed the migrants from the east, commented in 1867, "The whites are as numerous as the years."

Renewed pioneer migrations and returning regular troops to the West after the Civil War increased the velocity of change sweeping over Native Americans. Nor could Indians of the Plains, north and south, know that government officials and military leaders were now planning new strategies to force Indians to abandon their nomadic ways and move onto reservations. President Lincoln sent additional troops west and built forts to protect residents as well as incoming settlers. In 1867–68, the U.S. military launched a three-pronged attack. Negotiators at the Medicine Lodge Treaty (1867) and the Ft. Laramie Treaty (1868) also pressured tribes to relocate to reservations, accept government annuities of food and clothing, and begin the steps to become self-sufficient farmers. Older, more peaceful leaders like Chief Red Cloud reluctantly accepted these agreements, but younger warriors such as Sitting Bull, Crazy Horse, and Gall personified growing intratribal divisions on the peace agreements by refusing to come to reservations. Third, the military began winter campaigns, hoping to destroy Indian power by attacking tribes at their most vulnerable times. In the most notorious of these winter assaults, on November 27, 1868, on the Washita River in present western Oklahoma, General George Custer attacked Chief Black Kettle's camp (the chief had survived the Sand Creek conflict of 1864), where the Indian leader, his wife, and more than one hundred other Cheyennes were killed. Later Colonel

Ranald Mackenzie caught combined bands of Southern Cheyennes, Kiowas, and Comanches in Palo Duro Canyon in the Texas panhandle and destroyed their lodges and more than 1,400 ponies. Custer had done the same with Indian ponies at Washita, hoping to unhorse the Plains Indians and drive them on to reservations.

The Indians valiantly fought back. Protecting their homelands, they hoped to hold off the rising tide of white settlers and soldiers. In the late 1860s they opposed and succeeded in closing a series of newly built forts along the Bozeman Trail that cut sharply through Indian lands on the way to the Montana gold fields. Native leaders also complained when treaty previsions were not followed and when settlers invaded areas set aside as reservations. Most of all, a new group of warrior leaders simply refused to move to the reservations.

~

Sitting Bull (Tatanka Iyotake) became the best-known of these Native leaders. A member of the Hunkpapa band of the Teton Sioux (Dakota), Sitting Bull gained leadership among his people through his military prowess and his powerful visions. Resolutely remaining separate from whites, he fought against their expansion into the northern Plains and opposed all treaties that threatened to alienate Indian lands. When Red Cloud of the Teton Sioux chose to make peace with the whites, the northern Teton, in an extraordinary decision given the individualism of these Indians, selected Sitting Bull as their headman. When the Great Sioux War broke out in 1876, Sitting Bull began to lead those Indians refusing to come in to treat with government officials and military men.

Crazy Horse (Tashunca-uitco) gained his reputation as an astute military leader of the Oglalas of the Teton Sioux. By his mid-twenties, he was taking part in attacks on soldiers in the Powder River country of eastern Wyoming. A short, light-skinned, shy man, Crazy Horse exhibited his daring and courage against the soldiers and his rivals the Crows. When the noted Indian fighter General George Crook pursued the nontreaty bands in their traditional hunting areas, Crazy Horse and more than one thousand Oglala and Cheyenne warriors attacked Crook's men on June 17, 1876. Crazy Horse's unusually sharp attack and his followers' hand-to-hand fighting, untypical as they were, confused Crook and his troops. Although Crook claimed victory when the Indians left the battlefield at Rosebud River, Crazy Horse had obviously blunted Crook's offensive and sidelined him from the major battle that took place eight days later with General George Custer. After Rosebud, Crazy Horse led his warriors north to join Sitting Bull's massed bands on the Little Bighorn River.

The Battle of the Little Bighorn on June 25, 1876, brought together in one dramatic confrontation several important participants on the Indian and military sides of the Great Sioux War. Among the Native Americans were Sitting Bull, Crazy Horse, Gall, and the young holy man Black Elk. Their major opponent was General George Custer, the most notorious of the frontier military officers, who led his famed Seventh Cavalry into battle. Just thirty-six, George Armstrong Custer had gained a large if controversial reputation as a bold, fearless but sometimes erratic and nearly foolhardy commander. Breveted (an honorary promotion) as the youngest general in the Civil War at age twenty-five, Custer later marched his troops into several combats with Indians in the late 1860s and early 1870s. But on the fateful day in June 1876, Custer displayed more limitations than strengths. Dividing his troops into three groups and attacking without knowing much about his massing opponents, Custer precipitously led his troops to their deaths. Within a few hours, by late in the afternoon, all the troops immediately fighting around Custer—about 250 men—lay dead near the Greasy Grass, as the Indians called the Little Bighorn.

The sensational story of Custer's violent demise at the Little Bighorn jolted Americans gathered about a thousand miles away in Philadelphia to celebrate the country's centennial (July 4, 1876). They were stunned—even astounded—at the unbelievable news. How could a band of "savages" annihilate a crack frontier military force like the Seventh Cavalry? What had happened, who was to blame, what could be done? Whipped into greater action by these troubling questions, military leaders redoubled their efforts and went after the northern tribes, invading and destroying their winter havens. By May 1877, Crazy Horse, accompanied by his tired, discouraged, and hungry people, threw down his guns and surrendered. Four months later he lay dead at a reservation in Nebraska, held by another Indian and probably bayoneted by a scared, overzealous soldier. After the battle on the Greasy Grass, Sitting Bull retreated to the safety of Canada, but in July 1881, with but forty families remaining under his leadership, he too gave up. Nearly naked and starving, Sitting Bull handed his rifle to his son Crow Foot and told the presiding officer at Fort Buford, "I wish it to be remembered that I was the last man of my tribe to surrender my rifle. This boy has given it to you, and he now wants to know how he is going to make a living."

The story of Chief Joseph (Hin-mah-too-yah-lat-kekt) and the Nez Perce Indians provides another sorry episode in the tragic story of Indian-white conflict in the post–Civil War decades. The Nez Perce (Nee-Me-Poo, or Nimipu) lived in the beautiful, verdant meadows and valleys of the Wallowa Mountains on the converging boundaries of Oregon, Washington, and Idaho. They had been friends with whites since the time of Lewis and Clark. But the discovery of gold in the Nez Perce country in the 1860s and the flood of illegal miners who trespassed on Indian lands soon thereafter ended the decades of good feelings. Gradually, some of the "treaty" Nez Perce moved onto a much reduced

FIGURE 8:2. *Chief Joseph of the Nez Perce.* In 1877 this remarkable
Indian chief helped lead nontreaty members of his tribe in their
courageous if ultimately unsuccessful retreat toward freedom in
Canada. Courtesy Historical Photographs, Manuscripts, Archives and
Special Collections, Washington State University, Pullman, WA, 79–027.

reservation carved out from their expansive lands, but "nontreaty" Nez Perce
like Chief Joseph refused to do so. Government officials then demanded the
chief move to the reservation. As he began to do so, a small group of young
Nez Perce, incensed at these stipulations and spurred on by alcohol, attacked
and murdered nearly twenty nearby settlers. Other farmers were driven from
their homes. These were the first shots of the Nez Perce War of 1877.

Chief Joseph and other nontreaty Nez Perce hoped a peaceful compromise and settlement could be reached. It was not to be. General O. O. Howard and other military commanders drove the Nez Perce from their homelands in a series of skirmishes and battles. For more than three months and 1,400 miles the redoubtable Nez Perce retreated from and outwitted the pursuing soldiers. As a camp or domestic chief rather than a military leader, Joseph coordinated and helped direct his people in their strategic retreat through Idaho, Wyoming, and Montana. The Nez Perce were in northern Montana, within forty miles of sanctuary in Canada, before soldiers under the command of Colonel Nelson A. Miles ended their valiant journey toward freedom. At the final surrender, Chief Joseph is rumored to have said, "Tell General Howard I know his heart. What he told me before, I have in my heart. I am tired of fighting. . . . Hear me, my chiefs! I am tired. My heart is sick and sad. From where the sun now stands I will fight no more forever."

The postwar years for Chief Joseph and the Nez Perce were even more depressing. The Nez Perce thought they had been promised a return to their beloved Wallowas if they surrendered. Government officials in Washington, D.C., quickly disavowed any such promises and sent the Nee-Me-Poo first to a reservation in Kansas and then to another in Oklahoma. More than one hundred tribal members, including many children, died in these dry, hot, and unfamiliar places. Finally after numerous petitions from Joseph and his friends (and now supported by Generals Howard and Miles), the Nez Perce returned to the Pacific Northwest. Joseph was not allowed to reenter the Wallowas, however, unless he settled on a reservation there. When he refused to do so, he was sent to another reservation in north-central Washington. He and his followers were greatly disappointed and continued to contend for their freedom and a return to the Wallowas. The dream never materialized before Joseph's death in 1904. Joseph's story is a tragedy—a story of conflict that led only to compromise and accommodation to the terms of the military victors.

In the desert Southwest other kinds of conflicts between Indians and whites were taking place. Although most southwestern tribes had been defeated and placed on reservations, the Apaches continued their centuries-old conflicts with non-Indians. In the nineteenth century Apache leaders like Mangas Coloradas, Cochise, and Victorio were worthy opponents for General Crook (the Gray Fox) and other frontier military leaders. But the most competitive challenge came from Geronimo (Goyakla), the Chiricahua warrior and medicine man. Stern, tireless, and valiant, Geronimo eluded and outwitted his pursuers time and again. He was a superb warrior, with an unquenchable thirst for battle. "War is a solemn religious matter," he once told an interviewer. On at least one occasion, four thousand to five thousand Mexican and American soldiers were in the field trying to corner Geronimo and his small band of warriors and women. For a while, it looked as if the Gray Fox had won over Geronimo when the Apache leader surrendered and moved to the San Carlos Reservation in Arizona. But that hot, arid place was too confining for Geronimo and his followers. He broke out, surrendered, and broke out once more from 1884 to 1886. Finally, through the skillful use of Apache scouts, the tireless pursuit of the demoralized Chiricahua band, and the friendly persuasion of Lieutenant Charles Gatewood, Geronimo gave in to General Nelson A. Miles, who had replaced Crook after Geronimo's penultimate escape. With the surrender of Geronimo on September 4, 1886, the Indian Wars had ended.

~

Even as frontier troops tried militarily to defeat western Indians, reformers and government officials were attempting to transform Native Americans into another kind of people. During his administrations (1869–77), President U. S. Grant endeavored to effect positive change by selecting Quakers and other religious persons to administer Indian policies. Some of the corruptions and crassness of this cumbersome system disappeared. Other reformers pushed for reservations for all Indians and individual plots of land for all Natives. The latter effort led eventually to the Dawes Severalty Act (1887). This legislation was intended to "civilize" Indians by providing them land and encouraging all tribal members to take up farming. Under this act heads of households received 160 acres, other adults 80 acres, and minors 40 acres. Double that acreage was given for grazing land. Once these grants were awarded, the remainder of the reservations was to be opened for white settlers. Despite the good intentions of most supporters of the Dawes Act, nearly all the consequences of the legislation were disastrous for Indians. In 1887, Native Americans held 138 million acres of land; by 1934, once all allotments were given out, reservations lands had dwindled to 52 million acres. Indian inexperience with landholding, corrupt whites pressuring Indians to sell their lands, and the involvement of speculators likewise undermined the system. As historian Francis Paul Prucha has argued, the land allotment system "failed miserably," with the results "disappointing and damaging."

By 1890 American Indian existence was at a nadir. Native hunting grounds were gone, their cultures were under increasing threats, and they had been herded onto reservations. But new hope seemed to arise when a self-proclaimed Paiute Indian prophet, Wovoka, began to preach renewal and revitalization. He promised Native Americans that if they followed his teachings, danced the Ghost Dance, and wore so-called Ghost Shirts (said to protect them from all enemy bullets), everything would become new. The buffalo would return, Indians would get back their lands, and the whites would disappear. The

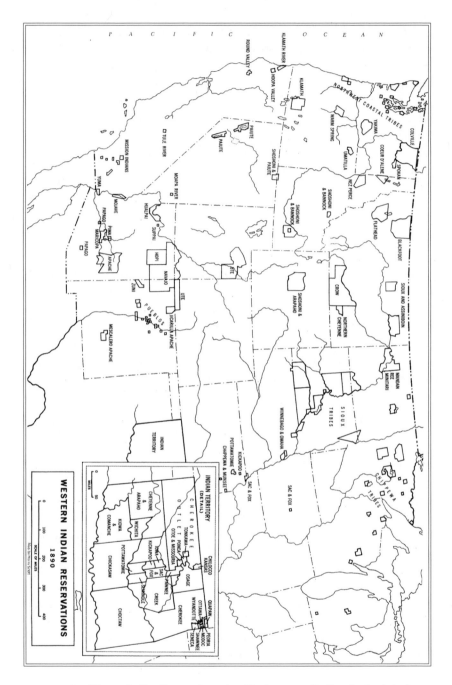

FIGURE 8:3. *Western Indian Reservations, 1890.* By 1890, most Indians in the American West had been placed on reservations. From Robert M. Utley, *The Indian Frontier of the American West 1846–1890* (Albuquerque: University of New Mexico Press, 1984), 233.

Ghost Dance spread like an emotional revival across the northern Plains. But two events quickly quashed the new religion. On December 15, Sitting Bull was killed in an angry melee on the Standing Rock Reservation following his attempted arrest. Two weeks later at Wounded Knee Creek, near the Pine Ridge Agency in South Dakota, the last major armed confrontation between Indians and U.S. troops took place. Big Foot, a Miniconjou Sioux leader, had agreed to come in from an unauthorized movement off the reservation, but his continuing independent actions scared a weak agent, who called for troops. When remnants of the Seventh Cavalry surrounded Big Foot's bands and attempted to disarm them, chaos resulted. It began with an accidental shot, and then a battle that no one planned or wanted erupted. At the end of the shooting, two hundred Indians were dead or wounded and about sixty-five soldiers.

The Massacre at Wounded Knee on December 29, 1890, signaled the end of Indian battles with whites. That year also represented another low point in Indian population, with only 228,000 remaining of the Native population of the estimated 360,000 in 1850. Warfare, disease, the disappearance of the buffalo, and traumatic disruptions of Indian lifestyles and social patterns had taken huge tolls. True, Indians were no longer on the warpath, but at what devastating costs to their cultures. For the next two generations, Native Americans seemed adrift as they tried to accept the end of one vision and attempted to dream a new one.

≈

Some say the birth of the Wild West began with a dramatic story. When eastern writer George Ward Nichols lionized James Butler ("Wild Bill") Hickok as a frontier demigod armed with unerring pistols and limitless bravery in the February 1867 issue of Harper's New Monthly Magazine, he helped launch an Old West school of storytelling that flourished well into the twentieth century. Indeed, in the quarter-century from 1865 to 1890, the frontier was often depicted as wild and wooly, seething with border warfare, street fights, and sensational shootouts. In these lurid tales, such worthies as Wild Bill, Billy the Kid, Wyatt Earp, and Calamity Jane, among others, became notorious heroes, heroines, and sometimes villains. Building on these dramatic narratives from the frontier, in the 1880s William F. ("Buffalo Bill") Cody organized a spectacular arena show, which he titled Wild West and which enjoyed enormous notoriety in depicting the pioneer West as a wild, untamed place. If one remembers, too, that added to these Wild West stories were numerous tales of Indian wars, it is not surprising that the West became for many easterners a land of nonstop action, adventure, and conflict.

The lives and reputations of these legendary characters married fiction and

FIGURE 8:4. *Billy the Kid*. This obscure print is the only authenticated image of Billy the Kid, the youthful and much-celebrated outlaw of the Southwest. Courtesy Lincoln Heritage Trust, Lincoln, New Mexico.

fact. As we shall see in chapter 10, all these frontier figures starred in unbelievable dime novels, melodramatic road shows, and outrageous journalistic tall tales. But they also were historical actors, revealing important strains of conflict and accommodations that marked the late-nineteenth-century West. In his apt phrase "the Western Civil War of Incorporation," historian Richard Maxwell Brown provides a useful interpretative framework for viewing such protagonists and the dramas in which they participated. In Brown's formulation, men like Wild Bill, Earp, and Pat Garrett were "incorporation" figures, representing a central homogenizing power of federal, state, and local officials. Their opponents, such as Billy the Kid and Jesse James, were individualistic, sometimes anarchic frontiersmen challenging those who wished to concentrate control in the hands of the elite.

Most of the Wild West figures sprang to notoriety in the interior West, usually emerging from nascent cow towns or mining camps and sometimes with links to the Civil War. Wild Bill Hickok left home as a teenager, wandered the frontier, and then gained his first attention in 1861 when he killed David McCanles and two others in a gunfight over a reputed unpaid debt. During the Civil War, Hickok served as a scout and gained his name Wild Bill through his bravery and courage. Four years later he killed a friend, Davis Tutt, over a card game. In 1867, Nichols's essay in *Harper's* transformed Hickok into the frontier's best-known gunman. His reputation as a fearless pistoleer led to his employment as a U.S. deputy marshal, a guide for visiting dignitaries, and in 1871 marshal of Abilene, Kansas, the famed cow town at the end of the Chisholm Trail. In the last five years of his life he seemed unable to settle down and stick to one job even after marrying in early 1876. On August 2, 1876, he was gunned down in Deadwood, South Dakota, while playing cards in a saloon. Hickok's life obviously reflected the unsettled social conditions of cattle and mining towns, but, even more significantly, his larger-than-life reputation resulted more from the American need for a Wild West than from any noteworthy accomplishments.

Billy the Kid (aka Henry McCarty, Kid Antrim, William H. Bonney) lived "a short and violent life." Coming to New Mexico territory as a teenager in 1873, Billy retreated to Arizona after an altercation with the law before returning to New Mexico. Soon after entering lawless Lincoln County, the largest county in the United States in 1877–78, Billy became part of the John Tunstall–Alex McSween–John Chisum faction in its deadly conflicts with "The House" partisans, headed by Lawrence Murphy and later James Dolan. After Tunstall and McSween died during the Lincoln County War of February–July 1878, Billy became the leader of the so-called "Regulators." He and his gang made their livings stealing horses and cattle. Tiring of the Regulators' actions, large cattlemen helped elect Pat Garrett as sheriff of Lincoln County. Garrett captured Billy in December 1880, but the next spring the young outlaw, after killing two deputies, escaped in a daring break from the Lincoln jail. Garrett tracked Billy to nearby Ft. Sumner, and on the hot summer night of July 14, 1881, shot Billy. In his pursuit of Billy, Garrett clearly reflected the interests of cattlemen and landowners ("incorporators") who wanted to end the frontier disorder and uncontrolled violence Billy the Kid represented.

Wyatt Earp, like Wild Bill Hickok, illustrated the narrow, murky lines often separating western lawmen and outlaws. When Wyatt's first wife died in 1870, his life rapidly veered in a new direction. He crisscrossed the West, served as a successful but sometimes violent lawman in Kansas cow towns, and then moved to the new mining boomtown of Tombstone, Arizona, in December 1879. With several of his brothers, Wyatt bought property, acted as a law officer, and hobnobbed with leading citizens. He and the other Earps gained reputations as solid businessmen and Republicans. Gradually, however, the Earps began to conflict with the "cowboys," especially Old Man Clanton, his sons, and the McLaurys. They were ranchers, southerners, Democrats, and sometime rustlers. Fueled by the growing hostility between the Clanton faction and the Earps, the controversy exploded in the West's most notorious gun battle, the Shootout at the OK Corral (actually in a vacant lot near the OK Corral) on October 26, 1881. After a few bloody seconds of wild, staccato gunfire, several of the Clanton-McLaury group lay dead and two of the Earp brothers wounded. The infamous shootout divided Tombstone. Some residents, considering the Earps the more guilty party, attempted to jail Wyatt and his brothers. When those efforts failed, assassins later severely wounded Virgil Earp and killed Morgan Earp. At this point, writes biographer Casey Tefertiller, Wyatt "became a vigilante, a marshal, and an outlaw all at the same time." Earp and his followers pursued and shot down several men they thought had wounded or killed the Earp brothers. Rather than face criminal charges, Wyatt, part of his family, and his shotgun-toting sidekick Doc Holliday shook off the dust of an increasingly unfriendly Tombstone and left for other Wests. Wyatt lived long enough into the 1920s to consult with Hollywood moviemakers to make sure they told the "truth" about his Old West. In the twentieth century, Hollywood and other popularizers capitalized on Earp as well as other Wild West figures to people their films, novels, and exhibits with dozens of larger-than-life frontier heroes and villains.

On the other hand, social expectations in the Gilded Age made it difficult for writers to depict Wild West women. One could, without much problem, write tongue-in-cheek about disreputable women "on the line" in houses of prostitution. Journalists often did that. But what to do about other women was more vexing. Because late-nineteenth-century women were not to be profane, outlaws, adulteresses, or law abusers, western females who bruised these societal guidelines were often depicted as consorts of bad men rather than as evil themselves. That meant Calamity Jane, Belle Starr, and Pearl Hart, among others, were frequently described as falling in with unsavory male companions, not as essentially loose women, drunkards, or outside the law. Later, in the twentieth century these heroines were considerably cleaned up in films, fiction, and other forms of popular culture. Energetic Jean Arthur in *The Plainsman* (1936) and bubbly Doris Day in *Calamity Jane* (1953) portray vibrant, vivacious Calamity Janes, in love with Wild Bill Hickok, and who are guilty of no more than an occasional "oh sassafras."

The most influential of the Wild West popularizers, Buffalo Bill Cody capitalized on the widespread interest and belief in a frenetic frontier in launching his arena show, *Wild West*, in 1883. This spectacle began at an auspicious

FIGURE 8:5. *Calamity Jane (Martha Canary).* Although Calamity Jane is usually depicted, as above, as a buckskin-clad woman of the Wild West, she also often expressed her true desire to be a typical pioneer wife and mother. Courtesy American Heritage Center, University of Wyoming, Laramie.

moment. During the previous half-dozen years from 1876 to 1882, a clutch of sensational events—Custer's dramatic demise (1876), the assassination of Wild Bill Hickok (1876) , the killing of Billy the Kid (1881), and the Shootout at the OK Corral (1881)—brought interest in a Wild West to a near fever pitch. It was in these traumatic times of rumor and bold headlines that Buffalo Bill Cody started his *Wild West.*

Cody created a show that featured a competitive Wild West. Indians and cowboys raced horses, competed on foot, shot at one another, and participated in other contests. The huge scenes of an Attack on a Settler's Cabin, the Emigrant Train, the Deadwood Stage, and Custer's Last Stand were also spectacular dramatizations of frontier conflict and competition. One person spotlighted in the shooting contests was Annie Oakley, "Little Missie" as Cody called her. A shy farm girl and sometime orphan from Ohio, Anne became a superb shootist and featured attraction in Cody's *Wild West.* Although modest in dress and never unfeminine in her actions, Annie nonetheless represented a West that called for competition and courage as necessary for success.

In addition to featuring conflict and competition, Cody's show also dramatized accommodations and new combinations. Buffalo Bill brought Indians into his entourage, befriended them, encouraged the sincere friendship between Sitting Bull and Annie Oakley, and generally served as a peaceful negotiator between Indian and white competitors. Indeed, in one emblematic publicity photo taken in 1885, Cody and Sitting Bull stand together grasping the chief's upright rifle. The photo's caption read "Foes in '76, Friends in '85." Displaying his penchant for pageantry, Buffalo Bill kept alive the conflict theme central to the Wild West even as he worked to effect cultural compromises between Indian and white visions of the pioneer West.

~

Well-organized, durable labor unions developed slowly in the nineteenth-century West. The large needs for workers in the mines and on farms, ethnic diversity on the frontier, and the dominating power of companies and corporations were impediments to the rise of unions. Yet a few scattered labor organizations began in the decades after 1850.

The city of San Francisco hosted the first notable western labor unions. "From the start," writes cultural historian Kevin Starr, "there was something volatile about San Francisco, something that welcomed radical dissent and warred against an equally persistent bourgeois style." A few short-lived unions and strikes popped up and disappeared in the city in the 1850s and 1860s. But Chinese returning from the mines and railroad building, the arrival of other immigrants to flood the job market, and the depression that struck the nation and the West in the early 1870s dramatically changed the situation.

Enter Denis Kearney, Irish immigrant, anti-Chinese agitator, sandlot orator. Organizing the Workingmen's Party of California (WPC) in October 1877, Kearney fiercely attacked "the Celestials" as California's major problem. "The Chinese must go," Charles Crocker's financial empire must be brought down, the streets must run in blood—these attacks and threats became parts of Kearney's incendiary street-corner harangues. Soon under attack from cooler heads, Kearney and his brand of labor radicalism gradually weakened and disappeared. But not the power of labor organizations in San Francisco. Other unions, less radical than the WPC, lobbied for workers in the 1880s and 1890s in San Francisco, preparing the way for active unionism there in the early twentieth century.

Elsewhere in the West unions representing miners and railroad workers surfaced by the 1870s. Indeed, vague outlines of a working-class culture began to develop as tight times pinched laborers, and they increasingly felt that mine owners and railroad companies paid little heed to wage earners and their difficulties. From the 1870s into the 1890s western railway workers became active in unions and strikes, as for example the nationwide railroad strikes in 1877, the Knights of Labor in the Southwest in the mid-1880s, and Eugene Debs's American Railway Union and its strike against the Great Northern Railroad in 1893. Even cowboys struck for higher wages in the Texas panhandle in 1883, but their strike too was quickly broken up. None of these unions or strikes was, in fact, greatly successful in the West. The reasons for failures of unions in the West are several. For one, unions and strikes were unable to attract most of the West's workers and were particularly weak in Idaho, Utah, and New Mexico, where Mormon and ethnic communities did not support strong union activities. It also became increasingly clear that in the West the craft and more exclusive unions like the American Federation of Labor were too tied to the interests of skilled, more elite workers. That meant the AF of L did not fare as well among the predominately unskilled laborers of the West as the inclusive, industrial unions like the Knights of Labor and the later Western Federation of Miners.

A galvanizing event for western labor in the 1890s took place in the Coeur d'Alene mining district of the Idaho panhandle. In 1892 when mine owners hired replacement miners ("scabs") and posted notice of a wage cut, union miners in the area quickly struck. Within a few weeks, a vicious labor-capital war had broken out. Union members and guards for the owners were killed and the Frisco mill dynamited. The Idaho governor called in troops, and hundreds of strikers and their sympathizers were herded into giant bullpens. Over time, tensions slowly subsided in Coeur d'Alene, but the next year in Butte (dubbed the "Gibraltar of Unionism") the most activist of the nineteenth-century western unions, the Western Federation of Miners (WFM), organized as a direct result of the violence laborers experienced in Idaho in 1892.

The aggressive WFM immediately launched strikes. In Cripple Creek and Leadville, Colorado (1894), again in Coeur d'Alene (1899), and in Telluride, Colorado (1901), the WFM led strikes in classic examples of class warfare between owners and workers. The conflict in Idaho raged on from 1899 to 1901 and resulted in the return of troops, bullpens, and protracted violence. Soon, the number and strength of the imported federal troops quashed the strikers in the Coeur d'Alene district. Indeed the lack of victories in Idaho and Colorado impelled hard-rock miners toward a more direct-action union. In 1905, the organization of the Industrial Workers of the World (IWW, or Wobblies), the most radical of all western labor unions, signaled a swing left in the union activities of miners, loggers, and agricultural workers in the early twentieth century. It was in the late 1890s in the WFM and especially later in the IWW that William "Big Bill" Haywood quickly emerged as a militant labor leader. Along with several others, Haywood helped lead union members toward the IWW and thus prepared the way for more active industrial unionism in the early twentieth-century West.

～

Political stances and party organizations at the end of the nineteenth century present still another example of conflicts and complexities that emerged in the West. In 1850 only Texas (1845) and California (1850) had become states in the area west of 95°. By 1900 all western territories save Indian Territory/ Oklahoma (1907), New Mexico (1912), and Arizona (1912) had become states. In this half-century, turbulent territorial politics were an important ingredient in the mix of the American West. During these decades westerners struggled to keep political control at home and out of the hands of eastern appointees, to avoid paralyzing intraterritorial squabbles and to address a growing number of pressing concerns.

The organization of western territories followed the system for turning unsettled areas into official territories and states established in the 1780s. The Land Ordinances of 1784 and 1785 and the Northwest Ordinance of 1787 laid out plans by which territories were organized, lands surveyed and made ready for settlers, and governmental and political structures outlined. The goal of these enactments was idealistic: the orderly transfer of unorganized areas to statehood on parity with earlier states.

The body of legislation for the erection and operation of territories was both brief and general. U.S. presidents nominated territorial governors, secretaries, and judges; Congress confirmed these nominations. Once named, federally appointed officals would work with a territorial legislature and a territorial delegate to Congress elected by the male voters in each territory. Other federal appointees included land surveyors, revenue collectors, and U.S. attorneys. When a territory achieved a population of 60,000 residents, it could apply to Congress for statehood. This cut-and-dried, but distinctly hybrid, system of federal appointees and popularly elected territorial officials left room for creative organization and cooperation—and for fractious arguments, misgovernment, and corruption. All were displayed with a flare during the western territorial period from 1850 to 1912.

The presidential selections for territorial governors, secretaries, and judges often resulted from pressures endemic to the American patronage system. Loyal Republicans and Democrats, friends of the president and congressmen, and scions of leading national and territorial families—all found their places conspicuously among the territorial appointees. That meant many inappropriate appointees came west. For example, Lew Wallace and his wife, Susan, arrived in New Mexico in September 1878 while that territory was still trembling from the aftereffects of the violent Lincoln County War. Wallace made feebly inadequate gestures to put down the rebellion and then returned to his back office in the Palace of the Governors in Santa Fe to write what became his best-selling novel *Ben-Hur* (1880). Susan Wallace reportedly told friends that the United States should force Mexico to take back what she considered backward, uncivilized New Mexico. The territory of Idaho seemed even more susceptible to short-lived, incompetent appointees. In its twenty-seven years as a territory, Idaho went through sixteen governors. Four failed to come west, six others lasted less than a year, and one resigned when he heard his salary was but $2,400 to live and work in the far-off territory. The most flamboyant of the governors, Caleb Lyon of New York, never could explain how $46,000 in funds for Indian aid went missing.

Truth to tell, territorial organization included too many unresolved conflicts to be a satisfactory system. Not unlike governors of the original thirteen colonies, territorial governors rode two diverging horses. They were expected to represent the nation's interests in the West, and they owed their appointments and salaries to the president and Congress. Yet they were also to govern and satisfy local residents. Often opposing them were popularly elected territorial legislatures, who served local groups, tried to keep federal officials from dominating the territory, and were forced to fund most of the territory's expenses. It is understandable that "appointed officials had divided loyalties," writes historian Earl Pomeroy, because territorial residents "wanted Federal money, but not Federal Government."

After the quick moves to statehood of Kansas (1861), Nevada (1864), and Nebraska (1867), only Colorado (1876) made the transition in the next twelve years. Before 1862, slavery and land were the complicating issues; afterwards, mining squabbles, national Reconstruction policies, Indian wars, and competition for political patronage were the most troubling matters. Even more problematic were the tugs-of-war between Republicans and Democrats on letting in only new states that would support the "right" party in Washington. The notoriously dull, issueless politics of the American Gilded Age meant that the possibilities of statehood were more linked to the vagaries of national policies than to the readiness of territories for that next stage. National elections were so close that both parties hesitated to admit new states that might swing the outcome of the vote. In the 1870s and 1880s territories made haste slowly toward statehood because their support or nonsupport of a national party determined their political futures.

The dam of hesitation and delay broke in the late 1880s. Republicans and Democrats, each wanting to be known as the party bringing in new states, finally agreed to support the so-called Omnibus Bill. It allowed in the new states of

Washington, Montana, North Dakota, and South Dakota in 1889. One year later Wyoming and Idaho also became states. When Mormon president Wilford Woodruff issued his Manifesto in 1890 officially forbidding new LDS polygamous marriages, Utah turned the corner toward statehood and joined the Union in 1896. The chaos of Indian-white conflicts, intertribal competitions, and the recentness of land rushes in Oklahoma delayed statehood for the Indian Territory/Oklahoma area until 1907. New Mexico and Arizona, territories since 1850 and 1863, languished in limbo largely because of ethnic and cultural prejudices visited upon southwestern residents. Senator Albert Beveridge, the powerful and imperious chairman of the Senate Committee on Territories, by himself delayed statehood for the two territories. For Beveridge and his supporters, New Mexico and Arizona were "backward areas," "stifled by their Spanish heritage," and residents there were "not equal in intellect" or "sufficiently American in their habits and customs." Such supercilious attitudes blocked statehood for New Mexico and Arizona until Congress finally relented and accepted the two territories as states in 1912.

For nearly all westerners statehood symbolized a badge of heightened respectability. Territorial status, for them, suggested a second-class, backward position they wished to avoid. No matter how much territories might squabble with one another and within themselves, they agreed that being a state and joining the union represented coveted cultural advancement. Gentiles might look down on Mormon Utah, non-Indians might think Oklahoma not yet civilized because of its Indian populations, and Anglo Arizona residents might scorn Hispanics of New Mexico, but all wanted statehood. Strong, long-standing conflicts in western territories melted away in the face of the strong common desire to become states and thus achieve hoped-for respectability and parity with the East.

≈

Growing numbers of western farmers in the post–Civil War years felt their livelihoods were increasingly out of their control and in the hands of nonagrarian forces in the United States. Farmers began to grumble like tourists certain they are being overcharged and duped by nefarious, greedy outsiders. These discontents bubbled up in sociocultural associations and then reached a boiling point in the third-party Populist organization in the 1890s. Widespread, diverse dissenters coalesced into "a movement culture," a powerful reform coalition calling for radical changes in late-nineteenth-century America. Although the Populists failed to gain the White House in the famed election of 1896, they bequeathed important legacies to later reform groups.

The sudden land booms and flood of westward-migrating setters to the plains in the years after the Civil War helped set the scene for Populism. Finding themselves isolated and hungry for socializing, farmers and their families set up groups to help alleviate the separation and isolation they felt. As a result, the National Grange or Patrons of Husbandry, begun in 1867, and the Farmers' Alliance groups in the 1870s and 1880s were organized. Ostensibly nonpartisan and nonpolitical in their purposes, these organizations, as well as the Greenback Party (so named because of its support for paper money) in the 1870s and 1880s, began to mount platforms that spoke for farmers and others feeling similarly dislocated. These groups, and the issues they came to speak for, culminated in the People's or Populist Party of the 1890s.

Farmers from the 1860s onward were increasingly convinced they were being excluded from the American Dream. For many agriculturists, industrial and financial behemoths like the railroads, grain elevators and milling companies, bankers, and other "middlemen" were robbing tillers of the soil of their rightful place in American society. In retrospect, this growing discontent was following in the traditions of Thomas Jefferson in its call for more rights of "the common man," especially the agrarian yeoman; but it also reflected the views of Jefferson's opponent Alexander Hamilton in its demand for the uses of federal government power to achieve these democratic goals.

By the early 1890s reformers were organizing third parties. Kansans founded a People's Party in June 1890; similar parties in other states offered tickets to voters. Encouraged by the outcome of the 1890 elections, the People's Party—now calling itself the Populist Party—held its first national convention on July 4, 1892, at Omaha, Nebraska. Nominating James B. Weaver, a Civil War veteran and Greenback Party member, as their presidential candidate, the Populists pulled together the famous Omaha Platform that reflected their desire to unite farmers, laborers, and other reforming groups. The platform called for federal government ownership of railroad, telephone, and telegraph systems; it also stipulated that all lands "in excess" of railroad needs should be returned to the government and made available to bona fide settlers. Also included was a call for an "independent treasury" system, allowing farmers to store their crops in government-owned warehouses and to borrow on those stored crops. This plan, as well as a more flexible circulating medium of gold, silver, and paper currencies, would give more elasticity to American credit systems.

Other political planks joined these economic proposals. For example, initiative, referendum, and recall measures, all intended to keep political power in the hands of voters rather than with corporation-dominated legislatures, were added. So were the Australian (secret) ballot, the direct election of U.S. senators by voters instead of by state legislatures, and single-term limitations on the U.S. presidency. These political proposals were clear attempts to appeal to groups beyond agrarian voters.

The Populists achieved some successes in the election of 1892. They carried

Kansas, Idaho, and Nevada and won more than one million votes nationally. Populists were elected to Congress, and Colorado and Kansas selected Populist governors. In fact, a lively cast of Populist characters emerged on the national scene in the early 1890s. Kansan Mary Elizabeth Lease, a superb stump orator, called upon farmers "to raise less corn and more *hell*"; and "Sockless" Jerry Simpson, also from Kansas, gained notoriety as a tireless agitator. Ignatius Donnelly, the novel-writing politician from Minnesota, added color and wit to Populist campaigns.

Buoyed by their successes in 1892, the Populists began planning a great crusade to capture the presidency in 1896. To win over dissident Republicans and Democrats, the Populists decided to delay their nominating convention until the two major parties had met and chosen their candidates. That decision, probably, was a fatal mistake. Not unexpectedly the Republicans named the conservative, sound William McKinley as their candidate, but the Democrats surprised most observers by nominating William Jennings Bryan of Nebraska to head their ticket. Bryan was also the candidate many Populists favored

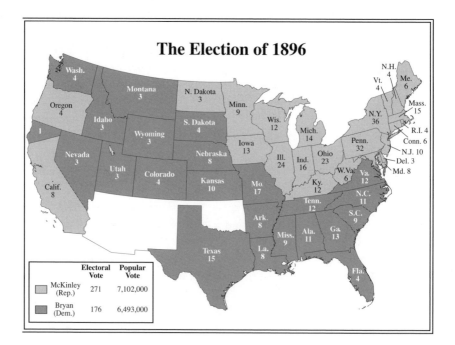

FIGURE 8:6. *The Election of 1896.* This notable presidential election pitted the Democratic and Populist candidate William Jennings Bryan, a westerner, against the eastern Republican William McKinley. Map by Robert Pace.

for their party's nominee. The Populists were now in a quandary: should they nominate their own candidate or "fuse" with the Democrats by also nominating Bryan? They chose the second option and joined the Democrats in running Bryan as their presidential candidate.

Just thirty-six years old in 1896, William Jennings Bryan had already gained a large reputation as a political orator. An attorney who had won two terms to the U.S. Congress (1890, 1892), Bryan earned recognition for his support of agricultural issues, rural values, and the free (inflationary) coinage of silver. At the Democratic national convention Bryan electrified delegates and garnered their enthusiastic support through his "Cross of Gold" speech, shot through with biblical rhetoric: "You shall not press down upon the brow of labor this crown of thorns"; "you shall not crucify mankind upon a cross of gold." A warm and sincere man, Bryan was a spirited campaigner, traveling throughout the country stumping for the Democratic and Populist tickets. Although unfriendly critics said Bryan's mind was like the Platte River, a mile wide at the mouth and a half-inch deep at the head, such harpoonings missed Bryan's sympathetic regard for common Americans. More friendly historians pointing to Bryan as the American political leader between Abraham Lincoln and Franklin D. Roosevelt most in tune with the aspirations of middle-class and lower-class Americans are much closer to the truth.

Unfortunately, the fused "Demo-Pops" were unable to win over eastern and city voters. Bryan did well in the rural South and West, but not in the towns of the West. Republican businessmen reportedly warned workers that if Bryan won they could expect to go home with empty dinner pails and perhaps lose their jobs. Bryan's call for "free silver" also worried others; they feared that this inflationary proposal would upset the economy, which was then beginning to recover from the dire effects of the Panic (depression) of 1893. In the election of 1896, McKinley won without much trouble, Bryan lost, and the Populist insurgence melted away.

But even in losing the Populists raised issues that subsequent political groups embraced. Those who later argued that the Progressives of the early twentieth century caught the Populists in swimming and stole all their clothes but their frayed underdrawers of free silver went too far in their assertions. Yet the initiative, referendum, recall, and direct election of senators had become important planks in Progressive campaigns. Other political activists agreed with the Populist demand for more federal government control of corporations and the national economy. Still others followed Populist calls for regulation of railroads, the adoption of a national income tax, and legislation to broaden relief for agriculturists in depressed times. Even though the Populists lost their bid for the White House in 1896, they advocated ideas that profoundly influenced national and western political groups for much of the next half-century.

Alberts, Don E. *The Battle of Glorieta: Union Victory in the West.* College Station: Texas A&M University Press, 1998.

Ambrose, Stephen E. *Crazy Horse and Custer: The Parallel Lives of Two American Warriors.* New York: Doubleday, 1975.

Brown, Richard Maxwell. *No Duty to Retreat: Violence and Values in American History and Society.* New York: Oxford University Press, 1991.

Coletta, Paolo E. *William Jennings Bryan.* 3 vols. Lincoln: University of Nebraska Press, 1964, 1969.

Debo, Angie. *Geronimo: The Man, His Time, His Place.* Norman: University of Oklahoma Press, 1976.

Dippie, Brian W. *The Vanishing American: White Attitudes and U.S. Indian Policy* Middletown, CT: Wesleyan University Press, 1982.

Etulain, Richard W., and Glenda Riley, eds. *Chiefs & Generals: Nine Men Who Shaped the American West.* Golden, CO: Fulcrum Publishing, 2004.

———. *With Badges & Bullets: Lawmen & Outlaws in the Old West.* Golden, CO: Fulcrum Publishing, 1999.

Goodwyn, Lawrence. *The Populist Moment: A Short History of the Agrarian Revolt in America.* New York: Oxford University Press, 1978.

Greene, Jerome A. *Nez Perce Summer, 1877: The U. S. Army and the Nee-Me-Poo Crisis.* Helena: Montana Historical Society Press, 2000.

Hicks, John D. *The Populist Revolt.* Minneapolis: University of Minnesota Press, 1931.

Hutton, Paul Andrew. *Phil Sheridan and His Army.* Lincoln: University of Nebraska Press, 1985.

Jameson, Elizabeth. *All That Glitters: Class, Conflict, and Community in Cripple Creek.* Urbana: University of Illinois Press, 1998.

Johnson, David Alan. *Founding the Far West: California, Oregon, and Nevada, 1840– 1890.* Berkeley: University of California Press, 1992.

Josephy, Alvin M. *Civil War in the American West.* New York: Alfred A. Knopf, 1991.

Kazin, Michael. *Godly Hero: The Life of William Jennings Bryan.* New York: Knopf, 2006.

Lamar, Howard R. *The Far Southwest, 1846–1912: A Territorial History.* 1966; Albuquerque: University of New Mexico Press, 2000.

Larson, Robert W. *Red Cloud: Warrior-Statesman of the Lakota Sioux.* Norman: University of Oklahoma Press, 1997.

McLaird, James D. *Calamity Jane: The Woman and the Legend.* Norman: University of Oklahoma Press, 2005.

McMurtry, Larry. *The Colonel and Little Missie: Buffalo Bill, Annie Oakley, and the Beginnings of Superstardom in America.* New York: Simon and Schuster, 2005.

Michno, Gregory. *Encyclopedia of Indians Wars: Western Battles and Skirmishes, 1850–1890.* Missoula, MT: Mountain Press, 2003.

Morrison, Michael A. *Slavery and the American West: The Eclipse of Manifest*

Destiny and the Coming of the Civil War. Chapel Hill: University of North Carolina Press, 1997.

Moses, L. G. *Wild West Shows and the Images of Indians, 1883–1933*. Albuquerque: University of New Mexico Press, 1996.

Moulton, Candy V. *Chief Joseph: Guardian of the People*. New York: Forge, 2005.

Nerburn, Kent. *Chief Joseph and the Flight of the Nez Perce: The Untold Story of an American Tragedy*. New York: HarperSan Francisco, 2005.

Nolan, Frederick. *The Lincoln County War: A Documentary History*. Norman: University of Oklahoma Press, 1992.

Ostler, Jeffrey. *The Plains Sioux and U.S. Colonialism from Lewis and Clark to Wounded Knee*. New York: Cambridge University Press, 2004.

Pomeroy, Earl. *The Territories and the United States 1861–1890: Studies in Colonial Administration*. Philadelphia: University of Pennsylvania Press, 1947.

Prucha, Francis Paul. *The Great Father: The United States Government and the American Indians*. 2 vols. Lincoln: University of Nebraska Press, 1984.

Reddin, Paul. *Wild West Shows*. Urbana: University of Illinois Press, 1999.

Riley, Glenda. *The Life and Legacy of Annie Oakley*. Norman: University of Oklahoma Press, 1994.

Robinson, Charles M. III. *The Plains Wars 1757–1900*. New York: Routledge, 2003.

Rosa, Joseph G. *They Called Him Wild Bill: The Life and Adventures of James Butler Hickok*. 2nd ed. Norman: University of Oklahoma Press, 1974.

Russell, Don. *The Lives and Legends of Buffalo Bill*. Norman: University of Oklahoma Press, 1960.

Schwantes, Carlos A. *Radical Heritage: Labor, Socialism, and Reform in Washington and British Columbia, 1865–1917*. Seattle: University of Washington Press, 1979.

Smoak, Gregory. *Ghost Dances and Identity: Prophetic Religion and American Indian Ethnogenesis in the Nineteenth Century*. Berkeley: University of California Press, 2006.

Tefertiller, Casey. *Wyatt Earp: The Life Behind the Legend*. New York: John Wiley, 1997.

Utley, Robert M. *Billy the Kid: A Short and Violent Life*. Lincoln: University of Nebraska Press, 1989.

———. *Custer: Cavalier in Buckskin*. Norman: University of Oklahoma Press, 2001.

———. *The Indian Frontier of the American West, 1846–1890*. Albuquerque: University of New Mexico Press, 1984.

———. *The Lance and the Shield: The Life and Times of Sitting Bull*. New York: Henry Holt and Company, 1993.

West, Elliott. *The Contested Plains: Indians, Goldseekers, and the Rush to Colorado*. Lawrence: University Press of Kansas, 1998.

———. *The Way to the West: Essays on the Central Plains*. Albuquerque: University of New Mexico Press, 1995.

Wrobel, David M. *Promised Lands: Promotion, Memory, and the Creation of the American West*. Lawrence: University Press of Kansas, 2002.

CHAPTER NINE

Frontier Social Patterns

~

THINK OF A VISITOR TO THE AMERICAN WEST IN 1850, TRYING TO DISCOVER and understand social patterns emerging in the region. Even after viewing the rural and urban populations, examining the racial and ethnic makeup of westerners, and studying frontier families, the visitor might have difficulty summarizing what he or she had seen. Quite possibly the varieties of frontier societies might have been clear, but the traveler would not have known how much those patterns had changed in the past generation and how the pace of transformation would accelerate in the next two generations. The quick changes and diversity of the second half of the nineteenth-century American West are both revealing and complicating elements in attempting to understand the region's emerging social mixes.

~

The first census of western population in 1850 furnishes an eye-opening portrait of settlement in the region. Roughly 392,000 of the nation's 23 million residents (Native Americans were not enumerated in the census) lived west of the 98th meridian, stretching from the eastern sections of present North Dakota south to Texas. Almost 80 percent of these persons resided in the only two western states: California and Texas; the remainder congregated in the territories of New Mexico, Utah, and Oregon. The population was 95 percent rural (unincorporated communities of less than 2,500 residents), with California and New Mexico pacing the region in urban population.

Racial, ethnic, and gender imbalances were also apparent. Yet conclusions must remain suspect and hazy since census-takers in 1850 did not count Indians or identify persons of Hispanic heritage. As a result, only Texas had a significant nonwhite population with 59,000 of its 213,000 residents listed as

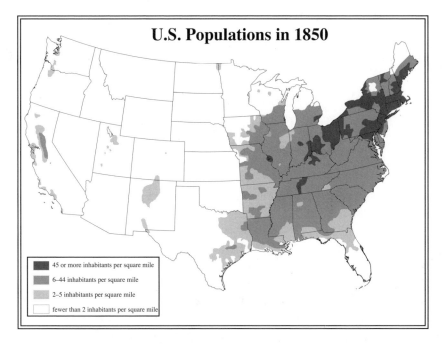

U.S. Populations in 1850

45 or more inhabitants per square mile

6–44 inhabitants per square mile

2–5 inhabitants per square mile

fewer than 2 inhabitants per square mile

FIGURE 9:1. *U. S. Populations in 1850*. This map demonstrates how small and rural-based western population was in 1850. Map by Robert Pace.

"Negroes," nearly all of whom were slaves. Almost two-thirds of westerners were male, but gender divisions were nearly even in New Mexico and Utah and markedly out of balance only in California, where the Gold Rush skewed the ratios to twelve men for each woman. The portrait that emerges from the census of 1850 is that of an isolated, rural, predominately male and white society.

Western pioneer society was transformed in the next fifty years. In 1900, more than 11 million of the nation's 76 million people lived in the West, with all but three continental areas—Oklahoma (1907), New Mexico (1912), and Arizona (1912)—having become states. Although 74 percent of western population remained rural, urban population had jumped from 5 to 26 percent, and now more than half of California's residents were urban. The ethnic and racial mixes of western society were increasingly diverse. In 1870, nearly 30 percent of westerners were foreign-born, with more than half of the adult male population in Utah, Nevada, Arizona, Idaho, and California born abroad. As late as 1900 nearly 40 percent of San Francisco (the largest city in the West at 343,000) remained foreign-born. Gender divisions had also notably changed, with the population of 1900 becoming 54 percent male and 46 percent female. The highest percentage of women was in the agricultural Plains states, with men dominating in California and in the new states of Wyoming and Montana. No western state or territory had yet achieved a numerical balance of the sexes.

～

Most of the West's nonurban population lived on farms. Social conditions in these agricultural areas were seldom similar and often changed. The most widely known segment of the rural frontier was that settled in the upper Great Plains. During the first decades after the Civil War hundreds of thousands of Americans and European immigrants swarmed west to take up land on this sod-house frontier.

The Great Plains surprised many of these newcomers. They spoke often of the new, strange spaces they encountered, the novel kinds of houses being built, and the unusual modes of living they experienced. One pioneer woman, Grace Snyder, who moved to Custer County, Nebraska, as a three-year-old, remembered the lonesome, isolated sod houses her father erected for their family after they moved from Missouri. The flat plains that surrounded her small, bleak house aroused fear in the child, perhaps causing anxiety about a home and landscape that seemed so alien and forbidding.

Another immigrant, twenty-year-old Seth Humphrey, a mortgage collector recently moved to Dakota Territory from Minnesota, also reacted negatively to the Plains. He found their vastness, silence, and anonymity disturbing. Traveling across the wide, flat miles of the upper Midwest, Humphrey found hundreds of abandoned "soddies" (sod houses), mute symbols of settlers who had given up in the battle to find a home on the Plains. Everywhere he heard stories of pioneers who reacted negatively to the seas of waving grass that confronted them. Their tales of woe were like the despairing and traumatizing realities writers such as Willa Cather (*My Antonia*, 1918), Ole Rölvaag (*Giants in the Earth*, 1927), and Conrad Richter (*Sea of Grass*, 1937) depicted later in their novels.

If the featureless plains and the crude dugouts and sod houses were reasons for discontent among farmers and their families, so were the drudgery of their work and their isolation from relatives and neighbors. The work of most farmers was daily dull, despite the changes that brought increased mechanization in new kinds of plows, reapers, and threshers. For farm wives, there were endless domestic tasks of cooking, washing, caring for their children—in addition, sometimes, to having to help with plowing and harvesting. The menial and monotonous details would have been less onerous if friends and families had been nearby. But in the earliest years of Plains settlement, farm families were often distant from neighbors, with their personal letters and diaries betraying frequent feelings of isolation and lonesomeness.

Distance and separation brought still other problems. Illness seemed a constant boarder at many farm homes. In others new babies came often and under difficult circumstances. Doctors were few and frequently too far away to help—and sometimes too expensive. So farm families had to "make do" in nursing one another through cholera, pneumonia, or injuries from accidents. Imagine the fearfulness of a woman approaching childbirth, which, if complications arose, often led to the death of the baby, or even of the mother and baby.

Uncertain weather, fires, and pests also took their toll. Inadequate rainfall, hot summer winds, and killing early frosts destroyed promising crops, whereas prairie fires wiped out grain fields and nearby frame homes and outbuildings. In other years, grasshoppers descended in voracious hordes, devouring all crops and even chewing away sideboards of wagons and ax handles or piling up so deeply on rails that train engines were unable to get traction to move along tracks.

~

These problems, real and dramatic as they were, can be overplayed. A majority of the settlers stayed on, with many becoming successful homesteaders. Even though some newcomers were alienated by the flat, treeless plains, others delighted in it. One pioneer wrote to his mother in the East, "You can see just as far as you please here and almost every foot in sight can be plowed." Moreover, a homesteader could begin with little capital. It usually took about $500 to $600 annually to sustain a farm family, but a bachelor from Pennsylvania with less than $100 settled in Kansas and built his sod house for less than $10. Others got by on even less. Within a few years, after much hard work, economizing, and help from Mother Nature, they were able to erect frame houses. Houses and homes were important to pioneers; they referred to them repeatedly in letters. "If we find any peace or happiness on this earth," one sodbuster told his new bride, "I suppose 99 per cent of it will be within our own home."

Nor should one exaggerate the daily labors of farmers. Agriculturists expected to work hard. The custom of the country told them that their work would sanctify their lives and provide useful outlets for the energies of their children. A few fortunate homesteaders had cash, but a system of bartering and labor exchange allowed most settlers to pay off their debts for seed and feed and to take care of expenses for plowing and harvesting.

Within a short period of time, other newcomers usually moved nearby. For example, six months after the Homestead Act of 1862 was enacted, thousands of settlers filed on more than a quarter-million acres in eastern Kansas and Nebraska. With the new neighbors came the possibility of visiting—on weekends and holidays. If settlers arrived in sufficient numbers, as they usually did, schools and churches sprang up to become social centers the year round. Several other possibilities for socializing followed once an area became settled: auctions and Grange meetings for men and sewing and quilting bees for women were particularly popular, as well as a variety of religious, educational, and recreational gatherings for parents and children. Farmers and wives wrote much about visiting and socializing as respites from the demanding daily duties that otherwise ordered their lives.

Settlers sometimes came to terms with their difficulties through stories or tall tales. One sodbuster opined that Kansas summers were always 118° in the shade—and all that in the next county. Another, referring to the crop-destroying hot winds of the Plains, told of a wicked Kansan being buried in his overcoat so he could survive in Hades. Still another told of a farmer writing to a barbed wire company, saying, "Send me your terms for fence wire. I am thinking of fencing in Kansas." The company representative, answering in kind, replied, "Have consulted the best authorities, and made an approximate calculation of the amount of wire it will take to 'fence in' Kansas. We find that we have *just* enough if you order at once."

Rural society exhibited different patterns in the West Coast states. Here the quickly commercialized nature of farming and agriculturists' ties to nearby urban centers brought about less isolation for farmers. The arrival of railroads in the 1870s and 1880s quickly opened new markets for farm produce in addition to those that mining camps provided. Indeed, some Californians became suitcase farmers, living in towns and cities but farming in adjacent fertile areas. Farmers in the Willamette Valley in Oregon, separated as a result of the generous parcels of land available under the Donation Land Act of 1850, rarely organized towns. Only in California did more than half of the population live in cities by 1900. Still, farmers on the coast looked to cities, whether to Seattle, Portland, or Eugene in the coastal or western valleys or to Spokane, Boise, and Salt Lake City in the interior areas. The rural social patterns of the Far West, as a result of differing terrain and an altered mix of immigration, varied a good deal from those that took root on the Great Plains.

Still other social patterns emerged in rural parts of the West. Across the Southwest, from Texas to California, the dominant rhythms of society rippled out from ranches and small farmsteads, particularly the cattle ranches of Texas and southern California and the smaller Hispanic *ranchos* of New Mexico. Here men and women and their families were centripetally tied to ranch houses, adobe homes, and small crossroad towns and pueblos that punctuated the region. These cattle kingdom and pastoral ways continued well into the 1880s and 1890s in many parts of the Southwest, before railroads brought

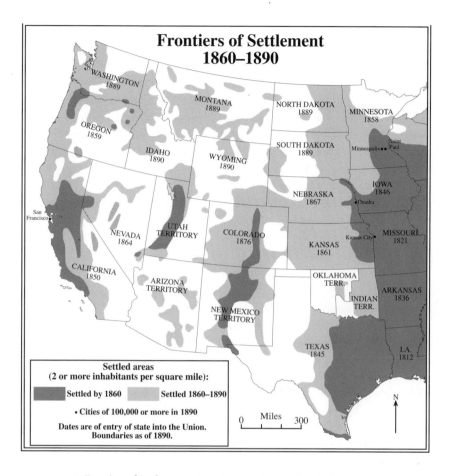

FIGURE 9:2. *Frontiers of Settlement, 1860–1890.* By 1890, settlers had spread across most of the West, save in desert, mountainous, and less fertile areas. Map by Robert Pace.

quick, gear-grinding changes and the precipitous rise of urban centers like Albuquerque, El Paso, and Los Angeles. Despite these new cities, the smaller "corralled communities" continued to typify much of the Southwest well into the twentieth century.

At the same time, the West gained a nonurban work force that fluctuated markedly in numbers and occupational types. Railroad hamlets, almost like portable towns, rose and fell even more rapidly than the early mining rush towns. Similar to the mining sites, these railroad towns ("hells on wheels") were inhabited primarily by young, male workers rarely known for establishing stable law-and-order communities. In addition, toward the end of the century, a new kind of mining town—like those in northern Idaho, western Montana, and western Colorado—replaced the fly-by-night Gold Rush camps. In these later mining towns a growing labor consciousness frequently solidified workers, leading to a series of confrontations between miners and operators in the 1890s and into the new century in such areas as the Coeur d'Alenes in Idaho, Butte in Montana, and Cripple Creek in Colorado. In fact, early in the twentieth century the laboring men of these mining towns joined their brethren in the lumbering camps and the bindlestiffs from the grain fields to form the Industrial Workers of the World (IWW), the most notorious union organization in the West.

The cow towns and earliest mining rush camps were halfway points between the rural and urban Wests. As end points of the cattle trails snaking up from Texas, most of the cattle towns nose-dived with the ending of the long trails. Towns such as Abilene, Dodge City, Caldwell, and Ellsworth (all in Kansas) never became notable cities, but Wichita, Kansas City, and Fort Worth, three towns benefiting from cattle trailing and shipping, rose to urban status by the end of the nineteenth century. Like the disappearing cow towns, most of the earliest mining camps lost out in the rush to populate the West. Where San Francisco and Denver became instant cities, dozens of other mining camps and towns rose and fell almost in union with the boom and bust of western mining rushes.

For every western town that mushroomed to become a dark, urban circle on a demographer's map, many others failed to gain after an original spurt. Or, worse yet, they lost their residents to become, as one commentator noted, "relics of lost opportunities for greatness." Some naysaying American writers like Sinclair Lewis, Thorstein Veblen, and Sherwood Anderson painted negative portraits of the provincial and materialistic sides of midwestern towns; others such as William Allen White and Edgar Watson Howe saw much to praise in western towns. On balance, the farm, railroad, and ranching towns were both narrow- and broad-minded; for every bigoted Babbitt there were community-motivated citizens ready to support sociocultural institutions aiming at bettering the town.

∽

The pioneer West has too often been stereotyped as a remote, isolated, and rural region. Even though primarily rural and agricultural during the last half of the nineteenth century, the frontier West was also surprisingly urban—and increasingly urbanized from 1850 to 1900. At the end of the century the New West was about one-fourth urban, compared to nearly 40 percent for the nation.

FRONTIER URBAN POPULATIONS, 1850–1900

City	1850	1860	1870	1880	1890	1900
San Antonio	3,396	8,235	12,256	20,550	37,673	53,321
Houston	2,396	4,845	9,382	16,513	27,557	44,633
Galveston	4,177	7,307	13,818	22,248	29,084	37,789
Austin	2,000	3,494	4,428	11,013	14,575	22,258
Dallas	250	2,000	4,500	10,358	38,067	42,638
El Paso		428	764	736	10,338	15,906
Oklahoma City					4,151	10,037
Santa Fe	4,846	4,635	4,765	6,635	6,185	5,603
Albuquerque		1,203	1,307	2,315	3,785	6,238
Phoenix			240	1,708	3,152	5,544
Tucson	400	915	3,224	7,007	5,150	7,531
Los Angeles	1,610	4,385	5,728	11,183	50,395	102,479
San Francisco	34,870	56,802	149,473	233,959	298,997	342,782
Sacramento	6,820	13,785	16,283	21,240	26,386	29,282
Oakland		1,442	10,500	34,555	48,682	66,960
San Jose	3,500	4,579	9,089	12,567	18,060	21,500
Portland	821	2,868	8,293	17,577	46,385	90,426
Tacoma			73	1,098	36,006	37,714
Seattle			1,107	3,533	42,837	80,671
Boise			995	1,899	2,311	5,957
Helena			3,106	3,624	13,834	10,770
Fargo			400	2,693	5,664	9,589
Sioux Falls			1,000	2,164	10,177	10,266
Omaha		1,883	16,083	30,518	140,452	102,555
Lincoln			2,441	13,003	55,154	40,169
Leavenworth		7,429	17,873	16,546	19,768	20,735
Kansas City				3,200	38,316	51,418
Topeka		759	5,790	15,452	31,007	33,608
Denver		4,749	4,759	35,629	106,713	133,859
Cheyenne			1,450	3,456	11.690	14,087
Salt Lake City	6,157	8,236	12,854	20,768	44,843	53,531
Virginia City (NV)	2,345	7,048	10,917	6,433	2,695	
Reno			1,035	1,302	3,563	4,500

Includes populations of largest cities and other towns in all western states and territories.

SOURCES: U.S. Bureau of the Census, *Historical Statistics of the United States: Colonial Times to 1970.* 2 vols. (Washington, D.C.: Government Printing Office, 1975); Riley Moffat, *Population History of Western U.S. Cities and Towns, 1850–1990* (Lanham, MD: Scarecrow Press, 1996).

Well before the Gold Rush and other mining strikes attracted hordes of miners to frontier camps, numerous small towns had sprouted in scattered areas of the West. As historian Gunther Barth has shown, four kinds of nascent urban places popped up: the "economic town" (Santa Fe) and "colonial outpost" (Monterey, California) illustrated the early hegemony of Spain and Mexico in the Southwest; the "marketplace" (Champoeg, Oregon) epitomized the trapper-farmer settlements in the Willamette Valley; and the "temple city" (Salt Lake City) reflected Mormon dominance in the Great Basin.

In addition, Texas cities such as Houston, Galveston, Austin, and San Antonio were well-established urban areas by the 1850s. Developed before or concurrent with agricultural settlements, these Texas cities became cultural centers attracting immigrants from the South and East. At the end of the Mexican-American War in 1848, well before the arrival of railroads, they had become economic, social, political, and culture cores for the new state. But other western cities would soon soar beyond these earlier pioneer towns, in size and importance.

No western city better illustrates the rapid urbanization of the Far West and the sway urban areas held over their hinterlands than San Francisco. First known as Yerba Buena, the hamlet hosted less than 1,000 inhabitants when upstart Americans renamed it San Francisco in 1847. The Gold Rush brought, immediately, thousands of Americans and world citizens to the area. By the early 1850s, San Francisco was already the largest city in the West, and remained so until World War I. Indeed, in 1880 with one-third of California's burgeoning population, San Francisco hosted more residents (234,000) than all western *states*, save the combined populations of Texas, Nebraska, and Kansas. From the Mexican border north to Canada and east to nearly Salt Lake City, westerners looked to San Francisco as "the city" for their business affairs.

San Francisco also pulsed as a sociocultural center for far-westerners. The best-known of the western "instant cities," San Francisco rivaled Boston, New York, and other eastern metropolises as a center of fashion and social life within a generation after the Gold Rush. Despite a wide gulf between its rich and poor, San Francisco had the highest per capita wealth of any American city. A communal city of hotels, boardinghouses, and families, "Baghdad by the Bay" was also more eastern (core-centered) than western (core- and suburb-centered) in its appearance, layout, and social life.

What San Francisco was as the urban hub of the Far West in the second half of the nineteenth century, Portland became—to a lesser extent—in the Pacific Northwest, that is, until the arrival of the transcontinental railroads propelled Seattle past Portland for regional dominance. In 1850 Portland was little more than a clearing alongside the Willamette River, but by 1890 it had swelled to 46,000 and nearly doubled to 90,000 at century's end. Like San Francisco,

Portland betrayed its eastern, conservative, and commercial origins from its founding years. "Portland had seemed old even when it was young, respectable when it was still crude," one historian writes. Although situated inland and up the Willamette, Portland became the first sizable port in the Pacific Northwest and until at least the 1880s commanded the commercial and transportation networks of the region. By 1860s the farmers and commercial interests in Oregon were tied to Portland merchants and financiers, and later the city provided banking and shipping support, particularly through the Oregon Steam Navigation Company, for mines in Idaho and Montana. Not surprisingly, Portland became known as the "city that gravity built" since its strategic location near the confluence of the Columbia and Willamette rivers ensured the city's control of the economies of Oregon and Washington and, later, the interior Northwest.

To the north, Seattle's fortunes were tied to the slower development of Washington territory between the 1850s and the late 1880s. Good fishing, nearby timber and a small sawmill, and growing coastal trade first boosted the town's hopes. But when the Northern Pacific Railroad chose Tacoma as its western terminus, Seattle boomers had to wait until James J. Hill's Great Northern track arrived in 1893 to enjoy the blessings of a transcontinental railroad. Trade routes to the Orient and gold rushes to the Yukon and Alaska in the 1890s compounded Seattle's growth. Its population sprang from 3,500 in 1880 to 43,000 in 1890 and on to 81,000 in 1900. But within the next decade, spurred on by Asian and Alaska connection and Hill's outstanding railroad, Seattle exploded to 237,000, surpassing Portland's 207,000. Seattle's amazing rate of growth from 1880 to 1910 could only be matched by Denver's and Los Angeles's expansion among the largest of western cities. As the West's third largest city in 1910, Seattle was poised to dominate the Pacific Northwest, which it has done since to the consternation of Portland's less opportunistic city fathers.

Similar to San Francisco, Denver became an instant city, zooming to urban status in a few short years. Located near the Rocky Mountain mining booms of the 1850s and 1860s, the tent town quickly turned into an important trade center and became the largest city between Omaha and the West Coast and second only to San Francisco in the West in size in 1900. At first Denver was a supply point for miners and others moving farther west, but the arrival of thousands of farm families in the area and railroads in the 1870s solidified the center's trade and financial importance to the central Rockies.

More than other interior western cities, Denver, with its ambitious business leaders pledging necessary support, backed railroads and commercial projects that linked nearby areas to the central city. By 1890 it was the third largest city in the West with 107,000 residents, capturing more than one fifth of Colorado's population. Soon Denver became known for its salubrious climate and attracted thousands of visitors annually by the end of the century, encouraging the development of hotels and the tourist industry. In 1900, Denver, although a decade younger than Salt Lake City, was two and a half times larger than the Utah capital. The Mormon ethos of Salt Lake City cut it off from some of the dynamic changes transforming Denver.

In the Midwest, Omaha rivaled Denver as the most important western city after San Francisco. Perched on the west bank of the Missouri, Omaha became, like most leading pioneer urban spots, an important freighting site, a major link on the first transcontinental railroad, and later a notable center for agriculturalists that swarmed into Nebraska and Kansas in the 1870s and 1880s. Omaha also grew to be a well-known packing plant site, another revelation of its regional ties to dirt farmers and livestock ranchers. These diverse industries drew a gathering stream of job-hungry immigrants, who made up nearly one-third of city's population in 1890. Omaha surged from 16,000 in 1870 to 140,000 in 1890, increasingly recognized as a grain and livestock center and as the headquarters of the Union Pacific Railroad. But when an agricultural depression undercut Omaha's economy, the city's population shrank 27 percent to 103,000 in 1900. In the first decades of the next century Omaha would regain most of its economic dynamism.

In a little more than five short decades, from 1850 to 1900, the West made clear strides toward becoming an urban society. With these trends continuing unabated, the region was more than half urban by the mid-1920s. But the patterns of urbanization were not uniform. If the largest city in the pre–Gold Rush West was Salt Lake City, Santa Fe, or one of the emerging Texas urban areas at 4,000 to 5,000, by 1900 more than thirty cites had grown to at least 5,000. Most of the largest cities were on the outer edges of the West—San Francisco, Portland, and Seattle on the coast, Omaha and San Antonio on the eastern borders of the West. Only Denver and Salt Lake City hosted populations of more than 50,000 in the interior West. In the early twentieth century Los Angeles became *the* western city, much as San Francisco had been in the nineteenth and Las Vegas threatened to be at the opening of the twenty-first century. By 1900, the demographic pattern of the West had been established: it would be a region of urban oases, widely scattered cities dominating the western social and economic landscape. These burgeoning cities—along with the earlier rapid setting of agricultural areas—drew a racially and ethnically mixed population to the West. Together, they produced a varied, complex society.

∾

When the present Southwest became part of the United States at the end of the Mexican-American War, about 80,000 persons of Mexican or mestizo heritage lived in Texas, New Mexico (including Arizona), and California. Although specific outcomes differed in each subregion, the general pattern in the next half-century was similar: Anglo-Americans pushed aside Spanish-speaking peoples and gained control of these newly acquired areas. Only in New Mexico was the turn of events substantially different.

In Texas on the eve of the Texas Revolution in 1835, Anglo-Americans and their slaves already outnumbered Mexicans, perhaps as much as six to one (30,000 to 5,000). Following the Texas victory in 1836 and formation of the Lone Star Republic, to be Mexican was a ticket to obscurity or, worse, to become a target for discrimination. Spanish-speaking peoples (*tejanos*) rapidly lost status, even in their heavily concentrated places like San Antonio. Increasingly Anglo farmers and sheep and cattle raisers hired Mexicans for manual labor on their farms or to herd their livestock. Only in border regions and towns like Laredo were tejanos able to retain a semblance of their previous sociopolitical dominance. A few other elite tejanos retained status when their daughters married Anglo men. In 1900 approximately 5 percent of Texas was Spanish-speaking, with about 25 percent black. Regrettably, many of the newly arrived English-speaking immigrants, with American southern backgrounds, treated both groups as social undesirables.

At the other end of the Southwest in California, the Gold Rush immediately transformed racial and ethnic patterns. In 1848 before the rush, original *Californios* were a large majority of the 14,000 or so non-Indians residents. Two years later about 100,000 newcomers had invaded the new state, and by the mid-1850s new tax and land laws had scrambled previous Hispanic control. Californios held on longer in southern California, but a combination of Anglo incursions, unwise expenditures, costly court cases dealing with clouded land grants, and disastrous weather and droughts alienated most Californio land holdings by the 1880s. The Yankees had come—and conquered.

In New Mexico, *nuevomexicano* dominance lasted longer. The two and one-half centuries of Spanish and Mexican control there could not be reversed as quickly. Although the poor farmers (*pobres*) in the northern part of the territory fell under Anglo hegemony, a few well-known, affluent (*rico*) families such as the Oteros and Chavezes retained their political power and social eminence well past the 1860s, often through intermarriage or other connections with Anglos. The most disastrous change for pobres and ricos alike was the loss of large portions of their lands. Persons of Mexican heritage, often unable to prove the validity of their land grants, were forced into long, costly legal battles to win their title. Anglo lawyers often undertook these cases for large shares—sometimes more than half—of a land grant. Most of the grants, meanwhile, had been subdivided among large families. Between exorbitant legal fees and repeated subdivisions of their holdings, nuevomexicanos had lost much of their land by 1900. Sometimes visitors to New Mexico spoke loudly and negatively of Mexican influences there, largely withholding statehood until 1912 because of this alleged sociocultural backwardness. Early in the twentieth century Hispanic domination in New Mexico was everywhere in retreat and near collapse in economic and political matters.

In Arizona (part of New Mexico until 1863) and Colorado, Mexican influences were noticeable in town and country life. From the 1850s to the 1870s Arizona remained more Hispanic than Anglo, but thereafter Anglo businessmen increasingly maneuvered for control of financial and political affairs. A small coterie of Spanish-speaking families intermarried with Anglos in the Tucson area, but the majority of the Mexican-heritage residents of the territory were forced into menial jobs to sustain their families. In southern Colorado, settlement patterns followed the small-farm and community traditions of northern New Mexico, with Spanish-speaking residents there maintaining their religious, family, and community traditions during the late nineteenth century.

By 1900, Anglo groups had, by and large, shouldered aside Hispanics in the competition to control the Southwest. Several hundred thousand Spanish-speaking people continued to reside in the region, but they had forfeited much of their land and most leadership positions in sociocultural affairs. In contacts between the two cultures, New Mexicans, retaining their lengthy traditions, held out longest against the Yankees, but they too had lost a good deal of status. But evidences of another major change were on the horizon; a few Mexican immigrants were crossing the U.S. border to find low-paying employment on southwestern farms and ranches and in towns. Even though this stream of immigrants was but a trickle at the turn of the century, it would soon swell to flood stage and redirect the ethnic mix of the Southwest.

∽

In the mid-nineteenth century Chinese began arriving in the United States just as other economic opportunities in Asia and South America also beckoned them. Simultaneously upheavals and social dislocations in China impelled them elsewhere to search for new jobs and homes. The inviting areas were the mines and railroad camps of the American frontier, places hungry for cheap labor. Before 1882, when the Chinese Exclusion Act effectively stopped their immigration, more than 320,000 Chinese came to the United States. Most settled in the West. They worked played-out mines extracting precious minerals from claims that other skip-and-run miners had abandoned, served as railroad workers, or took jobs in San Francisco or other western urban areas. Even though Chinese were never more than one-tenth of California's population, they sometimes filled one-fourth of its labor force.

FIGURE 9:3. *Chinese in the Mines.* Chinese laborers were important parts of
the western workforce on railroads and, as this photo of a hydraulic operation
shows, in the mines. Courtesy Idaho State Historical Society, 76–119.2/A.

Negative reactions to the Chinese quickly surfaced. The California census of
1850 listed only 500 Chinese, but by 1852 their presence had such impact that the
Foreign Miners' Tax—first aimed at the Sonorans (Mexicans)—was redirected
toward the Chinese. But the immigrants from China persisted and succeeded,
working in mining camps as far east as the Dakota Black Hills and as far north
as the Pacific Northwest and western Canada. Even larger groups—perhaps as
many as 12,000 to 14,000—were imported to work on the Central Pacific and
other railroads. After the completion of these projects, the Chinese—mostly
male workers—settled in mining or railroad towns. In 1880 more than 105,000
Chinese were living in the United States, primarily in California. There they
made up one-third of the truck gardeners in the state and filled the ranks of
urban laborers making shoes, cigars, and woolen goods.

By the late 1870s and early 1880s California seemed to have a surfeit of
workers for its farms and cities. Not surprisingly, other workers and the unemployed hatched plans to demand an end to Chinese competition. Rallying the

support of these dissidents and the Workingmen's Party in California, Irish labor agitator Denis Kearney maneuvered his forces behind the slogan "The Chinese Must Go." These demagogic actions, the Chinese Exclusion Act of 1882, and subsequent legislative enactments cut off further Chinese immigration and sparked riots and other violent acts against the Chinese throughout the Far West. Condemning the labor practices, the lifestyles, and the reputed clannish tendencies of the Chinese, many far-westerners were convinced that exclusion was the only answer. They followed that policy well into the twentieth century.

With Chinese immigration falling off in the 1880s and 1890s, labor contractors in Hawai'i and the mainland began focusing on Japan as a new source for cheap, tractable laborers. Concurrently, Japanese workers—following the earlier opening of Japanese society and economy by Commodore Matthew C. Perry's visit in 1855—were searching for new work opportunities. The convergence of these pull and push factors brought Japanese workers to Hawai'i and the Far West in the last two decades of the nineteenth century. In 1900, 24,000 Japanese lived in the United States, with about 75 percent of that number residing in California, Washington, and Oregon and more than 20 percent of the total living in Seattle, San Francisco, and Portland. Although a few far-westerners objected to this new influx of workers from Asia, the major conflicts involving Japanese did not erupt until the early twentieth century.

⁓

For many African Americans life in the American West seemed bittersweet. Although blacks played significant parts in the fur trade, mining camps, cattle drives, and frontier military, most came as slaves or newly freed poor farmers to Texas, and later to Kansas and Oklahoma. From 1850 to 1900 African Americans living in Texas made up more than half of the black population in the West. First slaves, they became poor farmers or laborers after the Civil War. At the end of the century Texas blacks made up 25 percent of the state's population and slightly more than 80 percent of all western blacks.

Other African American farmers migrated from the South to Kansas and Oklahoma to take up homesteads. Sometimes called Exodusters because their movements paralleled the Old Testament journey from Egypt to the Promised Land, black immigrants to Kansas in the 1870s and 1880s numbered in the thousands. Unhappily, insufficient cash, the negative reactions of white neighbors, and international disagreements impeded their progress. The most energetic of the Exoduster leaders was Benjamin "Pap" Singleton, who told his followers that Kansas could be a new Canaan for them. Settlements such as Nicodemus in Kansas and several others in Oklahoma began with promise and enthusiasm, but difficult times lurked like hungry tax collectors and kept the black towns from extraordinary growth or economic success.

Most African Americans found that although the West had trumpeted its antislavery views in the 1850s, westerners were also, by and large, anti-Negro. In fact, several western states and territories were not only reluctant to ratify the 14th and 15th amendments to the Constitution (protecting citizenship and voting rights), they also passed local and state ordinances forbidding blacks rights of residence, intermarriage with whites, and other constitutional rights. Generally speaking, blacks, like many westerners of Mexican descent or newly arrived Asian immigrants, did not find the American West a notable land of freedom and opportunity in the late nineteenth century.

≈

From the 1860s through the 1890s, new farming land available on the Great Plains was a magnet for several European immigrant groups. Many of these newcomers were Germans, whose first- and second-generation members made up from 10 to 20 percent of the population of Nebraska, South Dakota, and North Dakota in 1900. From varied geographical, occupational, and religious backgrounds, the Germans usually settled in fertile farming areas, the eastern and more humid sections of these states. Other Germans from Russia made an important contribution to western agriculture in importing Turkey Red wheat, a hard and hearty variety that survived the harsh Plains winters. A few other Germans, especially merchants and craftsmen, moved into midwestern towns and cities. Abundant lands, tantalizing colonization schemes, and generous immigration policies of the Mexican and Texas governments also attracted sizeable groups of German farmers to Texas. They moved to verdant lands along the Brazos River, particularly near New Braunfels and Fredericksburg.

Scandinavians also found the upper Plains to their liking. Norwegians immigrated to North Dakota, Swedes to Nebraska, and a few Danes to the northern areas. Coming primarily in family groups and usually settling near one another, Norwegians first stopped in Wisconsin and Minnesota and then spilled over into the Dakotas in the 1880s. Conditioned to work together, they often formed cooperative economic and political efforts in the late nineteenth and early twentieth centuries. When the earlier Scandinavian immigrants described the United States positively in their "American letters" as a symbol of freedom, those messages encouraged many more Old World residents to emigrate. In the 1880s and 1890s children of the first generations or other newly arrived immigrants pushed farther west and peopled the Pacific Northwest, where the Puget Sound area, some said, was "just like Norway." There, many Norwegians followed their old-country occupations in fishing or working in cities as laborers or craftsmen. By 1900 Seattle could boast of one of the largest concentrations of Norwegians in the United States.

English-speaking immigrants from England, Wales, Ireland, and Canada were another major ethnic ingredient on the Plains. Except for the Irish and a few Welsh, these groups easily assimilated and by 1900 were integral parts of their new host society. Some came as farmers, others worked on railroads, and still others were common laborers. Although most of these immigrants were poor, a few more well-to-do Englishmen tried to set up Runnymede, an idealistic community in Kansas. It failed, one former resident concluded, because it combined "British inexperience, credulity, some money, considerable cockneyism"; "champagne and venison," evidently, were not enough to survive. Other sons of titled Englishmen attempted to colonize Victoria, but polo, tennis, hunt clubs (where coyotes replaced foxes), and yachts were somehow out of place on the Kansas flatlands. These colonies soon disappeared.

≈

Like the Chinese, the first large groups of Irish to the American West came to work as miners or to lay railroad track. By 1870 they were the largest foreign-born group in California and among the top three in most other western states and territories. In the nonurban West, as miners, railroad workers, laborers, or soldiers, the Irish led transient lives. In San Francisco, however, where they made up 16 percent of the population in 1860 (9,363) and 10 percent in 1890 (30,718), the Irish were primarily unskilled laborers, with Irish women working as servants.

It was in California where the Irish gained most attention. Jasper O'Farrell of San Francisco and John G. Downey of Los Angeles were notable Irish leaders, with Downey serving as the first Irish-born western governor. More sensational were the contributions of Denis Kearney, the Irish firebrand orator of the California Workingmen's Party, who rallied his fellow ethnics and other workers against the Chinese. Kearney's actions were a portent of the later radical activities of other such Irish leaders as Mother Jones, Elizabeth Gurley Flynn, and Big Bill Haywood, all notorious labor figures of the early twentieth century.

Still other European groups spiced western social experiences with their presence. Northern Italians, settling in northern California, worked as merchants, truck gardeners, dairy farmers, grape growers, and wine makers. In 1860, California had the largest population of Italian-born Americans, and throughout the next decades San Francisco's Italians were the most prosperous group of that heritage in the United States. Other Italians worked in mining camps and farmed in Oregon, Washington, and Colorado. Greeks came later in the nineteenth century. They too were miners but also established restaurants, sidewalk businesses, and shoeshine parlors in western urban settings. Late in the century Finns settled in states of the northern West and worked as fishermen in Oregon and laborers in Washington and California. Equally small groups of central Europeans, Czechs and Poles for example, settled as farmers in the eastern Great Plains. And the sturdy Basques, first arriving during the Gold Rush, gradually spread over California, Nevada, Oregon, and Idaho as sheepherders and stock ranchers by 1900.

The Jews, like so many other ethnic groups, were drawn west during the Gold Rush. In California and other far-western mining camps, they served as merchants, wholesalers, and peddlers, establishing much-needed commercial links with eastern suppliers. Once mining booms cooled, Jews settled primarily in western urban areas as businessmen. In 1876, about 16,000 of the more than 22,000 Jews in the West lived in San Francisco, with most of the rest residing in Portland, Denver, Salt Lake City, and Virginia City, Nevada. These early arrivals, primarily from northern Europe, melted easily and well into western society. So well, argues one scholar, that "they had, for the most part, become Americanized in their language and culture and had assimilated with the majority of the population," and "enjoyed almost complete freedom from anti-Semitic prejudice." Other Jews such as the Ilfeld, Spiegelberg, and Goldwater families would become important merchants in the Southwest, while Sephardic Jews, with a different language and set of customs, would be notable in the Pacific Northwest.

≈

American families migrating west in the nineteenth century brought with them fairly well-defined beliefs about the nature of family. Between 1770 and 1820 the modern family emerged, including the charting of new standards of behavior for men, women, and children. Often referred to as the Cult of True Womanhood or the doctrine of two spheres, this ideology called for a man to provide a living for his wife and family and to protect them from a surrounding amoral and materialistic man's world or outer sphere. The woman's or inner sphere was to be domestic, home-centered, in which she nurtured their children and helped her husband to gain victory over the pressures of his nondomestic sphere. Children were not to be treated as small adults but as children, to be loved and protected. Unified and whole, the family was to be a companionate unit based on love and mutual respect. Families moving west seemed to adhere more to this ideology than to fashion fresh ideas for a new setting.

Generally, families were at the center of frontier society, as they were in most social settings in nineteenth-century America. Aside from the numerous single young males (white and Chinese) traveling to mining camps, westward-moving pioneers came as parts of families. Judging from the sketchy evidence available, families in the West experienced much the same problems and pressures that perplexed Americans elsewhere.

～

Ironically, even though the history of the American West has been frequently depicted in masculine terms—as a region often uncivilized, uncouth, rough, and two-fisted—little is known about men's reflections concerning western life. But a few scattered glimpses are coming into focus.

True, many of the first happenings in the West were male-directed. Women were not the leaders in western exploration and trapping in the mountains, even though the importance of Sacagawea to Lewis and Clark, the wives and companions of trappers, and the partners of early overlanders like Susan Shelby McGoffin must not be underestimated. In the first mining camps, especially those in California, Nevada, and Colorado, men sometimes outnumbered women more than 12 to 1. Men were also numerically superior in the cattle and sheep businesses. The ideology of the times ruled out most of these activities for women even while suggesting that their presence was needed to curb the acquisitive and violence-prone tendencies of men.

The doctrine of two spheres could not always be adapted to pioneer conditions, however. Isolation, changes in socioeconomic status, and other shifts forced men to deviate from their expected behavior. Distance from other farmers did not keep men from helping neighbors with plowing and harvesting, attending auctions and sales, or going to town for machinery and necessary supplies. Left at home with young children, some wives argued that there were too many men in the West and that they were not as thoughtful of their women as they should be. In this vein one farm woman, Molly Stanford, complained to her diary, "We do not see a woman at all. All men, single or bachelors, and one gets tired of them." Yet some men broke with traditions in carrying out household duties, helping with childbirth, and providing much of the disciplining and rearing of their children. As one farmer pointed out, "I assisted my wife all I could—probably did as much housework as she did." These invasions into the woman's sphere were so atypical they frequently provoked comments in women's diaries.

Other circumstances caused men to break with expected traditions. Where the greatest numbers of men congregated, prostitution often flourished. When men visited houses of ill repute, especially young single males, women accused them of not only abandoning their pledged duties of cherishing good women but also of supporting immoral women, thereby undermining western society.

Sarah Royce in a California mining community delighted in telling the story, for example, of a successful man and his "splendidly dressed woman, well known . . . as the disreputable companion of her wealthy escort" being asked to leave an entertainment because they obviously "tramped upon the institutions which lie at the foundation of morality and civilization." In these criticisms, western women were railing, in fact, against a double standard that, unacceptable to guardians of the doctrine of two spheres, nonetheless occurred widely on the nineteenth-century frontier.

In addition to furnishing a means of living for their families, men were also to establish and maintain institutions that fostered community in the West. Many frontiersmen did just that; they aided in the formation of schools, churches, and volunteer fire and police organizations. Yet even though men were involved in the establishing of schools and churches, women more often than their fathers, husbands, and brothers kept these institutions in operation. If women seemed content to allow their men to head up schools and churches, they did more than men to make these institutions the agents of moral and social order in frontier communities that women wished them to be.

When men were unable to fulfill their expected roles, western families experienced a good deal of tension and frustration. Arthur De Wint Foote, an engineer, was frustrated when unable to provide satisfactorily for his family and wife, Mary Hallock Foote, a well-known writer and illustrator. Even more embarrassing, Mrs. Foote, through her contributions to *Century Magazine* and other eastern literary journals, financially sustained the family. Mary Foote could not easily accept these changed roles, either, defending her husband from the possible criticism of her eastern, genteel friends. Similar tensions arose between men and women in Kansas when women of the state tried to organize relief efforts for destitute farm families. Men pooh-poohed the difficulties these families faced and the relief organizations of their women, suggesting that women's efforts embarrassed men unable to support their families and implying, too, that if help were needed it should come from men's, not women's, actions.

≈

Only recently have histories of the West begun to emphasize appropriately the huge contributions of women to western life. In the nineteenth century, for example, women were more numerous than most early historical accounts indicated. Men outnumbered women two to one in 1850, but women made up 46 percent of the population in 1900. In fact, by the turn of the century the ratio of men to women was substantially the same in the West as in most eastern states. Only in the mining camps and in the earliest stages of other far-western settlements did men greatly outnumber women. In agricultural regions and in other western communities more than a generation old, a near balance of sexes obtained. The West was not devoid of women, the popular stereotypes notwithstanding.

Women played richly diverse roles. Often frontierswomen have been stereotyped as Madonnas of the Prairie, Gentle Tamers, Drudges, and Bad Women. A few western women did fit these images; most did not. Instead, diversity and change over time were the hallmarks of women's experiences in the West. Their actions, too, should be viewed within the constraining ideology of True Womanhood: women were to be pious, pure, submissive, and domestic, the expected roles of women in American society during most of the nineteenth century.

The initial decision to move west was most often a family determination. As families became increasingly companionate and less patriarchal in the 1800s, a momentous decision like leaving home for the West was not to be made by father or husband alone, as it might have been in the eighteenth century. In these increasingly equitable families, the views of wives were solicited and weighed. After some discussion, husbands usually made most of the final decisions about moving. But the style of frontier women, historian Julie Roy Jeffrey writes, "was to respond, to influence, even to argue."

This does not mean, of course, that all women were eager to go west. Many were reluctant pioneers, understandably not wanting to leave their relatives and friends. In 1850, Margaret Hereford Wilson, the grandmother of General George Patton, wrote her mother that she had joined her husband in the trek west because there was "no other alternative. . . . I thought that I felt bad when I wrote you . . . from Independence, but it was nothing like this." Another frontier woman told of her sadness in leaving her Ohio relatives and starting "on this long & . . . perilous journey. . . . It proved a hard task to leave them but still harder to leave my children buried in . . . graveyards." Still another woman, Mary Jane Hayden, emphatically told her husband he had better not go to California without her—and she was unable then to go; and if he did, he "need never return for I shall look upon you as dead."

Even more numerous, however, were those women less reluctant to go west. Perhaps these pioneers wanted to keep their families intact and shared with their husbands the dream of finding a more rewarding life in the new country. One mother, her daughter reported, "was always ready and willing to go." We had nothing to lose, and we might "gain . . . a fortune," another wrote. A third pioneer woman bound for the West Coast enthusiastically recorded, "Ho for California . . . We are off to the promised land." Teenager Mollie Dorsey was even more positive when she related that moving to a new frontier home would provide "a freedom from restraint, and I believe it will be a blessing to we [sic] girls."

Some women were every bit as adventuresome as any frontiersman. Louise

A. K. S. Clappe, better known as Dame Shirley and authoress of revealing letters about remote California mining camps, went willingly—even daringly—with her physician husband to several mining hamlets cockleburred into the gravel bars and hillsides surrounding the Feather River. "This strange, old life fascinates me," she wrote, during a more-than-a year stay. Without children, she could be a "regular Nomad in [her] passion for wandering." Condemning the raw racism and violence of the mining camps, she could also celebrate their freedom from restraint and the beauty of the surrounding mountains. The isolated and rude qualities of the frontier mining camps did not alienate an adventurous woman like Dame Shirley.

Once families arrived in farming areas, women found an endless round of tiring tasks before them. Not only must they keep house—often in dugouts, tents, tar-paper shacks, or sod houses in the first years, they had to work long and hard helping their husbands and fathers prepare the new land and plant the first crops. They also had to "make do," cooking with primitive and limited utensils and stoves until better ones came after a modicum of financial success. No less difficult were the jobs of sewing and mending clothes for their families. There was also the washing of family clothes, which pioneer homemakers unanimously deemed the worst and most taxing of their duties.

More rewarding were hours spent rearing children. Yet attempting to mind toddlers in the midst of preparing meals and helping with farm tasks was nearly more than some women could bear. Most frontier mothers did not complain a good deal about their nurturing duties—except when a new pregnancy threatened to add another burden. Idaho pioneer Emma Thompson Just, for instance, despaired of being able to cope and even thought of suicide when new babies continued to arrive nearly every other year. An impending childbirth for a frontier woman, already with several children and isolated from a doctor and separated from other women, sent paroxysmal attacks of fear into the hearts of some pioneer women.

Despite the pressures of a new and forbidding frontier, women sought to carry out the pledge they made to carry civilization with them to the "barbaric" West. In the opening pages of her journal, eighteen-year-old Mollie Dorsey, although sad about leaving her home and friends in Indianapolis, promised herself that she would make certain there were churches in remote, faraway Nebraska, even if she had to accomplish that goal through her personal missionary work. After she married, Mollie lived in a tent and other rude abodes. Her spirits were considerably lifted, however, when she and her husband later found a comfortable home, one fit for her children and for other women with whom she could set up a network of visits and socialization. Like so many other women in the West, Mollie Dorsey Sanford felt at home when she could replicate on the frontier much of what she had known and relished earlier.

Other western women clearly moved beyond the restrictions of the domestic ideology. Some did so reluctantly, others with the relish of a newly freed captive. Not only did they break with expectations in working out-of-doors in farming; they also forged new traditions by filing for their own land claims as single, adult women. In frontier Colorado and Wyoming between 10 and 20 percent of the homestead entrants were female and perhaps as many as one-third of all homesteaders in the Dakota Territory in 1877 may have been women. In some areas, a higher percentage of women than men "proved up" and gained their homesteads. A few others became ranch women and, in extraordinary cases, cowgirls.

Nowhere were these western working women more obvious as tradition breakers than in urban areas. In the late nineteenth century in California where half of the population lived in cites, women—especially single women, widows and divorcees, and childless married women—worked as domestic servants and factory workers, or became petty proprietors by establishing boarding houses or small businesses in their homes. At the turn of the century, the numbers of women involved in domestic service and needlework dropped off, but those in factories, offices, and stores went up. In West Coast cities and other urban areas, women worked too as teachers, following Catharine Beecher's tenet that teaching was an extension of women's role in their homes as moral and religious instructors.

Women took part in outside-the-home activities that illustrated their breaks from the bond of domesticity. In addition to becoming advocates for churches and schools, they supported measures to curb gambling and drinking. These activities upset some men, who spoke of the reforming women as "meddling females." Men were even more disgruntled with women's efforts to destroy prostitution. Frontier men frequently looked upon prostitution as a necessary evil, neither to be opposed nor supported. But frontier women, often joining with ministers and other moral reformers, attacked the institution as an unnecessary, unacceptable evil. In some areas of the West, prostitutes were numerous yet still well-to-do. This situation occurred particularly in early mining camps in California, where prostitutes were about 20 percent of the female population and outnumbered other California women 25 to 1. But these ratios and stable livelihoods for prostitutes were exceptions; most led hazardous and outcast lives. Often they were victims of brutal male violence, and nearly all were ridiculed or lampooned in local newspapers. Even frontier men who disagreed with women's irritating attacks on prostitution were unwilling to escort "soiled doves" or "ladies of the night" to public social affairs. If women broke well-defined social prescriptions to become prostitutes, they did so with great cost to themselves and to those associated with them.

Toward the end of the nineteenth century, more than a few women in the West became much involved in movements to gain woman suffrage. At first no large, well-organized groups of western women lobbied for their voting rights, but some western women encouraged their husbands and sympathetic male friends to support woman's suffrage through various organizations: the Grange and Farmers' Alliances, women's clubs and other voluntary associations, and women's coalitions for reform. In some situations, particularly in Wyoming and Utah, men seemed to support the vote for women because they were convinced that with this right women voters would support traditional or conservative measures and thus help refurbish the tarnished images of a "wild" Wyoming or a polygamous Utah.

The best known of the woman's suffrage leaders in the West was Oregonian Abigail Scott Duniway. If unusual among western women in her strong support of woman suffrage, Duniway was quite typical of outspoken national leaders favoring the vote for women. Born and reared in Illinois, she moved to the Pacific Northwest in 1852. Married early, Abigail was the wife of Benjamin Duniway, an upstanding but unhealthy and unsuccessful farmer. She had several children and, eventually, became the author of even more books and essays. Always independent and—it is said—hot tempered and sometimes difficult, Abigail early on became known as a person with many strong opinions but specifically those on women's rights. First as a teacher, then as a writer, and finally as an ardent activist, Duniway built a reputation as stalwart advocate of more freedoms and additional rights for frontier women. She faced strong opposition from evangelical and middle-class westerners and, ironically, from her brother Harvey Scott, the well-known editor of the Portland *Oregonian*, the most influential newspaper of the Pacific Northwest. Duniway edited the feminist periodical *New Northwest* and wrote hundreds of fiery essays in behalf of her causes. A person no one could ignore, she became a "rebel for rights," the most notable western feminist of the pioneer era.

One must ask key questions at this point: Were women's experiences in the frontier West liberating? Did their lives in the new country encourage them to break with the systems of thought and culture they had followed in the East or that their eastern parents and communities had taught them? Some pioneer women obviously thought so. Those who agree and stress the innovating power of the West cite historian Frederick Jackson Turner's arguments that the frontier often broke the cake of eastern customs. Other observers, beginning from a feminist perspective, assert that active—not passive—women liberated themselves in their assertive, risk-taking actions.

Bulking just as large, however, were the persisting influences of eastern

FIGURE 9:4. *Abigail Scott Duniway, Western Suffragist.* No one did more than Oregonian Abigail Scott Duniway to further woman's suffrage in the West. In her later years she witnessed her diligent efforts come to fruition. Courtesy Idaho State Historical Society, 461.

experiences and the domestic ideology. Women often took part in community reform activities not because they wish to become tradition-breakers but because they feared their communities were fragmenting and needed further support to ensure retention of traditional values and morals. These women were convinced that they must expand their spheres of moral leadership from their homes to their neighborhoods. At the same time, women who adhered to the conservative domestic ideology were not necessarily passive. Indeed, they actively sought for and supported measures by which they could ensure tranquility and more order in a wider sphere. Even when women went to the Far West in the tradition-breaking capacity of single missionaries, they went to the far country to civilize the West, to make sure that the new region would be safe for families, that it would live by the preconceived notions of the domestic ideology. In the end, whatever one concludes about women's experiences in the pioneer West, their lives and deeds were pivotal, molding parts of the frontier social order.

~

If women received little attention in early western histories, children were even more invisible. The usual picture is of large families with numerous children who were forced early on to work as adults because of the large labor needs on the frontier. For these children there was no childhood, only the early, quick transition to adulthood. Census and personal records tell a more complex story.

First of all, families of white, native-born westerners were substantially the same size as other American families, which diminished in the average number of children from 7.04 in 1800 to 4.24 in 1880 and 3.56 in 1900. Pioneer women undoubtedly used their growing power within families to limit the number of their children, and a few private, personal sources indicate that they used a variety of birth control devices—including abortions—particularly after they had borne two or three children.

Nor did pioneers marry as young as the stereotypes suggest. Texas and Oregon males were often in their thirties or forties before they married, with their wives considerably younger, usually in their twenties. Families with fewer children allowed mothers to spend more time in nurturing each offspring, which nineteenth-century Americans began increasingly to expect.

Childhood took on new meaning too. Instead of viewing the earliest years as merely a brief prologue to adulthood, Americans in the 1800s began to see childhood as a separate time to be cherished. Children were to be encouraged to play, to enjoy times of leisure, but their early years were also to be a period in which they were schooled and trained for adult work. Families on the frontier were coming to agree with the adage that "all work and no play makes Jack [and Jill] a dull boy [and girl]."

Travelers to the Rocky Mountains camps saw vestiges of both systems at work. Children had time for play, and yet many were already working at a tender age. Narratives of mining camp life, like those of the overland trails, depict children playing and attending parties and holiday festivities as well as going to church and school. Even those youngsters lacking a father or mother found many adults, especially lonesome miners thinking of their own children left behind, as surrogate parents. Sarah Bixby-Smith remembered rounds of visits, holidays, and school days during her girlhood on a southern California sheep ranch in the 1870s. "Young people did not have time to be lonely," she wrote; there were too many interesting activities before her mid-teen years. Edith Stratton Kitt also had pleasant memories about growing up in Arizona in the 1880s and 1890s. In addition to playing outdoor games with an Indian boy and her brothers and sisters, she recollected fondly the series of houses in which her family lived. Her rough-and-tumble, tomboyish life was not much different from that of Agnes Morley Cleaveland, who came to adulthood on a ranch in central New Mexico. She too relished girlhood memories that included many escapades, particularly long horseback rides and a variety of competitive games.

Other accounts of frontier life portray a less carefree side to childhood. Many children soon realized that their fathers and mothers, with numerous farm and town chores, needed the help of all family members to keep up with mountains of work. Boys began feeding work animals, caring for other livestock, and weeding fields; girls were quickly introduced to cooking, cleaning, and sewing. Many frontier boys and girls knew the differences between masculine and feminine work roles by their early teens because they had already experienced these sexual divisions of labor for several years. One traveler in the Rockies discovered what seems incredible from more than a century later: preschool children working alongside adults in the mines. Laboring next to rough miners and other hardscrabble men and women was hardly positive for children. They often took up the habits of these companions—chewing tobacco, swearing, gambling, and fighting—and too early adopted the acquisitive and boisterous ways of their elders. In families where a single parent or both father and mother were forced to work away from home, children were allowed to fend for themselves. Even prostitutes bore children, and one can only imagine how early some of these frontier "young folks" were introduced to adult-like problems.

Anglo-American children's experiences in the pioneer West illustrated the tensions between ideal and real families of the nineteenth century. Americans might be becoming more convinced that childhood should be a separate, happy time for young people, but they also believed that work was good for people and that children should learn this valuable lesson. Pressing labor needs and a lack of money forced many western families to deviate from the ideal, carefree childhood they hoped for their children. The ambiguities, the conflicts, between these two views of childhood shaped the experiences of many young westerners. As western historian Elliott West writes, "the key to understanding the uniqueness of pioneer childhood is not in the children's special kinship with the new country. Nor is it in their elders' obsession with passing on their own values. Rather, it is in the mingling of these two powerful, contrasting influences."

FIGURE 9:5. *Frontier Black Family*. Frontier families, here the Nebraska African American family of J. W. Speese in 1888, often gathered in front of their sod houses to pose for photographers. Courtesy Nebraska State Historical Society, RG 2608. PH:1345.

≈

When Harvard philosopher Josiah Royce prepared in the 1880s an analytical history of his natal California, he concluded that the state and its early Anglo residents exhibited most of the imperfections hindering a sense of community in the American West. Royce asserted that a self-aggrandizing individualism, an incipient racism, an abdication of social responsibility, and a tendency to glorify unheroic leaders undermined efforts to establish a spirit of community in California. Not surprisingly, Californians were displeased with Royce's probing comments, and these comments rarely attract addicts to a romantic Old West more than a century later. But his wise, revealing observations help us to understand much of pioneer society.

Many of the fragmenting forces Royce identified in California's past were endemic in other sections of the West. These impulses, including competition between rural and urban parts of the frontier, conflicts between native-born westerners and immigrants as well as between whites and other races, and struggles among classes, were large barriers to those pioneers hoping to foster strong feelings of social unity in the West.

Another trend undermined efforts aimed at western unification. Toward the end of the nineteenth century, western farmers, as they did elsewhere in the nation, began migrating to cities. They went for adventure, for jobs, and for what they thought would be a better future. But two capable hands, a strong back, and a willingness to work were not always sufficient. Incoming rural migrants became a glut on urban labor markets and stirred up urbanites' animosities toward them. Many farm families in the 1880s and 1890s were also convinced that urban residents cared little about the hard times that came to agricultural areas and were uninterested in helping farm families. Differences between western farmers and urban dwellers were also clarified in the election of 1896 when William Jennings Bryan garnered the votes of most Plains farmers, but he was unsuccessful, by and large, in gaining support among urban workers of the West.

Even more dramatic were conflicts among whites and other racial and ethnic groups. As we have seen, whites generally backed all military and political efforts to place Native Americans on reservations and turn them into farmers. In California, tax and land laws favored whites and often dispossessed Hispanics and barred Asians from immigrating. If these enactments failed to achieve exclusionist purposes, vigilantes, riots, and lynchings were more direct—and sometimes deadly. These attitudes and actions toward Hispanics and Asians, particularly, were common in several parts of the Southwest and along the West Coast. On occasions Hispanics fought back, sometimes through social bandits such Joaquín Murrieta (California) and Juan Cortina (Texas) or through the united efforts of *Las Gorras Blancas* (white caps), who tried to fight off Anglos and ricos threatening their lands in New Mexico.

Class differences likewise forestalled a sense of social community. From the first contacts, Anglo immigrants rarely considered lowly Indians and downtrodden Hispanics as sociocultural equals in western society. By the end of the nineteenth century mine workers as well as urban laborers or the poor were also clearly at the opposite end of the social ladder from mine owners and magnates such as Charles Crocker, Mark Hopkins, and Leland Stanford, ensconced in their huge mansions on San Francisco's Nob Hill. Seeing these disparities of wealth and power firsthand in California, writer Henry George attacked monopolistic control of land and urged its return to common people in his trenchant treatise *Progress and Poverty* (1879).

Other observers of the nineteenth century infrequently talked of another barrier to community-building: incessant mobility. Westerners in cities and towns and on farms moved on, rarely staying in one location for long periods of time. With social and economic life retaining an essential fluidity, frontier men and women, particularly Anglo immigrants, could rise from near-poverty to middle-class status in scarcely one generation. In addition, the West was peopled so rapidly, it moved so quickly from Indian-dominated areas to agricultural or urban settlements in the nineteenth century, that community builders were hard pressed to establish traditions that outlasted the disintegrating pressures of the next wave of newcomers. Boston took two centuries to reach a population of 100,000, a size San Francisco attained in less than twenty years. Denver and Seattle zoomed from little more than forest clearings to cities of 100,000 in about three decades. If pioneers seemed born with itchy feet and ever on the move, new people stampedes followed so quickly and directly on the heels of earlier migrants that community traditions were difficult to establish, let alone maintain. Clearly the physical, economic, and social mobility of large numbers of westerners was often an insurmountable barrier to a settled, orderly social life on the frontier.

Still, one should not think of life in the West as a steady, unending series of disruptive social hiccups. No matter how much popularizers, chiefly fictionists and film-makers, depict the frontier as a Wild West of violence and chaos, it was not just the home of Billy the Kid, Calamity Jane, and Geronimo. Indeed, the West was not more—if in fact as—violent as other regions of the United States. Cattle towns in Kansas and mining camps in Nevada and California, to take two examples, were less violence-riven than eastern cities and much less so than modern American urban areas. Yet images of an antisocial, conflictual frontier dominate our visions of the pioneer American West.

To the contrary, feelings of community existed in many parts of the West. In the Great Basin, the strong sense of group identity among the Mormons struck many travelers. Writers also commented on the cohesion among immigrants and racial and ethnic groups. Observers mentioned Sunday schools, churches, schools, and voluntary organizations as symbols of community consciousness in rural and urban sections of the West. At the end of the nineteenth century in western cities, groups of diverse reformers were beginning to sense, in common, the need to take on the bloated railroad, mining, and other corporations stealing from the middle and lower classes. Their growing unity became apparent in the Progressive reform movements of the early twentieth century. And in New Mexico and some other parts of the Southwest, Spanish and Indian groups had intermarried to produce Mexican or other mestizo populations. These mixed-race peoples became a new native-born ethnic group of the American Southwest and of countries to the south. Despite these selective evidences of community-building, it must be admitted that these widely separated "island communities" rarely spread beyond their religious, racial, ethnic, occupational, or town or city groups to forge a larger regional identity. Such expanding, unifying efforts would have to wait until the twentieth century.

~

So, if the West of the late nineteenth century was not entirely a society of conflict and chaos, neither had it become a close-knit, well-defined community. Tensions between rural and urban areas, conflicts among diverse racial and ethnic elements, and geographical and economic mobility conspired to keep the West from establishing long-lasting, unifying social traditions. The region's social character by 1900 was an intriguing mosaic of diversity, nascent societies attempting to capture and homogenize varied social experiences. Similar changes and complexities challenged westerners searching for a coherent regional cultural identity.

Armitage, Susan, and Elizabeth Jameson, eds. *The Women's West.* Norman: University of Oklahoma Press, 1987.

Barth, Gunther. *Instant Cities: Urbanization and the Rise of San Francisco and Denver.* 1975; Albuquerque: University of New Mexico Press, 1988.

Basso, Matthew, Laura McCall, and Dee Garceau. *Across the Great Divide: Cultures of Manhood in the American West.* New York: Routledge, 2001.

Butler, Anne M. *Daughters of Joy, Sisters of Misery: Prostitutes in the American West, 1865–90.* Urbana: University of Illinois Press, 1985.

Chan, Sucheng, et al., eds. *Peoples of Color in the American West.* Lexington, MA: D. C. Heath, 1994.

Daniels, Roger. *Asian America: Chinese and Japanese in the United States since 1850.* Seattle: University of Washington Press, 1988.

Deutsch, Sarah. *No Separate Refuge: Culture, Class, and Gender on an Anglo-Hispanic Frontier in the American Southwest, 1880–1940.* New York: Oxford University Press, 1987.

Deverell, William. *Whitewashed Adobe: The Rise of Los Angeles and the Remaking of Its Mexican Past.* Berkeley: University of California Press, 2004.

Garceau, Dee. *The Important Things of Life: Women, Work, and Family in Sweetwater Country, Wyoming, 1880–1929.* Lincoln: University of Nebraska Press, 1997.

Hampsten, Elizabeth. *Settlers' Children: Growing Up on the Great Plains.* Norman: University of Oklahoma Press, 1991.

Hine, Robert V. *Community on the American Frontier: Separate But Not Alone.* Norman: University of Oklahoma Press, 1980.

Holt, Marilyn Irvin. *Children of the Western Plains: The Nineteenth-Century Experience.* Chicago: Ivan Dee, 2003.

Jameson, Elizabeth, and Susan Armitage, eds. *Writing the Range: Race, Class, and Culture in the Women's West.* Norman: University of Oklahoma Press, 1997.

Jeffrey, Julie Roy. *Frontier Women: "Civilizing" the West? 1840–1880.* Rev. ed. New York: Hill and Wang, 1998.

Larsen, Lawrence H. *The Urban West at the End of the Frontier.* Lawrence: Regents Press of Kansas, 1978.

Lotchin, Roger W. *San Francisco, 1846–1856: From Hamlet to City.* New York: Oxford University Press, 1974.

Luchetti, Cathy. *Children of the West: Family Life on the Frontier.* New York: W. W. Norton, 2001.

Luebke, Frederick C., ed. *Ethnicity on the Great Plains.* Lincoln: University of Nebraska Press, 1980.

Luebke, Frederick C., ed. *European Immigrants in the American West: Community Histories.* Albuquerque: University of New Mexico Press, 1998.

May, Dean L. *Three Frontiers: Family, Land, and Society in the American West, 1850–1900*. New York: Cambridge University Press, 1994.

Mitchell, Pablo. *Coyote Nation: Sexuality, Race, and Conquest in Modernizing New Mexico, 1880–1920*. Chicago: University of Chicago Press, 2005.

Montejano, David. *Anglos and Mexicans in the Making of Texas, 1836–1986*. Austin: University of Texas Press, 1987.

Montoya, María E. *Translating Property: The Maxwell Land Grant and the Conflict Over Land in the American West, 1840–1900*. Berkeley: University of California Press, 2002.

Myres, Sandra L. *Westering Women and the Frontier Experience 1800–1915*. Albuquerque: University of New Mexico Press, 1982.

Nugent, Walter. *Into the West: The Story of Its People*. New York: Alfred A. Knopf, 1999.

Pascoe, Peggy. *Relations of Rescue: The Search for Female Moral Authority in the American West, 1874–1939*. New York: Oxford University Press, 1990.

Pomeroy, Earl. *The Pacific Slope*. New York: Alfred A. Knopf, 1966.

Riley, Glenda. *Women and Indians on the Frontier, 1825–1915*. Albuquerque: University of New Mexico Press, 1984.

Takaki, Ronald. *Strangers from a Different Shore: A History of Asian Americans*. Boston: Little, Brown and Company, 1989.

Taylor, Quintard. *In Search of the Racial Frontier: African Americans in the American West, 1528–1990*. New York: W. W. Norton, 1998.

Tsai, Shih-Shan Henry. *The Chinese Experience in America*. Bloomington: Indiana University Press, 1986.

West, Elliott. *Growing Up with the Country: Childhood on the Far Western Frontier*. Albuquerque: University of New Mexico Press, 1989.

Wheeler, Kenneth W. *To Wear a City's Crown: The Beginnings of Urban Growth in Texas, 1836–1865*. Cambridge, MA: Harvard University Press, 1968.

Zhu, Liping. *A Chinaman's Chance: The Chinese on the Rocky Mountain Mining Frontier*. Niwot: University Press of Colorado, 1997.

CHAPTER TEN

Culture in the Frontier West

∿

WHEN THE YOUTHFUL BUT ALREADY CELEBRATED AUTHOR AND REPORTER Stephen Crane swung west across the Great Plains and Texas in 1895, he encountered a country that failed to live up to the tall tales he had heard about the West. Believing that the West was wild—if not primitive and barbaric—he found instead a region that seemed more mild than wild. The East and civilization had already invaded the frontier. In Nebraska, "yellow trolly-cars with clanging gongs" were "an almost universal condition," convincing him that "travelers tumbling over each other in their haste to trumpet the radical differences between Eastern and Western life" had "created a generally wrong opinion." Crane's contemporary, journalist and traveler Richard Harding Davis, had sounded a similar note three years earlier in *The West from a Car-Window*. Travelers to the West, Davis wrote, too often "show the differences that exist between the places they have visited and their own home. Of the similarities they say nothing."

Most other visitors, however, spoke of a tradition-breaking West. When eastern writer Owen Wister began going west in the mid-1880s, he was impressed with its novel qualities. He was drawn to the remoteness of Wyoming, the free-and-easy ways of people in the Southwest and Northwest, and differences, generally, between East and West. In 1889, the brilliant young English writer and traveler Rudyard Kipling ventured up the Pacific Coast, across Montana and Utah, and finally through Denver and Omaha. Like Wister, he enthusiastically embraced western scenery, celebrated what he considered the free and open spirit of much of the West, and especially noted its go-ahead, tub-thumping patriotism and progressive spirit. Yet in his *American Notes* (1891) he also hinted that westerners had been inflicted with American materialism, that they were inclined to sell off their abundant natural resources, and that they catered too willingly to the hordes of builders and tourists who swarmed like angry ants over sections of the region.

These conflicting reactions are keys to understanding the complexities of culture in the nineteenth-century American West. Crane and Davis were on target in viewing the West as something of a cultural colony of the East, in which eastern and European influences traveled west with immigrants. Conversely, the unique terrain and space, the novel social and ethnic mixes, and the rapidity of settlement in the West that Wister and Kipling noted were also shaping factors in the region's culture. Although most Americans of the nineteenth century—and perhaps a majority in the twentieth and twenty-first centuries—looked upon the West as a section distinctly different from the rest of the United States and acted on the assumed correctness of these observations, a close look at the literature, art, religion, and education of the pioneer West reveals a more complex, often ambiguous experience. Clearly the struggle of the West to find its identity—as an offshoot of the East; as a separate, unique region; or as an amalgam of these two traditions—is the major characteristic of western pioneer culture during the nineteenth century.

~

The image of the American frontier as a Wild West gradually emerged over the course of several centuries. Well before Europeans visited the American West in the sixteenth century, they had dreamed of it. Some of their dreams drew upon age-old visions of the West as Eden, as paradise, as the destiny of nations, or as the direction of all great empires. Other European visions, more closely tied to their first experiences in the New World, envisioned the West as Cíbola (the fabled Seven Golden Cities of the Spanish), as a Passage to India, as the home of larger-than-life heroes, or as the Great American Desert or the Garden of the World.

American experiences on the earliest frontiers of the New World added other ingredients to the cluster of ideas that grew up around the American West. New England Puritans, for instance, spoke of the frontier as a howling wilderness, infested with a dark Devil and his minions and with barbaric Indians. Yet they and others were gradually forced by economic circumstances to move out onto that evil frontier. In facing this necessity, Puritans constructed Indian captivity narratives that depicted these experiences as a test of one's spirituality. Gradually, these accounts were transformed into non-Puritan narratives with military or hunter heroes like Daniel Boone serving as civilization bringers to a remote region inhabited by uncivilized Indians.

These complex, varied images colored the visions of travelers to or writers about the West in the nineteenth century. Despite their variety, these myths about the West had a unifying core: since the West was less advanced than the East, it needed civilizing agents, and progress dictated that less advanced people and ideologies must give way to higher laws of progress and civilization. The West was truly wild—in need of giant doses of society and culture, which the East alone could provide.

This Wild West ideology powered much thinking and planning about the West in the nineteenth century. Religious and educational leaders such as Lyman Beecher and his daughter Catharine pointed to the frontier as a vital part of the country's future, but a territory that needed to be "saved" through an infusion of ministers and teachers. Political and economic elites reiterated this need to win the West from lesser peoples and to preserve it for worthy Americans. Given this rather widespread consensus about the West, it is not surprising that much writing about the region in the nineteenth century depicted it as a wild, unsettled section.

In the decades after the Civil War, these depictions of a Wild West took two forms. One was the treatment of historical figures as larger-than-life characters in history, biography, and fiction. The other was the creation of legendary figures, based usually on oral traditions, who figured prominently in folklore and literature. Biographers and historians often used historical figures such as Billy the Kid, Calamity Jane, Wild Bill Hickok, and Kit Carson to create the sensational heroes and heroines needed to capture a Wild West. In these romantic accounts Billy the Kid kills a bad man for each of his twenty-one years, Calamity Jane rides and shoots like a hellcat, Wild Bill is flashingly quick with his fists and guns, and the small, wiry Kit Carson becomes a ring-tailed roarer, a gigantic Samson. Since for these writers the West was a wild, forbidding place, only historical persons depicted as strong-armed demigods could be victorious and thus pave the way for western settlement.

The most significant of the historical figures who became legends in their own time was William Frederick "Buffalo Bill" Cody. A former pony express rider, buffalo hunter, scout, and Indian fighter, Cody also fathered the Wild West show, which probably did more than any other attraction to popularize the West as a wild frontier. As western novelist Larry McMurtry perceptively notes, Cody and his best-known Wild West performer, Annie Oakley, became "the first American superstars . . ." In Cody's becoming a superstar, McMurtry adds, he and "his audience were one": "they wanted the West, the gloriously dangerous West, the mythic romantic West, the cowboy-and-Indian West, and Cody came closer to giving it to them than anyone else. . . ." Cody was an experienced frontiersman, a compelling dramatist of his exploits, and a perceptive judge of Americans' instincts. He marshaled all these experiences and talents when he opened the first Wild West exhibition in 1883. He dramatized one frenetic scene after another: stagecoach holdups, trick riding and shooting, Indian fights, and appearances of Annie Oakley ("Little Sure Shot"), Buck Taylor ("King of the Cowboys"), and Chief Sitting Bull. So successful was Cody's *Wild West* show that it toured the United States for many years and even made appearances in several European cities. It also inspired competitors. Others, seeing the popularity of Buffalo Bill's extravaganzas, copied his program, and together they began a tradition of similar frontier exhibitions that lasted well into the 1930s. If audiences had questions about the nature of the American West, Cody and his *Wild West* and other such blowouts assured them that it was indeed a land of riders, ropers, and renegades—superheroes of the sagebrush. Conversely, there were no places for farmers and city citizens.

In the fertile twilight zone between fact and imagination legendary frontier heroes took root late in the nineteenth and early twentieth centuries. In the northern West, the gigantic lumberjack Paul Bunyan and his enormous bovine companion Babe the Blue Ox stalked through forests and lumber camps like

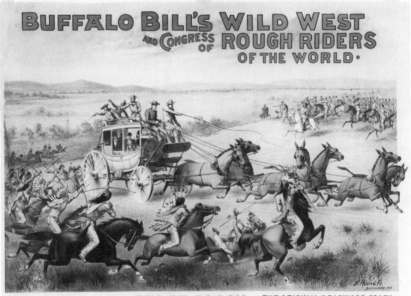

FIGURE 10:1. *On the Stagecoach, circa 1887.* Buffalo Bill's arena show *Wild West*, dramatizing dozens of memorable stories of competition, such as this action-filled scene of Indians attacking the Deadwood Stage, provided a pioneering cultural narrative for later western stories. Courtesy Buffalo Bill Historical Center, Cody, Wyoming; Gift of the Coe Foundation; 1.69.107.

a whirlwind armed with sharp axes. When Paul mistakenly dragged his spiked pole he gouged out the Grand Canyon. Together Paul and Babe hollowed out Puget Sound—Paul used a glacier for a scoop—so they could have a place to store their logs. Following in Bunyan's seven-league strides was Pecos Bill, the supercowboy of the Southwest who rode a mountain lion with barbed wire reins, or Febold Feboldson, the titanic Nebraska farmer who fashioned knots in the tails of tornados as they flashed over the plains. Here was a pantheon of manufactured gargantuan western heroes whose mien and deeds illustrate the fearless, mighty people needed to save and settle the West.

At the same time that popular histories, biographies, newspaper stories, and such events as the Wild West shows were launching the careers of several historical and legendary Wild West heroes and heroines, the dime novel Western arose to provide a new outlet. The discovery of an inexpensive method of printing newspapers and books, especially nickel and dime novels from pulp paper, allowed publishing firms to turn out thousands of cheap novels for the tidal wave of new readers after the Civil War. More than half of these sensationalized novels dealt with the frontier of the American West, thereby greatly increasing the possibilities for overly dramatic and sentimentalized depictions of the Wild West.

From the 1860s on dozens of authors, nearly all of whom were easterners with little knowledge of the West, utilized such new heroes as Kit Carson, Billy the Kid, Calamity Jane, and Buffalo Bill for their dime novels. No matter that the lives of these protagonists were created without fear or research; eastern readers bought dime novels by the hundreds of thousands and evidently believed much of what they were reading about a region and society foreign to them. Not content with revising and tinkering with the lives of historical characters, other writers created fictional frontier figures such as Deadwood Dick, Rattlesnake Ned, and the Black Avenger. They too were endowed with the physical prowess, stamina, and derring-do that characterized their historical brothers and sisters. Authors of dime novels were more than happy to provide whatever kind of characters satisfied the wish-needs of their readers.

But the pell-mell actions of these stereotyped characters who could ride like the wind, kill several Indians with one hand, and also win the heroine's attention could become tiresome. By the 1890s sales of dime novels had fallen off rapidly—just as the cowboy, the newest, most romantic figure, galloped onto the scene. Even though some of the earliest literary and artistic depictions of the cowpuncher treated him as unruly and in need of a dose of refinement, by the time novelist Owen Wister and artist Frederic Remington became his champions in the 1890s they pictured him as a buoyant, romantic hero stripped of the excessive heroics of earlier Wild West characters but sufficiently vivacious and charming to gain large audiences for theirs and similar works dealing with the

FIGURE 10:2. *Deadwood Dick on Deck.* Dime novels feverishly attracted
hundreds of thousands of readers by featuring sensational stories
of a Wild West. This dime novel by E. L. Wheeler starred detective
Deadwood Dick and heroine Calamity Jane. Author's collection.

cowboy. The publication of Wister's cowboy stories in leading magazines of the 1890s—often accompanied by Remington illustrations—and the eventual appearance of his classic Western *The Virginian* (1902) prepared the way for a long line of popular Westerns stretching from the works of Zane Grey, Ernest Haycox, and Luke Short down to the Westerns of the most popular writer of them all, Louis L'Amour. Although these popular Westerns were more literary than the dime novels, they too capitulated before the hunger for a Wild West that arose well before 1900 and continues to the present. Even though the Wild West tradition has not exclusively dominated the literary West, it has outstripped another western literary tradition of the nineteenth century.

∾

Not all explorers, travelers, and writers fell victim to the strong-armed and hairy-chested school of Wild West literature. Indeed, beginning early in the nineteenth century, other travelers and authors attempted to depict what they considered the real West, or at least one ostensibly based on fact. These efforts, appearing throughout the century, provide an alternative vision of the far frontier.

In the opening decades of the nineteenth century such explorers as Meriwether Lewis and William Clark, Zebulon Pike, and Stephen H. Long (Long's account was written by Edwin James) produced factual records of their expeditions into the West, emphasizing first of all what they saw and did. Rather than primarily providing imaginative reshapings of their experiences, these writers stressed the flora and fauna they encountered, described the terrain they crossed, and furnished rather straightforward descriptions of western Indian groups. Although nearly two-thirds of the Lewis and Clark journals were excised by the prudish Philadelphia lawyer Nicholas Biddle before they were published and much of their freshness emasculated, and although James's account of the Long expedition misled many Americans for nearly a half-century into thinking the central and lower Plains were a Great American Desert, these accounts were much less romanticized and exaggerated than the works of the Wild West tradition.

Three other well-known eastern literary figures—James Fenimore Cooper, Washington Irving, and Francis Parkman—published notable works about the West in the generation from the 1820s to the 1840s. A man of country gentry backgrounds who had never traveled west of his native New York, Cooper created the most notable frontier hero of the nineteenth century, Natty Bumppo, or the Deerslayer, in his five-volume Leatherstocking Saga. Obviously drawn to his hero and the wilderness he inhabited, Cooper also betrayed ambivalence about Natty's uncivilized and sometimes boorish behavior. As English writer and critic D. H. Lawrence explained, Cooper loved Natty but seemed afraid that he would belch at dinner.

The historical volumes of Irving and Parkman, who both made short visits to the West, contain similar ambivalences. During a month-long stay in what is present-day Oklahoma, Irving took copious factual notes and later read widely in appropriate historical works for his writings on the West, but when he prepared such works as *A Tour of the Prairies* (1835), *Astoria* (1836), and *The Adventures of Captain Bonneville* (1837) for publication, he "shaped" his notes, separating the uncivilized West from the cultured East, romanticizing the wilderness through which his explorers trudged, and making explicit social distinctions between his unpolished frontiersmen and their sophisticated eastern companions.

Upper-class Bostonian Francis Parkman followed this pattern of love for a primitive and pristine wilderness but snobbish distaste for many who inhabited this Eden. From his earliest years Parkman cultivated a "cult of masculinity," much as three other easterners—Teddy Roosevelt, Owen Wister, and Frederic Remington—would do at the end of the century. Yet once in the wilderness with Indians and frontiersmen—"the society of savages and men little better than savages"—Parkman produced his classic account *The Oregon Trail* (1849). It was as much a work illustrating the ethnocentrism of a Proper Bostonian as a factual account of the frontier in the late 1840s.

By the outbreak of the Civil War, literature about the West had fallen into two recognizable patterns. Some travelers had written factual records of what they had seen and done; other narratives, like those of Irving and Parkman, were as much revelations of the writer's biases as historical narratives. All these books were by outsiders, the West through eastern eyes. Although exhibiting no single viewpoint, these writings often revealed an ambivalence that embraced the open landscapes and freedom of the West on the one hand but hesitated to accept frontier characters and sociocultural life on the other.

Before the Civil War Europeans and easterners produced the bulk of literature about the West, but by the mid-1860s writers with extensive western experiences or backgrounds began to treat the West. When Mark Twain's lively sketch "The Celebrated Jumping Frog of Calaveras County" appeared in a New York journal in 1865 and Bret Harte's local stories in California's *Overland Monthly* in the 1860s, these writers were immediately hailed as something novel on the American literary scene. They were labeled authentic new voices from the West.

And they were pathbreaking in combining three particulars of western culture: dialect, frontier settings, and local customs. In their attempts to capture the resonances of western life, local colorists like Twain and Harte were setting important precedents. Eschewing many of the idealized settings and characters in American romantic literature of the pre–Civil War era, Local Color writers moved toward the greater verisimilitude of the realists of the late nineteenth century. But these two authors—and other Local Color writers such as Joaquin Miller, Mary Hallock Foote, and Alfred Henry Lewis—were also reluctant realists. Harte wrote about prostitutes and gamblers, Twain about uncouth miners and frontier people, and Lewis about awkward cowboys and cow-town citizens, but these ungenteel characters are treated romantically. They are given clean hearts and pure motives beneath rough and crude exteriors. Western Local Color writers compromised their realism by idealizing their undesirables so as not to affront eastern drawing-room and editorial sensibilities. Foote admitted, for example, that she sometimes revised the content and endings of her stories to please her editor.

The palpable center for much western Local Color writing was San Francisco. As the leading city of the West in the 1860s, San Francisco became the site for a throbbing western urban culture. The city featured numerous newspapers and several literary magazines. When in 1868 the *Overland Monthly* began publication as the western imitation of New England's *Atlantic Monthly*, San Francisco had its important regional journal. Twain's presence in the Mother Lode country and in San Francisco in the 1860s, his popular sketches of the 1860s, and his humorous account of overland trail and mining camp life in *Roughing It* (1872) pointed to San Francisco and California as the vortex of western literary activity. So did Harte's stories such as "The Luck of Roaring Camp," The Outcast of Poker Flats," and "Tennessee's Partner." Twain soon left for Hawai'i, the Holy Land, and Connecticut, with Harte removing to the East Coast and then Europe. But San Francisco drew other writers. By the turn of the century newcomers Frank Norris and Jack London became the Bay Area's new literary lions.

By the late 1890s the appearance of Norris, London, and—even earlier— Hamlin Garland signaled the birth of a new literary movement. It would come to fruition in the early twentieth century. Dissatisfied with the reluctant realism of the Local Color writers and abhorring the Wild West literary tradition, this triumvirate of western realists called for more veracious fictional treatments of farmers and ranchers, hoboes and sailors, and western city folk. Read from the perspectives of a century later, their works seem not so realistic and sometimes even lugubriously sentimental, but in demanding that western fiction demonstrate the shaping power of setting and environment on character development they were moving a giant step beyond the Local Color writers. In addition, in Garland's stories in *Main-Travelled Roads* (1891), Norris's novels *McTeague* (1899) and *The Octopus* (1901), and London's fiction *Call of the Wild* (1903), *The Iron Heel* (1908), and *Martin Eden* (1909), these writers were veering toward the naturalists and regionalists of the twentieth century. Writers in these two groups were even more certain that setting must form—perhaps even bruise or abuse—character. In their stress on this new relationship between environment and character, Garland, Norris, and London became a bridge between the Local Color writers of the nineteenth century and the regionalists of the 1920s and 1930s.

By the close of the nineteenth century authors had introduced a new West. They had shown to eastern readers—as well as to a growing number of followers in the West—a vast, unpeopled region, containing eye-stretching plains and mountains, a host of varied Indian groups, and new character types such as trappers, miners, and cowboys. The Local Color writers pioneered in dealing with the novel speech patterns, customs, and lifestyles of this new country, but they overlooked the activities of the most numerous westerners: farmers and city dwellers. Also, their sketches and stories owed as much to their ties to the European and eastern American literary traditions of Charles Dickens, Robert Louis Stevenson, and Nathaniel Hawthorne as to the new frontier life they encountered. As a result, western American literature hung balanced between the new and the old, the West and the East, as the new century dawned.

~

Eastern and foreign artists in the early nineteenth century endeavored to capture the flora and fauna, the animals, and the Indians and earliest white men for their viewers. Yet like the earliest depictions of the New World in the sixteenth and seventeenth centuries, the art produced in both cases seems to be as much what the painters were predisposed to see as what appeared before their eyes. To expect otherwise, however, is to misunderstand the staying power of social conditioning and cultural baggage. The American West of these artists, like that of their literary brothers and sisters, was an amalgam of what they already believed as well as the new scenes and people they encountered.

Since a variety of artists with diverse backgrounds came west to paint, one should expect that the West became a richly varied region transfixed or transformed in their artistic works. It was. From the earliest paintings in the nineteenth century through the artworks of Frederic Remington and Charles Russell at the century's end, diversity and change were the key ingredients of art about the West. In addition, these artists, like those who wrote most of the literature about the region, were nonwesterners. Every notable painter of the nineteenth century who emphasized the West—with the possible exception of Russell—was a European or an American from the East.

The painters of the 1830s—George Catlin, Karl Bodmer, and Alfred Jacob Miller—produced the first memorable art about the West. The least well-trained of the triumvirate, American George Catlin, visited the Mandans and other Plains Indians early in the decade and made later trips to the southern

Plains and West Coast. He is best known for his series of remarkably descriptive and sympathetic images of Plains Natives, which epitomize his raw talents as a painter. His first exhibitions in the 1830s and the publication of his two-volume *Letters and Notes on the Manners, Customs and Conditions of the North American Indians* (1841) and *North American Indian Portfolio* (1844) illustrate his profound interests in color and Indian dress. Conversely, he was unable to depict Natives in action or to catch their emotions.

Swiss draftsman Karl Bodmer rivaled Catlin as the first notable artist of western Indians. He came west initially as a companion to Prince Maximilian of Wied-Neuwied in a memorable tour of the upper Missouri in 1833–34. Painting in the bitter cold and in awkward conditions that limited the range of his palette, Bodmer nonetheless drew notable battle scenes of Indians in such paintings as *Assiniboine-Cree Attack on a Piegan Camp Outside Fort McKenzie* (1833) and a scene rich in ethnographic detail, *Interior of a Mandan Earth Lodge* (1833).

Catlin and Bodmer were intrigued with Plains Indians, but American artist Alfred Jacob Miller painted the only noteworthy group of portraits dealing with the mountain men. Miller traveled west with his wealthy Scots sponsor Sir William Drummond Stewart in the summer of 1837. The artwork from that trip and others drew on Miller's training in European Romantic art to place his trappers, as well as his depictions of Indians, against romantic backdrops that sometimes overshadowed his subjects. Miller also used his oils and watercolors to sketch out the spacious expanses of western land and thereby betrayed his limited interest in the details of people and specific settings, ingredients that so intrigued Catlin and Bodmer. On the other hand, his romantic notions about frontiersmen and landscapes were a notable prefigurement of Albert Bierstadt's compelling scenes.

Other artists accompanied government-sponsored explorations or railroad survey parties. In the days before cameras or extensive, detailed maps of western terrain, artists provided government officials—and general viewers—with descriptive, visual images of the routes and sites explorers and surveyors traversed. Traveling with the noted explorer John C. Frémont, such artists as Edward and Richard Kern contributed significant topographical and scientific details to the Frémont reports. John Mix Stanley did much the same for several explorers of the West and for a railroad survey into the Pacific Northwest.

The premier representative of the landscape art craze that spread among European and American artists during the middle decades of the nineteenth century is Albert Bierstadt. Born in Germany but reared in the United States, Bierstadt returned in 1853 to his natal land for artistic training. Imbued with the proper enthusiasm for Romanticism while in Europe, he returned to the United States and first traveled west in 1859 as part of the Lander expedition to the South Pass and the Rockies. Later he also visited California and Yosemite.

Not unexpectedly, Bierstadt was astounded with the "grandeur and magnitude" of western mountains, transformed by their power and awesomeness. Caught up in the currently popular ideas of the sublime and picturesque, Bierstadt produced gigantic oils of the Rockies, the Yellowstone area, and Yosemite, with some of his paintings—like *The Rocky Mountains* (1863) and *The Domes of the Yosemite* (1867)—measuring six by twelve or nine by fifteen feet. These huge, wall-covering landscapes captured the fancy of Europeans and Americans and commanded astounding prices in the 1860s and 1870s, but they seemed too romantic and unrealistic toward the end of the century. By the time of Bierstadt's death in 1902, he had been forgotten, his gigantic canvases no longer sought after by collectors and patrons.

Thomas Moran was also born abroad, raised in the United States, and then trained in Europe. Much influenced by the English landscape artist J. M. W. Turner, Moran's first artistic works about the West following his trip with the Hayden expedition to the Yellowstone region in 1871–72 betrayed Turnerian influences in his uses of light and color and in his appealing descriptions, particularly in his sunrises and sunsets. Moran's watercolors of the Yellowstone— along with the valuable photographs of W. H. Jackson—helped establish the area as a national park in 1872. Arguing that art should present the "scenic grandeur" of the West, Moran made his paintings conform more to his vision of the frontier than to the scenes that lay before him.

Less well known and much less feted than these previous artists, Mary Hallock Foote, also a Local Color writer, produced numerous significant illustrations and paintings during the late nineteenth century. The talented Quaker wife of a diligent but largely unsuccessful mining engineer who moved throughout the Far West, Foote absorbed and understood more of the diverse domestic life of the West than any other artist of her time. In such renderings as *Between the Desert and the Sown* (1895) and *The Engineer's Mate* (1895), and in a series titled *Pictures of the Far West* (1888–89), Foote painted scenes illustrating settled society impinging on an uncultivated West, the isolation of the wife in the rural West, and the solitude of numerous western home and farm settings. In these revealing sketches, Mary Hallock Foote presented vistas of pioneer life that escaped most other artists and writers.

More so than works of other artists of the nineteenth century, the paintings of Frederic Remington and Charles Russell have remained popular since they first appeared. Of the two artists, Remington was more eastern, decidedly less western, and yet much more accepted than Russell in eastern art circles as a better-than-adequate painter of western subjects. Born in New York and trained at the Yale School of Fine Arts and the Art Students League in New York City, Remington first went west in 1880, the same year Russell escaped to Montana. Remington spent much of the next decade traveling sporadically

FIGURE 10:3. *The Engineer's Mate.* Mary Hallock Foote's woodcut artwork represented a domestic West that lost out in the twentieth century to the more masculine, adventure-driven paintings by such artists as Frederic Remington and Charles Russell. *Century Magazine* 50 (May 1895): 90.

throughout the West, particularly visiting military posts and organizations. His lively depictions of cavalrymen and other western scenes began appearing in the mid-1880s; within a decade he was widely known for his paintings of cowboys, Indians, military figures, and other western riders. In the last decade of his brief life, Remington also fashioned nearly two-dozen bronze sculptures illustrating active, hard-riding westerners in several poses.

No artist better epitomizes the tendency of many nineteenth- and twentieth-century artists to dramatize and romanticize the Old West than Charles M. Russell. Born and reared in a suburb of St. Louis, Russell dreamed of becoming an artist and of going west from his earliest days. He finally convinced his parents to send him to Montana, which quickly became his home and where he lived until his death. Through a variety of jobs and experiences, including night riding and general ranch work, Russell learned the ways of the northern cattle industry and the lifestyles of nearby Indian tribes. His emblematic depiction of the ravages of the deadly winter of 1886–87, *Waiting for a Chinook* (1887; later titled *The Last of Five Thousand*), and his other western action scenes made him a much-admired Old West painter by the 1890s. Soon after his marriage in 1896, Charlie became more professional about his art and established a work routine that continued for the next three decades. His *A Bronc to Breakfast* (1908) and *In Without Knocking* (1909) illustrate his nonpareil talents in depicting lively cowboy scenes. Equally noteworthy are his numerous, sympathetic treatments of Indians, with whom Charlie lived for a few months soon after coming to Montana.

Yet Charlie Russell—like Remington and many other authors dealing with the Old West—displayed an ambivalent attitude about the region. Although Russell lived well into the 1920s and saw automobiles, modern roads, electricity, and even airplanes invade his beloved West, he remained emotionally tied to a frontier of cowboys, Indians, and other pioneer subjects. Indeed Remington and Russell were like the Local Color writers who depicted a romantic, descriptive West but who were unwilling or unable to portray a West undergoing notable economic shifts transforming its sociocultural life in the 1890s. These artists and writers, working in an atmosphere of nostalgic longing for a frontier quickly disappearing, tried to recapture what they considered the heroic and free ways of earlier generations, even as the West cantered into the twentieth century. In their reluctance to face these transformations, in their bent toward holding on to an earlier, vanishing frontier, they helped keep alive a Wild West that earlier writers, artists, and tourists had invented and that would continue well into the twentieth century. That Old West stayed alive in the art of Remington and Russell, in the fiction of Owen Wister and Zane Grey, and in the films of William S. Hart and Tom Mix. For the most part these purveyors of a romantic, idyllic Old West have been more popular than those who have portrayed a mild, realistic, and much less frantic West.

Unfortunately, this love affair with a disappearing frontier discouraged many talented, creative writers and artists from treating a more realistic West in their works. Easterners, the largest audience for literature and art about the West, voted with their dollars. That meant dime novelists, writers of popular biographies of Wild West figures, and artists depicting a West of limitless horizons and lively and heroic cowboys and Indians dominated much of western literature and art before the 1890s and on into the next century. This fascination with a romanticized frontier stunted the growth of a truly regional culture for more than a generation. Even though such western authors as Frank Norris, Jack London, and Willa Cather avoided most of these literary clichés, many others were unable to do so. Regional art by western painters was even slower to develop. By the end of the century, westerners had not yet freed themselves from stultifying, mythic images of their section; the realization of a notable regional literature and art was more than a generation in the future.

~

Religion was a central human experience for many pioneers. Although the works of novelists, artists, and a plethora of publications might entice immigrants west, priests, pastors, and rabbis and their churches and synagogues dealt directly with their personal lives. These religious leaders and institutions nourished pioneers' spiritual lives, consoled them in times of need, and often provided a lion's share of social life in some areas of the rural West. Although easterners may have emigrated west more often for economic than religious reasons, churches, like schools, were early and important institutions on far-western frontiers.

Nearly two and a half centuries before English-speaking settlers arrived in Texas and Oregon, before the Mormons came to the Great Basin, and before the Gold Rush drew hordes of newcomers west, the Roman Catholics had established Spanish missions among southwestern Indian groups. These religious institutions, as well as a few by French Catholics in the Great Lakes and Mississippi Valley areas, had spread by the opening decades of the nineteenth century along the southwestern rim from east Texas to northern California and into scattered areas in the northern West. Although the Franciscans in New Mexico, Texas, and California and the Jesuits in Arizona and California led by such giants as Eusebio Francisco Kino and Junípero Serra, labored heroically to minister to Natives and to European and Mexican immigrants, the Catholics achieved only partial success. True, Indian neophytes were exposed to the rudiments of Christianity and some became converts, but the disastrous Pueblo Revolt of 1680 in New Mexico and the quick loss of believers after secularization in the mid-1830s in California suggest that the achievements of the mission system were quite limited. On the other hand, many Indians in the Southwest to this day remain Catholics and adhere to the beliefs and practices of the church.

Before the United States obtained the Oregon Country from the British in the 1840s and took the Southwest from Mexico in the Mexican-American War, missionaries, pastors, and priests had invaded these territories. These evangelists hoped to win the souls of Indians as well as to minister to newly arrived immigrants. Spearheading the Protestant efforts in the Pacific Northwest were Jason Lee, Marcus and Narcissa Whitman, and Henry and Eliza Spalding. Although working diligently among the Indians of the region and defending their spiritual and secular efforts to eastern church supporters, none of these missionaries gained many converts. By the 1840s and 1850s, they were all gone from the Pacific Northwest. Meanwhile the Roman Catholics, under the dynamic leadership of Jesuit Pierre-Jean De Smet, a man of abundant energy and charm, raced past the Protestants in the competition to convert Indians of the region. By the 1850s, few religious signs remained of Protestant missionary efforts in the Northwest, but ironically the missionaries had helped to open the West in another way: they blazed the way for settlers who came up the Oregon Trail by the thousands in the 1840s and 1850s.

Other religionists marched into the Great Basin, California, and other parts of the West. Urged on by the conviction of many eastern churchmen that the West symbolized the future of the United States, these missionaries, pastors, and laypeople were also sometimes fired by Manifest Destiny, a belief that the frontier was a God-given gift that needed to be protected and saved. As we have seen in chapter 6, the Mormons also swarmed west into Utah in the 1840s and 1850s. In the rush for souls Protestant missionaries and ministers appeared in California even before 1849—but largely after the Gold Rush—and on the Plains in the 1850s.

By the end of the nineteenth century, Protestant groups were most numerous in several parts of the West. The Methodists were the largest denomination in Kansas, Oklahoma, Colorado, Oregon, and Washington. The Baptists led in Texas and the Lutherans in North and South Dakota and rivaled the Methodists for numerical superiority in Nebraska. Congregationalists, Presbyterians, and the Disciples of Christ were not far behind in several areas. Still, no church dominated the entire religious scene on the frontier, except the Catholics in the Southwest and in other areas and the Mormons in Utah and Idaho. Revealingly, ministers from all denominations, seemingly in ecumenical unity, often complained of their untrained colleagues, low salaries, inadequate housing, and the unceasing mobility of their parishioners. But they also agreed that more churches were needed to quell the rampant secularism in the West. As one Kansan quipped, there is "no Sunday west of Junction City and no God west of Salina." Another onlooker concluded that "California had more churches and less religion than any state in the Union." On the other hand, ministers rejoiced with new believers won in revivals and camp meetings and encouraged their regular members to support the work of the church and the faltering faith of many fresh converts.

Different kinds of problems faced Roman Catholic missionaries and priests who continued to play major roles in the religious life of the West in the second half of the nineteenth century. After the American takeover of the Southwest in 1848, Catholic missionaries tried to rebuild on the shaky foundations established during Spanish and Mexican rule. In New Mexico, under the able but Eurocentric rule of Jean Baptiste Lamy, the Catholics achieved a good deal and remained by far the dominant religion in New Mexico and Arizona for at least the next two generations. In widely scattered mining camps from California to Colorado and on to Idaho and South Dakota, priests took notable social and cultural, as well as spiritual, parts in ministering to large Irish, Italian, and other immigrant populations. In the first in-depth census of religion in the United States in 1906, Roman Catholics made up more than half of the church-affiliated population or were the largest denomination in eleven of the seventeen western states and territories.

Elsewhere Catholic missionaries continued to work with Indians, before and after reservations were established. Few if any of the black robes succeeded as well as the dynamic De Smet, who converted thousands of Indians, served as peacemaker between Natives and whites, and ensured Catholic dominance in much of the northern West. Also notable were the financial support and missionary effort of Katharine Drexel, who expended more than twelve million dollars of her family's fortune to establish schools for Indians and blacks. She also founded the missionary order of the Sisters of Beloved Sacrament. No other denomination came near to matching Catholic achievements among the Indians, about one-third of whom were members of the Roman church in 1900.

Except for the Episcopalians and a few other mainline traditionalists, most of the Protestant clergy who entered the West in the first generation after the Civil War were evangelicals. With a few differences separating Calvinists (Presbyterians and Baptists) and Arminians (Methodists) concerning the roles of God and man in the salvation process, most ministers preached that Christ died for a person's sins and that one could be saved by accepting Christ's forgiveness for one's misdeeds. They agreed further that the Bible was God's word, that all persons were equal before God, and that damnation awaited those who did not accept salvation. On a few other matters denominations squabbled, with, for instance, Congregationalists arguing that Presbyterians milked Congregational cows but to make only Presbyterian cheese. Rivalries between these and other Protestant groups were a major reason for sending missionaries west. Yet their shared animosity toward Roman Catholics and Mormons and their fear that these two groups might dominate the religious frontier were much more potent factors than interdenominational conflicts in urging Protestants to support evangelical efforts in the New West.

Like most other Americans who moved west, ministers and other religious leaders first tried approaches that had worked on earlier frontiers. In the Plains, Rockies, and other interior areas where rural settlements were sparse and widely scattered, denominations utilized circuit riders, revivals, and camp meetings to gather the faithful as well as to convert nonbelievers. Dozens of circuit riders and itinerant ministers logged thousands of miles crisscrossing large areas, sometimes preaching three or four times on Sunday and holding Bible studies during the week. Such was the hardy reputation of Methodist circuit riders that when bitterly cold weather struck the Plains the saying was "there is nothing out today but crows and Methodist preachers."

The sermons of these hardy frontier ministers illustrate their serious and

FIGURE 10:4. *Sod-house Church.* Early westerners build widely diverse kinds of church buildings. Here a congregation, including a row of children, gathers in front of their sod-house church in Nebraska. Courtesy Nebraska State Historical Society, RG 3035. PH:137.

straightforward demeanor. But the emotional content of their pulpit offerings and of revival and camp meeting services can be—and often is—exaggerated. Few preachers aped the Kentucky and Illinois exhorter Peter Cartwright, an emotional and uneducated revivalist who sometimes vaulted out of his pulpit to throttle disturbers of his meetings. True, most often preachers told listeners they were sinners, in need of God's forgiveness before they could enter heaven, but only an occasional pulpiteer in the West was a Bible-thumping Son of Thunder. Audiences complained more of the length and dryness of frontier sermons than of their emotional excesses.

Nor should one overplay the democratic and leveling influences of western Protestantism. These forces were indeed at work among frontier religionists, but Methodists, for example, led by powerful bishops, were hardly excessively democratic. In addition, they and other denominations often won as many— or more—converts in the East as on the western frontier. In addition, the eye-stretching and sometimes mind-numbing spaces, terrain, and climate of the West, even though prompting minor innovations in the strategies and techniques of ministers and churches in the West, did not change dramatically the beliefs or inner spirit of these groups. Distances, the paucity of stable and large congregations, and the meagerness of weekly offerings forced western ministers to tinker with systems of organization and financial support employed in the East, but these were not major innovations or dislocations. "Far more remarkable than the primitive and rudimentary aspects of frontier religion," wrote distinguished religious historian Sydney Ahlstrom, "was the persistence with which the thought, institutions, and practice of Europe and the settled East crossed the mountains and penetrated the life of the newly settled areas"

If churches in the West owed less to the novel atmosphere and experiences of the frontier than to their eastern precedents, they nonetheless clearly influenced societies and cultures of the New West. Often the sociocultural life of small frontier towns revolved around Sunday and midweek services, Sunday schools, Ladies Aid societies, youth groups, and a variety of bazaars, fairs, and other gatherings churches sponsored. Frontier life would have been much different had not missionaries, ministers, and priests come and churches been planted throughout the nineteenth century. Churches—and schools—provided important institutional underpinnings for frontier people in search of themselves.

≈

In the nineteenth century, westerners replicated eastern educational models but also adopted new educational measures introduced during the century. Even though new circumstances gave birth to some innovations, pioneers were more conservative than bold in the development of their schools. As educational historian Ronald Butchart has argued, "Western education faithfully mirrored contemporary Eastern practices." Schools in the West were "predicated upon ideas formulated in the contemporary urban and industrializing East." Even before the mid-nineteenth century, frontier residents attempted to set up a variety of educational institutions. The Spanish opened, soon after their arrival in New Mexico at the end of the sixteenth century and later in other parts of the Southwest, schools to convert as well as to Hispanicize Indians and to educate young Spaniards. These were not sophisticated, elite schools. Still, in addition to doctrinal classes, they tried to provide basics in reading, writing, and arithmetic and introductory training in the manual arts. Although a few teachers successfully built on Native experiences, most endeavored to Christianize and "civilize" Indians. Conversion and Americanization of Indians were also the stated purposes of Catholic and Protestant mission schools established in the Oregon Country before 1850.

A variety of forces influenced the organization of schools in the second half of the century. The religious aims of denominations and the dreams of political and cultural democrats were two powerful molding pressures, but a parallel desire of many easterners, chiefly women, to save the West from cultural barbarism was also a noteworthy force for education on the frontier. Nor can one overlook the enormous interest of westerners to prove their cultural maturation as an impetus for schools and schooling in the region. Sometimes interested groups forged surprising combinations between churches and schools. In small-town Cottage Grove, Oregon, the Freethinkers invited the Cumberland Presbyterian pastor to begin a school. For the Freethinkers, an evangelical leader for their school was much better than no school or teacher. In other western areas nuns, priests, and Protestant ministers taught in the public schools. As one scholar has noted, "everywhere, 'church' and 'school' overlapped."

Throughout the West religious groups lost little time in founding schools. Mormons in Utah and the Great Basin; Roman Catholics in mining camps, in immigrant farming areas, and in cities; and a welter of Protestant groups throughout the West established schools. They imported missionaries, teachers, and others claiming to be teachers to take over jerry-built schools to convert unbelievers, educate the converted, and supply a modicum of schooling for young people. These varied goals were a tall order and not often fully achieved, but denominational schools, even if of a decidedly religious cast, frequently provided the first or only education in many pioneer communities.

Pioneers in the West, like Americans generally in the nineteenth century, viewed education as a force for upward socioeconomic mobility as well as a clear badge of respectability. These predilections often inspired westerners to set up schools within weeks or months after their arrival. Yankee immigrants to the Bay Area spoke of establishing public schools even before the area was American, and after statehood, demands for schools in the 1850s far outran the buildings, personnel, and financing available. In Denver, new residents established schools within a few months after settlement. The same was true of the sod-house frontier of Kansas, Nebraska, and the Dakotas. Like their eastern forebears, newcomers wanted schools—immediately.

But these motivations and dreams were often unrealistic and led to major problems. In many agricultural areas, for example, a low tax base or the unwillingness of farmers to further squeeze their finances made funding for new schools improbable if not impossible. Since new homesteads were not taxed until purchased or "proved up" after five years, agricultural regions were particularly hard put to build schools. In Dakota, for instance, the public school system, five years after the territorial legislature ostensibly provided funding, was little more than words on a paper. Until dozens of settlers entered an area and began to pay taxes, officials found it difficult to establish and financially support adequate public schools.

Complicating school efforts was westerners' interest in funding institutions other than schools. In California between 1853 and 1858 residents spent $754,000 on prisons but about one-third that sum on its schools—meaning

FIGURE 10:5. *Frontier Schools.* Children gather with their teacher, benches, books, and even a dunce cap outside a log cabin school built in Idaho in the late nineteenth century. Courtesy Idaho State Historical Society, 73–215.1.

$2,000 on each convict but only $9 for each student. Still, with private support, quasipublic funding, and finally with territorial or state revenues, most western areas established and supported a system of public schools by the 1880s, with special circumstances in New Mexico and Utah proving the exceptions.

Another problem that plagued pioneers in the early years of settlement was the paucity of educated and trained teachers. Since teacher-training institutions were not yet available in the West, elementary and common-school teachers were often young, single women or married women without much training. Few of these instructors in rural, one-room schools or in later urban schools were educated beyond high school. Nor had they attended a teacher-training college (this lack of training was true also of many teachers outside the West). So when the young heroine of Laura Ingalls Wilder's widely read novels about the Dakota frontier began teaching as a teenager without teacher training she was more the norm than the exception.

Other women teachers came west as a result of the conviction that the crude and uncivilized West needed to be saved, religiously and culturally. Catharine Beecher, an eastern woman active in women's affairs in the early nineteenth century, represented these opinions. She urged women to carry out their civilizing and moralizing duties by infiltrating the teaching profession and thereby redeeming the untutored West. Beecher's admonition helps clarify why so many young, unmarried women, wives and daughters of missionaries and ministers, and other women elected to come west as teachers or to become teachers once they arrived. Like Beecher, many of these women viewed the classroom as an extension of their female spheres, in which they were expected to mold the minds and spirits of children.

In addition to following eastern precedents in schooling, western pioneers enthusiastically embraced other happenings in the field of education. Similar to other Americans, settlers in the frontier West thought of colleges and universities as symbols of cultural achievement. They often supported, at least verbally, the founding of a college in their locale even though they might be reluctant to tax themselves to fund the institution. The period from 1830 to 1860 was a boom time for establishing denominational colleges in the United States with more than 140 church-related schools begun during these three decades. Some of these colleges were launched in the West, with denominations hoping that their institutions would train members of their faiths while they attended classes in a religious atmosphere. A few of these early schools are still in operation: the Methodists established Willamette University in Oregon in 1842; the Baptists, Baylor University in Texas in 1845; the Roman Catholics, Santa Clara University in California in 1851; and the Lutherans, Augustana College in South Dakota in 1860. In addition, a combined group of college-educated New England Congregationalists and Presbyterians founded the College of California in Oakland in 1855, with the state taking over the college in 1868 and converting it to the University of California in Berkeley.

But after 1860, most colleges and universities in the West began as public institutions. Territories and states, copying the provisions of eastern constitutions, provided for colleges in the new states west of the 98th meridian. Federal support also became available in the Merrill (or Land Grant) Act of 1862. In this legislation to encourage the establishment of colleges to provide instruction in agriculture and the mechanical arts, Congress gave states a land grant of thirty thousand acres for each of the state's representatives and senators. Within the next thirty years, every western state or territory utilized the provisions of the Morrill Act—a second Morrill act of 1890 added $25,000 cash to each of the land-grant colleges—as well as earlier stipulations supporting education in their state constitutions to launch state universities and land-grant colleges. Although not all states furnished additional much-needed financial support for their new colleges, nearly all survived as important symbols of the West's desire to organize their system of higher education. More than westerners were willing to admit, however, these nascent educational institutions owed much to eastern organization and curricula.

Toward the end of the century, positive effects of this emphasis on education were becoming apparent. A higher percentage of school-age westerners, for example, were attending schools in 1883 than they were nationally. And by 1900 in the Pacific Slope states, where the level of literacy had always been higher than elsewhere in the country, the illiteracy rate was less than half that of the national average. Sometimes observers commented on the pathbreaking changes in western schools. They noted, for example, that newly established public schools accepted women students and that private institutions such as Mills College (1852), the oldest women's college in the West, were being founded.

Not all the picture was positive, however, in the field of education. Similar to other American schools, those in the West did little to educate racial or ethnic minorities. Schools for Indians, Hispanics (outside the Southwest), and Asians were nonexistent or, at best, third rate. In addition, westerners often supplied better verbal than financial support for their schools and colleges. Other pioneers, too, were reluctant to rally for educational efforts when they believed practical "education" received on the farm or at home was better preparation for life than the "book-learning" schools supplied.

If westerners tended to follow eastern precedents in establishing common schools, colleges and universities, and high schools, they likewise took part, perhaps unconsciously, in one trend in American urban education toward the end of the nineteenth century. In such cities as San Francisco and Portland, professional educators gained increasing control of public school systems, arguing that the "one best system" was that which took "schools out of politics" (meaning the control of parents and community officials) and placed it in the hands of educational specialists. This gradual professionalization of schools, which accompanied the gear-grinding changes of modernization in American society and culture, meant that urban educationists became less and less responsible to local citizens. The emergence of these professional educators markedly impacted regional and national schools. These new leaders promoted school systems as part of a search for order based on urban-educational values rather than those of an older, rural frontier society. This transformation was neither immediate nor complete, for too many western pioneers opposed the new order for it to gain full control. Still, by the early decades of the next century, observers of western urban as well as national schools could see that large, notable transitions had occurred in the leadership and administration of schooling in the United States.

Throughout the nineteenth century westerners clearly tried to imitate earlier eastern experiences in education. They adopted the format of common schools and colleges and universities in the East, and they attempted to emulate the curricula and philosophies of these schools. Even though the Morrill Act encouraged a unique stress on higher education for farmers and mechanics in the Midwest and Far West and the rural, sparsely populated interior West called for innovations, schools and schooling in the American West owed more to eastern precedents than to western uniqueness of experience or setting. A spokesman in Portland, Oregon, summed up this reiterative tendency when he said, "Education is guided by Americans from New England and the northern states." What he had seen in the Pacific Northwest was true for schools in several subregions of the West in the late nineteenth century.

~

At the end of the nineteenth century, the American West, like a swiftly turning kaleidoscope, had not settled into any static, persisting cultural patterns. Continual changes, and resulting complexities, disrupted most desires for western cultural stability. Disagreements among westerners about what achievements they should strive for also divided culture makers. Some Local Color writers and a few historians, emphasizing local subjects and encouraging home-grown voices, favored the development of a unique western culture. Others, less enthralled with frontier achievements, preferred to replicate in the West what they considered to be the higher culture of Europe and the American East. Similar differences between local chauvinists and cultural traditionalists divided artists, religionists, and educators. These cultural complexities and the controversies surrounding them continued well into the twentieth century.

Berkhofer, Robert F., Jr. *The White Man's Indian: Images of the American Indian from Columbus to the Present*. New York: Alfred A. Knopf, 1978.

Bogue, Allan G. *Frederick Jackson Turner: Strange Roads Going Down*. Norman: University of Oklahoma Press, 1998.

Bold, Christine. *Selling the Wild West: Popular Western Fiction, 1860–1960*. Bloomington: Indiana University Press, 1987.

Butchart, Ronald E. "Education and Culture in the Trans-Mississippi West: An Interpretation." *Journal of American Culture* 3 (Summer 1980): 351–73.

Cordier, Mary Hurlburt. *Schoolwomen on the Prairies and Plains: Personal Narratives from Iowa, Kansas, and Nebraska, 1860s–1920s*. Albuquerque: University of New Mexico Press, 1992.

Cremin, Lawrence A. *The Transformation of the School: Progressivism in American Education, 1876–1957*. New York: Alfred A. Knopf, 1961.

Cristy, Raphael James. *Charles M. Russell: The Storyteller's Art*. Albuquerque: University of New Mexico Press, 2004.

Dippie, Brian W. *Catlin and His Contemporaries: The Politics of Patronage*. Lincoln: University of Nebraska Press, 1990.

Etulain, Richard W. *Re-imagining the Modern American West: A Century of Fiction, History, and Art*. Tucson: University of Arizona Press, 1996.

———. *Telling Western Stories: From Buffalo Bill to Larry McMurtry*. Albuquerque: University of New Mexico Press, 1999.

———, ed. *Writing Western History: Essays on Major Western Historians*. 1991; Reno: University of Nevada Press, 2002.

Ewers, John. *Artists of the Old West*. Garden City, NY: Doubleday, 1965.

Goetzmann, William H., and William N. Goetzmann. *The West of the Imagination*. New York: W. W. Norton, 1986.

Guarneri, Carl, and David Alvarez, eds. *Religion and Society in the American West*. Lanham, MD: University Press of America, 1987.

Hendrick, Irving G. *California Education: A Brief History*. San Francisco: Boyd and Fraser, 1980.

Jones, Daryl. *The Dime Novel Western*. Bowling Green, OH: Bowling Green University Popular Press, 1978.

Kasson, Joy S. *Buffalo Bill's Wild West: Celebrity, Memory, and Popular History*. New York: Hill and Wang, 2000.

Kaufman, Polly Welts. *Women Teachers on the Frontier*. New Haven, CT: Yale University Press, 1984.

McMurtry, Larry. *The Colonel and Little Missie: Buffalo Bill, Annie Oakley, and the Beginnings of Superstardom in America*. New York: Simon and Schuster, 2005.

Miller, Darlis A. *Mary Hallock Foote: Author-Illustrator of the American West*. Norman: University of Oklahoma Press, 2002.

Nash, Gerald D. *Creating the West: Historical Interpretations 1890–1990*. Albuquerque: University of New Mexico Press, 1991.

Riley, Glenda. *The Life and Legacy of Annie Oakley*. Norman: University of Oklahoma Press, 1994.

Rischin, Moses, and John Livingston, eds. *Jews of the American West*. Detroit: Wayne State University Press, 1991.

Slotkin, Richard. *The Fatal Environment: The Myth of the Frontier in the Age of Industrialization, 1800–1890*. New York: Atheneum, 1985.

———. *Regeneration through Violence: The Mythology of the American Frontier, 1600–1860*. Middletown, CT: Wesleyan University Press, 1973.

Smith, Henry Nash. *Virgin Land: The American West as Symbol and Myth*. Cambridge, MA: Harvard University Press, 1950.

Starr, Kevin. *Americans and the California Dream 1850–1915*. New York: Oxford University Press, 1973.

Szasz, Ferenc Morton. *The Protestant Clergy in the Great Plains and Mountain West, 1865–1915*. Albuquerque: University of New Mexico Press, 1988.

Taylor, J. Golden, and Thomas J. Lyon, et al., eds. *A Literary History of the American West*. Fort Worth: Texas Christian University Press, 1987.

Truettner, William H. *The West as America: Reinterpreting Images of the Frontier, 1820–1920*. Washington, DC: Smithsonian Institution Press, 1991.

Tyack, David B. *The One Best System: A History of American Urban Education*. Cambridge, MA: Harvard University Press, 1974.

Warren, Louis S. *Buffalo Bill's America: William Cody and the Wild West Show*. New York: Alfred A. Knopf, 2005.

White, G. Edward. *The Eastern Establishment and the Western Experience: The West of Frederic Remington, Theodore Roosevelt, and Owen Wister*. New Haven, CT: Yale University Press, 1968.

Wrobel, David M. *The End of American Exceptionalism: Frontier Anxiety from the Old West to the New Deal*. Lawrence: University Press of Kansas, 1993.

CHAPTER ELEVEN

Social and Economic Patterns, 1900–1940

~

WHEN THE FICTIONAL JOAD FAMILY IN JOHN STEINBECK'S MASTERFUL novel *The Grapes of Wrath* (1939) piled into their overloaded jalopies in Oklahoma, they were headed for the Promised Land. Optimistic rumors, enthusiastic handbills, and diligent liars urged them to go to California, where a country overflowing with milk and honey awaited them. As one yarn-spinner told the Joads, "Why don't you go on west to California? There's work there, and it never gets cold. Why, you can reach out anywhere and pick an orange. Why, there's always some kind of crop to work in. Why don't you go there?"

What awaited the Joads in the midst of a deepening depression on the West Coast, however, were gut-twisting heartaches. The disappointments were enough to make a stone weep. Jobs were hard to find, California residents and recent migrants detested the Okies, and their families quickly began to disintegrate. After John Steinbeck visited migrant camps in California's rich agricultural regions, he concluded the Okies and many other newcomers were in dire straits. It was their depressing, heart-wrenching, and moving story he told in his Pulitzer Prize–winning novel.

The ups and downs of Steinbeck's Joad family epitomized the optimism of the early twentieth-century West and subsequent disappointments in the region during the Depression-era 1930s. Westerners and newly arrived immigrants began the new century with great hopes, and through World War I many of their dreams were realized. In the 1920s hundreds of thousands of new migrants moved west, especially into California. For these newcomers, the future still seemed bright. But in the same decade a harsh depression settled over much of the agricultural West and radiated out to the remainder of the region after 1929. By the early 1930s many of the earlier social and economic dreams had turned to dark, nightmarish realities.

~

Travelers to a varied West at the dawn of the twentieth century often reacted like the blind men touching the elephant. Each part was different. Sections of the West differed so decidedly that it was impossible to speak of it as a single, unified "region." Great open spaces separated the major population centers at the eastern, southern, and western edges. Except for Denver and Salt Lake City, no interior western city hosted more than 40,000 inhabitants. San Francisco, with 343,000 residents, was the only western city over 150,000, making it twice as large as any other western urban area. Most westerners still resided in agricultural areas or in small towns, with farming remaining the region's major occupation.

For many westerners, and perhaps for even more tourists, the West continued as a frontier or a frontier recently closed. Silent movies depicting horse-riding gunmen stopping trains or robbing banks seemed real enough since Butch Cassidy, the Sundance Kid, and other outlaws were still doing that. Wild West arena shows, rodeos, and other tourist attractions portrayed the West as a still-active frontier. Well into the 1930s Western films and popular Western novels, by authors such as Zane Grey, Max Brand, and Ernest Haycox, pictured a frontier West alive with cowboys, gunfights, and nomadic Indians.

In other areas the early twentieth-century West seemed underdeveloped. Western manufacturing lagged far behind the East, service industries were in their infancy, and eastern banking and other commercial headquarters dominated the West. Distance and inadequate transportation facilities still kept great expanses of the West isolated from the East and western urban cores. These limitations, in the words of historian Bernard DeVoto, caused the West to languish as a "plundered province" well into the twentieth century.

Yet other trends indicated the West was quickly moving beyond its frontier stage. Between 1900 and 1920, hundreds of thousands of newcomers invaded the West. The populations of California, Oklahoma, North Dakota, and Montana more than doubled; those of Washington and Idaho nearly tripled. In these two decades Los Angeles boomed from 102,000 to 577,000; Portland from 90,000 to 258,000; Seattle from 81,000 to 315,000; Dallas from 43,000 to 159,000. By 1920, more than half of California's population was living in cities, with nearly a quarter of California's dwellers foreign-born in 1910. These demographic explosions in western states and cities were accompanied by a dramatic expansion of western agriculture. More farming land was taken up, one writer has noted, during "the first two decades of the twentieth century . . . under the Homestead Act than all that had been disposed of in the nineteenth century." Among these incoming farm families were thousands of immigrants from Europe: Germans, Russians, Poles, Scandinavians, Czechs, and other extractions. Together they gave the upper Plains a definite multicultural cast.

FIGURE 11:1. *Agricultural Regions.* By the early twentieth century several types of agricultural regions had developed in the West, providing still another example of western diversity. From Warren A. Beck and Ynez D. Haase, *Historical Atlas of the American West*, map 63. Copyright © 1989 by the University of Oklahoma Press, Norman. Reprinted by permission of the publisher. All rights reserved.

Other indicators revealed that the West was becoming a postfrontier region. For example, the largest populations of Native Americans, Hispanics, and Asians in the United States resided in the West, giving western society a more distinct multiethnic flavor than that in other subregions of the country. New migrants to the West, many of middle-class backgrounds and well educated, spiced western society with their diverse experiences. Often with town, city, and midwestern backgrounds, they came to coastal cities looking for jobs, more salubrious climates, improvements in health, satisfying retirements, or the promise of a more fluid economy and society.

∾

The twentieth century opened with a burst of new expansion into the West's rural and urban areas. Agricultural and urban regions continued to expand until World War I, but after the world conflagration ended, expansion reached a plateau and then shrunk in the 1930s. Urban centers around the southern and Pacific rims of the West mushroomed in the 1920s, but the debilitating depression of the 1930s also slowed urban growth. These changes redefined the West, leading western subregions to take on increasingly varied social and economic faces.

Optimism, good weather, and blatant boosterism conspired to bring newcomers to the West's rural areas in the early twentieth century. Nearly all agricultural parts of the West attracted new migrants. Convinced that new methods of dry farming and irrigation meant fresh bonanza opportunities, farm families flooded into Plains areas that earlier migrants had leapfrogged on their way to the Far West. Western regions of Kansas, Nebraska, and the Dakotas received thousands of homesteaders. Others migrated into newly opened areas of Texas and Oklahoma. Agriculturalists, including considerable numbers of black farmers, took up lands available in Oklahoma after Native Americans received allotted lands under the Dawes Act and the remainders of their reservations were opened for other settlers. Even though negative "knockers" warned of looming disaster if lands west of the 98th to 100th meridians were farmed, before World War I thousands of farm families moved into these areas previously limited to grazing. Countering these warnings, hucksters, agricultural evangelists, and their disciples preached the dubious doctrine that "rain follows the plow." If farmers would simply turn over the soil in these marginal areas, rainfall would come.

The federal government, through several legislative enactments, also encouraged expansion into rural areas. The most significant of these was the Newlands, or National Reclamation, Act of 1902. This act called for setting aside payments from the sale of western public lands for a reclamation fund, which could be used to bankroll federally built dams and irrigation projects in the West. This "federalization" of reclamation or irrigation in the West, argues one historian, passed Congress because the Newlands Act "promised to augment wealth and muscle" in the West. In practical terms this landmark legislation made possible the opening of numerous rural areas previously thought too dry for settlement. Among the early projects developed under the Newlands Act were the Salt River area in Arizona, the Minidoka region in Idaho, the Truckee-Carson rivers in Nevada, and the Milk River in Montana. Other new legislation also encouraged a fresh crop of migrants west. In 1909 the Enlarged Homestead Act doubled homestead

FIGURE 11:2. *Irrigation in the West.* In the Newlands Act of 1902, the federal government helped finance new irrigation projects such as this one in Idaho. Courtesy Idaho State Historical Society, P 1984–101.6/B.

sizes from 160 to 320 acres. When a new immigrant heard of this windfall, he remembered thinking, "I was raised in Chicago without so much as a back yard to play in, and I worked 48 hours a week for $1.25. When I heard you could get 320 acres just by living on it, I felt that I had been offered a kingdom."

These federal enactments, as well as the promotional efforts of railroads, brought hordes of varied peoples into the rural West. In addition to African Americans moving into Oklahoma and Texas, Mexicans pushed out of a turbulent Mexico, particularly during the Mexican Revolution (1910–20), moved across the border to live in Texas or California. Even more diverse populations swarmed into the Dakotas, where Norwegians, Germans, and Canadians found available land. Other European groups, such as the Russians, Czechs, and Poles, migrated into the northern West before the 1920s. Farther west Basques arrived from northern Spain and southern France to herd sheep in California, Nevada, Idaho, and Oregon. Japanese, meanwhile, gravitated to West Coast urban areas, where they worked as laborers on suburban farms or truck gardens. In the years from 1910 to 1924 nearly 30,000 Japanese women arrived as picture brides, allowing Japanese to establish families before immigration restrictions of 1924 closed the door to these immigrants. Even though the Exclusion Act of 1882 cut off immigration from mainland China, the Chinese still outnumbered the Japanese in the early twentieth century. Many worked as farm laborers or in restaurants in small towns.

The earliest of westerners, the Native Americans, also lived in the rural West in the early twentieth century. Residing primarily on reservations, most Indians experienced bad times in these decades. Cut off from their nomadic, hunter-gatherer roots, American Indians were often reluctant agriculturists. In the words of one scholar, the goal of the Dawes Act of 1887—to turn individual Indians into farmers and stockraisers—"failed miserably." Tragically, Indian reservation lands of 138 million acres in 1887 had dwindled to 52 million in 1934. When the Meriam Commission filed its report, *The Problem of Indian Administration*, in 1928, that survey pointed to deplorable economic, health, and schooling conditions on nearly all reservations. Something must be done, quickly and thoroughly, the commissioners argued. Some of those changes would take place in the 1930s as part of the Indian New Deal.

The 1920s were a low point for many other rural westerners, especially those involved in agricultural pursuits. Farmers had enjoyed boom times during World War I as they fed and clothed American and Allied forces in Europe, but with the sudden end of the conflict, demand dropped off overnight. Farm prices plummeted nearly 40 percent between 1919 and 1921. Precipitous declines in wheat, cotton, and other crop revenues hit the rural West like a series of sledgehammer blows. Large sections of North Dakota, eastern Montana, and parts of other northern Plains and Rockies lost thousands of rural inhabitants because of the disastrous agricultural depression that settled over these states. Many of those areas newly plowed up during the frenzy of dryland farming early in the twentieth century were now abandoned. In Texas, under the onslaught of the agricultural hard times farm tenancy rose sharply among both whites (including people of Mexican descent) and blacks. Although the percentage of sharecroppers among black tenants was roughly double that of whites in Texas, the burden fell equally on the families of both groups in the 1920s. Under the drastic pressures of the agricultural depression, increasing numbers of wives, daughters, and sisters began to work alongside their men in fields. As one farmer confessed, "But for the women . . . we farmers would be ruined." In California, where the agriculture downturn was less harsh, new irrigation projects encouraged the expansion of cotton, fruit, and vegetable farms in the state's rich interior valleys. At the same time, even though these developments enlarged California agriculture, they also led to increasing agribusiness, thereby eliminating smaller farms and calling for increasing numbers of field workers. In this way the patterns of late-twentieth-century California agriculture were already being established in the 1920s.

Changes taking places in the urban West were even more dramatic. In 1900 only 25 percent of westerners lived in urban concentrations (incorporated towns or cities of at least 2,500 residents), but by the 1930s more than half of the region's inhabitants lived in urban areas. If populations in the rural areas of the West had hit a plateau by 1920, urban populations muscled past their rural counterparts. By World War II the West was well on its way to becoming the most urban region of the United States. Railroads, highways and automobiles, the promise of new jobs and opportunities, and rumors of more salubrious climates were all important draws to western cities in the first decades of the twentieth century.

Exploding urban centers along the Pacific Coast joined earlier cities perched on the eastern edge of the West as the major urban concentrations in the American West. These far-western cities drew hundreds of thousands of migrants westward from the southern and eastern United States. In accepting these waves of newcomers, coastal urban areas became hosts to the most dynamic and varied group of immigrants coming west. At the beginning of the twentieth century, San Francisco remained the most notable city in the West. It persisted as the largest and most influential western city until Los Angeles surpassed it in size and perhaps power around 1920. In the tale of these two cities, contrasting patterns of western urbanization become clear.

In the second half of the nineteenth century San Francisco became *the* city of the Far West. Known as a city of hotels and boardinghouses with a heavily male population and the region's largest Chinatown, San Francisco had become the region's dominant center by 1880. In addition to its varied Irish, Italian, and Asian populations, the city ruled over the Pacific Slope as a banking, trade, and cultural center at the beginning of the new century. Visitors, business leaders, and journalists celebrated the rich sociocultural diversity of the Bay Area city. But San Francisco was hemmed in by water, its inner core without space to expand. By 1920 the city seemed to have reached its limits, unable to take advantage of the thousands of immigrants arriving on the West Coast.

To the south Los Angeles raced by San Francisco, replacing it as the largest and most powerful western city by 1930. Founded as a sleepy Hispanic pueblo, Los Angeles was linked early on to the hide and tallow and wheat trade until the arrival of railroads in the late nineteenth century. The building of an impressive harbor at nearby San Pedro also opened the city to larger circles of national and international trade. A black bonanza in oil, which began to boom in the 1880s, and rumors of southern California's mild, warm, and healthy climate helped entice thousands of newcomers. Only 102,000 in population in 1900, Los Angeles more than tripled to 319,000 in 1910, and nearly doubled again to 577,000 a decade later. The next ten years, the 1920s, were an even more

Selected Western Cities and Their Populations, 1900–1950

City	1900	1910	1920	1930	1940	1950
Albuquerque	6,238	11,020	15,157	26,570	35,449	96,815
Billings	3,221	10,031	15,000	16,380	23,261	31,824
Boise	5.957	17,358	21,393	21,544	26,130	34,393
Cheyenne	14,087	11,320	13,829	17,361	22,474	31,935
Colorado Springs	21,085	29,078	30,105	33,237	36,789	45,472
Dallas	42,638	92,104	158,976	260,475	294,734	434,462
Denver	133,859	213,381	256,491	287,861	322,412	415,786
El Paso	15,906	39,279	77,560	102,421	96,810	130,485
Fargo	9,589	14,331	21,961	28,619	32,580	38,256
Fort Worth	26,688	73,312	106,482	163,447	177,662	278,778
Houston	44,633	78,800	138,276	292,352	384,514	596,163
Kansas City, KS	51,418	82,331	101,177	121,857	121,458	129,553
Las Vegas	25	945	2,304	5,165	8,422	24,624
Los Angeles	102,479	319,198	576,673	1,238,048	1,504,277	1,970,358
Oakland	66,960	150,174	216,261	284,063	302,163	384,575
Oklahoma City	10,037	64,205	91,295	185,389	204,424	243,504
Omaha	102,555	124,096	191,601	214,006	223,844	251,117
Phoenix	5,544	11,134	29,053	48,118	65,414	106,818
Portland	90,426	207,214	258,288	301,815	305,394	373,628
Reno	4,500	10,867	12,016	18,529	21,317	32,497
Salt Lake City	53,531	92,777	118,110	140,267	149,934	182,121
San Antonio	53,321	96,614	161,379	231,542	253,854	408,442
San Diego	17,700	39,578	74,361	147,995	203,341	334,287
San Francisco	342,782	416,912	506,676	634,394	634,536	775,357
San Jose	21,500	28,946	39,642	57,651	68,457	95,280
Seattle	80,671	237,194	315,312	365,583	368,302	467,591
Sioux Falls	10,266	14,094	25,202	33,362	40,832	52,696
Spokane	36,484	104,402	104,437	115,514	122,001	161,721
Tucson	7,531	13,193	20,292	32,506	35,752	45,454
Tulsa	1,390	18,182	72,075	141,258	142,157	182,740
Wichita	24,671	52,450	72,217	111,110	114,966	168,279

SOURCE: 1980 Census of Population, Bureau of the Census (corrected). Includes largest city of each Western state (urban centers, not Standard Metropolitan Statistical Areas).

dramatic decade of change for the City of Angels. In those years, more than 500,000 persons inundated the city. Counting those who settled in adjacent suburbs like Pasadena, Long Beach, Glendale, and Santa Ana, nearly 100,000 newcomers came each year to the Los Angeles area in the 1920s. A mushrooming community of migrants from Mexico, Asia, the American East and South, and many other places, Los Angeles in the years after World War I illustrated once more the changes and complexities that define the American West. In gaining more than a million new residents in the 1920s, the Los Angeles basin was the fastest-growing large urban area in the United States. A sociologist, observing this astonishing immigration to Los Angeles and California, concluded that "America is not finished, not static, not crystallized, but still evolving, still plastic, still pregnant, with nobler form and richer content."

The patterns of growth in Los Angeles provided a new model for western urbanization in the twentieth century. Nineteenth-century cities like San Francisco, Portland, Seattle, and Denver, for example, primarily grew up around central cores and maintained strong downtown centers. But Los Angeles decentralized, even fragmented. As one wag put it, Los Angeles was seven suburbs in search of a center. Unlike residents of San Francisco, those moving to southern California, often of midwestern backgrounds, wanted land of their own on which to build a comfortable bungalow home. Starting out as winter tourists and then becoming transplants, these newcomers scattered away from the central city and called for a transportation system that, while linking suburbs and downtown, would allow them to live distant from the city center. Boosters by the dozens built the necessary intercity transportation systems, like the Pacific Electric Railroad system that linked the suburbs, the central city, and the beach through its "Big Red Cars." The arrival of automobiles and a jerry-built street and highway system by the 1930s also provided linkages among the expanding suburbs and encouraged the booming real estate developers throwing up housing projects.

Immigrants to the Los Angeles area from 1900 to 1930 redefined the social makeup of southern California. Asians, Mexicans, blacks, and Jews might be ripples in the incoming stream, but the floods of middle-class whites seemed to dominate the new wave of immigrants to the Los Angeles area. Many migrants were midwestern families, bringing their farm and small-town backgrounds. They were often conservative Protestants with stern moral outlooks. One commentator thought these immigrants were perfect examples of Iowa on the loose, and another spoke of a "glacial dullness" resulting from their middle-class, moralistic outlooks. Another ingredient of the new social mix in Los Angeles was the uncompromising Reverend Robert Shuler. An ultraconservative Methodist minister and harsh opponent of other ministers and laypeople less reactionary than he, Shuler hammered adversaries and seemed to speak for mounting numbers of fundamentalist Protestants arriving in the Los Angeles area. Adding another component to the social mixture were newly arriving Mexicans. Mexican-heritage residents in Los Angeles in 1930 numbered nearly 300,000, making that the largest Mexican population in an American city. Protestant midwesterners might dominate the social scene in Los Angeles, but other groups were beginning to flavor the social makeup of Los Angeles with new racial and ethnic ingredients. This diverse social profile characterizes Los Angeles to this day.

To the north, the green urban places of Portland and Seattle were becoming the major centers of the Pacific Northwest. Portland grew from 90,000 to 302,000 between 1900 and 1930, but Seattle's expansion was even more spectacular, jumping in those three decades from 81,000 to 366,000. Railroads, rivers, and harbors were keys to the rise of these two northwestern cities. Seattle, profiting from its ties to Alaska, direct connections with the Orient, and ambitious city expansionists, shot by Portland for regional dominance. Before 1940 Seattle also played host to considerable numbers of Japanese and Scandinavians, whereas Portland became known for its predominately staid residents of European backgrounds.

At the eastern end of the West, Omaha, Kansas City (Kansas), and Wichita demonstrated steady if not spectacular growth. As railroad, milling, or general commercial centers, these cities were anchored primarily to agriculture, chiefly to cereal grains and livestock. As those economic sectors bit by bit tailed off in the post–World War I period, so did the urban centers that served them. Gradually Wichita took on a new reputation as an aircraft construction center. Unlike the far-western or southwestern cities, those in the Plains West hosted fewer minority people in the early twentieth century, but Mexicans were beginning to move into Denver and Kansas City and into smaller railroad and farming towns.

Although slower in their expansion than Pacific Coast cities, urban areas along the southern rim of the West nonetheless spread significantly from 1900 to 1930. Large urban clusters began to develop in the southwestern Sunbelt from Tulsa and Oklahoma City to Dallas, Houston, and San Antonio, and on to San Diego. Others like Albuquerque, El Paso, Tucson, and Phoenix boomed in later decades. Railroads, burgeoning manufacturing and commercial facilities, and later military establishments and rising tourism were the major stimuli for urban growth across the Southwest. In addition, tens of thousands of Mexican refugees, fleeing the horrendous Mexican Revolution (1910–20), relocated in American cities just north of the Mexican border. These escapees swelled the Hispanic populations, particularly, of San Antonio, El Paso, Tucson, and San Diego.

Only Denver and Salt Lake City ranked as substantial cities in the interior

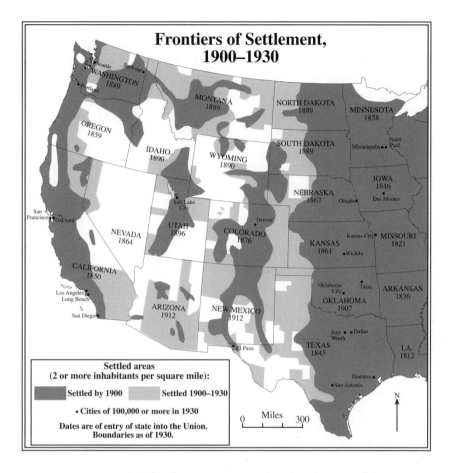

Frontiers of Settlement, 1900–1930

WASHINGTON 1889
Seattle
Spokane
Portland

OREGON 1859

MONTANA 1889

NORTH DAKOTA 1889

MINNESOTA 1858

IDAHO 1890

WYOMING 1890

SOUTH DAKOTA 1889

Minneapolis
Saint Paul

IOWA 1846

NEBRASKA 1867
Omaha
Des Moines

San Francisco
Oakland

NEVADA 1864

UTAH 1896
Salt Lake City

COLORADO 1876
Denver

KANSAS 1861
Kansas City
Wichita

MISSOURI 1821

CALIFORNIA 1850

Los Angeles
Long Beach

San Diego

ARIZONA 1912

NEW MEXICO 1912

El Paso

Oklahoma City
Tulsa

ARKANSAS 1836

OKLAHOMA 1907

Fort Worth
Dallas

TEXAS 1845

LA. 1812

Houston
San Antonio

Settled areas
(2 or more inhabitants per square mile):

Settled by 1900   Settled 1900–1930

• Cities of 100,000 or more in 1930

Dates are of entry of state into the Union.
Boundaries as of 1930.

Miles
0   300

N

FIGURE 11:3. *Frontiers of Settlement, 1900–1930.* The urban character of the West became increasingly clear by 1930, with nearly 50 percent of the region's population living in urban places (incorporated towns or cities of 2,500 inhabitants). Yet large unpopulated areas often separated these urban clusters. Map by Robert Pace.

West. Denver's central location in the Rockies, its early growth as a mining and trade hub, and its attractive climate helped bring migrants to the "Mile High City." In 1900 Denver was the second largest western city, with 134,000 residents. In the next three decades the Colorado capital, falling behind the dramatic growth rate of such cities as Los Angeles, Seattle, and Portland, nevertheless remained the major urban area of the Rockies. Five hundred miles to the west of Denver, Salt Lake City owed most of its urban dominance to its role as the administrative and cultural Mormon capital. It also became and remains an important transportation crossroads and commercial center. Revealingly the racial and ethnic diversity that flavored most southwestern and Pacific Coast cities had little impact on Salt Lake City.

During the 1930s the American West became a predominantly urban region, with more than half its population residing in cities. But other features of that growing urbanization need explanation. Even in the twentieth century western cities were situated, by and large, far apart, leading one historian to describe the American West as a series of urban oases. Separating western cities were large, eye-stretching spaces of mountains, deserts, and farms and ranches. California illustrated this unique combination of cities and spaces by becoming, later in the century, the most urban state in the nation but also its richest agriculturally. The urban centers, too, were not evenly scattered throughout the West. By the end of the 1920s, no city in the northern West between Spokane, Washington, and Minneapolis and north of Denver and Salt Lake City had reached a population of 100,000. In the next two decades, the Great Depression, the New Deal, and World War II would send another wave of newcomers west, again redirecting and transforming the urban places of the region. Like restless animals on the prowl, agents of change never seemed at rest in the West.

∾

Western cities enticed varied racial and ethnic groups, thereby enriching the social fabric of the West. Mexican populations fleeing the Mexican Revolution, or looking for better-paying jobs, moved to southwestern cities as well as to agricultural areas. By 1930 more than 50 percent of the Hispanics in the United States, immigrants or American-born, lived in *barrios*, or Chicano communities within large cities. More than half of El Paso, almost half of San Antonio, and about 20 percent of Los Angeles were Spanish-speaking peoples. At first they hired on as low-paid, unskilled factory laborers, worked as street vendors, or labored as railroad and construction workers. A steady flow of Mexicans continued moving into the Southwest despite mounting anti-Hispanic prejudices. Illustrating this negative vein, one Texas congressman attacked Mexicans as "illiterate, unclean, peonized." If they remain, he continued, their presence will lead to "a distressing process of mongrelization." Once the Depression struck, disparaging sentiments like this motivated American officials to deport Mexicans as well as to urge Mexican Americans to move to Mexico.

Asians experienced a variant ebb and flow of immigration. The Exclusion Act of 1882 effectively cut off Chinese entry into the West, but most of those remaining in the region (about 62,000 in 1920) lived in California. Once the Chinese ceased to come, the Japanese moved into some of the agricultural, small-town, and inner city jobs that the Chinese had held, with many living outside western cities. But the Immigration Act of 1924 closed the door to new Japanese immigration until after World War II. Before World War II, Filipinos worked in West Coast fields, whereas Koreans had arrived in only miniscule numbers by the Depression.

About 766,000 blacks lived in the West in 1900. They resided primarily in east Texas, the descendents of slaves and poor farmers. Growing numbers moved to Houston for better jobs, and another large group migrated to Los Angeles. Early in the century blacks thought they were treated more fairly in southern California than in Texas, but as their numbers grew in Los Angeles and they began to congregate in sections of the city, racism reared its ugly head. Those negative attitudes seemed to spiral upward when thousands of African Americans moved to California during World War II and immediately thereafter.

European ethnic groups also invaded western cities, but American attitudes toward their cousins from across the Atlantic seemed to diminish the notoriety of their presence. Greeks, Italians, Irish, and Cornish continued to work in mining towns. Scandinavians immigrated to the northern West from Minnesota to the Pacific Northwest, with notably large groups in the state of Washington. Germans and Russians settled in agricultural towns and cities across much the same area, but with larger numbers in the Dakotas. As they had in the nineteenth century, Irish and Italians enriched San Francisco with their foods, celebrations, and labor activism. Thousands of Canadians moved into northern parts of the West, but they seemed to melt without much strain into American culture.

≈

Not surprisingly, the arrival of millions of newcomers to the American West in the decades following 1900 was linked to the expanding economy of the region. When the West's economic motor roared into high gear in the late 1890s and remained at that momentum through World War I, migrants came west to profit from the region's economic expansion. When the same economic machine began to misfire in the 1920s and seemed on the verge of sputtering to a stop in the depression of the 1930s, the tide of immigration slowed accordingly.

In the years up through World War I, agriculture expanded dramatically in the West. Higher than usual rainfalls reversed the bad times of the early 1890s and motivated wheat and corn farmers to move out onto the Great Plains. The Campbell method of dry farming that called for careful, deep plowing to conserve moisture encouraged farmers to expand into areas previously reserved for grazing. The federal government, through the Newlands Act of 1902, which created the Bureau of Reclamation, provided funding for massive new irrigation projects. Such states as Idaho, Colorado, Arizona, Washington, and particularly California benefited from these huge reclamation and irrigation developments.

Thousands of farm families relocated to these newly watered areas. The U.S. government, under the leadership of Herbert Hoover as the head of the U.S. Food Administration during World War I, provided much aid to farmers. The administration offered bounties for farmers to up their production so as to feed U.S. forces and those of their European allies. Wheat and corn farmers, cattle and sheep raisers, and fishermen all greatly benefited from these subsidy programs.

Western agriculture was usually a family venture. True, bachelors and single men worked some farms, and in some western states between 10 and 15 percent of homesteaders were women. But by far the largest numbers of farms and ranches were family operations, with a clear sexual division of labor typifying their work patterns. Men tended the fields and did outside chores; women were homemakers and cared for their children. In 1912 one woman homesteader in southwestern Wyoming, Elinore Pruitt Stewart, explained her full but "truly happy" life in a letter to a friend: "It is true, I want a great many things I have n't got, but . . . I have my home among the blue mountains, my healthy, well-formed children, my clean, honest husband, my kind, gentle milk cows, my garden which I make myself. I have loads and loads of flowers which I tend myself. There are lots of chickens, turkeys, and pigs which are my own special care." In addition to these time-consuming chores, Stewart helped her husband in haying time and with other field duties.

But when the federal government withdrew its subsidies to agriculturists after World War I and less rain fell, farmers and ranchers entered a series of extremely lean years extending to the end of the 1930s. As crop surpluses piled up, prices plunged. So many tillers of the soil and keepers of livestock were in such bad shape that these normally individualistic, independent-minded agriculturalists even petitioned Washington, D.C., for special financial support. Congress listened to the so-called Farm Bloc and supported the congressional McNary-Haugen bills calling for government supports, but conservative presidents Calvin Coolidge and Herbert Hoover vetoed the legislation. Not until Franklin D. Roosevelt's New Deal in the 1930s was such tradition-breaking legislation passed.

≈

In the first decades of the twentieth century mining and oil industries experienced an up-and-down economic pattern much like that of agriculturists. Production expanded from 1900 to 1915, surged with federal support during World War I, and then fell on hard times in the 1920s. Gradually, too, western mining industries transitioned from precious metals (gold and silver) to the base metal of copper while the petroleum industry shot past others to become the most significant western extractive industry by the end of the 1920s. The spread of western mineral-producing sites in 1900 reveals the diversity and scattered locations of mining endeavors. Gold and silver mines dotted the states of California, Nevada, Colorado, Utah, and Idaho. Copper came from Montana, Arizona, Utah, and Nevada. Tungsten, molybdenum, zinc, and manganese were also found in the West. Rich oil fields ranged through Texas, Oklahoma, and California.

In the early twentieth century technological and scientific advances greatly aided in the development of novel mining techniques and in the refining of gold and copper. New electrical power was also harnessed to replace many earlier human and animal-driven operations, both in surface and underground mines. By the mid-teens copper had become the most important mineral in the West. Huge open-pit mines were carved out of the Rockies in areas of Montana, Utah, Arizona, and New Mexico. The largest of these cavernous pits, in the mountains near Salt Lake City in the Bingham Canyon, measured several miles from rim to rim. Dubbed the "richest hole in the earth," the Bingham mine proved that new technology could help produce massive amounts of copper from low-grade ore that beforehand was considered too costly to process. It took several decades, however, for westerners to realize the environmental costs of these mammoth open-pit mines.

If precious and base-mineral mining reigned supreme up and down the Rockies, the oil industry came to occupy that position in parts of the Southwest. A few oil strikes spouted in California in the 1890s, but the memorable gushers came in during the early twentieth century. The most sensational of these was in 1901 at Spindletop, in east Texas near Beaumont. In January of that year oil rushed out of the ground in an erupting flood, causing dozens of companies to plant oil derricks elbow to elbow in the Gulf Coast region. The next year Spindletop filled twelve million barrels of oil, more than 20 percent of the nation's petroleum output. Oil fields nearby in Texas, others in Oklahoma, and still others in California overflowed. In 1900 the West produced meager amounts of oil, but a decade later nearly 70 percent of the country's petroleum came from the region.

World War I, as it had for agriculture and other parts of the western economy, markedly influenced western extractive industries. The War Industries Board, guaranteeing high prices for much-needed war supplies, greatly stimulated wartime production. The war machine organized to fight the Central Powers and to aid European allies gobbled up needed western minerals and drank up hundreds of thousands of barrels of western oil. After the war, oil and gas industries gained new markets in the automobile craze sweeping the country. On the other hand, once the U.S. government ceased providing subsidies for the precious and base metals, those industries suffered a large dip in demand.

The slow development of manufacturing in the American West provides additional evidence of how much the region lay under the lion's paw of eastern interests in the early twentieth century. Typical of the older mercantile system, the West served as a dutiful colony, producing needed raw materials for the Mother Country (the American East) and in turn obligingly buying the East's manufactured goods. But the influx of population after the turn of the century and expanding western towns and cities encouraged the development of manufacturing in the West, even if most of this activity was initially limited to production of goods for local needs.

In California and the Pacific Northwest nascent manufacturing was linked to agricultural production and natural resources of those areas. Fruit, vegetable, and fish canneries, meat-packing plants, and flour mills served local needs. Along the coast from northern California to the Canadian border lumber mills were erected to process the timber that platoons of woods workers were beginning to harvest. A few ships were constructed in the Northwest, but most were still built in the East and brought to the Pacific.

Manufacturing developed even more slowly in the Rockies and on the Great Plains. Inadequate capital, insufficient demand, and a weak economic infrastructure were barriers to large, widespread industrial development in these areas. There were exceptions, however. These included the meat-packing and flour-milling companies already established on the eastern fringes of the West in Kansas City, Kansas, and Omaha. In these areas, most of the companies launched or expanded were processing rather than fabricating industries, with food-processing chief among them. Another exception in the interior West was the establishment of the Colorado Fuel and Iron Company in Pueblo, Colorado, which the Rockefellers later controlled. The volume of finished steel produced at the CF&I plant led to Pueblo's being dubbed the Pittsburgh of the West.

The infusion of government funds into the western economy in World War I aided in the rapid establishment of other manufacturing industries. In addition to stationing thousands of military personnel in the West and thereby ensuring a growing demand for goods, the federal government let contracts for ships and aircraft to be used in the war. Shipyards and airplane manufacturing hummed with new activity up and down the West Coast. The demand for goods from companies and their workers fired up lumber mills, canneries and food-processing plants, and smelters. Even though, statistically, the impact of World War I seems small in comparison with that of World War II, the clear, shaping influence of the earlier war on the West was evident throughout the region.

The lack of western investment capital retarded even larger industrial development. Aside from federal and state government funding, westerners could not muster much capital to establish industries. But that funding was on the horizon by the end of the 1920s. Instrumental in the gradual financial revolution that led to western funding for western industry was the westerner investor A. P. Giannini. The son of immigrant Italian parents, Giannini became, in the words of his biographer, "the West's leading banker in the twentieth century." Organizing and then expanding the huge, powerful Bank of America, the ambitious and indefatigable Giannini stood ready to finance the expansion of the West. By the end of the 1920s he controlled banking in California, poised to expand his financial empire. Although the Depression slowed the process, Giannini's bank and other western funding agencies, in partnership with the federal government, helped transform the West from a colony of the East into a region of burgeoning manufacturing from the late 1930s onward.

∾

Active labor unions accompanied the economic development of the early twentieth-century West. As agricultural, mining, and lumbering economies expanded up through World War I, workers began to organize and call for more benefits and rights for laborers. Laborers also lobbied for what they considered their share of the profits expanding companies enjoyed. In some parts of the West, unions organized workers with a minimum of confrontations. In other areas of the region competitions among owners, bosses, and workers led to violent conflicts.

In the late nineteenth century craft unions in the West, such as the railroad workers, organized successfully and retained their strength and leverage on owners well into the new century. Union organizations for longshoremen, oil and refinery workers, building trades, and other crafts also fared well. Many of these "labor aristocrats" belonged to the more cautious American Federation of Labor. That and other similar unions worked for shorter hours or higher wages, known then as "bread-and-butter" gains.

The armies of itinerant or unskilled workers who labored in the fields, mines, or forests of the West joined other kinds of unions. In the closing years of the nineteenth century the Western Federation of Miners, founded in 1893, served as a vehicle for more radical labor leaders and workers. When that union failed to satisfy growing numbers of militant laborers, the Industrial Workers of the World was organized in 1905. The IWW, or Wobblies as they became known, called for "one big union." They wanted to lump all the country's unskilled industrial workers into one huge union. The Wobblies denounced the capitalistic and democratic systems that, they asserted, fed the rich on the back of laborers.

Sometimes romantic troubadours, sometimes violent labor militants, the IWW was never a boring or inactive union. "Zealous, anarchical, and free from middle-class restraints," one author wrote, the "Wobblies acted with humor or fanaticism, out of idealistic motives or simple malice, but always with dash or spirit." Taking to street corners or soapboxes, engaging in free-speech campaigns, and participating in rallies and strikes, the Wobblies called for "solidarity forever," sang labor ditties set to popular hymns, and harpooned fat-cat capitalists. Led by the likes of "Big Bill" Haywood, the one-eyed, bluff, and determined radical, and egged on by others such as Mother Jones, Emma Goldman, and Elizabeth Gurley Flynn (the "Rebel Girl"), the IWW rallied

FIGURE 11:4. *Haywood Trial.* This famous courtroom drama in Boise in 1907 featured William Haywood (#11 in photo), a Western Federation of Miners leader; Harry Orchard (#1), a convicted bomber; Clarence Darrow (#9), nationally known trial lawyer; and William Borah, young Idahoan on his way to political prominence. Haywood later became active in the radical union, the Industrial Workers of the World (the IWW or "Wobblies"). Courtesy Idaho State Historical Society, 2005.

miners, lumber workers, and agricultural "bindle stiffs" to their cause. From its beginnings and into the 1920s the IWW stood at the center of radical labor activism in the West.

Sometimes this activism led to violence. In the first two decades of the twentieth century, a series of fierce confrontations, some engineered by the IWW, exploded across the West. In Idaho authorities accused Big Bill Haywood, then a leader of the Western Federation of Miners, of hiring dynamiter Harry Orchard to assassinate Frank Steunenberg, a former governor and opponent of radical laborites in Idaho. In a sensational trial in Boise in 1907 Haywood was acquitted under mysterious circumstances of the murder of Steunenberg, but Orchard was sentenced to life in prison. The dramatic courtroom battle pitted labor radicals against mine owners and their political supporters. When Wobblies engaged in free-speech fights and denounced capitalists as unworthy of their labor, that proved, their critics argued, that the union's initials— IWW—stood for "Imperial Wilhelm's Warriors" and revealed the union's ties to Germany's wartime leader, Kaiser Wilhelm. Others denounced IWW members as Reds or Bolsheviks, likening them to revolutionaries in Russia. Once Wobblies denounced World War I as a capitalist conflict waged to gain huge profits, the American press vilified the unionists as traitors, and popular opinion swung swiftly against the IWW. In November 1916 in the sawmill town of Everett, Washington, a boatload of Wobblies approaching a wharf were fired upon, with several of the labor activists killed. Three years later on Armistice Day, another bloody battle erupted in Centralia, Washington, between marching veterans and Wobbly members in front of the Wobbly hall. Several paraders and IWW members were killed. A few hours later, a group of vigilantes stampeded the jail, grabbed an imprisoned Wobbly, and then castrated and hanged him. The lumber town residents overwhelmingly supported the veterans in their attack on the Wobblies.

These and other tragic confrontations between capital and labor symbolized the class conflicts that simmered and sometimes broke out in the early twentieth-century West. As owners gained handsome returns on their investments, workers demanded their equitable share of these burgeoning profits. In contrast, businesses, viewing labor activism as antithetical to their entrepreneurial purposes, attacked unions and worker radicals as dangerous subversives to the American Way. In 1910 when the brothers John and James McNamara admitted setting off a bomb that killed more than twenty persons at the antiunion *Los Angeles Times*, the popular press attacked the bombers. Five years later in Utah, IWW troubadour Joe Hill was declared guilty of murdering a storekeeper in a dubious court decision. The next year, 1916, Tom Mooney was sentenced to life in prison for a bombing that killed ten persons in a war-preparedness parade in San Francisco. The most grievous of the violent conflicts occurred in Ludlow,

Colorado, in 1914. There members of the United Mine Workers struck against the Colorado Fuel and Iron Company. Weeks of vicious battles and shootings killed more than sixty people. The "Ludlow Massacre" sickened the Rockefeller owners, as well as stiffened the resistance of dedicated laborers.

World War I and the increasingly conservative early 1920s ended most militant labor activity in the West. The turn right in politics, the wartime patriotism, and the denunciation of all things German soured the atmosphere for the IWW and other unions or groups opposing the war. Probusiness and veterans groups, gaining the support of federal, state, and local officials, leveled harsh and successful attacks on labor activists. By the end of the war and certainly by the mid-1920s the IWW was nearly a moribund organization. Labor had lost momentum in its battle against owners and investors. Not until the 1930s, with the aid of Roosevelt's New Deal, did labor organizations win back what they lost—and more—between 1915 and 1925.

≈

In the fall of 1929 the Great Depression dropped on the United States like a heavy, wet blanket. This social and economic disaster, the most horrendous and far-reaching of its kind in American history, ushered in a dozen dark years of hard times for the nation. The Depression did not relinquish its hold on the United States until the country began to participate in World War II, allowing the economy to revive.

The West suffered through several of the worst disasters of the Great Depression. In fact, for agricultural sectors of the West, the crises of 1929–30 and thereafter were the second installment of economic hard times that blasted farmers from the end of World War I onward. The large social and economic readjustments forced on other Americans under the onslaught of the Depression were those that westerners faced too throughout the 1930s. There was a major difference, however: the impact of the Depression and the New Deal wrought different kinds of changes on the West than on other American regions. When the federal government launched President Roosevelt's New Deal in 1933, it set off a revolution that continued, and enlarged, during World War II and the later cold war. More than any other force, the federal government, through its social and economic programs in the West, helped transform that region from a dependent colony of the East to a new and powerful region.

≈

"Their houses [have] gone to ruins. . . . Their furniture, dishes, cook utensils— no replacements in years. No bed linen, and quilts and blankets all gone. A year ago their clothing was in rags. This year they hardly have rags." This dire report came from journalist Lorena Hickok, who in 1933–34 traveled west to visit the region and describe what she saw. Harry Hopkins, director of federal relief, asked Hickok to provide him an up-to-date profile of social conditions west of the Mississippi. What she viewed and wrote about here in North Dakota adjacent to the Canadian border was near disaster. Conditions were not much better in most parts of the West.

Everywhere Hickok went she found social and economic chaos. Farmers could not feed their families, let alone their livestock. Some farmers, on the edge of desperation, threatened county and local officials who attempted to foreclose on farmlands. Drought, grasshoppers, and the depressions were side-swiping thousands of agriculturists on the Great Plains. In New Mexico the Santa Fe Railroad employed 7,500 men (mostly Hispanics) in 1929; in 1933, only 3,200 were still working, and some of those part time. The situation seemed less pressing in the California valleys, but once Hickok returned to Wyoming she found ranchers without feed for their gaunt cattle. In nearly all parts of the rural West farmers and ranchers were in deep trouble.

Similar miseries were evident in western urban areas. Western cities along the famed Route 66 from Chicago to Los Angeles erected signs warning westering migrants they could expect no relief from these town officials. Oklahoma City was even more heartless, arresting the unemployed and driving them out of the city. Los Angeles leaders put up "bum barricades" at California's borders to warn away the jobless or indigent. In Houston unemployment shot up, relief funds disappeared, and more and more residents applied for government aid. In Colorado the heaviest demands for relief were in Denver. Typical of many other western cities, Seattle became the site of a large "Hooverville" (an ironic reference to President Herbert Hoover's unwillingness to provide aid), a jerry-built "community" where the jobless and hungry tried merely to exist.

In many western places minority peoples and poorer classes were hit especially hard. In eastern and coastal Texas government aid for blacks ran onto the shoals of discrimination; one relief administrator claimed that white attitudes forced him to reject "just as many Negroes as he" could. To the west, in New Mexico, 75 percent or more of persons on relief were Hispanics, particularly those living in rural areas. In Colorado relief officials found it difficult to place Mexican and Chicano clients because "an employer will often refuse to take a Spanish-speaking person unless a special effort is made by the placement officer." For most Mexican Americans that meant the available jobs were low-paying domestic positions. Mexican-heritage people of the Southwest suffered further indignities when owners and workers alike, looking for scapegoats, accused Mexicans of causing the Depression. As a result of these economic crises, thousands of Mexicans were repatriated (forcibly sent back) to Mexico.

FIGURE 11:5. *Dust Bowl West.* Human blunders in plowing up unsuitable farmlands, inadequate rainfall, and destructive winds combined to create a huge Dust Bowl spreading over expanses of New Mexico, Texas, Colorado, and Kansas. After turbulent storms blew thin topsoils eastward and many crops failed, thousands of homesteaders fled their fields and abandoned their homes. Courtesy National Archives.

Natural and human-made disasters added to the grief of many western-ers during the Depression. The worst of these was the Dust Bowl of the 1930s, which damaged thousands of acres in western Kansas and Oklahoma, east-ern Colorado and New Mexico, and the panhandle of Texas. The Dust Bowl resulted from exceptional climatic change and profound human error. Early in the 1930s rainfall was minimal in these Plains and southwestern areas, places expecting nearly twenty inches of rain each year getting only half that. Extremes in hot and cold also beat on the farm families already battling the Depression and joblessness. In 1936, north of the Dust Bowl in South Dakota, tempera-tures registered 121 degrees in the summer and 61 below zero in a frigid winter. Nature seemed to be working overtime to push farm families off the land and out of their homes.

But there were also human-induced reasons for the Dust Bowl. Thousands of acres too dry for farming had been plowed up in the frenzy of production during World War I. When the rain refused to fall and the dry, harsh winds blew with increasing velocity, black blizzards carried tons of valuable topsoil off to the east. The "dirty thirties" descended on large sections of the western Plains but particularly on the areas of what became the Dust Bowl. One *New York Times* reporter, traveling through Kansas, wrote, "Today I have seen the cold hand of death on what was one of the great breadbaskets of the nation . . ."

Some scholars point to a greedy capitalistic society as the main culprit for these ecological woes. The drive for profits, the reckless plowing of lands meant for grazing, and the planting each year of crops that took too much from the soil—these were the main reasons for the Dust Bowl disaster. Humans must learn, writes historian Donald Worster, to "satisfy [their] needs without mak-ing a wasteland." For like-minded historians the environmental calamity of the Dust Bowl should be a lesson to westerners that mindless, profit-driven agri-culture can often destroy "a fragile earth."

Whatever the causes, the Dust Bowl and other agricultural tragedies drove people off the Plains and sent them farther west. Their story is much like that of the Joad family in Steinbeck's novel *Grapes of Wrath*. Tractored off their farmlands in Oklahoma, the Joads limped down Route 66 hoping for better times in Edenic California. But in the Depression West there were no utopias, as these migrants and many others quickly realized

≈

The traumatic Depression that began in 1929 and sapped the economic vitality of the entire country in the next decade also directly impacted the West eco-nomically in the 1930s. As we have just seen, the Depression disrupted western social patterns, and in the next chapter we will see how the depression decade reshaped western politics and culture. The shock on western economic affairs was equally traumatic.

The link between supply and demand shifted sharply out of balance soon after the early fall of 1929. In the five years following the stock market crash, the economy of the West fell by half. Income, production, prices, and wages all plummeted. Farmers, already in dire straits in 1929, earned less than half their 1929 income in 1933. Crude oil selling for $3 a barrel in 1929 sold for only 10 cents a barrel in 1933. Also in 1933 lumbermen were selling only one-third of the forest products they marketed in the boom year of 1926. Fish canneries, mineral processors, cotton and wheat farmers, and cattlemen were all in a tight fix. Despite lessening demands, agriculturists produced too much, and that glut led to falling prices. Still in thrall to the East, the colonial West could not sell its raw materials to an East already bludgeoned by a deadly depression.

Westerners might have believed that the country was in good hands in 1929 since Herbert Hoover, the first western president, was in the White House. Born in Iowa, reared with an uncle in Oregon, and educated at Stanford, Hoover had shown leadership skills during World War I as director of the Food Administration and as secretary of commerce from 1921 to 1929 in the Harding and Coolidge administrations. He seemed the right person to help the country, including the West, out of its economic disaster. Unfortunately, that proved not the case. Hoover's incurable addiction to individualism, strongly tied to his own rise through difficult circumstances, convinced him that the American economy, if left alone, would correct itself, as it had in the past. Hedged in by his own conservative temperament, Hoover could not bring himself to use the full economic and administrative power of the central government to attack the Depression. Many other Americans, including more than a few members of Congress, agreed with the president. Let the economy alone; it would right itself. But as the Depression deepened, increasing numbers of observers called for some, even if guarded, actions. Hoover and Congress did act, even if too little and too cautiously. Those actions engendered mixed responses in the West.

The enactments influenced both western farmers and businesses. Even though Hoover opposed the McNary-Haugen Bill designed to boost agricultural prices through sales of foreign exports, and which many westerners favored, he backed the Agricultural Marketing Act of 1929 that promised to keep farm prices high so farmers would not overproduce. The bill did not work because farmers continued to produce far beyond demands. During his presidency Hoover also supported the Reconstruction Finance Corporation and its plan to provide monies to corporations and agricultural agencies that needed loans to avoid closure or bankruptcy. But Hoover could not support public power, favoring instead development by private companies. Truth to tell, even though Hoover used the power of the central government more than previous presidents to address some of the disasters of the Depression, he did not favor direct relief to citizens. In that way he opposed giving government funding directly to out-of-work or poverty-stricken laborers or farmers. Bit by bit westerners and other Americans began to blame Hoover, unfairly of course, for the onset of the Depression. That discontent mounted in the election of 1932 when the country, including the West, rose up to throw Hoover out of office and voted in the Democratic candidate, Governor Franklin D. Roosevelt of New York. The latter promised a New Deal to restore hope among the country's citizens and to end the Depression. Roosevelt's plans, once instituted, not only attempted to transform the economy of the American West but enlarged links between the federal government and the region that continue to this day.

~

Over time Franklin D. Roosevelt (FDR) became a master manipulator of the country's economy, its politics, and, by extension, its social patterns. Temperamentally an experimenter, he was willing to try a series of plans and proposals until something worked. Telling his fellow Americans that they had nothing to "fear but fear itself," Roosevelt plunged ahead in the spring of 1933 with the so-called 100 Days of legislation. Several of the legislative enactments of that period and in the later days of the New Deal directly impinged on the economy of the American West.

Roosevelt's "New Deal" included notable programs aimed at addressing several of the nation's economic ills. Among the New Deal measures, one would provide relief for those out of work and without incomes, another would recover the earning power of farmers and workers, and still another would organize government agencies to address other problems the Great Depression introduced. This legislation had large, lasting impact on the West. As one historian points out, "New Deal grant and loan programs had a greater relative impact in the West than in any other part of the United States." Revealingly, the fourteen states receiving the highest per capita federal assistance were all in the West.

Several agencies provided direct relief to westerners. Among the earliest of these was the Federal Emergency Relief Administration, which served as a conduit through which to funnel relief funds for the unemployed in all states. After 1935, the Works Progress (later, Projects) Administration (WPA) provided jobs for out-of-work laborers, who built roads, bridges, and public buildings, including Timberline Lodge at Oregon's Mount Hood. The WPA also paid writers to prepare WPA guides to states and artists to paint murals for post offices and other government buildings. Another giant infusion of government funds came through the Public Works Administration (PWA), which funded the construction of huge dams and other public works projects. Sometimes working closely with the Bureau of Reclamation and Army Corps of Engineers, the PWA and these groups erected Boulder (Hoover) Dam on the Colorado River, part of the sprawling Central Valley Project in California, the Bonneville Dam on the Columbia River, and, the largest of them all, the gigantic Grand Coulee Dam, also on the Columbia. These dams and reclamation projects put hundreds of thousands of westerners and immigrants on the payroll and, eventually, provided less expensive electricity, flood control, and irrigation water for farmers.

 CCC

But the most popular of the agencies of relief in the West was the Civilian Conservation Corps (CCC). Under this program armies of young men, primarily from the East and many from eastern cities, were sent west. They were put to work building roads and trails, clearing campgrounds and preparing rest areas, and helping conserve croplands and forests. In these work programs westerners saw federal funds providing jobs as well as helping preserve western forests and farming lands. CCC workers also constructed firebreaks, erected national park buildings, and prepared flood control areas. Living in remote areas of the West and receiving decent wages was an experience that many urban young men from the East would remember all their lives.

TAYLOR GRAZING ACT

The New Deal also tried to bring order to the chaos of grazing rights in the West. The Taylor Grazing Act of 1934 helped immensely in providing much-needed organization and protection for grazing areas. Previous to this legislation, the government intended to sell most public lands to individuals; after 1934, remaining public lands were withdrawn, put under close supervision, and carefully administered to avoid overgrazing. Not always popular with individualistic, go-ahead western stockmen, the act nonetheless systemized and protected the large, federally owned grazing areas of the West. The Soil Conservation Service and the Rural Electrification Act were two other federal attempts to aid farmers and ranchers with conserving their lands and bringing electricity to isolated rural areas of the West.

Through other major pieces of legislation, FDR moved to recover the livelihoods of many western farmers, businesses, and workers lost during the early years of the Depression. The Agricultural Adjustment Act (AAA) of 1933 greatly impacted the West by attempting to bring agricultural production into line with demand. To reduce surpluses and raise prices to "parity" with those before World War I, the government began paying subsidies to farmers to limit the size of their crops and their livestock holdings. For businesses and laborers, the New Deal created the National Industrial Recovery Act (NIRA). This agency, by placing limits on industrial output and cutthroat competitions, attempted to raise prices. Businesses were encouraged to subscribe to NIRA "codes" by affixing a Blue Eagle insignia on their office windows. Trying to

FIGURE 11:6. *The New Deal West.* The Civilian Conservation Corps, a popular and well-received part of President Franklin Roosevelt's New Deal, put thousands of young men to work reforesting lands, building roads, and contouring and protecting erosion-endangered farmlands. Courtesy Library of Congress.

"broker" something for all Americans, Roosevelt and Congress included the controversial section 7a in the NIRA, allowing collective bargaining for laborers and helping to raise wages and improve fringe benefits. The AAA and NIRA, although controversial and in their early forms declared unconstitutional by the U.S. Supreme Court, nonetheless survived in revised form later in the 1930s and furnished another clear indication of the increasingly strong links between Washington, D.C., and the West.

≈

In the two generations from 1900 to 1940 westerners experienced an undulating social and economic history. From the turn of the century to World War I, new immigrants invaded the West to take advantage of the region's reputed cornucopia. In those roughly two decades western farmers and city workers did quite well. But the war in Europe disrupted socioeconomic patterns in the American West, as it did elsewhere in the western world. Agriculturalists and laborers, riding high during wartime expansion, fell off the plunging economic steed of postwar times. Farmers especially experienced depressing social and economic times from the early 1920s through that decade and on into the 1930s. Workers in mines, forests, and oil fields suffered similar wage and benefit losses.

But the Great Depression beginning in 1929 took by far the largest toll on westerners. Agriculturists lost much of their purchasing power in crop-glutted markets. Concurrently, in some western areas nearly half of city dwellers had difficulty finding work. Even though President Roosevelt promised to turn the tide and make things better, Dr. New Deal did not successfully address most of the socioeconomic problems pressing the West. Dr. Win-the-War in the 1940s did much more than Roosevelt's domestic plans in the 1930s to solve the economic dilemmas of the West and, thereby, to better social conditions for many hard-pressed westerners. In these same four decades, as chapter 12 shows, the political and cultural configurations of the American West likewise displayed fluctuating and mixed forms.

Abbott, Carl. *The Metropolitan Frontier: Cities in the Modern West*. Tucson: University of Arizona Press, 1993.

Athearn, Robert G. *The Mythic West in Twentieth-Century America*. Lawrence: University Press of Kansas, 1986.

Boag, Peter. *Same-Sex Affairs: Constructing or Controlling Homosexuality in the Pacific Northwest*. Berkeley: University of California Press, 2003.

Deutsch, Sarah. *No Separate Refuge: Culture, Class, and Gender on an Anglo-Hispanic Frontier in the American Southwest, 1880–1940*. New York: Oxford University Press, 1987.

Egan, Timothy. *The Worst Hard Time: The Untold Story of Those Who Survived the Great American Dust Bowl*. Boston: Houghton Mifflin, 2005.

Etulain, Richard W., et al., eds. *The American West in the Twentieth Century: A Bibliography*. Norman: University of Oklahoma Press, 1994.

Fite, Gilbert C. *American Farmers: The New Minority*. Bloomington: Indiana University Press, 1981.

Foley, Neil. *The White Scourge: Mexicans, Blacks, and Poor Whites in Texas Cotton Culture*. Berkeley: University of California Press, 1997.

Gregory, James N. *American Exodus: The Dust Bowl Migration and Okie Culture in California*. New York: Oxford University Press, 1989.

Hurt, R. Douglas. *Problems of Plenty: The American Farmer in the Twentieth Century*. Chicago: Ivan Dee, 2002.

Limerick, Patricia Nelson. *The Legacy of Conflict: The Unbroken Past of the American West*. New York: W. W. Norton, 1987.

Lowitt, Richard. *The New Deal and the West*. Bloomington: Indiana University Press, 1984.

Malone, Michael P., and Richard W. Etulain. *The American West: A Twentieth-Century History*. Lincoln: University of Nebraska Press, 1989.

Meinig, D. W. *Transcontinental America, 1850–1915*. Vol. 3, *The Shaping of America*. New Haven, CT: Yale University Press, 1998.

Merrill, Karen R. *Public Lands and Political Meaning: Ranchers, the Government, and the Property Between Them*. Berkeley: University of California Press, 2002.

Milner, Clyde A. II, et al., eds. *The Oxford History of the American West*. New York: Oxford University Press, 1994.

Nash, Gerald D. *The American West in the Twentieth Century: A Short History of an Urban Oasis*. 1973; Albuquerque: University of New Mexico Press, 1977.

———. *The Federal Landscape: An Economic History of the Twentieth-Century West*. Tucson: University of Arizona Press, 1999.

Nugent, Walter. *Into the West: The Story of Its People*. New York: Alfred A. Knopf, 1999.

Pisani, Donald J. *Water and the American Government: The Reclamation Bureau, National Water Policy, and the West, 1902–1935*. Berkeley: University of California Press, 2002.

Pomeroy, Earl. *The Pacific Slope: A History of California, Oregon, Washington, Idaho, Utah, and Nevada*. New York: Alfred A. Knopf, 1965.

Prucha, Francis Paul. *The Great Father: The United States Government and the American Indians*. 2 vols. Lincoln: University of Nebraska Press, 1984.

Righter, Robert W. *The Battle Over Hetch Hetchy: America's Most Controversial Dam and the Birth of Modern Environmentalism*. New York: Oxford University Press, 2005.

Robbins, William G. *Colony and Empire: The Capitalist Transformation of the American West*. Lawrence: University Press of Kansas, 1994.

Rowley, William D. *Reclaiming the Arid West: The Career of Francis Newlands*. Bloomington: Indiana University Press, 1996.

Ruiz, Vicki L. *From Out of the Shadows: Mexican Women in Twentieth-Century America*. New York: Oxford University Press, 1998.

Sánchez, George J. *Becoming Mexican American: Ethnicity, Culture and Identity in Chicano Los Angeles, 1900–1945*. New York: Oxford University Press, 1993.

Schwantes, Carlos A. *The Pacific Northwest: An Interpretive History*. Lincoln: University of Nebraska Press, 1989.

Takaki, Ronald. *Strangers from a Different Shore: A History of Asian Americans*. New York: Penguin Books, 1989.

Taylor, Quintard. *In Search of the Racial Frontier: African Americans in the American West, 1528–1990*. New York: W. W. Norton, 1998.

Van Nuys, Frank. *Americanizing the West: Race, Immigrants, and Citizenship, 1890–1930*. Lawrence: University Press of Kansas, 2002.

White, Richard. *"It's Your Misfortune and None of My Own": A History of the American West*. Norman: University of Oklahoma Press, 1991.

Wishart, David J. *Encyclopedia of the Great Plains*. Lincoln: University of Nebraska Press, 2004.

Worster, Donald. *Dust Bowl: The Southern Plains in the 1930s*. New York: Oxford University Press, 1979.

CHAPTER TWELVE

Politics and Culture, 1900 to 1940

~

HIRAM JOHNSON WAS ANGRY. THE ENERGETIC, REFORM-MINDED CANDIDATE told his listeners he would "kick the Southern Pacific Railroad out of politics" if he were elected California's governor in 1910. Traveling from town to town throughout the state in a red roadster and announcing his coming with a cowbell, Johnson toured the California countryside like the vigorous campaigner he was. After being elected governor as a progressive Republican, Johnson initiated a reform agenda so thoroughgoing that President Theodore Roosevelt called California's progressive achievements "the most comprehensive program of constructive legislation" any state had enacted. What Johnson achieved in California paralleled what other like-minded progressive politicians were attempting elsewhere in the West. Throughout the region reformers were addressing the corruptions and inequities that had surfaced in the late nineteenth century. They also encouraged some of the region's initial participation in environmental conservation. Almost overnight, however, that progressive ardor cooled during World War I and in the twenties. Then, the social and economic dislocations of the Great Depression helped spark a new cycle of reform, the New Deal of President Franklin D. Roosevelt, in which much of the American West took part fully and enthusiastically.

In the first decades of the twentieth century the West also began to define itself, tentatively, as a region. Two opposing ideas pushed at novelists, historians, artists, and film-makers: (1) the West as a continuing or closing frontier, and (2) the West as a developing region with its own identity. Just as progressives like Hiram Johnson, Oregon's William S. U'Ren, and Nebraska's George Norris tried to bring reform politics to the West, so writers and artists such as Mary Austin, Willa Cather, John Steinbeck, Walter Prescott Webb, and Thomas Hart Benton attempted to portray the American West as a place redolent with regional identity. Religious and educational leaders, although much less interested in defining the West as region, nonetheless hoped to bring culture to the region through a system of vigorous, widespread religious and educational institutions.

~

Progressivism in American history spanned the first decades of the twentieth century, lapped over into the 1920s, and provided legacies and leaders for the New Deal in the 1930s. Although not a fully organized, coherent political group, the progressives, as members of both national parties and some as members of the Progressive Party formed in 1910, made notable contributions to American political history. Presidents Theodore Roosevelt (1901–9) and Woodrow Wilson (1913–21) were progressives and during their administrations enacted significant progressive legislation. Senator Robert La Follette of Wisconsin achieved prominence among the progressives, as did Jane Addams, the well-known founder of Hull House in Chicago. In several ways, the Progressive Era was a "catching up" period, attempting to control—even destroy—the "bloated capitalists" who

FIGURE 12:1. *Hiram Johnson, Progressive.* Elected California's governor in 1910, Johnson introduced a series of political reforms that made his state administration a model for national progressivism. Courtesy The Bancroft Library, University of California, Berkeley. Gubernatorial: 14. ID 14. POR Johnson, Hiram.

dominated the late nineteenth century. By and large, progressives were sympathetic to laborers (but not radical unions), urban reformers, advocates of women's rights, and conservation leaders. Often moralistic, many progressives also favored Prohibition and sometimes applied religious terminology to their political reforms. Conversely, they were usually blind to the inequities minority groups experienced and rarely pushed for reforms aimed at the poorest of poor in the United States.

Progressives in the American West participated in these national movements as well as pioneered regional efforts that influenced national leaders. Although the progressive impulse drew from many sources, it particularly attracted middle-class, well-educated urban dwellers worried about the excesses of big business and political machines. The progressives were optimistic, desirous of protecting their own status in American society, and convinced of the rightness of using the power of federal and state governments to mount reforms and bring change. In some sections of the interior West, the progressives drew on Populist ideas and leaders, providing a direct link between these two notable reform efforts missing in other parts of the region and nation. "Perhaps the most distinctive aspect of western progressivism," write two historians, "was its passion for the more democratic, antiinstitutional political reforms, such as the initiative, the referendum, and the recall, and a form of the direct primary which allowed voters to cross party lines. Not every western state adopted these measures, but they were more common there than anywhere else in the nation."

The ethos of progressivism in California and Oregon illustrates important ingredients in the reform effort. In 1908–9 Hiram Johnson catapulted to the forefront of California progressives after helping win the case against Abraham Ruef, the crooked political boss of San Francisco. Focusing on the Southern Pacific Railroad as the epitome of evil corporate control in the state's politics, Johnson set up a laboratory of direct democracy experiments in the use of the initiative, referendum, and recall. In addition, he stood for direct primaries and a cross-filing system, allowing candidates and voters to free themselves from party domination and to exercise innovative, individualistic political leadership. Drawing upon support from the reformist Lincoln-Roosevelt League and other insurgent Republicans, Johnson led a showcase state government from 1911 to 1917.

Oregon adopted similar measures, but its progressive leadership differed markedly from California's. The key figure in Oregon was the enigmatic William S. U'Ren. A political manipulator extraordinaire, U'Ren preferred to hold the political reins from backstage, serving as secretary of a group rather than as president or director. His wire-pulling and persuasive powers became so well known that Harvey Scott, editor of the *Portland Oregonian*, joked that Oregon had two legislatures—"one in Salem and one under U'Ren's hat."

FIGURE 12:2. *William S. U'Ren, Political Reformer.* Known as the father of the "Oregon System," U'Ren introduced initiative, referendum, and recall measures designed to rescue political control from the hands of big businesses and political bosses and to return voting power to ordinary citizens and their representatives. From Lincoln Steffens, *Upbuilders* (New York: Doubleday, Page, and Company, 1909), 286a.

Nationally, U'Ren became recognized as the father of the "Oregon System," which included the initiative, referendum, and recall, as well as legislation limiting women's working hours and their minimum wage. First a Populist and then a Republican, U'Ren favored, most of all, nonpartisan efforts. Through the years, he helped encourage Oregonians to vote on 107 measures in six elections, including taxes on utility companies and legislation to regulate transportation costs. National figures like Senator La Follette and President Theodore Roosevelt sought out U'Ren. Woodrow Wilson, looking for a model of progressivism after being elected New Jersey governor, singled out the Oregon System and U'Ren's indefatigable leadership when he said, "In the East I am counted intensely progressive. In Oregon, I am not so sure."

Progressivism surfaced in several other western states as well. In Kansas, progressives rallied to pass regulations on corporate stocks, elect reform governors, and support forward-looking senators. Some Kansas progressives also cheered on the fiery efforts of prohibitionist Carry Nation, who wielded a hatchet to destroy saloon bars, windows, and mirrors. (She called her sensational actions "hatchetations.") Nebraska progressives voted for bipartisan legislation, and in Oklahoma colorful William H. "Alfalfa Bill" Murray, a Democratic progressive, encouraged Native American–white alliances. In Colorado, progressive Judge Ben Lindsey pioneered reformist treatment of juveniles in Denver. Prohibition crusades were particularly strong in the Midwest among progressives with Protestant backgrounds. Woman suffrage also received progressive support in most western states, helping Jeannette Rankin of Montana, for example, to become the first woman elected to Congress. As the only person in Congress to vote against both World War I and World War II, Rankin, writes a biographer, "lived a life remarkable for its adherence to principle over political gain." Western progressives, generally, backed national progressive candidates: Roosevelt in 1904, both Roosevelt (the Progressive Party candidate) and Wilson (Democrat) in 1912, and Wilson in 1916.

Some western political reformers, particularly those in northern Plains states, moved farther left than the progressives. Chief among these were leaders of the Nonpartisan League. Organized in 1915, the League drew former Populists and socialists to its bandwagon, including A. C. Townley and William Lemke of North Dakota. Calling for state-owned banks and grain elevators, urging special tax breaks and other supports for agriculturists, and running on tickets avowedly socialistic, the League did well in farm states: the North Dakota elections in 1916 and 1918 and other campaigns in Minnesota, Montana, and Idaho, as well as across the line in Canada. When the League forcefully opposed U.S. entry into World War I, however, public opinion shifted quickly, abruptly ending the League's power and bringing about the recall of League officeholders in North Dakota. Another such radical organization of political dissidents in Oklahoma dubbed their efforts the "Green Corn Rebellion." To their ranks they drew poor sharecroppers, blacks, and Indians and betrayed their hatred for corporate power by smashing pipelines and bridges. When this group also opposed the draft and World War I, they too lost most of their public support.

$\sim$

Progressives also spoke out for conservation measures. In the nineteenth century only a few westerners worried about the mistreatment of their lands, animals, and other natural resources. For this small group of worried observers, the wilderness seemed to be disappearing at an alarming rate, along with the beaver and buffalo. In the early 1870s Californian Henry George, the noted author of the widely read book *Progress and Poverty*, declared, "A generation hence . . . our children will look with astonishment at the recklessness with which the public domain has been squandered. It will seem to them we must have been mad." But stronger desires to conserve the nation and the West began to emerge early in the twentieth century.

Some of the progressive enthusiasm for conservation began with Theodore Roosevelt, the ebullient New Yorker who owned a small ranch in North Dakota. When the terrible "die-off" year of 1886–87 destroyed much of Roosevelt's cattle herd and when he realized that buffalo, wild sheep, and antelope were rapidly disappearing—or already gone—he turned toward conserving big-game animals. Later, as president and with the help of Gifford Pinchot, whom he tapped as leader of the newly organized U.S. Forest Service, Roosevelt urged his colleagues and Congress to do more to conserve the nation's natural resources. "Conservation . . . under Roosevelt," writes one scholar, "was a major weapon of the progressive movement."

Western progressives agreed with Roosevelt that state and federal governments should take steps to encourage wiser uses of natural resources. In doing so, they would help thwart the wastefulness of destructive and excessively powerful corporations. With Roosevelt's support Congress passed the Reclamation Act of 1902, which funded several irrigation projects in the West through the sale of public lands. By and large westerners also supported Roosevelt's and Pinchot's successful efforts to set aside millions of acres of timber stands as forest reserves in the West. The president explained his act of conservation by telling the country in 1905, "a timber famine in the future is inevitable," to which the pragmatic Pinchot added, "forestry is handling trees so that one crop follows another."

Not all westerners agreed with the utilitarian views of Roosevelt and Pinchot. The high priest of western wilderness, John Muir, had quickly emerged as an advocate of a more spiritually based view of nature and resources even before Roosevelt came to the presidency in 1901. Muir, a transplant from Wisconsin to California, became deeply imbued with a spiritual, transcendent view of nature. Following his tramps across the continent and particularly after his experiences in the Sierra Nevada in California, Muir converted to an urgent,

FIGURE 12:3. *Theodore Roosevelt and John Muir in Yosemite.* Roosevelt and Muir illustrated the competing "wise use" and "preservationist" approaches to conservation. These differences underlay the stormy controversy surrounding the building of a dam in the beautiful Hetch Hetchy Valley in California. Courtesy The Bancroft Library, University of California, Berkeley. POR 65, Muir, John.

evangelical spokesman for preserving nature as close to its pristine existence as possible. The "wise use" policies of Roosevelt and Pinchot alienated Muir. Ideas like that, Muir asserted, allowed those destructive "hoofed locusts" (sheep) to destroy verdant high meadows and foul limpid mountain streams.

These two divergent views—the utilitarian position of Roosevelt and Pinchot, the preservation stance of Muir—clashed in the Hetch Hetchy Valley controversy beginning in 1907. When San Francisco, California, and Washington, D.C., officials backed a proposal to build a dam in Hetch Hetchy to provide water to San Francisco following a terrible earthquake and fire in 1906, Muir led the charge against the project. He quickly lined up support from the Sierra Club, which he had founded in 1892, the Society for the Preservation of National Parks, and other like-minded conservation groups in the fiery battle against Congress and Roosevelt's Secretary of the Interior, James Garfield. For nearly seven long years the emotional debate raged. But after numerous hearings and confrontations, in 1913 Congress supported the building of a dam in Hetch Hetchy. Muir was devastated and died the next year.

Those Americans and westerners who pushed for wiser use of western lands and landscapes and the end of despoliation and wanton destruction of western natural resources won other battles. Two years after Muir's death Congress passed and President Woodrow Wilson signed the National Park Service Act, which launched a new section of the Department of the Interior devoted to the conservation of parks and wildlife. Soon thereafter the first leader of national parks, Stephen Mather, forged a series of pragmatic agreements with railroads and new automobile clubs to encourage tourists to visit national parks, many of which were in the West. By the end of the twentieth century many westerners complained of the "selling of the West" and a "devil's bargain" between invading tourists and spreading tourism, but in the first two or three decades of the century links between tourism and the new parks seemed to many westerners a sensible and well-intended conservation effort.

These moves to make productive and pragmatic use of resources in the West spilled over into several areas in the progressive period and into the 1920s. Reclamation policies, forest preservation, and the national park system, though often driven by middle-class, capitalist motivations, nonetheless led to an idea only vaguely coming to focus for many westerners and other Americans. If they were to sustain life itself in their country, they had to be more careful with their lands, water, forests, and natural beauty. The dire socioeconomic demands of the Great Depression and World War II sidelined some of this growing impulse, but it would resurface stronger and more widely accepted in the 1960s and beyond.

~

Unintended consequences often follow major wars, with untoward events frequently disrupting domestic affairs as dramatically as international ones. Such was the case with the rapid changes that invaded the American West during World War I and in the years immediately following. Although not as transforming of the West as World War II was a generation later, World War I nonetheless clearly influenced the politics, as well as the other elements, of the region in the second and third decades of the twentieth century.

Progressives were optimists, thinking they could contain and redirect the excesses of corporations and party bosses of the late nineteenth century. But under the stresses and conflicts of World War I that optimism drained away. A narrower, more pessimistic spirit quickly replaced much of the progressive idealism. Mirroring national trends, western politics during World War I and the 1920s took a sharp turn right. That change in direction was illustrated in western reactions to radicals and war resisters, in the rise of the Ku Klux Klan, and in the changing pattern of western voting during the 1920s.

Once conflict broke out in Europe in 1914, and especially after the United States joined the war in 1917, Americans increasingly supported our involvement in Europe. Westerners displayed their divided opinions about the war soon after conflict broke out. German Americans and Irish Americans in the West disliked the pro-English positions of many U.S. leaders, and Scandinavians and Germans with socialist backgrounds generally opposed war. Reflecting some of these hesitations, Secretary of State William Jennings Bryan resigned from President Wilson's cabinet rather than support what he considered the president's push toward war. But by the time the United States entered the war in spring 1917, little room remained for strong antiwar sentiments. Several western states passed legislation supporting the war effort, punishing those who criticized federal or state governments and attacking those who openly opposed war. Many critics of the war were of European socialist backgrounds or members of activist labor organizations, making them especially suspect to veterans and other patriotic groups.

One of these suspect groups, the radical union known as the Industrial Workers of the World (the IWW or Wobblies), bore the brunt of some of these conservative reactions. When manufacturers began to profit greatly from supplying forces in the European war, workers thought they should share in these gains. Local unions of the American Federal of Labor (AFL) joined the IWW in a large strike of lumber workers in August 1917. Under intense pressure not to undermine the U.S. war machine, AFL workers returned to work, but the IWW continued its strike, raising antiwar voices to a much higher pitch. Some members turned to sabotage. Within weeks of the 1917 strike, the IWW was under attack from federal officials, who invaded Wobbly offices, arrested dozens of IWW members including leaders such as "Big Bill" Haywood and Elizabeth

Gurley Flynn, and quickly "rushed to justice" many Wobblies. Popular slogans also derided the IWWs. Those initials, critics said, stood for "I Won't Work." The ugly antiradical spirit surfaced in Bisbee, Arizona, where in July 1917 more than a thousand Wobblies and other strikers (mostly of Hispanic heritage) were rounded up, shipped out of town, and abandoned in the deserts of New Mexico. Even worse, in Centralia, Washington, on Armistice Day of 1919 a parade of veterans stopped in front of an IWW local office, shots rang out, and a gun battle ensued. Veterans and Wobblies both died there on the street.

Other concurrent events illustrated the sharp turn right in public opinion. Members of the Nonpartisan League, an organization also opposed to World War I, saw their political power fall sharply in the northern Plains states. In 1921 in North Dakota the Nonpartisan governor, Lynn Frazier, and the attorney general, William Lemke, were recalled from office. In like fashion the antiwar socialists of Oklahoma nearly dropped from the scene in the early 1920s. Other states like Montana and Nebraska passed Sedition Acts aimed at war protesters or German sympathizers.

When the Russian Revolution broke out in spring 1917 and the Bolsheviks took control, an American "Red Scare" rushed through the country. Groups like the IWW, Nonpartisan League, and socialists were quickly libeled as "Reds" or "Bolshevistic" for their antiwar stances. The near-hysteria of the times seemed to heighten near the end of the war. When unions in Seattle announced a "general strike" in February 1919, sympathetic workers shut down the city. Conservative Mayor Ole Hanson attacked the strike as the beginning of a revolution and broke up the work stoppage with the threat of bringing in troops. When laborers went back to work in a few days, Hanson was celebrated as a patriot of Americanism and a savior from left-wingers.

Westerners also demonstrated their clear move to the right in their voting patterns in the 1920s. Earlier they had supported progressives Roosevelt and Wilson, but they voted for conservatives Warren G. Harding (1920), Calvin Coolidge (1924), and Herbert Hoover (1928) in the next decade. A large part of that swing to the conservative camp resulted from the sour national mood following World War I. That war and its peace had not, as President Wilson promised, made "the world safe for democracy." The unsuccessful attempts to set up a League of Nations, the failure of the United States to achieve a signed peace agreement, and the economic disruptions following the dismantling of the war machine and the return of soldiers—all these failures upset Americans and sent them in new directions. When Harding as the Republican candidate in 1920 called for a "return to normalcy," meaning a move away from reform, Americans seemed to agree. They elected him to the White House and thus began a dozen years of Republican ascendancy.

The swing away from progressivism in the early 1920s did not take the West entirely to the far right, however. Some reforms continued, others were muted, even while counter-reform measures surfaced. For example, the Nonpartisan League dominated North Dakota politics until about 1923 before it lost control there and declined elsewhere in the northern Plains. Other western political leaders like Senator George Norris of Nebraska continued to champion reforms aiding farmers in the 1920s and 1930s. In Texas, "Pa" and "Ma" Ferguson tried to head off Ku Klux Klan (KKK) and other right-wing influences. In California, the midwesterners who moved to the southern part of the state turned the Los Angeles area into a region supporting Prohibition. Indeed, most rural areas of California, as well as in the West generally, favored Prohibition, whereas city dwellers did not, with Los Angeles as a notable exception.

The rise of the Ku Klux Klan in several areas of the West best represents the shift right away from progressivism. The first KKK appeared in the South immediately after the Civil War. In the 1860s and 1870s that organization tried to block efforts by northerners, liberal southerners, and blacks to further civil liberties for the freed slaves. But when the KKK resurfaced in the 1920s, it targeted Catholics, Jews, new immigrants, and minorities. In Texas,

IGURE 12:4. *Ku Klux Klan in the West.* The KKK gained considerable power in Oregon and other states in the West during the 1920s. The Klan wanted to disallow Catholic schools while championing what they considered Christian (Protestant) values. Courtesy Eckard V. Toy.

Colorado, and Oklahoma, KKK Klaverns quickly organized to intimidate and control members of these targeted groups. Most surprising was the emergence of the KKK in Oregon, the vaunted home of the West's aggressive progressives. Postwar discontents, new immigrants to the state, and antireform elements united to bring the KKK to center stage. The KKK dominated Oregon politics in 1922–23, influenced the state legislature to pass several nativistic laws (including no land ownership by noncitizens), and supported the initiative measure for compulsory public school attendance. The latter measure, ironically utilizing the direct democracy techniques of the progressives, would have meant the end of parochial education in the state. Before the legislation could be put in effect, however, the U.S. Supreme Court declared it unconstitutional. Still, the quick upsurge of KKK strength in Oregon illustrated the muted reform or conservative bent of western politics in the 1920s.

~

Even though the West voted for Republican Herbert Hoover in 1928, he soon lost the region's support. The first West-born president, Hoover and his administration did too little to address the West's most pressing needs after the Great Depression broke out in the fall of 1929. Finding Hoover unresponsive to their petitions, westerners in 1932 enthusiastically lined up behind Democratic candidate Franklin D. Roosevelt, who carried every western state in that election. Within hours after FDR took office in March 1933, he was on the move. Within days, he launched the first 100 Days of his New Deal program, which introduced a blizzard of bureaus, agencies, and administrations. New federal policies and programs emerged in the West like products from a high-speed, well-oiled assembly line. Seen in larger perspective, Roosevelt's New Deal forged close links between Washington, D.C., and the West, a linkage that, more than any other influence, has shaped the identity of the West since 1933.

At the same time Roosevelt and his Democratic Party altered the direction of western politics. Westerners had voted for Harding in 1920, Calvin Coolidge in 1924, and Hoover in 1928. But during Roosevelt's presidency from 1933 to 1945, he and the Democrats won over the West, as they did the rest of the country. The American West moved into the Democratic camp in 1932 and stayed there for several elections.

Not everyone, including members of Roosevelt's own Democratic Party, reacted enthusiastically to the large new impact of the New Deal on the West. Part of the discontent arose from New Deal demands for western matching funds to augment federal outlays. These stipulations and other strings attached to Washington funding did not sit well with ambitious, independent western leaders. One dissenter, Idaho's rambunctious Democratic governor "Cowboy

Ben" Ross, grudgingly ran in 1935 on a sales tax platform to raise matching funds and lost the election. In North Dakota and Oklahoma, governors William Langer and "Alfalfa Bill" Murray angered New Deal relief czar Harry Hopkins when they tried to take control of federal funding in their states. Similar wars erupted between Hopkins and Texas and Colorado politicians. Here were early evidences of the West's later tendency to tell Washington "Give us more money—and get out."

Most westerners realized, however, how much critical aid the New Deal provided. They also understood that the West, per capita, received more than any other region of the United States. These understandings usually led to friendly relations with Roosevelt's administration. Governors Culbert Olson of California, Charles Bryan of Nebraska, and Payne Ratner of Kansas were among those supporting FDR. Texans also played important roles in Washington during the 1930s. John Nance Gardner, the gruff and astute speaker of the House of Representatives, became Roosevelt's vice president from 1933 to 1941, and Congressman Sam Rayburn, much admired for his able leadership, became speaker of the House in 1940.

Not surprisingly, most of the West moved into the Roosevelt camp in the 1930s. His New Deal policies provided jobs, furnished public works projects, and, most of all, rekindled hope among Depression-blasted westerners. In turn, they flocked to the polls to support him. FDR won overwhelmingly in the West in 1936 and 1940. By the end of the decade and on the eve of World War II, westerners had switched their allegiances. If in 1930 they still looked to their state capitals in Sacramento, Austin, Denver, and Bismarck for direction and funding, by 1940 that connection had transferred to Washington, D.C. FDR's New Deal had facilitated the change.

～

The quick changes that typified western politics between 1900 and World War II also marked western culture during the same four decades. Many novelists and historians became interested in regional topics, and so did artists. Simultaneously, western religious affiliations and schools changed, becoming more multifaceted.

A defining moment in western cultural history occurred in the publication of Owen Wister's novel *The Virginian* (1902). First of all, the novel synthesized fictional ingredients inherited from Wild West stories of the nineteenth century. Wister drew on these familiar tales for his novel, which included the appealing story of a larger-than-life cowboy, a romance between the cowboy and his schoolmarm sweetheart, and the cowboy's participation in vigilante justice against villains. Second, in the coming decades Wister's work provided a popular fictional model that writers invoked again and again. But other western authors assiduously tried to ride in other directions, to avoid what they considered the numbing stereotypes that *The Virginian* stylized and made so popular. These innovators thought that realistic fictional treatments of the farming and urban Wests, the roles of women and families, and a developing regional consciousness should be the essences of western literature. From 1900 to 1940, these authors provided counter narratives to the popular Westerns cantering up Wister's well-worn trail. A parallel dichotomy appeared in historical works about the West. Although most western historians followed Frederick Jackson Turner in depicting the West as an evolving frontier, others like Herbert Eugene Bolton and Walter Prescott Webb depicted the West as an emerging region. Western artists also divided into two camps. In the first decades of the twentieth century, eastern artists coming west as well as western regionalists tried to break from the cowboy and wild Indian images that immensely popular artworks of Frederic Remington and Charlie Russell bequeathed to later painters.

~

Novelists such as Zane Grey, B. M. Bower, and Max Brand solidified the form and content of the popular Western novel by imitating Wister's *The Virginian*. Grey, a former baseball pitcher and bored dentist, crashed onto the literary scene with his best-selling *Riders of the Purple Sage* (1912). In that Western, Grey introduced the two-gun, black-clad Lassiter, a mysterious, brave rider who defeats the evil-hearted villains and wins the hand of the courageous, virtuous heroine. Grey's superhero, following in the path of Wister's cowboy hero, foreshadows the John Waynes, Shanes, and Louis L'Amour heroes of later times. In such novels as *Chip of the Flying U* (1906), B. M. Bower, the only well-known woman writer of Westerns, made a place for more significant roles for women even as she followed closely the other ingredients of the popular genre. Max Brand became the best known of twenty pennames of the prolific Frederick Schiller Faust, whose nearly five hundred novels included more than two hundred Westerns, often peopled by epic-like, supernatural heroes of a twilight zone West.

For many other writers these predictable plots of masculine cowboys and other valiant frontiersmen were literary betrayals of frontier and western materials. One very popular writer, Jack London, set many of his stories and novels in the Klondike. These included the best-seller *Call of the Wild* (1903), which portrayed the shaping power of the harsh Northland on character development. Frank Norris, chiefly in his novels *McTeague* (1899) and *The Octopus* (1901), likewise depicted the molding force of California's physical and social settings on city dwellers and wheat ranchers. On the northern Plains, Hamlin

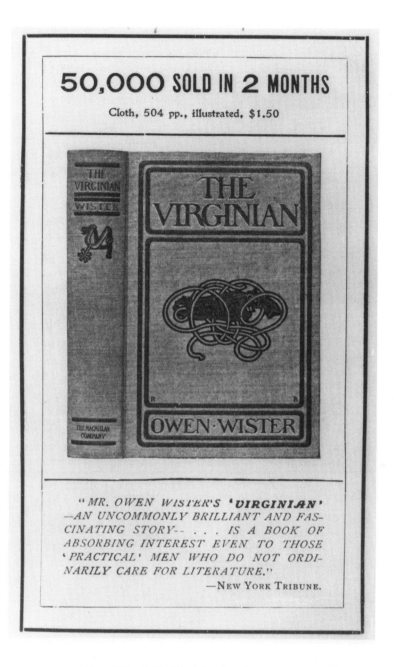

FIGURE 12:5. *Owen Wister's* The Virginian *(1902)*. More than any other novel about the West published in the early twentieth century, *The Virginian* synthesized the ingredients of Old West stories from James Fenimore Cooper through the dime novel. Courtesy Library of Congress.

Garland effectively treated the dilemmas and disappointments that led to farmers' involvements in Populist politics, or, worse, to defeat and despair.

The writings of two women authors, Mary Austin and Willa Cather, were even more notable as forerunners of the western literary regionalism that flowered beginning in the 1920s. Austin's work of nonfiction, *The Land of Little Rain* (1903), encapsulated the southern California desert and forest lands that, over time, hosted a variety of flora and fauna and human inhabitants. Her treatments of Indian and Hispanic reactions to these arid landscapes were particularly noteworthy. More influential were the Plains and southwestern novels of Nebraskan Willa Cather. One of the most significant of all western writers, Cather utilized a refined, clear style to create finely honed characters and skillfully plotted fiction. The heroines of *O Pioneers!* (1913) and *My Antonia* (1918) and the Catholic, Native American, and Mexican-heritage characters in *Death Comes for the Archbishop* (1927) illustrated what a talented literary artist could do with western regional materials.

Of all the western regional writers California novelist John Steinbeck remains the most widely recognized. In novels such as *Tortilla Flat* (1935), *In Dubious Battle* (1936), and *Cannery Row* (1945) Steinbeck drew hundreds of thousands of readers and positive critical attention from scholars. It is his Pulitzer Prize–winning novel *Grapes of Wrath* (1939) for which he merits most regard. A moving depiction of Okies driven out of their homes and off their farms by soulless agribusinesses, the novel traces their lonely journeys down Route 66 to find work in California. There the generic Joad family struggles to exist and by the end of the novel seems defeated by their depressing circumstances, save for the unremitting energy and hopefulness of Ma Joad, who passes on her undefeated spirit to her daughter, Rose of Sharon. The only western writer to be awarded the Nobel Prize for literature, John Steinbeck demonstrated how a regional writer—like William Faulkner and Robert Frost did for the South and Northeast—might use physical and sociocultural environments to shape the personalities of his characters.

~

Mary Austin, Willa Cather, John Steinbeck, and dozens of other writers, editors, and artists were part of the regionalist movement that swept across the United States in the 1920s and 1930s. Austin and Cather were forerunners, and initiators, of this growing emphasis on region; Steinbeck fully participated in the movement. Both the American West and South were awash in coteries of writers who turned inward to find in their regions solace as well as possible answers to dilemmas that swept across the United States after World War I.

In the West, regionalism particularly displayed itself in a group of small magazines. Editors of *The Southwest Review* (Texas), *The Midland* (Iowa), *The Frontier* (Montana), *Prairie Schooner* (Nebraska), *Folk-Say* (Oklahoma), and *The New Mexico Quarterly* urged contributors to abandon earlier Wild West yarns and to embrace new ideas and cultures emerging from varied subregions of the West. The editor of *The Southwest Review* wanted that journal to look "to the *milieu* from which it springs." B. A. Botkin, noted American folklorist and editor of *Folk-Say*, encouraged submissions that dealt with the lore of "the folk," and H. G. Merriam, editor of *The Frontier*, stated that the explicit goal of his magazine was making "readers and writers of this region [Pacific Northwest] conscious of its literary achievement."

Regionalists wanted western writing to move in several new directions. In subject matter, writers should eschew stereotyped cowboys and deal with farmers, other rural people, and the lore and life of minority people, including Negroes, Indians, and Mexicans. In point of view, regionalists should capitalize on the voices of common folk rather than writing for New York editors of pulp and slick magazines. Most of all, those of a regionalist bent must show how the physical and sociocultural landscapes of specific places placed their imprints on the characters, outlooks, and events of their novels, stories, and sketches. Throughout the interwar years, these tub-thumpers for regionalism were notable influences on creative writers, historians, and artists and provided a vision of the West different from that seen in the Old West or frontier school of western writing.

≈

If Austin, Cather, and Steinbeck illustrate breaks from the past and adherence to new currents pulsing through western literary regionalism, similar competing currents swirled around historians of the West. Early in the twentieth century most historians writing about the West belonged to the frontier school of historiography closely linked to the historian Frederick Jackson Turner. Regional challenges to that point of view began to emerge in the 1920s.

Frederick Jackson Turner was a buoyant, vivacious, and persuasive evangelist for his doctrine of the frontier interpretation of American history. He preached that frontier or Turner thesis in his seminal and widely circulated essay "The Significance of the Frontier in American History," first published in 1894. In the early years of the twentieth century, nearly all American historians writing about the West converted to Turner's thesis that the frontier became and remained the most significant shaping force in the American past. Although Turner failed to produce several book-length studies elaborating on his frontier thesis, his ideas dominated interpretations of the West up to World War II. A nonwesterner hailing from Wisconsin who spent his teaching career at the University of Wisconsin and Harvard University, Turner became the best-known American historian after serving as president of the American Historical Association in 1910 and succeeding to a chair of history at Harvard.

Turner's successor at the University of Wisconsin, Frederic Logan Paxson, also an easterner by background, preached much of the Turner doctrine throughout his career. In addition, Paxson, delivering on his promises, turned out Turnerian interpretations of the West in his book *The Last American Frontier* (1910) and his overview *History of the American Frontier, 1763–1893*

FIGURE 12:6. *Frederick Jackson Turner.* In 1893 the historian Frederick Jackson Turner spoke before a group of historians about "The Significance of the Frontier in American History." His "frontier" or "Turner" thesis shaped historical writing about the American West well into the twentieth century. Courtesy University Archives, University of Wisconsin, Madison.

(1924), the latter of which won a prestigious Pulitzer Prize. Paxson, like the early Turner, emphasized the West as a frontier experience, its history as a migration of peoples "to-the-West." Neither historian was much interested in examining what happened to pioneers once they arrived on the frontier; it was the movement to the West, the competition with "the Indian barrier," and the first settlements that meant most to Turner and Paxson.

But in the teens and twenties Turner himself encouraged a competing view of the western past. First in a series of lectures, then in a key essay entitled "The Significance of the Section in American History" (1925), and finally in a book of collected essays, *The Significance of Sections in American History* (1932), Turner advocated the study of the West as a "section," or region. Over time, he noted, new frontiers evolved and matured. Frontier experiences were laminated, regional identities forged, different from those in adjacent areas. It was time, Turner continued, for historians to move on to the next era of western history and to examine the postfrontier period of the West.

Even though Turner's frontier thesis remained in the saddle during the 1920s, regionalism began to challenge the frontier doctrine among western historians. In 1921, one of Turner's former graduate students, Herbert Eugene Bolton, published his influential book *The Spanish Borderlands*. In that volume and his numerous later publications Bolton called for an "Epic of Greater America," meaning a larger focus on regions where Spanish, Indian, and English-speaking cultures met, sometimes conflicted, and sometimes combined to form a "Borderlands" region. A decade after the appearance of Bolton's notable book, Texas historian Walter Prescott Webb issued his even more influential study *The Great Plains* (1931). Webb announced his regionalist thesis in his preface when he wrote "that the Great Plains environment . . . constitutes a geographic unity whose influences have been so powerful as to put a characteristic mark upon everything that survives within its borders." Kansas historian James Malin argued for similar emphases on regional themes in his essays on Kansas agricultural and cultural history. Trained both in history and the biological sciences, Malin wrote the first major books about the ecological influences shaping western history. In that regard, he became a major influence on later western environmental historians.

Although the regionalists challenged the frontier interpretations of the West, the earlier views still held sway at the outbreak of World War II. Indeed, the West as a frontier shaping influence on American society lasted well into the 1960s. Yet the regionalists planted seeds of an alternative view that bore fruit later in the twentieth century. Their argument that historians should see the region from an inside, in-the-West, perspective became increasingly popular after the 1960s. The regionalists urged students of the past to understand that the West as *place* was much more significant in western history than *process*, or the migration west. This regional emphasis on place rather than process became a central tenet of the New Western historians at the end of the twentieth century.

∾

When cowboy painter Charlie Russell died in 1926, an older era in western art seemed to disappear. Russell and Frederic Remington (until his death in 1909) represented the romantic cowboy-and-wild-Indian art that fascinated Americans from the 1890s onward. For Russell and Remington, and thousands of their admirers, the West was a frenetic frontier, alive with noble Indians, heroic soldiers, and galloping cowboys. What Owen Wister and Zane Grey were to popular Western fiction and John Wayne became to Western films, Russell and Remington were to western art. Their oil paintings, reproduced in a plethora of formats, adorned Old West hotels, taverns, train stations, and tourist facilities well into the twentieth century.

But early in the century eastern artists, discovering less-inhabited areas of the West, began to produced a different kind of western art. The most notable of these colonies of eastern artists coming west sprang up in Taos and Santa Fe, New Mexico. New York–trained and European-trained artists were particularly drawn to the bright colors, sparse spaces, and diverse peoples of the Southwest. For these easterners it seemed somehow more romantic to starve in an Indian or Hispanic adobe than in the cold, stuffy garrets of New York or Paris. Such artists as Ernest L. Blumenschein, Bert Geer Phillips, Oscar E. Berninghaus, W. Herbert "Buck" Dunton, and E. Martin Hennings began to spend several months each year living and painting in New Mexico.

These and later artists like Marsden Hartley, Robert Henri, and John Sloan painted artworks that married their training in modernistic art to scenes and peoples of the Southwest. For artists enamored with Impressionism and plein air (outdoor) painting, the southwestern sand tones, blue skies, and desert shrubs captured their attention. Of these attractions Blumenschein wrote, "No artist had ever recorded the New Mexico I was now seeing. . . . The color, the effective character of the landscape, the drama of the vast spaces, the superb beauty and serenity of the hills, stirred me deeply." In essence the Taos–Santa Fe artist produced oxymoronic cultural documents: paintings that combined European artistic techniques with southwestern settings and Pueblo Indian and Hispanic subjects to produce artworks part universal and part regional.

The most significant of the eastern artists who came west to paint new scenes and experiences was Georgia O'Keeffe. Reared in Wisconsin and trained in Chicago and New York City, O'Keeffe taught high school and college art classes in Texas between 1912 and 1914 and 1916 and 1918. In 1929 she made her first trip to New Mexico and fell under its spell. Throughout the 1930s she traveled frequently to the Southwest before moving there permanently in 1949 after the death of her husband, Alfred Stieglitz, the modernist photographer. The large, open skies, the brilliant colors of southwestern landscapes, and the churches and religious symbols—all appealed to O'Keeffe. Out of these strong, persisting attractions came O'Keeffe paintings such as *Taos Pueblo* (1929), *Rancho Church* (1930), and *Cow's Skull—Red, White and Blue* (1931). These works as well as dozens of others, in their stress on spaces, colors, and symbols rather than on specific places and concrete scenes, separated O'Keeffe from many regionalists. Like the artists of Taos and Santa Fe, O'Keeffe linked her training as a modernist artist to southwestern artifacts to produce artworks much different from the paintings of either frontier or regional painters.

A triumvirate of midwestern painters in the 1920s and 1930s became the premier regional artists of that period. Missourian Thomas Hart Benton, Iowan Grant Wood, and Kansan John Steuart Curry appeared in national magazines as the consummate regionalist painters in their notable depictions of midwestern scenes, people, and events. Benton's gigantic wall murals resembled pictorial histories of a mosaic of humans, and his oil and tempera paintings included redolent reproductions of Missouri, Texas, and other western settings. Other viewers found attractive Wood's well-known *American Gothic* (1930) and *Stone City* (1930), mixes of humor and midwestern small-town scenes. Wood's good friend Curry also filled his paintings *Baptism in Kansas* (1928) and *Tornado in Kansas* (1929) with lively, revealing portraits of Plains people and eye-catching landscapes of natural disaster. From these three midwestern artists came local and regional scenes overflowing with familiar and intriguing human and physical settings, paintings attractive and psychically healing.

A clutch of artists in other parts of the West also turned to regionalist and nonregional emphases in their paintings. In the 1930s southwestern artist Alexandre Hogue painted his stark *Erosion* series that depicted and scored the human-induced tragedies of the Dust Bowl. At the same time Peter Hurd executed several evocative treatments of the aridity, minimalistic terrain, and lyrical colors of southern New Mexico. His watercolors, oils, and egg tempera paintings, as two art historians note, "emphasize the vast spaces of the Southwest, with its bare hills and mountains. Only small intrusions—ranch houses and rickety fences—disturb the emptiness of the scene." In the Pacific Northwest, Mark Tobey, Morris Graves, and Kenneth Callahan, sometimes dubbed the "Northwest School of Art," shared interests in the Orient and used northwestern places, peoples, and animal life to treat regional experiences. But they also looked forward to the postregional interests of artists after World War II in employing universal themes and innovative techniques rather than focusing entirely on local and regional themes and artistic approaches.

The rise of Hollywood and the film industry furnishes still another example of the cultural diversities of the first half of the twentieth-century West. Although the movie industry began on the East Coast, by 1915 most film companies had relocated to California. Happy to avoid legal embroilments over patent infringements and speedily recognizing the merits of year-round sunny days in southern California, moviemakers established and soon expanded the Hollywood community adjacent to booming Los Angeles.

In its initial years Hollywood churned out all kinds of films. In the silent movie years stretching up to 1929, slapstick comedies, fairy tale fantasies, religious epics, and historical extravaganzas did well. By the mid-1920s the "star system" had emerged, featuring such leading men and ladies as Charlie Chaplin, Rudolph Valentino, Douglas Fairbanks, Mary Pickford, and Gloria Swanson. At the same time several big companies began to dominate the film industry: MGM, Warner Brothers, RKO, and Twentieth-Century Fox. Not everyone kowtowed, however, to the rumored licentiousness and tawdry lives of actors and hangers-on. Sedate Los Angelenos, living near Hollywood and deeply under the sway of moralistic midwestern immigrants, tried to keep "those weird people" at a distance by erecting "No Dogs or Actors Allowed" signs on the lawns of their rental apartments. When the movie industry boomed and many jobs—some well-paying—became available, these derogatory signs about actors quickly disappeared.

Once in the West, movie companies and ambitious directors promptly capitalized on the wide-open, attractive scenery of Los Angeles and its environs. A blizzard of Western films followed, with the Western becoming Hollywood's most popular movie type. From the first one-reeler (ten-minute) Western movie, *The Great Train Robbery* (1903), until well into the 1930s, film Westerns reinforced, rather than transformed, popular ideas about the West. Strong, masculine heroes; violent, malevolent opponents; and spacious, appealing settings—here were the familiar ingredients of Buffalo Bill's *Wild West*, dime novels, and Owen Wister's *The Virginian* in a new venue. Film directors and producers were not interested in depicting the West as a developing region with its own regional identity; they were satisfied to cater to their audiences' love of a romantic Old West.

Three sagebrush movie heroes dominated the early Hollywood Westerns. Broncho Billy Anderson, William S. Hart, and Tom Mix rode dramatically across hundreds of silent screens—and into the hearts of their viewers. They displayed what seemed inbred notions of defending women, children, and weak communities and their ever-active fast fists to fight off evil-doers. Hart and Mix were also skilled riders whose saddleback antics won ever-growing audiences. As Hart's career ended with his *Tumbleweeds* (1925), John Ford was winning his first spurs as a director in the Western epic *The Iron Horse* (1924) and John Wayne and Gary Cooper launched their long careers as Western heroes.

The advent of sound added a very important new ingredient to the film Western. Taking advantage of this addition in the 1930s, Gene Autry, Roy Rogers, and dozens of other movie cowboys strummed their ever-present guitars while warbling or yodeling their ways to stardom. Singing Westerns closely followed the frontier plot lines of heroes, villains, appealing scenery, and sometimes fetching heroines that earlier films and popular fiction had established and solidified by the 1920s. Audiences wanted these familiar ingredients, and the guitar-plucking cowboys and pliant directors gave them what they wanted in the singing Westerns.

The release of the classic Western film *Stagecoach* (1939) also proved that the West could be depicted much more realistically. Based on an Ernest Haycox

FIGURE 12:7. Stagecoach *(1939)*. This classic Western film, directed by John Ford and starring John Wayne, avoided many of the clichés of early Hollywood movies and proved that complex cinematic stories about the Old West were possible.

short story that director John Ford purchased and remade into a superb film, the movie featured a stagecoach overflowing with pilgrims journeying through dangerous Geronimo country. The lead actors played appealingly complex roles: John Wayne as the outlaw Ringo Kid, Thomas Mitchell as the drunken doctor (a role for which he won an Oscar), and Claire Trevor as Dallas the prostitute. Ford adeptly played on social class prejudices, conflicts between the military and Indians, and an improbable romance between two social outcasts, the outlaw (Wayne) and the prostitute (Trevor). While the stagecoach rumbled perilously through the forbidding Monument Valley setting and the threatening Geronimo country, the characters wonderfully displayed their flaws, biases, and courage. As runner-up to *Gone with the Wind* as the best film of 1939, *Stagecoach* gained deserved high laurels as a first-rate movie. More than anything this film, featuring the work of John Ford and John Wayne together for the first time, proved that mundane western materials might, in the hands of a skillful director and premier actors, be transformed into a sophisticated, complex, adult Western. *Stagecoach*, one of the classic films of all time, demonstrated that the Western had come of age by the end of the 1930s.

~

Religious patterns from 1900 to 1940 illustrated the diversity and change of western culture. Although often mimicking national tendencies, religious trends in the West also frequently broke from those familiar patterns. Religionists west of the 100th meridian wrestled with the controversial issues of the times: higher criticism of the Bible, Darwinism, immigration pressures, secularism, and the dilemmas of war and depressions. Yet the makeup of Protestant, Catholic, and Jewish populations greatly varied from subregion to subregion in the West, and gusts of change swept over religious groups before the outbreak of World War II. As the leading authority on western religion points out, "The religious history of the modern American West introduces a new cast of characters and often forges its own boundaries."

Several religious leaders in the West captured national headlines early in the century. The Reverend Mark Matthews of Seattle's First Presbyterian Church became a notoriously militant Fundamentalist attacking modernist doctrines, alcohol and imbibers, and liberal religious leaders. But he also supported reform efforts to "clean up" Seattle and built his flock into the largest Presbyterian church in the world. J. Frank Norris, pastor of the First Baptist Church in Fort Worth, took a similar approach to opponents and what he called the "fat cats" who criticized his conservative religious views. The Texas Tornado, as Norris became known, epitomized the slashing style of some Fundamentalists who

FIGURE 12:8. *Sister Aimee Semple McPherson.* The most popular and widely acclaimed
Protestant minister of the 1920s and 1930s, Sister Aimee loved to engage in ministerial
drama. These acts including dressing as a member of the police to STOP sinners from
misdeeds. *Foursquare Bridal Call,* March 1925. Used by permission of the Heritage
Department of the International Church of the Foursquare Gospel.

enlivened and made controversial Protestant stances in the 1920s and 1930s. William Jennings Bryan, the Populist and Democratic candidate for the presidency, was also a well-known Protestant layman early in the twentieth century. Although affable and sincere, Bryan's embarrassing actions toward the end of his life at the landmark Scopes Trial in 1925 shadow his lifetime accomplishments as a spokesman for Christian acceptance and charity.

The most famous of the Protestant leaders and preachers in the West was Aimee Semple McPherson. As a young woman, Aimee had converted to an enthusiastic brand of Pentecostalism and moved to California in 1918. A vivacious, attractive person and speaker, she soon attracted thousands in the 1920s to her Sunday services and revival meetings, established the Four Square Gospel Church, and built the sprawling Angelus Temple in Los Angeles. Her lively sermons, delivered with gusto, style, and a clear empathy for the frustrations and alienations newcomers to the West Coast often felt, attracted more headlines than most movie stars. Sister Aimee, as she was called, became "the most famous American woman of her day, a position she held until the appearance of Eleanor Roosevelt." Up to her death in 1944, Sister Aimee provided solace and hope for the thousands who flocked to her services or listened to her uplifting, revivalistic sermons on the new medium of the radio.

Most Protestant churches and pastors in the West were much less controversial, of course. The first religious censuses of the twentieth century revealed that mainline groups dominated several parts of the West. Methodists did well in Kansas and Oklahoma, Baptists in Texas, and Lutherans across the northern Plains. California hosted a variety of Protestant groups, but the Pacific Northwest manifested the lowest church-affiliated numbers of any region of the West. In the 1920s and 1930s, evangelical Protestant groups like the Assemblies of God, the Church of the Nazarene, and the Southern Baptists grew rapidly, soon becoming what *Life* magazine labeled the "Third Force of Christendom" (following the Catholics and mainline Protestants).

~

Roman Catholics, meanwhile, dominated church membership in most of the seventeen western states. In six of these states, Catholics made up more than 50 percent of church affiliation, with Catholic numbers especially strong across the Southwest, in old mining regions, and in the northern West. Hispanic, Irish, Italian, German, other immigrant groups, and many Native Americans were strongly Catholic. Overall, Catholic populations were also evident in many western urban areas.

The 1920s and 1930s were difficult times for many western Catholics. First, expanding migrations west in the 1920s consisted primarily of Protestants, which meant that non-Catholic populations surged to the forefront of some traditionally strong Catholic areas. Second, KKK attacks on Catholics obviously wounded the church in areas such as Oklahoma, Texas, California, and Oregon. Third, the Great Depression of the 1930s weighed heavily on the church, weakening its ability to provide support services in needy urban and rural areas. Fourth, with insufficient numbers of priests, the church was unable to minister to many isolated sections of the West; considerable "leakage" occurred as a result in rural areas of the region.

In other arenas Catholics experienced fewer difficulties than the Protestants. Higher criticism of the Bible and Darwin's theory of evolution had little impact generally on western Catholics, and Catholics felt none of the fractious disputes between Fundamentalists and mainline churches that shook Protestants in the interwar years. Also, continuing immigration of Spanish-speaking Catholics from south of the border swelled church numbers from Texas to California. Although large Catholic majorities melted away in some states, their church-going numbers still predominated in many western areas. Of all the western states, New Mexico retained most its Catholic profile, with nearly half of its population remaining loyal to the church.

Catholic institutions likewise persisted, and new ones were launched. Interestingly, non-Catholics swarming into California and the Southwest and looking for a common past on which to bond often romanticized the Catholic heritage of those areas, particularly its mission churches and church sites. Charles Fletcher Lummis, the son of an eastern Protestant minister and an indefatigable journalist and promoter, led the way in championing a new appreciation of Catholic missions and history in the Southwest. Mother Katharine Drexel, in addition to starting an order for nuns, continued to pour her family funds into missions for Indians and "Negroes." Additionally, Father Edward J. Flanagan established his soon-to-be-famous Boys' Town in Nebraska, an institution that drew Catholic, Protestant, and secular support for homeless, delinquent, and other poverty-stricken boys. Catholic mission work among Indian communities also remained strong. Finally, the organization of archdioceses in several areas—San Antonio (1926), Los Angeles (1936), Denver (1941), and Omaha (1945)—testified to continuing Catholic strength in those areas of the West.

~

Jews lived in a different kind of West from that of Christians. Although hundreds of Jews migrated to the West in the nineteenth century, most of them scattered throughout the region. By 1920, no western city could boast of more than 5 percent of its population as Jewish. Those scholars studying American Jewry in the West point to the important commercial and trade services they provided and their part in the popularity of German culture in the West. By and large, Jews experienced very little anti-Semitism in the late nineteenth or early twentieth centuries. In addition to playing major roles in the rise of Hollywood, Jews did well as candidates for political office. Governors Moses Alexander of Idaho (1915–19) and Simon Bamberger of Utah (1917–21), Senators Joseph Simon of Oregon (1898–1903) and Simon Guggenheim of Colorado (1907–13), and several western Jewish mayors held office well before eastern states elected equal numbers of Jews to similar offices.

Jewish populations continued to grow in the early twentieth-century West, although not as rapidly as elsewhere in the United States. Some came west as part of European and Russian migrations from the 1880s to the 1920s. The Askenazim Jews arrived from Germany and eastern Europe and the Sephardim from Spain and Portugal. Relations between these two groups as well as among the Reform, Conservative, and Orthodox branches of Judaism could be strained and sometimes divisive, but these tensions never completely divided Jewish westerners. In the post–World War II period, Jewish migration to the Far West experienced a high tide and allowed Los Angeles to become, after New York City, the largest center of Jews in the United States.

For another important western religious group, the Latter-day Saints (LDS or Mormons), a variant historical and cultural path emerged. After experiencing the traumas of federal legal and political attacks in the late nineteenth century that shook their church to its foundations, Mormons made, early in the twentieth century, adjustments and accommodations to the American mainstream. These changes included denouncing polygamy and abandoning some of their social and cultural isolation. But, two Mormon historians explain, LDS "adjustment did not mean a total melting into the national patterns. It [was] still a distinctive church, not liberal Protestant, not fundamental Protestant, not Catholic."

Mormon adherents and converts grew in numbers and strength in the first decades of the twentieth century. With about 200,000 members in 1900, the LDS Church exploded to nearly one million by World War II. It also became an international organization, with its first temples built outside the United States in 1919 and thereafter. Brigham Young University became an increasingly well-known institution of higher learning, and the church established a thoroughly organized and highly successful welfare plan for needy members in the 1930s. Yet in its high birth rates (twice the national average), its use of nonbiblical texts, and its lack of a professional clergy, the Mormons remained different from Protestant and Catholic Christians. Conversely, in their heavy emphases on families; their abstinence from alcohol, tobacco, and drugs; their church-centered entertainments; and their practice of tithing (10 percent of income to the church), the Mormons closely resembled evangelical Christians groups who were also enjoying rapid growth in the 1920s and 1930s.

Western education, like so many other aspects of the region's cultural life, simultaneously followed national as well as regional precedents. Schools and educational systems in the West were, at one and the same time, conservative and innovative. This bifurcated outlook meant that schools and schooling in the West build on well-known national educational foundations even as they erected pioneering structures that set the pace for other regions.

At the opening of the twentieth century, public school systems in the West were well in place. Drawing on a federal policy that set aside one of every sixteen sections of government lands for schools and additional support for schools at the state level, western states had organized public schools through the first eight grades. Early in the new century, California also experimented with junior high schools and junior colleges. Soon that state also divided schools into systems of six, three, and three grades through high school and then two years of junior college. No other western state—indeed of nearly all other states—was as forward-looking as California in its educational experimentation.

Even in following national precedents like the establishing of high schools, the West moved more quickly in this implementation than did other regions. Generally speaking, the most experimental, innovative reforms in schools came in rapidly changing urban areas of the West. Not surprisingly, California early gained a reputation for the strong, innovative quality of its statewide educational system—a reputation it maintained throughout the twentieth century.

Educationalist John Dewey's controversial new ideas about schooling, Progressive Education, also shaped western education in the decades before World War II. Pointing out the deficiencies in rote learning, Dewey and his disciples called for education through adventure. That is, students learned best by activity, and those activities should teach learners how to function in a democratic society. Dewey's Progressive Education program quickly influenced western schools, as it did teachers and schools throughout the country.

Westerners were also busy sustaining and establishing college and university systems in their region. Again, as was true with public schools, federal legislation aided greatly in funding western institutions of higher learning. Eighteenth- and nineteenth-century federal acts provided endowments of land for state universities and land-grant colleges; by 1900 all western states had established at least one state university or land-grant college. Increasingly, as was the case with elementary and high schools, westerners favored public universities over private ones. In that tendency they differed from residents of eastern states. Yet western colleges and universities were often tradition-bound in the course of studies they adopted, choosing the classical curricula of their eastern counterparts more often than establishing more innovative course offerings.

Despite the growing predominance of public colleges and universities, denominational and secular colleges persisted or were newly founded. The Catholics led the way in the numbers of their church schools. Among the large number of Catholic colleges were Creighton University in Nebraska, Gonzaga University and Seattle University in Washington, University of Portland in Oregon, Loyola in California, and Regis in Colorado. Protestant denominations launched competitors: Texas Christian University, Southern Methodist University, and Baylor University (Baptist) in Texas; the University of Southern California (Methodist) in California; Willamette (Methodist) and Linfield College (Baptist) in Oregon; and Augustana College (Lutheran) in South Dakota. Indeed, small, virtually unknown church-related colleges appeared and disappeared throughout the West like undulating bull and bear markets. Prestigious nonsectarian colleges and universities included Stanford University, Mills College, California Institute of Technology, Reed College, Whitman College, Colorado College, and Rice University.

~

Although western schools and colleges had opened their doors to all classes of white male and female students, they were slower to help immigrant children or students of minority racial backgrounds. Indeed, prejudices too often blinded western educators to the special needs of culturally different scholars. In 1906, for example, the San Francisco Board of Education stipulated that Japanese students must attend a separate school. Quickly, however, President Theodore Roosevelt's blustering attack on the inequities of the board's unfortunate decision, as well as a strong response from Japan, reversed the order. Segregation of white and black students was particularly blatant, too, in east Texas. There nearly all black students (making up more than 30 percent of the school population) were forced into inferior schools. Sometimes these two-tiered school systems resulted from corrosive racism, sometimes from inadequate funding, and perhaps most from inadequate attention being paid to students with large needs. Thankfully, a few necessary reforms began to appear in the 1930s. As part of the New Deal, John Collier, leader of the Bureau of Indian Affairs, established new day schools for Indians, added more reservation teachers, and began new bilingual educational programs for Native students. Two other New Deal agencies, the National Youth Authority and the Civilian Conservation Corps, provided training and part-time jobs for high school and college students.

President Franklin Roosevelt's generous support for educational programs and reforms were much needed to offset the huge impact of the Great Depression on schools and schooling in the West during the 1930s. Observant travelers visiting much of the West in 1933 found states despairing in keeping open their colleges and schools. In numerous western colleges, faculty members were let go, and those who remained had their salaries severely cut. Reductions were even more drastic for public schools. To keep schools operating, school boards eliminated everything in the curriculum considered nonessential (meaning everything but the three R's), reduced the length of the school year, increased loads for teachers, and slashed salaries. Oklahoma placed a lid on teachers' pay, Oregon threw out a minimum salary law for instructors, and Wyoming mandated a much-shortened school year. Sometimes money for salaries was so short that teachers were "boarded around" in student homes to save money. Other school districts issued promissory notes to teachers for salary monies they did not have. In New Mexico and Oklahoma the situation was so dire that some public schools were simply closed. In other western areas educational outlays were reduced by more than 30 percent.

What happened to western colleges and schools in the early 1930s was part of the disastrous impact of the Great Depression on the region. By the end of the decade, better economic times and growing hope for the future broke through the gloom like a sunburst on a rainy day. School boards, teachers, and students began to look forward to better days just as World War II broke out.

~

Visitors to the West in the first decades of the twentieth century often spoke of how quickly western people and places seemed to change. Nothing stood still, and within a generation or two western towns became cities, with waves of newcomers suddenly filling these mushrooming urban areas, especially on the West Coast. Uncle Sam seemed more and more present in the West, particularly as New Deal policies obviously changed western economic and social life. New political and cultural currents were also coursing through the West. But none of these observers could have predicted the tidal wave of change that swept over the West in the early 1940s. As we shall see, World War II truly transformed the American West.

Botkin, Daniel R. *Beyond the Stony Mountains: Nature in the American West from Lewis and Clark to Today*. New York: Oxford University Press, 2004.

Brown, Richard Maxwell. "The New Regionalism in America, 1970–1981." In *Regionalism and the Pacific Northwest*, edited by William G. Robbins et al., 37–96. Corvallis: Oregon State University Press, 1983.

Buscombe, Edward, ed. *The BFI Guide to the Western*. New York: Atheneum, 1988.

Deverell, William, and Tom Sitton, eds. *California Progressivism Revisited*. Berkeley: University of California Press, 1994.

Dorman, Robert L. *Revolt of the Provinces: The Regionalist Movement in America, 1920–1945*. Chapel Hill: University of North Carolina Press, 1993.

Dubofsky, Melvyn. *We Shall Be All: A History of the Industrial Workers of the World*. Chicago: Quadrangle Books, 1969.

Eldredge, Charles C. *Georgia O'Keeffe*. New York: Harry N. Abrams, 1991.

Etulain, Richard W. *Re-imagining the American West: A Century of Fiction, History, and Art*. Tucson: University of Arizona Press, 1996.

———. *Telling Western Stories: From Buffalo Bill to Larry McMurtry*. Albuquerque: University of New Mexico Press, 1999.

Etulain, Richard W., and Glenda Riley, eds. *The Hollywood West: Lives of Film Legends Who Shaped It*. Golden, CO: Fulcrum Publishing, 2001.

Goetzmann, William H., and William N. Goetzmann. *The West of the Imagination*. New York: W. W. Norton, 1986.

Harvey, Mark. "James J. Hill, Jeannette Rankin, and John Muir: The American West in the Progressive Era, 1890–1920." In *Western Lives: A Biographical History of the American West*, edited by Richard W. Etulain, 283–304. Albuquerque: University of New Mexico Press, 2004.

Heller, Nancy, and Julia Williams. *The Regionalists: Painters of the American Scene*. New York: Watson-Guptill, 1976.

Jameson, Elizabeth. *All That Glitters: Class, Conflict, and Community in Cripple Creek*. Urbana: University of Illinois Press, 1998.

Johnston, Robert D. *The Radical Middle Class: Populist Democracy and the Question of Capitalism in Progressive Era Portland*. Princeton, NJ: Princeton University Press, 2003.

Lowitt, Richard. *The New Deal and the West*. Bloomington: Indiana University Press, 1984.

McGerr, Michael. *A Fierce Discontent: The Rise and Fall of the Progressive Movement in America, 1870–1920*. New York: Free Press, 2003.

Mowry, George E. *The California Progressives*. Berkeley: University of California Press, 1951.

Nash, Gerald D. *Creating the West: Historical Interpretations 1890–1990*. Albuquerque: University of New Mexico Press, 1991.

Pomeroy, Earl. *In Search of the Golden West: The Tourist in Western America.* New York: Alfred A. Knopf, 1957.

———. *The Pacific Slope: A History of California, Oregon, Washington, Idaho, Utah and Nevada.* New York: Knopf, 1965.

Righter, Robert W. *The Battle Over Hetch Hetchy: America's Most Controversial Dam and the Birth of Modern Environmentalism.* New York: Oxford University Press, 2005.

Rothman, Hal K. *Saving the Planet: The American Response to the Environment in the Twentieth Century.* Chicago: Ivan Dee, 2001.

Shabecoff, Philip. *A Fierce Green Fire: The American Environmental Movement.* New York: Hill and Wang, 1993.

Sklar, Robert. *Movie-Made America: A Cultural History of American Movies.* Rev. ed. New York: Vintage, 1994.

Smith, Sherry L. *Reimagining Indians: Native Americans Through Anglo Eyes, 1880–1940.* New York: Oxford University Press, 2000.

Starr, Kevin. *Americans and the California Dream 1850–1915.* New York: Oxford University Press, 1973.

———. *Inventing the Dream: California Through the Progressive Era.* New York: Oxford University Press, 1985.

Steinberg, Ted. *Down to Earth: Nature's Role in American History.* New York: Oxford University Press, 2002.

Szasz, Ferenc Morton. *Religion in the Modern American West.* Tucson: University of Arizona Press, 2000.

Turner, Frederick Jackson. *The Frontier in American History.* New York: Henry Holt, 1920.

Webb, Walter Prescott. *The Great Plains.* Boston: Ginn, 1931.

Woodward, Robert C. "William S. U'Ren, A Progressive Era Personality." *Idaho Yesterdays* 4 (Summer 1960): 4–10.

Wrobel, David M. *The End of American Exceptionalism: Frontier Anxiety from the Old West to the New Deal.* Lawrence: University Press of Kansas, 1993.

CHAPTER THIRTEEN

The West Transformed

WORLD WAR II TO 1960

~

EARLY IN 1942, NORMA CANTRELL JOINED HUNDREDS OF THOUSANDS OF Americans flocking west to work in the war-related industries popping up all over the Far West. Just seventeen and one of eleven children of a disintegrating family in Texas, Norma had already served as a migrant worker in California. Then, she recalled, "all hell broke loose on the 7th of December"; "everybody was leaving to go [to] Seattle or California." Once west again, she began working for Lockheed near Los Angeles. "I didn't even have to go for the job; people were coming to me for jobs. Not only just me, but everyone. They were recruiting workers and they didn't care whether you were Black, white, young, old." Because hundreds of factories supplying war goods were frantic for workers, Norma remembered, "You were bombarded." "They were begging for workers."

Norma Cantrell's story became the norm for multitudes of workers coming west during World War II. War-driven factories and military installations demanded more laborers than the West could provide. News of the many good-paying jobs was like a gift from heaven for many depression-deprived families. As they flooded into the West, countless newcomers like Norma Cantrell swelled the region's population, redirected its urban patterns, and transformed its cultural and political identities. Truly, a Second Gold Rush, with all the attendant changes and complexities of a mighty rush, broke out during the early 1940s. But not all was glittering gold; there were manifold tensions and problems challenging the new westerners.

The Second World War revolutionized the American West. Much as the Gold Rush had a century earlier, World War II transformed the region. Social and economic patterns, as well as political and cultural life, felt the barrage of change reorienting large parts of the United States. But in addition, writes the leading authority on the history of the West during World War II, "In four short years [1941 to 1945] the war brought a maturation to the West that in peacetime might have taken generations to accomplish. It transformed an area with a self-image that emphasized colonialism into one boasting self-sufficiency and innovation."

~

Even before the attack on Pearl Harbor in December 1941, the West experienced an infusion of federal funds and power into the region. From 1933 onward New Deal policies injected billions of dollars into reclamation, Civilian Conservation Corps, business, and agricultural projects. After World War II broke out in Europe in 1939 and the United States moved to help its European allies, early war contracts sent west another transfusion of government funding. But these were as small streams compared to the river of federal monies flowing out from Washington, D.C., after the United States entered the Atlantic and Pacific war theaters between 1941 and 1945. In those four tumultuous years, as much as $70 billion flew west.

This huge influx of federal monies made possible the hasty erection of hundreds of war-support industries and the opening of millions of war-related jobs. A veritable deluge of families flowed west, going after promised jobs like a school of trout chasing new lures. Overnight Pacific Coast and Southwest cities mushroomed with these burgeoning hordes. Indeed, nearly every far-western state felt the wave of migrants. California topped the list with one million new residents between 1940 and 1945. The exceptions to this incoming flood were interior states like the Dakotas, Nebraska, and Montana, which lost as much as 10 percent of their populations when jobseekers went to the coast. Above all, those western cities, towns, and rural places most closely linked with the emerging military behemoth felt strongest the dramatic changes rippling over the region.

Government spending for military installations and bases triggered much of the transformation of the West in the early 1940s. Massive amounts of funding established or expanded shipyards, airplane factories, and military bases. Since President Roosevelt wanted to disperse government spending, as well as to avoid placing all military complexes in one area, he viewed the West as a new, innovative region ready for military expansion. Also, because much of World War II took place in the Far East, the West became an important staging area for launching military support in the Pacific.

Most spending on military expansion funded shipbuilding sites, airplane construction plants, and military bases. Working through important industrialists like Henry J. Kaiser, a bluff, hard-working administrator, the federal government contracted for hundreds of new ships to be built in Kaiser's booming

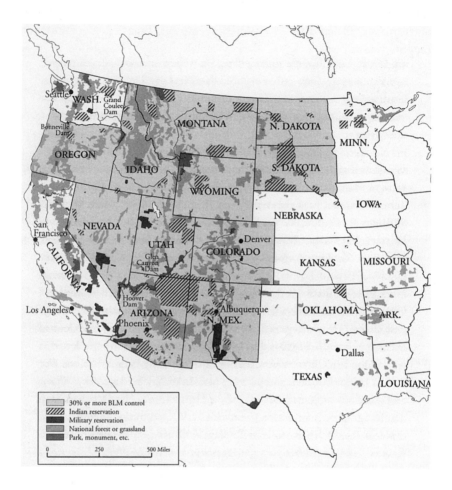

FIGURE 13:1. *The Federal Landscape in the West.* The federal government became a growing presence in the West, especially from the 1930s onward. Agencies like the Bureau of Land Management, national park and national forest systems, and Indian and military reservations illustrated this expanding federal presence. "The Federal Landscape in the West" is based on a map by Randy Wallace and Mary Wyant, with data from the Environment Systems Research Institute, Redlands, California, from Gerald D. Nash, *The Federal Landscape: An Economic History of the Twentieth-Century West.* © 1999 The Arizona Board of Regents. Reprinted by permission of the University of Arizona Press, frontispiece.

shipyards in Los Angeles, San Francisco (Richmond), and Portland. At one time, Kaiser employed more than 250,000 men and women in his sprawling plants, with shifts of laborers working around the clock. A man of immense energies and business acumen, Kaiser produced thousands of ships for multiple uses. Although eastern shipyards might need a year to construct a 10,000-ton vessel, Kaiser turned them out in a few weeks.

Aircraft factories also sprang up. Southern California and Seattle established or expanded major airplane construction plants. Douglas, Lockheed, and North American Aviation in California and Boeing in Washington became important sites for airplane production. Although these West Coast plants turned out as many as one thousand planes in 1939, they upped production to forty thousand planes annually between 1942 and 1945. Plane engines were still built in Detroit, but the completed planes came from the Far West sites. President Roosevelt made this industrial "take-off" possible when he called for fifty thousand planes to be built each year and pushed Congress into handing out billions of dollars in wartime contracts.

The growing military presence in the West became clear in the mounting number of bases throughout the region. The federal government scattered army bases from Kansas (Fort Riley), Oklahoma (Fort Sill), and Texas (Fort Hood and Fort Bliss) to California (Fort Ord and the San Francisco Presidio) and Washington (Fort Lewis) on the coast. Numerous air force bases were situated from Minot and Ellsworth in the Dakotas to Edwards, Williams, Kirtland, and Lackland across the Southwest. Naval installations stretched along the West Coast from San Diego in the south to Bremerton, Washington, in the north. Meanwhile, several Marine Corps bases dotted the California terrain. Not surprisingly, the numbers of military personnel stationed in the West soared. In the 1930s fewer than 100,000 servicemen were in the West; by 1945, as many as 10 million men and women had been stationed in the West. In the same period fewer than 1,000 planes deployed in the West grew to a force of more than 75,000 planes.

These new or expanded ship- and airplane-building facilities and the military bases laid the foundation for what became known as the military-industrial complex. The billions of dollars made available to build this infrastructure turned the region into Uncle Sam's West. And with the factories and bases came jobs, and to fill those openings millions of newcomers moved west during World War II.

≈

The unprecedented deluge of migrants changed and diversified the social patterns of the West. Already more than half urban by the 1930s, the West became increasingly a region of cities during the wartime. Most of the incoming populations arrived from the American East or South, beginning what later was described as the "westward tilt." But others came from within the West, moving from rural areas to take advantage of newly opened jobs in urban factories or installations fueling and supporting the war. These flocks of new westerners, from a welter of racial and ethnic backgrounds, wrought enormous changes on the social mosaic of the region.

In the 1940s, more than 8 million persons relocated to the trans-Mississippi West, most of them before 1945. California alone gained 3.6 million of the newcomers, swelling the state's population to 10.5 million in 1950. The migrants to the West Coast were but a portion of those who inundated other areas of the West, especially those hosting new military installations and wartime production plants. Western ethnic, gender, and family profiles were transformed as a result of this gigantic people movement.

Newcomers to the West during World War II were as varied and shifting as a shimmering rainbow. The velocity of change was highest, of course, near war production sites and military installations. West Coast cities from San Diego to Seattle sometimes grew more than 10 percent annually. Interior western cites such as Albuquerque, Denver and Colorado Springs, Tucson and Phoenix, and Dallas and El Paso also expanded rapidly as a result of their close proximity to air bases or other military sites. Others like Salt Lake City, Reno, and Wichita were hubs for subregions also experiencing economic and social expansion.

~

Housing was a major dilemma for incoming wartime families. In San Diego, one labor leader noted, "There seems to be little doubt that adequate housing is the most pressing problem facing the war workers in our area. Even a cursory inspection makes it evident that our facilities are woefully inadequate." Between 1940 and 1943 San Diego built more houses than in the previous thirty years, but from 1940 to 1945 the population of the city jumped from 202,000 to 380,000, not counting the 130,000 military personnel also crowded into the area. Similar housing problems vexed Los Angeles and also Oakland and the East Bay in the north. War workers and their families camped out in tents, trailers, virtually any kind of space, waiting for adequate housing. A headline story in the *Oakland Tribune* in 1942, titled "Nomads But Not By Choice," told of one Richmond shipyard worker whose family lived out of their car for several weeks.

That family's story of woe was repeated thousands of times up and down the West Coast, even though numerous flimsy housing projects rolled out like school children tumbling into recess. For example, between Portland, Oregon, and Vancouver, Washington, a gigantic, hastily erected housing area, Vanport, accommodated more than forty thousand residents at its peak. In 1940, the area was virtually open space; three years later it contained ten thousand housing units. Residents complained that these jerry-built houses hosted more cockroaches and bedbugs than people, and women found the cooking and washing facilities inadequate for daily living. Concrete floors, muddy streets, and faulty drainage were added drawbacks for residents in Vanport. Other cities in the interior West, including Denver, Wichita, and Tulsa, were also deluged with new workers and faced similar housing problems. .

These rapid, complex transformations brought manifold stresses to relocating families. Job shifts, increasing numbers of women working outside their homes, and new schools, friends, and neighborhoods for children heightened the traumas of transition. Eastern, rural, and other western laborers faced new occupations as skilled and unskilled workers in urban or suburban airplane, shipbuilding, or other war-production facilities. Incessant and demanding orders, frenzied deadlines, and insecure positions impacted nearly all new laborers in the West.

Especially pathbreaking was the unprecedented number of women taking factory jobs. Indeed, a new name, "Rosie the Riveter," was coined to denominate women now working on assembly lines and in war-production factories. For many women, this change meant they were doing double shifts: one working in war-related industries, one at home tending their homes and families. A western political leader, understanding these new dilemmas for women, observed, "We have hundreds of thousands of women who are working in our war factories . . . who are keeping homes for their husbands and children. . . . They may be able to stand the gaff for 60 days or 6 months, but then they are exhausted and quit . . ." The California politician was only half right: western women experienced a good deal of stress in their jobs, many looked for less burdensome employment, and they often retreated from their new, taxing positions. More impressive, however, were the thousands of women who gradually adapted to their demanding workloads, outside and within their homes. One study of American women during World War II found that western women were more adaptable to change than other women. More educated and forward-looking, less religious, western women accepted major transitions more readily than other American women.

Other fallout from their novel circumstances buffeted new western families in the early 1940s. How were day care and schooling to be worked out, for example, if both parents were working outside their homes? For many families these were entirely new problems, without precedent. Attempted solutions to this new dilemma were several. In some homes older children tried to parent their younger sisters and brothers. In other families older preadolescent

FIGURE 13:2. *Rosie the Riveter.* During World War II women in
unprecedented numbers worked in war-related industries. Their presence
in these factories was so widespread that, as a group, they became known
as "Rosie the Riveter." Courtesy Franklin D. Roosevelt Library.

children were left alone. Difficulties if not outright failures followed many of
these ill-conceived solutions. In Los Angeles, arrests for juvenile delinquency
doubled between 1940 and 1943. One social worker in California discovered
nearly fifty children locked in cars in the parking lot of a war-related industry.

Other answers proved more positive and long-lasting. Industrialist Henry J.
Kaiser, knowing that in thousands of families both parents were working at
his factories, realized he must do something about the care of their children.
Near his factories in Portland and Vancouver he established day-care centers
for toddlers to six-year-olds. These facilities featured playrooms, swimming
pools, and prepared meals that working parents could take home to their families. To accommodate parents working on swing and night shifts, the child-care
centers were open around the clock. Seattle and Wichita, two other western cities booming with wartime contracts, also quickly discovered how ill-prepared
they were to address the problems of families flooding into their urban spaces.

So many families moved into Seattle to work at the Boeing Aircraft Company and other war industries that workers, at first, had to delay bringing their families to the Pacific Northwest because there were no houses for them. Between 1940 and 1943 Wichita grew faster than any other western urban concentration save San Diego. At first new families coming to Wichita to work at aircraft factories or stationed at nearby bases also faced housing problems as well as heightened racial conflicts, but those problems gradually diminished toward the end of the war.

~

World War II profoundly impacted specific groups in the West. Among these were the traumatic changes shaping the lives of Native Americans scattered across the region. New Deal policies of the 1930s had encouraged Indians to return to their reservations, their land-based societies, but the global war reversed these trends, bringing thousands of Natives off reservations into American society. One anthropologist concluded, after interviewing dozens of Indian war veterans, that "this Second World War has exerted a great impact on the cultures of these peoples, perhaps the greatest since the arrival of the Spaniards 500 years ago." As many as 25,000 Indians joined the war effort. One story circulated that a group of Apaches, volunteering for the service, asked a recruiter, "Why do Apaches need training to make war?" Another group of Native soldiers attracted special attention. When the Marines wished to set up a means of secret communication in the Pacific theater, they employed a group of Navajos who became known as "code talkers." The little-known Navajo language became the code of the Signal Corps, keeping messages secret from American enemies. Perhaps as many as 40,000 other Indians left reservations to take war-related jobs in cities such as Los Angeles, Denver, Albuquerque, and Tucson. After the war, many veterans, as well as those working in western urban areas, returned to their reservations, bringing back experiences that challenged earlier Native traditions. Even though not all these experiences were positive for Indian societies, World War II had clearly wrought powerful, lasting alterations to Native American life.

No less marked was the wartime impact on Hispanics. Growing demands for military hardware and foodstuffs opened hundreds of thousands of unskilled jobs for Spanish-speaking Americans as well as for Mexican-born residents of or immigrants to the United States. Thousands of other Mexican Americans joined the service. One estimate suggests that of the nearly three million Mexican-heritage Americans in the United States, nearly 500,000 saw duty in the war. As one Hispanic veteran stated, "We believed that by joining the service, we could lay to rest the idea that Mexicans were disloyal to the United States." Front-line casualties were particularly high for Mexican Americans. In Los Angeles, Chicanos were 10 percent of the city's population but suffered 20 percent of its losses. In south Texas, 50 to 75 percent of the war casualties had Spanish surnames. And in the tragic Bataan Death March in the Philippines fully 25 percent of the prisoners of war were Hispanics. Mexican American women were also on active duty during the war, although much larger numbers worked in war industries, sold war bonds, organized patriotic associations, or provided child care for Chicanas laboring in war-support factories.

Wartime changes for Hispanics were not without their tensions. As Mexican American numbers mounted across the Southwest from Texas to California, prejudices surfaced and sometimes turned violent. In 1943 in southern California conflicts broke out between servicemen and the exotically clad Mexican American youth known as "zoot-suiters." Sometimes with—and often without—provocation, white servicemen set upon these "pachuco" gangs, beating the young Chicanos and stripping them of their distinctive hats, coats, pegged pants, and heavy shoes. There were some obvious grievances, writes author Wallace Stegner; servicemen had been attacked and beaten. But, Stegner adds, the pachuco-hunters made the same mistake as many police: "they drew no distinction between innocent and guilty but blamed every zoot-suiter, in some districts every Mexican. A majority of those beaten undoubtedly were innocent victims."

≈

Changes in the 1940s were equally traumatic for African Americans, but these shifts also offered blacks opportunities in the West to protect and expand their civil rights. In the decade from 1940 to 1950, African American populations in the West jumped from 1.3 to 1.7 million, a gain of 33 percent, while the total population of the West expanded only 26 percent. Most of this increase came in the Pacific Coast states, where the numbers of California blacks expanded 338,000 or 272 percent during the decade. Even with this explosion on the West Coast, however, there were more African Americans residing in Texas in 1940 and in 1950 than in all the other western states combined.

The largest transformations took place in occupational status. Before World War II, western blacks worked largely at menial jobs, in fields and as domestics. The war soon changed that. Blacks joining the service were stationed all over the West, and new jobs opened up at factories and shipyards, particularly in California. Unfortunately, with the influx of African Americans into the West came mounting racial tensions and sometimes conflicts. Blacks soon realized that they would have to battle ingrained prejudices to gain fair housing, defeat job discrimination, and ensure their political rights. Gradually African Americans organized associations to protect themselves from occupational and residential discrimination. Black women also pushed to receive fair treatment, from white and black male workers alike. One African American woman working at North American Aviation in California in 1943 reported that "[t]he War made me live better"; "Hitler was the one that got us out of the white folks' kitchen."

Asians faced other kinds of barriers, particularly those resulting from a Pacific war. In the century from the Gold Rush to World War II, the American West remained a bittersweet adopted home for Asians. Chinese and Japanese were coveted as railroad and field workers but kept isolated from mainstream America and discouraged from becoming landowners, establishing families, and reestablishing their traditions in these new lands. The Chinese Exclusion Act of 1882 and the anti-Japanese Immigration Act of 1924 all but shut down the immigration of these two groups. Filipinos had similar experiences, laboring as valued agricultural workers in California and other coastal areas but systematically excluded from full citizenship legally or socially. Fortunately, when as many as 30 percent of all Filipinos in the United States joined the service and Americans heard of the valiant Filipino opposition to the Japanese occupation of the Philippines, American opinion switched, becoming much more friendly toward the Filipinos. In truth Americans up through World War II tended to lump all Asian groups as "Orientals," as people to be kept at arm's length.

∿

The worst discrimination toward Asians targeted Japanese. After the attack on Pearl Harbor in December 1941, many Americans became increasingly fearful of Issei (foreign-born Japanese) and Nisei (American-born Japanese). Of the roughly 120,000 mainland Japanese Americans, 100,000 lived in California, the rest in Oregon and Washington. Jittery and agreeing with others afraid of a Japanese attack on the West Coast, California Governor Culbert Olson and his attorney general Earl Warren urged the federal government to round up and intern Japanese Americans in fortified assembly areas and detention camps. These and other officials were convinced that Japanese were a clear threat to the United States. One leader of the Western Defense Command probably spoke for many others, unfortunately, when he warned, "A Jap's a Jap. . . . It makes no difference if he is an American citizen."

On February 19, 1942, President Franklin Roosevelt, heeding reports that expressed these fears and that favored Japanese relocation, issued Executive Order 9066 calling for removal of "all persons . . . as deemed necessary or desirable." In the next two years about 110,000 Japanese, most of whom were

FIGURE 13:3. *Japanese Relocation.* The relocation of Japanese Americans to the inland West remains a shameful blot on the American past. Here Japanese internees gather in front of their bleak, barrack-like habitations at Camp Minidoka in Idaho. Courtesy Idaho State Historical Society, 73–184.1.

native-born Americans, were incarcerated in relocation camps throughout the trans-Mississippi West. These hastily erected camps were purposefully located in areas away from the Pacific Coast and isolated from western population centers. Many Japanese families, crammed into tar-papered, primitive barracks without proper sanitation, privacy, or adequate food and medical care, began to disintegrate under the mounting pressures. In time rules were loosed, visitors allowed, freedoms gained, but in August 1945, at war's end, 44,000 Japanese remained in the enclosed camps.

The months and years in the relocation camps scarred the lives of detainees. Remembering when she was a girl of eight in the camp at Manzanar, California, one Nisei woman recalled that her family, "after three years of mess hall living, collapsed as an integrated unit. Whatever dignity or feeling of filial strength we may have known before December, 1941, was lost." Another young Nisei also interned at Manzanar, when visiting the camp thirty years later, thought she "had nearly outgrown the shame and guilt and sense of unworthiness." But the return trip "made comprehensible, finally, the traces that remained and would always remain, like a needle."

There were other more tangible losses. In the relocation process many Japanese Americans lost their homes, lands, and businesses or were forced to sell them at disastrous prices. To make matters worse, sometimes in the months following the closing of the relocation sites and their attempts to return to pre-detainee homes or newly established homes, Japanese faced hostile opposition. When Japanese American families expressed a wish to return to their homes in small-town Oregon, headlines in the local newspaper read, "So sorry please, Japanese not wanted in Hood River." But gradually, despite lingering prejudices, transitions back to homes, schools, and prewar routines were reestablished. Meanwhile Japanese American young men had distinguished themselves as soldiers in World War II. One group of Japanese American soldiers, the 442nd Regimental Combat Team, earned a Medal of Honor for their valorous fighting and became the most decorated army unit in the war. But from a perspective of more than half a century, the treatment of Japanese Americans during World War II, especially the horrific Relocation experience, remains the darkest sociocultural tragedy in the West resulting from the tensions and traumas of a world war.

∾

Fueled by the infusion of the New Deal funds in the later 1930s, the engine of the West's economy began to sputter into life at the end of the decade. The injection of richer, larger government funds during World War II kicked the West's economy into high gear. Massive federal investment kept the war machine throbbing at high capacity throughout the 1940s. Some of the federal largesse went directly to government contractors; other dollars passed through the hands of highly visible persons like the entrepreneur Henry Kaiser and banker A. P. Giannini. Nearly all these monies, through a "trickle down" route, directly encouraged the West's economic development. The burgeoning military-industrial West provided jobs, and new employees created new demands and markets for manufacturers. An expanding scientific community emerged alongside and often intertwined with the sprawling military-industrial complex. "After World War II," writes one historian, "the West was obviously a very different place than it had been before." The conflict, he adds, led to a new kind of future: "The heritage of World War II endowed the West with a new economic structure that would serve it for a generation."

Industries tied closely to the expanding war machine grew the most rapidly and clearly exerted the largest influence on the western economy. Among these huge plants were the shipbuilding and aircraft industries. In fact, much of the roughly $70 billion the federal government funneled into the West went to build ships and planes. Shipbuilders such as the energetic Kaiser garnered remunerative contracts to turn out thousands of ships in California, Oregon, and Washington. S. D. Bechtel put his construction and administrative expertise to work in operating Calship in Los Angeles. In the interior West, even

Denver yards produced barges, landing craft, and ship parts sent to the coast for assembling. Observers marveled at the unusual sight of mammoth sections of ships making their way by rail from Denver to the West Coast.

Gargantuan sums of government money likewise led to the rapid expansion of aircraft factories. Most of these companies, including Consolidated-Vultee, Lockheed, Douglas Aircraft, North American Aviation, and Northrop, built sprawling factories in California. The Boeing Company also expanded its facilities in the state of Washington, as well as in Wichita. Other airplane-building factories were located in Tulsa and testing or assembly plants in Tucson and

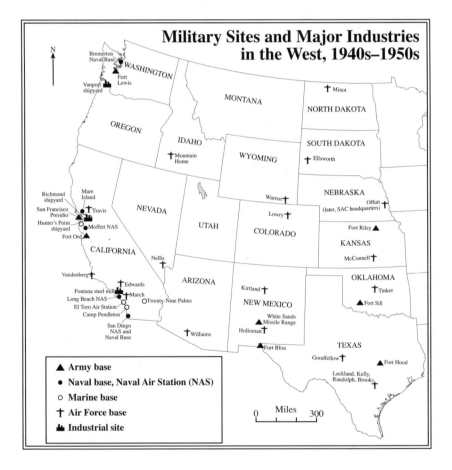

FIGURE 13:4. *Military Sites and Major Industries in the West, 1940s to 1950s.* Clear evidence of Uncle Sam's presence appeared throughout the West in military bases and war-related industries. Map by Robert Pace.

Cheyenne. Obviously these companies, like many others involved in wartime production, reaped large profits. Yet most of the funding turned into wartime jobs by the hundreds of thousands. By 1945, on the West Coast alone, nearly a half-million Americans were working at aircraft plants.

Federal expenditures for military installations and bases also spurred the western economy. As we have seen, these training facilities and sites were scattered throughout the West and thus revitalized the economies of nearly every part of the region. Of the fifteen million servicemen and women serving during World War II, possibly half were stationed in the West. Even the economic stimulus from government funding of military bases was spread over the West. California—and after it, Oregon, Washington, and Texas—received the lion's share of the financing. Of all the monies the government spent in the West from 1940 to 1945, about 50 percent went to California.

If government funding trickled down to corporations and contractors, to states and cities, and to millions of individuals, it also flowed outward to nearby factories, manufacturers, and bases serving as suppliers for the huge industries. Builders of planes and ships needed aluminum, magnesium, steel, and a host of other processed minerals. Large demands for oil and processed rubber also became apparent, to take care of military needs and to supply the fuel and tires of surging populations moving west. These growing desires for manufactured goods encouraged western manufacturers to move rapidly to fill these demands. The expansion of steel production at the Geneva Steel Works near Provo, Utah, and the erection of the Fontana steel manufacturing complex close to southern California shipbuilding yards illustrated the economic spillover of government funds into support industries. So did the construction of Alcoa and Reynolds aluminum production facilities in the Pacific Northwest; that location allowed the aluminum plants to be near shipbuilding facilities and to take advantage of the subregion's low-cost hydroelectric power. A magnesium plant situated at the edge of the fledgling town of Las Vegas, Nevada, and the expansion of oil production in California, Texas, and Oklahoma were other evidences of subsidiary industrial expansion in the West. For the same reason factories producing synthetic rubber were soon established in California and the Texas Gulf area to meet mounting demands for processed rubber.

~

World War II also helped spawn a new network of scientific centers. Here too the federal government provided most of the funding for scientific advancements, just as it did for military-industrial complexes. Through the Office of Scientific Research and Development, headed by the energetic, skilled administrator Vannevar Bush, funds from Washington, D.C., flowed west for dozens of scientific projects. Between 1941 and 1945, about $100 million went to universities and science laboratories and to research centers usually linked to them. Additional federal funding poured into nuclear research sites such as Los Alamos, New Mexico, and Hanford, Washington. Still other government dollars arrived at scientific agencies within the government, for example the U.S. Geological Survey. Not surprisingly, because of mounting war needs, increasing numbers of dollars were channeled into scientific projects tied to military and defense projects. These efforts made the American West a swiftly developing region for research and scientific development.

Like military bases and war industries, these research projects were spread over the West but with a heavy preponderance on the Pacific Coast. In Pasadena, California, the Jet Propulsion Laboratory at the prestigious California Institute of Technology received support to develop and test rocket motors and to carry out other projectile experiments. The University of Southern California and labs of the University of California located in the southern part of the state used their funding for experiments with oceanic and naval detection of submarines and for aviation medicine. In the Bay Area, the Radiation Laboratory at the University of California pushed ahead with nuclear research. To the north the Boeing Company and the University of Washington in Seattle undertook aeronautical and torpedo research. Two hundred miles to the east, the largest plant for producing plutonium was established at Hanford, Washington, employing upwards of twenty thousand workers in 1944. In the Southwest scientists at the University of Texas and Rice University undertook a variety of scientific projects related to the war effort.

~

Quite possibly the most notorious complex of scientific and research groups was established in the isolated deserts of New Mexico. In addition to rocket work in the southern part of the state and the atomic and other scientific laboratories near Albuquerque, a huge secret laboratory was established in Los Alamos. In the Land of Enchantment the federal government funded a highly secret project that changed the course of the world's history. President Roosevelt, warned by Albert Einstein and other leading scientists about Germany's experiments with a possible atom bomb, decided to establish a nuclear program in the United States, code-named the Manhattan Project. The president and the scientists wanted to separate the project into several research sites to speed up the process, isolate it from population centers, and protect it from possible sabotage. As a result, Oak Ridge, Tennessee; Hanford; and sites in Idaho, Colorado, and Nevada played roles in the development and testing of an atom bomb. But the most important of the scientific sites established to work on the bomb was Los Alamos.

In the piñon-covered mountains of north-central New Mexico, the world's most advanced scientific effort to harness the atom came rapidly into existence. Selected to head the new and closely guarded installation at Los Alamos was J. Robert Oppenheimer, a world-renown California physicist. Choosing the site and many of the top-ranked scientists to work at what became know as "Site Y," Oppenheimer proved to be a superb choice for director. In 1943 hundreds of scientists, nearly a dozen of whom would win Nobel Prizes, began to move into quickly erected houses and laboratory buildings on "the hill." By 1945, about 5,000 men, women, and children called Los Alamos home. No one knew much about what was going on at the labs. All sorts of rumors circulated about the weird "long hairs" "up there." One wag maintained that the scientists were "making windshield wipers for submarines." More ingenious, "another speculated that the site was constructing the front end of donkeys for shipment to Washington, D.C., for final assembly."

Maintaining silence and secrecy, the scientists worked around the clock fashioning the first atomic bombs. By early summer 1945, all was ready for the explosion of the first bomb, the much-awaited "fishing trip." Scientists were still uncertain what "Jumbo," the 214-ton casing with its 15-inch banded sides

FIGURE 13:5. *Trinity Site.* In July 1945 the first atomic bomb exploded at the Trinity Site in New Mexico. That explosion quickly and dramatically ushered in a new era in human history. Courtesy Palace of the Governors (MNM/DCA), 147362.

wrapped about the nuclear core, would do. They held their breath when the world's first nuclear bomb was exploded just before dawn on July 16, 1945, at an obscure site in the New Mexico desert. The gigantic blast hurled a brilliant, "multicolored cloud" 38,000 feet into the sky. "At ten miles away people felt a blast of heat equivalent to standing about three feet from a fireplace. Where the fireball touched the ground, it created a crater half a mile across." Truly, it was "the day the sun rose twice." At the Trinity Site in far-off New Mexico and later that summer in the two horrendous nuclear bombs exploded over Japanese cities, the world had whirled explosively into the Atomic Age.

The Trinity detonation signaled how much the American West had become home to numerous scientific, industrial, and military projects. In four brief but frenetic years the West made a giant leap forward in shaking eastern dominance and in establishing its identity as an independent, powerful economic region in its own right. During this astounding restructuring of its society and economy, the West shifted into overdrive. As one historian has concluded, World War II "in four short years . . . accomplished more than forty years in peacetime. . . . And the pattern created by the war dominated the western economy for the next three decades."

≈

Postwar eras are often marked by years of socioeconomic and political uncertainty—if not the chaos of postwar depression. Such was the case following the American Civil War and World War I. But that was not so in the period immediately after World War II. For a number of reasons, both domestic and international, the late 1940s and 1950s spawned an era quite different from that of the early 1920s. Unlike the post–World War I American West, the post–World War II West exhibited as much continuity as change.

The booming times following World War II did not affect the western economy or region equally, however. Those industries most closely linked with the large governmentally funded war machine continued to do well in the postwar West. The politics of water development also became increasingly complex—and controversial. Conversely the growth of extractive industries like mining grew, reached a plateau, and then began to decline. Concurrently service and high-tech industries arose to new prominence. Political and cultural trends exhibited similar contradictions. Even though some western politicians maintained their allegiance to the post–New Deal liberal politics, others moved right and initiated conservative political stances that marked western politics in much of the late twentieth century. Similarly, treatments of the West on radio and television, in the movies, and in fiction and historiography also betrayed a divided stream between clichéd plots and characters and probing, realistic themes of cultural analysis. In these ways the West between 1945 and 1960 proved to be a very complex region.

Even before Germany and Japan were defeated at the end of World War II, the United States faced a new, dangerous opponent. English Prime Minister Winston Churchill's warning that the Soviet Union would be the Allies' next opposition proved to be true. Mounting conflict with Russia led to a long cold war (nonfighting war) that lasted from the mid-1940s until the end of the 1980s. That war of words and bad feelings kept the American war machine throbbing throughout most of those decades. Add in the Korean War (1950–53), the later war in Vietnam (1964–73), and persisting tensions with China from the 1940s forward. Then one understands why the military bases and military-industrial complexes continued to play such large roles in the economic and social history of the post–World War II American West.

The federal government was the key player in all this activity. So persistent was the central government's support of military bases, airplane- and ship-building facilities, and scientific centers that the region continued to be known as Uncle Sam's West. Convinced that their administrations should help Americans avoid a postwar depression, Presidents Roosevelt and then Harry Truman spent large sums of money, keeping Americans employed and industries humming. Soon after the war's end, bureaucrats also sold factories, business buildings, and machinery for giveaway prices, sometimes for only 10 percent of actual cost. The Geneva Steel Works near Provo, Utah, went as a bargain to U.S. Steel. The ambitious and canny Henry J. Kaiser snapped up plants at Fontana, California, and several aluminum works in the Pacific Northwest went at greatly reduced prices. The federal government even encouraged the widespread air conditioning that began to appear in the Southwest by giving tax incentives to employers and homeowners who installed air conditioners.

Full employment, an appealing climate, increased amenities, and less expensive housing drew another flock of newcomers to the West from 1945 to 1960. The Pacific Coast cities that grew so rapidly during World War II exploded again. San Diego, Los Angeles, Portland, Seattle, and inland Denver hosted hundreds of thousands of immigrants. But cities across the Southwest also sprang into life. Tucson, Phoenix, Albuquerque, and El Paso mushroomed. Dallas and Houston continued to spread out. So did smaller cities like Reno and Boise. All these cities expanded in part as a result of the federal government's financing of military-industrial endeavors.

Other urban areas profited from special circumstances. Las Vegas, only 30,000 in 1945, jumped to nearly 130,000 in 1960, a city already known for its gambling, lively entertainment, and fully air-conditioned facilities. By 1960, Del Webb and other developers had built Sun City, a suburb of Phoenix, as a retirement community for the "snowbirds" visiting or relocating to the sunny Southwest. Five years earlier, in 1955, Disneyland opened as a prime tourist attraction in southern California, a model for other tourist sites popping up in several appealing subregions of the West. Still another of the "magic lands" flourished in the Bay Area after the Industrial Park was established near Stanford University in Palo Alto. Research and development industries clustered around one another, bringing together scientists, investment capitalists, and a plethora of electronics, computer, and other light-manufacturing firms. As a forerunner of the much-vaunted Silicon Valley, these early industries produced about half their goods for the government and the rest for consumers. With only seven tenants in 1955, the Industrial Park had exploded to nearly one hundred in 1980.

∼

When World War II hero Dwight D. ("Ike") Eisenhower, a Kansan, replaced Harry Truman as president in 1953, national and western politics turned in a new direction. If Truman represented the more liberal New Deal tradition of Democrat Franklin Roosevelt, Eisenhower ushered in a politics of moderate to conservative Republicanism. With the exception of Texan Lyndon Baines Johnson in the 1960s, the moderate to conservative Republicans have dominated most of western politics in the past half-century. In this regard, Eisenhower belonged more to the conservative political tradition of the first western president, Herbert Hoover, than to the liberal tradition of Theodore Roosevelt and Franklin Roosevelt.

So influential and popular was President Eisenhower, the second western president, that the 1950s have often been labeled the Eisenhower Era. The political leader from Kansas favored lessened federal government control, more political power at the local level, and fewer central government restrictions and welfare programs. Westerners played important roles in the Eisenhower cabinet carrying out these policies. Secretary of Agriculture Ezra Taft Benson, a Mormon from Utah and a strong conservative, helped roll back government subsidies on agricultural products. Douglas McKay, a former Oregon car dealer and Ike's secretary of the interior, supported reclamation projects, expanded tourism, and advocated the controversial policy of termination, removing Indians from federal support and encouraging them to be independent, self-sustaining groups. Oveta Culp Hobby, a wealthy Texan, served as secretary of health, education, and welfare. Most important of all, Californian Richard Nixon, a staunch conservative and self-defined opponent of communists, was selected as vice president. Not since Hoover and his Kansas and Native American vice president Charles Curtis had both the president and vice president been westerners.

Several westerners became politically well known before 1960. None was more powerful in congressional circles than Lyndon Johnson, the Democratic senator from Texas. A shrewd, adept political manipulator, Johnson became the senate majority leader in the 1950s and helped deliver government largesse to Texas and the West. Arizonan Carl Hayden, also a Democrat, served for a half-century in Congress and chaired the important Senate Appropriations Committee. He too made sure that Arizona received extraordinary federal funding and helped secure increasing amounts of much-needed water from the Colorado River. Senator Barry Goldwater, also from Arizona, began to gather support from the conservative wing of the Republican Party, whereas Senator Mike Mansfield of Montana served as a leader of moderate to liberal Democrats and became senate majority leader when Johnson was elected vice president on the Democratic ticket with John F. Kennedy in 1960. Senators Wayne Morse of Oregon and Frank Church of Idaho were also becoming widely known for their outspoken and charismatic qualities of leadership.

Emblematic of this emerging western political pattern was Earl Warren of California. Warren, serving as governor from 1943 to 1953 before President Eisenhower named him chief justice of the U.S. Supreme Court, became an able, popular leader for a bipartisan, middle-class, and suburban electorate of California. He argued, as did President Eisenhower, that political leaders should be above politics, beyond partisan biases. The nonpartisan, consensus, and person-focused political stances that Warren and other far-western politicians adopted appealed to West Coast voters from Seattle to San Diego. These new views also illustrated the West's gradual abandonment of an earlier frontier politics linked to confrontation, agrarian policies, and radical labor issues. In the Plains states, however, the shift was even more markedly to the right. The earlier progressive and New Deal liberalism of Senator George Norris of Nebraska and other reform candidates in the Dakotas paled before the rise of new conservative political leaders, mostly Republicans, from the Dakotas south to Oklahoma.

The election of 1960 showcased the rising importance of the West in the national political arena. After a closely contested runoff campaign between liberal Governor Nelson Rockefeller of New York and conservative Vice President Richard Nixon of California, Nixon was nominated, meaning westerners had been the Republican nominees in 1952 (Eisenhower), 1956 (Eisenhower), and 1960 (Nixon). Nixon had gained a large reputation as a communist-fighter before his vice presidency and as a man who could stand up to the United States' most notable cold war opponent, Nikita Khrushchev of Russia. Oregon Senator Mark Hatfield nominated Nixon at the Republican convention. The Democrats nominated Kennedy as their standard bearer, and he, in turn, chose Johnson of Texas as his running mate. That choice angered liberal Democrats, including the nominee's brother Robert Kennedy, but Kennedy's plan that

Johnson could carry important southern and western votes and thus win the election proved true. In that Democratic convention another up-and-coming western politician, Senator Frank Church of Idaho, gave the keynote address. In a very close election, Kennedy defeated Nixon. In 1952 and 1956 Eisenhower had won every western state, and all but three western states—Nevada, New Mexico, and Texas—supported Nixon in 1960. The West became even more prominent politically in 1964 when Texan Democrat Johnson ran against and defeated the conservative Republican candidate Barry Goldwater of Arizona. It was the first American election in which the two major parties ran western candidates for the presidency.

≈

One of the hottest issues embroiling western politicians was the controversy over water use. Who would control much-needed water supplies in many parts of the West, especially in the competition between agriculturalists and urban dwellers? It was, of course, a long-range problem, stretching back into the nineteenth century. By the mid-twentieth century, major competitors, once thought to be easily recognizable, continued to shift, like a game of musical chairs. Conflicts over water sometimes threatened to break out in mini–civil wars.

Especially contentious were the tug-of-wars over water sources in the Colorado River basin. Beginning in 1922 with the Colorado River Compact, through the building of Hoover/Boulder Dam (1931–35), and continuing well past 1960, state, federal, and local politicians tried to negotiate equitable divisions of water supplies for lower Rocky Mountain and southwestern areas. The vast farms of the rich interior valleys of California called for more and more water, even as the incoming populations of the Los Angeles basin threatened to use up large amounts of available water. At first imperial California gained ascendancy with an inordinate share of the Colorado's waters. Later, Senator Hayden almost single-handedly forced Congress to provide more water for his state of Arizona. Quarrels over Colorado River water led to several fractious political and legal debates. In the words of one journalist, westerners were threatening to turn the Southwest, as well as other portions of the West, into a "Cadillac desert" by excessively selfish, wasteful uses of water for huge agricultural and human uses.

One sign of the mounting controversy among dam builders, water users, promoters of tourism, and environmentalists was the conflict surrounding the proposed dam at the Dinosaur National Monument area at Echo Park on the Green River in northwestern Colorado. A coterie of environmental activists, reform politicians, and members of the Sierra Club helped block the reclamation project that would have spoiled this marvelous landscape. The same group gave way on the Glen Canyon Dam on the Colorado so that they might save Echo Park. Had they known their true strength, Sierra Club supporters later argued, both dams might have been stopped. Similar controversies boiled up around reclamation and irrigation projects planned for the Columbia, Snake, and Missouri river systems. Throughout the 1950s dam builders seemed to win most of the controversies, but the winds of opinion then shifted, with environmentalists and their supporters blocking most dam-building efforts after 1960.

∼

The booming postwar economy, expanding cities, and increased emphases on the West as the land of opportunity profoundly impacted social patterns in the West. Not surprisingly, the continuing influx of heterogeneous populations also enriched the region's ethnic diversity. For instance, African American populations in California jumped from 124,000 in 1940, to 462,000 in 1950 and 884,000 in 1960. In Texas, the western state with the largest black population, African American numbers expanded from 924,000 in 1940, to 977,000 in 1950 and up to 1.2 million in 1960. Most of these incoming African Americans were flooding into cities, including Houston and Los Angeles. By this time Houston hosted more black millionaires than any other American city. Still, blacks experienced a persisting segregation in Texas, forcing them into inferior schools and substandard modes of transportation. Not until the late 1960s were some of these barriers partially dismantled.

For Native Americans the immediate postwar years brought special challenges. When Indian veterans returned to reservations, they discovered that their wartime experiences often placed them at odds with tribal traditions. As Tayo, the hero of Leslie Silko's novel *Ceremony* (1977), soon learns, the scarring traumas of fighting in the Pacific have unbalanced him, alienating him from his Native beliefs. Adjustments come gradually and laboriously for Tayo, like a deep wound slowly healing. For other returnees, service in the military brought knowledge of a wider, more complex world that they quickly put to work as new leaders at their pueblos and reservations.

Other changes marked Native Americans. By 1960, Indian numbers had expanded to almost one million, nearly four times the Native population in 1900. Despite this demographic expansion, Indians were still the poorest Americans, often isolated without jobs on poverty-stricken reservations. Another major dilemma faced Natives in the new policy known as "termination." Under termination, the Eisenhower administration urged Indians to accept "withdrawal programming," which meant that Natives would move off reservations, end communal land ownership, and enter the American mainstream. A few Indians tribes, including the Klamaths of Oregon, the Menominee of Wisconsin, and small groups in Utah and Oklahoma, were "terminated." Nearly all of these decisions led to disaster, with Indian groups and their supporters quickly moving for reversal. Meanwhile, nearly 35,000 Indians left reservations to move to cities, but up to a third soon returned. By 1960, Native Americans clearly were not yet ready to leave their reservations. Most Indians were still closely linked to government policies and support and insufficiently organized to speak out for their own rights.

Wartime adjustments also brought notable changes to the lives of many Hispanics. In addition to those who flocked to unskilled jobs in war industries, hundreds of thousands of Mexican Americans and Mexicans served as migrant agricultural workers. After many farm laborers entered the service during World War II and the Japanese were relocated to internment camps in the interior West, ranch and farm owners lobbied the federal government for much-needed agricultural replacements. A series of agreements between the U.S. and Mexican governments brought more than 200,000 bracero ("strong-armed") unskilled Mexican workers north to American ranches and farms between 1942 and 1947. These contracts worked fairly well. True, Mexican workers were often subjected to difficult jobs in unsatisfactory conditions, but they also earned much more than they had south of the border, allowing them to send home thousands of dollars to their families in Mexico. Both governments agreed on an expansion of the program in the 1950s. Revealingly, a much higher percentage of Mexican and Mexican American women worked in the fields than women from other minority groups.

Asian experiences in the postwar years followed and yet also broke from those of other ethnic groups in the West. During World War II Chinese men served in considerable numbers in the armed services and took jobs in war-related industries. Chinese populations expanded, too, when exclusionary acts were repealed and refugees fled mainland China after the communist takeover in 1949. Many of the Chinese settled on the West Coast, with nearly 10 percent of their numbers congregated in San Francisco, primarily in its Chinatown, the country's largest. As economic and social conditions in the United States improved in the 1950s, larger groups of Chinese women came from Taiwan and elsewhere, allowing nearly balanced numbers of Chinese men and women in 1960 for the first time in the United States. Filipino status also notably changed when the U.S. government granted independence to the Philippines in 1946. When other restrictions were lifted, a new wave of Filipino males immigrated into California, where they worked alongside Chinese in the state's rich, expanding agricultural economy. As we have seen the Japanese faced a far different set of circumstances when many returned from internee camps in the mid-1940s. Theirs were the most tragic and disruptive of all ethnic experiences in the American West during the war and immediately thereafter.

In the Eisenhower 1950s the popularity of the American West in radio and television, movies, and popular fiction reached a new high point. At the beginning of the decade, radio programs such as *The Lone Ranger*, *Tom Mix*, and Gene Autry's *Melody Ranch*, among others, drew large listening audiences. So did the first of the "adult Westerns," *Gunsmoke*, launched on radio in 1952. Most of these programs transitioned to television, which surpassed radio in the 1950s as the most popular medium for Westerns. The television program *Gunsmoke* pioneered with a cluster of more complex characters. In its central protagonists, the heroic marshal Matt Dillon (James Arness), Doc (Milburn Stone), Kitty the dance hall proprietress (Amanda Blake), and sidekick Chester (Dennis Weaver), the series provided more realistic fare. The program's complicated protagonists and plots were more convincing than the ingredients of the singing and grade B "horse-opera Westerns," which usually featured nonstop action by stereotyped figures. *Cheyenne*, *Have Gun Will Travel*, and, later in the decade, *Bonanza* challenged *Gunsmoke* for supremacy among TV Westerns.

The same popular and "adult" categories characterized many Hollywood Westerns. The low-budget "B," cowboy, and singing Westerns, showcasing such stars as Gene Autry, Roy Rogers, and Hopalong Cassidy, continued to be released well into the 1950s. But a clutch of remarkable "adult" or "classic" Western films became the memorable movies about the West in the 1940s and 1950s. John Wayne in *Red River* (1948) and *The Searchers* (1956), Gary Cooper in *High Noon* (1952), and Alan Ladd in *Shane* (1953) starred in high-caliber, probing roles depicting the corrosive impact of violence and racism and the redemptive qualities of courage and strong leadership. Other contemporary Westerns like *The Ox-bow Incident* (1943) and *Broken Arrow* (1950) provided masterful depictions of the dangers of vigilantism and prejudice. These "adult" Westerns, particularly when in the capable hands of noted directors like John Ford, proved that Hollywood could move well beyond the clichés and stereotypes of too many cinematic treatments of the West. By avoiding excessive emphases on cowboy heroes and in dealing with the darker sides of frontier violence, racism, and extralegal activities, moviemakers furnished fuller, more human portraits of the western past.

≈

Novelists and historians seemed equally caught between these romantic and more realistic accounts of the West. Fiction writers such as Luke Short (Frederick Glidden), Ernest Haycox, and Will Henry (Henry Wilson Allen) continued to produce their annual novels treating the West as a dramatic, dangerous terrain peopled with cowboys, gunslingers, evil villains, supportive females, and occasional well-known historical figures like General Custer, Sitting Bull, and Crazy Horse. In 1953, the best known producer of popular Westerns, Louis L'Amour, launched his stunningly successful financial career with his first well-known Western, *Hondo*.

Other novelists were motivated to portray the western past as much more complex. John Steinbeck followed his classic *Grapes of Wrath* with *Cannery Row* (1945), *East of Eden* (1952), and other novels overflowing with well-rounded characters and appealing sociocultural details. Also widely recognized were the historical novels of Montanan A. B. Guthrie, Jr. His fictional trilogy, *The Big Sky* (1947), *The Way West* (1949, which won a Pulitzer Prize), and *These Thousand Hills* (1956), traced western history from the mountain men through the Oregon Trail and on to early frontier ranching. Guthrie's deft handling of history, many-sided protagonists, and vibrant landscapes won many readers. Novelist Wallace Stegner, who came to adulthood on the tail-ends of the Canadian and American frontiers, was also gathering increasing attention as a skilled stylist and dramatic storyteller. Among his early novels was *Big Rock Candy Mountain* (1943), a powerful coming-of-age story of a boy and young man. Stegner drew much on his own life for this realistic, memorable novel about the early twentieth-century West.

Historians, too, were divided into the camps of those portraying romantic and realistic western pasts. The grand master of western historical narrative, Utahan and Harvard man Bernard DeVoto, published his triplex of superbly written historical narratives in the 1940s and 1950s: *The Year of Decision: 1846* (1943), *Across the Wide Missouri* (1947), and *The Course of Empire* (1952). DeVoto's sense of historical drama, his apt use of literary devices, and his grasp of detail proved that narrative history could also provide dependable, analytical stories of the frontier West. Ray Allen Billington followed somewhat in this tradition with his *Westward Expansion* (1949), a smoothly written history that, in subsequent editions, remained the leading western history text until the 1970s. Billington's clear narrative skills displayed his training as a journalist.

Two other scholars, Henry Nash Smith and Earl Pomeroy, portrayed a much more complicated western heritage in their writings. An American Studies specialist, Smith pointed students of the American West in a new direction in his classic work *Virgin Land: The American West as Myth and Symbol* (1950). Viewed by some as the most important book on the American West published in the twentieth century, Smith's study urged readers to understand that "myths" (stories not necessarily true but having the power to motivate) of the West had shaped its history just as powerfully, if not more so, as verifiable facts. *Virgin Land* forced students of the West to rethink the shaping power of myths such as "Passage to India," "The Sons of Leatherstocking," and "The

Garden of the World" in the history of the West. Also eschewing a romantic approach to the West was historian Earl Pomeroy. In a key essay, "Toward a Reorientation of Western History" (1955), and in his major book, *The Pacific Slope* (1965), Pomeroy asserted that rather than viewing the frontier West as a radical, tradition-breaking set of experiences, readers should realize how much the West replicated rather than broke from eastern and European traditions. He saw numerous carryovers from earlier legal-constitutional, political, social, and cultural precedents into the West. In his contentions, Pomeroy argued against the ideas of frontier historian Frederick Jackson Turner and his disciples, who continued to point to the frontier experience as a major source of America's exceptionalism.

≈

The Beatniks, though a very small group, proved a notable exception to the argument that the United States and the American West in the 1950s were primarily placid places. The origins of the Beats, especially as seen in the first writings of authors Jack Kerouac and Allen Ginsberg, were eastern. Kerouac and Ginsberg met and became close acquaintances at Columbia University in New York City. They soon found, however, that San Francisco and other western sites like Venice, California, and Denver, Colorado, were more accepting communities for their bohemian, nose-thumbing lifestyles. In their smoke-filled coffeehouse readings and in their antisocial actions, the Beats celebrated frenetic, experience-driven lives greatly at odds with Eisenhower America. In some ways they were more *in* the West than *of* it. In his widely read novel *On the Road* (1957), Kerouac depicted life as a series of nonstop "trips" from coast to coast and from one unorthodox experience to many others. But Ginsberg's poem *Howl* (1956) was more explicit and conflictive. It railed against what Ginsberg and the other Beats considered the smugness, materialism, and meaninglessness of the 1950s. The opening lines of *Howl* make clear the distance between the Beats and other Americans of the 1950s:

> I saw the best minds of my generation destroyed by madness,
>   starving hysterical naked,
> dragging themselves through the negro streets at dawn looking for
>   an angry fix . . .

Here were dissenting voices, sounding chiefly from the yeasty Bay Area, foreshadowing western countercultures that emerged in the 1960s.

≈

The two decades of western history between 1940 and 1960 displayed *both* rapid change and clear continuity. World War II disrupted nearly every economic and sociocultural pattern of the West that had been in place during the earlier 1930s. Wartime expansion brought millions of people west. The region boomed, with numerous western cities rapidly expanding and the ethnic-racial profile of the West transformed. These disruptive trends, becoming more familiar and expected, continued by and large into the 1950s. Ongoing government funding during the early years of the cold war allowed the West to continue expanding economically and numerically.

But there were other hints of coming changes. When the Supreme Court decided in *Brown v. Board of Education of Topeka* (1954) that segregated schools were inherently unequal and must be ended, that decision foreshadowed momentous sociocultural changes that swept over the West and the rest of the nation in the 1960s and 1970s. Political trends were also moving right, toward the Republican Party, by the end of the 1950s. In cultural developments, tradition and change also jostled one another. Even as filmmakers and writers continued to capitalize on popular cowboy themes, films like *Shane* and *High Noon* and authors such as Steinbeck, Guthrie, and Stegner were portraying a more complicated West. The appearance of the Beatniks, with their dismissive attacks on a placid Eisenhower America, suggested that some parts of the West in the late 1950s were less tepid than previously thought. Clearly, these events and writings adumbrated the 1960s and 1970s, which proved to be a transformative period in western history. Continuing to swiftly change in these decades, the American West had become, by 1980, something of a pacesetter for the entire nation.

SUGGESTED READINGS

Abbott, Carl. *The Metropolitan Frontier: Cities in the Modern American West.* Tucson: University of Arizona Press, 1993.

Anderson, Karen. *Wartime Women: Sex Roles, Family Relations, and the Status of Women During World War II.* Westport, CT: Greenwood Press, 1981.

Bernstein, Alison B. *American Indians and World War II: Toward a New Era in Indian Affairs.* Norman: University of Oklahoma Press, 1991.

Campbell, D'Ann. *Women at War with America: Private Lives in a Patriotic Era.* Cambridge, MA: Harvard University Press, 1984.

Daniels, Roger. *Asian America: Chinese and Japanese in the United States since 1850.* Seattle: University of Washington Press, 1988.

Ford, Larry R. *Metropolitan San Diego: How Geography and Lifestyle Shape a New Urban Environment.* Philadelphia: University of Pennsylvania Press, 2004.

Foster, Mark S. *Henry J. Kaiser: Builder in the Modern American West.* Austin: University of Texas Press, 1989.

Gluck, Sherna Berger. *Rosie the Riveter Revisited: Women, the War, and Social Change.* Boston: Twayne Publishers, 1987.

Hayashi, Brian Masaru. *Democratizing the Enemy: The Japanese American Internment.* Princeton, NJ: Princeton University Press, 2004.

Hundley, Norris, Jr. *The Great Thirst: Californians and Water, 1770s–1990s.* Berkeley: University of California Press, 1992.

Hunner, Jon. *Inventing Los Alamos: The Growth of an Atomic City.* Norman: University of Oklahoma Press, 2004.

Johnson, Marilynn S. *The Second Gold Rush: Oakland and the East Bay in World War II.* Berkeley: University of California Press, 1993.

Kesselman, Amy. *Fleeting Opportunities: Women Shipyard Workers in Portland and Vancouver During World War II and Reconversion.* Albany: State University of New York Press, 1990.

Lotchin, Roger W. *The Bad City in the Good War.* Bloomington: Indiana University Press, 2003.

———. *Fortress California 1910–1961: From Warfare to Welfare.* New York: Oxford University Press, 1992.

Malone, Michael P., and Richard W. Etulain. *The American West: A Twentieth-Century History.* Lincoln: University of Nebraska Press, 1989.

Martínez, Oscar J. *Mexican-Origin People in the United States: A Topical History.* Tucson: University of Arizona Press, 2001.

Maynard, John Arthur. *Venice West: The Beat Generation in Southern California.* New Brunswick, NJ: Rutgers University Press, 1991.

Nash, Gerald D. *The American West Transformed: The Impact of the Second World War.* Bloomington: Indiana University Press, 1985.

———. *World War II and the West: Reshaping the Economy.* Lincoln: University of Nebraska Press, 1990.

Nugent, Walter. *Into the West: The Story of Its People.* New York: Knopf, 1999.

Patterson, James T. *Grand Expectations: The United States, 1945–1974.* New York: Oxford University Press, 1996.

Pitti, Stephen J. *The Devil in Silicon Valley: Northern California, Race, and Mexican Americans.* Princeton, NJ: Princeton University Press, 2002.

Reisner, Marc. *Cadillac Desert: The American West and Its Disappearing Water.* New York: Viking Penguin, 1986.

Rogers, Everett M., and Judith K. Larsen. *Silicon Valley Fever: Growth of High-Technology Culture.* New York: Basic Books, 1984.

Schwantes, Carlos Arnaldo. *Going Places: Transportation Redefines the Twentieth-Century West.* Bloomington: Indiana University Press, 2003.

Starr, Kevin. *The Dream Endures: California Enters the 1940s.* New York: Oxford University Press, 1997.

———. *Embattled Dreams: California in War and Peace, 1940–1950.* New York: Oxford University Press, 2002.

Szasz, Ferenc Morton. *The Day the Sun Rose Twice: The Story of the Trinity Site Nuclear Explosion, July 16, 1945.* Albuquerque: University of New Mexico Press, 1984.

Taylor, Quintard. *In Search of the Racial Frontier: African Americans in the American West, 1528–1990.* New York: W. W. Norton, 1998.

CHAPTER FOURTEEN

The Cold War West, 1960 to 1980

∼

WHEN BARBARA JORDAN BECAME A TEXAS STATE SENATOR IN 1966 AND A U.S. congresswoman in 1972, and gave the keynote address at the Democratic National Convention in 1972, she set several important precedents. She was the first African American to serve in the Texas Senate, the first black woman from Texas in the U.S. Congress, and the first woman to deliver the keynote address at a national political convention. Jordan later became a well-known member of the House Judiciary Committee that voted for the articles of impeachment against western president Richard Nixon.

For another African American woman in the West, activist Angela Yvonne Davis, the path to national attention followed a much different direction. Educated at Brandeis University and in Germany and clearly influenced by the ideas of radical thinker Herbert Marcuse, Davis also took part in civil rights activities in the 1960s, joined the Black Panthers, and became a member of the Communist Party. Although Davis was offered a position in the Philosophy Department at UCLA, the university's regents fired her before she began to teach. Jailed and tried on charges of kidnapping, conspiracy, and murder, Davis gained a not-guilty verdict in 1972. Thereafter, she took up her teaching and remained a highly visible member of the activist contingent of the University of California professoriate.

The careers of Barbara Jordan and Angela Davis illustrate both major changes and the diversity of those transformations taking place in the American West during the 1960s and 1970s. These two decades were one of the most yeasty periods of American history. Minority ethnic groups, increasingly organized and vocal, spoke out more vociferously for their rights. Probably Jordan and Davis and Chicano/as like César Chávez and Dolores Huerta could not have surfaced as major western figures as late as the 1950s. Additionally, the 1960s saw important new developments in women's activism. In those years and the next decade increasing numbers of women worked outside their homes. They also became more active in reform movements and political organizations, becoming, as the later term indicated, "feminists." At the same time, youthful Americans reacted strongly to what they considered the numbing qualities of American suburban and campus life, society's mistreatment of racial minorities, and the country's wrong-headed involvement in the Vietnam War. In the words of one historian, for many Americans living through the 1960s, the decade seemed "a revolutionary time awash in unanticipated and inexplicable conflict," but these years were also "very much the culmination of an era that began with the Great Depression and the New Deal and continued with World War II and its aftermath."

The lives of Barbara Jordan and Angela Davis also reflected other socioeconomic changes taking place in the West. In 1962 California surpassed New York as the most populous state, and the Golden State's population continued

FIGURE 14:1. *Barbara Jordan*. A political activist from Texas, Barbara Jordan later served with distinction as a congresswoman in the U.S. House of Representatives. Courtesy of the Prints and Photographs Collection, Barker Texas History Center, University of Texas, Austin, CN 02268.

to soar well into the 1990s. In Texas, populations also mushroomed, making it the third most populous state in 1980, behind only California and New York. Between these two behemoths, the Southwest grew rapidly, and so did cities situated along the coast from San Diego to Seattle. In all, the West became more populous, urban, and suburban. Caught in these dramatic changes, westerners displayed deeply ambivalent attitudes. A majority seemed cautiously optimistic about the future, accepting the incoming populations and resultant economic and social shifts. Barbara Jordan represented these westerners. But for others, neither the status quo in the West nor the changes ushered in were dealing with needed reforms. For radical activists like Angela Davis, the West needed to face up to its inequities, prejudices, and profit-driven lifestyles. For Davis, the Black Panthers, many campus activists, and a growing number of environmentalists, the West faced a bleak future if it failed to reorient its mistreatment of minority groups and western landscapes. As a result of these conflicting attitudes, the West of the 1960s and 1970s became a region of increasingly ambivalent anxieties, leading to what some called the New Gray West.

～

A bird's-eye view of western subregions clearly reveals the existing diversity and rapid change reshaping these varied parts of the West. From 1940 to 1980 many parts of the northern Plains and Rockies did not experience the barrage of transformations sweeping across much of the Southwest and Pacific Coast. In the eastern and northern sections of the West, agriculture remained king. The corn-and-hogs pattern of the Midwest spilled over into the more humid and eastern ends of the Dakotas, Nebraska, and Kansas. In the central parts of these states wheat still dominated. In the western subregions of the Plains states, ranching prevailed, as it did in eastern Montana, Wyoming, and Colorado. In Wyoming and parts of Montana cattle ranching was widespread. Potatoes were the crop of choice in southern Idaho, particularly in irrigated farms along the Snake River. When droughts destroyed most wheat and rice crops in Russia and China in the early 1970s and those countries bought millions of bushels of wheat to feed their people, Plains farmers were euphoric with the high prices for their crops. But most trends for agriculturists were in the opposite direction: overproduction led to lower prices, and larger "agribusiness" firms crowded out family farmers. Fewer and fewer jobs were available in the upper Plains and Rocky Mountain states for agricultural families.

Metal mining likewise declined in these western subregions. Even though the Homestake mine in South Dakota continued to produce gold, the Sunshine and Bunker Hill and Sullivan mines of Idaho silver and lead, and the Bingham Canyon mine in Utah huge amounts of copper, most mining was collapsing in the 1970s in the northern West. Mounting competition from South Africa and South America, escalating production costs, and increasing environmental restrictions undercut the mining industry. By the 1980s most of the mines in the northern West, and many in the remainder of the region, had closed.

During these times of rapid change, federal footprints were in evidence across the northern West. The U.S. government, first of all, owned more than half of the land in these thinly populated states. In addition, federal monies paid farmers to take their lands out of production, attempting to balance yield and demand. The government also provided price supports for planting alternative crops and loans for crops stored. Even more notable was Uncle Sam's sponsorship of dams and water projects. The Army Corps of Engineers and the Bureau of Reclamation joined forces, in the Pick-Sloan Plan, to erect several dams on the Missouri River and its tributaries. Canyon Ferry and Yellowtail dams were built on the upper reaches of the Missouri system, and Garrison in North Dakota and Oahe in South Dakota. Surrounded by controversies, the latter two projects were never totally completed. To the west, the Colorado–Big Thompson Project diverted water east to the Platte River. A few other new water projects were built without large government outlays. In another part of the interior West, beneath large spaces of western lands stretching from South Dakota to Texas, the Ogallala Aquifer began to supply water for thousands of center-pivot sprinklers. So heavy was the draw on this underground water supply, however, that by the early 1980s environmentalists were warning of dire results from continued overuse.

Uncle Sam also funded dozens of military-industrial complexes in the northern Plains and Rockies. By the 1960s, several air bases had been established in North Dakota, making the area, one writer noted, "the world's third-ranking nuclear power." Later in the Nixon administration an anti-ballistic missile system (ABMs) spread across North Dakota and Montana grain fields, armed with a sophisticated radar system designed to intercept any incoming missiles with nuclear warheads. Cold war competition also helped fund the sprawling Strategic Air Command installation near Omaha. At the same time, the Department of Defense continued funding airplane-building operations in Wichita, where nearly twenty thousand workers were employed in the early 1980s.

Federal monies supporting military-industrial sites were particularly important, too, in northern Utah and Colorado Springs. By the 1960s more than 10 percent of Utah's workers were Uncle Sam's employees. The state's largest employer was Hill Air Force Base near Ogden. Thiokol Corporation, a major firm building rocket missile motors and linked to federal funding, hired perhaps as many as fifty thousand employees for defense work. In Utah in the 1960s and 1970s, 30 percent or more of the state's labor force worked on defense projects. As one scholar has written, "the military-industrial complex was the West's biggest business in the cold war years."

Even more notable was the large federal impact on the Colorado Springs area. From the 1940s to the early 1980s Colorado Springs turned into a federal city. In addition to the army's Camp Carson and Peterson Army Air Base, the city became in 1966 the site for the North American Air Defense Command (NORAD), the hub of the complicated defense system to intercept or ward off enemy bombs or missiles. Colorado Springs also became home to the Air Force Academy, which was completed in 1958. In establishing NORAD and the Academy, the federal government expended nearly a billion dollars. As a result, the economy and social life of Colorado Springs boiled over with new activity during these decades.

Despite these pockets of action, expansion in most of the Plains and Rockies remained static for much of the cold war. From 1940 to 1980, North Dakota and South Dakota gained only 10,000 and 48,000 new residents, respectively. In Nebraska and Kansas, the growth was a bit more impressive, as it was in Montana, Wyoming, Utah, and Idaho. But only Colorado truly boomed in the years between 1940 and 1980, jumping from 1,123,000 residents in 1940 to 2,890,000 in 1980. Most of the largest cities in the Plains and Rockies states—for example, Fargo, Sioux Falls, Kansas City, Salt Lake City, and Cheyenne—experienced moderate growth or remained under 100,000 in size. On the other hand, Omaha, Boise, and Denver rapidly expanded during these decades. Seen another way, the four upper Plains states—North Dakota, South Dakota, Nebraska, and Kansas—and the five northern Rockies states— Montana, Wyoming, Colorado, Utah, and Idaho—together gained only 4.3 million in population from 1940 to 1980. In these same years, California alone soared from 6.9 to 23.7 million, Texas from 6.4 to 14.2 million. Even though the northern Plains and Rockies states all gained new residents, won scattered government funding, and experienced at least a modicum of economic growth, they experienced the smallest gains of any western subregion during the cold war era.

~

In the 1960s and 1970s the Southwest, building on its expansion during World War II and the immediate postwar years, became a dynamic, pulsating subregion. The states of Texas, Oklahoma, New Mexico, and Arizona and overlapping sections of surrounding states increasingly became known as the Sunbelt of the West. Continued government funding for hundreds of firms, expansion of high-tech and service industries, and the rising popularity of amenity tourism added much to the enlargement of the Southwest during these two decades. Gradually settling into patterns in this region and along the Pacific Coast were the ingredients of a new American West: less emphasis on agriculture and extractive industries, less reliance on eastern investors; and more dependence on federal monies, heightened emphases on military-industrial connections, and mounting stress on high-tech businesses, tourism, and service industries. The increasingly powerful sections of the West, chiefly the Southwest and West Coast, were beginning to compete with, if not surpass, other regions of the nation.

If Uncle Sam built a modest financial home in the Southwest during the New Deal 1930s and expanded it during World War II, he added several new rooms during the cold war years. By the 1960s and 1970s, government expenditures clearly exceeded taxes gathered in most parts of the Southwest. Congress continued to fund military bases like Fort Sill in Oklahoma; Fort Bliss near El Paso, Texas; Kirtland Air Base in Albuquerque; Holloman in Alamogordo, New Mexico; and four air and one army base in Houston. Millions of government dollars also bankrolled aerospace industries in Dallas–Fort Worth; the Johnson Space Center in Houston; and several projects near Tucson and Phoenix in Arizona. Even more impressive was the funding rolling into New Mexico for its research-science-military contracts at Sandia Corporation in Albuquerque, Los Alamos, and other installations in the southern part of the state. By the 1970s, New Mexico had the highest per capita number of science PhDs of any state in the country. Still other federal monies went to fund the Central Arizona water project, dams on the Rio Grande, and irrigation projects in Oklahoma and Texas.

The factories, bases, and scientific installations that government funding continued to sustain drew hundreds of thousands of workers to the Southwest. Most of the newcomers, running a gamut of racial and ethnic groups, moved to cities, causing those southwestern urban areas to grow by leaps and bounds. Most urban centers of the Southwest—Houston, Dallas-Fort Worth, San Antonio, El Paso, Oklahoma City, Tulsa, Albuquerque, Phoenix, and Tucson— rapidly expanded in the 1960s and 1970s. In fact, most grew by 50 percent or more during these two decades; some, like Phoenix and El Paso, mushroomed even more rapidly. These southwestern states and their sprawling cities soon became increasingly known for their sunshine, inviting climates, abundant jobs, and tourist amenities. Most of the southwestern urban areas, following twentieth-century Los Angeles more than nineteenth-century San Francisco, became sprawling metropolises rather than urban-centered cities.

The rapid growth of Arizona cities illustrates the predominant patterns of southwestern urbanization. Between 1940 and 1960, Tucson expanded from 36,000 to 213,000, and then to 332,000 in 1980. The changes in Phoenix were even meteoric: 56,000 in 1940, 439,000 in 1960, and up to 790,000 in 1980. These were just the urban center populations of Tucson and Phoenix; when the metropolitan areas clustered around the two Arizona cities were factored in, that meant 80 percent of the state's residents lived in or near Tucson or Phoenix. More than half of the state—55 percent—lived in Phoenix, the fastest growing of the thirty leading Standard Metropolitan Statistical Areas in the United States. Similar to other parts of the Southwest, Arizona was clearly urban—and becoming quickly more so in the second half of the twentieth century.

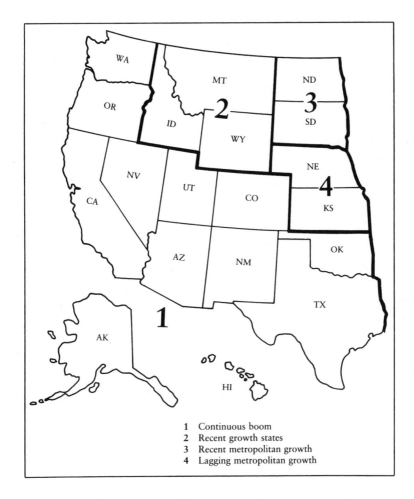

1 Continuous boom
2 Recent growth states
3 Recent metropolitan growth
4 Lagging metropolitan growth

FIGURE 14:2. *Population Growth Regions in the West.* As this map indicates, California, the Pacific Northwest, and the Southwest surged with new population booms in the postwar West, while growth in the northern Rockies and Plains lagged behind. Courtesy Carl Abbott.

City planners and real estate developers, often reacting to the demands of newcomers for more space, allowed suburbs to expand and sprawl like the contents of a spilled container. Suburbs quickly surrounded, and thus expanded the size of, such metropolitan areas as Houston, Dallas-Fort Worth, and Phoenix. These burgeoning urban and suburban populations pressed for, and got, a spreading network of airline connections so that the rising behemoths of the West—Texas and California—were closely linked through the airways. The construction of the country's largest airport at Dallas–Fort Worth illustrated the rising importance of the booming Sunbelt Southwest. Another symbol of the region's growing eminence came when the national freeway system, launched in the Eisenhower 1950s, completed its last link on Interstate 40 in Arizona, replacing much of the fabled Route 66 stretching from Chicago to Los Angeles.

The Southwest also benefited from much of the so-called Westward Tilt that sent millions of newcomers into the West during these two decades. Most of all, new jobs, many of them remunerative and challenging, enticed willing workers. In addition to positions at government-funded bases and military-industrial sites, new jobs opened in expanding high-tech fields. Increasingly after 1950, as part of the cold war buildup, high-tech and electronic firms in the Southwest joined hands and relied on a steady stream of government funding. Once truly partners in the 1960s and 1970s, these new kinds of industries increasingly called the shots in the Southwest, as they would up and down the Pacific Coast. A new economic order in the West was coming to the fore.

Even though no center in the Southwest could be called the equal of California's powerful Silicon Valley, several high-tech industries found homes and expanded in the Southwest. In areas surrounding the sprawling University of Texas campus in Austin, dozens of companies established offices, including Texas Instruments and Motorola. To the north near Dallas and Fort Worth, another cluster of high-tech industries gathered and served as support for the area's aerospace firms. One entrepreneur, H. Ross Perot, gained international headlines—and later political notoriety—as the leader of Electronic Data Systems. Farther north, Tulsa, Oklahoma, landed several telecommunication and data-processing firms that kept its unemployment rates lower than nearly all leading U.S. cities. Motorola also established a huge electronics plant in Phoenix, and Arizona captured new Honeywell, Sperry-Rand, and General Electric firms. In New Mexico, the sophisticated, high-tech industries linked up with atomic, nuclear, and other scientific institutions in Albuquerque and Los Alamos, and near Alamogordo. Electronics, computer, and other high-tech firms were revolutionizing the economics and workforce of many southwestern areas.

The new forces were transforming other, older parts of the southwestern economic patterns as well. In mineral production, for example, copper peaked in the 1970s, only to crash in the 1980s. Low-cost foreign production and lessened uses of copper in high-tech and fiber-optic industries have forestalled a revival of copper mining since the 1980s. Huge mines in Arizona and New Mexico closed or maintained a very low level of productivity. Oil production also peaked in the mid-1950s, with more than 80 percent of the nation's total supply coming from western wells. Fully three-quarters of that U.S.-produced oil came from the states of Texas (the largest producer), California, Oklahoma, and Louisiana. Offshore drilling added new sources of oil in the 1950s and 1960s. U.S. production rose in the energy crisis that plagued the world in the 1970s, but then dropped in the 1980s. This up-and-down pattern of oil production and refining created an uneasiness in Houston and other oil refining centers.

Agriculture in the Southwest also experienced transitions. In the 1960s and 1970s ranchers, other livestock raisers, and farmers took their hits, but the detrimental impact was not as damaging as elsewhere in the West. The markets for Texas sheep and goats—for their meat and wool—dropped precipitously. Cattle-raising, twice as large in Texas as in the next competing state, became more diversified when feedlots and fattening pens were added to the traditional forms of cattle ranching. Beef production, in lesser quantities, also limped along in Oklahoma and Arizona. In Texas, where agribusinesses expanded rapidly, cotton, rice, citrus fruits, and vegetables remained major crops. Arizona farmers also continued to raise notable crops of fruit and vegetables on expanding irrigated farms.

A new surge in tourism and incoming floods of retirees reshaped parts of the Southwest. Increasing numbers of tourists visited amusement parks in Texas and the state's expansive beaches and coastline. Fort Worth's Amon Carter Museum, the Gilcrease Institute in Tulsa, and the National Cowboy Hall of Fame (now the National Cowboy and Western Heritage Museum) in Oklahoma City drew thousands of visitors. In New Mexico, tourists were drawn to art galleries in Santa Fe and Taos, as well as to Native American and Hispanic dances, festivals, and fiestas throughout the year. The Indian pueblos in New Mexico and the Hopi sites in Arizona were also popular tourist locations. Over the years retirees found the sunshine, warm weather, and low taxes of Arizona particularly attractive. The "snowbirds" also flooded into southern Texas and New Mexico to avoid the winter months of northern Frost Belt states.

Even though a new Southwest featured expanding cities, high-tech jobs, and modern conveniences of all sorts, visitors to the region, as well as residents of the area, remained in love with the Old West. In that dreamscape Southwest, John Wayne still rode high, silhouetted against Monument Valley monoliths; the Earp brothers and Doc Holliday engaged in OK Corral shootouts in Tombstone; and the Apache leader Geronimo still outsmarted the pursuing military. Those addicted to a Wild West continued to visit Lincoln and Fort Sumner, New Mexico, and Tombstone, Arizona, to relive the dramatic lives of their heroes, Billy the Kid, the Earps, and Doc Holliday. As western films, novelists, and journalists depicted this go-go Old West, job seekers, government workers, and tourists were coming into a new Southwest. So even as federal funding, air conditioning, and modern conveniences drew hundreds of thousands of newcomers, millions continued to dream of a romantic old Southwest.

$\sim$

Throughout recent decades California has repeatedly proven alarmists wide of the mark. Bashers of the Golden State often predict that jobs, the state's economy, and the inward flow of population will taper off and eventually reverse. But migrants persist in coming—for good-paying positions and appealing climate and to participate in the centuries-long California Dream. Despite sprawl, smog, horrendous commutes for workers, and escalating charges for housing and other living costs, California grows. From 1950 to 2000 population in California has expanded an average of more than four million persons each decade. Population growth in the 1960s and 1970s stayed at that average. When California became the most populous state in 1962, Los Angeles was also replacing New York City as *the* entry point, the nation's new Ellis Island. Although at a less frantic pace, several parts of the Pacific Coast states and Nevada experienced similar expansion. These sections of the West, along with Texas, were its most dynamic subregions.

Cold war government funding continued to stoke the engines of expansion on the West Coast. Ongoing federal monies kept aerospace, nuclear, and military sites humming in the 1960s and 1970s. As one scholar has pointed out, "arms contractors and military leaders, gladly reinforcing talk about a missile gap, stepped up their demands for ever-larger defense expenditures." Interestingly, Democratic and Republican presidents both supported this defense spending. John F. Kennedy (D), Lyndon B. Johnson (D), Richard Nixon (R), Gerald Ford (R), and Jimmy Carter (D) led their administrations in urging continuing support for military and other defense-related industries. This bankrolling from Washington, D.C., helped bring about what journalist Kirkpatrick Sale called the "power shift," the increasing transference of political power, demographic expansion, and industrial might from the northeastern United States to the southern rim, from Florida to southern California. Other writers expanded their definitions of the Sunbelt to include the northern Pacific Coast.

Unquestionably federal largesse encouraged the expansion of California cities. Los Angeles, the San Francisco area, and San Diego particularly benefited from government funding, becoming more and more "martial metropolises."

In the early 1960s some labeled Los Angeles a "federal city" because of its numerous strong links to Washington, D.C. Perhaps as many as 40 percent of the city's workers in manufacturing were tied to government spending on military or space projects. At the same time nearly one-quarter of all government military contracts were awarded to California firms. As parts of this expanding military-industrial complex, the aerospace firms of McDonnell Douglas, North American, TRW, and Hughes located adjacent to the Pacific Ocean, on the west side of Los Angeles; Lockheed was in the San Fernando Valley north of Los Angeles; and others were proximate to Cal Tech and Pasadena northeast of central Los Angeles. These firms and other R&D (Research and Development) companies found times rough going in the late 1960s and early 1970s and yet kept afloat even during these uncertain economic times. Government bailouts, loans, and other special favors were instrumental in saving some companies from bankruptcy during downturns in military spending.

A different kind of defense-technological-urban matrix rapidly expanded in the Bay Area of northern California. There in the Silicon Valley, in Santa Clara County, dozens of electronic firms established themselves. These firms relied on the scientific emphases at Stanford University and followed the leadership of Frederick E. Terman, an expansive-thinking electrical engineer at the university. Soon such entrepreneurial-minded students as David Packard and William R. Hewlett were at work near Stanford. In 1954 the Hewlett-Packard partnership became part of the Stanford Research Park (launched in 1951) and helped to attract several other firms. "This idea of an industrial park near a university was completely foreign," Terman noted. It became "Stanford's secret weapon." The idea quickly caught on. With only seven companies in 1955, the park had thirty-two in 1960 and sixty ten years later. By the mid-1980s nearly one hundred firms occupied all of the 655 acres in the Stanford park. Other industrial parks, modeled after Stanford's, sprang up throughout Silicon Valley. In 1980, forty such parks employed nearly 200,000 workers in electronics, defense, aerospace, and other high-tech industries. From these high-tech parks would come the computer giants that rushed to the forefront of West Coast industries in the 1970s but especially thereafter. Most of the firms relied heavily on federal contracts for their annual budgets.

The Pacific Northwest, although participating in the continuing government support for military-industrial firms, never experienced as many dramatic upsurges as those that characterized California's economic growth in the 1960s and 1970s. Until the early 1970s, Seattle seemed a one-industry city, with the ups and downs of Boeing dominating the city's economic scene. But by 1978 Bill Gates and Paul Allen had located their Microsoft Corporation in a suburb of Seattle and immediately began to impact the regional—even national and global—computer industry. As we shall see in chapter 15, the story of Gates and

Allen and Microsoft is the tale of one company reshaping a regional economy. Gates was soon on an upward trajectory to become the world's richest person. In Portland, Tektronix had become Oregon's largest company. Launched shortly after World War II, the firm had established, by the early 1980s, a reputation for manufacturing test, measurement, and informational display products used in computer, electronics, and communications industries. When Intel, a leading maker of computer chips, built one of its "fab" (manufacturing) plants just west of Portland, that city had already joined the high-tech scene. Continuing to expand, Intel became Oregon's largest employer by the end of the century.

Oregon, Washington, and Nevada experienced steady population growth in the 1960s and 1970s. With 1.8 million residents in 1960, Oregon expanded to 2.6 million in 1980. In the same period Washington grew at a faster rate from 2.9 million in 1960 to 4.1 million in 1980. Nevada's much smaller population enlarged at an even higher percentage rate. Only 285,000 in 1960, Nevada surged to 800,000 in 1980. These population growths were primarily in suburban areas. For example, between 1960 and 1980 the central cores of Portland and Seattle lost population, but their "Metropolitan Statistical Areas," which include urban cores and surrounding suburbs, experienced steady growth. In 1962, the Century 21 world's fair in Seattle introduced the Space Needle and monorail to the city's skyline and refurbished the civic center. Even more dramatic in its impact was another world's fair in 1964 in Spokane, the hub city of eastern Washington and the Inland Empire, which lapped over into Idaho and Montana to the east and Canada to the north. Both fairs brought hordes of visitors to the two Northwest cities. In Nevada, newcomers came primarily to the state's only two sizeable cities, Reno and Las Vegas. By 1960, Las Vegas became the state's largest city, on its way to explosive growth in later decades that made it the country's fastest growing large city by the end of the century. Gambling, legalized in 1931, and expanding tourism keyed Nevada's steady and Las Vegas's phenomenal growth.

While high-tech industries and urban centers expanded, other sections of the economy in Oregon, Washington, and Nevada declined or moved in other directions. The forest and mining industries particularly felt the brunt of change. The lumber industry peaked in the 1950s in the Pacific Northwest, then gradually declined, and fell off precipitously in the 1980s and thereafter. Lumbermen moved elsewhere to cut costs of production and labor, leaving thousands of loggers out of work. The closing of mines in northern Idaho and Montana added other economic woes to Spokane and nearby areas. By the end of the 1970s, the overproduction of wheat had also glutted the market and driven down prices. Farmers and ranchers in the Northwest and livestock raisers in Nevada were feeling an economic pinch that workers in high-tech and service industries had not experienced. It was clear that the economy of the New West had invaded and taken over much of the Pacific Northwest.

~

The nonstop, blistering changes of the 1960s raised welts of discontent on many westerners. Voices of discontent and reform were raised throughout the region. Civil rights activists complained that western states and their large cities were overlooking or discounting inequities in housing policies, workplaces, and political arenas. Western youth charged that life in middle-class suburbs and on university campuses, shaped by profit-driven parents and cold-hearted college administrators, must be changed to prepare students for society's needs. Increasingly, too, western environmentalists pointed to the reckless use of natural resources that needed to be curbed. For these discontented westerners, the dramatic expansion of the West in the postwar years led to unexpected consequences. Cities had grown too large, technocrats were running the region, and the interests of common people were falling before the juggernaut of progress and development. For critics, these dark sides of western life must be recognized and reformed. In the midst of growth and expansion the West thus experienced a new discordant chorus of criticism and discontent. At the same time all the minority groups in the West discovered new leaders to speak for their interests. Blacks, Native Americans, Asian Americans, and Chicanos became more active in advocating for their cultures.

~

The growing and increasingly powerful African American presence in Texas and California undoubtedly made possible the emergence of new black leaders like Barbara Jordan and Angela Davis in the West during these decades. Although black populations continued to mount in several areas of the West, most of the growth took place in Texas and California. By 1980, more than 75 percent of the West's African Americans resided in these two states. Historically, Texas had hosted large black numbers, but with World War II and cold war booms on the West Coast, by 1980 California's black population topped that in Texas. Thousands of unskilled black laborers found work in humming military-industrial plants, and hundreds of thousands of other men and women stationed in the region stayed on to become westerners after their service obligations.

Many African Americans experienced a bittersweet West. Even if they enjoyed more job opportunities and perhaps less discrimination during World War II than in other regions of the country, racial barriers kept them from

HUEY NEWTON
FOR U.S. CONGRESS

BOBBY SEALE
FOR STATE ASSEMBLY
black panther candidates

Register TODAY in the
Peace & Freedom Party

FIGURE 14:3. *Black Panther Candidates.* Huey Newton and Bobby Seale
were leaders of the controversial Black Panthers group. The two men ran
for political office and helped establish community aid organizations, but they
were also involved in violent, antiestablishment actions. Courtesy
The Bancroft Library, University of California, Berkeley, 86/157 Ctr. 5:2.

attending integrated schools even after school segregation was outlawed in
the mid-1950s. In both Texas and California, blacks tended to congregate in
cities, and there they also encountered discriminatory housing laws. In Los
Angeles, mounting discontent exploded in the Watts Riot of August 11–16, 1965.
Residential racism, police harassment, and rising national tensions over ethnic
and racial differences led to the riot. When a white policeman attempted to

arrest a black man for intoxication, a brutal battle broke out. For several days, a virtual war burned red hot in Watts. More than thirty people, primarily blacks, died in the violence, with $40 million worthy of damage to the area. It was the most costly racial conflict to date in the West and clearly proved that racial prejudice simmered in the region.

Blacks reacting to these pressures and events in the early 1960s took varying paths. In Texas, African Americans like Barbara Jordan became politically active and gradually brought racial issues before Texas voters, bit by bit helping to overthrow discriminatory laws and practices. California black leaders like Augustus Hawkins, Ronald Dellums, and Yvonne Braithwaite Burke also supported legislation to set aside residential, occupational, and real estate barriers based on race. But other Californians turned farther left to rally for their demands. Angela Davis was among these activists.

The most controversial of the African American groups was the Black Panther Party. In October 1966 Huey Newton helped found the Black Panthers in Oakland. He and Bobby Seale, the other principal Panther leader, urged young urban blacks particularly to move beyond civil rights organizations, which Newton and Seale saw as too conservative, too linked to white reformers. Disappointments, frustrations, and anger drove the Panthers to radical positions. Newton evidenced his bitterness in indicting California public schools that, he said, had tried "to [rob] me of my worth . . . and nearly killed my urge to inquire." In a series of confrontations, sometimes violent, Panther members disrupted white urban and suburban communities, which they described as inhabited by packs of oppressive racists. Panther party membership peaked in the late 1960s and early 1970s, but the party's inability to gain widespread black support, their disagreements over gender issues, and their failures at forging strong, lasting alliances with other reformers, minority or majority, doomed the party. By the 1980s, in a far different West, the Black Panthers were nearly moribund.

~

Many Native Americans also became more active in speaking out for their rights in the 1960s. With termination and relocation policies of the 1950s obviously failing, young Indians, advocates of Red Power and spurred on by civil rights activities of other minority groups, began calling for a number of reforms. These included (1) ending federal government assaults (through the Bureau of Indian Affairs [BIA]) on tribal traditions; (2) holding the government to its treaty promises; (3) involving more Indians in decisions about Native Americans; and (4) accepting and supporting Indian ways of life.

New organizations and activities were launched to help achieve these goals.

In 1960, in Gallup, New Mexico, a large group of young Native Americans met and founded the National Indian Youth Council (NIYC), calling especially for more Indian participation in policy-making decisions. Later, Vine Deloria, who became a well-known Indian writer through his book *Custer Died for Your Sins* (1969), noted that if the NIYC and similar organizations achieved their goals "for the first time tribes can plan and run their own programs for their people without someone in the BIA dictating to them." In the Pacific Northwest, Indians and their supporters gathered to participate in "fish-ins" designed to remind all Americans of tribal fishing rights assigned to Indians in nineteenth-century treaties. Another group of activists seized Alcatraz Island in San Francisco Bay, symbolizing direct action as a tool for asserting Indian rights and deciding their own future.

The most controversial of the new Native organizations, the American Indian Movement (AIM), was established in 1968. AIM also called for Indian self-determination and an end to BIA attempts to control tribal decisions and policies. Eventually, AIM activism led to a violent clash in early 1973 among militant activists, traditional Indians, and FBI and government officials in the village of Wounded Knee on the Pine Ridge Reservation in western South Dakota. Traditionalists banned AIM from the reservation, but under the forceful leadership of Dennis Banks and Russell Means, AIM took over Wounded Knee. A tense siege lasted for more than two months, during which two Indians were killed. Two years later, with tempers still red hot and after two FBI agents had been slain, AIM leader Leonard Peltier was arrested, tried, convicted, and sentenced to life imprisonment for the killings. His continuing imprisonment remains a contested case of international controversy.

Other factors led to heightened Indian activism. By 1980, a majority of Native Americans lived off the reservation, with large contingents in Los Angeles, Albuquerque, Phoenix, Denver, and Seattle in the West. These urban Indians, often coming back to reservations to attend powwows and other celebrations, returned to their city homes with ethnic batteries recharged and more inclined to take to the streets in support of Indian rights. At the same time a new generation of Indian writers and artists encouraged Indian cultural recovery. Writers N. Scott Momaday, who won a Pulitzer Prize for his novel *House Made of Dawn* (1968), and Leslie Silko, author of *Ceremony* (1977), provided first-rank, provocative treatments of Indian experiences. Painters Oscar Howe, R. C. Gorman, and Fritz Scholder added to the Native cultural renaissance with their important, complex artistic treatments of Native cultures. They too encouraged Native Americans to be proud of their history and to realize that their cultural heritage remained a unique part of American traditions.

~

The presence and reactions of Asian Americans also became more evident in the postwar American West. The Immigration Act of 1965 keyed the explosion of Asian population in the United States and the West in the late twentieth century. This new law and subsequent amendments ended the favored status of European immigrants and allowed in increasing numbers of Asian newcomers. Between 1960 and 1970, Japanese and Chinese populations nearly doubled in the United States, and much the same occurred in the next decade. Smaller numbers of Filipinos, Koreans, and East Indians likewise rapidly grew. Beginning in the late 1970s and thereafter Vietnamese refugees also began flowing into the United States. At least half of these immigrants—sometimes well more than half—moved to the American West.

As they expanded in power and learned from other minority groups, Asians began to speak up for their rights. Japanese Americans, rebounding from their tragic relocation experiences during World War II, worked to overturn discriminatory laws and to achieve redress from losses suffered during relocation. The Japanese American Citizens League (JACL), founded in 1930, took on more activist roles after the war, pushing for repeal of biased laws and organizing for repayment of dispossessions. With the JACL as a major motivating force, Congress enacted legislation in 1988 to pay $20,000 to each individual who had suffered incarceration in relocation camps. In the postwar years, Filipinos joined unions to fight for better wages and working conditions in California's fields and canneries. In the 1960s, they worked with Chicano leader César Chávez in a long but ultimately successful strike to gain higher pay and other rights for field workers in California's valleys.

Minority authors participated in these calls for larger recognition and acceptance of the cultural differences they represented. Filipino writer Carlos Bulosan, drawing extensively on his life as an immigrant field worker and alien newcomer, indicted America's racism in his "personal history" *America Is in the Heart* (1946). These oppressive experiences, Bulosan added, taught immigrants to assert their rights in America, join unions, and urge other Americans to accept their society's racial and ethnic differences. In his dark novel *No-No Boy* (1957), Japanese author John Okada scored Americans for their ill treatment of loyal Nisei (U.S.-born Japanese) but also plumbed the complexities of his protagonist's love-hate for the United States. Chinese American novelist Amy Tan focused on the generational conflicts among Old World Chinese mothers and their American-born daughters. Her probing novel *The Joy Luck Club* (1989) delineated the bittersweet experiences of younger Chinese women trying to please their mothers and yet fit into the sociocultural milieu of their America. These works by Asian writers, like those of so many other western novelists, revealingly depicted the conflicts and convergences that buffeted many racial and ethnic minorities in the postwar American West.

In the 1960s and 1970s César Chávez emerged as the primary Chicano leader in the West and took his place among the most important Americans of the second half of the twentieth century. A leading reformer, a major activist, and a well-known minority spokesperson, Chávez became the country's most-recognized Chicano before his death in 1993. In the West, Chávez became a dynamic field general for Hispanics as well as for others championing equitable rights for agricultural workers and other unskilled laborers.

Chávez drew repeatedly on his own experiences as a migrant worker. After several years working in southwestern agricultural fields and then serving two years in the navy, Chávez became a community organizer in the Bay Area. Working for the Community Service Organization (CSO), he gained invaluable experience as a social planner. When the CSO refused his request to establish a union solely for farmworkers, Chávez resigned, moved to the small California valley town of Delano, and founded the Farm Workers Association (later better known as the United Farm Workers [UFW]). With his only financial support his inadequate $50-a-week salary from the union, Chávez had to return to field work to support his wife and large family. But his bulldog tenacity and quiet courage won hundreds—even thousands—to his fledging organization. "We didn't have any money at all," Chávez wrote later of those starving days, so he "went to people and started asking for food."

In the fall of 1965 Chávez took a huge gamble. He ordered a farmworker strike against the powerful grape growers of the Delano area with only $100 in the union strike fund. For five long years Chávez indefatigably led the strike. Gradually gaining support from the AFL-CIO, the United Automobile Workers, Catholic and Protestant groups, and thousands of strikers who held steady despite the large challenges, Chávez and his farmworkers claimed a surprising victory when the growers in summer 1970 agreed to negotiate. Chávez and his cohorts had taken on the Goliaths of the California grape industry, and ultimately won.

The year of 1970 was the high point of Chávez's career. *Time* magazine named him "Man of the Year," he already was the best-known Chicano in the United States, and he emerged as an international champion for social justice. Rallying the farmworkers with other boycotts, fasts, marches and pilgrimages, and nonviolent strikes, Chávez stayed in the limelight from the 1960s through the 1980s. But his narrow focus on fieldworkers and his nonviolent tactics, drawn from the teachings of Henry David Thoreau and the East Indian leader Mahatma Gandhi, put him at odds with other Chicano leaders. Among these was the fiery Reies López Tijerina, who rallied New Mexico Hispanics in an attempt to regain family lands lost after the Mexican-American War. Also Chávez was not much interested in two other Chicano happenings: the attacks Denver activist Rodolfo

"Corky" Gonzales launched on socioeconomic inequities in urban barrios, and the Chicano political party that José Angel Gutiérrez organized in Texas. The ethnic nationalism of La Causa (the Cause) and La Raza (people of Mexican heritage) attracted Chávez much less than the bread-and-butter issues of field workers of all ethnic and racial backgrounds.

On the other hand, no one worked more closely with Chávez than Dolores Huerta. A well-educated, attractive, and forceful Chicana, Huerta became a stalwart lieutenant in Chávez's cause. She was a dynamic, tough-minded negotiator and could stand high-pressure confrontations without folding or losing her wits. Although Huerta and Chávez vigorously differed on many issues, though they sometimes vociferously argued over which tactics to use and which goals to attain, they respected each other. Huerta marveled at Chávez's "commitment, cooperation, perseverance, and integrity." In turn, Chávez thought of Huerta as a "fighter" who "knew everyone" and who used these strengths to advance the UFW cause. Occasionally Chávez would question Huerta about paying too little attention to her large family (she had eleven children), but he also valued, praised, and depended on her leadership talents and superb skills as a labor negotiator.

Throughout the late 1970s and on to the early 1990s Chávez, Huerta, and other farmworker leaders faced new difficulties and barriers. When Ronald Reagan was elected California's governor in 1966 and later the U.S. president in 1980, Chávez lost much of the political support from Democratic leaders he had enjoyed at state and national levels. The general swing to the right in western politics also undercut the strength of Chávez's labor movement. The mounting numbers of Mexican workers flooding across the U.S. southern border—some illegally, some with work permits—provided another challenge. These workers, available as strikebreakers, effectively hamstrung some of Chávez's strike and boycott efforts. On several occasions he supported moves to stem the tide of these undocumented workers. The arrival of these illegal workers posed then, as now, an unresolved dilemma.

The dynamic leadership of César Chávez illustrated the advancements Chicanos made in the 1960s and 1970s but also illuminated ongoing difficulties facing them. Chávez's achievements with the UFW and other farmworkers revealed what Chicanos might gain through skillful organization, strong leadership, and class and ethnic solidarity. At the same time, problems of illiteracy, crime, and urban unemployment continued to plague Chicanos in East Los Angeles and in other barrios spread across the Southwest. Too many young Chicano/as were also dropping out of school. On balance, Chicanos were making progress slowly—a stride forward, but sometimes it was a faltering step.

∾

The dislocations and discontents that became increasingly evident in the United States in the 1960s and 1970s deeply affected western young people. Fallout from the divisive Vietnam War, rising expectations of civil rights movements, the traumatic assassinations of political leaders, and the new assertiveness of racial and ethnic groups clearly influenced the attitudes of younger westerners. More vociferous activists joined so-called New Left organizations such as the Students for a Democratic Society (SDS) or the even more radical Weathermen bent on the destruction of the American system. Most did not, however. Still, clear manifestations of student discontents erupted in several parts of the West, especially in California in the Bay Area and on several college campuses. During the 1960s and early 1970s the American West gained a reputation as a pacesetter for social activism, as a country of the young.

FIGURE 14:6. *Mario Savio and the Free Speech Movement.* This student-led movement erupted on the campus of the University of California, Berkeley, in late 1964. Spokesman Mario Savio, here standing on a police car, helped lead this movement challenging university leadership and criticizing curricular content. It quickly spread to other campuses in the West and nation. Courtesy The Bancroft Library, University of California, UARC PIC 24B:3.

Western young people coming of age in these two decades, like other young Americans, found the value systems of their Depression-age and World War II parents increasingly unsatisfactory. The growing affluence of American families, an enlarging sense of the meaninglessness of high school and college curricula, and mounting concern with environmental problems added fuel to adolescent discontents. Youthful westerners raised their voices to challenge American societal values.

In 1964, the howl of discontent broke out quickly and forcefully at the University of California in Berkeley. The Free Speech Movement that formed on the Berkeley campus was an important part of the yeasty 1960s and, more specifically, the youth revolt of that decade. Drawing on earlier civil rights protests, marches against university hiring practices, and mushrooming discontent with suburban and campus life, University of California students, with the aid of nonstudent agitators, mounted a series of protests that virtually closed the Berkeley campus. In early December 1964, student Mario Savio harangued a gathering in front of the university's administration building. "There is a time when the operation of the machine becomes so odious," he told his listeners, that "you've got to put your bodies upon the gears and upon the wheels, upon the levers, upon all the apparatus and you've got to make it stop. And you've got to indicate to the people who run it, to the people who own it, that unless you're free, the machine will be prevented from working at all."

Savio and the Free Speech Movement spoke for increasing numbers of American students in the early-to-mid-1960s. He also represented student alienation from California's huge, sprawling university and college system. Four years earlier, the state had formalized its three-tier organization of dozens of universities, colleges, and junior or community colleges. This Master Plan for High Education, while providing system to the welter of higher education units in California, also seemed to depersonalize it for students. Mario Savio and his fiery colleague Bettina Aptheker, the daughter of a noted American Marxist historian, inspired fellow students to protest the inadequacies of the California system and then shut down the Berkeley campus with "sit-ins." Across the bay at San Francisco State University a student strike against university policies and in support of a black studies program led to weeks of chaos, including a closed university and campus violence. Similar disruptions took place at Stanford and the University of California at Santa Barbara. Student "revolts" similar to these in California broke out throughout the West on college campuses scattered from Washington to Texas. If panty raids, telephone-booth stuffing, and bedstead races of fraternities and sororities characterized student life in the 1950s, in the 1960s college students were notable for their rebellions against campus policies, social and racial prejudices, and the Vietnam War.

San Francisco helped spawn yet another youth movement in the 1960s, the so-called "Hippies." The Hippies were part of the larger countercultural move-ment that emerged in the 1960s calling for alternatives to the "American Way of Life." Although owing some to the separatist legacies, "hip" stances, and drug use advocacy of the earlier Beats, the Hippies were influenced even more by the rising feminist, environmental, antiwar, and civil rights movements of the early 1960s. Toward the end of the decade and well into the 1970s, scattered Hippie communes dotted California, northwestern, and southwestern landscapes.

The Hippie movement reached its zenith of notoriety in 1967. Thousands of "flower power children" gathered in the North Beach and Haight-Ashbury dis-tricts of San Francisco for a "Summer of Love," or a gigantic "love-in." Rock-and-roll music, drug ingesting sessions (especially LSD "trips"), and sexual couplings ("make love, not war") filled the ecstatic summer. "Getting stoned," "dropping out," and "doing your own thing" were slogans the Hippies attempted to live out in those wild summer months of 1967.

But there were more serious sides, too, of the Hippies. Rationality, profit motives, political machinations, and sexual prudishness were ruining American society, the Hippies argued. Instead, they "saw themselves as the people of zero, the vanguard who would build a new society on the ruins of the old, corrupt one." They would abandon an overly commercialized, technocratic, and power-hungry society and establish a counterculture with more attention to the natural, agrarian, organic, and mystical. On these values, Hippie communities flourished for a few years. As the mood of the country shifted in the 1970s, however, so did support and participation in the counterculture. Their own excesses, violence, mistreatment of women, and impracticalness combined to lead to the virtual demise of the Hippie movement by the end of the 1970s.

∾

In the 1960s and 1970s politics in the West migrated to the right, in the oppo-site direction from the youth movements. During this period Governor Ronald Reagan of California (1967–75) was the most influential western politician. Identifying with Republican political leaders in the West like Richard Nixon and Barry Goldwater, Reagan solidified the conservative Republican swing to the right taking place in these years. For many westerners—and later, for many other Americans—Reagan represented the answer to what they considered the excesses of the New Left and the disastrously liberal tendencies of students, civil rights reformers, and other left-leaning politicians of the 1960s. By time he left the governor's office in Sacramento, Reagan had become a national political leader. He completed that ascendancy when elected to the U.S. presidency in 1980.

Reagan came to the California governorship by an unusual path. Raised in the Midwest, he took up radio announcing before moving in the 1930s to

FIGURE 14:7. *President Ronald Reagan Horseback Riding at Rancho del Cielo.* The most important western politician in the second half of the twentieth century, Reagan served as governor of California (1967–75) and then as president of the United States (1981–89). He both followed and led the turn to the right that characterized politics in the post–World War II West. Courtesy Ronald Reagan Library, C3606–21A.

Hollywood to become an actor. Eventually starring in many films, including several Westerns, Reagan was named president of the Screen Actors' Guild. Meanwhile he changed his politics from liberal Democrat to conservative Republican. In 1966, without any experience in elected public office, he ran against incumbent Pat Brown, accusing his opponent of being responsible for the "mess in Berkeley," violence in California cities, and the state's mounting taxes. Easily winning the election, Reagan promised a conservative agenda of smaller budgets, reduced spending, law and order, and sound government. Without long ties to the Republican Party and facing Democratic majorities in the California assembly and senate, Reagan achieved few of his campaign pledges. In his first term, state budgets reached new heights, and the largest tax increase in the state's history was enacted. On the other hand Reagan did cut higher education support, tried to whittle down welfare costs, and attempted to ram through tax limitations. Although he achieved few of his promises and his actions were primarily negative—attempting to roll back expenditures— California voters loved him. Smooth, usually cheerful, and smilingly telling his opponents "there you go again," Reagan displayed the self-confidence, patriotism, and reputed fiscal conservatism that won him mounting popularity. In the end, Ronald Reagan projected a many-sided image: a model of dependability and tradition, he also became recognized as an opponent of the frothy and radical 1960s that Californians wanted to disavow in the early 1970s. When former Californian and sitting president Richard Nixon fell under the cloud of the Watergate scandal and resigned in August 1974, Reagan became the Republican leader of the West.

Other western politicians followed trails similar to Reagan's cautious conservatism. In Oklahoma, voters elected Republican governors in the 1960s, and John Connally, after serving three terms as Texas governor, joined the Nixon administration and became a Republican. Arizona continued to be a bulwark of conservativism in the 1960s and 1970s, and by the early 1980s New Mexico, traditionally Democratic, was supporting Reagan as president. In Montana and Wyoming, residents sent liberal senators like Mike Mansfield, Joseph O'Mahoney, and Gale McGee to the U.S. Senate but retained conservative governments at home. Republican loyalties were particularly strong in the northern Plains states of North Dakota, South Dakota, Nebraska, and Kansas. Conservatives also did well in Utah, Idaho, Colorado, and Nevada.

A few western politicians broke from this conservative mold. In Washington, Democratic senators Henry "Scoop" Jackson and Warren Magnuson and progressive Republican governors Arthur Langlie and Dan Evans represented the more nonpartisan politics of the northern coast. The independent senator Wayne Morse, who became a Democrat, and the later Republicans Mark Hatfield and Robert Packwood gave Oregon one of the most liberal contingents in the U.S. Senate of any western state. In Idaho, maverick Glen Taylor and then the very popular Frank Church, both liberal Democratic senators, proved that politicians left of center could win in a conservative state. Remaining safe on local issues dealing with agriculture, gun control, and nuclear energy, Church became one of the country's most outspoken opponents ("doves") on the Vietnam War, as were Morse and Hatfield in Oregon, but still repeatedly won one of Idaho's U.S. Senate seats until the Reagan national landslide victory in 1980.

The political move to the right in the 1970s and thereafter revealed a good deal about westerners. Civil rights reformers and student activists might attack the prejudices, stuffiness, and shortsightedness of the American middle class, but rural and suburban middle-class westerners won at the ballot box in the 1970s. By and large they elected governors and national representatives and senators who seemed to promise security, balance, fiscal soundness, and conservative leadership in a diverse society and constantly changing times. Their leaders, in general, symbolized the spirit and stances of Ronald Reagan.

∾

The conflicting moods that characterized so much of the American West during the 1960s and 1970s marked its historical writings, fiction, and films as well. Even as historian Ray Allen Billington, novelist Louis L'Amour, and actor John Wayne portrayed the western past as adventuresome, heroic, and positive, other writers and filmmakers were portraying an Old West shot through with ambiguity, as a less-than-upbeat place. For the first time numerous authors and directors were depicting the region as a New Gray West, as a placed of blurred perspectives and values.

In his pioneering revisionist book, *Bury My Heart at Wounded Knee* (1970), librarian Dee Brown startled readers with his scathing treatment of a vicious frontier military murdering Indians and preparing the way for avaricious white pioneers. Some academic historians denounced Brown's history as based on shoddy research and slanted evidence, but lay audiences took to his account as if irrefutable truth. In the 1960s and 1970s, other writers, although less critical of the nineteenth-century western past than Brown, nonetheless pointed to the lack of attention paid to women and families, ethnic and racial groups, and the environment in western histories. Noting the difficulties pioneer women often faced, the virulent racism aimed at minority groups, and the rapaciousness of settlers vis-à-vis the environment, these scholars urged western historians to tell more complex stories about the western past that included darker elements.

More than a few western writers moved in the same direction in the 1960s and 1970s. In doing so they were following in the steps of historical novelist A. B. Guthrie, Jr., who castigated the environmental destructiveness of frontier mountain men in his novel *The Big Sky* (1947). More pointed in his criticism of environmental despoliation was Edward Abbey, especially in his work of fiction *Monkey Wrench Gang* (1975). The most important of the environmentally aware writers, Wallace Stegner, urged westerners and policy makers to think of wilderness areas as a "geography of hope." A host of other western authors pointed to a unified and sustaining ecological vision as the largest need in historical and fictional writings about the West.

In their writings, novelists Ken Kesey and Joan Didion captured much of the doubting mood of the 1960s and 1970s about the western present and future. In 1962, Kesey provided the quintessential novel of the counterculture in his *One Flew Over the Cuckoo's Nest*. The novel's hero, Randle Patrick McMurphy (RPM), thumbs his nose at a nameless, bureaucratic "fog machine" that threatens the mental institution where he has taken refuge. Eventually, the technocratic institution, run by a dictatorial and unwavering Big Nurse, catches and lobotomizes him, leaving him a pathetic vegetable. Only Chief Bromden, the huge Indian chief, escapes. Energized by RPM's courage, the chief flees to the outside to keep hope alive. In Joan Didion's first novel set in her native California, *Run River* (1963), residents blindly and dangerously worship a false, romantic past. In a later novel, *Play It As It Lays* (1970), Didion's heroine wanders clueless, bereft of a moral or historical compass in a blighted, colorless world of endless California freeways. Nothing in Kesey's or Didion's novels suggests that the West, past or present, embodies the heroic, adventurous spirit that drives most of L'Amour's fiction and John Wayne's films.

Western movies also invoked the New Gray West. By the end of the 1960s, it was apparent how far Western films had moved away from the classics *High Noon* and *Shane* of the early 1950s. In Arthur Penn's *Little Big Man* (1970), starring Dustin Hoffman as a wandering western roustabout, George Custer is portrayed as an arrogant, blind, and dangerous fool rather than as a heroic military leader. Turning the tables on earlier Westerns, this film depicts Native Americans as the new heroes, with the white military and pioneers the villains. In the late 1960s and early 1970s college audiences, demonstrating their sympathies for these reversed roles, often stood to cheer when Custer was wiped out at the Little Bighorn. Director Sam Peckinpah presented an even more vicious, violent West in his *Wild Bunch* (1969), a film about aging gunmen driven by power, money, and rootlessness. Dubbed a "ballet of blood" by critics because of its extensive treatment of mindless violence, the movie depicted a West without morality, love, or communal spirit. Concurrently the spaghetti Westerns directed by Italian Sergio Leone and starring Clint Eastwood (for example, *A Fistful of Dollars* [1964] and *For a Few Dollars More* [1965]) dramatized an equally amoral West driven by dollars, promiscuity, and greed; this West lacked any sense of unity or hope. By the mid-1970s, moviemakers moved beyond these more pointed socially critical films to seriocomic Westerns like *Blazing Saddles* (1974). This very popular, high-grossing film, directed by Mel Brooks and starring African American Cleavon Little, satirized pioneers, gunmen, and racism while it poked fun at nearly all ingredients of the well-known Westerns of John Wayne and John Ford.

∼

The emergence and flowering of the New Gray West revealed how uncertain many westerners were about their region, its heritage as well as its future. Some, like politician Barbara Jordan, committed themselves to avenues of service to help protect and improve the West. Others, like Angela Davis, seeing so many unanswered questions facing the modern West, advocated radical reforms to dramatically redirect the region and thus achieve justice and balance in western life. Some writers and moviemakers chose to work in more traditional modes of western fiction and film, but others broke with those more optimistic outlooks to depict a rudderless West in need of large reorientation. This bifurcated view, divided into accepting and challenging views of the West, continued to shape and stimulate strong reactions to the region in the final decades of the century.

Abbott, Carl. *The Metropolitan Frontier: Cities in the Modern American West.* Tucson: University of Arizona Press, 1993.

Berlin, Leslie. *The Man Behind the Microchip: Robert Noyce and the Invention of Silicon Valley.* New York: Oxford University Press, 2005.

Etulain, Richard W., ed. *César Chávez: A Brief Biography with Documents.* Boston: Bedford Books, 2002.

Farber, David. *The Age of Great Dreams: America in the 1960s.* New York: Hill and Wang, 1994.

Fernlund, Kevin J., ed. *The Cold War American West 1945–1989.* Albuquerque: University of New Mexico Press, 1998.

Findlay, John M. *Magic Lands: Western Cityscapes and American Culture After 1940.* Berkeley: University of California Press, 1992.

Foster, Mark S. *A Nation of Wheels: The Automobile Culture in America Since 1945.* Fort Worth, TX: Harcourt, 2003.

Gómez, Arthur R. *Quest for the Golden Circle: The Four Corners and the Metropolitan West 1945–1970.* Albuquerque: University of New Mexico Press, 1994.

Griswold, Richard del Castillo, and Richard A. Garcia. *César Chávez: A Triumph of Spirit.* Norman: University of Oklahoma Press, 1995.

Hagstrom, Jerry. *Beyond Reagan: The New Landscape of American Politics.* New York: W. W. Norton, 1988.

Harvey, Mark. *Wilderness Forever: Howard Zahniser and the Path to the Wilderness Act.* Seattle: University of Washington Press, 2005.

Hurt, R. Douglas. *Problems of Plenty: The American Farmer in the Twentieth Century.* Chicago: Ivan Dee, 2002.

———, ed. *The Rural West Since World War II.* Lawrence: University Press of Kansas, 1998.

Indergaard, Michael. *Silicon Alley: The Rise and Fall of a New Media District.* New York: Routledge, 2004.

Iverson, Peter. *Barry Goldwater: Native Arizonan.* Norman: University of Oklahoma Press, 1997.

Lowitt, Richard, ed. *Politics in the Postwar American West.* Norman: University of Oklahoma Press, 1995.

Matthews, Glenna. *Silicon Valley, Women, and the California Dream: Gender, Class, and Opportunity in the Twentieth Century.* Stanford, CA: Stanford University Press, 2003.

Miller, Timothy. *The Hippies and American Values.* Knoxville: University of Tennessee Press, 1991.

Nash, Gerald D. *A Brief History of the American West Since 1945.* Fort Worth, TX: Harcourt, 2001.

———. *The Federal Landscape: An Economic History of the Twentieth-Century West.* Tucson: University of Arizona Press, 1999.

Nugent, Walter. *Into the West: The Story of Its People*. New York: Knopf, 1999.

O'Mara, Margaret Pugh. *Cities of Knowledge: Cold War Science and the Search for the Next Silicon Valley*. Princeton, NJ: Princeton University Press, 2005.

Rorabaugh, W. J. *Berkeley at War: The 1960s*. New York: Oxford University Press, 1989.

Sale, Kirkpatrick. *Power Shift: The Rise of the Southern Rim and Its Challenge to the Eastern Establishment*. New York: Random House, 1976.

Schwantes, Carlos A. *The Pacific Northwest: An Interpretive History*. Lincoln: University of Nebraska Press, 1989.

Self, Robert O. *American Babylon: Race and the Struggle for Postwar Oakland*. Princeton, NJ: Princeton University Press, 2003.

Sides, Josh. *L.A. City Limits: African American Los Angeles from the Great Depression to the Present*. Berkeley: University of California Press, 2004.

Slotkin, Richard. *Gunfighter Nation: The Myth of the Frontier in Twentieth-Century America*. New York: Atheneum, 1992.

Taylor, Quintard. *In Search of the Racial Frontier: African Americans in the American West, 1528–1990*. New York: W. W. Norton, 1998.

Tygiel, Jules. *Ronald Reagan and the Triumph of American Conservatism*. New York: Longman, 2004.

Wills, Garry. *Reagan's America*. New York: Penguin Books, 1988.

Wrobel, David M., and Michael C. Steiner, eds. *Many Wests: Place, Culture, and Regional Identity*. Lawrence: University Press of Kansas, 1997.

CHAPTER FIFTEEN

In Search of Region

THE AMERICAN WEST, 1980 TO THE PRESENT

~

THEY WERE TWO NERDY COLLEGE DROPOUTS. RAISED IN THE PACIFIC Northwest and graduates of a prestigious high school in Seattle, they had gone off to college with strong academic backgrounds. Drawn more to technology and computers than to the regimentation of college courses and campus life, they abandoned lecture halls and in 1975 moved to the Southwest, hoping to found and expand a company of their own. Unable to fund their dream in Albuquerque, they retreated in 1978 to Seattle, their hometown. Drawing on their parents' connections and initially working with IBM and other firms, the two young entrepreneurs quickly turned the corner on their own visions. By the early 1990s, scarcely more than a decade after launching Microsoft and still under age forty, Bill Gates and Paul Allen had become two of the world's richest and most widely known persons.

The astounding rise of Gates and Allen illustrates again the rapid changes and diverse economies that continued to mark the history of the American West. At the end of the twentieth century and at the beginning of a new one these two computer enthusiasts had enriched the economy of the Pacific Northwest. That region, long known as the domain of Boeing and aircraft building, assumed a new identity as the home of Microsoft Corporation, which employed in excess of twenty thousand workers and was capitalized at more than $500 billion in 2000. The simultaneous emergence of Starbucks Coffee and of Amazon.com, the huge Internet bookseller, added new items to the region's expanding economic menu. Recognized as one of the West's most livable cities, Seattle assumed a new, more complex identity as also one of the region's most entrepreneurially alive urban areas. It likewise became more crowded, beset with mounting housing, traffic, and air pollution problems.

What happened in Seattle and the Pacific Northwest at the end of the twentieth century illustrated the rapid transformations overtaking several parts of the modern American West. Indeed, expansion of jobs and economic possibilities and attendant social and environmental problems seemed the inseparable twins of the contemporary American West. With demographic and occupational growth came urban dilemmas and increasing pollution. Change and diversity, the hallmarks of the western past, continued to mark the region in the late twentieth century. They were also barriers to the West's search for a coherent regional identity in the years following 1980.

∼

For the most part population expansion in the West during the 1980s and 1990s followed familiar trends. California and Texas were once again the boom states. After surpassing New York as the most populous state in the early 1960s, California had jumped to 33.9 million residents in 2000. Jobs, sunshine, and promise of the "good life" remained the primary lures to the Golden State. Even though naysayers continued to predict that California would cease drawing migrants, in the 1980s and 1990s hundreds of thousands of newcomers continued to flock to the state. Only in the first years of the twenty-first century did more Californians leave than new U.S. residents arrive, but even then new births and foreign immigration continued to increase California's total population.

In the mid-1990s Texas became the second most populous state in the United States. It too had leapfrogged over New York, as California had earlier. In 2000 Texas boasted of 20.1 million residents, compared to New York's 19 and Florida's 16 million. Texas was even growing faster than California. But the places of expansion in Texas were the same as those in California—in cites and suburbs. Both states also drew sizable numbers of immigrants from Mexico, the nation sending the largest number of newcomers to the United States at the end of the century. In 2000, Texas and California, together, made up 54.9 of the West's total of 91.5 million residents, with nearly six out of ten westerners residing in those two states and only four of ten in the other fifteen western states.

The social makeup of the West stood out in other ways besides its continual demographic growth. It was also the most urban region of the United States and yet in some areas one of the least densely populated. The continued expansion remained unbalanced, with some areas booming, others losing population.

∼

During the 1980s and 1990s long-held myths about the American West still collided with reality. Even though western movies and fiction and other popular media frequently depicted the region as sparsely settled and replete with open spaces, the West became increasingly urban, especially if one considers

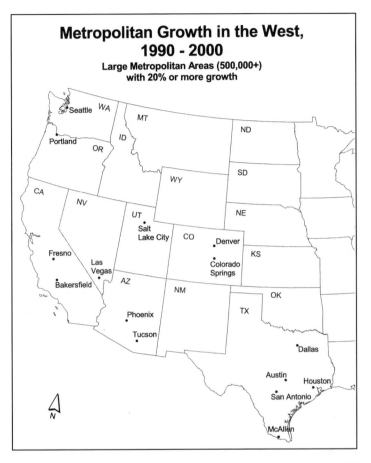

FIGURE 15:1. *Metropolitan Growth in the West, 1990–2000.* In the last years of the twentieth century, urban expansion in the West continued where it had for three to four decades: across the Southwest and up the Pacific Coast. Courtesy Carl Abbott.

expanding suburbs along with long-existing urban centers. As a leading urban historian notes, many western cities not only continued to grow rapidly in the second half of the twentieth century, they also organized the West's "vast spaces and connect[ed] them to the even larger sphere of the world economy." Western cities have taken on additional significance as "national and even international pacesetters." By 1990, about 90 percent of westerners lived in cities and towns of more than 2,500 population. Western urban areas also expanded more rapidly than those in the East. Together the six largest western metropolitan areas grew more than 380 percent in the five decades following 1940, whereas the six largest in the East expanded but 64 percent. In fact, in this half-century the dozen largest western metropolitan areas made up 28 percent of the nation's growth. In 1990, 80 percent of westerners lived in metropolitan areas of 60,000 or more, compared to 76 percent in other parts of the United States.

The patterns of western cities were also changing. In the nineteenth century western urbanization tended to follow the centralized city model of San Francisco. In the next century, Los Angeles became the typical city, even though its sprawl has often been overemphasized. By end of the twentieth century, "edge cities" had sprouted alongside several western metropolitan areas. These multicentered cities featured a large urban area that incorporated suburbs— nearly small cities in themselves—with all the business, shopping, recreational, school, and health-care facilities of earlier, single-centered cities. Among these new edge cities in the West were Phoenix, Denver, Dallas–Fort Worth, Las Vegas, Los Angeles, San Diego, Portland, and Seattle.

Demographic trends in the recent West were more diverse than merely adding hordes of newcomers to the region's most populated states and largest cities. Indeed, aridity remained a powerful shaping force in the contemporary West, even though technology and government funding redirected some of aridity's molding power. Except for its humid eastern and western edges, the West was by and large dry country, where the lack of sufficient rainfall limited the kinds of agriculture and hence human habitation possible in these subhumid areas. As Texas historian Walter Prescott Webb often noted, the American West was a land of urban oases. That meant most sections of the West still featured a good deal of open space, with larger cities separated from one another by eye-stretching landscapes. A paradox existed: the West might be the most urban section of the country, but it also retained more open areas than any other region of the United States.

~

The numbers of minority peoples in the West continued to expand in the last two decades of the twentieth century. Increasingly, the West became the meeting ground for an ever more diverse array of racial and ethnic cultures. By the year 2000, the West was home to about two-thirds of the nation's Native Americans, most of the country's Hispanics, half its Asians, and growing numbers of African Americans.*

In these recent years not only had Los Angeles become the new Ellis Island

---

*Beginning with the census of 2000, Americans were allowed to list themselves as members of more than one race.

for immigrants to the United States, the West served as the most yeasty example of America's ethnic pluralism.

The most surprising growth among racial groups was that of Native Americans. Between 1980 and 2000, those denoting "Indian" as their racial identity on the national census report jumped from 1.4 to 2.5 million, a 44 percent gain. Every western state saw a healthy expansion of Indian population between 1980 and 1990 and again between 1990 and 2000. Most states experienced at least a 10 percent gain in each of the decades. By the end of the century more than half of the region's Indians had moved off reservations and lived in cities. During these two decades several Native American tribes in the West augmented and diversified their investments, became more involved in expanding efforts for better education for Indians on reservations and in cities, and greatly enlarged their tourist industries. In 2000 nearly one-third of the western tribes had established casinos, and whatever the moral and ethical ramifications of these gaming institutions, they attracted thousands of visitors and gamblers and earned a great deal of money. Many Indian communities made good use of casino income to provide better schooling, health care, and other amenities for enrolled tribal members.

Unfortunately, darker sides of Indian life in the West also remained. At the end of the twentieth century Indians were the poorest, sickest, and least-educated minority in the West. Their median income was about two-thirds that of other Americans, with one-third of Indian households below the poverty line. One in eight Indians also had diabetes, with their death rate from this disease three times that of Caucasians. Native Americans had the lowest life expectancy of any American group, and their infant mortality rate was the highest in the country. Alcoholism remained a large problem, too, with five to six times as many Indians likely to die from the disease as other Americans.

Despite all these persisting dilemmas, among some Indians hope for the future had not disappeared. "We've got a new generation with a different attitude," one Crow woman observed. In the political arena Ben Nighthorse Campbell (Northern Cheyenne) served as a Republican senator from Colorado for more than a decade. Powwows, tribal dances, arts and crafts fairs, and a florescence of Indian writing were also important evidences of a Native American cultural revitalization. Many problems continued, but surging population growth and less defeatist attitudes were good signs for the next generation.

Change seemed to buffet African Americans less notably than it did Native Americans. Of the more than seven million blacks residing in the West, California and Texas claimed by far the largest populations. Sizeable groups of blacks were also living in Nevada, Oklahoma, and Kansas. Los Angeles, Houston, Dallas, Oakland, and San Diego all boosted more than 100,000 black residents. In the 1980s and 1990s African Americans in the West were much less inclined to join fiery reform groups as they had the Black Panthers in the 1960s and 1970s. Indeed, in the last decades of the twentieth century increasing numbers of African Americans were finding white-collar jobs and joining the middle class.

These advances might imply that most western blacks were living out the American Dream. Such was not the case. There were as many "down" as "up" experiences for blacks in the West. The horrendous incident of police brutality in March 1991 in which four Los Angeles officers allegedly beat African American motorist Rodney King tragically revealed the consequences of black inner-city poverty and how far a racial Eden was in the future. Months later in April 1992 when the courts declared the policemen not guilty of beating King, riots broke out, and as one African American historian writes, "south Central Los Angeles exploded in a maelstrom of rage." At the corners of Florence and Normandie streets in Los Angeles, black youths dragged white driver Reginald Denny from his truck and violently beat him, in retaliation for what the police had allegedly done to King a year earlier. The resulting violence from April 29 to May 1, 1992, which ended in fifty-one deaths and the looting and burning of local businesses, indicated the intense racial hatred that existed among whites, blacks, Asians, and Latinos. Rioters destroyed nearly two thousand Korean businesses, and almost twelve thousand people, 41 percent African American and 45 percent Hispanic, were arrested.

The frustrations that quickly surfaced had deep, long economic and social roots. For many inner-city blacks in Los Angeles, as well as in other large western cities, jobs had been hard to find. The rate of poverty among blacks in south Los Angeles, at more than 30 percent, was more than twice the national average, and nearly 40 percent of black males were unemployed. Many felt that competition from other ethnic and racial groups was forcing African Americans from positions rightfully theirs. The atmosphere in Los Angeles remained charged for several months.

The riots of 1992 revealed what westerners were gradually learning. Competitions and conflicts were not just between whites and minority groups but also increasingly evident *among* as well as *within* minority groups themselves. For instance, as several Asian groups moved into predominantly black areas of Los Angeles, racial tensions mounted, particularly when African Americans saw job opportunities waning and their incomes falling. These conflicts in Los Angeles in spring 1992 were but one more indicator of the growing complexity of life in the American West.

～

Asian experiences in the late-twentieth-century West took several new directions. Although strong economic times in Japan and an assertive political

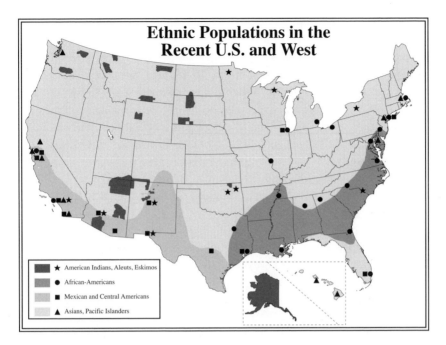

FIGURE 15:2. *Ethnic Populations in the Recent United States and West.* Most Asians, Hispanics, Indians, and increasing numbers of African Americans in the United States resided in the West by the end of the twentieth century. Map by Robert Pace.

regime in Mainland China discouraged emigrants from leaving those two countries, new cohorts of immigrants arrived from Hong Kong and Taiwan, the Philippines, Korea, and Southeast Asia. Even the phrases employed for describing these newcomers changed: the ethnocentric epithet "yellow peril" had disappeared, and the denomination "Oriental" was no longer acceptable. These peoples were now known simply as "Asians" by those other than themselves. Yet they were the most diverse of minority groups in the West, with more than a half-dozen groups identified as Asian.

Not only were patterns of Asian immigration shifting in the last few decades of the twentieth century, the sheer volume of Asians arriving had increased dramatically. If in the 1950s only 5 percent of immigrants to the United States were Asians, by the 1990s they made up more than 50 percent of the newcomers. Between 1980 and 1990, Asian populations in the United States more than doubled from 3.5 to 7.2 million. Perhaps as many as 10 million Asians resided in the United States in 2000, with about half living in the American West.

Since the booming economy of Japan during much of the 1980s and 1990s lessened Japanese immigration to the United States, Japanese American communities, unlike other Asian communities, were not experiencing a new influx of immigrants. As one Japanese American ruefully noted, "Many second- and third-generation Japanese have moved to the suburbs," and "there are too few new immigrants from Japan to fill their places in Japantown." Meanwhile many Japanese who had lived through the depressing circumstances of Japanese Relocation during World War II were coming to terms with their horrific memories. By the end of the 1980s, the U.S. government had issued a long-delayed apology for those untoward wartime actions and provided a payment of $20,000 to each relocation survivor. Meanwhile Japanese immigration, by the year 2000, had fallen to about four thousand annually, far below the yearly immigrant quota of twenty thousand for Japanese.

Chinese immigrants followed other routes. Even though restrictions in Mainland Communist China virtually cut off legal immigration from that location, newcomers from Hong Kong and Taiwan swelled the Chinese population in the United States. Most Chinese Americans, as well as the incoming Chinese, settled on the West Coast. Nearly 10 percent of the nation's Chinese lived in San Francisco's buoyant Chinatown. In fact, in 1980 the number of Chinese in the United States had surpassed the Japanese. Chinese Americans diligently encouraged their sons and daughters to attend college, with a result that by 1970 fully one-quarter of Chinese American men had college degrees, the highest rate in the country. Chinese students in California did so well on college entrance exams that officials at prestigious institutions like the University of California, Berkeley; Stanford University; and Cal Tech felt compelled to limit the number of top-ranked Chinese students so as to achieve ethnic balance in entering classes.

Other Asian groups came in even greater numbers. Filipinos arrived first as field and other unskilled workers, but increasing numbers of middle-class professionals immigrated in the 1960s. From the mid-1960s to the mid-1970s more than 250,000 Filipinos came to the United States. With the economy of the Philippines in disarray, larger numbers of immigrants moved across the Pacific. Between 1980 and 1990 Filipino numbers more than doubled from 774,000 to 1.5 million. Ten years later Filipino population in the United States was up to 2.5 million. Most Filipinos in the West, which comprised about two-thirds of the nation's total, gravitated to Pacific Coast cities. Especially noteworthy were the more than 30,000 Filipino nurses working in Los Angeles, San Francisco, and Houston. With as many as 40,000 to 50,000 Filipinos entering the United States each year and most settling in the West, they are likely to become the largest Asian group in the region early in the twenty-first century.

Koreans also arrived in increasingly large numbers in the second half of the twentieth century. The Immigration Act of 1965, as it did for many Asian groups, encouraged a new influx of Koreans. Between 1970 and 1980 Korean numbers soared from about 70,000 to 354,000. This rapidly expanding migration continued, with Korean population zooming to more than one million in 2000. The percentage growth rate for Korean immigration was higher than for any other Asian group. They too congregated on the West Coast, with Los Angeles as the major center and numbering more than 145,000 Koreans in Los Angeles County in 1990. Koreans often operated small businesses, including mom-and-pop groceries, gas stations, and liquor stores. Their economic successes as entrepreneurs were not without their problems, however. Korean stores, as we have seen, became prime targets for looting and burning during the 1992 riots in Los Angeles.

Concurrently, sizable groups of immigrants from Southeast Asia arrived. As a result of military conflicts and oppressive regimes in Southeast Asia, chiefly the Vietnam War, hundreds of thousands of refugees fled their homelands, frantically searching for safety. The South Vietnamese received special treatment when they immigrated to the United States after abandoning their country following the American withdrawal and the collapse of South Vietnam in 1975. As supporters of American efforts in Vietnam, the South Vietnamese were brought to the United States, dispersed throughout the country, given some financial support, and urged to adjust to American culture as rapidly as possible. But this dispersal caused problems for close-knit, extended Vietnamese families in a new, alien society. Gradually federal restrictions loosened, after which most Vietnamese moved to California, particularly to its cities. Nearly fifty thousand Vietnamese had congregated in Los Angeles alone.

Smaller numbers of other groups also came from Southeast Asia. Several legislative acts passed from the 1960s into the 1980s encouraged and supported these immigrants, notably those from war-torn countries. In addition to the Vietnamese thousands of refugees arrived from Cambodia and Laos. These immigrants scattered over the United States, after stops in Asian or American refugee camps. Over time, most of these Southeast Asians, like the Vietnamese, moved to the warmer climates of California and Texas. Still another Asian group, the East Indians, came in much larger numbers after the passage of the Immigration Act of 1965. East Indian population in the United States doubled between 1980 and 1990 and did so again in the next decade, reaching a total of about 1.7 million in 2000. The act of 1965 allowed immigrants to bring their families, helping to establish more stable communities among these newly arrived people. Nearly all the East Indians also spoke English as a result of their having been part of the British Commonwealth. Because of their language facility, they were able to move more quickly into better-paying jobs and to work directly with other Americans. Nearly one-fourth of the East Indians in the United States, or about 400,000, lived in the West, primarily in metropolitan areas.

The largest minority group in the West at the end of the century was the Hispanics. Indeed, at the beginning of the twenty-first century Hispanics (often called Chicanos or Latinos) had become the most numerous minority people in the entire country, making up 35.3 million or 12.5 percent of the American population. Between 1980 and 2000 Hispanic numbers in the United States had exploded from 14.6 to 35.3 million. In 2000 about two-thirds of the country's Hispanics lived in the West, with California hosting 10.9 and Texas 6.7 million. The Hispanic population not only surpassed the totals of other minority groups in the West, the numbers of their annual migrations, as much as they can be determined, also dwarfed others. This growing influx was not without its problems. Undocumented or illegal immigrants surreptitiously crossed the U.S.-Mexican border to work in fields, as roofers, and in other unskilled areas. Many western agriculturists, wanting a cheap labor source, often turned their heads to the clandestine border crossings. The largest portion of the newly arrived Mexicans, who eventually stayed on, crowded into the urban *barrios* (Hispanic neighborhoods) of southwestern cities such as San Antonio, El Paso, Tucson, and San Diego. Expanding groups clustered in East Los Angeles, where the largest group of Mexican-heritage people outside Mexico City has congregated.

At the beginning of the twenty-first century, several problems challenged Hispanic communities. Class and heritage differences caused divisions. Many long-time Mexican American residents, not wanting to become involved with the difficult problem of undocumented workers, kept the newcomers at arm's length. In New Mexico some residents with Spanish surnames whose families have lived for centuries in that area thought of themselves as Spanish, not as Chicanos. Still other Hispanics in the West did well economically, became middle-class, moved into upwardly mobile neighborhoods, and were not inclined to speak warmly of *La Raza* (a nationalistic term referring to Mexican-heritage people). These divergent backgrounds and interests made it increasingly difficult for Hispanic leaders to forge strong, ethnic-wide, activist or reform programs. Indeed, since the death of César Chávez in 1993 and the declining influence of other notable Chicano leaders of the 1960s and 1970s, no other Hispanic leader has stepped forward to gain wide approval from the West's growing numbers of Chicanos.

Still, even though difference and change complicated Hispanic experiences in the American West in 2000, the group achieved a great deal in the closing decades of the twentieth century. In addition to financial and educational advancements, Hispanics also enjoyed a cultural revival. Historians such as Juan Gómez Quiñones, Vicki Ruiz, and Richard Griswold del Castillo; novelists Rudolfo Anaya and Ana Castillo; and artists like Judith Baca and the muralistas involved in the gigantic mural *The Great Wall of Los Angeles* (1967–) provided rich evidences of a Chicano culture percolating with activity. In the political arena more than three thousand Hispanics held political office, including the mayoralties of Denver and San Antonio, the governorship of New Mexico (twice), and more than a dozen seats in the U.S. Congress. These economic, cultural, and political successes bode well for the increasing power of Hispanics in the new century.

~

Demographic patterns and racial and ethnic diversity were but part of the story of the recent West. Modern westerners were also people of the mind and spirit. Religious experiences and western writers and thinkers likewise revealed much about the West at century's end. In these areas, too, westerners showed many, divergent faces.

In the twentieth century, writes the leading authority on religion in the West, Ferenc M. Szasz, "the modern American West participated in all national religious trends." Yet religious organizations in the region often defined that participation on their own terms. One would have expected, adds Szasz, with "the onset of the interstate highway system and the ongoing media revolution . . . that the religious history of the West would become more like that of the rest of the nation. In fact, almost the opposite has occurred." The weakening hegemony of Mainline Protestants and Roman Catholics, the expanding populations of Jews, Mormons, and evangelicals, and the rise of new faiths typified religious developments in the recent West. As Professor Szasz concludes, "the American West has never produced any religious mainstream"; instead, "with a few exceptions, the celebrated individualism of western life has remained preeminent" in its religious life.

In the late twentieth century, although the numbers of Mainline Protestants did not expand, those groups retained their traditional areas of strength in the West. Methodists were strong in Kansas, Oklahoma, and other Plains areas, with Presbyterians and Lutherans challenging them for numerical superiority in those western subregions. Only the Baptists, particularly the Southern Baptists, grew rapidly. As southerners moved across the Southwest, many took their conservative Baptist faith with them, establishing Southern Baptist congregations from Texas into California.

Roman Catholics, still the largest religious group in the West, lost ground with some competitors in the second half of the twentieth century. Still numerous in Mexican-heritage areas, old mining regions, the northern Plains, and some western cities, the Catholics seemed to have reached a plateau. By the 1980s, the national percentage of Catholics (21 percent nationwide) ranked above that in the seventeen western states (16 percent). In that decade Catholic numbers in only two states, New Mexico (34 percent of its population) and North Dakota (27 percent), ranked above national averages of Catholics. Still, Catholics provided many social services in southwestern urban and rural areas and in other western urban places, refuge for thousands of Latin Americans fleeing repressive regimes in countries like El Salvador and Guatemala, and support for reformers like César Chávez and his farmworkers.

~

Jews in the recent West became increasingly urban and were particularly drawn to southern California. By 1948, 225,000 Jews had congregated in Los Angeles, making it the fifth largest Jewish community in the United States. Three decades later Los Angeles Jews numbered nearly a half-million, second only to the New York Jewish community in size. Sizable Jewish communities formed in Phoenix and Dallas, with smaller Sephardic groups settling in the Pacific Northwest. By 1990, nearly 600,000 Jews were living in the Los Angeles area, making up about three-fourths of the western Jewish population. Observers noted, too, that the business-minded, informal, self-fulfillment, and outdoor lifestyles of southern California Jewry were influencing most western Jews. As one scholar concluded, "other western Jewries are merely imitating southern California patterns, even while they are breaking away from them."

The Church of Jesus Christ of Latter-day Saints (LDS), popularly known as the Mormons, experienced astounding growth in the last decades of the twentieth century. By mid-century most of the controversies swirling around obscure Mormon origins, their exclusiveness, and their alleged secret temple rites had abated, but not the church's evangelistic zeal and enthusiasm for expansion. Numbering 1.5 million members worldwide in 1960, the Mormons exploded to about 11 million in 2000, with about 5 million in the United States. At the end of the century there were more Mormons than Jews or Presbyterians in the United States and twice as many LDS as Episcopalians. The LDS were particularly strong in the intermountain West areas and California, with a large presence in Utah, Idaho, Nevada, and Wyoming. Utah, with the highest religious affiliation of any American state (75 percent), was Mormon-led. From their western crossroads location in Salt Lake City, the Mormons sent out annually more than thirty thousand young missionaries throughout the world, vying with Pentecostal groups for new converts in Latin America and elsewhere. Mormons in the West exhibit higher birth rates (twice the national average), maintain strong church attendance, follow traditional lifestyles, support conservative politics, and follow lay leadership at the local level. In most of these areas, Mormons and evangelicals have much in common.

No religious group in the West, except the Mormons, has grown as dramatically as evangelical/fundamentalist groups. Indeed, if one adds the first range of states west of the Mississippi, this enlarged West surpasses the South as the U.S. region with the largest number of churchgoers. This larger West also becomes home to more evangelicals than the South, long known as the Bible Belt of America. Such groups as the Southern Baptists, the Pentecostals (especially the Assemblies of God denomination), the Church of the Nazarene, and nondenominational denominations like Calvary Chapel, Vineyard Fellowship, and Church of the Rock experienced steady if not phenomenal growth, chiefly along the Pacific Coast and across the Southwest. Although these conservative Protestant groups sometimes differed on doctrinal matters, they often united in supporting national and international evangelizing efforts. Charles E. Fuller's radio broadcast "The Old Fashioned Revival Hour" in the 1940s, the Fuller Theological Seminary in Pasadena (1947–), Bill Bright's Campus Crusade for Christ (1951–), Chuck Smith's Calvary Chapel (1960s–), and James Dobson's Focus on the Family (1976–) illustrate the rise of important evangelical organizations in the second half of the twentieth century. Most of these western evangelical leaders were less controversial than the earlier fundamentalists like William Jennings Bryan, Sister Aimee Semple McPherson, "Fighting Bob" Shuler, and the Reverends Mark Matthews and J. Frank Norris. Political evangelicals like Senator Mark Hatfield (R) of Oregon might speak out against the Vietnam War, but they avoided reputations as contentious Bible-pounders or narrow-minded bigots.

Other western evangelicals did stir up controversy. Pentecostal revivalist Oral Roberts, an energetic even stem-winder as a preacher, filled his charismatic and healing services to overflowing. Roberts and other Pentecostal tent revivalists stormed through the Southwest and up the West Coast, igniting healing and deliverance revivals that burned red hot in the 1940s and 1950s and into the next generation. Later, Roberts stirred up other critics when he established Oral Roberts University in Tulsa, Oklahoma, with its law and medical schools. On one occasion, Roberts told listeners that the Lord would "call him home" if he did not raise a large amount to fund the university's financially depressed medical school.

At the opposite extreme, some observers thought, was Robert Schuller, whom a few competitors dismissed as little more than a Pied Piper of New Thought. Coming to southern California in 1955, at age twenty-nine, Schuller began a new congregation of the Reformed Church in America in a drive-in theater. In four years, the church expanded rapidly from forty to four hundred in attendance. Already fired with the first flames of "possibility [or positive] thinking," Schuller dreamed large and quickly built large foundations for his dreams. To house his booming congregation, which was on its way to ten thousand members, Schuller erected the magnificent Crystal Cathedral in the Garden Grove suburb of Los Angeles. Costing $20 million to construct (journalist Norman Cousins once quipped, "This is the kind of church God would build; if he could afford it."), the Cathedral became identified with Schuller's positive uplift program "The Hour of Power," heard around the globe on hundreds of radio and television stations. Sometimes critics, including skeptical evangelicals, denounced Schuller as a theatrical possibility thinker rather than a committed conservative Protestant, but Schuller's mission and outreach continued to grow. He remained one of the most widely known—and controversial—ministers whose presence signaled the Westward Tilt of Protestantism to the Southwest and California.

~

Not all westerners were Protestant, Catholic, Jewish, or Mormon, however. A variety of churches, spiritual organizations, and other religious centers began in the West as a result of the "revolution of consciousness" that swept through the

FIGURE 15:3. *Crystal Cathedral.* This imposing church edifice hosts one of the largest Protestant congregations in the American West. Pastor Robert Schuller provided warm, encouraging messages in his Sunday morning services, the "Hour of Power." Courtesy Crystal Cathedral ministries.

United States from the 1960s onward. The Hare Krishna, Moonie, Scientology, People's Temple, and Children of God groups found fertile soil in southern California. In other parts of the West the Church Universal and Triumphant moved to western Montana under the dynamic leadership of Elizabeth Claire Prophet, the utopian community Rajneeshpuram organized around an East Indian mystic in isolated central Oregon, and the Branch Davidian group settled near Waco, Texas. A startling variety of other survivalist, antigovernment, countercultural, and "alternative faith" groups rose and fell in the West from the 1960s through the 1980s. Tragically, as in the case of Jim Jones's People's Temple or the Branch Davidians, clashes between these communes' leaders and federal and state officials led to mass suicide, shootouts, or fiery destruction.

Illustrating the diversity of western culture, the region's religious groups notably differed. Evangelicals continued to expand across the Southwest and in California, Mormons spread throughout the central Rockies and expanded worldwide, and Catholics and Mainline Protestants held on to their dominions. If religious affiliations were unusually high in states like Utah, New Mexico, and North Dakota, where Mormon and Catholic numbers or percentages were large, religiously affiliated westerners were revealingly low in Washington, Oregon, and Nevada, where no one denomination predominated. Religious faith and church affiliation continue to be important to many westerners, even though the meaning of religion in western life remains complex and constantly changing.

∾

Novelists and historians during the last decades of the twentieth century were equally complex—and sometimes pessimistic—in their treatments of the American West. With a notable exception in Louis L'Amour, whose numerous works of uplifting frontier historical fiction sold in the millions and made him the best-selling western writer of all time, western authors avoided the simplistic, positive, and adventuresome depictions so popular in western writing earlier in the twentieth century. Rather, they portrayed the West as a complicated, varied region with a multifaceted past and present. On occasion students of recent western writing spoke of novelists and historians as postregionalists, meaning that they emphasized primarily racial and ethnic, gender, and class topics. Unlike the earlier regionalists, postregionalists were interested in these influences and seemed less intrigued with the shaping power of place on the West's fiction and historical writing. Postregional authors also seemed taken with an ambivalent or negative Gray West, introduced in the 1960s and gaining popularity in following decades.

∾

A host of new ethnic writers dealing with their cultures were clear evidence of the shifts in western fiction. Rudolfo Anaya, in the most widely read Chicano novel *Bless Me, Ultima* (1972), told the coming-of-age story of a young Hispanic. Like a Chicano Huck Finn, Antonio (Tony) Márez learns about religion, sex, war, family, and especially the larger mysteries of life from a *curandera* (healer) named Ultima. Written in clean, well-lighted prose, Anaya's first novel remains a rich reservoir of Hispanic lore and wisdom. A Chicana writer, Ana Castillo, expertly mined women's places as wives, mothers, daughters, and sisters in a series of novels. Utilizing the technique of magic realism (mixing fact and fantasy) so popular among Latin American writers, Castillo also invoked the *telenovela* format (a novel utilizing television techniques) in her widely acclaimed book *So Far from God* (1993). It is a lyrical, quirky, and humorous work of fiction, displaying the tone, characterizations, and plot formats increasingly popular with Chicana authors like Castillo, Denise Chávez, and Sandra Cisneros.

Similar themes and moods characterized the novels of African American novelist Terry McMillan. In *Waiting to Exhale* (1992), for example, McMillan depicts four African American young women, independent and adventuresome, hopscotching through jobs, marriages, and one-night relationships. Although set in modern Arizona, the novel illustrates the postregional tendency of emphasizing ethnicity, gender, and class more than setting or place. Another black writer, Walter Mosley, took a different tack in utilizing his detective hero Ezekial "Easy" Rawlins to illuminate the dilemmas facing many African Americans in southern California. Los Angeles, Mosley told an interviewer, is an ideal setting for detective fiction since the city "just doesn't want to be known. L. A. is a big secret." In such novels as *Devil in a Blue Dress* (1990), *White Butterfly* (1992), or *Black Betty* (1994), Mosley added, he tried to deal with "black migration from the Deep South to Los Angeles and this blue-collar existential hero ["Easy" Rawlins] moving through time." Like McMillan's fiction, Mosley's novels provide more probing pictures of racial, gender, and class experiences than those of setting and the shaping power of a specific region, the central emphases of many regional writers.

Native American and Asian novelists likewise furnished varied examples of the fiction about the recent West. As we have seen in chapter 14, American Indian writers Vine Deloria, N. Scott Momaday, and Leslie Silko turned out important nonfiction and novels in the 1960s and 1970s treating Native American experiences. All continued to write significant works in the next two decades. Joining them as leading American Indian writers, among many others, were Louise Erdrich (Chippewa), James Welch (Blackfeet/Gros Ventre), and Sherman Alexie (Spokane/Coeur d'Alene). In a series of intricately plotted novels about mixed bloods in the upper Midwest, including *Love Medicine* (1984), *The Beet Queen* (1986), and *Tracks* (1988), Erdrich dealt with complications within Indian societies as well as their depressing, nearly always tragic connections with a white society. Welch's best-known novel, *Winter in the Blood* (1974), features a nameless Indian man who, after years of mistreatment at the hands of whites, reconnects with his Indian heritage and seems on the road to recovery at the end of the story. Welch's later novels *The Death of Jim Loney* (1979) and *The Indian Lawyer* (1990) and his work of nonfiction *Killing Custer* (1994) were darker narratives, more critical of whites and less optimistic about Indian survival. The writings of the youthful, prolific Sherman Alexie, often critical of whites, sometimes overflow with welcome humor. In his first notable collection of stories, *The Lone Ranger and Tonto Fist Fight in Heaven* (1993), Alexie satirized the Lone Ranger, allowing his faithful scout Tonto repeatedly to outwit his masked partner. One of the stories in this widely cited collection, "This Is What It Means to Say Phoenix, Arizona," became the basis for the script of the very successful film *Smoke Signals* (1998), which Alexie codirected and for which he wrote the script. Alexie's clever, witty, and bleak fiction, exemplified in his later novels *Reservation Blues* (1995) and *Indian Killer* (1996), greatly appealed to Indians and non-Indians alike.

Asian writers were less numerous than Native American authors, but the works of Maxine Hong Kingston, Amy Tan, and Ronald Takaki illustrated the complexity of their contributions. Kingston gained much attention with her pioneering work *The Woman Warrior* (1976), part autobiography, part fiction, and part Chinese myth. In this important work and in its literary twin, *China Men* (1980), Kingston reclaimed the Chinese past as an overlooked subject of western history even as she dealt with the tensions of Chinese mother-daughter relations. These generational differences, as well those between Old World and New World Chinese, were at the center of Amy Tan's novels *The Joy Luck Club* (see chapter 14) and *The Kitchen God's Wife* (1991). The most outspoken of the Asian historians in the West was Ronald Takaki, the author of numerous works on race relations in the United States. In volumes such as *Strangers from a Different Shore: A History of Asian Americans* (1989) and *Iron Cages: Race and Culture in 19th-Century America* (1990), Takaki pointed to the repeated racism that kept Chinese, Japanese, Koreans, and other Asian minorities from fully participating in the economic abundance of the American West. These works by Native American and Asian writers provided still other examples of literary figures charting the varied and changing meanings of the contemporary American West.

≈

In the 1980s the *New York Times* declared Wallace Stegner the "dean" of western writers. It was a wise, defensible choice. In addition to his numerous influential writings on environmental matters, Stegner produced more than a dozen

FIGURE 15:4. *Wallace Stegner, Western Writer.* Often referred to as the "Dean of Western Writers," Wallace Stegner wrote superb fiction, as in his Pulitzer prize–winning novel *Angle of Repose* (1971), and in his polished and provocative essays and books on the western environment. Courtesy Mary Page Stegner and Page Stegner.

important novels, histories, and biographies. His biographies of John Wesley Powell and Bernard DeVoto, his histories of the Mormons, and his travel and personal essays on many parts of the West won wide acclaim. But his western novels, including *The Big Rock Candy Mountain* (1943), *All the Little Live Things* (1979), *The Spectator Bird* (1976), and *Recapitulation* (1979), were even more impressive as remarkable fictional renditions of California and other regions of the twentieth-century Canadian and American Wests. The apex of Stegner's literary output was *Angle of Repose* (1971), a novel that won the Pulitzer Prize.

A panoramic work with a complicated plot and large cast of characters and settings, the novel features a wheel chair-bound historian dissatisfied with his life and in search of meaning in the lives of his frontier grandparents. The narrator wants to achieve his grandparents' "angle of repose" (the incline where rocks cease to roll) in his life. Based extensively on the lives of the talented Local Color writer and artist Mary Hallock Foote and her engineer husband (see chapter 6), the novel addresses large, important themes of western history: (1) the impact of eastern America on the West; (2) the imprint of the nineteenth century on the modern West; and (3) the central roles of women and families in western society and culture. In *Angle of Repose* Wallace Stegner produced a classic western novel, the most important fictional work about the West since John Steinbeck's *Grapes of Wrath* (1939).

Two other writers from other western subregions, Larry McMurtry and Ivan Doig, also worked the rich lode of connections between earlier and contemporary Wests. Texan McMurtry, beginning with his first novel, *Horseman, Pass By* (1961, made into the much-acclaimed film *Hud*) and on through a series of new West settings in *The Last Picture Show* (1966), *Moving On* (1970), and *Terms of Endearment* (1975), produced several classic Gray West novels. In McMurtry's fiction, many westerners, particularly Texans, reared on the myths of the cowboy Old West, were unable to deal with the dark, depressing sides of a Cadillac, oil-soaked, unheroic West. These conflicts between romantic and realistic frontiers powered McMurtry's best novel, *Lonesome Dove* (1985), which also won a Pulitzer Prize. Sending his cowboy protagonists on a long, tortuous cattle drive, the author shows them to be valiant and courageous but also vicious and amoral men. Most of the novel's supporting cast, except for an African American drover and the wife of a dying cowman, are also deeply flawed. *Lonesome Dove* overflows with the postregional emphases on gender, ethnicity, and a depressing, dark West.

Montana novelist Ivan Doig was less inclined to see a debased West. His tetralogy of Montana novels, *English Creek* (1984), *Dancing at the Rascal Fair* (1987), *Ride with Me, Maria Montana* (1990), and *Prairie Nocturne* (2003), included disappointments and tragedies, but his heroes and heroines were courageous survivors, winning out against demanding environments and their own less admirable personal traits. Adroitly treating the multiple, varied pressures of passing time on his characters, Doig dealt extensively and revealingly with a rural West so often mistreated in cliché and stereotype. Doig's most appealing nonfictional work, *This House of Sky* (1978), told his boyhood story of growing up the son of a hard-working, itinerant, not very financially successful sheepherder in Montana.

Several western women novelists, in addition to those ethnic women writers previously mentioned, added much to a more complex, gendered literary West.

Barbara Kingsolver, a transplant from the South to the Southwest, drew provocative portraits of strong, single women caught in vexing circumstances. Featuring realistic, antimythic settings, plots, and western characters, several of them Native American and Hispanic, Kingsolver's novels, including *The Bean Trees* (1988), *Animal Dreams* (1990), and *Pigs in Heaven* (1993), pulsated with strong woman characters. Another writer, Marilynne Robinson, in her probing novel *Housekeeping* (1981) set in northern Idaho, built on women's networks, in this case the link between the adolescent narrator Ruth and her lonely but nurturing Aunt Sylvie. At the end of the novel, aunt and niece leave their fractured home together, to find meaning in a life of wandering. The author set out to show that "at a certain level housekeeping is a regime of small kindnesses, which, together, make the world salubrious, savory, and warm." Even more impressive are Robinson's achievements in *Gilead* (2004), which won a coveted Pulitzer Prize. A quiet, meditative, deeply moving work of fiction, Robinson's second novel is ostensibly a letter that a seventy-seven-year-old pastor leaves for his seven-year-old, much-loved son. This notable novel, full of spiritual insights and expressed in polished, elegant prose, solidifies the author's ranking as a leading western writer.

∾

The most significant change in western historical writing in these decades was the rise to prominence of the New Western historians. This small group of younger historians and their historical works, building on trends in western historical writing of the 1960s and 1970s, emphasized racial, ethnic, gender, class, and environmental themes. In the 1980s and 1990s the New Western historians provided fresh syntheses of the western past. Influenced too by their own experiences in growing up in the complexities of the 1960s and 1970s, these scholars stressed the darker, less triumphal features of the American West. Gaining increasing popularity by the early 1990s, the New Western history became the most talked-about approach in dealing with the West, but by the turn of the new century an even newer, complex view of the West was emerging.

The most prominent of the New Western historians were Patricia Nelson Limerick, Richard White, and Donald Worster. Limerick, more than any other person, deserves credit for launching the New Western movement. Her widely cited book *Legacy of Conquest: The Unbroken Past of the American West* (1987), her coedited volume *Trails: Toward a New Western History* (1991), and her numerous smoothly written essays and lively oral presentations helped push the New Western history to the forefront of western historical studies. In *Legacy of Conquest* Limerick argued that a desire for dominance and conquest drove European-heritage settlers, frequently leading to their mistreatment

FIGURE 15:5. *Patricia Nelson Limerick, Western Historian.* The major figure in the New Western history movement, Patty Limerick called for more realistic stories about the West that addressed racism, environmental despoliation, and pioneer greediness. A lively speaker and writer, Limerick wrote essays and books attractive to general readers as well as scholars. Courtesy Patricia Nelson Limerick.

of Indians, Mexicans, Asians; destruction of the environment; and acts of selfishness, cupidity, and aggrandizement. For Limerick, too many earlier historians had told a triumphal story of unrelenting progress and adventure; she wished to see more of the underside of the western story.

At the same time, Richard White and Donald Worster furnished superb environmental histories of the West. White reminded westerners that Indians had clearly put their marks on large sections of the West before Europeans came. But once Anglo Americans arrived they followed the Judeo-Christian ethic of making the "desert [or wilderness] blossom like a rose." In doing so, settlers often misused the land, rivers and streams, and other natural resources, at the same time pushing aside Natives or forcing them into a coercive economic system leading to their dependency on foreign economic empires. In his widely cited work *"It's Your Misfortune and None of My Own": A New History of the American West* (1991), a mammoth synthesis of western history, White did not mention Frederick Jackson Turner, his thesis, or the frontier, emphasizing instead the complex interplay of race, ethnicity, class competitions, and environmental contacts and competitions in the West. The most erudite of recent western historians, as were Henry Nash Smith and Earl Pomeroy in earlier years, White urged historians to think more broadly and analytically about the West.

Of all the New Western historians Donald Worster was the most closely linked to the field of environmental history. A historian of immense breadth and strong opinions, Worster asserted in his thought-provoking book *Rivers of Empire* (1985) that world water empires often led to oppressive political regimes. He also contended in *The Dust Bowl* (1979) that American selfishness and greed, not nature's random actions, were the major causes of the disastrous dirt storms and agricultural disasters that plagued the West in the 1930s. Adding to his reputation as a first-rank historian, Worster then produced a hugely successful biography, *A River Running West: The Life of John Wesley Powell* (2001). Here, as he had done in his earlier works, Worster warned westerners of their limited natural resources and their need to know and respect those limitations. Early on, Powell had learned several of these important lessons, Worster asserted; now contemporary Americans had to relearn them.

What were the central themes of the New Western history, and how were they supplanting earlier interpretations of the American West? When the author of this book asked Professor Limerick to define the New Western history, she provided a succinct answer in her brief essay entitled "What on Earth Is the New Western History?" The fresh approach was a more realistic, complex, and multicultural way of examining the West, she replied. New Western historians, Limerick added, would "break free of the old model of 'progress' and 'improvement,' and face up to the possibility that some roads of western development led directly to failure and to injury." In her own early writings, the shadowy side of the western past, including the failures and the injuries, occupied the limelight. More recently, Limerick seemed less inclined to target Frederick Jackson Turner and the frontier school as mistaken in their judgments.

≈

Just as the New Western historians appeared safely in the saddle to lead historians into the twenty-first century, another viewpoint about the western past came increasingly into view. This more complex western history had emerged earlier, but in the hoopla surrounding the New Western history, the alternative perspective had been overshadowed. A key work in this more complex view of the region was Elliott West's superb volume *The Contested Plains: Indians, Goldseekers, and the Rush to Colorado* (1998). A balanced, thorough, and imaginative work, West's gracefully written synthesis showed how Indians, as well as the later pioneers pulled by the Colorado Gold Rush, misused natural resources. Even before the hordes of miners and later families arrived, the fragile ecosystem of the west-central Plains was in trouble with too many demands on it from Natives and their animals. West also pointed out the racial, sexual, and economic complexities that marked the region in the mid-nineteenth century. His was indeed a "messy" West of competing societies and cultures, not a dichotomy of white and black hats massacring one another. As one reviewer discerningly wrote, West had diligently covered competitors without "scold[ing] or trash[ing] any culture."

Other western historians were presenting similarly complicated stories of the region. James P. Ronda, in the best book written on the subject, *Lewis and Clark among the Indians* (1984), provided another valuable example of complex western history. Americans have known much about the Lewis and Clark Expedition up the Missouri and down the Columbia rivers, and back, Ronda noted, but we knew too little about the Indian groups with which the Corps interacted. His memorable volume urged readers to study the riverbanks as well as the river boats, and connections between them, and thus grapple with the larger contexts of cultures that both motivated and surrounded Lewis and Clark in their trek west. The most voluminous writer about women's experiences in the West, Glenda Riley, also called for a larger, more layered look at contacts between Indians and whites. In her revealing study *Women and Indians on the Frontier, 1825–1915* (1984; revised and republished as *Confronting Race: Women and Indians on the Frontier, 1815–1915* [2004]), Riley demonstrated that pioneer women and Indians often got along well, trading goods and helping one another on the frontier. Her story belied so many accounts of Indian-white contacts as little more than brutal pioneer attacks on Natives and the reciprocal, savage forays of Indians. Those earlier stories were oversimplified and misleading, in Riley's view. More recently James F. Brooks supplied another intricate, valuable account of the contact, conflict, and intermingling of cultures in his prize-winning *Captives and Cousins: Slavery, Kinship, and Community in the Southwest Borderlands* (2002). Focusing on the zone of interactions between Indians and the Spanish, Brooks revealed how complex these interrelations were, leading to kinship and community as often as to conflict and violence.

Like other recent historians producing multifaceted accounts of western history, Brooks avoided stereotyping either side and furnished, instead, a rewarding and involved story of societies and cultures meeting along a new frontier.

~

To comprehend the fast-paced changes and increasing complexity that define the American West in the opening years of the twenty-first century, send an imaginative, astute observer on an extended trip through the major sections of the American West. Allow that traveler to know the major currents of western history since World War II. At the end of this extensive, thorough journey ask the visitor to provide a brief evaluation of what he or she has seen and experienced.

The traveler will undoubtedly observe the twin shaping influences of the modern American West: change and complexity. Between 1940 and 2000, the West experienced remarkable expansion, jumping from 36.7 to 91.4 million people, a population growth of 150 percent. Cities all over the region, fueled largely by federal defense expenditures during World War II and the cold war, kept growing and growing. Uncle Sam's West first boomed in California, then up the Pacific Coast and across the Southwest. The Silicon Valley in the Bay Area (high-tech), Bellevue/Seattle (Microsoft Corp.), and Las Vegas (gambling and tourism) were but three examples of the overnight urban growth that swept across the West. Denver, Albuquerque, Phoenix, Austin, and Dallas–Fort Worth represented other western urban areas that expanded rapidly in the second half of the twentieth century. With that population growth came larger economic booms; in some subregions, thousands of jobs begged for workers. Military industrial complexes, air and army bases, scientific/educational laboratories, and tourism fired up the western economy. Midway through these sixty years, high-tech and other "footloose" industries such as electronics and computer firms brought a new surge of urban and technological growth.

Waves of newcomers, like a sharply shifting kaleidoscope, continually recreated the social patterns of the modern West. African Americans came to work in war-related industries, Native Americans increasingly moved off reservations and into towns and cities to find employment, new crops of Asians came, particularly after the Immigration Act of 1965, and Mexicans provided the steadiest, largest flow of newcomers during these three generations. The highest numbers of immigrants and earlier minority residents settled in the Southwest and California, the subregions with the largest Hispanic populations. The smallest minority numbers were in the northern Plains and Rockies. In some western subregions in 2000, minorities had become majorities (more than 50 percent of the population) in New Mexico and California. But they made up less than 15 percent of the population in the Dakotas, Montana, Idaho, and Wyoming.

The West's expanding economy and the new social mixes in the region helped to reshape its cultural and political life. Ethnic and women writers portrayed a more diverse racial and gendered West than previous European-heritage males had suggested. Burgeoning numbers of Mormons, evangelicals, and alternative faiths also leavened the "inner" West. Expanded higher education systems in states like California and Texas evidenced the gathering strengths of western education. The University of California, Berkeley; Stanford University; Cal Tech; Reed College; the University of Texas; and Rice University, for example, took their places among the nation's most elite universities and colleges. Our observer would see, too, that western politics shifted to the right after World War II. Richard Nixon, Barry Goldwater, Ronald Reagan, and George W. Bush, as leading regional and national politicians, reflected this upsurge of western conservative politics.

But, of course, the all-wise reporter would move beyond these changes to point to the West's complexities as well. Like a fraternal twin, complications seemed always to follow changes in the West. The economic development and growth patterns were unequally distributed throughout the region. The upper Plains and Rockies did not share in much of the wealth that brought rocketing changes to the Pacific Coast and Southwest states. Indeed, one outspoken academic couple from the East and a few of their enthusiastic disciples called for a return of the sparsely populated High Plains to a Buffalo Commons, keeping out people and reintroducing nature. That suggestion played in sections of Montana, Wyoming, and the Dakotas like a vegetarian commercial at a convention of angry cattle ranchers. In other areas, pockets of poverty dotted the West. Unemployment or low wages plagued many Indian reservations, small Hispanic towns in northern New Mexico, and ghettoes in many large western cities. And in several agricultural areas of the West agribusinesses had taken over huge farmland areas, pushing aside individual small farmers.

Sometimes more friction than fusion accompanied these rapid multiracial and multicultural shifts in the West. Nonminority westerners bristled at what they considered special privileges given to minority workers, students, and businesses. In another contested area, English-only legislative efforts across the Southwest often reflected a desire to undermine or cut back on multicultural influences. Our observer would point to the Japanese Relocation, the Watts Riot, the second battle at Wounded Knee, and the Rodney King episode as but a few tragic examples of a much larger problem. He or she would also note the ongoing disagreements within and among Native American tribes, Hispanic groups, and Asian peoples.

Other difficulties leaked in around the edges of expansion, growth, and progress. In several of the areas of largest growth, southern California for instance, pollution, hectic commutes, and traffic jams reared their ugly heads.

It seemed as if the rapid, headlong pursuit of expansion left heaps of detritus, dangerous to bodies and souls. In other areas of the West, huge allotments of water for cities and sprawling farms dried up rivers, streams, and underground water supplies. The drive to lure tourists, gamblers, and investors often led to the unexpected consequences of garish casinos, falsified Old West sites, and chancy developments that crashed even before they were launched.

The booming city of Las Vegas represents these conflicting impulses even as it illustrates the nonstop changes transforming the modern West. In the early 1930s Las Vegas was the jumping-off place for the building of the Hoover/ Boulder Dam, and later it became the supply point for the Nevada nuclear test site, about seventy miles north of the city. But gambling, legalized in Nevada in 1931, brought most of the newcomers to Las Vegas. From the 1960s forward the

FIGURE 15:6. *Las Vegas, Fremont Street, Looking East, 1991.* Early twenty-first-century Las Vegas illustrated the challenges facing much of the larger American West—how to balance astounding growth against mushrooming urban sprawl, social tensions, and mounting environmental dilemmas. By the year 2000, Las Vegas had become the fast-growing large American city. Courtesy Sarah Vinci Collection University of Nevada, Las Vegas Library, 0268–0022, Sarah Vinci Collection.

city became a gambling hotspot and then a family entertainment center. First, southern Californians drove to Las Vegas for a weekend of "fun, excitement, and a bit of danger"; then improved transportation brought in the hundreds of thousands—eventually the millions. By the late 1980s a huge complex of casinos and entertainment centers dotted the famous Las Vegas Strip, but in the next decade high rollers remade the city. Earlier Old West themes were pushed aside in the rush to throw up gigantic, internationally themed casinos. The reinvention of Las Vegas became the best-known example of entertainment tourism in the United States. The theme-driven and fantasy casinos and hotels provided something for all ages—from toddlers to grandparents. As one scholar has written, the reinvented Las Vegas "can always be whatever you want it to be as long as you're willing to pay for it." Millions of tourists and new residents were.

But at what costs? How might more traditional residents in Las Vegas build sound families, a strong sense of community, and moral integrity in an economy based primarily on gaming, tourism, and attendant industries? True, new crops of retirees, business operatives, and professionals were migrating to Las Vegas to take advantage of its pulsating economy. Taxes were low, jobs were available, and newcomers flooded in like a series of tidal waves. Still, the gaming industry seemed unfortunately to encourage the shadier elements of society: prostitution, higher rates of divorce and broken families, and large socioeconomic chasms yawning between owners and unskilled workers in casinos and hotels. Had the gaming and tourist industries made a "devil's bargain" with expansion and profit, and were now the evil bargainers of those questionable agreements rending the social and moral fabric of Las Vegas?

If our adventurous observer visited Las Vegas, California, Texas, and many other parts of the urban West, he or she would likely report change and complexity as twin hallmarks of the recent and present West. Our traveler might also speak of the schizophrenia that characterizes much of the region. New West and Old West jostle alongside one another in which greater Los Angeles encompasses both high-tech and sociocultural achievement on one side and yet Old West addictions featured in Hollywood Westerns, the Gene Autry Museum (now the Autry National Center), and the Frontierland of Disneyland on the other. Even as westerners utilized the advanced technologies of cell phones, fax machines, and the Internet, allowing them to live where they wished while carrying on their business affairs hundreds of miles away, they often dreamed of an Edenic West of the great outdoors and endless open spaces, home of Louis L'Amour novels, John Wayne films, Buffalo Bill and Annie Oakley, outlaws and lawmen like Billy the Kid and Wyatt Earp, and rodeos and Wild West enactments. These varied, complex emphases continued to be the major barriers to establishing anything like a coherent western regional identity.

Truth to tell, our insightful traveler would remind us that the American West continues to be defined by change and complexity. Like two horses harnessed together, the West of change and the West of complexity alternatively gallop and prance, slip and stumble. For every clear advancement, a resulting dilemma of complexity seems to follow. So it has been, so it is likely to remain.

SUGGESTED READINGS

Abbott, Carl. *The Metropolitan Frontier: Cities in the Modern American West.* Tucson: University of Arizona Press, 1993.

Brooks, James F. *Captives & Cousins: Slavery, Kinship, and Community in the Southwest Borderlands.* Chapel Hill: University of North Carolina Press, 2002.

Comer, Krista. *Landscapes of the New West: Gender and Geography in Contemporary Women's Writing.* Chapel Hill: University of North Carolina Press, 1999.

Davis, Mike. *City of Quartz: Excavating the Future in Los Angeles.* New York: Verso, 1990.

Egan, Timothy. *Lasso the Wind: Away to the New West.* New York: Knopf, 1998.

Etulain, Richard W. *Re-imagining the Modern American West: A Century of Fiction, History, and Art.* Tucson: University of Arizona Press, 1996.

Etulain, Richard W., and Ferenc M. Szasz, eds. *The American West in 2000: Essays in Honor of Gerald D. Nash.* Albuquerque: University of New Mexico Press, 2003.

Flores, Dan. *The Natural West: Environmental History in the Great Plains and Rocky Mountains.* Norman: University of Oklahoma Press, 2001.

Garreau, Joel. *Edge City: Life on the New Frontier.* New York: Doubleday, 1991.

Gutiérrez, David G. *Walls and Mirrors: Mexican Americans, Mexican Immigrants, and the Politics of Ethnicity.* Berkeley: University of California Press, 1995.

Johnson, Michael L. *New Westers: The West in Contemporary American Culture.* Lawrence: University Press of Kansas, 1996.

Klein, Kerwin Lee. *Frontiers of Historical Imagination: Narrating the European Conquest of Native America, 1890–1990.* Berkeley: University of California Press, 1997.

Limerick, Patricia Nelson. *The Legacy of Conquest: The Unbroken Past of the American West.* New York: W. W. Norton, 1987.

———. "What on Earth Is the New Western History?" In *Trails: Toward a New Western History,* edited by Patricia Nelson Limerick et al., 81–88. Lawrence: University Press of Kansas, 1991.

Lotchin, Roger. "Angels and Apples: The Late-Twentieth-Century Western City, Urban Sprawl, the Illusion of Urban Exceptionalism." In *The American West in 2000: Essays in Honor of Gerald Nash,* edited by Richard W. Etulain and Ferenc M. Szasz, 143–63. Albuquerque: University of New Mexico Press, 2003.

[Lyon, Thomas J., et al., eds.] *Updating the Literary West.* Fort Worth: Texas Christian University Press, 1997.

Malone, Michael P., and Richard W. Etulain. *The American West: A Twentieth-Century History.* Lincoln: University of Nebraska Press, 1989.

Moehring, Eugene. *Resort City in the Sunbelt: Las Vegas, 1930–2000.* Rev ed. Reno: University of Nevada Press, 2002.

Nash, Gerald D. *A Brief History of the American West Since 1945.* Fort Worth, TX: Harcourt, 2001.

Olson, James S. *Equality Deferred: Race, Ethnicity, and Immigration in America Since 1945.* Fort Worth, TX: Harcourt, 2003.

Rawls, James J. *Chief Red Fox Is Dead: A History of Native Americans Since 1945.* Fort Worth, TX: Harcourt, 1996.

Rich, Laura. *The Accidental Zillionaire: Demystifying Paul Allen.* New York: Wiley, 2002.

Riley, Glenda. *Confronting Race: Women and Indians on the Frontier, 1815–1915.* Rev ed. Albuquerque: University of New Mexico Press, 2004.

Robbins, William G. *Landscapes of Conflict: The Oregon Story, 1940–2000.* Seattle: University of Washington Press, 2004.

Ronda, James P. *Lewis and Clark among the Indians.* Lincoln: University of Nebraska Press, 1984.

Rothman, Hal K. *Devil's Bargains: Tourism in the Twentieth-Century American West.* Lawrence: University Press of Kansas, 1998.

———. *Neon Metropolis: How Las Vegas Started the Twenty-First Century.* New York: Routledge, 2003.

Ruiz, Vicki L. *From Out of the Shadows: Mexican Women in Twentieth-Century America.* New York: Oxford University Press, 1998.

Starr, Kevin. *Coast of Dreams: California on the Edge, 1990–2003.* New York: Alfred A. Knopf, 2004.

Stegner, Wallace. *The American West as Living Space.* Ann Arbor: University of Michigan Press, 1987.

———. *Angle of Repose.* Garden City, NY: Doubleday, 1971.

Szasz, Ferenc Morton. *Religion in the Modern American West.* Tucson: University of Arizona Press, 2000.

Takaki, Ronald. *Strangers from a Different Shore: A History of Asian Americans.* New York: Penguin Books, 1989.

Taylor, Quintard. *In Search of the Racial Frontier: African Americans in the American West, 1528–1990.* New York: W. W. Norton, 1998.

Topping, Gary. *Utah Historians and the Reconstruction of Western History.* Norman: University of Oklahoma Press, 2003.

Wallace, James, and Jim Erickson. *Hard Drive: Bill Gates and the Making of the Microsoft Empire.* New York: Wiley, 1993.

West, Elliott. *The Contested Plains: Indians, Goldseekers, and the Rush to Colorado.* Lawrence: University Press of Kansas, 1998.

White, Richard. *"It's Your Misfortune and None of My Own": A History of the American West.* Norman: University of Oklahoma Press, 1991.

Worster, Donald. *A River Running West: The Life of John Wesley Powell.* New York: Oxford University Press, 2001.

———. *An Unsettled Country: Changing Landscapes of the American West.* Albuquerque: University of New Mexico Press, 1994.

Index

Lone Star Republic, 100, *101*, 251
Los Alamos, New Mexico, 376–68
Los Angeles: 111, 249, 300, 306–8, 426;
    development as urban center, 306–8;
    early importance of, 306–7.
Los pobres, 251
Los ricos, 43, 109, 251
Louisiana, 66, 68
Louisiana Purchase, 68, 77
Love, Nat, *185*
Ludlow, Colorado, 317–18
Lumber industry and logging. *See* Forestry
    and lumbering
Lutherans, 354, 431
Lux, Charles, 184

McCoy, Joseph, 180, 182
Mackenzie, Alexander, 64, 70, 77
McKinley, William, 236, 237
McLoughlin, Dr. John, 74–76, *75*, 123, 124,
    130, 132, 134
McMillan, Terry, 436
McMurtry, Larry, 275, 439
McNary-Haugen bills, 312, 322
McPherson, Aimee Semple (Sister Aimee),
    353, 353–54
McWilliams, Carey, 107, 108
Magoffin, Susan Shelby, 103, 258
Malin, James, 347
Malone, Michael P., xii, 206
Mammoths, 16
Mandans, 78, 282
Manifest Destiny, 88, 112, 113, 118, 288
Manufacturing and industry, 300, 314–15,
    373–75. *See also* Federal government
    economic supports
Marcos de Niza, Fray, 40
Marshall, James, 161
Martínez, José Antonio (Padre), 106
Masculinity, 258–59
Master Plan of Education (California), 412
Matthews, Mark, 352
Means, Russell, 406
Measles. *See* diseases
Meat-packing industries, 250, 314
Megafauna, 16, 18
Meriam Commission and report, 304
Mesa Verde, 21
Mestizos, 59, 93, 94
Methodist missions, 130–31
Methodists, 289, 290, 307, 354, 431. *See also*
    Lee, Jason
Metís, 66, 69, 85

Metropolitan West, 422–24, *423*. *See also*
    Urbanization; Urban populations
Mexican Americans: 310, 319, 370, 384,
    408–10, 430–31. *See also* Chicanos;
    Hispanics
Mexican-American War, 100, 112–16, 117
Mexican-heritage peoples, 250–52, 308,
    310, 369–70, 430. See also *Barrios*
Mexican immigration, 308, 310, 384, 430,
    444
Mexican politics: in Mexican period,
    93–95, 99, 105, 111–12
Mexican provinces, 94–112
Mexican Revolution, 308, 310
Mexico, 40–41, 117–18, 319, 430; and the
    Southwest, 92–118, *96*
Mexico City, 99, 104, 115
Microsoft Corporation, 401–2, 421
Middle class influences, 94, 307, 331, 336
Migrant labor, 299, 408, 410, 430
Migrations, 138, 299, 398, 430
Miles, Nelson A., 222, *223*
Military-industrial complex, 365, *374*, 375,
    394
Military installations and operations,
    363–65, *374*, *375*, 396; operations
    against Indians, 218–19
Miller, Albert Jacob, 282, *283*
Miller, Henry, 184
Milling industries, 314
Mineral resources, 11, 312, 393–94. *See also*
    Gold; Silver
Miners, 163, 168, 173. *See also* Prospectors
Mines and mining, 160–76, *162*, *253*,
    393–94, 402
Mining towns and communities, 160–61,
    163–76, 245–46
Ministers, 287, 288, 280–91
Minorities, racial and ethnic, 2, 424–25,
    426, *427*, 430, 444,; and schools, 358;
    as writers, 436–37. *See also specific
    minority groups*
Missionaries, 66, 129–37, 287–89, 292.
    See also Franciscans; Missions;
    Secularization
Mission Dolores, 52, *108*
Missions: American, 129–37; schools
    operated at, 292; French, 66; Mexican,
    107–9; Spanish, 44, 52, 56–57
Mississippi River, 65, 77
Mississippi River valley, 65, 68, 138
Missouri, 102–3, 214–15
Missouri Compromise, 213, 214

ABOUT THE AUTHOR

Richard W. Etulain is professor emeritus of history and former director of the Center for the American West at the University of New Mexico, where he taught from 1979 to 2001. He also taught at Northwest Nazarene College (University) and at Idaho State University and served as Distinguished Professor of Humanities at the University of Nevada, Reno, and as the Pettyjohn Distinguished Lecturer at Washington State University. He holds bachelor's degrees in English and history from Northwest Nazarene and a master's in English and a doctoral degree in history from the University of Oregon. Etulain is the author or editor of more than forty books, most of which focus on the history and cultures of the American West. His books include *Conversations with Wallace Stegner* (1983, 1996), *The American West: A Twentieth-Century History* (1989), *Writing Western History* (editor 1991), *Re-imagining the Modern American West: A Century of Fiction, History, and Art* (1996), *Telling Western Stories: From Buffalo Bill to Larry McMurtry* (1999), and *Western Lives: A Biographical History of the American West* (editor, 2004).

Professor Etulain has been president of both the Western Literature and Western History associations. He has also lectured abroad on U.S. history and the American West in several countries, most recently as a Fulbright Lecturer in Ukraine. On his retirement in 2001, the University of New Mexico established the Richard W. Etulain Lectureship in Western History and Culture. He currently edits four series of books on the American West and is working on a study of Abraham Lincoln and the American West.